Famous Pianists & Their Technique

to Connie

Reginald R. Gerig

Famous Pianists & Their Technique

Robert B. Luce, Inc.   Washington - New York

Second Printing 1975

Gerig, Reginald, 1919-
Famous pianists & their technique.

    Bibliography: p.
    1. Pianists.   2. Piano music—Interpretation (Phrasing,
dynamics, etc.)   I. Title.

ML700.G44   1976   786.1'092'2 [B]   75-37789
ISBN 0-88331-066-X

Contents

Foreword

Throughout the history of music the great keyboard teachers, many of them equally celebrated as virtuosos, have freely passed along to their students the insights and procedures deemed necessary for the acquisition of a fine performance technique. A substantial number have been moved to leave written records, and from time to time a student has set down his explanation of the master's comprehension of his art. Furthermore, other contemporaries have written accounts of how these accomplished pianists and harpsichordists played or taught. During a period of over three and a half centuries, a large, significant body of technical literature has accumulated for the piano and its predecessors. Some sources rightfully deserve to be forgotten; but most warrant a better reception than they have been given in recent years. Much of this bibliography is lost to the present-day piano student, and even to his teacher, through unawareness, lack of time, or inaccessibility.

The failure of many pianists to claim and then assimilate this part of their musical heritage is a serious one. Often horizons are restricted: the student's learning achievement usually will not go beyond the limited understanding and provincialisms of his teacher and his other immediate influences. Where his resources are excellent, the loss may not appear so great. But, even here, a sense of historical perspective will be missing. A master teacher may discover a technical truth through personal comprehension and even proclaim it as a special revelation. Had he looked into the historical literature, he might have found that another master from a different school and an earlier century had declared the same truth in a more convincing manner. Both student and teacher would have been enriched thereby.

For his fullest development the pianist must not neglect these resources. The author recalls a conversation several years ago with Nathan Broder, the former editor of *The Musical Quarterly*, during which he stated that pianists do not read books. This is surely an exaggeration and there is reason to believe that the situation has improved in recent days. But pianists should take note of a well-known musicologist's evaluation.

Admittedly the piano is not mastered by holding a textbook in the comfort of a lounge chair. There are no easy short cuts to reduce materially the endless number of hours that must be spent at the keyboard. The music itself is the best teacher of both interpretation and technique, and it best instructs at the keyboard. But reading can open up new vistas. It can help the student to a greater understanding of style, composers, and periods. It can help him to become his own teacher. And it can help him to apply his mental powers to the solving of practical keyboard problems, to a more perfect comprehension of technical truth. This in turn leads to even greater creative freedom and inspiration.

The organization of this study is a chronological one. An alternate scheme might well have been to treat each aspect of piano technique separately with an in-depth topical approach. However, an over-all unity of the field would not have been as well preserved. Various schools of technical thought from the harpsichord period to the present day are surveyed. An extensive amount of source material has purposely been quoted; the book is partially in the nature of a technical anthology. Hopefully such first-hand contact will be valuable to the reader and stimulate him to go directly to the original materials.

Because *Famous Pianists and Their Technique* is concerned with actually helping the student in his technical development, it differs very substantially from such recent books as Harold Schonberg's *The Great Pianists* and Arthur Loesser's *Men, Women, and Pianos*. There is a closer relationship to *A History of the Pianoforte and Pianoforte Players* by Oscar Bie, written nearly four generations ago.

While the inclusion of biographical data may add to the readability of the text, its presence should serve a far more useful purpose: to help explain the nature of the pianists' technical contributions to the field. Human personality is uniquely revealed in a performer's approach to the keyboard. Technique and personal interpretation are absolutely inseparable. The selection of pianists within the book was guided to a large extent by the significance and scope of the written record. It was impossible to include every important teacher and performer, especially those from the twentieth century, without the manuscript assuming encyclopedic dimensions. The summary chapter on harpsichord technique is basic to an understanding of the Mozart-Hummel school of piano technique. Furthermore, the teaching of François Couperin, C.P.E. Bach, and others of their era is of relevance to pianists today because of the renaissance of interest in the baroque keyboard instruments and because of the technical problems which arise from transcribing this pre-piano literature to the piano. When the technical treatises of such major performers and teachers as C.P.E. Bach, Couperin, Hummel, Czerny, Matthay, and the many others are viewed in retrospect and their lasting value fully assessed, one hopes that the masters of today will continue to leave written accounts of their views on piano technique and performance for future generations of students.

A project as extensive as this one could not have been possible without the encouragement and advice of many. Foremost thanks must go to Wheaton College and its administration for sustained and tangible assistance. The Wheaton College Alumni Association, so ably guided by senior director, Mr. Edward A. Coray, and executive director, Dr. John F. Taylor, provided several grants including two one-semester faculty research awards for the 1963-1964 and 1966-1967 school years. The Wheaton College Scholastic Honor Society also provided assistance. A debt of gratitude is freely acknowledged to the able musicians who read all or portions of the manuscripts and gave inspiration and helpful suggestions: Mr. Josef Raieff and Mr. Irwin Freundlich, my former teachers and members of the piano faculty at the Juilliard School in New York City; Dr. Vincent Persichetti, chairman of the composition department at the Juilliard School; Prof. Walter Robert, a member of the graduate faculty of the School of Music of Indiana University at Bloomington; musicologists Nicolas Slonimsky and Kurt Stone; Mr. Joseph Prostakoff, president of the Abby Whiteside Foundation, New York City; Dr. William S. Newman, director of graduate music studies at the University of North Carolina at Chapel Hill; Mr. Otto Ortmann, former director of the Peabody Conservatory of Music, Baltimore, Maryland; and the late Mr. Arnold Schultz, Chicago piano teacher and theorist.

Valued correspondence was also received from Dr. Halsey Stevens, chairman of the department of composition in the School of Performing Arts of the University of Southern California at Los Angeles; Mr. Gyorgy Sandor, director of the doctoral piano program at the School of Music of the University of Michigan at Ann Arbor, regarding study with his teacher Béla Bartók; and from

Prof. A.A. Nikolaev of the Moscow Conservatory concerning contemporary Russian study. Thanks are due to Dr. Clarence B. Hale, Dr. William A. Henning, Dr. Helmut Ziefle—all of the Wheaton College faculty, and Mrs. Carl Swenson for the English translations of a number of foreign sources; also to concert pianist Jacob Lateiner, Mrs. Ralph A. Johnson, and associates too numerous to mention. And, for assistance in obtaining research materials, appreciation must be expressed to the Newberry Library in Chicago, the New York Public Library, the Library of Congress in Washington, D.C., and the following school libraries: Wheaton College, the Eastman School of Music of the University of Rochester, the Peabody Conservatory of Music, the School of Music of Northwestern University, Evanston, Illinois, and the University of Iowa at Iowa City.

Mrs. Robert L. Goddard, secretary to the Vice President in charge of Academic Affairs at Wheaton College, spent many hours on her own time carefully checking and typing the manuscript for which I will always be most grateful. My wife Connie and son Reginald, Jr. assisted in many helpful ways in seeing that the project moved steadily forward. Words of personal appreciation would not be complete without directing thanks to Mr. Fernando Laires, of the piano faculties of the Peabody Conservatory of Music and the National Music Camp at Interlochen, Michigan, and Ms. Virginia Wheaton, my book editor at Robert B. Luce, Inc. Without their devoted efforts the publication of this book would not have been possible.

Finally, thanks must be extended to the following publishers for kindly granting permission to reproduce copyrighted material:

Abelard-Schumann, Ltd., New York — Cortot, Alfred. *In Search of Chopin*. 1952.

Associated Music Publishers, Inc., New York — Cowell, Henry. *Piano Music*. 1922, 1950.

Bärenreiter-Verlag, Kassel, West Germany — Harich-Schneider, Eta. *The Harpsichord*. 1954.

Belwin-Mills Publishing Corp., Melville, N.Y. — Maier, Guy. *The Piano Teacher's Companion*. 1963.

Boosey & Hawkes, Ltd., London — Matthay, Jessie Henderson. *The Life and Works of Tobias Matthay*. 1945.

Bosworth & Company, Ltd., London — Ching, James. *Piano Playing*. 1946.

— Coviello, Ambrose. *What Matthay Meant*. n.d.

Breitkopf & Härtel, Wiesbaden, West Germany — Couperin, François. *The Art of Playing the Harpsichord*. 1933.

Cambridge University Press, London — Harding, E.M. Rosamond. *A History of the Piano to 1851*. 1933.

Collet's Holdings, Ltd., London — Gát, Jozsef. *The Technique of Piano Playing*. 1974.

Curtis Publishing Co., Indianapolis — Chasins, Abram. "The Return of Horowitz." October 2, 1966.

J.M. Dent & Sons, Ltd., London — Levinskaya, Marie. *The Levinskaya System of Pianoforte Technique*. 1930.

E.P. Dutton & Co., Inc., New York — Ortmann, Otto. *The Physiological Mechanics of Piano Technique*. 1962, paperback.

Editio Musica Budapest, Budapest — von Dohnanyi, Ernst. *Essential Finger Exercises*. 1963.

Carl Fischer, Inc., New York — Schultz, Arnold. *The Riddle of the Pianist's Finger*. 1936.

Heinemann Educational Books, Ltd., London and McGraw-Hill, New York — Chopin, Fryderyk. *Selected Correspondence of Fryderyk Chopin*. 1962.

Macmillan, London and Basingstoke — Fielden, Thomas. The Science of Pianoforte Technique. 1927.

The New Yorker, New York — "Prepared Pianist," An Interview with John Cage, from *The Talk of the Town*, Feb. 24, 1945.

— Sargeant, Winthrop. "The Leaves of a Tree." Jan. 12, 1963.

W.W. Norton & Co., Inc., New York — Bach, C.P.E. *Essay on the True Art of Playing Keyboard Instruments*. Translated and edited by William J. Mitchell. 1949.

— *The Bach Reader*. Edited by Hans T. David and Arthur Mendel. 1945.

— *The Mussorgsky Reader*. Edited by Jay Leyda and Sergei Bertenson. 1947.

Novello & Co., Ltd., London and University of Washington Press, Seattle — Dolmetsch, Arnold. *Interpretation of Music of the Seventeenth and Eighteenth Centuries*. 1946.

Oxford University Press, London — Matthay, Tobias. *The Visible and Invisible in Pianoforte Technique*. 1932.

Pantheon Books, New York — Schumann, Robert. *On Music and Musicians*. Translated by Paul Rosenfeld and edited by Konrad Wolff. 1946.

C.F. Peters Corp., New York (Henmar Press, Inc.) — Cage, John. *Amores*. 1943. *Sonatas and Interludes*. 1960.

Philosophical Library, Inc., New York — Bonpensiere, Luigi. *New Pathways to Piano Technique*. 1953.

Philosophical Library, Inc., New York and Cassell and Co., Ltd., London — Sitwell, Sacheverell. *Liszt*. 1955.

Prentice-Hall, Inc., Englewood Cliffs, N.J. and Barrie and Rockliff, London — Jacob, H.E. *Felix Mendelssohn and His Times*. 1963.

Theodore Presser Co., Bryn Mawr, Pa. — Hofmann, Josef. *Piano Playing with Piano Questions Answered*. 1920.

— Lhevinne, Josef. *Basic Principles of Pianoforte Playing*. 1924.

The Etude (Presser) — Balogh, Erno. "Bartók, The Teacher—As I Knew Him." January 1956.

— Copp, Laura Remick. "Should the Piano Have Two Keyboards?" Interview with Winifred Christie. April 1931.

— Dumesnil, Maurice. "Teacher's Round Table." September 1949.

— Godowsky, Leopold. "The Best Method Is Eclectic." November 1933.

— Schmitz, E. Robert. "A Plea for the Real Debussy." December 1937.

Record Treasures, Inc., Hollywood, Calif. — Hall, Ben. Brochure accompanying record albums, "The Welte Legacy of Piano Treasures." 1963.

St. Martin's Press, Inc., New York — *The Letters of Beethoven*. Edited by Anderson. 1961.

— *The Letters of Mozart*. Edited by Anderson. 1966.

— Badura-Skoda, Eva and Paul. *Interpreting Mozart on the Keyboard*. 1962.

— Schnabel, Artur. *My Life and Music*. 1963.

— *Grove's Dictionary of Music and Musicians*. 5th edition by Eric Blom.

Saturday Review, New York — Holcman, Jan. "An Interview with Horowitz." April 20, 1960.

— Holcman, Jan. "Keyboard Left to Right." July 25, 1959.

G. Schirmer, Inc., New York — *Impressions of Contemporaries* — Beethoven. 1926.

— Whiteside, Abby. *The Pianist's Mechanism*. 1929.

— *The Musical Quarterly* (Schirmer).

— Bauer, Harold. "Self-Portrait of the Artist as a Young Man." April, 1943.

— Boise, Otis. "An American Composer Visits Liszt." July, 1957.

— Czerny, Carl. "Recollections from My Life." July, 1956.

— Parrish, Carl. "Criticisms of the Piano When It Was New." October, 1944.

Simon &Schuster, Inc., New York — Schonberg, Harold. *The Great Pianists*. 1963.

— Wierzynsky, Casamir. *The Life and Death of Chopin*. 1949.

Summy-Birchard Co., Evanston, Ill. — Kochevitsky, George. *The Art of Piano Playing*. 1967.

— *The Piano Teacher* (Summy-Birchard).

— Boissier, Auguste. "Liszt as Pedagogue." May-June, 1961. July-August, 1961.

— Dumesnil, Maurice. "Coaching with Debussy." Sept.-Oct., 1962.

— Goldberger, David. "Arthur Schnabel's Master Classes." March-April, 1963.

— Jonas, Oswald. "Beethoven's Piano Technique." Nov.-Dec., 1960.

— Schultz, Arnold. "Contest Standards—Are They Logical?" May-June, 1963.

Taplinger Publishing Co., Inc., New York—Freidheim, Arthur. *Life and Liszt; The Recollections of a Concert Pianist.* 1961.

Under the doctrine of fair use, the author also wishes to thank the following publishers for the use of further quotation material:

American Mercury, Torrance, Calif. — Ortmann, Otto. "Piano Technique in the Light of Experiment." December 1927.

Appleton-Century-Crofts, New York — Newcomb, Ethel. *Leschetizky as I Knew Him.* 1921.

Argo Record Co., Ltd., London — Gueroult, Denys. "The Golden Age of Piano Virtuosi." (Brochure with recordings of Ampico Piano Rolls) 1966.

The Atlantic Monthly Press, Boston and Harold Ober Associates, New York — Bowen, Catherine Drinker. *Free Artist: The Story of Anton and Nicholas Rubinstein.* 1939.

The Bobbs-Merrill Co., Inc., Indianapolis — Harding, Bertita. *Concerto, the Glowing Story of Clara Schumann.* 1961.

J.&W. Chester, Ltd., London — Safonov, Wassili. *New Formula for the Piano Teacher and Piano Student.* 1916.

Clavier Magazine, Evanston, Ill. — Fleischer, Leon. "About Practicing and Making Music." September 1963.

— Newman, William S. "On the Special Problems of High-Speed Playing." May-June 1963.

— Robert, Walter. "In Defense of Scales." Nov.-Dec. 1962.

Continental Book Co., Stockholm — Onren, Frank. *Maurice Ravel.* n.d.

Denman & Farrell, New York — Merrick, Frank. *Practising the Piano.* 1958.

J.M. Dent & Sons, Ltd., London and Farrar, Strauss and Giroux, New York — Demuth, Norman. *Ravel.* 1947.

Dial Press, Inc., New York — Schumann, Eugenie. *The Schumanns and Johannes Brahms.* 1927.

Dodd, Mead & Co., New York and Manne and Ross, New York — Thompson, Oscar. *Debussy, Man and Artist.* 1937.

Doubleday & Co., Inc., New York — Geiringer, Karl. *Haydn, A Creative Life in Music.* 1963.

— Slenczynska, Ruth. *Music at Your Fingertips.* 1961.

Dover Publications, Inc., New York — Mellers, Wilfred. *François Couperin and the French Tradition.* 1950.

Gerald Duckworth & Co. Ltd., London — Myers, Rollo H. *Ravel, Life and Works.* 1960.

Editions Salabert, Paris — Cortot, Alfred. *Rational Principles of Pianoforte Playing.* 1928.

— Long, Marguerite. *Le Piano.* 1959.

Foreign Languages Publishing House, Moscow — Prokofiev, S. *Autobiography, Articles, Reminiscences.* Edited by Shlifstein. c. 1954.

Harper & Brothers, New York — Newman, William S. *Pianist's Problems.* 1956.

Harvard University Press, Cambridge, Mass. — Bodky, Irwin. *The Interpretation of Bach's Keyboard Works.* 1960.

Harvill Press, London—Moreux, Serge. *Béla Bartók.* 1953.

Henry Holt & Co., New York — Seroff, Victor I. *Maurice Ravel.* 1953.

—Goss, Madeleine. *Bolero, Life of Maurice Ravel.* 1940.

Journal of the American Musicological Society — Parrish, Carl. "Haydn and the Piano." Fall 1948.

Journal of Research in Music Education — Syllabus of Special Classes in Piano for Music Schools approved by the Department of Education of the Ministry of Culture of the USSR, Moscow 1960. Fall 1964 reprint.

The Juilliard Review Annual 1966-1967, New York — Farmer, John. "Josef Lhevinne on Ampico Piano Rolls."

— Limon, José. "Dancers Are Musicians Are Dancers."

R. Julliard, Paris and J.M. Dent, London — Long, Marguerite. *Au piano avec Claude Debussy.* 1960.

— Long, Marguerite. *Au piano avec Gabriel Fauré.* 1963.

Kegan Paul, Trench, Trubner & Co., Ltd., London — Ortmann, Otto. *The Physical Basis of Piano Touch and Tone.* 1925.

Alfred A. Knopf, New York — Turner, Walter James. *Mozart, the Man and His Works.* 1938.

— Schenk, Erich. *Mozart and His Times.* 1959.

— Hutcheson, Ernest. *The Literature of the Piano.* 1948.

— Chasins, Abram. *Speaking of Pianists.* 1961.

— Niemann, Walter. *Brahms.* 1937.

London Daily Telegram, Feb. 7, 1931 — Description of Matthay student recital cited in Jessie Matthay: *The Life and Works of Tobias Matthay.*

London Sunday Telegram — Moisewitsch quote about Leschetizky in *The Piano Teacher* for January-February 1963.

Louisiana State University Press, Baton Rouge, Louisiana — Loggins, Vernon. *Where the World Ends.* 1958.

The Macmillan Co., New York — Liszt, Franz. *Life of Chopin.* 1963.

— Mason, Daniel Gregory. *Music in My Time and Other Reminiscences.* 1938. Estate of D.G. Mason, Stamford, Connecticut.

— Murdoch, William. *Chopin: His Life.* 1935. John Murray, London.

— Lockspeiser, Edward. *Debussy: His Life and Mind.* 1962.

Musical America, New York — Whiteside, Abby. "Successful Piano Teaching: The Physical Sensation Comes First." Dec. 15, 1951.

Music Teachers National Association Proceedings — Haake, Charles J. "Modern Piano Technic—How New Is It?" 1921.

— Ortmann, Otto. "Tone Quality and the Pianist's Touch." 1936.

— Schultz, Arnold. "The Riddle of the Pianist's Finger." 1936.

The Musician — Lhevinne, Josef. "Good Tone Is Born in the Player's Mind." July 1923.

— Brower, Harriette. "Where Technique and Mechanics Differ." September 1923.

— Hinderer, J.G. "We Attend Godowsky's Master Class." July 1933.

— Campbell, LeRoy B. "Wischnegradzky's Quarter-Toned Piano." May 1937.

— "New Piano Effects Created by Double-Keyboard." August 1930.

The New York Times — Kamm, Henry. "The Grande Dame of French Music." January 31, 1965.

— Schonberg, Harold C. "The Cluster Man." March 11, 1962.

The University of North Carolina Press, Chapel Hill — Schindler, Anton Felix. *Beethoven as I Knew Him.* 1966.

University of Oklahoma Press, Norman — Helm, Ernest Eugene. *Music at the Court of Frederick the Great.* 1960.

Oxford University Press, New York — Einstein, Alfred. *Schubert, a Musical Portrait.* 1951.

— *The Collected Correspondence and London Notebooks of Joseph Haydn.* 1959. Edited by H.C. Robbins Landon.

— Stevens, Halsey. *The Life and Music of Béla Bartók.* 1964. Included in Stevens is a letter from a collection entitled *Bartók Béla levelei.* Edited by János Demény. Published by Magyar Muvészeti Tanács in Budapest. 1948.

Philosophical Library, New York — Busoni, Ferruccio. *The Essence of Music and Other Papers.* 1957.

The Piano Quarterly, New York — Boulanger, Nadia. "Sayings of

Great Teachers." Winter 1958-1959.

— Lassimonne, Denise. "Tobias Matthay 1858-1945." Summer 1961.

Sir Isaac Pitman & Sons, Ltd., London — Harrison, Sydney. *Piano Technique.* 1953.

Prentice-Hall, Inc., Englewood Cliffs, N.J. — Galamian, Ivan. *Principles of Violin Playing and Teaching.* 1961.

Princeton University Press, Princeton, N.J. — Thayer, Alexander Wheelock. *The Life of Ludwig van Beethoven.* Edited by Elliott Forbes. 1964.

Proceedings of Royal Music Association, London — Fielden, Thomas. "The History of the Evolution of Pianoforte Technique." January 17, 1933.

Schroeder & Gunther, Inc., New York — Dumesnil, Maurice. *How to Play and Teach Debussy.* 1932.

Scientific American — No author listed. "Recording the Soul of Piano Playing." November 1927.

Charles Scribner's Sons, New York — Whiteside, Abby. *Indispensables of Piano Playing.* 1955.

Stanford University Press, Stanford, Calif. — Deutsch, Otto Erich. *Mozart, a Documentary Biography.* 1965.

— Nestyev, Israel V. *Prokofiev.* 1960.

— *American Composers on American Music,* a symposium edited by Henry Cowell, 1933.

Stein & Day, New York — Landowska, Wanda. *Landowska on Music.* 1964. © Denise Restout.

Steinway & Sons, New York — Steinway, Theodore E. *People and Pianos.* 1953.

Syracuse University Press, Syracuse, New York — Bacon, Ernst. *Notes on the Piano.* 1963.

Tudor Publishing Co., New York — Bidou, Henri. *Chopin.* 1927.

The University Society, New York — Pecher, W.F. "The Emotional Legacy of the Classical School: Reminiscences of the Teaching of Moscheles," from the *International Library of Music for Home and Studio.* Vol.III. 1948.

Neuman, Vitaly. Unpublished article on Isabelle Vengerova based on material from the Vengerova Music Archives. Translation and permission by Nicolas Slonimsky. c. 1968.

1. The Meaning of Technique

"Music is technique. It is the only aspect of music we can control." So states Nadia Boulanger. She believes that "one can only be free if the essential technique of one's art has been completely mastered."[1]

The thorough development of the basic physical tools has been of the most vital concern to keyboard performers and pedagogues across the centuries. It is hardly necessary to argue its importance. The historical piano technical literature abounds with admonitions from the great; and while they all stress the urgency of attaining this goal, they do not lose sight of the fact that there is something more. The technical objective at the same time becomes *the* means to a far greater end—the projection of a meaningful interpretation, the re-creation of fine piano literature with heart and mind, as well as the physical element, totally involved. The spiritual and the physical interweave, even interfuse. There cannot be a truly great performance without a masterful physical technique. It becomes the great liberating force for the pianist.

Note the following descriptions and definitions of technique scattered throughout the literature:

Tobias Matthay:

Technique means the power of expressing oneself musically . . . Technique is rather a matter of the Mind than of the "fingers". . . . To acquire Technique therefore implies that you must induce and enforce a particular mental-muscular association and co-operation for every possible musical effect.[2]

Josef Hofmann:

Technic represents the material side of art, as money represents the material side of life. By all means achieve a fine technic, but do not dream that you will be artistically happy with this alone. . . .

1

Technic is a chest of tools from which the skilled artisan draws what he needs at the right time for the right purpose. The mere possession of the tools means nothing; it is the instinct—the artistic intuition as to when and how to use the tools—that counts. It is like opening the drawer and finding what one needs at the moment.

There is a technic which liberates and a technic which represses the artistic self. All technic ought to be a means of expression. It is perfectly possible to accumulate a technic that is next to useless.[3]

Ferruccio Busoni:

NO, technique is not and never will be the Alpha and Omega of pianoforte playing any more than it is with any other art. Nevertheless, I certainly preach to my pupils: provide yourselves with technique and thoroughly too. Various conditions must be fulfilled in order to make a great artist, and it is because so few are able to fulfil them that a true genius is such a rarity.

Technique, perfect in and for itself, may be found in any well-constructed pianola. Nevertheless a great pianist must first of all be a great technician; but technique, which constitutes only a part of the art of the pianist, does not lie merely in fingers and wrists or in strength and endurance. Technique in the truer sense has its seat in the brain, and it is composed of geometry—an estimation of distance—and wise coordination. [4]

Thomas Fielden:

"Technique can be defined as the acquired skill in physical craft which an artist brings to bear in expressing his own spiritual individuality." [5]

Sidney Harrison:

"I am satisfied that we cannot make a sharp division between technique and interpretation. As the technique gains in command and confidence, it actually seems to prompt the imagination to bolder and bolder flights." [6]

Ivan Galamian:

Technique is the ability to direct mantally and to execute physically all of the necessary playing movements of left and right hands, arms, and fingers. A complete technique means the development of all the elements of . . . skill to the highest level. In short, it is the complete mastery over all of the potentialities of the instrument. It implies the ability to do justice, with unfailing reliability and control, to each and every demand of the most refined musical imagination. It enables the performer, when he has formed an ideal concept

2

of how any work should sound, to live up to this concept in actual performance. A technique which fulfills these ultimate requirements can be called an accomplished *interpretative technique*. It is the fundamental goal for which one must strive, because it, and it alone, opens the way to the highest artistic accomplishment.[7]

While the famous pianists and theorists of the past and present have all attempted to ascend Mt. Parnassus — some with greater vision than others — they have not agreed on the specific road to be used in acquiring a fine interpretative technique. Most, perhaps all, would agree in principle with Ivan Galamian, the master violin teacher, that "naturalness" should be the "first guiding principle" and that "'right' is only what is natural for the particular student, for only what is natural is comfortable and efficient."[8] He goes on to express his distress at the number of unnatural technical theories that have come and gone. The history of piano technique includes numerous examples of such methods, proclaimed the only right road—the natural way. They enjoyed great vogue but, under the test of time, fell into disrepute.

Naturalness is, without a doubt, the final determinant of a valid piano technique. Such a technique operates in harmony with the laws of nature—with a special regard for those laws concerned with physiological movement and muscular coordination. The great pianists, with their almost supernatural musical and physical endowments, often discovered them by instinct. But, throughout the course of piano technical history, those not so blessed frequently sought in vain for a natural technique that the great pianists themselves could not fully explain. Prejudiced against or simply indifferent to objective intellectual inquiry, the many followed systems erected upon preconceived technical notions—biased methods, contrary to natural law and distorted in perspective.

It is hoped that this historical study of the development of piano playing — through the examination of the contributions of many of the most famous pianists and influential theorists — will help to guide present-day pianists into a broader perspective of piano technique and into a sound recognition and understanding of its fundamental, "natural" principles.

Surely more than one system has effectively presented technical truth and no one method holds a patent right to truth. Perhaps it might be said that there is a more or less absolute body

3

of technical truth and each theorist and master teacher of integrity has tried in his own way to discover it, to make it his own, to pass it on to posterity. These means have differed greatly, but can be grouped freely into two broad categories. We can discern both an empirical and an analytical approach to piano technical knowledge. Too often the proponents of one have fought the other and failed to see that both are valid and even complementary.

Many of our finest master teachers are or have been empiricists. Mozart, Beethoven, Chopin, and Liszt all found technical truth through practical, intuitive experience. They passed it along without labeling it or exploring its ramifications. In more recent days Rosina and Josef Lhevinne, Artur Schnabel and Vladimir Horowitz could be cited, along with a large number of others, as being primarily empirical in their teaching. One of Schnabel's students wrote of his approach: "It was his constantly expressed belief that if you knew exactly what you wanted, you would find — invent if necessary — the means to achieve it."[9]

Another Schnabel student, Leon Fleisher, puts it in this way:

It's your musical ideas that form or decide for you what kind of technique you are going to use. In other words, if you are trying to get a certain sound, you just experiment around to find the movement that will get this sound. That is technique.[10]

After an interview with Horowitz, Jan Holcman discovered Horowitz's position:

It is a mistake to suppose that Horowitz has some mysterious "tricks" for learning technique. Despite long years spent with his instrument, he is not able to explain how he attained his own stupendous mastery, "as I can't explain how I learned languages." There are some hints, however. While studying with Blumenfeld (who in turn studied with Anton Rubinstein), Horowitz received no recipes for technique. The way to technical perfection led, in a significant measure, through various purely musical approaches.[11]

Sometimes the empiricists have a dread of any detailed analytical approach for fear it may spoil the freedom, the spontaneity, the freshness of the musical interpretation. Almost a hundred years before Horowitz, Modeste Mussorgsky (1839-1881) wrote along these lines:

Maybe I'm afraid of technique, because I'm poor at it? However, there are some who will stand up for me in art, and in this respect as well. For example, I cannot bear it when a

4

hostess serves a good pie she has prepared and, while we are eating, says: "A million *puds* of butter, five hundred eggs, a whole bed of cabbages, 150¼ fish. . . ." You are eating the pie and it tastes good, then you hear all about the kitchen . . . and well, the pie grows less tasty.[12]

Ernst Bacon, the contemporary composer and pianist, expresses a somewhat similar point of view today:

Learned books have been written on the *physical aspects* of piano playing, notably those of Matthay, Breithaupt, Ortmann, and Schultz, all of them rewarding to whomsoever is given to probing into the anatomy, physiology, neurology, and the mechanics of the arm and hand, as they affect piano technique. But while they may stimulate and satisfy "scientific" curiosity, they help the student of piano no more than would an analysis of the larynx, the lungs, the diaphragm, and the sinuses, help the singer to sing. In aiming to enlighten, too much mechanical self-knowledge mostly confuses. Piano playing will never be a science. If it were, it would cease to be an art.

A good rule is that *the teacher should introduce conscious devices only when they are needed,* just as the doctor prescribes medicines only when the body cannot take care of itself.[13]

The theorists Bacon quotes might well answer in rebuttal that, while it is perfectly true that piano playing will never be a science, there is no reason that its technique cannot be based upon scientific knowledge. And where do you draw the line in determining which of these facts should be utilized and which not? Why should not all pertinent information be employed by the mature student in developing an enlightened piano technique? Conscious, physiological introspection applied in the practice periods can surely lead to sound technical habits that do not need to be given a second thought in public performance. Many analytical treatises exist in the historical literature which may well speak for their rightful place in the student's consideration. Writing twenty-seven years before Bacon, Arnold Schultz summarized well the analytical point of view:

The general hostility to the idea of method derives much of its vitality, I believe, from a half-conscious and almost universal suspicion that there is a fundamental incompatability between a mind interested in the mechanical phases of playing and a mind filled with what is loosely known as musical temperament. There is a fear, furthermore, that a persistent

5

use of the reasoning mind in reference to the objective phenomena of technique results finally in the deterioration and atrophy of the subjective emotions upon which the interpreter's art depends. This is not, I believe firmly, too bald a statement of the case. It explains the widespread custom of camouflaging purely technical instruction with references to expression marks and with what are often entirely gratuitous rhetorical flights on the beauty of the music in hand.[14]

Schultz freely accepted the introspective nature of music—an objective, analytical view of technique is of vital importance, but must be complemented by a mind which continually "looks inward rather than outward."[15] He further wrote:

... And even so far as the thought processes involved in the analysis of technical touch-forms are concerned, I myself am anxious to concede—in fact, to insist—that few things are more grotesquely alien to the meaning of, say, the Beethoven *Appassionata* than the concept of a fixed fulcrum.

Nevertheless, anyone who has puzzled at all deeply over the personal aspects of his art knows the rich complexity of the problems he encounters and the relative uselessness of broad distinctions. It is one thing to recognize the extremely objective personality and to dismiss him from music, and it is another thing to assert that all personalities showing strong objective interests are unadapted to musical expression. It is one thing to say that scientific curiosity is vastly different from subjective sensibility, and quite another to imply that an extreme curiosity and an abundant sensibility cannot coexist in the same personality. If one's own intuitions do not rebel, then the facts of history afford the proof against too facile thinking. Leonardo da Vinci was not only a painter, a sculptor, and an architect, but he was also an engineer; and although the spiritual subtlety of his "Mona Lisa" has overshadowed his mechanical achievements in popular fame, nevertheless he is recognized as the first to have formulated the laws of the lever—laws which are integral to the analysis of piano technique which follows. The giant among German literary figures, Goethe, made valuable contributions to the fields of botany, anatomy, and physics, some of which he himself regarded as equal in importance to his poetic achievement. Closer to home is Johann Sebastian Bach, who, in his invention of "equal temperament" for instruments of fixed intonation, surely served his art as a scientist; and Alexander Borodin, whose name remains almost as important in the annals of chemistry as it does in the history of music. It

6

would be folly to assume that the creativeness of these men was impaired by their scientific activity; it would be only open-mindedness to assume that they were the better artists for it.[16]

In the chapters which follow, both empirical and analytical technical approaches are thoroughly explored and shown to be entirely compatible. It is hoped that the reader's desire may be strengthened to study in greater depth and breadth the original source writings sampled in these pages.

Notes

[1] Nadia Boulanger, "Sayings of Great Teachers," *The Piano Quarterly*, No. 26, Winter 1958-1959, p. 26.

[2] Tobias Matthay, *The Visible and Invisible in Pianoforte Technique being a digest of the author's technical teachings up to date*, p.3.

[3] Josef Hofmann, *Piano Playing with Piano Questions Answered*, pp. 80-81.

[4] Ferruccio Busoni, *The Essence of Music and Other Papers*, p. 80.

[5] Thomas Fielden, *The Science of Pianoforte Technique*, p. 162.

[6] Sidney Harrison, *Piano Technique*, p. 57.

[7] Ivan Galamian, *Principles of Violin Playing and Teaching*, p. 5.

[8] *Ibid.*, p. 1.

[9] David Goldberger, "Artur Schnabel's Master Classes," *The Piano Teacher*, Vol. 5, No. 4, March-April, 1963, p.6.

[10] Leon Fleisher, "About Practicing and Making Music," *Clavier*, Vol. II, No. 4, September 1963, p.12.

[11] Jan Holcman, "An Interview with Horowitz," *The Saturday Review of Literature*, Vol. XLIII, No. 18, April 30, 1960, p.60.

[12] Jay Ledya and Sergei Bertensson, eds., *The Mussorgsky Reader*, p. 192.

[13] Ernst Bacon, *Notes on the Piano*, p. 77.

[14] Arnold Schultz, *The Riddle of the Pianist's Finger and Its Relationship to a Touch-Scheme*, p. vi.

[15] *Ibid.*, p. vii.

[16] *Ibid.*, pp. vii-viii.

2. The Early Clavier Methods

Before the technique of the early piano can be adequately studied, it is mandatory to investigate that of its predecessors, the harpsichord and the clavichord. In fact, the clavier touch was transferred directly to the early piano. The harpsichord, which achieved its greatest influence and usage during the eighteenth century, has an action in which the string, when the key is depressed, is plucked by a plectrum attached to an upright jack. The plectrum, also called the quill, early was made from the quills of bird feathers and even from small pieces of metal. Leather has been most frequently used, even down to the present day. Recently plastic has been used with considerable success. The tone quality will vary with the material used.

The point of tone is reached very quickly in the key's descent—a third to a half of the way down. Little force is needed to pluck the string; the action of the fingers is adequate for most of the literature. If two or more sets of strings are coupled to the same manual or keyboard, more plectra will have to be activated simultaneously. Thus more resistance will need to be overcome in the touch. Volume is largely predetermined by the registration and the construction of the instrument and cannot be significantly increased by the application of greater force. Some hand and arm movement is needed in chord production, but with no more of the weight of the arms brought to bear than is necessary. Too much force, even with a finger action, is undesirable because of the loss of sensitivity and control and also because of the resulting percussive noises which are more noticeable than those heard in the piano action. The arm needs to be suspended over the keyboard in a weightless manner. It serves as a stationary base for the action of the fingers. The movement of the arm, necessary in controlling horizontal placement of the hand, should be executed in a quiet, graceful, and curvilinear manner.

The nature of the harpsichord tone — bright, shimmering, incisive, well-defined, and more easily sustained than generally realized — requires the most careful attention to articulation. Keyboard music of the Elizabethan and baroque periods, with its polyphonic lines and embellishing features, is perfectly suited to the harpsichord, in tone and in action. There is no room at all for vagueness of touch—every tone stands out in sharp relief. A legato is completely controlled by the fingers—the slightest deficiency is immediately evident. Varying the length of sound duration of individual notes can produce a sense of accent or increasing intensity within a tonal line. The instrument has an infinite capacity for subtle rubato and this should be achieved with the lightest possible degree of pressure in the finger tips. The fingers must be held close to the keys and move in as precise a manner as possible. The plectrum action against the string can be felt in the keyboard touch to a very remarkable degree and in itself presents a great challenge to the performer.

The little sister of the harpsichord, the clavichord, reached its greatest popularity a century earlier than the harpsichord. It was especially prized in Germany and greatly loved by Johann Sebastian Bach. The clavichord's small, intimate tone suited it ideally to the home. Its lovely "beseelter Ton," soulful sound and tender expressive quality, is produced by small brass tangents or wedges which press against the strings and vibrate them in much the same manner as a violinist's bow presses against the string. Wanda Landowska described its tone as "a timid sound, melancholy and infinitely sweet."[1] The tone can be sustained and even renewed with a tremolo-like finger pressure. This haunting effect, which will cause a slight variance in the pitch, is termed *Bebung.* Since the dynamic intensity of the tone may be controlled by the fingers from the softest degree of pianissimo to a moderate mezzo forte, its touch is even more sensitive than that of the harpsichord. The early writers advocated that harpsichordists perfect their technique at the clavichord: the subtle coloring that they would be able to achieve would be most beneficial to their musicianship. Eta Harich-Schneider commented that "It is not that the clavichord *technique* should be transplanted, but rather that the quality of tone colour of this extremely rich and sensitive instrument should *nourish the creative imagination of the harpsichordist.*"[2] Pianists today should likewise perfect and discipline their touch, as well as sharpen their listening powers, by working at both the harpsichord and the clavichord.

10

There is great value in studying what the clavier writers had to say about the technique and performance of their instruments. The earliest clavier method of any real importance, *Il Transilvano* by Girolamo Diruta, was written in Venice in about 1600. He wrote:

The rule of how to play with dignity and grace is based on certain main points. . . . The first thing is that the organist should sit with his body exactly before the middle of the keyboard, the second that he must not make gestures or movements with his body, but hold himself, chest and head, erect and poised. The third thing is to know that the arm leads the hand, and the hand must be held strictly on the same level as the arm, neither higher nor lower. The fourth, that the fingers stand all evenly on the keyboard, although slightly arched. . . . Besides all this the hand must be placed on the keyboard with ease and facility — otherwise the fingers cannot move with agility and promptitude.... Let the arm guide the hand — this is the most important rule before all the others.[3]

And lastly, the keys should be gently depressed, never struck, and the fingers withdrawn in lifting the key. Although these precepts may appear of little or no moment, they are nevertheless of very great utility in rendering the harmony smooth and sweet, and freeing the organist from all impediments in his playing.

The discussion is in the form of a dialogue and the pupil, Il Transilvano, replies:

I allow that these rules may be useful, but what can that do to the Harmony, whether your head be straight or awry, or your fingers flat or curved?

Diruta answers: They do not affect directly the Harmony, but the gravity and elegance of the organist: they are the cause of that admirable combination of charm and grace so noticeable in Signor Claudio Merulo. He who twists and turns about shall be likened to the ridiculous actor in the Comedy. Besides, the work of such a man will not succeed as it might; he prefers his own caprice, and scorns true art, rendering difficult many things which would otherwise be easy. . . .

And how to hold the hands lightly and loosely on the keys, I shall give you an example: when you want to give an angry slap, you use strength; but if you mean to caress, you use no strength, but on the contrary relax your hand as for fondling a babe.[4]

Diruta's remarks were directed to harpsichordists as well as

11

organists, and were no doubt badly needed as the harpsichord and its performers in Italy at this time were not nearly as advanced as those in England. The English could boast of such incomparable musicians as William Byrd, John Bull, and Orlando Gibbons; highly refined instruments; and a golden era of magnificent original literature.

The Italian harpsichord was used largely to accompany dancing. In order to produce more sound, its plectra were more rugged in character. The tendency was to strike the keys in rough fashion rather than to use a gentle pressure after the manner of the English virginalists. Even in this early period the matter of keyboard attack was a vital issue. In a lively discussion with his student, Diruta questioned the ability of his contemporary virginalists to play in a refined manner:

Diruta: The Council of Trent wisely forbade the playing in churches of "passemezzi" and other light dances, and all lascivious songs. The profane should not be mixed with the sacred, and such performances should not be tolerated on the organ. If by any chance some dance-player adventures to try something musical on the organ, he cannot refrain from striking the keys, whilst on the contrary an organist finds no difficulty in playing dance-tunes on the virginals.

Transilvano: But I cannot see why dance-players could not succeed in playing music on the organ whilst organists can play dance-tunes well?

Diruta: . . . Because the Sonatori who want to play music on the organ have to observe all the rules I have given about keeping the hands quiet and relaxed, holding the notes, and so forth, which are unfamiliar to them; whilst the organist who wishes to play dances can easily make an exception to the rules, especially that about the jumping of the hands and the striking of the keys; and in due reason he should do so, for the jacks and quills act better when struck, and this manner of playing is required by the particular style of the dances.[5]

The early methods allotted much space to fingering. A major concern was determining which were the "good" or accented notes. Diruta explained the Italian system of fingering, which was also shared by the early Germans:

Now it remains for me to say which are the good and the bad fingers, which will similarly play the good and the bad notes, for this is as necessary to the organist as to the virginal player. This knowledge is really the most important thing of all. There are five fingers in each hand, the thumb being

12

accounted the first, and the little finger the fifth. The first plays a bad note (*noto cattivo*), the second a good note (*noto buono*), the third a bad note, the fourth a good note, and the fifth a bad note. The second, third and fourth fingers do most of the work; what I say about one hand applies equally to the other.[6]

This meant that pairs of fingers such as 2 3 and 3 4, were used many times in succession with the resulting crossing over of the fingers. The use of the thumb and fifth fingers was largely avoided. Although such patterns strike us as awkward today, considerable agility must have been developed.

The English virginalists of the late Renaissance and early baroque did not agree with the Italian view of fingering. In fact, they advocated an opposing scheme: the thumb, third, and fifth fingers were considered to be the better fingers.

In comparing the two systems, Arnold Dolmetsch stated:

At first sight there does not seem to be much difference between the Italian fingering and that of the English virginalists. . . . In the right hand we have the same crossing of the third finger over the fourth in ascending, and of the third over the second in descending. But in reality there is a radical opposition between the two systems. It is possible, in theory at least, to cross the fingers smoothly and evenly, just as in theory the fingers of the modern pianist are supposed to be all equally strong and independent. But in practice there is a strong tendency . . . to induce wrong accents by the instinctive shortening of the fourth finger note, ascending, and the second finger note, descending. No doubt it suited the music, or the music suited it. But play the same passage with the English fingering, and . . . it rings right and true, both for rhythm and phrasing, and naturally falls in with the "Harmonic System of Fingering."[7]

Many of these English fingerings can be seen in the famous *Fitzwilliam Virginal Book*. The superiority of English fingering was no doubt an important factor contributing to the supremacy of English virginalists. The influence of the English school was so great that it was widely felt in Germany in the seventeenth century—and even touched J.S. Bach.

But after Diruta, the important clavier books are found at the beginning of the eighteenth century in France at a time when the harpsichord there was reaching its zenith. We first meet with Michel de Saint Lambert's *Les Principes du Clavecin* (*The Principles of the Harpsichord*), published in Paris in 1702, and then

L'Art de Toucher le Clavecin (*The Art of Playing the Harpsichord*)
by François Couperin (1668-1733), also first issued in Paris in 1716.
St. Lambert commented on keyboard posture:

> The hands must stand parallel to the keyboard, which
> means that they must not have any inclination to fall, either to
> one side or the other. The fingers should be curved and stand
> all in line, in accordance with the length of the thumb. The
> wrist should be on the same level as the elbow, which position
> is achieved by adjusting the player's seat to the proper height.
> Palm, wrist, and elbow must form one straight line — they
> must be exactly on the same level.[8]

This position calls for a fairly high seat and helps to free the
elbow. Harich-Schneider amplified St. Lambert's instructions:
"The weight of the elbow, or its stiffness, must not by any means
hinder the agility of wrist and hand."[9]

The *Art of Playing the Harpsichord* by Couperin is a major
work in the literature. The first English translation, by Mevanwy
Roberts, became available in 1933. In the preface, written by Anna
Linde, we read of the tardy fulfillment of a Couperin request:

> The lasting significance of François Couperin as a com-
> poser, which rests on the keyboard style peculiar to himself, is
> fully equalled by his work, "The Art of Playing the Harpsi-
> chord." With this he gave to the musical world the first real
> "Pianoforte Tutor."
>
> The translation carried out today, after more than 200
> years, Couperin's own wish: "I wish someone would take the
> trouble to translate us for the benefit of foreigners, and would
> thus give them the possibility of judging for themselves of the
> excellence of our instrumental music."[10]

Couperin, sometimes called "le Grand," was of excellent
musical lineage. He early proved himself by becoming one of the
royal court organists and teacher of the royal children while still in
his twenties. Couperin ranks as one of France's greatest harpsichordists and composers of harpsichord music, much of it pro-
grammatic in character and romantic in spirit.

Every student of the piano should own his treatise on harpsichord playing. Although somewhat rambling in character (and
because of that delightful reading), it contains much valuable
material. The first section gives numerous study suggestions.
Couperin believed a child should begin study at six or seven, as the
hands are more easily molded at that age. He stated:

People who begin late, or who have been badly taught must be careful; for as the sinews may have become hardened, or they may have got into bad habits, they should make their fingers flexible, or get some one else to do it for them, before sitting down to the Harpsichord; that is to say, they should pull, or get someone to pull their fingers in all directions; that, moreover, will stir up their minds, and they will have a feeling of greater freedom.[11]

This may well be the first reference to the use of hand gymnastics as a part of technical preparation. Regarding position, Couperin wrote:

To be seated at the correct height, the under-surface of the elbows, wrists, and fingers should all be on one level: therefore a chair must be chosen which will allow this rule to be observed.

It will be necessary to place some additional support under the feet of young people, varying in height as they grow, so that their feet, not dangling in the air, may keep the body properly balanced.

The distance at which an adult should be seated from the keyboard is about nine thumb-lengths (inches), measured from the waist, and less in proportion for young people.

The centre of the body and that of the keyboard should correspond.

When seated at the Harpsichord, the body should be turned very slightly to the right, the knees not pressed too closely together; the feet should be kept side by side, but the right foot, especially, well out. . . .

If a pupil holds one wrist too high in playing, the only remedy that I have found, is to get someone to hold a small flexible stick which is passed over the faulty wrist, and at the same time under the other wrist. If the defect is the opposite, the reverse must be done. But this stick must not absolutely hinder the freedom of the player. Little by little this fault will correct itself; and this invention has been of great service to me.[12]

Here also is one of the first references in pedagogic history to the use of mechanical aids in teaching position at the keyboard. It sounds more sensible than the contrivances which were used a century later by Logier and Kalkbrenner.

Couperin was very conscious of appearance:

With regard to making grimaces, it is possible to break oneself of this habit by placing a mirror on the reading desk of the Spinet or Harpsichord. . . . It is better and more seemly

15

not to beat time with the head, the body, nor with the feet. One should have an air of ease at one's Harpsichord; not gazing too fixedly at one object, nor yet looking too vague; in short, look at the assembled company, if there be one, as if not occupied with anything else. This advice is only for those who play without the help of their books.[13]

For the young he recommended using a one-keyboard, lightly quilled harpsichord because "dexterity in execution depends much more on suppleness and great freedom of the fingers than on force."[14] Using two keyboards in the beginning would cause the hands to be badly placed and result in a hardness of touch. He noted also that

Delicacy of touch depends also on holding the fingers as close to the keys as possible. It is reasonable to assume (apart from experience) that a hand falling from a height, gives a sharper blow than if it strikes from quite near, and that the quill will produce a harder tone from the string.[15]

Although always concerned about achieving musical ends, Couperin was not averse to practicing pure technique:

I have always given my pupils little finger-exercises to play, either passages, or strings of shakes or tremolos of various intervals, beginning with the simplest, and on the most natural intervals, and gradually leading them to the quickest and to those most transposed. These little exercises, which cannot be too varied or too multiplied, are, at the same time, material all ready to be put in place, and may prove serviceable on many occasions.[16]

Later he included a series of *Evolutions* or *Little Exercises for Forming the Hands*. Near the close of the book are eight excellent preludes which he deemed useful for loosening the fingers and "in trying over instruments upon which one has not yet practiced."[17]

It is significant that the larger portion of Couperin's method book is devoted to the matter of fingering. Fielden felt that this emphasis, also shared by other of Couperin's contemporaries, shows that the early pedagogues were more concerned "with the mental side of technique than with the mechanical, and that they considered that a knowledge of the keyboard and also of harmony was a very important part of training."[18] Couperin fingered in great detail numerous excerpts from his major harpsichord works, thus providing insight into the best performance practices of the period. He did not hesitate to caution that as "the better fingers"[19] improve in the practice of embellishments they should be employed

16

in preference to "the poorer ones, without any regard for the old way of fingering, which must be given up in favour of the proficiency in execution expected today."[20]

Most significant was his direct repetition of the same finger—on the last note of one phrase and the beginning note on the next, making correct phrasing inevitable. Here was a remarkable correlation between fingering and phrasing, just as was so clearly evident among the English virginalists in the previous century. Couperin also used the third and fourth fingers (or the second and third) several times in succession—and with excellent results. The thumb was frequently employed, but not as a pivot in scale passages. Couperin achieved a fine legato through the frequent use of organ-type finger substitutions.

Wilfred Mellers commented that Couperin's fingering

> ... clearly establishes the principle of finger-substitution to secure a legato. Moreover, we must remember that the fingering and the phrasing of old music were interdependent. It may be more difficult to play Couperin's music with his own than with modern fingering, but the performer who does so can be sure that he will be phrasing the music correctly. Couperin's fingering is a means of revealing as clearly as possible the musical sense of a composition.[21]

Couperin was more than mere technician. His treatise is an authoritative guide to the ornamentation practices of his period. It also contains interpretative suggestions in keeping with his own advice, ". . . let the style of playing be directed by the 'bon-gout' (good taste) of today, which is incomparably purer than the old."[22]

The writings of Jean Philippe Rameau (1683-1764) followed shortly after those of Couperin. A leading composer and theorist of his day, he was most exacting and demanding in his approach to the harpsichord. Concerned with securing a true harpsichord touch, Rameau wrote in his *Méthode sur la Mécanique des doigts sur le Clavessin* (Paris, 1724):

> Perfection of touch results from proper finger action. Any ability can be acquired by simple mechanical practice, cleverly done. The ability to walk or run derives from the flexibility of the knee-joint; the ability to play the harpsichord from the flexibility of the fingers at their roots. A larger movement is only admissible when a smaller is not sufficient: so long as a finger can reach a key without any other movement of the hand than a slight opening or stretching, one is not allowed to make a movement which goes beyond what is

17

necessary. Every finger must preserve its own particular action, independent of the rest, so that even when the hand is moved to a more distant part of the keyboard, the striking finger none the less must fall upon the key solely from its own independent action. Observe a great regularity in the finger movements, and before everything, never be rash and uncontrolled, because velocity and speed are attained only by the practice of regularity. When you practice trills, lift the fingers alternately as high as possible, but the more you advance in training, the less you need this lifting and finally it is transformed into an easy and rapid action.[23]

In a later treatise published in Paris in 1760, *Code de Musique Pratique*, Rameau gave further technical description with emphasis on freedom and suppleness.

Contemporary with these illustrious Frenchmen was the greatest musician of his time, the German Johann Sebastian Bach (1685-1750). By far the outstanding organist of his day, there were few who could rival him on the harpsichord — Scarlatti being a notable exception. Bach has left us little direct comment. What we know regarding his own performances and his thoughts on technique must be gotten largely from his associates and particularly his son, Carl Philipp Emanuel.

All who heard him were astounded at his gift of improvisation and his complete ease and fluency at any keyboard. Johann Matthias Gesner in 1738 commented that

> . . . either playing our clavier, which is many citharas in one, with all the fingers of both hands, or running over the keys of the instrument of instruments [the organ]. . . with both hands and, at the utmost speed, with his feet, producing by himself the most various and at the same time mutually agreeable combinations of sounds in orderly procession.[24]

He also very significantly remarked that Bach was "full of rhythm in every part of his body."[25] Johann Adolph Scheibe, the year before, reacted similarly:

> One is amazed at his ability and one can hardly conceive how it is possible for him to achieve such agility, with his fingers and with his feet, in the crossings, extensions, and extreme jumps that he manages, without mixing in a single wrong tune, or displacing his body by any violent movement.[26]

Joachim Quantz without a doubt referred to Bach when he wrote the following description of harpsichord technique in his *Versuch:*

Experience proves that if two musicians of unequal skill perform on the same harpsichord, the tone will be much better with the better player. There can be no other cause for this than the difference in the touch, and on this account it is necessary that all the fingers should act not only with the same strength, but with the right strength; that the strings be allowed sufficient time to vibrate without impediment, and that the keys be not depressed too slowly, but, on the contrary, with a certain snap which sets the strings vibrating for a long time. . . . It is important to see whether one finger presses more strongly than another, which can come from the habit of curving some fingers more than others. This not only causes unevenness in the tone, but it prevents the passages from being round, distinct, and agreeable; in this manner, should a rapid scale occur, the fingers will do no more than tumble upon the keys. If, on the contrary, the habit has been acquired of curving the fingers equally, we shall not fall so easily into this fault. Moreover, in the performance of such rapid passages, the fingers should not be suddenly raised; their tips should rather be slid up to the forward end of the key, and thus withdrawn, for this will ensure the clearest possible execution of the runs. My opinion in this is based on the example of one of the most highly skilled harpsichord players, who followed this method, and taught it.[27]

In an authoritative obituary thought to have been written by C.P.E. Bach, with the assistance of Johann Friedrich Agricolo, we have this statement:

How strange, how new, how beautiful were his ideas in improvising. How perfectly he realized them! All his fingers were equally skillful; all were capable of the most perfect accuracy in performance. He had devised for himself so convenient a system of fingering that it was not hard for him to conquer the greatest difficulties in the most flowing facility. Before him, the most famous clavier players in Germany and other lands had used the thumb but little.[28]

As related earlier, this was particularly true in Italy and to a large extent in the other European countries as well. Although they may not have originated the system of fingering they employed, Bach and his son (in his *Essay*) did more than any other to establish the function of the thumb in its pivotal capacity in our modern scale and arpeggio fingerings. Philipp Emanuel gave his father full credit:

My late father told me about having heard great men in his

youth who did not use the thumb except when it was necessary for large stretches. Since he lived at a time in which there gradually took place a quite remarkable change in musical taste, he was obliged to think out a much more complete use the fingers, and especially to use the thumb (which apart from other uses is quite indispensable especially in the difficult keys) in such a manner as Nature, as it were, wishes to see it used. Thus it was raised suddenly from its former idleness to the position of the principal finger.[29]

The first important biography of Johann Sebastian Bach was published by Johann Nicolaus Forkel (1749-1818) in 1802 and appeared in an English translation by an unknown Mr. Stephenson in 1820. Forkel was personally acquainted with both Philipp Emanuel and Wilhelm Friedemann Bach and based much of what he wrote upon information received from them. His chapters on "Bach the Clavier Player," and "Bach the Teacher," are valuable source materials. Writing fifty-two years after Bach's death, Forkel could well have colored some of the details, yet it is the best early material we possess.

Forkel described Bach's finger technique in the following paragraphs:

According to Sebastian Bach's manner of placing the hand on the keys, the five fingers are bent so that their points come into a straight line, and so fit the keys, which lie in a plane surface under them, that no single finger has to be drawn nearer when it is wanted, but every one is ready over the key which it may have to press down. What follows from this manner of holding the hand is:

(1) That no finger must fall upon its key, or (as also often happens) be thrown on it, but only needs to be *placed* upon it with a certain consciousness of the internal power and command over the motion.

(2) The impulse thus given to the keys, or the quantity of pressure, must be maintained in equal strength, and that in such a manner that the finger be not raised perpendicularly from the key, but that it glide off the forepart of the key, by gradually drawing back the tip of the finger towards the palm of the hand.

(3) In the transition from one key to another, this gliding off causes the quantity of force or pressure with which the first tone has been kept up to be transferred with the greatest rapidity to the next finger, so that the two tones are neither disjoined from each other nor blended together.

20

The touch is, therefore, as Carl Philipp Emanuel Bach says, neither too long nor too short, but just what it ought to be.[30]

Earlier, Forkel had referred to C.P.E. Bach's statement in his *Essay:*

Some persons play too stickily, as if they had glue between their fingers; their touch is too long, because they keep the keys down beyond the time. Others have attempted to avoid this defect and play too short, as if the keys were burning hot. This is also a fault. The middle path is the best.[31]

Continuing his description, Forkel wrote at length:

The advantages of such a position of the hand and of such a touch are very various, not only on the clavichord, but also on the pianoforte and the organ. I will here mention only the most important.

(1) The holding of the fingers bent renders all their motions easy. There can therefore be none of the scrambling, thumping, and stumbling which is so common in persons who play with their fingers stretched out, or not sufficiently bent.

(2) The drawing back of the tips of the fingers and the rapid communication, thereby effected, of the force of one finger to that following it produces the highest degree of clearness in the expression of the single tones, so that every passage performed in this manner sounds brilliant, rolling, and round, as if each tone were a pearl. It does not cost the hearer the least exertion of attention to understand a passage so performed.

(3) By the gliding of the tip of the finger upon the key with an equable pressure, sufficient time is given to the string to vibrate; the tone, therefore, is not only improved, but also prolonged, and we are thus enabled to play in a singing style and with proper connection, even on an instrument so poor in tone as the clavichord is.

All this together has, besides, the very great advantage that we avoid all waste of strength by useless exertion and by constraint in the motions. In fact, Sebastian Bach is said to have played with so easy and small a motion of the fingers that it was hardly perceptible. Only the first joints of the fingers were in motion; the hand retained even in the most difficult passages its rounded form; the fingers rose very little from the keys, hardly more than in a shake [trill], and when one was employed, the other remained quietly in its position. Still less did the other parts of his body take any share in his play, as happens with many whose hand is not light enough.

A person may, however, possess all these advantages, and

yet be a very indifferent performer on the clavier, in the same manner as a man may have a very clear and fine pronunciation, and yet be a bad declaimer or orator. To be an able performer, many other qualities are necessary, which Bach likewise possessed in the highest perfection.

The natural difference between the fingers in size as well as strength frequently seduces performers, wherever it can be done, to use only the stronger fingers and neglect the weaker ones. Hence arises not only an inequality in the expression of several successive tones, but even the impossibility of executing certain passages where no choice of fingers can be made. Johann Sebastian Bach was soon sensible of this; and, to obviate so great a defect, wrote for himself particular pieces, in which all the fingers of both hands must necessarily be employed in the most various positions in order to perform them properly and distinctly. By this exercise he rendered all his fingers, of both hands, equally strong and serviceable, so that he was able to execute not only chords and all running passages, but also single and double shakes with equal ease and delicacy. He was perfectly master even of those passages in which, while some fingers perform a shake, the others, on the same hand, have to continue the melody.[32]

It may well be that Bach preferred the clavichord. The piano, even though it was making its way, was still too new and unrefined an instrument to please him fully. Forkel pointed out:

He therefore considered the clavichord as the best instrument for study, and, in general, for private musical entertainment. He found it the most convenient for the expression of his most refined thoughts, and did not believe it possible to produce from any harpsichord or pianoforte such a variety in the gradations of tone as on this instrument.[33]

How much teaching Bach did at the harpsichord and clavichord we do not know. His most famous pupils were his children Carl Philipp Emanuel and Wilhelm Friedemann. The *Little Clavier Books* for Anna Magdalena Bach and Wilhelm Friedemann, and the *Two and Three Part Inventions* provide ample evidence that he believed in thorough musical preparation. The preface to the *Inventions* (1722) in Bach's own words is sufficient proof:

A proper introduction, whereby lovers of the Clavier and especially those with thirst for true knowledge are shown a clear way not only (1) of learning to play clearly in two voices, but (2) also with further progress to proceed with three obligato parts correctly and well—at the same time not only receiving good ideas (i.e., inventions) but also utilizing them for the development of a cantabile style of playing and for the procurement of a thorough foretaste of composition.[34]

In the chapter entitled "Bach the Teacher," Forkel tells us:

The first thing he did was to teach his scholars his peculiar mode of touching the instrument, of which we have spoken before. For this purpose, he made them practice, for months together, nothing but isolated exercises for all the fingers of both hands, with constant regard to this clear and clean touch. Under some months, none could get excused from these exercises; and, according to his firm opinion, they ought to be continued, at least, for from six to twelve months. But if he found that anyone, after some months of practice, began to lose patience, he was so obliging as to write little connected pieces, in which those exercises were combined together. Of this kind are the six little Preludes for Beginners, and still more the fifteen two-part Inventions. He wrote both down during the hours of teaching, and, in doing so, attended only to the momentary want of the scholar. But he afterwards transformed them into beautiful, expressive little works of art. With his exercise of the fingers, either in single passages or in little pieces composed on purpose, was combined the practice of all the ornaments in both hands.[35]

Two other outstanding harpsichordists of Bach's time were Domenico Scarlatti (1685-1757) and George Frederick Handel (1685-1759). Judging from the color and virtuosity, the wide range of skips, and the many chordal and figural devices of his own keyboard works, we can conclude that Scarlatti's technique was extraordinary. He must have used much arm activity as well as a quiet hand and finger position. His playing overwhelmed a traveling Irish harpsichordist by the name of Thomas Roseingrave (1690-1766). Charles Burney, the famous eighteenth century music historian, related Roseingrave's reaction:

Being arrived at Venice on his way to Rome, as he himself told me, he was invited, as a stranger and a virtuoso, to an academia at the house of a nobleman, where, among others, he was requested to sit down to the harpsichord and favour the company with a toccata, as a specimen *della sua virtu*. And, he says, "Finding myself rather better in courage and finger than usual, I exerted myself, my dear friend, and fancied, by the applause I received, that my performance had made some impression on the company." After a cantata had been sung by a scholar of Fr. Gasparini, who was there to accompany her, a grave young man dressed in black and in a black wig, who had stood in one corner of the room, very quiet and attentive while Roseingrave played, being asked to sit down to the harpsichord, when he began to play, Rosy said, he thought ten hundred devils had been at the instrument; he never had heard such passages of execution and effect before. The performance so far surpassed his own, and every degree of perfection to which he thought it possible he should ever arrive, that, if he had been in sight of any instrument with which to have done the deed, he should have cut off his own fingers. Upon enquiring the name of this extraordinary performer, he was told that it was Domenico Scarlatti, son of the celebrated Cavalier Alessandro Scarlatti. Roseingrave declared he did not touch an instrument himself for a month...[36]

Although Handel, the writer of many excellent harpsichord suites, did not possess J.S. Bach's all-encompassing harpsichord technique, his playing still was excellent enough for Burney again to remark, "His touch was so smooth and the tone of the instrument so cherished that his fingers seemed to grow to the keys. They were so curved and compact that when he played no motion and scarcely the fingers themselves could be discovered."[37]

J. Mainwaring compared the harpsichord styles of Scarlatti and Handel when he wrote in 1760 in his *Memoirs* of Handel:

Though no two persons ever arrived at such perfection on their respective instruments, yet it is remarkable that there was a total difference in their manner. The characteristic excellence of SCARLATTI seems to have consisted in a certain elegance and delicacy of expression. HANDEL had an uncommon brilliancy and command of finger: but what distinguished him from all other players who possessed these same qualities was that amazing fulness, force, and energy which he joined with them.[38]

Moving along one generation, we come to Carl Philipp Emanuel Bach (1714-1788), who owed much to his father. In his autobiography he states: "In composition and keyboard performance, I have never had any teacher but my father."[39] His indebtedness was more apparent in his achievements as a clavier performer than in his style of composing. His works are among the best examples of the "empfindsamer Stil" (sensitive style) of the period that broke away from the polyphony of J.S. Bach. It strived to present a more "true and natural" feeling and foreshadowed the romantic period. C.P.E. Bach's keyboard sonatas are of major importance — his handling of the early sonata form helped to lay the foundations for the works of Haydn, Mozart, and Beethoven. Within this form we also see the younger Bach's creation of a true piano keyboard idiom. Burney said that Emanuel Bach told him

... that of all his works those for the clavichord and pianoforte are the chief in which he has indulged his own feelings and ideas. His principal wish has been to play and compose in the most *vocal* style possible, notwithstanding the great defect of old keyed-instruments, except the organ, in not sustaining their tone. But to make a harpsichord or piano-forte sing, is not easily accomplished; as the ear must not be tired by too thin a harmony, nor stunned by too full and noisy an accompaniment. In his opinion music ought to touch the heart and he never found that this could be effected by run-ning, rattling, drumming, or arpeggios.[40]

In the *Essay* he advised that "The whole approach to per-formance will be greatly aided and simplified by the supplementary study of voice wherever possible and by listening closely to good singers."[41]

His treatise *Versuch über die wahre Art das Clavier zu spielen* (*Essay on the True Art of Playing Keyboard Instruments*) is the most important one from the entire harpsichord period, and the first thoroughly organized one—overshadowing other fine method books from the period such as those by Marpurg and Quantz.[42] C.P.E. Bach wrote it while serving Frederick the Great in Berlin as chamber cembalist, a position he had assumed in 1740. In this post he had contact with the musical notables of his day and thus wrote from wide experience. He himself stated in the foreword to Part Two of the *Essay:* "The observations are not speculative but rest in experience and wisdom. With no desire to boast, it may be said that this experience can hardly be rivaled, for it has grown out of many years of association with good taste in a musical environment which could not be improved."[43]

The *Essay,* first published in two parts in 1753 and 1762, is the work of a first-rank musician. Its objective throughout is sensitive musical performance. The influence of the work soon was wide-spread; so much so that Haydn called it "the school of all schools"[44] and Beethoven had his pupil Czerny work from it. Johann Friedrich Rochlitz (1769-1842), probably the first pro-fessional music critic, quoted Mozart as saying: "He is the father, we are the children. Those of us who do anything right learned it from him. Whoever does not own to this is a scoundrel."[45] The

25

early pianists like Clementi, Cramer, and Hummel built directly upon it—it is the connecting link between the harpsichord and the early piano.

In the introduction to Part One, Bach stated that the true art of playing keyboard instruments is dependent upon three factors: correct fingering, good embellishments, and good performance. He treated each of these in a separate chapter. He immediately objected to keyboardists whose "playing lacks roundness, clarity, forthrightness, and in their stead one hears only hacking, thumping, and stumbling. All other instruments learned how to sing. The keyboard alone has been left behind, its sustained style obliged to make way for countless elaborate figures."[46]

Toward the end of the introduction, he wrote:

> The more recent pianoforte, when it is sturdy and well built, has many fine qualities, although its touch must be carefully worked out, a task which is not without difficulties. It sounds well by itself and in small ensembles. Yet, I hold that a good clavichord, except for its weaker tone, shares equally in the attractiveness of the pianoforte and in addition features the vibrato and portato which I produce by means of added pressure after each stroke. It is at the clavichord that a keyboardist may be most exactly evaluated.[47]

Then he spoke of the relationship of harpsichordist and clavichordist:

> Every keyboardist should own a good harpsichord and a good clavichord to enable him to play all things interchangeably. A good clavichordist makes an accomplished harpsichordist, but not the reverse. The clavichord is needed for the study of good performance, and the harpsichord to develop proper finger strength. Those who play the clavichord exclusively encounter many difficulties when they turn to the harpsichord. In an ensemble where a harpsichord must be used rather than the soft-toned clavichord, they will play laboriously; and great exertion never produces the proper keyboard effect. The clavichordist grows too much accustomed to caressing the keys; consequently, his wonted touch being insufficient to operate the jacks, he fails to bring out details on the harpsichord. In fact, finger strength may be lost eventually, by playing only the clavichord. On the other hand, those who concentrate on the harpsichord grow accustomed to playing in only one color, and the varied touch which the competent clavichordist brings to the harpsichord remains hidden from them. This may sound strange, since one would think

26

that all performers can express only one kind of tone on each harpsichord. To test its truth ask two people, one a good clavichordist, the other a harpsichordist, to play on the latter's instrument the same piece containing varied embellishments, and then decide whether both have produced the same effect.[48]

Philipp Emanuel's contemporary, Johann Friedrich Reichardt, also commented on his high regard for the clavichord:

Bach's manner of playing would not have been devised at all without the clavichord, and he devised it only for the clavichord. But he who once masters this instrument plays the harpsichord quite differently from those who never touch a clavichord. For him harpsichord compositions may be written which under the hands of the mere harpsichordist become insipid, often unintelligible, and disconnected. . . .

Soul, expression, feelings, these things Bach gave first to the clavichord, and the harpsichord could not receive the smallest degree of them save from the hand of him who knew how to animate the clavichord.[49]

In the section on fingering in the *Essay,* Bach wrote first regarding good posture: forearm slightly above the keyboard, fingers arched, muscles relaxed. He related good finger and thumb action to good fingering:

In playing, the fingers should be arched, and the muscles relaxed. The less these two conditions are satisfied, the more attention must be given to them. Stiffness hampers all movement, above all the constantly required rapid extension and contraction of the hands. All stretches, the omission of certain fingers, even the indispensable crossing of the fingers and turning of the thumb demand this elastic ability. Those who play with flat, extended fingers suffer from one principal disadvantage in addition to awkwardness; the fingers, because of their length, are too far removed from the thumb, which should always remain as close as possible to the hand. As we shall see later, the principal finger is thereby robbed of all possibility of performing its services, whence it comes about that those who seldom use the thumb play stiffly, something that those who use it correctly cannot do even willfully. For the latter, everything is easy. This can be observed immediately in a performer: If he understands the correct principles of fingering and has not acquired the habit of making unnecessary gestures, he will play the most difficult things in such a manner that the motion of his hands will be barely noticeable; moreover, everything will sound as if it presented no obstacles to him. Conversely, those who do not understand these principles will often play the easiest things with great snorting, grimacing, and uncommon awkwardness.[50]

Then he made a strong defense for the use of the thumb:

Those who do not use the thumb let it hang to keep it out of the way. Such a position makes even the most moderate span uncomfortable, for the fingers must stretch and stiffen in order to encompass it. Can anything be well executed this way? The thumbs give the hand not only another digit, but the key to all fingering. This principal finger performs another service in that it keeps the others supple, for they must remain arched as it makes its entry after one or another of them. Those passages which, without the thumb, must be pounced upon with stiff, tensed muscles, can be played roundly, clearly, with a natural extension, and a consequent facility when it lends its assistance.[51]

After this statement there follows an exhaustive, but orderly presentation of Bach's principles of good fingering. All of the major and minor scale fingerings are presented, frequently with alternate solutions. Many of our commonly used ones today are found here, but there is still some crossing over of fingers (such as 3 4). The thumb has a true pivotal function, but appears frequently on keys uncommon to us. He felt the thumb is best used immediately before black keys. Perhaps his solution for the right hand in the ascending A melodic minor scale was a better one than the fingering generally used today:

1	2	3	4	1	2	3	1
A	B	C	D	E	F#	G#	A [52]

Altogether sixty-six illustrations of fingering are given, including chordal, broken chordal, arpeggiated, polyphonic, and scale-line passages.

In the famous section on embellishments, Bach suggested practical execution and development of the trill, which after all is *the* basic finger exercise:

In practicing the trill, raise the fingers to an equal but not an excessive height. Trill slowly at first and then more rapidly but always evenly. The muscles must remain relaxed or the trill will bleat or grow ragged. Many try to force it. Never advance the speed of a trill beyond that pace at which it can be played evenly. This precaution must be heeded in practicing rapid as well as difficult passages so that they may

28

be performed with fitting lightness and clarity. Through intelligent practice it is easy to achieve that which can never be attained by excessive straining of the muscles. When the upper tone of a trill is given its final performance it is snapped; after the stroke the upper joint of the finger is sharply doubled and drawn off and away from the key as quickly as possible.

The trill must be practiced diligently with all fingers so that they will become strong and dexterous. However, let no one believe that all of the fingers can be made to trill equally well. For one thing, there are natural differences among them, and for another, compositions usually offer more trills for certain fingers than for others; hence these are unwittingly given more practice . . .

No one can succeed without a minimum of two good trills in each hand: The second and third, and the third and fourth fingers of the right hand; and the thumb and second, and second and third fingers of the left. It is because of this normal fingering of trills that the left thumb grows so agile and along with the second finger becomes about the most active of the left hand.[53]

The final chapter in Part One is on "Performance." Bach once again stressed that technique without musicianship is of no value:

Most technicians do nothing more than play the notes. And how the continuity and flow of the melody suffer, even when the harmony remains unmolested! . . .

What comprises good performance? The ability through singing or playing to make the ear conscious of the true content and affect of a composition. Any passage can be so radically changed by modifying its performance that it will be scarcely recognizable.

The subject matter of performance is the loudness and softness of tones, touch, the snap, legato and staccato execution, the vibrato, arpeggiation, the holding of tones, the retard and accelerando. Lack of these elements or inept use of them makes a poor performance.

Good performance, then, occurs when one hears all notes and their embellishments played in correct time with fitting volume produced by a touch which is related to the true content of a piece. Herein lies the rounded, pure, flowing manner of playing which makes for clarity and expressiveness.[54]

Other pertinent words of wisdom are quoted herewith:

In order to become oriented at the keyboard and thus make easier the acquisition of a necessary skill at sight reading, it is

29

a good practice to play memorized pieces in the dark.[55]

A well-rounded manner of performance can be most readily discerned from the playing of rapid pieces which contain alternating light and heavy runs of equal speed. Keyboardists are often found whose ready fingers serve them well in loud runs, but desert them through lack of control in the soft ones, thereby making for indistinctness. They grow nervous, speed onward, and lose control.[56]

Play from the soul, not like a trained bird! A keyboardist of such stamp deserves more praise than other musicians. And these latter should be more censured than keyboardists for bizarre performance.[57]

All difficulties in passage work should be mastered through repeated practice. Far more troublesome, in fact, is a good performance of simple notes. These bring fretful moments to many who believe that keyboard instruments are easy to play. Regardless of finger dexterity, never undertake more than can be kept under control in public performance, where it is seldom possible to relax properly or even to maintain a fitting disposition. Ability and disposition should be gauged by the most rapid and difficult parts in order to avoid overexertion, which will surely result in a breakdown of the performance. Those passages which are troublesome in private and come off well only occasionally should be omitted from public performance unless the performer finds himself in a particularly favorable frame of mind . . .

As a means of learning the essentials of good performance it is advisable to listen to accomplished musicians. Above all, lose no opportunity to hear artistic singing. In so doing, the keyboardist will learn to think in terms of song. Indeed, it is a good practice to sing instrumental melodies in order to reach an understanding of their correct performance. This way of learning is of far greater value than the reading of voluminous tomes or listening to learned discourses . . .

It is principally in improvisations or fantasias that the keyboardist can best master the feelings of his audience. Those who maintain that all of this can be accomplished without gesture will retract their words when, owing to their own insensibility, they find themselves obliged to sit like a statue before their instrument. Ugly grimaces, of course, are inappropriate and harmful; but fitting expressions help the listener to understand our meaning. Those opposed to this stand are often incapable of doing justice, despite their technique, to their own otherwise worthy compositions.[58]

Part Two of Bach's *Essay* does not deal with physical technique, but is of great practical value in the study of thorough bass, accompaniment and improvisation. We do find him referring to the piano as one of the most common of accompaniment instruments.[59] He felt that the piano and the clavichord are best for performances that call for "the most elegant taste," yet he hastened to add that "some singers prefer the support of the clavichord or harpsichord to the pianoforte."[60]

After surveying these early clavier method books, we may well re-emphasize the true nature of the clavier touch that shortly was to be transferred to the early piano. Physically, it was achieved through a very close finger action with minimal arm activity. Rameau cautioned, "Never weigh down the touch of your fingers by an effort of the hand. . . . On the contrary, let your hand sustain your fingers and thus make the touch lighter; this is of great consequence."[61] This does not mean that the arm is relegated entirely to a passive role in the harpsichord and clavichord technique. Its graceful, flowing movement will control horizontal placement of the fingers upon the keys and assist in the shaping of the phrase line. The arm is also inevitably involved in a chordal technique.

The articulation of the clavier technique is a combination of both staccato and legato. Too often the harpsichord touch is envisioned as essentially a staccato one. Mme. Landowska tried to correct this impression in her own case:

It has been said that my touch is a perpetual staccato. This is a fundamental misunderstanding. The great precision required to strike the keys at the harpsichord is sometimes misconstrued for staccato touch. This error also stems from the elasticity of my bouncy touch, with its precise and neat outlines. I use perfect legato, however, as harpsichord touch requires. This is a condition *sine qua non*. Even when staccato is required for certain effects, the basis of harpsichord touch remains the legato.[62]

Erwin Bodky, after making an intensive study of articulation as revealed in the writings and editorial indications of Quantz, Marpurg, Couperin, and both J.S. and C.P.E. Bach, came to the following conclusions:

From the results of our study we can formulate the following guide to articulation: In an *allegro* piece nonlegato to staccato playing is more probable; in an *adagio* piece a legato atmosphere generally prevails; in *moderato* the close intervals (the second and third, but the latter not without exceptions)

31

are slurred, and the large intervals are detached. That the distinction between small and large intervals is very often valid in *allegro* and even *presto* situations as well is proved by the slurs in the first and last movements of the Italian Concerto. In addition to these suggestions, there is a supplementary principle that takes into account the characteristic qualities of the harpsichord and the clavichord. In the *allegro* and *moderato* categories, designation of a piece for the harpsichord increases the tendency toward nonlegato or staccato playing, and designation for the clavichord increases the chances of quasi legato to legato playing. *Adagio* implies basically a quasi legato performance on the harpsichord, molto legato on the clavichord.[63]

Notes

[1] Wanda Landowska, *Landowska on Music*, p. 125.

[2] Harich-Schneider, *The Harpsichord, An Introduction to Technique, Style and the Historical Sources*, p. 18.

[3] *Ibid.*, p. 12.

[4] Arnold Dolmetsch, *The Interpretation of the Music of the Seventeenth and Eighteenth Centuries*, p. 373.

[5] *Ibid.*, pp. 374-75.

[6] *Ibid.*, pp. 375-76.

[7] *Ibid.*, pp. 380-81.

[8] Harich-Schneider, *The Harpsichord*, p. 12.

[9] *Ibid.*

[10] François Couperin, *The Art of Playing the Harpsichord*, p. 8.

[11] *Ibid.*, p. 12.

[12] *Ibid.*, pp. 10-11.

[13] *Ibid.*, p. 11.

[14] *Ibid.*, pp. 11-12.

[15] *Ibid.*, p. 12.

[16] *Ibid.*, p. 12.

[17] *Ibid.*, p. 28.

[18] Thomas Fielden, "The History of the Evolution of Pianoforte Technique," *Proceedings of the Royal Music Association*, Session 59, January 17, 1933, p. 37.

[19] Couperin, *The Art of Playing the Harpsichord*, p. 13.

[20] *Ibid.*

32

[21] Wilfrid Mellers, *François Couperin and the French Classical Tradition*, p. 308.

[22] Couperin, *The Art of Playing the Harpsichord*, p. 33.

[23] Quoted by Harich-Schneider, *The Harpsichord, An Introduction to Technique, Style and the Historical Sources*, p. 15.

[24] Hans T. David and Arthur Mendel, eds., *The Bach Reader, A Life of Johann Sebastian Bach in Letters and Documents*, p. 231.

[25] *Ibid.*

[26] *Ibid.*, p. 238.

[27] Johann Joachim Quantz, *Versuch einer Anweisung die Flöte traversiere zu spielen (An Experimental Method for Playing the Transverse Flute)*, Cited in *Grove's Dictionary of Music and Musicians*, 5th ed., IV, p. 106.

[28] David and Mendel, *The Bach Reader*, p. 223.

[29] *Ibid.*, p. 254.

[30] *Ibid.*, pp. 307-308.

[31] *Ibid.*, p. 307.

[32] *Ibid.*, pp. 308-309.

[33] *Ibid.*, p. 311.

[34] Cited in Preface to Hans Bischoff edition of J.S. Bach, *Two and Three Part Inventions*.

[35] David and Mendel, *The Bach Reader*, p. 328.

[36] Charles Burney, *A General History of Music, from the Earliest Ages to the Present Period* (1789), II, p. 704.

[37] Cited in *Grove's Dictionary of Music and Musicians*, 5th ed., VI, p. 745.

[38] J. Mainwaring, *Memoirs*, p. 61.

[39] William J. Mitchell's Introduction to Carl Philipp Emanuel Bach, *Essay on the True Art of Playing Keyboard Instruments*, p.5.

[40] Burney, *A General History of Music*, II, p. 955.

[41] C.P.E. Bach, *Essay on the True Art of Playing Keyboard Instruments*, p. 39.

[42] In about 1750 Friedrich Wilhelm Marpurg (1718-1785) had written his influential *Die Kunst das Clavier zu spielen* (*The Art of Playing the Harpsichord*). Johann Joachim Quantz (1697-1773), celebrated flutist at the court of Frederick the Great, in 1752 published his *Versuch einer Anweisung die Flöte traversiere zu spielen* (*An Experimental Method for Playing the Transverse Flute*), a widely used work of which only about one eighth of its contents was concerned specifically with flute instruction. The rest dealt with general musical interpretive practice of the period.

33

[43] C.P.E. Bach. *Essay on the True Art*, p. 169.

[44] Cited by Wm. J. Mitchell in Introduction. *Ibid.*, p. 2.

[45] *Ibid.*, p. 4.

[46] *Ibid.*, p. 30.

[47] *Ibid.*, p. 36.

[48] *Ibid.*, pp. 37-38.

[49] *Ibid.*, p. 38.

[50] *Ibid.*, pp. 42-43.

[51] *Ibid.*, p. 43.

[52] *Ibid.*, p. 48.

[53] *Ibid.*, pp. 101-102.

[54] *Ibid.*, pp. 147-148.

[55] *Ibid.*, p. 39.

[56] *Ibid.*, p. 149.

[57] *Ibid.*, p. 150.

[58] *Ibid.*, pp. 151-152.

[59] *Ibid.*, p. 172.

[60] *Ibid.*

[61] Wanda Landowska, *Landowska on Music*, pp. 168-169.

[62] *Ibid.*, p. 375.

[63] Erwin Bodky, *The Interpretation of Bach's Keyboard Works*, p. 222.

3.   The Beginnings of the Piano

It was during C.P.E. Bach's lifetime that the pianoforte began to come into its own, but its hammer action can surely be traced back to the invention of the pantalon by Pantaleon Hebenstreit about 1690. This was a dulcimer-like instrument played with two small hammers. Although letters and records from the sixteenth and seventeenth centuries indicate usage of the term *Piano e forte,* Bartolommeo Cristofori (1655-1731) from Florence, Italy is generally credited with the first pianoforte. Cristofori's instrument dates from 1709 and was called a *Gravicembalo col piano e forte.* In outward appearance, its shape was much like the large harpsichords from the period, although inwardly its action in many ways remarkably resembled our modern piano. A description of Cristofori's instrument was written in 1711 by Francesco Scipione, Marchese de Maffei, after he had seen one that belonged to Prince Ferdinand:

> It is known to everyone who delights in music, that one of the principal means by which the skilful in that art derive the secret of especially delighting those who listen, is the piano and forte in the theme and its response, or in the gradual diminution of tone little by little, and then returning suddenly to the full power of the instrument; which artifice is frequently used and with marvellous effect, in the great concerts of Rome. . . .
>
> Now, of this diversity and alteration of tone, in which instruments played with the bow especially excel, the harpsichord is entirely deprived, and it would have been thought a vain endeavour to propose to make it so that it should participate in this power. Nevertheless, so bold an invention has been no less happily conceived than executed in Florence, by Signor Bartolommeo Cristofali of Padua, harpsichord player, in the service of the most serene Prince of Tuscany.

He has already made three, of the usual size of other harpsichords, and they have all succeeded to perfection. The production of greater or less sound depends on the degree of
power with which the player presses on the keys, by regulating
which, not only the piano and forte are heard, but also the
gradations and diversity of power, as in a violoncello . . . This
is properly a chamber instrument, and it is not intended for
church music, nor for a great orchestra.... It is certain, that to
accompany a singer, and to play with one other instrument, or
even for a moderate concert, it succeeds perfectly; although
this is not its principal intention, but rather to be played
alone, like the lute, harp, viols of six strings, and other most
sweet instruments. But really the great cause of the opposition
which this new instrument has encountered, is in general, the
want of knowledge how, at first, to play it; because it is not
sufficient to know how to play perfectly upon instruments
with the ordinary finger board, but being a new instrument, it
requires a person who, understanding its capabilities, shall
have made a particular study of its effects, so as to regulate
the measure of force required on the keys and the effects of
decreasing it, also to choose pieces suited to it for delicacy,
and especially for the movement of the parts, that the subject
may be heard distinctly in each . . .[1]

Two Cristofori pianofortes still exist: one from 1720 is in the

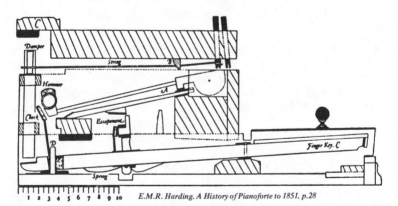

E.M.R. Harding, A History of Pianoforte to 1851, p.28

Pianoforte by Cristofori, 1726 (Leipzig, No. 170).   Inscription printed in Roman
lettering: BARTHOLOMAEVS DE' CHRISTOPHORIS PATAVINVS INVENTOR
FACIEBAT FLORENTIAE M. DCCXXVI.

A, intermediate lever; *B*, wrest-block bridge; *C*, 'Ruler', a strip of wood to prevent
the dampers jumping out; *D*, one of two wood guide posts to keep the key steady.
The natural keys are faced with box.

36

Metropolitan Museum of Art in New York City and the other from 1726 in the Heyer Collection in Leipzig. The former has a keyboard of four-and-a-half octaves (C-f^3) and the latter four (C-c^3). The action of the 1726 instrument, considerably perfected over the 1709 model, is shown opposite.

The source of our present-day escapement action, which permits the hammer to fall back from the string while the key is still depressed, and also the check of the hammer's return to its original resting place (thus allowing faster repetition) are clearly evident. The heads of the hammers were covered with leather just as the harpsichord plectra were frequently made of leather.

No Italians of note furthered the development of Cristofori's remarkable invention — it remained for the Germans to do this. The first major German harpsichord maker who was directly influenced by the Cristofori piano was Gottfried Silbermann (1683-1753), Dresden organ and clavichord maker. He was motivated by a translation of Scipione's article which appeared in Mattheson's *Musikalische Kritik* in 1725. He submitted one of his early piano-fortes in 1736 to the judgment of Sebastian Bach's penetrating mind and critical ear. Johann Friedrich Agricola in his notes from a *Treatise on the Organ and Other Instruments* (1768) gave an interesting account of Bach's contact with Silbermann:

Mr. Gottfried Silbermann had at first built *two* of these instruments [pianofortes]. One of them was seen and played by the late Kappelmeister, Mr. Joh. Sebastian Bach. He had praised, indeed, admired, its tone; but he had complained that it was too weak in the high register, and was too hard to play [i.e. the action was too heavy]. This had been taken greatly amiss by Mr. Silbermann, who could not bear to have any fault found in his handiworks. He was therefore angry at Mr. Bach for a long time. And yet his conscience told him that Mr. Bach was not wrong. He therefore decided—greatly to his credit be it said—not to deliver any more of these instruments, but instead to think all the harder about how to eliminate the faults Mr. J.S. Bach had observed. He worked for many years on this. And that this was the real cause of this postponement I have the less doubt since I myself heard it frankly acknowledged by Mr. Silbermann. Finally, when Mr. Silbermann had really achieved many improvements, notable in respect to the action, he sold one again to the Court of the Prince of Rudolstadt. Shortly thereafter His Majesty, the King of Prussia, had one of these instruments ordered, and when it met with His Majesty's Most Gracious approval, he had several more ordered from Mr. Silbermann. Mr. Silbermann also had the laudable ambition to show one of these instruments of his later workmanship to the late Kapellmeister Bach, and have it examined by him; and he had received, in turn, complete approval from him.[2]

It was on a visit to the court of Frederick the Great in 1747 that Bach performed on a number of the Silbermann pianos. This time Bach's reaction was more favorable. A.J. Hipkins examined the existing Silbermann pianos and wrote in 1896 that Silbermann "was following Cristofori."[3] However, Silbermann did not use the Cristofori hammer check.

After Silbermann, we can move almost directly to the most famous of German piano manufacturers: Johann Andreas Stein (1728-1792) and his son-in-law, Johann Andreas Streicher (1761-1833). Stein used a hopper (escapement) action from 1770 on, which was quite similar to Silbermann's. It differed in that, where before a long rail or ledge had been used, now there was a separate escapement for each of the keys.

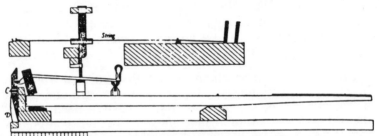

1 2 3 4 5 6 7 8 9 10   *E.M.R. Harding: A History of Pianoforte to 1851. p.25*

German Action by Stein for grand pianoforte, 1773 (Stuttgart, No. C 25).
A, the wooden Kapsel; *B*, the escapement—a transformed Prelleiste; *C*, one of two guide wires to keep the escapement steady; *D*, the escapement spring; *E*, the damper. This type of damper, the *Kastendämpfer*, is typical of the German Action.

Under Streicher and his wife Nannette's direction, the Stein piano continued to be perfected, including reinstatement of the hammer check device. Even before they moved their operation to Vienna, their instruments were in great demand. They were much favored by Mozart and other musicians of the day. The Stein-Streicher pianoforte, with its elegant tone, its smooth, fluent action, and its lovely, graceful outward appearance, was the instrument of the famous German or Viennese action.

Earlier, Mozart had visited Stein at his workshop in Augsburg and wrote the celebrated letter to his father on October 17 and 18,

38

1777 in which he gave his enthusiastic reaction to the Stein instruments:

This time I shall begin at once with Stein's pianofortes. Before I had seen any of his make, Spath's claviers had always been my favourites. But now I much prefer Stein's, for they damp ever so much better than the Regensburg instruments. When I strike hard, I can keep my finger on the note or raise it, but the sound ceases the moment I have produced it. In whatever way I touch the keys, the tone is always even. It never jars, it is never stronger or weaker or entirely absent; in a word, it is always even. It is true that he does not sell a pianoforte of this kind for less than three hundred gulden, but the trouble and the labour which Stein puts into the making of it cannot be paid for. His instruments have this special advantage over others that they are made with escape action. Only one maker in a hundred bothers about this. But without an escapement it is impossible to avoid jangling and vibration after the note is struck. When you touch the keys, the hammers fall back again the moment after they have struck the strings, whether you hold down the keys or release them. He himself told me that when he has finished making one of these claviers, he sits down to it and tries all kinds of passages, runs and jumps, and he polishes and works away at it until it can do anything. For he labours solely in the interest of music and not for his own profit; otherwise he would soon finish his work. He often says: "If I were not myself such a passionate lover of music and had not myself some slight skill on the clavier, I should certainly long ago have lost patience with my work. But I do like an instrument which never lets the player down and which is durable." And his claviers certainly do last. He guarantees that the sounding-board will neither break nor split. When he has finished making one for a clavier, he places it in the open air, exposing it to rain, snow, the heat of the sun and all the devils in order that it may crack. Then he inserts wedges and glues them in to make the instrument very strong and firm. He is delighted when it cracks, for he can then be sure that nothing more can happen to it. Indeed he often cuts into it himself and then glues it together again and strengthens it in this way. He has finished making three pianofortes of this kind. To-day I played on one again.

. . .the device too which you work with your knee is better on his than on other instruments. I have only to touch it and it works; and when you shift your knee the slightest bit, you do not hear the least reverberation.[4]

Other Viennese makers who followed closely in the Stein tradition in the 1780s and later were Anton Walter and J. Wenzel Schanz. Mozart was also very fond of the Walter piano and had one specially made for him before 1784. It had hammers covered with leather, a five-octave range, and a keyboard with the key colors the reverse of our modern pianos, similar to the harpsichords of the period. Two knee-pedals served to dampen the strings and a manual device controlled *una corda* effects. In outward appearance it resembled a beautiful large harpsichord. This instrument can be viewed in the Mozart Museum in Salzburg, Austria.

In clarity of tone these Viennese instruments somewhat resembled the harpsichord. Eva and Paul Badura-Skoda commented:

It should not be supposed that our piano is capable of subtler nuances; the Mozart pianos of Stein and Walter, for instance, were clear and very bright in the upper register, and this made it easier to play cantabile and with full colour. The lower notes had a peculiar round fullness, but none of the dull, stodgy sound of the low notes of a modern piano. Whereas the tone becomes steadily thinner toward the top, the highest register sounding almost as if pizzicato, the full sound of the bass is by far the most satisfying register of the Mozart piano. The strings are so thin that chords in the bass can be played with perfect clarity even when they are very closely spaced.[5]

It is interesting to note too that the weight of the Walter piano was about 140 pounds while that of a modern Steinway concert grand is more than 1000 pounds.

Joseph Haydn (1732-1809), whose sonatas were greatly influenced by Emanuel Bach, favored the Schanz piano. Never the outstanding performer that Mozart was, he did not study the clavier until after he had gone to St. Stephen's choir school in Vienna in 1740; he did use it later in teaching and as an aid in his composing. Philip James speaks of his having worked on the *Creation* (1799) at a clavichord made by Johann Bohak in 1794.[6] Haydn himself at one time told Georg August Griesinger how he went about the process of sharpening his creative powers: "I sit down, I start to extemporize—according to whether my mood is sad or cheerful, serious or gay. When I had captured an idea, then my whole desire was to mould it according to the rules of the art of composition."[7]

Various items of his correspondence prove that he whole-heartedly adopted the new pianoforte. On October 26, 1788 he told his publisher, Artaria: "In order to compose your three pianoforte Sonatas particularly well, I had to buy a new fortepiano."[8] Then voicing the woe shared by so many composers, he continued, "Now since no doubt you have long since realized that scholars are sometimes short of money — and that is my situation at present — I should like to ask you, Sir, if you would be kind enough to pay 31 gold ducats to the organ and instrument maker, Wenzl Schanz [as a loan]."[9]

Haydn's royal friend, Maria Anna von Genzinger, received a letter from him dated June 27, 1790, in which he told her:

> Your Grace will certainly have received the new pianoforte Sonata, but if not, you will perhaps receive it along with my letter. . . . It's only a pity that Your Grace doesn't own a Schanz fortepiano, on which everything is better expressed. I thought that Your Grace might turn over your still tolerable piano to Fraulein Peperl, and buy a new one for yourself. Your beautiful hands and their facility of execution deserve this and much more. I know I ought to have composed this Sonata in accordance with the capabilities of your piano, but I found this impossible because I was no longer accustomed to it.[10]

He wrote her one week later (July 4) and clearly showed his preference of instruments:

> I have just received your letter, and this very moment the mail goes out. I am simply delighted that my Prince intends to give Your Grace a new fortepiano, all the more so since I am in some measure responsible for it: I constantly implored *Mademoiselle* Nanette to persuade your husband to buy one for Your Grace, and now the purchase depends entirely on Your Grace and simply consists in Your Grace choosing one to fit your touch and suit your fancy. It is quite true that my friend Herr Walther [Anton Walter] is very celebrated, and that every year I receive the greatest civility from that gentleman, but between ourselves, and speaking frankly, sometimes there is not more than one instrument in ten which you could really describe as good, and apart from that they are very expensive. I know Herr von Nikl's fortepiano: It's excellent, but too heavy for Your Grace's hand, and one can't play everything on it with the necessary delicacy. Therefore I should like Your Grace to try one made by Herr Schanz, his fortepianos are particularly light in touch and the mechanism very agreeable. A good fortepiano is absolutely necessary for Your Grace, and my Sonata will gain double its effect by it.[11]

With a technique inferior to Mozart's, Haydn no doubt also found a lighter touch much more agreeable to him.

By this time fine pianos were also being constructed in France by such well-known builders as Sebastian Érard (1752-1831) and Pascal Taskin (1723-1793). In 1801 Haydn received an Érard piano with an English-type action as a gift, but this he also found too difficult to play. Érard's earliest piano was dated 1777; three years earlier John Brent manufactured America's first in Philadelphia. The Germans, however, were making the greatest impact. Their influence had already been felt strongly in England after the devastation of the Seven Years' War (1755-1762) in Germany. By 1760 many German craftsmen had emigrated to London, the most influential of these being Johannes Zumpe (dates unknown). Johann Christian Bach also had recently arrived in London. It was he who gave the first solo pianoforte performance in public on June 2, 1768, on an instrument manufactured by Zumpe. Music for the keyboard now began to have both harpsichord and pianoforte printed on the title sheet in that order. By the late 1770s the term *pianoforte* for the first time in England was listed alone on a piece of music. Soon, when both were mentioned, the pianoforte was first. Beethoven's very early keyboard works of the early 1780s were for harpsichord. The three Sonatas, Opus 2 (1795) were written for either harpsichord or pianoforte; the term *pianoforte* was first indicated by itself in 1799 on the title page of Opus 13, the *Pathétique* Sonata. The first German method book to use the word in its title was *Die Wahr Art das Pianoforte zu Spielen* (*The True Art of Playing the Pianoforte*), published in Dresden in 1787 by Johann Peter Milchmyer.

Many of Haydn's keyboard works are clearly for piano alone—such as the great Sonata in E flat major, the Variations in F minor, and the lively Fantasia in C major published by Artaria to whom he wrote on March 29, 1789: "In my leisure hours I have completed a new *Capriccio* for the pianoforte which, from its taste, singularity, and careful execution cannot but fail to be received with approbation from professional and non-professional alike."[12] Karl Geiringer elaborated further upon this work:

The fantasia shows, better even than the sonatas, the colorful character of Haydn's piano-playing. We seem to hear in this piece the tone of violins and double basses, of horns and flutes; moreover the rapid crossing of the hands, the arpeggios, and the distribution of passages between the hands exhibit the composer's concern for purely pianistic devices.

The effect that Haydn achieved by holding notes in the bass until they die away (*tenuto intanto finchè no si sente più il sono*) is rather notable. This fantasia was written by a master who exploited the possibilities of piano technique in transcribing ideas of an essentially orchestral nature.[13]

Johannes Zumpe, while working in London for a harpsichord maker of Swiss background, Burkat Shudi (Swiss spelling: Burkhardt Tschudi), began making the square pianoforte about 1769—the instrument which became very popular for use in the home. Daniel Gottlob Türk in his *Klavierschule,* published in 1789, states that the design for the square piano came from the clavichord and that for the grand piano from the harpsichord.[14] In 1761 a Scotch cabinet maker by the name of John Broadwood (1732-1812) also began to work for Shudi. In 1770, after marrying Shudi's daughter, Barbara, he became a partner in the firm which then was known as Shudi and Broadwood. Broadwood became sole proprietor in 1782, nine years after Shudi's death. After 1795, the Shudi name was dropped from the firm's title when Broadwood's sons began to come into the business. Today Broadwood and Sons is the oldest maker of keyboard instruments in existence.

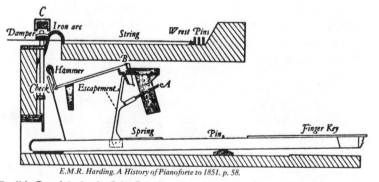

E.M.R. Harding, A History of Pianoforte to 1851, p. 58.

English Grand Action by John Broadwood and Sons, dated 1795 (formerly in the possession of Messrs Miller and Son, Cambridge).

A, screw to regulate the play of the escapement or hopper; *B,* screw binding the hammer to a wire pivot: by unscrewing it the hammer çan be removed; *C,* ruler or rail to regulate the action of the dampers (a relic of the harpsichord ruler to prevent the jacks from jumping out). The check catches and holds the hammer after it has fallen from the strings, to prevent it from rebounding against them. The check acts only so long as the key is pressed down.

John Broadwood did not begin to construct pianos himself until 1773—and these were square instruments similar to Zumpe's.

By the 1780s, he had made and patented a square piano of his own which greatly helped to separate the piano from the more fragile construction of the clavichord and the harpsichord. Pedals similar to the modern damper and *una corda* or soft pedals were introduced. The first known Broadwood grand piano was constructed in 1781. In 1788, the bass strings were strung over their own separate bridge. In the harpsichord there had been only a single continuous bridge. The Broadwood piano was evolving into a much heavier, sturdier, and more sonorous instrument than the Viennese piano — the Broadwood which the dynamic Beethoven would soon come to prefer.

The Broadwood piano had three strings for every two on the Viennese instruments and the diameter of the strings was twice as great. The English sounding board was thicker; the strings over it were attached directly to the case and could take a greater pull than in the Viennese piano where the strings were fastened to a solid base. The hammers in the English piano were heavier and its action not capable of velocity as great as that in the Viennese piano. The dampers in the latter instrument worked more effectively.

By 1800 pianos in Europe were being turned out by the thousands. In 1809 the last English harpsichord, a Kirkman, was constructed. Along with the piano's popularity came many perversions in the early nineteenth century. In addition to the damper and *una corda* pedals, one might find an astonishing variety on some instruments. Czerny objected to "such as the Fagotto and harp pedals, or the Drum and Bells, or Triangle, etc."[15] He thought they were "childish toys of which a solid player will disdain to avail himself."[16] Czerny did speak of another pedal which he felt had legitimate usage:

> The buff-pedal or Piano-pedal properly so called [indicated *Il pedale del Piano* or *Flauto*]. This pedal which is not at present used in English Piano fortes, is placed in the center of the other pedals; by moving of a strip of cloth situated between the hammers and strings, it causes the tone to become weak and of a flute-like quality. It is much seldomer used than the other pedals, and chiefly in a soft *Tremolando* passage, in combination with the damper-pedal.[17]

Then there were manual stops that would operate various types of gadgetry in the piano's action. For example, bits of leather tipped with a hard substance like ivory might come between the

44

hammers and the strings to create a harpsichord-like sound. Or parchment or stiff paper might be inserted instead, especially in the bass register, to give a "bassoon-like" tone.

The reasons for the popularity of the piano can easily be seen. The great dynamic range and possibilities for shading (Philip James thought the name should have been shortened to forte rather than piano[18]) fitted the melodic classical style well. With the rise of the middle class following the French Revolution and other significant political and industrial developments, there was a much larger music public. The piano was well suited for mass production; it became less costly than the harpsichord. It also took much less care and it was particularly well-suited for the larger concert halls.

Typical of criticism of the harpsichord were these remarks written in the *Encyclopédie Méthodique* in 1780 by the composer Nicolas-Joseph Hüllmandel, who had studied with C.P.E. Bach:

All these complications indicate the imperfection of this instrument. It demands too much patience from those who play it. . . . Are we tied to this instrument by such false and puerile imitations [imitative stops]? There is an instrument that far better fulfils the purpose of music and possesses evenness and purity of sound in any desired degree of strength or sweetness, and speaks to the heart without hurting the ear.[19]

But many lovers of the harpsichord and clavichord viewed the piano's takeover of the keyboard scene with alarm and regret. Voltaire called the piano a "cauldron-maker's instrument"[20] and the organist Balbastre told Taskin: "You toil in vain, this newcomer will never dethrone the majestic harpsichord."[21] Carl Cramer in his *Magazin* in Germany in 1783 lamented:

It is indeed a sad thing for music to find this sort of instrument so widespread in every country, even in Germany, the real home of the clavichord, and especially in the southern districts, where there are twenty good *Pianofortes, Fortpiens, Clavecin royals,* and whatever else this species of *Hackbrett* is called, to a single tolerable clavichord.[22]

With its own expressive powers and emotional qualities of tone, the clavichord did outlast the harpsichord — particularly in Germany. Emanuel Bach's strong influence and his deep love for the clavichord no doubt helped to prolong its existence in Germany. Carl Parrish has written about the German musician's outlook:

45

An interesting concept that persisted for a while in Germany was that each of the three stringed keyboard types performed a definite function and that each would continue to be cultivated. The clavichord was regarded as best fitted for solo playing of an intimate character, for the instruction of beginners, and for composing. The piano was preferred for accompanying a singer and for use in small chamber groups, while the harpsichord was ordinarily employed only for *continuo* playing by the conductor of an operatic or concert orchestra. A composer, in writing a keyboard piece, was supposed to bear in mind the nature of the instrument for which it was intended and to write accordingly.[23]

The Germans were so reluctant to let the clavichord go that as late as 1804 August Eberhard Müller called his technical treatise a *Klavier und Fortepiano Schule.*

The situation got so bad for the harpsichord that during the bitter winter of 1814 many of the instruments which had been stored at the Paris Conservatoire since they were confiscated from the aristocracy during the French Revolution, were broken up for firewood. However, there were still those who valued and began to collect many of the priceless old harpsichords and clavichords. Throughout the nineteenth century these instruments were played privately and a limited number of recitals, often accompanied by lectures, were given by such discerning musicians as Ignaz Moscheles, Charles Salaman, Ernst Pauer, Carl Engel, Louis Diémer, and Arthur Hipkins, who realized that the baroque keyboard music could only sound authentic upon the instruments for which it was conceived. Thus, in spite of the overwhelming popularity of the piano, the harpsichord and the clavichord did not completely die out—although for most musicians and the general public they did for a time.

Toward the close of the nineteenth century, a significant event occurred. The present-day renaissance of the harpsichord can be traced to about 1882 when the French piano manufacturer Érard borrowed a 1769 Pascal Taskin harpsichord from the Taskin family. Érard studied this instrument and then began commercial production of a model based on it.

Just as the baroque era had produced such outstanding harpsichord virtuosos as Domenico Scarlatti, J.S. Bach, C.P.E. Bach, the classic period and the emerging piano shortly thereafter began to bring forth the first of the famous pianists such as Mozart, Hummel, Clementi, and Beethoven.

Notes

[1] *Giornale dei Letterati d'Italia,* 1711, vol. V, 144, cited by Rosamond E.M. Harding, *The Piano-Forte, Its History Traced to the Great Exhibition of 1851,* pp. 5-6.

[2] Hans T. David and Arthur Mendel, eds., *The Bach Reader, A Life of Johann Sebastian Bach in Letters and Documents,* p. 259.

[3] A.J. Hipkins, *A Description and History of the Pianoforte and of the Older Keyboard Stringed Instruments.* p.103.

[4] Emily Anderson, ed., *The Letters of Mozart and His Family,* I, pp. 328-29.

[5] Eva and Paul Badura-Skoda, *Interpreting Mozart on the Keyboard.* p.10.

[6] Philip James, *Early Keyboard Instruments from their Beginnings to the Year 1820.* p.18.

[7] Carl Parrish, "Haydn and the Piano," *Journal of the American Musicological Society,* Vol. 1, No. 3, Fall 1948, quoted in German and translated by Helmut Ziefle, p. 27.

[8] H.C. Robbins-Landon, *The Collected Correspondence and London Notebooks of Joseph Haydn,* p. 79.

[9] *Ibid.*

[10] *Ibid.,* p. 106.

[11] *Ibid.,* p. 107.

[12] *Ibid.,* p. 83.

[13] Karl Geiringer, *Haydn, A Creative Life in Music,* p. 306.

[14] Cited in Raymond Russell, *The Harpsichord and Clavichord: An Introductory Study,* p. 121.

[15] Carl Czerny, *Complete Theoretical and Practical Piano Forte School, from The First Rudiments of Playing, to the Highest and most Refined state of Cultivation; with The requisite numerous Examples, Newly and Expressly Composed for the Occasion; in 3 Volumes.* Opus 500, III, p. 65.

[16] *Ibid.*

[17] *Ibid.,* III, p. 57.

[18] Phillip James, *Early Keyboard Instruments,* p. 47.

[19] Carl Parrish, "Criticisms of the Piano When It Was New," *Musical Quarterly,* Vol. XXX, No. 4, pp. 433-34.

[20] *Ibid.,* p. 433.

47

[21] *Ibid.*
[22] *Ibid.*, p. 436.
[23] *Ibid.*, p. 437.

4.   Mozart and the Early Piano Technique

Wolfgang Amadeus Mozart (1756-1791) was the first of the great pianoforte players. In his early years in Salzburg he was brought up on the harpsichord and clavichord, but from the time of his initial contact with Stein in 1777 the pianoforte became his favorite. Because of the light action of the Stein and Walter pianos, it is not likely that Mozart's technique on the pianoforte varied greatly from that which he used on either the harpsichord or the clavichord.

Keyboard proficiency came early and easily for Mozart. In all of music history there is no child prodigy to compare with him. At the age of three when hearing his sister Maria Anna (called Nannerl by her family), who was four-and-a-half years older than he, play the clavier, he would amuse himself by picking out thirds at the keyboard. Their father, Leopold, was a capable musician. In 1756, the year that Wolfgang was born, he had published his famous *Versuch einer gründlichen Violinschule (A Treatise on the Fundamental Principles of Violin Playing)*. Then for Nannerl he had compiled a collection of clavier pieces containing small dances, marches, themes and variations and the like by well-known composers of the day and inscribed it *Pour le clavecin, ce Livre appartient à Mademoiselle Marie-Anne Mozart 1759*. It was from this notebook that Wolfgang began to study under his father at the age of four. That he was a most apt student is evident from Leopold's comments written on some of the pieces. By the eighth minuet he noted that "the preceding minuet was learned by Wolfgangerl in his fourth year."[1] In another place there was the notation that "This minuet and trio Wolfgangerl learned in half an hour at half past nine o'clock on January 26, 1761, one day before his fifth birthday."[2] Soon Leopold compiled another volume and inscribed it: "To my dear son Wolfgang Amadee on his sixth birthday from his father Leopold Mozart. Salzburg, October 31,

1762."[3] It was at this time that Wolfgang began to compose. He also learned to sing well and to master both the violin and the organ.

The best source of information regarding Mozart's early abilities is Andreas Schachtner, court trumpeter in Salzburg from 1754. After Mozart's death in 1791, his sister Nannerl wrote him asking him certain questions about Wolfgang's childhood. His answer is noteworthy:

> ... no sooner had he begun to busy himself with music than his interest in every other occupation was as dead, and even children's games had to have a musical accompaniment if they were to interest him; if we, he and I, were carrying his playthings from one room to another, the one of us who went empty-handed always had to sing or fiddle a march the while. But before he had begun music, he was so ready for any prank spiced with a little humour that he could quite forget food, drink and all things else.
>
> Whatever he was given to learn occupied him so completely that he put all else, even music, on one side; e.g. when he was doing sums, the table, chairs, walls, even the floor, was covered with chalked figures.[4]

In June of 1763 when Nannerl was eleven and Wolfgang nearly seven, they left with their father on a concert tour of Europe that was to last until November of 1766 and take them to Brussels, Paris, London, Amsterdam, and Zurich. As early as 1762 they had already performed in both Munich and Vienna. Astonished reactions followed their every appearance; witness the account which appeared in Melchior Grimm's journal on December 11, 1763, twelve days after the Mozart family arrived in Paris:

> True prodigies are sufficiently rare to be worth speaking of, when you have had occasion to see one. A Kapellmeister of Salzburg, Mozart by name, has just arrived here with two children who cut the prettiest figure in the world. His daughter, eleven years of age, plays the harpsichord in the most brilliant manner; she performs the longest and most difficult pieces with an astonishing precision. Her brother, who will be seven years old next February, is such an extraordinary phenomenon that one is hard put to it to believe what one sees with one's eyes and hears with one's ears. It means little for this child to perform with the greatest precision the most difficult pieces, with hands that can hardly stretch a sixth; but what is really incredible is to see him improvise for an hour on end and in doing so give rein to the

inspiration of his genius and to a mass of enchanting ideas, which moreover he knows how to connect with taste and without confusion. The most consummate Kapellmeister could not be more profound than he in the science of harmony and of modulations, which he knows how to conduct by the least expected but always accurate paths. He has such great familiarity with the keyboard that when it is hidden for him by a cloth spread over it, he plays on this cloth with the same speed and the same precision. To read at sight whatever is submitted to him is child's play for him; he writes and composes with marvellous facility, without having any need to go to the harpsichord and to grope for his chords. I wrote him a minuet with my own hand and asked him to put a bass to it; the child took a pen and, without approaching the harpsichord, fitted the bass to my minuet. You may imagine that it costs him no trouble at all to transpose [*transporter*] and to play the tune one gives him in any key one may ask; but here is something more I have seen, which is no less incomprehensible. A woman asked him the other day whether he was able to accompany by ear, and without looking at it, an Italian cavatina she knew by heart; and she began to sing. The child tried a bass that was not absolutely correct, because it is impossible to prepare in advance the accompaniment to a song one does not know; but when the tune was finished, he asked her to begin again, and at this repeat he not only played the whole melody of the song with the right hand, but with the other added the bass without hesitation; whereafter he asked [her] ten times to begin again, and at each repeat he changed the style of his accompaniment; and he could have repeated this twenty times, if he had not been stopped. I cannot be sure that this child will not turn my head if I go on hearing him often; he makes me realize that it is difficult to guard against madness on seeing prodigies. I am no longer surprised that Saint Paul should have lost his head after his strange vision. M. Mozart's children have excited the admiration of all who have seen them. The Emperor and Empress have overwhelmed them with kindnesses; and they have already met with the same reception at the Court of Munich and the Court of Mannheim. It is a pity that people are so ignorant of music in this country. The father proposes to go on from here to England, and afterwards to take his children back through lower Germany. . . .[5]

Throughout much of his brief lifetime, Mozart traveled widely. The years from 1769 to 1772 were spent largely in Italy. In 1777 and 1778 he journeyed to Mannheim and Paris. From 1781 on he settled in Vienna. Wherever he played, he was received with the same remarkable enthusiasm which had marked his appearances as a child. Mueller von Asow wrote from Augsburg in 1777:

Everything was extraordinary, tasteful and remarkable. . . . his performance on the fortepiano so pleasing, so pure, so full of expression, yet at the same time so extraordinarily fluent that one hardly knew what to listen to first, and the whole audience was moved to ecstasy. . . .[6]

His mother accompanied him on his visit to Mannheim the same year and wrote to Leopold on December 28, 1777:

Everyone thinks the world of Wolfgang, but indeed he plays quite differently from what he used to in Salzburg—for there are pianofortes here, on which he plays so extraordinarily well that people say they have never heard the like. In short everyone who has heard him says that he has not got his equal. Although Beecke has been performing here and Schubart too, yet everyone says that Wolfgang far surpasses them in beauty of tone, quality and execution. And they are all positively amazed at the way he plays out of his head and reads off whatever is put before him.[7]

Surely it was Mozart who defined the ideal Viennese piano technique in superlative fashion: an extremely smooth-flowing touch — leggiero, immaculate, clear; a tone quality that was always refined and cantabile in melody passages; a physical approach that ruled out all affectation and unnecessary movement — still largely the finger and hand technique of the harpsichord; an interpretation always in the best of taste with moderation shown in matters of tempo, rubato and dynamics, and elegance in phrasing. It should be emphasized that Mozart inherited a basic non-legato style of playing from the harpsichord era. Eva and Paul Badura-Skoda cautioned:

He does indeed often demand a legato for melodic passages, but for whatever instrument, he almost always wanted virtuoso passage-work played "non-legato." At least we have never come across any extended passage of triplets or semiquavers that should be played legato.[8]

Mozart's performance style is clearly seen in the many letters to his family while away on recital tours. On October 23-24, 1777, he wrote from Augsburg to his father:

. . . When I was at Stein's house the other day he put before me a sonata by Beecke — I think that I have told you that already. That reminds me, now for his little daughter.

Anyone who sees and hears her play and can keep from laughing, must, like her father, be made of stone. [Mozart puns on the word "Stein," which means "stone"]. For instead of sitting in the middle of the clavier, she sits right up opposite the treble, as it gives her more chance of flopping about and making grimaces. She rolls her eyes and smirks. When a passage is repeated, she plays it more slowly the second time. If it has to be played a third time, then she plays it even more slowly. When a passage is being played, the arm must be raised as high as possible, and according as the notes in the passage are stressed, the arm, not the fingers, must do this, and that too with great emphasis in a heavy and clumsy manner. But the best joke of all is that when she comes to a passage which ought to flow like oil and which necessitates a change of finger, she does not bother her head about it, but when the moment arrives, she just leaves out the notes, raises her hand and starts off again quite comfortably—a method by which she is much more likely to strike a wrong note, which often produces a curious effect. I am simply writing this in order to give Papa some idea of clavier-playing and clavier-teaching, so that he may derive some profit from it later on. Herr Stein is quite crazy about his daughter, who is eight and a half and who now learns everything by heart. She may succeed, for she has great talent for music. But she will not make progress by this method — for she will never acquire great rapidity, since she definitely does all she can to make her hands heavy. Further, she will never acquire the most essential, the most difficult and the chief requisite in music, which is time, because from her earliest years she has done her utmost not to play in time. Herr Stein and I discussed this point for two hours at least and I have almost converted him, for he now asks my advice on everything. He used to be quite crazy about Beecke; but now he sees and hears that I am the better player, that I do not make grimaces, and yet play with such expression, that, as he himself confesses, no one up to the present has been able to get such good results out of his pianofortes. Everyone is amazed that I can always keep strict time. What these people cannot grasp is that in *tempo rubato* in an Adagio, the left hand should go on playing in strict time. With them the left hand always follows suit. Count Wolfegg, and several other passionate admirers of Beecke, publicly admitted at a concert the other day that I had wiped the floor with him.[9]

In Mannheim Mozart met the celebrated pianist Abbé Vogler at a party. He could not tolerate sham; he wrote his reactions to his father on November 13, 1777:

The whole orchestra, from A to Z, detest him. He has caused Holzbauer a great deal of annoyance. His book is more useful for teaching arithmetic than for teaching composition. He says he can turn out a composer in three weeks and a singer in six months, but so far no one has seen him do it. He disparages the great masters. Why, he even belittled Bach to me.[10]

And again he said of Vogler on January 17, 1778:

I should mention that before dinner he had scrambled through my concerto at sight (the one which the daughter of the house plays—written for Countess Lützow). He took the first movement *prestissimo,* the Andante *allegro* and the Rondo, believe it or not, *prestississimo.* He generally played the bass differently from the way it was written, inventing now and then quite another harmony and even melody. Nothing else is possible at that pace, for the eyes cannot see the music nor the hands perform it. Well, what good is it? . . . Well you may easily imagine that it was unendurable. At the same time I could not bring myself to say to him, *Far too quick!* Besides, it is much easier to play a thing quickly than slowly: in certain passages you can leave out a few notes without anyone noticing it. But is that beautiful?—In rapid playing the right and left hands can be changed without anyone seeing or hearing it. But is that beautiful?—And wherein consists the art of playing prima vista? In this: in playing the piece in the time in which it ought to be played, and in playing all the notes, appoggiaturas and so forth, exactly as they are written and with the appropriate expression and taste, so that you might suppose that the performer had composed it himself. Vogler's fingering too is wretched; his left thumb is just like that of the late Adlgasser and he does all the treble runs downwards with the thumb and first finger of his right hand.[11]

Adlgasser had been Mozart's predecessor as court organist in Salzburg and had used the old harpsichord style of fingerings to which Mozart objected. Also while in Mannheim, a Barbara Cannabich studied with Mozart for a time. He wrote on November 14, 1777 that, if he were to work with her as her regular teacher, he would

. . . lock up all her music, cover the keys with a handkerchief and make her practice, first with the right hand and then with the left, nothing but scales, trills, mordants and so forth, very slowly at first, until each hand should be properly trained. I would then undertake to turn her into a

54

first-rate clavierist. For it's a great pity. She has so much talent, reads quite passably, possesses so much natural facility and plays with plenty of feeling.[12]

Another letter by Mozart to his father on April 28, 1784 gives vivid insight into his own technique while he described that of the Dutch-born pianist, Georg Friedrich Richter:

> He plays well so far as execution goes but as you will discover when you hear him, he is too rough and laboured and entirely devoid of taste and feeling. Otherwise he is the best fellow in the world and is not the slightest bit conceited. When I played to him he stared all the time at my fingers and kept on saying, "Good God! How hard I work and sweat—and yet win no applause—and to you, my friend, it is all child's play." "Yes," I replied, "I too had to work hard, so as not to have to work hard any longer."[13]

But Mozart's most pointed remarks were reserved for the contemporary pianist next greatest in importance to himself, Muzio Clementi (1752-1832). Born in Rome, he had his early musical study in Italy, but went to England for further training in 1766. There he was sponsored by an English nobleman, Peter Beckford. From 1773 on he was a brilliant success in London as both composer and pianist. He embarked upon a tour of the Continent in 1781, beginning first in Paris (an entry in the records of Broadwood and Sons from this time indicates: "Shipped a harpsichord and a pianoforte for Mr. Clementi to Paris"),[14]thence by way of Strasbourg and Munich to Vienna by the end of the same year. The Emperor Joseph was not long in arranging a musical duel at the royal palace on December 24 between Clementi and Mozart, who had just settled in Vienna the same year. Clementi described their meeting some years later to his pupil, Ludwig Berger:

> Scarcely had I been present in Vienna for a few days when I received an invitation from the Emperor to perform for him on the pianoforte. Entering his music room, I found there someone whom I took to be, on account of his elegant appearance, one of the imperial chamberlains. However, we had barely struck up a conversation when this person promptly turned to musical subjects, and we soon recognized one another as colleagues—as Mozart and Clementi—and greeted one another in the most friendly manner. . . .[15]

The account of the actual engagement comes to us best from Mozart's pen:

After we had stood on ceremony long enough, the Emperor declared that Clementi ought to begin. *"La Santa Chiesa Cattolica,"* he said, Clementi being a Roman. He improvised and then played a sonata. The Emperor then turned to me: "Allons, fire away." I improvised and played variations. The Grand Duchess produced some sonatas by Paisiello (wretchedly written in his own hand), of which I had to play the Allegros and Clementi the Andantes and Rondos. We then selected a theme from them and developed it on two pianofortes. The funny thing was that although I had borrowed Countess Thun's pianoforte, I only played on it when I played alone; such was the Emperor's desire—and, by the way, the other instrument was out of tune and three of the keys were stuck. "That doesn't matter," said the Emperor. Well, I put the best construction on it I could, that is that the Emperor, already knowing my skill and my knowledge of music, was only desirous of showing especial courtesy to a foreigner. Besides, I have it from a very good source that he was extremely pleased with me. . . .[16]

Mozart had every right to feel so since we have a record of a conversation the Emperor had following the competition with the composer Dittersdorf:

Emperor: Have you heard Mozart play?
Dittersdorf: Three times already.
Emperor: Do you like him?
Dittersdorf: Yes; all musicians do.
Emperor: You have heard Clementi, too?
Dittersdorf: Yes.
Emperor: Some prefer him to Mozart and Greybig is at the head of them. What do you think? Out with it!
Dittersdorf: Clementi's playing is art simply and solely; Mozart's combines art and taste.
Emperor: I said the same.[17]

Nor were they the only ones that felt Clementi's playing lacked Mozart's taste. In biting words and in a manner that was hardly objective, Mozart said the same thing to his father on January 16, 1782 in the above letter in which he had described the meeting with Clementi:

Now a word about Clementi. He is an excellent cembalo-player, but that is all. He has great facility with his right hand. His star passages are thirds. Apart from this, he has not a farthing's worth of taste or feeling; he is a mere *mechanicus*.[18]

56

Six months later to his father, he re-echoed these sentiments and included some technical advice for his sister (June 7, 1783):

Well, I have a few words to say to my sister about Clementi's sonatas. Everyone who either hears them or plays them must feel that as compositions they are worthless. They contain no remarkable or striking passages, except those in sixths and octaves. And I implore my sister not to practise these passages too much, so that she may not spoil her quiet, even touch and that her hand may not lose its natural lightness, flexibility and smooth rapidity. For after all what is to be gained by it? Supposing that you do play sixths and octaves with the utmost velocity (which no one can accomplish, not even Clementi) you only produce an atrocious chopping effect and nothing else whatever. Clementi is a *ciarlatano,* like all Italians. He writes *Presto* over a sonata or even *Prestissimo* and *Alla breve,* and plays it himself *Allegro* in 4/4 time. I know this is the case, for I have heard him do so. What he really does well are his passages in thirds; but he sweated over them day and night in London. Apart from this, he can do nothing, absolutely nothing, for he has not the slightest expression or taste, still less, feeling. . . .[19]

Clementi was much more charitable in his reaction and seems to have profited greatly from the experience. Regarding Mozart's performance, he said:

I had never before heard anyone play with such intelligence and grace. I was particularly overwhelmed by an adagio and by several of his extempore variations for which the Emperor chose the theme, and which we were required to vary alternately, accompanying one another.[20]

Surely Clementi's playing became less mechanical in the years following. His pupil Berger, recalling Mozart's harsh words, later remarked:

I asked Clementi whether in 1781 he had begun to treat the instrument in his present [1806] style. He answered *no,* and added that in those early days he had cultivated a more brilliant execution, especially in double notes, hardly known then, and in extemporized cadenzas, and that he had subsequently achieved a more melodic and noble style of performance after listening attentively to famous singers and also by means of the perfected mechanism of English pianos, the construction of which formerly stood in the way of a cantabile and legato style of playing.[21]

This more brilliant style of execution may have been tasteless for

Mozart, but it was, nevertheless, pointing straight in the direction of Beethoven. It contained something of the true virtuoso piano style.

At the time that Mozart had rubbed shoulders with him, Clementi's influence as a pianist and composer was just beginning to be widely felt. In fact, he was not only to outlive Mozart, but Beethoven as well. Returning to England, Clementi continued to perform and to write his many keyboard works. He also became involved in the music publishing business and in the manufacture of pianos by his own firm, Clementi & Co., which was responsible for further improvements in the English piano. Here he amassed a large personal fortune, notwithstanding the loss of £40,000 to his establishment by fire in 1807.

As a teacher he had even greater success: in England his students included John Field, who was widely heralded for his singing tone and legato playing, John Cramer, and even the "Wunderkind" Hummel for a time. Field (1782-1837) demonstrated Clementi's pianofortes for him. His manner of playing, with its exquisite shading, nuances, and quiet manner, foreshadowed Chopin's pianistic style. Field's pioneer work in the nocturne style greatly influenced Chopin. Ludwig Spohr painted an unforgettable picture of a visit to Clementi's piano showroom:

> . . . In the evening, I sometimes accompanied him [Clementi] to his large pianoforte warehouse, where Field was often obliged to play for hours, to display the instruments to the best advantage to the purchasers. The diary speaks with great satisfaction of the technical perfection and the "dreamy melancholy" of that young artist's execution. I have still in recollection the figure of the pale, overgrown youth, whom I have never since seen. When Field, who had outgrown his clothes, placed himself at the piano, stretched out his arms over the keyboard, so that the sleeves shrunk up nearly to his elbows, his whole figure appeared awkward and stiff in the highest degree; but as soon as his touching instrumentation began, everything else was forgotten, and one became all ear. . . . many anecdotes of the remarkable avarice of the rich Clementi were related. . . . It was generally reported that Field was kept on very short allowance by his master, and was obliged to pay for the good fortune of having his instruction with many privations.[22]

After travelling to Russia with Field in 1802 and playing before enthusiastic audiences, Clementi taught such pianists as Berger, Klengel and Meyerbeer in Germany. After a period in Italy and

Russia, he returned permanently to England in 1810. His later years were spent much more in composing than in performing.

Beginning in 1773, Clementi wrote over sixty solo pianoforte sonatas. They are full of great virility and are ideally suited to the early piano. In our present day Vladimir Horowitz has done much to revive interest in this remarkable literature. Its influence was very strong on Beethoven as well. Beethoven's biographer, Anton Schindler, tells us that the music library belonging to Beethoven was not very extensive, but that it did contain nearly all of Clementi's sonatas. He wrote:

> These he cherished above all others, and placed them in the first rank of works adapted for beautiful piano playing; this as much because of their lovely, fresh and attractive melodies as in view of the definite, therefore easily understandable form, in which all the movements progressed. Beethoven was not much drawn to Mozart's piano music. Hence for several years in succession the master had the musical education of the nephew he loved carried on almost exclusively through the medium of the Clementi sonatas. This was something which by no means pleased Karl Czerny, who was teaching his nephew at the time, and was far less prepossessed in favor of Clementi than Beethoven.[23]

While Mozart made the first major keyboard transition from harpsichord to the pianoforte, it was Clementi who was responsible for the early beginnings of a true pianoforte technique. With Clementi, passage work is naturally played legato. In the Mozartian era, it would be played *leggiero* — non-legato — unless the text specifically called for legato with the appropriate slurs. Clementi's works of a pedagogical nature give us considerable insight into his keyboard style. Two that must be mentioned are his *Introduction to the Art of Playing the Pianoforte* which dates from about 1803 and the influential *Gradus ad Parnassum*, published in sections between 1817 and 1827. The 1803 method book, besides containing the routine details of music fundamentals, fingering directions, and a number of one-measure finger exercises, is chiefly distinguished by the excellent collection of fifty moderately easy pieces for piano, either original or transcribed. Oscar Bie pointed out that it "is noteworthy as one of the first important attempts to make use of already existing pieces, not the work of the collector, as materials for studies."[24] We have compositions by Couperin, Rameau, Corelli, Haydn, and Beethoven represented, not to mention Mozart's "Away with Melancholy" and Handel's "Airs" from *Atalanta, Saul,* and *Judas Maccabaeus.*

Clementi gave little but superficial physical technical direction, but the importance of legato was emphasized:

> When the composer leaves the staccato and legato to the performer's taste the best rule is to adhere chiefly to the legato, reserving the staccato to give spirit occasionally to certain passages, and to set off the higher beauty of the legato.
>
> The hand and arm should be held in an horizontal direction; neither depressing nor raising the wrist; the seat should therefore be adjusted accordingly. The fingers and thumb should be placed over the keys, always ready to strike, bending the fingers in, more or less in proportion to their length. All unnecessary motion should be avoided. . . . Let the pupil now begin to practice, slowly at first the following passage; observing to keep down the first key till the next has been struck, and so on.[25]

This is the kind of finger technique that allows a penny to rest undisturbed upon the wrist. The finger action will be a little more vigorous (notice the word *strike*) and the tone larger on the English piano than on the Viennese, but the arm is not actively involved.

With his achievement in the *Gradus ad Parnassum,* Clementi assured himself a place of distinction in piano technique history. The original, completed work contained one-hundred compositions of various kinds including not only etude-type selections but movements of sonatas, canons, fugues, rondos, adagios, and others. It was Carl Tausig, at about mid-nineteenth century, who maligned Clementi's reputation by publishing his own version of the *Gradus ad Parnassum*—a selection of twenty-nine of the hundred that were more etude-like in character and less musical in content. This is the Clementi which has been widely known for the last hundred years. Nevertheless here are some of the earliest pieces of any importance which make use of five-finger scale patterns and all manner of arpeggiated and broken chord figurations, and help to define the piano idiom. A particular pattern is used in each study and then is employed consistently and intensively throughout. It is equality of finger action and evenness of tone that Clementi desires to achieve through the practice of these etudes, not to mention the increase of strength and fluency in the hands and fingers.

It is impossible to mention Clementi's *Gradus* without referring to the numerous studies by his very gifted pupil, Johann Baptist Cramer (1771-1858). The first forty-two of the famous eighty-four were published by Cramer in 1803-04 as Opus 39 and in 1810, the other half as Opus 40. This would make them forerunners of the *Gradus ad Parnassum*. Many of the technical figurations which Cramer uses are similar to those of Clementi. Sometimes they are shorter, but Cramer assimilates them into the musical structure so as to make them less stereotyped and more refined than Clementi. Schindler said that

Beethoven possessed the two books of Etudes by John Cramer which thus far had been published. These Etudes, our Master declared, were the chief basis of worth-while playing. Had he ever realized his own intention of writing a piano method, these Etudes would have supplied the most important portion of the practical examples in it, for he regarded them as the preparatory school best suited for the study of his own works because of the polyphony which so largely dominated in them.[26]

Beethoven had no less a regard for Cramer's pianistic abilities. Beethoven's pupil Ferdinand Ries remarked: "Amongst the pianoforte players he [Beethoven] had praise for but one as being distinguished—John Cramer. All others were but little to him."[27] Other of Cramer's contemporaries also spoke of the grace and beauty with which his hands and fingers glided about the keyboard.

The polyphonic structure referred to by Schindler reflected the deep love of Cramer, the classicist, for the music of J.S. Bach and Mozart. His musical development had begun at an early age. It was solid and thorough. His German father had brought him to England when he was only two years of age. In addition to violin and theory study with his father, he had worked in his youth for two years with Clementi. His first public performance came at the age of ten. At thirteen, in March of 1784, together with Clementi he performed a "Duetto for Two Pianofortes"—the first public two-piano presentation on record. Thereafter he developed on his own. Like Clementi, Cramer had his own publishing business and toured the Continent as a successful virtuoso. "Glorious John," as he came to be called, must have had some of the electrifying public appeal of Franz Liszt. Robert Schumann recorded an interesting anecdote:

While playing Kalkbrenner's four-part one-handed fugue, I thought of the excellent Thibaut, author of the book *On the Purity of Music*, who told me that once, at a concert given by Cramer in London, a polite Lady Somebody, an art amateur, actually rose, against all English convention, and stood on tiptoe to stare at the artist's hands. The ladies near her imitated her example, until finally the whole audience was standing, and the lady whispered ecstatically into Thibaut's ear: "Heavens, what trills!—what trills! and with the fourth and fifth finger!—and with both hands at once!" The whole audience murmured in accompaniment: "Heavens! what a trill! what trills!—and with both," etc.[28]

Cramer also wrote a piano method book and gave it the comprehensive title, *Instructions for the Pianoforte in which the first Rudiments of Music are clearly explained and the principal rules on the Art of Fingering, illustrated with numerous and appropriate Exercises to which are added Lessons in principal major and minor keys with a Prelude to each key.* His technical explanation reads much like Clementi:

> Let the performer sit in a graceful manner opposite the centre of the keyboard, neither too near, nor too far from the Instrument, so as to be able to reach with facility the highest and lowest keys.
> The height of the seat must be suited to that of the Performer, who, when seated, should have the elbows a little above the Keyboard, and the feet resting firmly on the ground near the pedals, to be ready to press them down, the arms must not be kept too close to the body, nor too distant from it; the shoulders should be rather depressed; the wrists must be nearly on a level with the arms and elbows, the knuckles being kept somewhat elevated, the first, second and third fingers must be bent, so as to bring the thumb and the little finger on a line; each finger must be placed over its respective key, and remain in that position whether used or not.
> The extremity of the fingers, but not the nails, must strike the keys, their motion should be so smooth as not to be noticed, the thumb must be kept over the keys so as to bring the other fingers close to the black keys, ready to strike them, this will prevent the wrist moving uselessly backwards and forwards.[29]

Clementi and Cramer both lived to be octogenarians and anachronisms in the romantic period. The more advanced styles of Beethoven, Chopin, and Liszt passed them by. But even in his old age when he occasionally performed, Clementi could still show flashes of his youthful vigor and improvise in delightful fashion. Cramer did not fare so well. Wilhelm von Lenz in 1842 found it a painful experience to hear him play several of his Etudes: "It was dry, wooden, harsh, with no *cantilena* in the third one, in D major. . . . Was *that* Cramer? Had the great man lived so long, only to remain so far behind the times?"[30] Nevertheless, in their prime Clementi and Cramer did much to establish and advance the course of an early legitimate piano technique.

Notes

[1] Walter James Turner, *Mozart, the Man and His Works,* p. 28.

[2] *Ibid.,* p. 29.

[3] *Ibid.*

[4] Otto Erich Deutsch, *Mozart, A Documentary Biography,* pp. 451, 454.

[5] *Ibid.,* pp. 26-27.

[6] Mueller von Asow, *Briefe W.A. Mozarts,* I, p. 271, cited by Eva and Paul Badura-Skoda, *Interpreting Mozart on the Keyboard,* p. 9.

[7] Maria Anna Mozart's letter to her husband, cited by Emily Anderson, ed., *The Letters of Mozart and His Family.* I, p. 436.

[8] Badura-Skoda, *Interpreting Mozart,* pp. 54-55.

[9] Anderson, ed., *Letters of Mozart,* I, pp. 339-40.

[10] *Ibid.,* I, p. 370.

[11] *Ibid.,* I, pp. 448-49.

[12] *Ibid.,* I, p. 374.

[13] *Ibid.,* II, p. 875.

[14] *Grove's Dictionary of Music and Musicians,* 5th ed., II, p. 345.

[15] Erich Schenk, *Mozart and His Times,* p. 309.

[16] Anderson, ed., *Letters of Mozart,* II, p. 793.

[17] Karl von Dittersdorf, *Autobiography,* p. 251.

[18] Anderson, ed., *Letters of Mozart,* II, p.793.

[19] *Ibid.,* p. 850.

[20] Schenk, *Mozart and His Times,* p. 309.

[21] *Grove's Dictionary,* 5th ed., II, pp. 345-46.

[22] Ludwig Spohr, *Ludwig Spohr's Autobiography,* pp. 39-40.

[23] O.G. Sonneck, ed., *Ludwig van Beethoven, Impressions of Contemporaries,* p. 173.

[24] Oscar Bie, *A History of the Pianoforte and Pianoforte Players,* p. 209.

[25] Muzio Clementi, *Introduction to the Art of Playing the Pianoforte,* pp. 14-15.

[26] O.G. Sonneck, ed., *Beethoven, Impressions of Contemporaries,* p. 173.

[27] Alexander Wheelock Thayer, *The Life of Ludwig van Beethoven,* I, p. 219.

[28] Robert Schumann, *On Music and Musicians,* p. 50.

[29] John Cramer, *Instructions for the Pianoforte,* p. 10.

[30] Wilhelm von Lenz, *The Great Piano Virtuosos of Our Time from Personal Acquaintance (Liszt, Chopin, Tausig, Henselt),* p. 43.

5.   Hummel: the Culmination
of the Viennese Era

In the direct line of musical descent from both Mozart and Clementi stands Johann Nepomuk Hummel (1778-1837), as the consummation of the Viennese school of pianoforte playing. Possessing the precocity of a Mozart, he developed very rapidly at the keyboard under his father's tutelage. In 1786 the family went to Vienna where his father became conductor at Schikaneder's theatre. Herr Hummel did not waste any time in getting his son to Mozart for an audition. Wolfgang's initial reluctance soon turned to enthusiastic praise as he heard the boy perform. Johann's father described the scene:

> Mozart was in the midst of work when we entered. Nevertheless, he received me with a friendly greeting: "Well, well, my dear Hummel, where have you been, how are you? So glad to see you. Sit down, and you too, my boy, find yourself a chair." The little man then had me sit down beside him on the sofa. "Well, what's on your mind?" he asked me. A bit hesitantly I came out with my request. He listened patiently to me, but when I was finished he looked dubious, and said: "You know, my dear friend, I'm not very fond of teaching; it takes too much of my time and interrupts my composing. But let's see and hear what's in the boy and whether it's worth taking trouble with him.—All right, sit down at the clavier and show us what you can do," he said to Nepomuk. The boy took out a few small pieces by Bach which he had practiced well, and set them on the clavier. Mozart made no comment, and he began. Wolfgang had sat down beside me again, arms folded, and listened. He became more and more attentive, his expression keener; his eyes lit up with delight. During the playing he nudged me gently once or twice and nodded his head in approval. When my boy was finished with the Bach,

65

Mozart put before him a none too easy composition of his own, to see how he did on sight-reading. It came off quite well. . . . Shortly thereafter my Nepomuk moved into Mozart's home, where he was treated like a child of the family.[1]

During his short life, Mozart had little time or inclination for piano teaching. Nevertheless, financial need made a certain amount of it necessary and he suffered the insecurity that many a private piano teacher of our day still encounters. A letter to his father, dated December 22, 1781, shows how he had tried to solve his problem:

Every morning at six o'clock my friseur arrives and wakes me, and by seven I have finished dressing. I compose until ten, when I give a lesson to Frau von Trattner and at eleven to the Countess Rumbeck, each of whom pays me six ducats for twelve lessons and to whom I go *every day,* unless they put me off, which I do not like at all. I have arranged with the Countess that she is never to put me off, I mean that, if I do not find her at home, I am at least to get my fee; but Frau von Trattner is too economical for that.[2]

On January 23 he wrote again that he had solved his problem:

. . . I have three pupils now, which brings me in eighteen ducats a month; for I no longer charge for twelve lessons, but monthly. I learnt to my cost that my pupils often dropped out for weeks at a time; so now, whether they learn or not, each of them must pay me six ducats. I shall get several more on these terms, but I really need only one more, because four pupils are quite enough.[3]

Although his lessons may not have been too regular, young Hummel absorbed the musical atmosphere of the Mozart home for the next two years and, greatly inspired, made very rapid progress in his piano studies. Mozart is said to have told the nine-year-old Nepomuk that he would soon be better than himself. This must have put ideas in Herr Hummel's head because the following year father and son set out on a concert tour of Germany and then Scotland and England. The sojourn in England lasted until 1792; during this time he had some study under Clementi and twice performed in public with Cramer. The story also goes that he received a kiss of appreciation from Haydn for being a last minute substitute for an ailing concert pianist.

The decade preceding the year 1803 passed quietly for Hummel in Vienna where in theory and composition he was under the tutelage and influence of Albrechtsberger, Salieri, and Haydn. Throughout his lifetime he was to compose extensively, but few of his pieces have survived the test of time or come close to matching the classic charm and flawless structure of his well-known Rondo in E flat major.

After a trip to St. Petersburg, he became Kapellmeister to Prince Esterhazy in Eisenstadt in 1804. He succeeded the aging Haydn. It was here that Hummel unwittingly incurred Beethoven's wrath. Beethoven had come to Eisenstadt in September of 1807 to hear his Mass in C major performed at the court. Following the performance the guests adjourned to the Prince's private chambers, according to Schindler,

> . . . for the purpose of conversing with him about the works which had been performed. When Beethoven entered the room, the Prince turned to him with the question: "But, my dear Beethoven, what is this that you have done again?" The impression made by this singular question, which was probably followed by other critical remarks, was the more painful on our artist because he saw the chapelmeister [Hummel] standing near the Prince laugh. Thinking that he was being ridiculed, nothing could keep him at the place where his work had been so misunderstood and besides, as he thought, where a brother in art had rejoiced over his discomfiture. He left Eisenstadt the same day. Thence dates the falling-out with Hummel, between whom there never existed a real intimate friendship. Unfortunately they never came to an explanation which might have disclosed that the unlucky laugh was not directed at Beethoven, but at the singular manner in which the Prince had criticized the mass.[4]

Hummel and Beethoven had known each other before this episode. Schindler goes on to say that there may have been other contributing factors involved including Beethoven's previous dislike of Hummel's style of piano playing and their simultaneous interest in the same girl. Hummel was the victor. This strained relationship continued until Beethoven's final illness when they effected a reconciliation.

By 1811 Hummel was back in Vienna teaching and performing. The Grand Duke of Saxony asked him to come to Weimar in 1819 to be his Kapellmeister, a position which Hummel held until his death. During this time, he was to make further trips to St. Petersburg, Paris, and London, but after 1822 he performed infrequently in public. But while in Weimar, he often played at

Goethe's house. With his polished, facile style he was greatly admired by the Biedermeier culture of the day.

This was even more the case in Hummel's youthful days spent in the elegance and refinement of the Viennese atmosphere. Even Czerny, the devoted pupil and disciple of Beethoven, fell under the musical spell of the youth in his early twenties whose physical appearance seems to have been somewhat of a contradiction. Czerny wrote in "Recollections from My Life":

> For several years (c. 1801-04) my father and I visited Mozart's widow; every Saturday there were musical soirees at her house, where Mozart's younger son (a pupil of Streicher's) gave very skillful performances. On one occasion the party was a good bit larger than usual, and among the many elegant persons I was especially fascinated by a very striking young man. His unpleasant, common-looking face, which twitched constantly, and his utterly tasteless clothing (a light-gray coat, a long scarlet vest, and blue trousers) seemed to indicate that he was some village schoolmaster. But the many valuable diamond rings he wore on almost all fingers provided a most peculiar contrast. As usual there was music, and finally this young man (he might have been somewhat older than twenty) was asked to play. And what an accomplished pianist he turned out to be! Even though I had already had so many opportunities to hear Gelinek, Lipavsky, Wölffl, and even Beethoven, the playing of this homely fellow seemed like a revelation. Never before had I heard such novel and dazzling difficulties, such cleanness and elegance in performance, nor such intimate and tender expression, nor even so much good taste in improvisation; when later he performed a few of Mozart's sonatas with violin (he was accompanied by Krommer) these compositions, which I had known for a long time, seemed like a completely new world. The information soon got around that this was the young *Hummel* once Mozart's pupil and now returned from London, where for a long time he had been Clementi's student. Even at that time Hummel had reached the pianistic proficiency—within the limits of the instruments of that time—for which he became so famous later.[5]

Czerny proceeded to compare the pianism of Hummel with that of Beethoven. He spoke of the rivalry which the two generated — seemingly not a deliberate thing fostered on the part of either personally:

> While Beethoven's playing was remarkable for his enor-

mous power, characteristic expression, and his unheard-of virtuosity and passage work, Hummel's performance was a model of cleanness, clarity, and of the most graceful elegance and tenderness; all difficulties were calculated for the greatest and most stunning effect, which he achieved by combining Clementi's manner of playing, so wisely gauged for the instrument, with that of Mozart. It was quite natural, therefore, that the general public preferred him as pianist, and soon the two masters formed parties, which opposed one another with bitter enmity. Hummel's partisans accused Beethoven of mistreating the piano, of lacking all cleanness and clarity, of creating nothing but confused noise the way he used the pedal, and finally of writing wilful, unnatural, unmelodic compositions, which were irregular besides. On the other hand, the Beethovenites maintained that Hummel lacked all genuine imagination, that his playing was as monotonous as a hurdy-gurdy, that the position of his fingers reminded them of spiders, and that his compositions were nothing more than arrangements of motifs by Mozart and Haydn. I myself was influenced by Hummel's manner of playing to the extent that it kindled in me a desire for greater cleanness and clarity.[6]

In spite of his brilliant manner of playing, it seems that Hummel was not taken up with any false admiration of himself. He appraised himself realistically in a moment of truth, faced during his youthful Vienna days. Years later in Weimar he told his pupil, Ferdinand Hiller, that

. . . it was a serious moment for me when Beethoven appeared. Was I to try to follow in the footsteps of such a genius? For a while I did not know what I stood on; but finally I said to myself that it was best to remain true to myself and my own nature.[7]

And that nature produced interpretations and improvisations of rare beauty, sometimes on rather frivolous tunes to be sure, but employing a superb technique built upon both Mozart and Clementi and perfectly suited to the light action and exquisite tone of the Viennese piano.

Hummel, the teacher, matched and very likely surpassed Hummel, the performer. His students (Hiller, Henselt, Pauer, Pixis, and Thalberg) enjoyed successful concert careers. It must also be mentioned that his three volume work, *A Complete Theoretical and Practical Course of Instruction on the Art of*

Playing the Piano Forte commencing with the Simplest Elementary Principles, and including every information requisite to the Most Finished Style of Performance, published midway during his tenure at Weimar in 1828, was undoubtedly one of the most important works on technique and piano playing of the entire nineteenth century. In size alone it must have achieved some kind of a record.

There are over 2,200 technical exercises and musical examples, most of them a few measures in length. By 1899, when the high finger school was beginning to be held in disrepute, Oscar Bie had labeled it "a monument of misguided diligence, great in its patient calculation of permutations, but a dead curiosity."[8] Much of its usefulness had undoubtedly been outgrown. However, in the light of present-day musicological research, it does deserve consideration because of what it tells us of the study practices of the period. An abridged version would still be of value to today's student.

In his preface to both parents and teachers of music, Hummel advocates a daily hour of instruction for the beginner for the first six months and if possible even for a full year! This seems to have been a common practice of the period. He thinks that girls should not begin their instruction before seven years of age and boys not before eight. He also feels that three hours a day of practice at the most should be enough for the advancing student to achieve excellence. Then follows a list of "chief qualities that a good master should possess." They are worth recalling today:

1) That the master should feel the most zealous interest in all that relates to his pupil's progress in the art.

2) That he must not allow him to contract any bad habits.

3) That as soon as the pupil has acquired the preliminary knowledge absolutely necessary, he should not exclusively occupy him with merely dry examples, but should occasionally intermingle with them, short and pleasing pieces, composed for the Piano-forte and for this express purpose, that the Pupil's amusement and his desire of learning may be encouraged.

The custom of many masters of tormenting beginners with difficult compositions is absolutely injurious.

4) That he should accustom the pupil betimes to direct his eyes to the notes only, and to find the keys by the feel of the fingers, according to their distance from one another. Many pupils, particularly children, endeavour at first to play from

70

memory, by which means they never attain to any readiness in reading the notes; let the master by all means use them to name aloud the notes quickly, one after the other; if he should observe that the pupil has committed a piece too much to memory, let him proceed no further with it, but at once give him something new, that he may be compelled to play by note and not by ear.

5) Let him never allow the pupil to play too fast; for this is the first step towards an unintelligible and incorrect style of performance.

6) Let him endeavor, from the very outset, to give the pupil a clear and correct manner of marking time by his touch, and a strict and well-measured observance of it.

7) Let the master, as far as possible, attend to the proper tuning of the instrument, that the ear of the pupil may not be spoiled but rather improved, and refined.

If he wishes to see his Pupil make a rapid progress, he must demonstrate the warmest interest in his so doing; must treat him with indulgence, and not urge him too quickly forward, but nevertheless be strict in his instructions. From the first, he must not allow the pupil to keep his fingers on the keys, either a longer or shorter time than is necessary; he must accustom him to hold out syncopated notes, and to play short ones lightly and detached, that he may have his hands and fingers under control, and avoid a lame and heavy style of performance. Let the master also, from the very commencement, habituate the pupil to the strict observance of time, and to count while playing; let him shew the pupil how he should play a passage, and cause him to imitate and practise it, till he can perform it with perfect correctness. By this method the pupil will play well what he attempts, and in the end reap the best fruits from his labours.[9]

The first volume, or Part I, deals largely with fundamentals and their illustrations and includes no less than 617 one-measure five-finger patterns covering the range from a fifth up to and including the octave. Completing Part I are 60 Practical Pieces illustrating the previous material and graded as to difficulty. Written in Hummel's polished style, they contain many interesting melody lines and classical figurations. They would be better suited for use today than the large proportion of our contemporary teaching materials which are only poor imitations of the past. Hummel's instructions on the physical approach to the piano are also included:

PART I.[10]

SECTION FIRST.

Elementary Instructions.

CHAPTER I.

ON SITTING AT THE PIANO FORTE.

§1.

The pupil must sit opposite to the middle of the key board, at a distance of from six to ten inches, according to his stature, and the length of his arms; so that the right hand may conveniently reach the highest, and the left hand the lowest keys, without altering the position of the body.

§2.

The seat must neither be too high nor too low, and such that both hands may rest on the keys, natural and without effort. Children should have their feet supported, that their seat may be steady and secure.

CHAPTER II.

ON HOLDING THE BODY, THE ARMS, THE HANDS, AND THE FINGERS.

From the outset, particular attention must be directed to these points, since any negligence on this head, drags in its train the most disadvantageous results, such indeed as are scarcely to be amended at a future period; and facility, gracefulness, neatness, expression, and strength of performance will thereby suffer materially.

§1.

The *body* must be *held* upright, neither bending forwards nor sideways, and the elbows rather turned towards the body, yet without pressing against it.

§2.

The *muscles* of the arms and hands must act without any stiffness, and with so much force only, as is necessary to move the hands and fingers without languor.

§3.

The *hands* must be held in a somewhat rounded position and turned rather outwards like the feet, yet freely and without effort;

72

by this means the employment of the thumb on the black keys will be much facilitated. Their position must not be either higher or lower than is necessary to bend the finger joints, so as to strike the keys with the middle of the tips of the fingers and so that the thumb may form a horizontal line with the little finger on the key board.

Extending the fingers flat on the keys and as it were boreing into them by letting the hands hang downwards are altogether faulty positions and give rise to a lame and heavy manner of playing.

§4.

Excepting in extensions, the fingers must neither stand too far apart nor be drawn too close together; each finger should lie naturally over its proper key. They ought not likewise, to rest longer on the keys than the prescribed time, as a habit of so doing, greatly diminishes the clearness of the performance.

The *thumb* touches lightly the surface of the keys with the edge of its top joint. As it is shorter than the fingers, the pupil must accustom himself to hold it somewhat bent and inclining towards the first finger, that it may always be ready to pass under the fingers but it must not be permitted to touch the fingers, nor be allowed to drop below the keys.

In general, to attain the necessary facility, steadiness and certainty in playing, we must avoid every violent movement of the elbows, and the muscles must not be exerted beyond what a free and quiet position of the hand requires. The quickness of motion lies only in the joints of the fingers, which should move with lightness and freedom, and not be lifted up too high from the keys.

§5.

The *touch* or mode of striking the key must be decisive and equal; all pressure and thumping are to be avoided; neither hands nor fingers should change their naturally bent position, and the keys must be struck rather forwards than backwards on the key board, that the tone may be more powerful, and the passage delivered with more roundness and finish.

§6.

Lastly, unbecoming habits should be carefully avoided; as, holding the face too near the book, biting the lips, nodding the head to mark the time, opening or distorting the mouth &c. &c. as they are prejudicial to the health and contrary to gracefulness of demeanour.

73

At the end of Part I, Hummel has a supplementary chapter suggesting graded pieces for the aspiring student. It bears marked resemblance to a modern-day study program:

As the uninterrupted study of the foregoing exercises and lessons might somewhat abate the energy of the Beginner, I should advise the Master to mix with them, from time to time, compositions of a light and pleasing character; avoiding only flimsy extracts from Operas, ballets, overtures, dances, &c: because they are not suited to the Piano-forte, form neither the hands nor the fingers, employ the left hand too little, spoil the taste for genuine Piano-forte music, and interrupt the progress of a serious and rational study of music.

I conceive, therefore, that it will not be unacceptable to the Master if, upon this opportunity, and as a termination to this part of the work, I add a select list of compositions, known to me; which, suited to the increasing powers of the Pupil, begin with pieces purposely written for him, and advance gradually towards the highest stage of execution and refinement.

SELECTION FOR THE BEGINNER

A.C. MÜLLER'S,	instructive Lessons—6 books.
_____	3 Sonatines progressives. Op: 18.
HUMMEL,	6 pieces faciles.
PLEYEL,	18 pieces faciles.
WANHALL'S,	works for beginners.
DUSSEK'S	6 Sonatines progressives. Op 20. Books 1 & 2.
KUHLAU,	little Rondos
CLEMENTI'S	Sonatinas fingered. Op 36, 37, 38.
C. CZERNY	_____
GELINEK,	Sonatine facile, 1 & 2.
LIKL,	Sonatines, Nos: 1.2.3. with Violin Acct.
HASLINGER'S	Youth's Musical friend.
HÄSER,	little pieces for beginners in all the keys.
_____	musical diversions.

IN A MORE ADVANCED STAGE

PLEYEL,	
KOZELUCH,	
HUMMEL,	
HAYDN,	
MOZART,	and
CLEMENTI'S	easier works, with or without accompaniments.

When the Pupil shall have attained a still greater power of execution, place before him:

MOZART,
CLEMENTI,
DUSSEK,
BEETHOVEN, and
CRAMER'S,   more difficult compositions; and if, in the meanwhile, he has sufficiently studied the practical examples contained in the second part of this school, then

CLEMENTI'S   Preludes and Exercises,
——————   Gradus ad Parnassum
CRAMER'S   Studies &c:

and the more difficult compositions of distinguished composers, ancient and modern. And, as a termination to the whole, as a practice in the strict or fugued style of composition, and as a means of forming the taste for the loftiest departments of the art:

J.S. BACH   and HANDEL'S WORKS.[11]

The remaining hundreds of exercises in his method are mostly contained in the second book. They work out problems in fingering in exhaustive fashion. Hummel prepares the way for our modern system of rational fingering when he says that, excepting to avoid the use of the thumb on a black key, ". . . we must employ the same succession of fingers when a passage consists of a progression of similar groups of notes."[12] Almost 200 exercises follow which work out this one principle alone.

In the final volume of Hummel's *Art of Playing the Piano Forte,* he treats the interpretative side of performance: such topics as ornamentation (he preferred the trill to begin on the principal note), pedaling (only in slow movements), beauty in performance, and matters of good taste. Two selections from Part II are quoted herewith because they show so clearly how Hummel would relate his philosophy of beauty and expression to one's physical technique:

ON MUSICAL PERFORMANCE IN GENERAL

§1

It is usual, and very properly so, to discriminate between a *correct* and a *beautiful* performance. The latter is frequently termed *expressive,* but, as it appears to me, not with sufficient accuracy.—Correctness of performance relates to the mechanism of playing, as far as it can be indicated by musical notation. Beauty of performance supposes every thing nicely

75

rounded off, and actually suited to any given composition, and to every passage in it; it includes whatever is tasteful, pleasing, and ornamental. Expression relates immediately to the feelings; and denotes in the player a capacity and facility of displaying by his performance, and urging to the heart of his audience, whatever the composer has addressed to the feelings in his production, and which the performer must also feel; points which can be intimated only by general terms, having but little precision in them, and which usually are of service to those only who have these things already within them. If such be the case, it will follow, that expression may be awakened indeed, but, properly speaking, that it can neither be taught nor acquired; it dwells within the soul itself, and must be transfused directly from it into the performance; for which reason we shall not treat of expression in this place. It follows also, that beauty of performance cannot be perfectly taught or acquired; though much that relates to it may be explained by means of circumstances connected with it. This we shall endeavor to do; and, on the whole, we must conclude, that correctness of performance alone admits of a thorough development.

§2

What relates to beauty and taste in performance will be best cultivated, and perhaps, ultimately most easily obtained, by hearing music finely performed, and by listening to highly distinguished musicians, particularly singers gifted with great powers of expression. Indeed, among those musicians and composers, who in their youth have received instructions in singing, there will generally be found more pure, correct, and critical musical feeling, than among such as have only a general and extrinsic idea of melody and good singing.

§3

It is, no doubt, meritorious to overcome great difficulties upon the instrument; but this alone is not sufficient to entitle any one to the reputation of a complete master of it; such dexterous players surprise the ear, to be sure (as Ph. Em. Bach expresses himself), but do not delight it; they astonish the understanding without satisfying it.

In the present day, many performers endeavor to supply the absence of natural inward feeling by an appearance of it; for example,—

1. By distortions of the body, and unnatural elevations of the arms;
2. By a perpetual jingle, produced by the constant use of the pedals;

3. By a capricious dragging or slackening of the time, (*tempo rubato*), introduced at every instant, and to satiety;

4. By an overloaded decoration of the passages of melody, till the air and character are often no longer perceptible.

But I caution every player against falling into these impure and tasteless excesses, and advise him to give to every thing *that* which really belongs to it. By excessive dragging in the time, the *allegro* loses its brilliancy, neatness, and unity. By being overcharged with embellishments, the *adagio* is deprived of its genuine solemn and pathetic character, and of its beauty, sweetness, and grace.

In his performance, the player ought not to let it be for a moment doubtful, even to the uninitiated, whether he is playing an *adagio* or an *allegro*. I do not, by any means, intend to say that we may not occasionally retard the time in an *allegro,* or that we ought not to introduce embellishments into an *adagio;* but this must be done with moderation, and in the proper place. That an *adagio* is much more difficult to perform with propriety than an *allegro* is a fact acknowledged by everyone.

SOME LEADING OBSERVATIONS RESPECTING BEAUTY
OF PERFORMANCE

§1

To arrive at a correct and beautiful style of performance, it is requisite that the player should be perfectly master of his fingers,—that is, that they should be capable of every possible gradation of touch.

This can be effected only by the finest internal sensibility in the fingers themselves, extending to their very tips, by which they are rendered capable of increasing their pressure on the keys, from the most delicate contact to the utmost degree of power. Consequently, the fingers must obey the player in the gentlest touch, and in the most natural and easy position of the hand, equally as in the finest stroke, and in the most extended state of the muscles.

When he has obtained this delicate feeling so far as to be able to produce these various gradations, this power will manifest itself, not only by its advantageous effect upon his ear, but, by degrees, it will also shed its influence upon his sensibility, become, by its means, purer and more delicate, and thus implant in his soul the seeds of a true, beautiful, and expressive style of performance.

I am unable to give any better rule than this, drawn from nature herself. Any remaining observations belong rather to the mechanical part of execution, with which the feelings of the individual come less into contact.

§2

Let the player study the character of the composition, as, otherwise, he cannot possibly awaken in his audience the same emotions as the composer has endeavored to excite by his music. Let him also keep in mind, steadily, which he is performing, an *adagio* or an *allegro,* for each requires a particular style, and that which is proper for the one is injurious to the other.[13]

And lastly it should be pointed out that in this same section we have from a very authoritative original source in the classical period one of the most eloquent descriptions of the differences in action and tone between the Viennese and English pianos—and indirectly between these two schools of pianoforte playing. Hummel writes:

ON TOUCH PROPER TO DIFFERENT PIANO-FORTES
OF GERMAN OR ENGLISH CONSTRUCTION

§2

Pianofortes, generally speaking, are constructed on two different plans, the *German* or *Vienna,* as it is termed, and the *English,* the former is played upon with great facility as to touch, the latter with considerably less ease. Other modes of construction are compounded of these two, or are merely partial variations of them.

§3

It cannot be denied, but that each of these mechanisms has its peculiar advantages. The German Piano may be played upon with ease by the weakest hand. It allows the performer to impart to his execution every possible degree of light, and shade, speaks clearly and promptly, has a round, flute-like tone, which, in a large room contrasts well with the accompanying orchestra, and does not impede rapidity of execution by requiring too great an effort.* (Footnote: *By this, I do not merely understand a somewhat shorter and a stiffer touch; for every player should possess this much power over the instrument.) These instruments are likewise durable, and cost but about half the price of the English Piano Forte.

§4

To the English construction, however, we must not refuse the praises due, on the score of its durability and fullness of tone. Nevertheless, this instrument does not admit of the same facility of execution as the German; the touch is much heavier, the keys sink much deeper and, consequently, the return of the hammer upon the repetition of a note, cannot take place so quickly.

Whoever is yet unaccustomed to these instruments, should not, by any means allow himself to be disconcerted by the deep descent of the keys, nor by the heaviness of the touch; only let him not hurry himself in the time, and let him play all quick passages and runs with the usual lightness of finger; even passages which require to be executed with strength, must, as in the German instruments, be produced with the power of the fingers, and not by the weight of the arms; for as this mechanism is not capable of such numerous modifications, in force of tone, as ours, * (Footnote: *It is self-evident that we speak here only of the instruments of the most celebrated Vienna and German makers.) we gain no louder sound by a heavy blow, than may produced by the natural strength and elasticity of the fingers.

In the first moment, we are sensible of something unpleasant, because in forte passages, in particular on our German instrument, we press the keys quite down, while here, they must be only touched superficially, as otherwise, we could not succeed in executing running passages without excessive effort and double difficulty. As a counterpoise to this, however, through the fullness of tone of the English Piano-Forte, the melody receives a particular charm and harmonious sweetness.

In the meantime, I have observed, that, powerfully as these instruments sound in a chamber, they change the nature of their tone in spacious rooms; and that they are less distinguishable than ours, when associated with complicated orchestral accompaniments; this, in my opinion, is to be attributed to the thickness and fullness of their tone.[14]

When the Hummel achievement is seen for what it is — the final flowering of the Mozartean culture and not something competing directly with the genius of a Beethoven — Hummel emerges as a figure of genuine musical stature, one of the truly great pianists of the early nineteenth century. Schumann placed him in the company of Chopin as one of the important "many-sided, cultured composer-performers"[15] of the day. Hummel's compositional style influenced both Schumann and Chopin. And his pianoforte school, although going into far more detail than was necessary to help pianists of the day cope with the keyboard figurations of the classic literature, was a notable contribution to the study literature—unique and amazingly original. Oscar Bie was forced to admit after surveying the ground:

79

And thus comes to pass the great miracle, that by means of the utmost conceivable combinations, by means of the hundred chromatic subleties, musical figures are formed which no composer had previously invented, and which lead on to sound-effects never before suspected. In the examples of an exercise-book lay undreamed-of novelties in piano composition.[16]

But in spite of giving more technical detail and instruction material than either Clementi or Cramer, even Hummel did not make any significant advance toward a true science of piano technique. He supplied a wealth of finger technique material, but no adequate blueprint as to how to use it.

Notes

[1] Erich Schenk, *Mozart and His Times*, p.366.

[2] Emily Anderson, ed., *The Letters of Mozart and His Family*, II, p. 789.

[3] *Ibid.*, II, p. 795.

[4] Quoted in Alexander Wheelock Thayer, *The Life of Ludwig van Beethoven*, II, p. 108.

[5] Carl Czerny, "Recollections From My Life," *The Musical Quarterly*, XLII, No. 3 (July, 1956), pp.308-309.

[6] *Ibid.*, p. 309.

[7] Oscar Bie, *A History of the Pianoforte and Pianoforte Players*, p. 212.

[8] *Ibid.*, p. 187.

[9] Johann Nepomuk Hummel, *A Complete Theoretical and Practical Course of Instruction, on the Art of Playing the Piano Forte Commencing with the Simplest Elementary Principles, and including every information requisite to the Most finished Style of Performance*, I, pp. iv-v.

[10] *Ibid.*, I, pp. 12-13.

[11] *Ibid.*, I, pp. 109-110.

[12] *Ibid.*, II, p. 3.

[13] *Ibid.*, III, pp. 39-41.

[14] *Ibid.*, III, pp. 64-65.

[15] Robert Schumann, *On Music and Musicians*, p. 83.

[16] Bie, *A History of the Pianoforte and Pianoforte Players*, p. 212.

6.   The Dynamic Beethoven Technique

There is no more fascinating personality in music history than Ludwig van Beethoven (1770-1827). With this spiritual giant and fighter for the rights and dignity of the musician in the court society of the European aristocracy, we have the true beginnings of modern pianism. The pianoforte became a means to an end in expressing the deepest human emotions; previous rules and traditions of piano technique meant nothing to him if they in any way hampered his inner feeling at the keyboard. Here is the first major pianist directly to oppose the finger school and its harpsichord ancestry. The man, who struggled intensely with the mundane while creating the most sublime, who could show the deepest sympathy and kindness and then again vast ill will, simply had to play the piano with his entire physical body. Here was the intensely human being who comforted his pupil, the Baroness Dorothea von Ertmann, in the loss of her child by saying not a word, but by playing the piano from his heart to hers uninterruptedly for over an hour ("He told me everything, and at last brought me comfort").[1] Here was also the impatient, ill-mannered diner who, when the waiter brought the wrong dish, took the serving of meat and gravy, threw it on the waiter's head, and then laughed heartily with his friends at the ridiculous sight of gravy running down his face.

The young Beethoven came from a background where circumstances worked against him and had much to do with the formation of his later character and personality. His heritage from his grandfather on his father's side seems to have been honorable enough — he was Kapellmeister in Bonn, Germany — but the grandmother was addicted to strong drink. This trait was passed on to their son Johann, a singer and Ludwig's father. Johann's wife, Maria Magdalena, was a kindly, serious soul and doubtless was a comfort to Ludwig when her husband's unstable, sometimes irascible nature manifested itself. Lacking Leopold Mozart's qualifications, the father did recognize his son's enormous talent at a very early age, however, and gave him limited training in both violin and piano. The prospect of financial gain surely helped to motivate Johann.

From the age of eight Ludwig received sporadic music teaching from several others, including the seventy-year-old court organist, Heinrich van den Eeden, and an opera singer, Friedrich Pfeiffer, who was also a pianist. He made rapid progress, but stable, systematic study did not come until he became the pupil of Christian Gottlob Neefe. This was sometime shortly after Neefe came to Bonn in 1779 where he became Vice-Kapellmeister and then court organist at van den Eeden's death in 1781. Neefe's influence on the young boy was major and of lasting proportions. A man of learning and culture, he introduced Ludwig not only to the great musical classics, but the literary ones as well—Shakespeare, Goethe, Schiller, and the ancients of Greece and Rome.

The first printed mention of Beethoven came from the pen of Neefe and was written for *Cramer's Magazin,* dated March 2, 1783:

> Louis van Beethoven, son of the tenor singer mentioned, a boy of eleven years and of most promising talent. He plays the clavier very skilfully and with power, reads at sight very well, and — to put it in a nutshell — he plays chiefly "The Well-Tempered Clavichord" of Sebastian Bach, which Herr Neefe put into his hands. Whoever knows this collection of preludes and fugues in all the keys—which might almost be called the *ne plus ultra* of our art—will know what this means. So far as his duties permitted, Herr Neefe has also given him instruction in thorough-bass. He is now training him in composition and for his encouragement has had nine variations for the pianoforte, written by him on a march — by Ernst Christoph Dressler — engraved at Mannheim. This youthful genius is deserving of help to enable him to travel. He would surely become a second Wolfgang Amadeus Mozart were he to continue as he has begun.[2]

He soon became Neefe's assistant. Neefe also saw to the publication of Ludwig's three *Bonn* Sonatas. In 1787 Beethoven determined to go to Vienna for further study; but after being there only a matter of weeks during which time he had several lessons with Mozart, he had to return to Bonn because of his mother's serious illness. While passing through Augsburg, he visited Streicher and inspected his instruments. Saddened by the death of his mother and the continued moral deterioration of his father, he continued on in Bonn for four more years—bearing the family burdens, but also developing rapidly as both performer and composer.

By the time Beethoven was able to return to Vienna in 1792, Mozart had died. Study followed with Haydn, Albrechtsberger, Schenk, and Salieri. Haydn and Beethoven never got along very well: there was probably too much of the revolutionary in the young Beethoven and not enough time and patience available from the older Haydn. Beethoven was not long in making a place for himself in the musical culture of Vienna. His initial reputation there seems to have been achieved to a large degree by his excellent performances of Bach's *Well-Tempered Clavier*.[3] He was soon in demand as a pianoforte performer and improviser in palatial homes of the royal community. It was in these settings, as well as at court, that Viennese musical life flourished. It was not unusual for a count to have his own orchestra and chamber groups; one nobleman invited his friends to hear string quartets performed before breakfast! It was to these circles that Beethoven, the man and artist, was cordially welcomed — notwithstanding his sometimes uncouth appearance and coarse manners. As a musical aristocrat, Beethoven considered himself an equal and was accepted as such.

The composer Johann Schenk in his autobiography described his first meeting with Beethoven in 1792:

> After the customary courtesies he offered to improvise on the pianoforte. He asked me to sit beside him. Having struck a few chords and tossed off a few figures as if they were of no significance, the creative genius gradually unveiled his profound psychological pictures. My ear was continually charmed by the beauty of the many and varied motives which he wove with wonderful clarity and loveliness into each other, and I surrendered my heart to the impressions made upon it while he gave himself wholly up to his creative imagination, and anon, leaving the field of mere tonal charm, boldly stormed the most distant keys in order to give expression to violent passions.[4]

It seems highly unlikely that Beethoven had any formal piano instruction after he returned to Vienna in 1792. There is reason to believe that at this stage of his development, in spite of the respect he was already commanding at the keyboard, his playing lacked refinement and control. Schindler said that Beethoven himself admitted that "his own usual way of playing the piano was hard and heavy, owing, not to his want of feeling, but to his practising a great deal upon the organ, [particularly in Bonn] of which instrument he was very fond."[5] Then, too, at the very beginning of his Viennese career, he had had little opportunity to hear the greatest, most polished performers of the day. The closing years of the eighteenth century were years of seasoning and growth. Doring recorded Beethoven's own dumb-founded reaction to the playing of the pianist Sterkel, celebrated in his day for an easy and graceful approach to the piano. Beethoven was reluctant to perform before him; but when Sterkel insinuated that Beethoven could not play a set of his own variations, he immediately proceeded to play not only this set, but several others, ". . . to the great amazement of the listeners, in the same graceful manner, by which he had been so much struck in Sterkel. He thus gave a proof how easy it was for him to learn his manner of piano-playing from another."[6] Surely by the year 1798, when Tomaschek referred to him as the giant among pianoforte players,[7] many of the rough edges had been rubbed smooth. But perhaps not quite to Beethoven's own satisfaction, because later in 1801, he wrote that he had greatly perfected his playing.[8] This period found him at the pinnacle of his performance career.

One of the most eloquent descriptions of Beethoven's superlative creative powers at the piano at this time was recorded about 1799 by Ignaz von Seyfried, one of the conductors at Schikaneder's Theatre. This is the account of his pianistic duel with the popular bravura pianist Joseph Wölffl, (1773-1812), from Salzburg:

Beethoven had already attracted attention to himself by several compositions and was rated a first-class pianist in Vienna when he was confronted by a rival in the closing years of the last century. Thereupon there was, in a way, a revival of the old Parisian feud of the Gluckists and Piccinists, and the many friends of art in the Imperial City arrayed themselves in two parties. At the head of Beethoven's admirers stood the amiable Prince Lichnowsky; among the most zealous patrons of Wölffl was the broadly cultured Baron Raymond von Wetzlar, whose delightful villa (on the Grunberg near the Emperor's recreation-castle) offered to all artists, native and foreign, an asylum in the summer months, as pleasing as it was desirable, with true British loyalty. There the interesting combats of the two athletes not infrequently offered an indescribable artistic treat to the numerous and thoroughly select gathering. Each brought forward the latest product of his mind. Now one and anon the other gave free rein to his glowing fancy; sometimes they would seat themselves at two pianofortes and improvise alternately on themes which they gave each other, and thus created many a four-hand Capriccio which if it could have been put upon paper at the moment would surely have bidden defiance to time. It would have been difficult, perhaps impossible, to award the palm of victory to either one of the gladiators in respect of technical skill. Nature had been a particularly kind mother to Wölffl in bestowing upon him a gigantic hand which could span a tenth as easily as other hands compass an octave, and permitted him to play passages of double notes in these intervals with the rapidity of lightning. In his improvisations even then Beethoven did not deny his tendency toward the mysterious and gloomy. When once he began to revel in the infinite world of tones, he was transported also above all earthly things; — his spirit had burst all restricting bonds, shaken off the yoke of servitude, and soared triumphantly and jubilantly into the luminous spaces of the higher aether. Now his playing tore along like a wildly foaming cataract, and the conjurer constrained his instrument to an utterance so forceful that the stoutest structure was scarcely able to withstand it; and anon he sank down, exhausted, exhaling gentle plaints, dissolving in melancholy. Again the spirit would soar aloft, triumphing over transitory terrestrial sufferings, turn its glance upward in reverent sounds and find rest and comfort on the innocent bosom of holy nature. But who shall sound the depths of the sea? It was the mystical Sanscrit language whose hieroglyphs can be read only by the initiated. Wölffl, on the contrary, trained in the school of Mozart, was always equable; never superficial but always clear and thus more accessible to the multitude. He used art only as a means to an end, never to exhibit his acquirements. He always enlisted the interest of his hearers and inevitably compelled them to follow the progression of his well-ordered ideas. Whoever has heard Hummel will know what is meant by this. . . .[9]

At about this same time, the *Allgemeine muskalische Zeitung*, in its first year of publication, 1798, remarked about Beethoven's brilliant, free improvisations and the wonderful way in which he was "able to perform impromptu on any given theme a graceful and at the same time closely knit development of ideas, not merely a variation of the figure, which so many virtuosi do so well—and so emptily."[10] The reviewer did not overlook, however, that "he sometimes lacks delicacy and clarity."[11]

During these years Beethoven's playing did achieve greater refinement, but his temperament had not undergone any change. His playing always remained freely expressive, exceedingly dynamic and emotional. Reis relates Beethoven's meeting with another famous pianist of the day, the charlatan and tremolo specialist, Daniel Steibelt (1765-1823), at a concert at the home of Count Fries during the spring of 1800. Steibelt performed in his own quintet and then played an obviously prepared "improvisation," a set of variations on one of Beethoven's own themes. This so irritated Beethoven that he felt he had to go to the piano himself and improvise. Reis, Beethoven's pupil, continues:

> He went in his usual (I might say, ill-bred) manner to the instrument as if half-pushed, picked up the violoncello part of Steibelt's quintet in passing, placed it (intentionally?) upon the stand upside down and with one finger drummed a theme out of the first few measures. Insulted and angered, he improvised in such a manner that Steibelt left the room before he finished, would never again meet him and, indeed, made it a condition that Beethoven should not be invited before accepting an offer.[12]

If there was one thing that Beethoven respected above all others, it was musical integrity.

Two other pianists and far greater musicians, whom Beethoven met later in life and for whom he showed genuine appreciation, were Franz Schubert and Carl Maria von Weber. For both, playing the piano was incidental to their careers as composers, but their pianistic abilities helped them to create masterpieces for the piano which were unique contributions to the literature. Schubert (1797-1828) brought his song style to his sonatas. That he must have been a respectable pianist is evident from his own remarks following a performance he had given in 1825 of the variation movement of his Sonata in A Minor, Op. 42. He said that "several people assured me that my fingers had transformed the keys into singing voices. If this is really true, then I am highly delighted, since I cannot abide the damnable thumping which is peculiar to even the most distinguished pianists and which pleases neither the ear nor the mind."[13] There is no doubt that Weber (1786-1826) was a phenomenal pianist, even as a youth—a highly original, largely self-made performer. His keyboard style, brilliant, yet warmly romantic, is evident in his compositions for piano. It opened up new dimensions with the use of wide and rather startling skips and bravura passages in thirds, sixths, and octaves. Weber had gone to Vienna in 1823 for the first performance of his opera *Euryanthe*. While there he went to the suburb of Baden to pay his respects to Beethoven. That Beethoven showed admiration for Weber is seen in the following excerpt in a letter from Weber to his wife:

He received me with an affection which was touching; he embraced me most heartily at least six or seven times and finally exclaimed enthusiastically: "Indeed, you're a devil of a fellow!—a good fellow!" We spent the afternoon very merrily and contentedly. This rough, repellant man actually paid court to me, served me at table as if I had been his lady. In short, this day will always remain remarkable in my memory as well as of those present.[14]

Most of the performances in Vienna were in the salons of the rich, and Beethoven undoubtedly received stipends for many of these. There was very little of our system of concert management and admission fees. Orchestral concerts open to the public for the purpose of raising money for charitable enterprises were held from time to time. Only the truly great might risk a public performance for his own benefit.

Observations at close range by his pupils, Ferdinand Ries and Carl Czerny, give striking evidence of his mature ability and also his paradoxical nature. Ries thought

. . . he played his own compositions very freakishly, holding firmly to the measure, however, as a rule and occasionally, but not often, hurrying the tempo. At times he would hold the tempo back in his *crescendo* with *ritardando,* which made a very beautiful and highly striking effect. In playing he would give a passage now in the right hand, now in the left, a lovely and absolutely inimitable expression; but he very seldom added notes or ornaments.[15]

For Czerny, not even Hummel could match his virtuosity and speed in scales, double trills, and skips. He also rather surprisingly observed a serene facet in Beethoven's nature:

His bearing while playing was masterfully quiet, noble and beautiful, without the slightest grimace (only bent forward low, as his deafness grew upon him); his fingers were very powerful, not long, and broadened at the tips by much playing, for he told me very often indeed that he generally had to practise until after midnight in his youth.[16]

Czerny also realized that both his playing and his compositions were far ahead of his time, and that the pianos before 1810,

. . . still extremely weak and imperfect, could not endure his gigantic style of performance. Hence it was that Hummel's

87

purling, brilliant style, well calculated to suit the manner of the time, was much more comprehensible and pleasing to the public. But Beethoven's performance of slow and sustained passages produced an almost magical effect upon every listener and, so far as I know, was never surpassed.[17]

Both pupils marvelled at his improvisatory gifts. Czerny thought him less successful in performing his printed compositions, attributing this to the fact that "he never had patience or time to practise."[18] Ries said that "he played his own compositions very unwillingly."[19] He often had to be coaxed or tricked into performance. Seyfried observed:

When he did not feel in the mood it required repeated and varied urgings to get him to sit down to the pianoforte. Before he began playing he was in the habit of hitting the keys with the flat of his hand, or running a single finger up and down the keyboard, in short, doing all manner of things to kill time and laughing heartily, as was his wont, at the folly.[20]

Late in Beethoven's performance career, Louis Spohr was in the audience when he played with orchestra. Spohr's description also revealed anything but a quiet technique:

Beethoven was playing a new Pianoforte-Concerto of his, but forgot at the first *tutti*, that he was a Soloplayer, and springing up, began to direct in his usual way. At the first *sforzando* he threw out his arms so wide asunder, that he knocked both the lights off the piano upon the ground. The audience laughed, and Beethoven was so incensed at this disturbance, that he made the orchestra cease playing, and begin anew. *Seyfried*, fearing that a repetition of the accident would occur at the same passage, bade two boys of the chorus place themselves on either side of *Beethoven*, and hold the lights in their hands. One of the boys innocently approached nearer, and was reading also in the notes of the piano-part. When therefore the fatal *sforzando* came, he received from *Beethoven's* out thrown right hand so smart a blow on the mouth, that the poor boy let fall the light from terror. The other boy, more cautious, had followed with anxious eyes every motion of *Beethoven*, and by stooping suddenly at the eventful moment he avoided the slap on the mouth. If the public were unable to restrain their laughter before, they could now much less, and broke out into a regular bacchanalian roar. *Beethoven* got into such a rage, that at the first chords of the solo, half a dozen strings broke. Every endeavour of the real lovers of music to restore calm and attention were for the moment fruitless. The first *allegro* of

88

the Concerto was therefore lost to the public. From that fatal evening Beethoven would not give another concert.[21]

As Beethoven's hearing began to deteriorate, naturally his reticence to perform increased. When Czerny, as a child of about ten, auditioned for study with him about 1800, he "noticed immediately with the power of observation so typical of children that both his ears were stuffed with cotton which seemed to have been dipped in a yellow liquid. But at that time he certainly appeared to be not the least bit hard of hearing."[22] He was also struck by his "Robinson Crusoe" appearance: jacket and trousers of a grey furry material, jet-black hair — cut "à la Titus" and shaggy, and a swarthy, unshaven face. One of the great tragedies in all of music history was the steady decline of his hearing so that in his later years Beethoven could no longer hear his piano at all. Ludwig Rellstab recalled a moving incident that occurred during his visit with him in 1825, two years before his death. Beethoven still took pride in his Broadwood piano which had been received some seven years previously. While remarking to Rellstab that it was a handsome gift, he was, to quote Rellstab:

> . . . stretching his hands out toward the keys, yet without ceasing to hold my eye. He gently struck the C-major chord with his right hand, and played a B to it in the bass, his eyes never leaving mine; and, in order that it might make the soft tone of the instrument sound at its best, he repeated the false chord several times and—the greatest musician on earth did not hear its dissonance![23]

Throughout his teaching years, Beethoven exerted a strong influence on his piano students, many of whom came from the Viennese aristocracy. The Countess Gallenberg recalled the stress he placed on the smallest interpretative detail and the light manner of playing which he encouraged,[24] as did Countess Giulietta Guicciardi who also could not forget that "he was prone to excitement, flinging down music and tearing it up."[25] But with Therese Brunswick none of this temperament was necessary:

> He came assiduously, but instead of remaining for an hour, from 12 o'clock on, he would often stay until 4 or 5 and never wearied of holding down and bending my fingers, which I had learned to stretch up and hold flatly. The great man must have been well content; for sixteen days in succession he did not once fail to appear.[26]

With Ries, who did not possess a large talent, he showed extreme patience:

When Beethoven gave me a lesson he was, I might almost say, unnaturally patient. This, as well as his friendly treatment of me, which very seldom varied, I must ascribe principally to his attachment and love for my father. Thus he often would have me repeat a single number ten or more times. . . . When I left out something in a passage, a note or a skip, which in many cases he wished to have specially emphasized, or struck a wrong key, he seldom said anything; yet when I was at fault with regard to the expression, the *crescendi* or matter of that kind, or in the character of the piece, he would grow angry. Mistakes of the other kind, he said, were due to chance; but these last resulted from want of knowledge, feeling or attention. He himself often made mistakes of the first kind, even when playing in public.[27]

When Czerny first came to Beethoven, he had to secure immediately a copy of C.P.E. Bach's book and then begin a strong classical program of technical developments. He later recalled:

During the first lessons Beethoven made me work solely on the scales in all keys and showed me many technical fundamentals, which were as yet unknown to most pianists, e.g. the only proper position of the hands and fingers and particularly the use of the thumb; only much later did I recognize fully the usefulness of these rules. He then went through the various keyboard studies in Bach's book and especially insisted on legato technique, which was one of the unforgettable features of his playing; at that time all other pianists considered that kind of legato unattainable, since the *hammered,* detached staccato technique of Mozart's time was still *fashionable.* (Some years later Beethoven told me that he had heard Mozart play on several occasions and that, since at that time the forte-piano was still in its infancy, Mozart, more accustomed to the then still prevalent *Flügel,* used a technique entirely unsuited for the fortepiano, I, too, subsequently made the acquaintance of several persons who had studied with Mozart, and found that Beethoven's observation was confirmed by their manner of playing.)[28]

And at another time Czerny remembered that Beethoven

. . . could scarcely span a tenth. He made frequent use of the pedals, much more frequent than is indicated in his works. His playing of the scores of Handel and Gluck and the fugues of Seb. Bach was unique, in that in the former he introduced a full-voicedness and a spirit which gave these works a new shape.[29]

Schindler agreed with Czerny:

90

With regard to piano-forte playing, Beethoven always inculcated the following rule: "Place the hands over the keyboard in such a position that the fingers need not be raised more than is necessary. This is the only method by which the player can learn to *generate* tone, and, as it were, to make the instrument sing." He adjured the *staccato* style, especially in the performance of phrases, and he decisively termed it "finger-dancing," or "manual air-sawing." There are many passages in Beethoven's works, which, though not marked with slurs, require to be played *legato*. But this a cultivated taste will instinctively perceive.[30]

Beethoven was working for fullness of tone and was concerned that the power of the arm should back up the fingers. Schindler, devoted disciple and early biographer, said that the library of Beethoven contained a number of works by Bach: a worn copy of the *Well-Tempered Clavier*, three volumes of exercises, all of the *Two and Three Part Inventions*, and a Toccata in D Minor. The sonatas of Clementi and the etudes of Cramer also occupied major places. Twenty of the latter he had annotated for his nephew's study. These were finally published in England by Augener in 1893. Great emphasis was placed upon a complete and thorough legato. At one point, Beethoven gave these directions for the execution of a figurated sixteenth note sequence: "To obtain the strictest legato, the finger must not be lifted off the first note of each group until the fourth note is to be struck."[31]   He also stressed varying rhythmic accent patterns.

He approved of the C.P.E. Bach and Clementi method books. But Schindler said that he had a "pronounced aversion to all long-winded expounding of theory,"[32] and that he shook his head over Hummel's bulky volume. Dr. Gerhard von Breuning's first-hand experience with Beethoven and method books is quoted by Schindler:

I had a copy of the Pleyel *Method of Piano Playing*. He (Beethoven) was dissatisfied with this as with all the other methods. He once said to me as I sat by his bed, 'I wanted to write a textbook for piano students myself, but I never had the time. I would have written something very different.' Then he promised my father he would see about a text for me. Some time later he sent me the Clementi sonatas he had ordered for me, which were not available here (in Vienna). The following note accompanied the music:

'Dear friend:

At last I am able to break away from my negligence. I send herewith Clementi's *School of Piano Playing* for Gerhard. If he uses it in the way that I will show him, it will certainly produce good results.[33]

In one of his sketchbooks now in the British Museum, Beethoven wrote out a number of exercises for specific musical and physical purposes. These might well have gone into his proposed method book. A selection of them is included here.[34]

for dynamic range

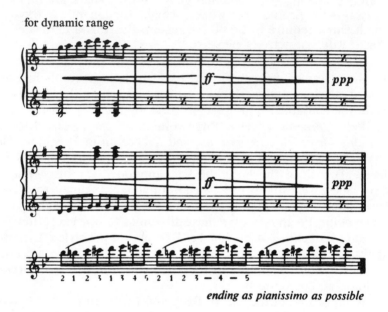

ending as pianissimo as possible

for great agility

to be thrown with the hand

for Beethoven's
special kind of legato and legatissimo

the hand contracted as much as possible

pp strictest legato

Andante

Here the 3rd finger must cross over the 4th and remain above it
until the 4th withdraws and the third assumes its place

for contraction of the hand

D.C.

for
a certain
sound effect

93

for arm carry

all these notes with the third finger only

all these notes with the third and fourth fingers kept together

for legato double notes

for leaps in the left hand

for double-note trills

trill is difficult

Beethoven indicated the 5-1 4-2 fingering for the double-note trill in Var. IV of Op.111. He preferred this fingering at all times, even when it was difficult.

94

It was to Czerny that he entrusted the musical education of his eleven-year-old nephew, Karl, in 1816. Beethoven's brother had died of tuberculosis the year before and Beethoven assumed the care of the young boy. There are two letters to Czerny in existence from the year 1816[35] that show concern over lesson arrangements and failure to make payment for lessons promptly. In February of 1817 Beethoven wrote to Cajetan Giannatasio del Rio, the cultured and kindly boarding schoolmaster in whose institution in Vienna Beethoven had placed young Karl, requesting that more piano practice time be arranged for his nephew.[36] Shortly thereafter Beethoven wrote the famous letter to Czerny in which he gave the often quoted suggestions as to how he should work in the lesson period with Karl:

[Vienna, 1817]

My Dear Czerny!

Please be as patient as possible with our Karl, even though at present he may not be making as much progress as you and I would like. If you are not patient, he will do even less well, because (although he must not know this) owing to the unsatisfactory timetable for his lessons he is being unduly strained. Unfortunately nothing can be done about that for the time being. Treat him therefore so far as possible with affection, but *be firm with him. Then there will be* a greater chance of success in spite of these really unfavourable circumstances where K[arl] is concerned—In regard to his playing for you, as soon as he has learnt the right fingering and can play a piece in correct time and the notes too more or less accurately, then please check him only about his interpretation; and, when he has reached *that point* don't let him stop playing *for the sake of minor mistakes,* but point them out to him when he has finished playing the piece. Although I have done very little teaching, yet I have always followed this method. It soon produces *musicians* which, after all, is one of the chief aims of the art, and it is less tiring for both master and pupil — In certain passages, such as

I should like him also to use all his fingers now and then, and in such passages too as

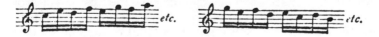

95

so that he may slip one finger over another. Admittedly such passages sound, so to speak, as if they were 'played like pearls (i.e. with only a few fingers) or like a pearl'—but occasionally we like to have a different kind of jewelry.—More of this some other time—I hope that you will take note of all these suggestions in the affectionate spirit in which I have ventured to make them and would like to have them interpreted—As it is, I am and must still remain your debtor—In any case may my sincerity serve as a guarantee to you that so far as possible I shall soon discharge that debt.—

Your true friend
BEETHOVEN[37]

Schindler speaks of a number of pedagogical disagreements between Carl Czerny and Beethoven. The nephew was finally placed with Joseph Czerny unrelated to Carl. A principal point of conflict was the exclusive use of Clementi sonatas with the young boy. Beethoven insisted upon them while Czerny was "much less devoted" to them. Schindler speaks of the great influence which Clementi exerted upon Beethoven and also the critical feeling he held at times for Czerny. The contrast he draws between the playing mannerisms of Beethoven and Czerny seems to run counter to other accounts. Schindler writes:

Even though his impaired hearing made it impossible for him to apply Clementi's principles himself, he was still able to recommend Clementi to others eager for instruction. Beethoven learned directly from Clementi how, after searching everywhere for positive rules governing performance, he finally found the key in vocal art. Himself a singer, he attempted to apply the rules of prosody even to certain instrumental passages where stressed and unstressed notes in endless sequence played an important role. . . .

I should like to name a few salient traits of our master's playing, and here I am fully supported by the accounts of Cramer and Clementi. His hands and the upper portion of his body were held quiet. His notes were sustained, and his accentuation was always very distinctive. In regard to his sustained style, in which we see the former organist, the master was said in earlier times to have surpassed Hummel, who was, like John Field, considered a model for this style. Here was another reason for Beethoven's argument with the modern trend in piano performance, for, with the exception of Hummel, it abandoned entirely the sustained style. Yet, irony of fate! the creator of so many noble works in all the musical media, with his vigorous opposition to all bodily motion at the piano, had to be content to see a herald of this style take an interest in his piano music and hold off for a few years its total disappearance from the concert repertoire. It was Carl Czerny whose contribution must be proclaimed aloud, even for the very piano style that the great master deplored.

It is no less true that Czerny was the only one among the Viennese virtuosi who took the trouble to hear Beethoven frequently when he was at his best. He deserves our praise up to the point where he began his attempts to improve upon Beethoven's music with the elaborations of the modern virtuosi; from that point on he deserves nothing but censure. These elaborations consist of indiscriminate use of the pedal, the transposition in the *cantilena* sections from the first and second octaves above middle C to the third and fourth (we are already familiar with Czerny's predilection for the highest register from all his compositions), the use of trills and other ornaments, and finally a metronome-like rhythmic regularity. . . .

Anyone who has seen Herr Franz Liszt play the piano has an accurate picture of the mannerisms he learned from his teacher Czerny: hands always in the air, sometimes even flung above the head, the keys struck from a height of two feet above the keyboard, and so forth. Liszt is merely imitating the didactic model that was held before him for two of his boyhood years. When in 1816 Beethoven wrote to his esteemed friend, Frau von Ertmann (we know the letter from the third period), that illness had prevented him from hearing a recent recital at Czerny's, a more plausible reason may have been his objection to Czerny's annoying mannerisms. By the winter of 1818, however, when Czerny played at his house for a group of admirers, Beethoven had brought himself, for other reasons, to the point of honouring the performer and his guests with his presence. It was fortunate for the sensitive listeners that, accustomed to Czerny's style, their pleasure was not disturbed by it. Even the exacting master's often repeated complaint: 'Czerny never sustains his notes and accentuates badly,' was incapable of disturbing the cult, for the group as a whole lacked depth of insight. For this author in particular, Czerny's performance provided excellent instruction, for they afforded the master a unique opportunity to express critical comments and highly interesting and instructive explanations of so many of his works.

As for Beethoven's particular style of accentuation, the author can speak partly from Beethoven's critical remarks on Czerny's playing and partly from the piano instruction that Beethoven gave to him directly. It was above all the rhythmic accent that he stressed most heavily and that he wanted others to stress. He treated the melodic (or grammatic, as it was generally called) accent, on the other hand, mostly according to the internal requirements. He would emphasize all retardations, especially that of the diminished second in *cantabile* sections, more than other pianists. His playing thus acquired a highly personal character, very different from the even, flat performances that never rise to tonal eloquence. In *cantilena* sections he adopted the methods of cultivated singers, doing neither too much nor too little. Sometimes he recommended putting appropriate words to a perplexing passage and singing it, or listening to a good violinist or wind player play it.

He set great store by the manner of striking the keys, and in double import: The physical or material, and the psychological of which Clementi made him aware. By its psychological import, Clementi meant the fullness of tone already conceived in the player's mind before the fingers strike the keys. One who is a stranger to this sense can never play an Adagio with feeling. Our master was a declared opponent of 'miniature painting' in all musical performance, and demanded strength of expression throughout.[38]

Pianist Ernst Pauer summarized the overall effect of Beethoven's playing in similar terms:

They say that his performance was not so much 'playing' as 'painting with tones,' while others express it as recalling the effect of 'reciting,' all of which are attempts to state the fact that in his playing, the means,—the passages, the execution, the technical appliances,—disappeared before the transcendent effect and meaning of the music. . . . He was not particular in polishing and refining his performance, as were Hummel, Wölffl, Kalkbrenner, and others: indeed, such 'special' artists he satirically calls 'gymnasts,' and expresses the opinion that 'the increasing mechanism of pianoforte playing would in the end destroy all truth of expression in music.'[39]

Beethoven's reactions to the use of Maelzel's metronome, invented in 1816, are interesting indeed. He wrote Ignaz von Mosel the following year that he would never again use "these senseless designations: *allegro, andante, adagio, presto*"[40] and proceeded to discuss ways of promoting the new little machine. But his ardor soon cooled. Schindler explained his later reaction:

Why did Beethoven neglect to use the metronome? Actually, he himself assigned metronome marks to only two of his works: The great sonata opus 106, at the explicit request of Ries for the London edition, and the ninth symphony at the request of the publishing house of Schott in Mainz and the

Philharmonic Society of London. In connection with the latter transaction, there occurred an event that illustrates the master's low opinion of the metronome. He asked me to make a copy for London of the metronome notations he had a few days before made for Mainz, but the list had been mislaid and we could not find it. London was waiting and there was no time to lose, so the master had to undertake the unpleasant task all over again. But lo! no sooner had he finished than I found the first version. A comparison between the two showed a difference in all the movements. Then the master, losing patience, exclaimed: 'No more metronome! Anyone who can feel the music right does not need it, and for anyone who can't, nothing is of any use; he runs away with the whole orchestra anyway!'[41]

A study of Beethoven must include a brief consideration of Beethoven's own pianofortes. With his dynamic manner of playing, he must frequently have felt some degree of frustration with the Viennese instruments with which he constantly came in contact in the society homes of Vienna. When Czerny first played for Beethoven about 1801 in Beethoven's own lodgings, he speaks of the instrument being a Walter, a Viennese contemporary of Streicher. Emily Anderson tells us that following this, he owned a French Érard pianoforte dated 1803 which was given to him by Prince Karl Lichnowsky.[42] In the fall of 1810 there is impatient correspondence with Johann Andreas Streicher regarding the new pianoforte he is eagerly awaiting from Streicher.[43] Beethoven laments the fact that "My French piano is no longer of much use; in fact it is quite useless."[44]

But the instrument for which he most anxiously waited, and unfortunately could hear and enjoy the least, was the six octave Broadwood grand pianoforte which the Broadwood firm shipped to him as a gift in late December, 1817. It arrived at the Streicher warehouse in Vienna early in 1818, coming by way of the Mediterranean port of Trieste. This beautiful instrument, with its split damper pedal—for individual dampening of treble and bass registers — was tried at the warehouse by some of the leading pianists of the day. Those, including Moscheles, who were unfamiliar with the English action, remarked about the beauty of its tone but found the touch to be heavy. The sole exception was Potter, a pianist already familiar with English pianos.[45] The touch of the Broadwood was much more to Beethoven's liking than the Viennese pianos. That Beethoven took great pride in it is evident from the fact that he would only allow it to be tuned by the English tuner, Stumpff, whom Broadwood had recommended. But its tone, at least in volume, still could not match the later instruments and its durability was not enough for a Beethoven. Stumpff, when he saw the instrument six years later, found that the treble sound was all gone and that the inside was a maze of broken iron strings.

How unfortunate that Beethoven, really the first of the great romantic period pianists, could not fully benefit from the improvements to the pianoforte already taking place during the closing years of his life and during those immediately following. It was the dynamic pianism of Beethoven and of the school which descended from him through Czerny to Liszt that helped to supply the impetus for the creation of bigger and better instruments during the nineteenth century. In 1821 Sebastian Érard in Paris first invented the double escapement action. This permitted a faster repetition by letting the hammer fall back to an intermediate position after being struck and not returning to its original resting place until the key was completely released by the finger. Then in 1825 the first complete cast iron frame was used by Babcock in Boston. This, of course, made possible the introduction of heavier, stronger strings, greater tensions, and more durable all-round construction with resulting increase in tonal amplitude and resonance. Innovations in cross stringing by Babcock followed in 1830. Steinway and Sons of New York, founded in 1853 by a branch of the German Steinweg family which had immigrated to America in 1850, took up these improvements as did the other great piano manufacturers.

Beethoven desired above all else to set nineteenth century piano technique upon a course of complete naturalness and freedom, totally serving the spiritual depths of the worthiest of the keyboard literature. The opposition which he encountered from the followers of Mozart and Hummel continued to exist far down into the century, particularly in the European conservatories. Unwittingly, the enigmatic Czerny aided the opposition's cause by providing it with a limitless supply of finger exercise material. But even after his death, Beethoven was not without his advocates.

Notes

[1] Alexander Wheelock Thayer, *The Life of Ludwig van Beethoven*, II, p. 83.

[2] *Ibid.*, I, p. 69.

[3] *Ibid.*, footnote, II, p. 355.

[4] *Ibid.*, I, p. 153.

[5] Ignace Moscheles, ed., *Life of Beethoven*, including the Biography by Schindler, Beethoven's Correspondence with his Friends, Numerous Characteristic Traits, and Remarks on His Musical Works, edited by Ignace Moscheles, to which is added *The Life and Characteristics of Beethoven* from the German of Dr. Heinrich Doring, p. 13.

[6] *Ibid.*, p. 328.

[7] Thayer, *Life of Beethoven*, I, p. 218.

[8] *Ibid.*, I, p. 219.

[9] *Ibid.*, I, p. 216.

[10] Quotation cited from *Allgemeine musikalische Zeitung* in Anton Felix Schindler, *Beethoven As I Knew Him*, p. 79.

[11] *Ibid.*, p. 80.

[12] Thayer, *Life of Beethoven*, I, p. 268.

[13] Alfred Einstein, *Schubert, a Musical Portrait*, p. 77.

[14] Thayer, *Life of Beethoven*, III, p. 137.

[15] *Ibid.*, II, p. 90.

[16] *Ibid.*, II, p. 91.

[17] *Ibid.*

[18] *Ibid.*

[19] *Ibid.*, II, p. 90.

[20] *Ibid.*, p.68.

[21] Ludwig Spohr, *Ludwig Spohr's Autobiography*, pp. 186-87.

[22] Czerny, "Recollections From My Life," *Musical Quarterly*, XLII, No. 3 (July, 1956), p. 306.

[23] O. G. Sonneck, ed., *Beethoven, Impressions of Contemporaries*, p. 188.

[24] Thayer, *Life of Beethoven*, I, p. 322.

[25] O. G. Sonneck, ed., *Beethoven, Impressions*, p. 33.

[26] *Ibid.*, p. 34.

[27] *Ibid.*, p. 52.

[28] Czerny, "Recollections from My Life," p. 307.

[29] Thayer, *Life of Beethoven*, II, p. 91.

[30] Moscheles, *Life of Beethoven*, p. 156.

[31] J.B. Shedlock, ed., Cramer *Etudes* including Beethoven's annotations.

[32] Schindler, *Beethoven as I Knew Him*, p. 380.

[33] *Ibid.*, pp. 379-80.

[34] Cited by Oswald Jonas, "Beethoven's Piano Technique," *The Piano Teacher*, Vol. 3, No. 2 (Nov.-Dec., 1960), pp. 10-11.

[35] Emily Anderson, ed., *The Letters of Beethoven*, II, pp. 292-300.

[36] *Ibid.*, II, p. 673.

[37] *Ibid.*, II, pp. 742-43.

[38] Schindler, *Beethoven As I Knew Him*, pp. 414-17.

[39] Henry C. Lahee, *Famous Pianists of Today and Yesterday*, quoting from an essay by Ernst Pauer, p. 50.

[40] Schindler, *Beethoven As I Knew Him*, pp. 423-24.

[41] *Ibid.*, pp. 425-426.

[42] Anderson, ed., *Letters of Beethoven*, I, p. 292.

[43] *Ibid.*, I, pp. 292, 300.

[44] *Ibid.*, I, p. 300.

[45] Thayer, *Life of Beethoven*, II, pp. 390-91.

7.   Czerny: Technique Personified

It is to the words of the man himself that we can best turn to gain insight into the life and times of Beethoven's most famous student, Carl Czerny (1791-1857). His reminiscences have only recently been published in their entirety. His Bohemian father had excellent training in his youth as a violinist, singer, and organist, but had joined the army at the age of seventeen because of his family's poverty. In his fifteenth and last year of artillery service he married a Moravian girl and then settled in Vienna as a teacher of piano. There Carl, an only child, was born in his father's forty-first year. Wenzel Czerny soon found his son to be most teachable and set out to make the most of it. Carl later recalled in "Recollections from My Life," written in 1842, that

> His study of Bach's works and others like them had helped my father to develop a good technique and a proper approach to the fortepiano, and this circumstance had a beneficial influence on me. My father had no intention whatever of making a superficial virtuoso out of me; rather, he strove to develop my sight-reading ability through continuous study of new works and thus to develop my musicianship. When I was barely ten I was already able to play cleanly and fluently nearly everything by Mozart, Clementi, and the other piano composers of the time; owing to my excellent musical memory I mostly performed without the music. Whatever money my father could set aside from the scant pay for his lessons was spent on music for me, and since I was carefully isolated from other children and thus was under my parents' constant supervision, diligence became a habit.[1]

A violinist friend of the family and Beethoven devotee, Wenzel Krumpholz, brought the ten-year-old Carl to Beethoven. Czerny recalled that he played the C major Mozart Concerto (K. 503) and that

103

Beethoven soon took notice, moved close to my chair, and played the orchestral melody with his left hand whenever I had purely accompanying passages. His hands were very hairy, and his fingers very broad, especially at the tips. When he expressed satisfaction I felt encouraged enough to play his recently published *Sonate Pathétique* and finally the *Adelaide,* which my father sang with his very respectable tenor voice. When I had finished, Beethoven turned to my father and said, "The boy is talented, I myself want to teach him, and I accept him as my pupil. Let him come several times a week."[2]

Although these lessons turned out to be very irregular in nature, Czerny developed greatly at the piano and also in composition, an area which came all too easily for him. Opus 1, a set of 20 Variations Concertantes for violin and piano (written for his friend Krumpholz) appeared in 1806. This was the first of over a thousand works to come from his facile pen. Extemporization was no problem for him either. Czerny recalled an incident in about 1804 which got him into trouble with Beethoven. Playing Beethoven's own Quintet with Wind Instruments, he allowed himself

> . . . in a spirit of youthful carelessness, many changes in the way of adding difficulties to the music, the use of the higher octave, etc.—Beethoven took me severely to task in the presence of Schuppanzigh, Linke, and the other players.[3]

It must have been quite a scene. By the next day Beethoven had cooled off and wrote to him by way of apology: "I burst forth so yesterday that I was sorry after it had happened; but you must pardon that in an author who would have preferred to hear his work exactly as he wrote it, no matter how beautifully you played in general."[4] Czerny had learned his lesson and was moved to comment: "This letter did more than anything else to cure me of the desire to make any changes in the performance of his works, and I wish that it might have the same influence on all pianists."[5]

Shortly after this experience, at the age of fifteen he turned to piano teaching, an occupation to which he was to devote a large portion of his life and one for which he was temperamentally better suited than performance. His reputation grew and he attracted many fine students. Czerny recalled that it was the famous piano maker, Andreas Streicher, who had helped him greatly in the beginning: "Since I had frequent opportunities to recommend his pianos, I, in turn, received many good students through him."[6] In

1810 Clementi came to Vienna and Czerny was able to observe much of his teaching with the result that "I became familiar with the teaching method of this celebrated master and foremost pianist of his time, and I primarily owe it to this circumstance that later I was fortunate enough to train many important students to a degree of perfection for which they became world-famous."[7] But he was equally indebted to Beethoven who had "showed me many technical fundamentals, which were as yet unknown to pianists."[8] Czerny's schedule became so full that he was giving as many as eleven and twelve lessons a day from 8:00 in the morning until 8:00 at night. And then after that he would spend his evenings composing.

It was in the year 1819 that Czerny met his most celebrated piano student. This meeting with Liszt and the manner in which he taught him are described by Czerny in considerable detail:

One morning in 1819 . . . a man brought a small boy about eight years of age to me and asked me to let that little fellow play for me. He was a pale, delicate-looking child and while playing swayed on the chair as if drunk so that I often thought he would fall to the floor. Moreover, his playing was completely irregular, careless, and confused, and he had so little knowledge of correct fingering that he threw his fingers over the keyboard in an altogether arbitrary fashion. Nevertheless, I was amazed by the talent with which Nature had equipped him. I gave him a few things to sight-read, which he did, purely by instinct, but for that very reason in a manner that revealed that Nature herself had here created a pianist. He made the same impression when I acceded to his father's wish and gave him a theme on which to improvise. Without the least bit of acquired knowledge of harmony he yet managed to convey a feeling of inspiration in his performance. The father told me that his name was Liszt, that he was a minor official at the court of Prince Esterhazy, and that up to that time he himself had taught his son; he was now asking me whether I would take charge of his little boy beginning the following year when he would come to Vienna. Of course I gladly assented and, by showing him scale exercises, etc., also instructed him how to continue the little boy's training in the interim. About a year later Liszt and his son came to Vienna and moved to the same street where we lived; since I had little time during the day, I devoted almost every evening to the young boy. Never before had I had so eager, talented, or industrious a student. Since I knew from numerous experiences that geniuses whose mental gifts are ahead of their physical strength tend to slight solid technique, it seemed necessary above all to use the first months to regulate and strengthen his mechanical dexterity in such a way that he could not possibly slide into any bad habits in later years. Within a short time he played the scales in all keys with a masterful fluency made possible by a natural digital equipment especially well suited for piano-playing. Through intensive study of Clementi's sonatas (which will always remain the best school for the pianist, *if one knows how to study them in his spirit*) I instilled in him for the first time a firm feeling for rhythm and taught him beautiful touch and tone, correct fingering, and proper musical phrasing, even though these compositions at first struck the lively and always extremely alert boy as rather dry.

Because of this method it was unnecessary for me to pay much attention to technical rules when a few months later we took up the works of Hummel, Ries, Moscheles, and then Beethoven and Sebastian Bach; instead I was able to acquaint him immediately with the spirit and character of the various composers. Since I made him learn each piece very rapidly, he finally became such an expert sight-reader that he was capable of *publicly* sight-reading even compositions of considerable difficulty and so perfectly as though he had been studying them for a long time. Likewise I endeavored to equip him with skill in improvising by frequently giving him themes to improvise on. The young Liszt's unvarying liveliness and good humor, together with the extraordinary development of his talent, made us love him as if he were a member of our family, and I not only taught him completely free of charge, but also gave him all the necessary music, which included pretty nearly everything good and useful that had been written up to that time. After only one year I could let him perform publicly, and he aroused a degree of enthusiasm in Vienna that few artists have equaled. In the following year his father, mindful of the advantages, arranged to have him give public concerts, in which the boy played Hummel's new Concertos in A minor and B minor, Moscheles's Variations, Hummel's Septet, Ries's Concertos, and a number of my compositions; in addition he would always improvise on motifs the public gave him, and people had indeed every right to see a new Mozart in him. Unfortunately his father wished for great pecuniary gain from the son's talent, and just when the latter had reached a most fruitful stage in his studies and had barely begun to receive from me some rudimentary instruction in composition, he went on tour, at first to Hungary and ultimately to Paris and London, etc. Everywhere he caused a sensation, as is confirmed by all the papers of that time. It is true that he made a great deal of money in Paris, where he and his parents settled, but he lost many years during which his life and his art became misdirected. When sixteen years later (1837) I went to Paris I found his playing rather wild and confused in every respect, the enormous bravura notwithstanding. The best advice I felt I could give him was to travel all over Europe, and when the following year he came to Vienna his genius received a new impetus. Showered with the boundless applause of our sensitive public, he developed that brilliant and yet more limpid style of playing for which he has now become so famous throughout the world. However, I am convinced that, had he continued his youthful studies in Vienna for a few more years, he would now likewise fulfill in the field of composition all the high expectations that were then rightly cherished by everyone.[9]

When it is considered that Theodor Leschetizky and Theodor Kullak also studied with Czerny, the impact of his contribution to nineteenth century piano pedagogy is apparent.

Czerny's industry as both a teacher and composer is almost past believing. He arranged many orchestral works for piano. He also wrote in nearly every form: masses, symphonies, concertos, string quartets—not to mention the countless number of studies aspiring young pianists have drilled down through the years. Czerny's writing streamed effortlessly, much of it in the light and superficial salon style of the day. There is no doubt that he had a fine musical gift, but the good was produced along with the bad— and the bad tended to dominate. Paul Henry Lang characterized him as "the victim of bourgeois frugality, sobriety, orderliness, and industry carried to the most fantastic extremes"[10] and goes on to cite Field's reaction that Czerny must have "manufactured models of passages, turns, and cadenzas which were carefully filed in the pigeonholes of a cupboard for further use whenever the need arose for a suitable chunk of music."[11] Had Czerny been able to judge himself more severely he might have avoided Schumann's scathing criticism of his Introduction and Brilliant Variations on an Italian Theme, Opus 302: "Not even with all one's critical speed is it possible to catch up with *Herr* Czerny. Had I enemies, I would, in order to destroy them, force them to listen to nothing but music such as this. The insipidity of these variations is really phenomenal."[12] But not all critics were quite so severe, as Chopin would indicate: "He is a good man, but nothing more."[13] He found him a warm-hearted person.

It is the better material which has survived, such as the Toccata in C Major, Op. 92, the Variations on a Theme by Rode (*La
Ricordanza*), Op. 33; and innumerable studies. The best of these
include The School of Velocity, Op. 299; 40 Daily Exercises, Op.
337; The School of the Virtuoso, Op. 365; and The Art of Finger
Dexterity, Op. 740. This literature has formed a significant part of
the practice diet of piano students everywhere the many years since
it was created, notwithstanding its often debated musical merits. It
is unfortunate that Czerny's exhaustive and valuable treatise, the
*Complete Theoretical and Practical Piano Forte School, from the
First Rudiments of Playing, to the Highest and most Refined state
of Cultivation; with The requisite numerous Examples, newly and
expressly composed for the occasion,* Opus 500, is not more readily
available today. Published in Vienna in 1839, it gives the clearest
picture available of Czerny the teacher and musician. From it he
emerges as something more than the popular conception of the dry
technician. Hermann Erler, in his clever *Little Music Lexicon,*
depicted him as "a man of sour disposition who disliked children
and therefore did nothing but write etudes."[14] Too many since
have shared the same view.

His *Piano Forte School* is made up of three principal volumes.
Volume I, comprised of nineteen lessons and 219 large size pages,
deals primarily with fundamentals and beginning technical
material. It provides a thorough grounding in scales in all the keys.
There are nearly 200 pages and sixteen chapters in Volume II
working out fingering patterns in many ways. Volume III contains
twenty chapters on interpretative details in its 130 pages. A fourth
volume, interpreting Beethoven, is sometimes appended, discussing fugal playing and styles of performers of the day. Czerny's
method book is no doubt the most important work of its era and as
Adolph Kullak remarked, "closes an epoch."[15] The early piano
method books culminate in it; it is of far more practical value than
Hummel's study book. All of the technique of the finger school is
presented in great detail. There are many pure finger exercises and
there are short study pieces, many of which contain chordal
material. The verbal guidance throughout is more extensive than
Hummel. Czerny provided no probing technical analyses, but the
etudes he included are exceedingly playable, fitting the hands well.
Constant repetition is the key to mastery. He eloquently exhorted
the student:

Practice is the great Magician, who not only makes apparent impossibilities performable, but even easy.

108

Industry and practice are the Creators and Architects of all that is great, good, and beautiful on the earth.

Genius and Talent are the raw materials; industry and practice are as the graver impelled by an expert hand, which from the rude block of marble, forms the beautiful statue.[16]

Fielden pondered along these lines when he wrote that "even with him there is no record of how he taught his pupils to cultivate right movements and conditions. One must suppose that they went on till their hands ached and hoped for the best, and that the fittest survived. Possibly massage was used, as advocated by Couperin."[17]

And yet there are veiled comments in Czerny's *School* that seem to anticipate later technical thought. Having observed Beethoven's technique which far surpassed the finger school, Czerny could not have remained unmoved. He must have passed along at least some suggestions on a more complete technique to his students. Opus 500 begins with observations and technical directions not unlike those found in Hummel, yet they are more explicit. The first two pages from Volume I are reproduced herewith from the original English version of 1839:

PRELIMINARY OBSERVATIONS

For the first three months, it is requisite that the Learner should receive one hour's lesson every week-day, or at least four lessons in the week; and in addition to this, that he should daily practise one hour by himself, as it is very necessary to abridge as much as possible the labour of acquiring the first principles of the art.

The subjects to be explained, are distributed into LESSONS, such that the contents of each LESSON may easily be read through and explained at length to a Pupil in one hour's attendance; this calculation will also include the time necessary for him to fix in his mind, and to practice the rules laid down in each Lesson.

It will naturally depend on the age, talent, and industry of the Pupil, as to how far the Teacher may find it necessary to lengthen or curtail the prescribed times. At the end of each month, a couple of days should be devoted to the recapitulation of all what has been already learned, and the Pupil should be made to repeat the principal rules by heart.

The practical exercises must be frequently and diligently played over; and they should not be laid aside, till the Pupil by his progress is enabled to proceed to the study of longer and more difficult compositions.

109

POSITION OF THE BODY, AND OF THE HANDS.

The movements of the body have so great an influence on PIANO-FORTE playing, that a good and graceful position must be the first thing to which the Pupil's attention should be drawn; and the rules on this head must be incessantly repeated, till the exact observance of them shall have grown into a settled habit. In playing, all unnecessary movements must be avoided, for every obliquity of position, every grimace, and every useless gesture, have a disadvantageous influence on the hands and fingers.

Before any thing else, the Pupil must be made acquainted with the following rules

§1 The seat of the player must be placed exactly opposite to the middle of the keyboard; and at such a distance from it, that elbows, when hanging down freely, shall be about four inches nearer the keys than the shoulders; so that the movements of the arms and hands over the whole length of the keyboard may not be impeded in any way by the chest.

§2. The height of the stool must be so exactly proportioned to the stature of the player, that the ends of the elbows may be about an inch higher than the upper surface of the keys; for a low seat impedes and fatigues the hands.

§3. While playing, the stool must never be moved either backwards or forwards; nor must the player wriggle to and fro' upon his seat.

§4. The position of the head and of the chest should be upright, dignified, and natural; a little inclining towards the key-board, so that the back of the chair or seat may not touch the body. But we must avoid assuming a bent and crooked position, as that is at once unsightly and injurious to the player; and if persisted in for any length of time, it may even become prejudicial to the health.

§5. Let the pupil, while playing, avoid accustoming himself to nodding, or any other movement of the head. It is only when both hands have to play in the highest octave on the right of the key-board, or in the lowest octave on the left, that the body may follow them by a gentle side-motion, but however without moving on the seat.

§6. The feet should rest on the ground, near the PEDALS, but without touching them; children must place their feet on a foot-stool adapted to their height.

§7. The arms ought neither to be pressed against the body, nor extended outwards, away from it; but they should hang freely down by their own natural weight, avoiding every perceptible and restless movement.

§8. The surface of the fore-arm, from the elbow to the knuckles of the bended fingers, must form an absolutely straight and horizontal line; and the wrists must neither be bent downwards, nor upwards, so as to resemble a ball. The preserving an exactly straight line with the knuckles and the upper surface of the hands is one of the principal requisites towards acquiring a fine style of playing.

§9. The fingers must be somewhat bent inwards. As the fingers are of unequal lengths, each finger (not including the thumb) must take such a part in this species of curvature, that all their tips as well as the thumb in its natural outstretched position, may form one straight line, when placed close together. In this case the knuckles will assume nearly the form of a semicircle.

§10. In playing, the fingers ought never to be pressed against one another; they must be kept so far apart, that when the hand is at rest, each for itself may freely and independently make the necessary movement upwards or downwards; for it is by this motion that the keys are to be struck.

§11. An oblique position of the hands and fingers, either inwards or outwards, is very injurious. In proportion to their lengths, the fingers must form a line with the length of the keys, and it is only in extensions or skips that this rule may be deviated from, so far as it may become necessary.

§12. The four fingers of each hand are respectively indicated by the figures 1, 2, 3, 4; the character + is used to indicate the thumb.

§13. The percussion of the keys is effected by means of the fleshy tips of the four longer fingers, and with the extreme side of the tip of the thumb, which for this purpose must be somewhat bent inwardly. We must avoid bending the other fingers inwardly, so much that the nails shall fall on the keys. The keys must not be struck near their edge, but at about half an inch from their end nearest the player.

§14. The player must keep his nails so short, that they may never project beyond the extremities of the tips of the fingers, as otherwise the clicking of them on the keys will become disagreeably audible.[18]

Throughout the three volumes, while acknowledging the necessity of freedom of movement, Czerny emphasizes a quiet, restrained keyboard approach. Although he continually speaks of "striking" the key, a high percussive finger action, so typical of the later Stuttgart school, bothers him: "As each finger, *previous* to its being used, must be held very near to its key (without however touching it); so, after the stroke, it must again return to its previous situation."[19] Then again: "The hand must ... be held as tranquilly as possible over the 5 keys, so that the reiterated percussion may be produced by the quiet movement of the single finger."[20] Happily, he also calls for pressing as well as striking: "The beginner must accustom himself to a moderately strong touch, so as to press down the keys firmly; he will naturally practice it, at first very slow, accelerating the movement by degrees, as the flexibility of the fingers develops itself, and without any strain upon the nerves."[21]

Freedom and quietness are essential to a smooth, even touch:

This equality in the touch can only be acquired, when both hands are kept perfectly still, and all the fingers held up equally high; for those fingers which are removed farther from the keys than the rest, or which are held with stiffness, naturally strike later, by which the perfect equality of the blow is destroyed.[22]

In the left hand, too, we must avoid any unnatural twisting or shaking of the arms or elbows in these passages; and endeavour to acquire that degree of flexibility, which is equally necessary in passing the thumb under the other fingers, or those fingers over the thumb, and which will be best attained by a light and yet firm touch.[23]

For very rapid passages Czerny describes a special type of finger action which he terms a mezzo staccato or dropped notes touch:

... it consists in this, that each finger with its soft and fleshy tip on the keys, makes movement like that used in *scratching* or in *tearing* off something, employs more or less of the rapid action of the nerves and muscles; and thereby obtains a very clear, pearly, and equal touch, by which, even in the quickest times, all passages may be executed with equal roundness and finish, with a full and not too harsh tone, and with the most perfect and pleasing tranquility of the hands.[24]

In discussing the technical requirements of a crescendo passage, he introduces the term so popular in the Breithaupt era, *weight:*

Before anything else, it must be observed that the crescendo should never be produced by a visible exertion of the hands, or by lifting up the fingers higher than usual, when we are playing legato; but only by an increased *internal action of the nerves,* and by a *greater degree of weight,* which the

112

hand receives therefrom, without however fettering the flexibility of the fingers.[25]

Where more emphatic arm action is needed, as in a martellato octave passage, he does not hesitate to call for it, but cautions against overuse:

For the Player must take especial care, that the fore-arm shall only be allowed so much movement, as is absolutely necessary to attain the desired effect, and to always maintain a fine equality of tone. Excess in this respect would be too laborious and exciting, and in very lengthy passages might even become prejudicial to the health.[26]

Czerny wrote a series of six *Letters to a Young Lady on the Art of Playing the Pianoforte.* The material in many respects is similar to that found in his *Piano Forte School.* Brief excerpts from the fourth letter to this mythical young lady reinforce the above thoughts:

You possess an excellent pianoforte by one of our best makers; and you will already have remarked, that the most gentle pressure of the finger on a key produces a perceptible alteration and modification in the tone; and that we may play with great power, without any excessive exertion, and without using any unnecessary and ridiculous movements of the hands, arms, shoulders, or head. For, unhappily, many, even very good pianists, are guilty of these and similar contortions and grimaces, against which I must warn you. . . . Do not suppose, however, that you are to sit at the piano as stiff and cold as a wooden doll. Some graceful movements are *necessary* while playing; it is only the excess that must be avoided.[27]

Czerny's views on fingering show his empirical approach to teaching. Volume II constitutes a thorough treatise on this subject. He first gives three fundamental rules which he grants "admit of many exceptions":[28] "(1) The 4 long fingers of each hand . . . must never be passed over one another. (2) The same finger must not be placed on two or more consecutive keys. (3) The thumb and the little finger should never be placed on the black keys in playing the scales."[29] These are followed by two more universal rules:

Every passage which may be taken in several ways, should be played in that manner which is the most suitable and natural to the case that occurs, and which is determined partly by adjacent notes, and partly by the style of execution . . . We must always call to our aid as many fingers, as are

113

necessary to enable us to take the most distant note in every passage with a convenient finger, and to avoid the superfluous passing of the thumb or the other fingers.[30]

All of these rules are then applied in every conceivable situation.

Glimpses of Czerny the musician, as well as the warmhearted teacher, are not hard to find in these volumes. Some of his concluding remarks in Volume I are as meaningful today as then and merit quotation. The reader may be surprised to find the suggestions in the final paragraph coming from Czerny:

An important means in this respect is a fortunate choice as to the musical pieces to be studied. We shall gain nothing by torturing the young Pupil with Compositions which must appear to him as old fashioned, unintelligible, and tasteless, or as too difficult and troublesome; every Pupil makes much greater progress when he plays all his lessons *willingly* and with satisfaction. That whatever is fundamental and solid in playing may be very well combined with this mode of teaching, I am able to assert from long and extensive experience.

Pieces which are adapted from orchestral music, such as Overtures and operatic pieces, as also Waltzes &c. are seldom advantageous to the Pupil. At present however, most of the striking and pleasing melodies even of the most celebrated Composers are arranged in almost countless numbers, as real piano forte pieces, in the form of Rondos, Variations, Pot pourris, &c: and that in a way perfectly suited to the instrument, so that every Teacher has in this respect an inexhaustible choice, from which to select and unite the useful with the agreeable in giving his instructions.

From among these compositions let him always choose such as are adapted to the development of execution, and in which therefore the melody frequently alternates with easy passages, and runs. Very often, Pupils are fatigued for years with pieces of an opposite description, because their masters attempt too soon to teach them expression and a knowledge of harmony. But experience shows that this end, if tried too early, will seldom be attained, and that in the mean time, we neglect that which every Pupil possesses sufficient talent to acquire, and what alone will give him facility at every sort of Exercise.

Nothing is more important for the Teacher than to form and develop as soon as possible *the taste of his Pupil.* This cannot be accomplished in any way better than by a good choice of pieces. Good taste is always a proof of good sense and a clear understanding; and the Teacher must not allow himself to be led away by pedantic views, to rob his Pupils of their time, by laying before them dull and tasteless pieces, and thus as too often happens, to give them a distaste for this fine art.

Useful as may be the practice of the numerous Exercises or Studies, now published; still the Teacher must not overload his Pupils with them. He must keep in mind, that each musical piece, even a Rondo, or an Air with Variations, etc. *is an Exercise in itself,* and often a much better one, than any professed Study; because it is a complete composition, in which melody is intermixed with passages; and because a Pupil will certainly practice such a Piece more willingly than any studies, which however good they may be in themselves, generally appear to youth dry and tedious. The best and most necessary Exercises will always be the scales and the other passages which are given at length in this part; for they are quite sufficient to develop the execution of the Pupil for the first year, and at the same time they are absolutely indispensable to the formation of any Pianoforte player.[31]

Volume III, which centers on expression, has chapters on dynamics, rhythm, tempo, touch, melody playing, style, memory, public performance, pedaling, sight reading, extemporaneous playing, and even tuning. It is most readable. Czerny cautioned the very light use of the damper pedal in composers before Beethoven. With Beethoven and even late Clementi it found regular usage. Then he said: "Almost all modern Composers employ it very often, as Ries, Kalkbrenner, Field, Herz, Moscheles (in his latter works) etc.; and it is self evident that the Player must use it whenever he finds it indicated."[32] Many of his musical examples from this volume are expressive and lyrical; they even seem to bear some resemblance to a Chopin or a Field nocturne. Czerny the musician continually put great emphasis on listening and tonal sensitivity. Here is one statement on beauty of tone:

Whoever possesses the art of always producing from the piano forte a beautiful, harmonious, and smooth tone; who never carries the forte or fortissimo to a disagreeable and excessive harshness; and further who combines the highest degree of volubility with perfect distinctness and clearness, will execute even the most startling assemblage of notes, so that they shall appear beautiful, even to persons unacquainted with music, and give them unfeigned delight.[33]

One of the most valuable sections in the whole Czerny treatise is the chapter on expression. It deals with the various performance styles before and throughout his own period and constitutes an appropriate summary at this point of our study. It also shows the full breadth and depth of Czerny's musical understanding and must explain, at least in part, why his influence as both teacher and composer has been so great. The passage is quoted in its entirety:

ON THE PECULIAR STYLE OF EXECUTION MOST
SUITABLE TO DIFFERENT COMPOSERS AND THEIR WORKS.

1. The object of this Chapter cannot be better explained, than by giving a short history of the development of Piano-forte playing:

2. In the commencement of the 18th century, the legato style of playing, as well as the execution of considerable difficulties on the Harpsichord and Clavichord, the instruments then in use, had already been carried to a high degree of perfection by *Seb. Bach,* Domenico Scarlatti, and others; and, indeed, Scarlatti may be looked upon as the founder of the brilliant or bravura style.

The *Piano-forte,* just then invented, (about 1770), gained a prodigious step in advance by *Mozart* and *Clementi,* two great practical Masters, and improvers of the art. Clementi, who devoted himself exclusively to piano-forte playing and Composition for this instrument, may with justice be looked upon as the founder of a regular School; as he first of all was able to unite brilliant bravura execution with tranquility of the hands, solidity of touch, correctness, distinctness, and grace of execution; and in his day he was always allowed to be the greatest Player on the Piano-forte.

The most distinguished masters on this instrument of the subsequent period were his Pupils, and formed according to their individual ideas, various styles and schools of playing.

The Pianos of that day possessed for their most distinguished properties, a full Singing quality of tone; but as a counter balance to that, they had also a deep fall of the keys, a hard touch, and a want of distinctness in the single notes in rapid playing; this naturally led *Dussek, Cramer,* and a few others to that soft, quiet, and melodious style of execution, for which they, and likewise their compositions are chiefly esteemed, and which may be looked upon as the Antipodes of the modern, clear, and brilliantly piquant manner of playing.

3. *Mozart's* style, which approached nearer to the latter mode, and which was brought to such exquisite perfection by Hummel, was more suited to those piano-fortes which combined light and easy touch with great distinctness of tone, and which were therefore more suited for general purposes, as well as for the use of Youth.

Meantime, in 1790, appeared *Beethoven,* who enriched the Piano-forte by new and bold passages, by the use of the pedals, by an extraordinary characteristic manner of execution, which was particularly remarkable for the strict Legato of the full chords, and which therefore formed a new kind of melody; — and by many effects not before thought of. His execution did not possess the pure and brilliant elegance of many other Pianists; but on the other hand it was energetic, profound, noble, and particularly in the Adagio, highly feeling and romantic. His performance like his Compositions, was a musical painting of the highest class, esteemed only for its general effect.

4. The subsequent improvements in the mechanism of the Piano-forte soon gave occasion to young professors of talent, who were rising to maturity, to partly discover and partly improve upon another mode of treating the instrument, namely, the *brilliant style,* which about 1814, was chiefly distinguished by a very marked Staccato touch, by perfect correctness in the execution of the greatest difficulties, and by extreme and striking elegance and propriety in the embellishments; and which was soon acknowledged to be the most favorite and most applauded style of all, through the skill of Hummel, Meyerbeer, Moscheles, Kalkbrenner, &c.

5. This style is now still further distinguished by even more tranquil delicacy, greater varieties of tone and in the modes of execution, a more connected flow of melody, and a still more perfect mechanism; and in future it must be considered as the most desirable manner of all.

6. We may therefore assume the 6 following styles of execution as so many principal schools.

a. *Clementi's style,* which was distinguished by a regular position of the hands, firm touch and tone, clear and voluble execution, and correct declamation; and, partly also, by great address and flexibility of finger.

b. *Cramer* and *Dussek's* style. Beautiful Cantabile, the avoiding of all coarse effects, an astonishing equality in the runs and passages, as a compensation for that degree of volubility which is less thought of in their works, and a fine legato, combined with the use of the Pedals.

c. *Mozart's School.* A distinct and considerably brilliant manner of playing, calculated rather on the Staccato than on the Legato touch; and intelligent and animated execution, the Pedal seldom used, and never obligato.

d. *Beethoven's style.* Characteristic and impassioned energy, alternating with all the charms of smooth and connected cantabile, is in its place here. The means of Expression is of-

117

ten carried to excess, particularly in regard to humourous and fanciful levity.

The piquant, brilliant, and shewy manner is but seldom applicable here; but for this reason, we must the more frequently attend to the total effect, partly by means of a full, harmonious Legato, and partly by a happy use of the Pedals. &c.

Great volubility of finger without brilliant pretensions, and in the Adagio, enthusiastic expression and singing melody, replete with sentiment and pathos, are the great requisites in the Player.

The compositions of *F. Ries* for the most part require a similar style of execution.

e. The modern brilliant School founded by *Hummel, Kalkbrenner,* and *Moscheles.* Its peculiar qualities are perfect mastery of all the mechanical difficulties; the utmost possible rapidity of finger; delicacy and grace in the various embellishments; the most perfect distinctness, nicely suited to every place of performance, whether small or large; and a correct declamation, intelligible to every one, united with refined and elegant taste.

f. Out of all these schools, a new style is just now beginning to be developed, which may be called a mixture of an improvement on all those which preceded it.

It is chiefly represented by *Thalberg, Chopin, Liszt,* and other young artists; and it is distinguished by the invention of new passages and difficulties, and consequently the introduction of new effects — as also by an extremely improved application of all the mechanical means, which the Piano-forte offers in its present greatly improved state, and which, like all former improvements in their day, will give a new impulse to the art of playing on this much cultivated instrument.

7. From this historical sketch, the reflecting Pianist will easily perceive that the works of each Composer must be executed in the style in which he wrote; and that the performer will assuredly fail, if he attempts to play all the works of the Masters above named in the self-same style.

The Player who desires to arrive at anything like perfection, must dedicate a considerable space of time exclusively to the Compositions of each Master who has founded a School; till he has not only accustomed his mind to the peculiar style of each, but also, till he is enabled to remain faithful to it, in the mechanical performance of their works. Thus, for example, the quiet, soft, and heartfelt elegance with which the Compositions of Dussek ought to be played, are not by any means sufficient for the execution of a work of Beethoven's, or of a brilliant Composition of the present day:—just as in Painting, there exists a great difference between Miniature, Crayon, Fresco, and Oil painting.[34]

Notes

[1] Carl Czerny, "Recollections from My Life," *The Musical Quarterly*, XLII, No. 3 (July, 1956), p. 303.

[2] *Ibid.*, pp. 306-7.

[3] Alexander Wheelock Thayer, *The Life of Ludwig van Beethoven*, I, p. 316.

[4] *Ibid.*

[5] *Ibid.*

[6] Czerny, "Recollections from My Life," p. 312.

[7] *Ibid.*, p. 313.

[8] *Ibid.*, p. 307.

[9] *Ibid.*, pp. 314-16.

[10] *Ibid.*, footnote, p. 314.

[11] *Ibid.*

[12] Robert Schumann, *On Music and Musicians*, p. 247.

[13] James Huneker, *Chopin, the Man and His Music*, p. 19.

[14] Quoted by Ernest Hutcheson, *The Literature of the Piano*, p. 128.

[15] Adolph Kullak, *The Aesthetics of Pianoforte-Playing*, p. 76.

[16] Carl Czerny, *Complete Theoretical and Practical Piano Forte School*, Op. 500, III, p. 115.

[17] Thomas Fielden, *The History of the Evolution of Pianoforte Technique*, p. 47.

[18] Czerny, *Piano Forte School*, I, pp.1-2.

[19] *Ibid.*, I, p. 7.

[20] *Ibid.*

[21] *Ibid.*

[22] *Ibid.*, I, p. 9.

[23] *Ibid.*, I, p. 58.

[24] *Ibid.*, III, p. 26.

[25] *Ibid.*, III, p. 15.

[26] *Ibid.*, III, p. 30.

[27] Carl Czerny, *Letters to a Young Lady on the Art of Playing the Pianoforte*, p. 33.

[28] Czerny, *School*, II, pp. 2-3.

[29] *Ibid.*, II, p.4.

[30] *Ibid.*, II, p.8.

[31] *Ibid.*, I, pp.216-217.

[32] *Ibid.*, III, p.64.

[33] *Ibid.*, III, pp.72-73.

[34] *Ibid.*, III, pp.99-100.

8. The Early Methodology

In a historical survey of piano technique, it is impossible to treat every famous pianist and teacher in depth. But in summing up the early decades of pianoforte playing, it is necessary to refer at least briefly to the contributions of certain lesser pedagogical figures who worked during the days of Mozart, Hummel, Beethoven, and Czerny. Even before Carl Philipp Emanuel Bach's death in 1788, the first pianoforte method books began to appear. One of the earliest and most popular to be published in England was the *Guida di Musica,* Op. 34, by James Hook (1746-1827), Part I of which appeared in 1785 and Part II nine years later. He subtitled it *A Complete Book of Instructions for Beginners on the Harpsichord or Piano Forte entirely on a new plan, calculated to save a great deal of time, trouble both to Master and Scholar to which is added Twenty-Four Progressive Lessons in Various Keys with the Fingering marked Throughout.* The work contained not more than a few pieces and an explanation of the fundamentals and the embellishments. Yet it must have enjoyed wide usage judging from England's acceptance of Hook's prolific trivia in the galant style and from his economic success as a pianoforte teacher. In his prime, he was making over £600 per year, a princely sum in those days.

Of far greater worth and very much in the C.P.E. Bach tradition was the *Klavierschule* for both pianists and harpsichordists by Daniel Gottlob Türk (1756-1813), published in 1789 in Germany. An exhaustive volume, it was one of the most important interpretative source books of the time with its extensive treatment of ornamentation and expressive details. It begins with a description of the various clavier instruments and then in rather typical fashion deals with matters of posture and physical execution. The player should be from ten to fourteen inches from the keyboard with hands a few inches lower than the elbows. The hand position is rather strange: the middle finger is bent inward, the thumb is straight, and the little finger is either straight or bent as necessary. Only the fingers should play; the hands and arms are allowed only a slight movement in leaps.

Following chapters on time and tempo, there is a detailed section on principles of fingering. Kullak felt "its precision is matched only by Czerny's method."[1] In summary, Türk states that the best and most convenient system of fingering is that in which the hand can remain most quiet. Much of the book is concerned with matters of expression. Maria Levinskaya thought that Türk could be viewed as "the spiritual forerunner of the trend of artistic piano teaching"[2] in the light of such statements as: "The characteristic expression is the highest aim of the player. He must try to identify himself with the general feeling of the composition, and endeavour to transmit this feeling to others through each spoken tone."[3] Then, to Türk, the most beautiful playing would be inspired by the singing voice. The player should experiment at the keyboard, practicing diligently for a good sound: "An absolutely beautiful tone must be clear, full, bright, excellent, but agreeable; even in the greatest force should it not become rough and harsh, and in the utmost softness it should remain distinct."[4] Türk also emphasized the subtle use of time nuances:

> Another means of accentuation, but one which must be used sparingly and with great caution, is that of lingering on certain notes. An orator not only emphasizes the most important syllables etc., but also lingers on them. Naturally, such lingering in music cannot always be of equal duration; for it seems to me that it depends chiefly on (1) the degrees of importance of the note itself, (2) the value of the note and its relation to other notes, and (3) the basic harmony.[5]

A highly respected contemporary of Türk was the Bohemian performer, pedagogue, and composer, Jan Ladislav Dussek (1760-1812). After thorough childhood training in piano and organ he went to Amsterdam in 1782 and shortly thereafter to the Hague where he established himself as a truly fine pianist. After a year of study at Hamburg at the age of twenty-three under C.P.E. Bach, he set out on a series of successful concert tours which took him to Berlin, St. Petersburg, Paris, Milan, and London. The years from 1790 to 1802 were spent in London with great success as both teacher and performer. An evidence of Dussek's musical stature is Haydn's affection for him during these years as indicated in a letter which

Haydn wrote in 1792 from London to Dussek's father, still in Czechoslovakia:

MOST WORTHY FRIEND — I thank you from my heart that, in your last letter to your dear son, you have also remembered me. I therefore double my compliments in return and consider myself fortunate in being able to assure you that you have one of the most upright, moral, and, in music, most eminent of men for a son. I love him just as you do, for he fully deserves it. Give him, then, daily a father's blessing, and thus will he be ever fortunate, which I heartily wish him to be, for his remarkable talents.[6]

In 1796 while still in London Dussek published his *Instructions on the Art of Playing the Piano-forte or Harpsichord*. Following ten lessons on fundamentals, he gives fingering suggestions that end with his "Rule the Last." It contains observations that show his sensitive musicianship and concern for refined phrasing:

We exhort our Pupils and Amateurs to be very attentive to avoid as much as possible changing the position of the Hand, and particularly near the end of a Passage. Ascending with the Right Hand, it is necessary to place (if possible) the Thumb in such a manner as to be able to end the Phrase with the Little Finger which will be as graceful for the hand, as agreeable to the Ear, because the last Notes of a Phrase are always the most interesting, and ought to be executed in the most natural and easy method.[7]

At the zenith of his performance career, Dussek returned to his native land and appeared in Prague in 1802 where he made a most profound impression. Johann Wenzel Tomaschek was present and recorded the event in his autobiography:

. . . my countryman, Dussek, came to Prague, and I very soon became acquainted with him. He gave a concert to a very large attendance, at which he introduced his own Military Concerto. After the few opening bars of his first solo the public uttered one general Ah! There was, in fact, something magical about the way in which Dussek with all his charming grace of manner, through his wonderful touch, extorted from the instrument delicious and at the same time emphatic tones. His fingers were like a company of ten singers, endowed with equal executive powers and able to produce with the utmost perfection whatever their director could require. I never saw the Prague public so enchanted as they were on this occasion by Dussek's splendid playing. His fine declamatory style, especially in *cantabile* phrases, stands as the ideal for every artistic performance — something which no other pianist since has reached.... Dussek was the first who placed his instrument sideways upon the platform, in which our pianoforte heroes now all follow him, though they may have no very interesting profile to exhibit.[8]

His handsome appearance and noble profile must have moved his audiences as well. Other firsts for him included playing a six octave Broadwood grand before the London public in 1794 and also indicating pedaling in his own music. He was a productive composer with works running to over seventy opus numbers.

While in England, Dussek may have met Johann Bernhard Logier (1777-1846), notorious inventor of the "Chiroplast," the first of a series of mechanical gadgets designed to assure a quiet hand and arm, a proper position at the keyboard, and the Viennese finger technique. As a child of ten, he had come from Germany to England where he studied the pianoforte and the flute. When he was old enough, he joined a military band and later became a band director. Duty took him to Ireland. After his release he settled in Dublin where he opened a music store and taught piano. It was while instructing his seven-year-old daughter that he hit upon the idea of the Royal Chiroplast which he patented in 1814. He must have been a very persuasive salesman; it was not long before many others besides his daughter were using the "miracle" gimmick. He built its usage into a method, *The First Companion to the Royal Chiroplast*. He also worked out a system (this is surely one of the first references to class piano) whereby groups of students could play special studies simultaneously at different pianos. The terms of his patent allowed him to license other teachers in his method. It soon became the vogue in London and then on the Continent. In 1822 he was invited to Germany by the Prussian government to set up a Chiroplast school for the purpose of training teachers to spread its usage throughout the country. Spohr, on a visit to England, described the operation of one of Logier's classes:

"Mr. *Logier*, a German by birth, but resident for the last fifteen years in England, gives instruction in pianoforte-play and in harmony upon a method of his own invention, in which he permits all the children, frequently as many as thirty or forty, to play at the same time. For this purpose he had written three volumes of studies, which are all grounded upon perfectly simple themes, and progress by degrees to the most difficult ones. While beginners play the theme, the more advanced pupils practice themselves at the same time in more

124

or less difficult variations: one might imagine that from this manner of proceeding great confusion must ensue, out of which the teacher would be able to distinguish very little; but as the children who play these studies, sit near each other, one hears, according to whichever part of the room one may be in, either one or the other of the studies very distinctly. The teacher also frequently makes half of the pupils, at times all but one, cease playing, in order to ascertain their progress individually. In the last lessons he makes use of his chiroplast, a machine by means of which the children get accustomed to a good position of the arms and hands, and which so soon as they have progressed so far as to know the notes and keys, is removed first from one hand and then from the other, and then for the first time they put their fingers to the keys and learn to play scales; but all this, in the respective studies, with all the children at once, and always in the strictest time. When they have then progressed to a new lesson they do not of course succeed in bringing out more than a few notes of each bar, in the quick movement which they hear being played near or around them; but they soon overcome more and more of them, and in a shorter time than might well be believed, the new lesson is played as well as the previous one. But what is most remarkable in Mr. *Logier's* method of teaching is, that, with the very first lessons in pianoforte playing he teaches his pupils harmony at the same time. How he does this, I do not know; and that is his secret, for which each of the teachers in England who give instruction on his system pay him one hundred guineas. The results of this method with his pupils are nevertheless wonderful; for children between the ages of seven and ten years solve the most difficult problems. I wrote down on the board a triad, and denoted the key in which they were to modulate it: one of the littlest girls immediately ran to the board, and after very little reflection wrote first the bass, and then the upper notes. I frequently repeated this test, and indeed with the addition of all manners of difficulties: I extended it to the most divergent keys in which enharmonic changes were required, yet they never became embarrassed. If one could not succeed, another immediately came forward, whose bass perhaps was corrected by a third; and for everything they did they were obliged to assign the reason to the teacher."[9]

Exactly what was the Chiroplast? Perhaps it would be best to let Logier himself describe it. In 1816 Logier published *An Explanation and Description of the Royal Patent Chiroplast or Hand-Director.* A portion of this pamphlet follows:

125

This then is the object accomplished by the Position frame, which consists of two parallel rails, extending from one extremity of the keys to the other; to the ends of these are fixed two cheek pieces, which, by means of a brass rod and extending screw, are attached firmly to the instrument: when adapted to square Piano Fortes, it will be in its proper situation, if the cheek pieces rest upon the keys at the two extremities of the key-board. In Grand Piano Fortes, it will rest upon the blocks.

The rails must be adjusted by means of the screws which will be found in the cheek pieces for that purpose, so as to admit the hands of the pupil passing between them nearly as far as the wrists; being so regulated as to prevent any perpendicular motion of the hand, though sufficiently wide to allow a free horizontal movement when required.

By this contrivance the learner is obliged to keep himself in a proper position, and with very little trouble becomes acquainted with the proper mode of conveying his hands gracefully to any part of the instrument; the awkwardness arising from every unnecessary motion is thus prevented.

By this part of the apparatus likewise the fingers are compelled to move independently, and thereby very soon acquire a freedom, strength, and equality of power, which cannot otherwise be accomplished but by incessant perseverance, length of time, and the unremitted attention of a good preceptor.

The Finger-guides are two moveable brass plates with five divisions, through which the thumb and four fingers are introduced. These divisions correspond perpendicularly with the keys of the instrument, and may be moved to any situation by means of the brass rod, on which they are made to slide. They are secured in the position required by two screws, which pass through them and press against the bracing bar.

To each Finger-guide will be found attached a brass wire, with its regulator, called the Wrist-guide, the use of which is to preserve the proper position of the wrist, and to prevent its being inclined outwards, which would necessarily withdraw the thumb from the proper command of its key.

In fixing the Finger-guides in any situation as directed before the lessons, let the projecting points range parallel with the front edge of the keys, as close as possible without actually touching them; for regulating this, graduated notches will be found in the cheek pieces.

When the learner, without the assistance of this apparatus, for the first time puts his fingers on the keys, it may be observed that they are found to be every where but in the right place. The hands of children exhibit the most unnatural appearance, the fingers being very often all crowded together over each other.

Let the thumb and fingers be put through the compartments of the Finger-guide, and they will be found exactly over those keys for which they are designed; nor is it in the power of the learner either to disengage, misplace them, or alter their position.

In this situation he might play the first lesson without knowing a note of music, by merely observing the marks 1, 2, 3, 4, engraved over the fingers, with a x over the thumb, and the corresponding marks over the notes of the lesson.

Having now no apprehension with respect to misplacing his fingers, hands, or arms, he finds it unnecessary even to glance at the keys, and turns all his attention to the music which is set before him.

In the Book of Instructions will be found a regularly arranged series of lessons and exercises calculated for the gradual advancement of the pupil, which will save the master much time and trouble.

The first are played with the Finger-guides. They consist of three different subjects, so varied and contrived, that whilst they please by their simplicity, they employ all the fingers alike, and carry the learner imperceptibly through the most useful keys and elementary part of time, &c. &c. He has, at most, only five notes to learn for each hand, and all other necessary instructions are communicated progressively as they are wanted.

Each lesson contains new matter for improvement. For example:

The Finger-guides being fixed so that the thumb of the right hand is over B, and the thumb of the left over C, the rest of the fingers will be properly disposed over the keys required for the 1st, 2d, 3d, and 4th lessons, which are all in the key of C.

The 5th, 6th and 7th lessons are in the key of G. The Finger-guides are moved, so that the thumbs of both hands are upon D, and the fingers, consequently, in their proper situations.

The pupil, during these three lessons, learns the nature of a sharp placed at the beginning of an air or lesson; acquires the names of two more notes in the treble, and one more in the bass, and is likewise introduced to an accidental sharp and natural.

When the pupil has thus gone through those lessons and

exercises with the Finger-guides, the subject of the first is again resumed, the Finger-guide of the left hand is moved away, which is done by loosening the screw, and turning it up; the bass is now altered so as to require a slight change of position in the hand.

In the lesson immediately following, the right hand Finger-guide is moved away and the left replaced, the subject of the treble is now so varied as to require a change of position of the right hand; after which both guides may, for a while, be laid aside. The subjects are now varied both in treble and bass, and a diatonic scale and prelude added to each lesson, which, together with the exercises with the Finger-guides, should be practised daily.

There can be no doubt that a series of lessons composed on the same subject, varied each time by alternate changes in the bass and treble, will tend to create a fancy in the pupil however young, raising a desire for composing (at least in the style of variations) which otherwise might for ever lie dormant; and whilst they are intended merely to improve the hand, may also unconsciously improve the head.

The master will, no doubt, add to the number of these lessons, according to his own judgment, and the abilities of his pupil.

By an early and frequent use of this apparatus it is evident that the learner must become habituated to a proper position of the body, and a graceful movement of the arms; and the fingers must acquire an independent motion and equality of power rarely accomplished by other means.

It happens generally that brilliant passages are found within the regular scales, in the different keys ascending or descending, and the hand when once confirmed by habit in the proper position as inculcated by the Finger-guides, will always return to it, however various passages may require its temporary extension, with satisfaction and confidence, as to a rallying point from which it set out.[10]

In this same booklet were included recommendations by some of the leading musicians of the day including Clementi (his firm manufactured the Chiroplast), Cramer, and the church musician, Samuel Wesley, who thought that it

. . . cannot fail of producing the two desirable consequences of *correct fingering,* with a *secure and graceful position of both hands in performing on a keyed instrument;* the universal and infallible utility of which, as well as an immense saving of time and trouble to masters cannot but be obvious and self-evident to all candid lovers of improvement and of truth.[11]

These same sentiments were echoed in America as late as 1834 by W. Nixon in *A Guide to Instruction on the Piano-Forte designed for the Use of Both Parents and Pupils in a Series of Short Essays, dedicated to the Young Ladies of the Musical Seminary, Cincinnati* when after describing the Chiroplast he extolled: "The great excellence of these *guides* is, that they present no hindrance, whatever, to the fingers, when properly directed; but merely prevent them diverging to wrong keys, or *guide* them to the right ones."[12] Then he added that the Hand-guide would help one to relax and set the mind at ease.[13] In the previous chapter, he had counseled the young ladies regarding the importance of placing coins on the back of the hand.[14]

Fortunately, almost from the beginning, there were those who were skeptical or at least cautious about the Chiroplast's usage. Written objections appeared as early as 1817 in scholarly musical publications,[15] followed by a heated rebuttal by Logier.[16] Even Czerny joined in the criticism in concluding remarks in his *Piano Forte School,* Op. 500:

> In modern time several mechanical aids have been invented towards attaining a well regulated facility and flexibility of finger; as for Ex. the *Chiroplast,* the *Hand-guide,* the *Dactylion,* etc.: To such Pupils as have at first been spoiled by improper instructions, these machines may be of great, and even striking utility.
>
> But to those Pupils whom from the very commencement, the Teacher has carefully and patiently accustomed to the observance of all the rules relating to the position of the hands, the acquirement of a good touch, and a correct mode of fingering, as those points have been explained in this School, we consider such machines as useless on the following grounds:
>
> 1st Because a long use of them must necessarily be relaxing both to the mind and to the feelings.
>
> 2ly Because they consume a great deal of time.
>
> 3ly Because they are by no means well adapted to encrease the love of the art in young Pupils and Amateurs.
>
> 4ly Lastly because they fetter by far too much, all freedom of movement, and reduce the Player to a mere Automaton.[17]

Carl Engel in *The Pianist's Hand-book, a Guide for the Right Comprehension and Performance of Our Best Pianoforte Music* (1853) felt much the same way: he would concede that these devices might be used to correct a bad habit, but if you had a good foundation, you would not want such a support. Then a little later, he spoke about the need for freedom of movement:

Nothing so much hinders a fine expression, as a thin, uncertain and stiff touch; and nothing is so often the cause of an indifferent or deficient performance.

If we compare the elastic walk of a horse with the stiff steps of a sheep, we see that the elasticity consists chiefly in the equal movements of all the joints, as if produced by a hidden spring. The touch should be similar.[18]

There were other mechanically inclined musicians whose fertile minds were set in motion by Logier's invention. One was Henri Herz (1803-1888), educated at the Paris Conservatoire and renowned for his book on scales. He came forward with the "Dactylion," a device that had ten wires hanging down attached to ten rings through which the fingers were to be inserted. Springs were fastened at the top of each wire. The fingers were then forced to lift high.

Not to be overlooked is Friedrich Kalkbrenner (1785-1849), if only because of his relationship, reported in the next chapter, with Chopin. It was he who invented the Hand-guide. A German by birth, he had gone to the Paris Conservatoire in 1798. It was here that he studied with Louis Adam (1758-1848) — although largely self-taught, the first important French pianoforte teacher. Appointed a professor of piano at the Paris Conservatoire, a post which he held for years, Adam wrote several early method books, including *Méthode ou principe général du doigté pour le Forte Piano* (*Method including General Principles of Fingering for the Pianoforte*) which was published in 1798. This rather large volume, besides its section of verbal directions, contained 150 pages of short exercises and an unusual "Dictionary of Passages," 359 excerpts from the works of Haydn, Mozart, Clementi, Dussek, Cramer, Steibelt, and others. In his explanation he said that there are a great many ways of "touching the key and drawing out the tone. Only through the touch can a fine tone be obtained; only the power and pressure of the finger are to be employed."[19]

Following his association with Adam and after a time of concertizing in his native land, Kalkbrenner settled in London in 1814 for a period of nine years. During this time he came in contact with Logier and became an enthusiast of his Chiroplast. Returning to Paris in 1824, he was made a partner in the pianoforte manufacturing firm of Pleyel & Co. This together with his other musical activities and shrewd business talents made him a wealthy man. His reputation as both teacher and performer grew exceedingly. His most outstanding student was Madame Pleyel. Evidence of his brilliant mind and great talent appeared early; when he was only eight years old he could speak four languages. Completing his course at the conservatoire in Paris in three years while capturing the first prize in pianoforte playing, Kalkbrenner was a pianist in the Hummel tradition and an exceptionally fine one. As a teacher he was very persuasive and certainly not lacking in egotism. The German pianist from Westphalia, Charles Hallé, was keenly aware of these traits when he encountered him in 1836:

> He took me into his sitting room, where there was the most beautiful grand piano, and I played him his own *Effusio musica*. He made several remarks about the tempo and said several times "very good," "first-rate," until I got to the part where both hands had scales in octaves during several passages; when I had finished them he stopped me, and asked why I played the octaves with my arms and not from my wrists? "You are quite out of breath," he said (which was the case); *he* could play scales in octaves for an hour without the least fatigue; and why had God given us wrists? He was sure, if the Almighty played the piano, He would play from the wrist! He made several other remarks. He said I held my fingers rather too high, I must hold them closer to the keys, especially in legato passages, to make them more finished and obtain altogether a rounder and more ringing tone. . . . He then played part of the piece I had played, to make it clear to me. After this he began another, and altogether played for me more than half an hour. You can imagine my delight. It was the first time I had ever heard a celebrated musician, and this half-hour has been of the greatest use to me. In Kalkbrenner's playing there reigns a clearness, a distinctness and a neatness that are astonishing. In octave scales he has an immense facility and precision, especially in the left hand; then he has a special mode of handling the piano, particularly in melodious passages, which made a great impression, but which I cannot describe to you; the reason of it lies mostly in that he keeps his fingers so closely over the keys.[20]

An anecdote which clearly reveals the charlatan in Kalkbrenner was told by Adolph Marx, the editor of the *Berliner Allgemeine musikalische Zeitung*. In 1834 Kalkbrenner came to visit him, bemoaning the fact that since the days of Hummel no one was carrying on the noble art of improvisation except himself. Then he went to the piano and improvised for fifteen minutes without interruption—impressing Marx with his use of various themes and the brilliance of his fugal treatment. But the next day Marx received a package of newly published music from Paris. What should he find included in it but the previous day's "improvisation" by Kalkbrenner note for note!

Kalkbrenner wrote piano concertos and sonatas as well as numerous other potpourris all lying easily under the hands, brilliant but meaningless and superficial in the salon style of the day. His best pieces are the etudes in his method book, *Méthode pour apprendre le Piano à l'aide du Guide-Mains* (*Method for Teaching Piano with the Help of the Hand-Guide*), Op. 108 and published about 1830. The study material is divided into six sections: exercises in five notes with quiet hand, as principal groundwork; scales in all forms; thirds, sixths, and chord-forms; octaves with the wrist; studies on the trill; crossing of the hands; and ease in the mastery of all difficulties combined. In this work Kalkbrenner advocates more use of the pedal than he feels can be secured from the German pianos with their dryer sound. He almost cancelled a concert in Vienna, he said, because of this; but finally he hit upon a plan whereby he could place a piece of cork under the treble damper rail so that there would be very little damping action in the upper two octaves. In this way he got the melodic sound and line that he wanted.[21]

Technically he stressed the use of the wrist in octave work and also sensitive qualities of finger action. From Logier he had gained a very close contact with the keys. He supplemented this, as Bie pointed out, with "that special kind of sensuously charming touch which differentiated the Parisian school from the brilliant playing of the Viennese and the emotional style of the English. That *carezzando,* or stroking of the keys, was a favorite practice of Kalkbrenner and Kontski in Paris."[22] Relating manner of attack to inner feeling, Kalkbrenner stated in his *Méthode:*

> The manner of striking the key must exhibit innumerable variations, corresponding to the various emotions to be expressed. One must now caress the key, now pounce upon it as the lion hurls himself upon his prey. Still, while drawing from the instrument all the tone possible, avoid striking it rudely and roughly. Bravura is not the highest aim; one should strike after higher ends — expression, emotion, and grand effects. In particular, variety of expression must prevail. The melody must always predominate; if one note has an expression-mark, the rest should not be likewise modified. One must at length attain to the expression of warmth without violence, strength without harshness, gentleness without weakness; that is, to be sure, the highest goal.[23]

In the preface of his *Méthode,* Kalkbrenner introduced his Hand-guide, actually a simplification of the Chiroplast. He had seen that development of passage work involving thumb-under movement was impossible when the Chiroplast was used. He no doubt was also keenly aware of the confining nature of the device in general. The Hand-guide was merely a railing or ledge, running parallel to the keyboard and attached at both ends, upon which the arms and wrists were to rest while practicing. Kalkbrenner's preface is a gem of persuasiveness and makes fascinating reading:

So many works have been published on the study of the piano that nothing less than the application of a thoroughly new procedure could make me decide to publish this method.

A long time ago I had virtually promised to let my friends know how I had succeeded in developing this independence of fingers which enables me without effort or tension to draw so much tone from the piano. Here is my secret:

What hinders beginners is the extreme tension which they show in all of their practice. This tension causes their fingers to become like claws at the keyboard and gives the hands a very ungraceful appearance. Very often a whole lifetime is scarcely long enough to correct the bad habits contracted during the first three months of lessons.

I had not escaped this same pitfall even after having attained the first prize at the Paris Conservatoire. My professor, Mr. Adam, used to admonish me all the time when I had trills to perform, for at that time my little finger got so stiff that my hand seemed to be paralyzed.

After a thousand fruitless efforts, the idea came to me that all technical practice at the piano could be facilitated by the aid of a mechanical device which would give the hands their true position at the very outset. I found that by supporting my right wrist with my left hand the force concentrated entirely in my fingers was augmented by the force which formerly had only served to stiffen the arms and the hands. The first result encouraged me greatly. All that remained was to find an appropriate point of support. In my impatience for the lack of something better, I took an old armchair, one of whose arms I sawed off. Then turning the other arm around in front of the piano keyboard and placing my legs through the space under the arm of the armchair, I found myself located in such a position as to take full advantage of my recently discovered secret. My forearms, thus supported on the arm of the armchair, permitted me to move my fingers without the least sign of tension. After several days, I fully realized the advantage which this new style of study afforded me. The position of my hands could no longer lead me into the previous error. And I did not have to concentrate on position, since I was playing only five finger exercises. Soon I decided to try reading while exercising my hands each day. During the first few hours, this seemed to be somewhat of a problem for me. But the next day I had gotten used to it. Since that time I have always read while practicing. I point out these details in the hope that others may profit from them. Life is too short for any artist to learn everything there is to know without taking certain short cuts. Raphael had materials read to him while he was painting; Voltaire dictated to his secretary from his bed and while he was getting dressed. These are all excellent examples to follow. Now let's get back to the piano.

From the moment when I discovered the possibility of studying with my arms supported, I grasped a new manner of practicing. It was observed that in most brilliant passage work, as well as in scales where the thumb passed under one or more times, that the ending was always a five finger sequence. I made these five notes my principal study, but varied them in as many ways as possible; this is the procedure which gave me, in the execution of the most difficult things, this quietness of hands and of body that one notices especially in my playing. I do not advise students to practice scales too soon. One runs the risk of developing tensions in their arms. It is necessary to make sure that their fingers have acquired a certain independence before trying to make them learn to pass the thumb under.

The Hand-guide which I am introducing with this method will take the place of the armchair. It will determine exactly the height of the piano bench so that the forearm of the person who is playing the piano is perfectly horizontal. With the Hand-guide it is impossible to contract bad habits. I recommend it especially to persons who are not too strong and tire easily at the piano. They will find their arms being supported and their fingers alone working during practice without the fear of physical harm. Persons who live outside of Paris and those who spend time in the country can benefit from this method; the mother who supervises her children's study will be able as well, while they are separated from their music teacher, not only to keep them from losing ground but to obtain further progress for them. With the Hand-guide and this method, everybody, in fact, who knows music can give piano lessons, and even those who wish to learn without a music teacher would be able to reach a certain degree of success without the fear of having someday in the future to

134

unlearn what they have taught themselves.

I have tried to make this method as short as possible by cutting out all the useless parts and by giving more rules than examples. As far as the Hand-guide is concerned, I could not recommend its usage too highly even for the finest musicians who desire to rid themselves of bad habits; it keeps people from making faces, from playing from the arm or the shoulder; it makes the fingers independent, corrects the position of the hand which it makes as graceful as possible. I shall add as a last recommendation the fact that I still use it myself all of the time.

There are some teachers who in order to perpetuate old ways of doing things or to promote other elementary teaching works have said that this method is too difficult for children. Let no one be deceived on this point. Four editions and more than 31,000 copies sold in Paris alone disprove such an assertion. Regarding the criticism directed against my pupils for not being able to read music very well—such may be the case during the early years of their study. My principle is to educate the hands before the eyes, to make them attack the notes well, to learn to finger well, to phrase well, to give the desired expression to lyrical passages and independence to the fingers. When these essential qualities are once acquired, I pay exclusive attention to teaching them to read. My procedure is much shorter, and the result is more sure. It is clear that the teacher who is only a fairly good musician and not a brilliant performer himself cannot apply himself to the details which he does not understand. All that he can do is to show his pupils how to read music fluently. He produces mediocre musicians.

I urge those who read this method not to judge the rules which I give here by those which they already know; several roads lead to the same goal; mine is the shortest. Unfortunately many people approve only of that which fits in with their way of looking at things, and they condemn in a vague sort of way every good or faulty innovation for the simple reason that they have not been the ones to discover it. It is not for them that I write. I am counting on conscientious teachers who try a new invention out before they condemn it; my experience assures me of their support.[24]

Kalkbrenner's Hand-guide had a wide acceptance for a time, but not so great as that received by Logier's contraption. The experiences which a young American in Paris had with Kalkbrenner and his Hand-guide are reconstructed by Vernon Loggins in his biography of Louis Moreau Gottschalk (1829-1869). Born in New

Orleans of English-Jewish and French-Creole ancestry, Gottschalk had shown such progress at the piano as a child that at the age of thirteen it was arranged for him to study in Paris. Destined to be America's first internationally known concert pianist, he first became the pupil of Hallé. After five months he went to Camille Stamaty, Kalkbrenner's pupil whom Kalkbrenner called his "musical son." During the very first lesson Stamaty introduced Gottschalk to the Hand-guide which he had to use for many months. It was a very trying time for him after the great advancement he had made during his early years of study. Gottschalk found at least a little inspiration in observing Stamaty's prodigy of seven years, Camille Saint-Saëns, use the Hand-guide "as if he were amusing himself with a game."[25] Saint-Saëns later was to comment:

> I also was put upon the regime of the *guide-mains*. It was a bar fixed in front of the keyboard, upon which the forearm rested, in such a fashion as to get rid of all muscular action except that of the hand itself. This system is excellent for forming the young pianist in the execution of works written for the clavecin and for the earliest pianofortes, of which the notes spoke without effort on the player's part, though insufficient for modern works and instruments. It is thus, however, that we should begin developing first firmness of touch and finger, and suppleness of wrist, and adding progressively the weight of the forearm and that of the arm. It was not only strength of finger that one acquired by this method, but also the production of tone-quality by the finger only, a precious expedient that has become rare in our days.[26]

Finally the day came in March of 1845 when Gottschalk was to play his debut program, including the Chopin E Minor Concerto, at the Salle Pleyel. Following the concert, Chopin went backstage to congratulate him, but it was beneath Kalkbrenner's dignity to do such a thing. Stamaty suggested that Louis call on his "musical grandfather" Kalkbrenner the next day. He was well enough received by Kalkbrenner, who credited his fine technique completely to the Hand-guide and then remarked: "But I don't like the music you played — Chopin, Liszt, Thalberg. They're not classical. You and Stamaty should have chosen *my* music. It *is* classical. And, besides, *everybody* likes it."[27]

The last great pianist and teacher born in the eighteenth century was Ignaz Moscheles (1794-1870), a sterling musician who spanned both the classical and romantic periods. Born in Prague, he early became acquainted with the keyboard works of Mozart and Clementi during his study at the Prague Conservatory under Dionys Weber. He later went to Vienna where in 1814 Beethoven permitted him, under his own supervision, to make a piano reduction of his opera *Fidelio*. Two years later when Beethoven was asked what he thought of Moscheles' playing he remarked brusquely: "Don't ever talk to me again about mere passage players;"[28] but Beethoven's ears were in such poor condition that he could not have judged him fairly. During the following years Moscheles developed greatly as a virtuoso, appearing in London, Paris, and Berlin. In 1824 while in Berlin, Mendelssohn became his pupil. Two years later he settled in England; but in 1846, at Mendelsshon's invitation, he became the first professor of piano at the newly formed Leipzig Conservatory, a post he held with great honor.

A man of utmost integrity and nobility of character, his playing in his prime was characterized by purity, clarity, and attention to minute detail, and his teaching by great devotion. Moscheles' wife spoke of how he began as a bravura player, but then "gradually took broader views of his art both as a composer and player."[29] But he was basically a pianist of the old school of finger action. Pecher described his playing position as one with the knuckle joints slightly depressed, the wrist about level, an inflexible wrist for octave playing often executed with considerable power, and at other times with lightness, but never arm movement for single notes. He spoke of his "astonishingly round and full" tone and of the manner in which he played Bach:

> . . . not the dry, pedantic Bach, but a living Bach, played on the principle of part-singing, in which expression and accent found full room for development amid the interlacing of the strands of counterpoint. Moscheles' Bach-playing was vocal in the perfect enunciation of each of the voices.[30]

In October 1835, when Moscheles was forty-one and beginning to lose his youthful performance powers, Schumann gave his own evaluation in a review:

> No one who has ever heard this master can be in doubt as to his mode of playing, the elasticity of his touch, his healthy power of tone, his poise and certainty in the higher style of expression. And what has been lost of youthful enthusiasm and general sympathy with this newest imaginative way of performance has been replaced by the mature man's sharpness of characterization and intellectual grasp. There

137

were some gleaming moments in the improvisation which concluded the evening.[31]

Schumann always wrote very respectfully of Moscheles' abilities. In the same review he remarked that the audience had grown enthusiastic

... after the duo played by Moscheles and Mendelssohn not only like two masters, but like two friends resembling a pair of eagles — rising and falling in turn and alternately encircling one another. We consider this composition, which is dedicated to Handel's memory, as one of the most successfull and original of Moscheles' works. . . .[32]

When the music of Chopin and the other romantics came along, he had difficulty playing it with his previously formed technique as well as understanding it. In 1833 Moscheles wrote:

I gladly pass some of my leisure hours of an evening in cultivating an acquaintance with Chopin's Studies and his other compositions. I am charmed with their originality, and the national coloring of his subjects. My thoughts, however, and through them my fingers, stumble at certain hard, inartistic, and to me inconceivable modulations. On the whole I find his music often too sweet, not manly enough, and hardly the work of a profound musician.[33]

By around 1838 he had mellowed a bit and then commented:

I play all the new works of the four modern heroes, Thalberg, Chopin, Henselt and Liszt, and find their chief effects lie in passages requiring a large grasp and stretch of finger, such as the peculiar build of their hands enables them to execute. I grasp less, but then I am not of a grasping school. With all my admiration for Beethoven, I cannot forget Mozart, Cramer and Hummel. Have they not written much that is noble, with which I have been familiar from early years? Just now the new manner finds more favor, and I endeavor to pursue the middle course between the two schools, by never shrinking from any difficulty, never despising the new effects, and withal retaining the best elements of the old traditions.[34]

Moscheles' account of his first meeting with Chopin in 1839 shows his open-mindedness toward Chopin and his music:

. . . His appearance is completely identified with his music — they are both delicate and sentimental (schwärmerisch). He played to me in compliance with my request, and I now for the first time understand his music, and all the raptures of the lady world become intelligible. The *ad libitum* playing, which in the hands of other interpreters of his music degenerates into a constant uncertainty of rhythm, is with him an element of exquisite originality; the hard inartistic modulations, so like those of a *dilettante*—which I never can manage when playing Chopin's music—cease to shock me for he glides over them almost imperceptibly with his elfish fingers. His soft playing being a mere breath, he requires no powerful forte to produce the desired contrasts; the consequence is that one never misses the orchestral effects that the German school demands of a pianoforte-player, but is carried away as by some singer who troubles himself very little about the accompaniment, and follows his own impulses. Enough; he is perfectly unique in the world of pianoforte-players. He professes a great attachment for my music, and at all events knows it perfectly. He played me some of his Studies, and his latest work, "Preludes"; I played in return several things of my own.[35]

As a composer Moscheles' works ran to Opus 142, besides other light unclassified pieces long since forgotten. His better works are of a more serious nature than Kalkbrenner's; among them would be named the 24 Etudes, Op. 70 and the Characteristic Studies, Op. 95. His *Méthode des Méthodes*, which was published in 1837 in collaboration with François Joseph Fétis (1784-1871), musicologist, teacher, and composer, contains excellent technical material including the three etudes in cross rhythms which Chopin composed for it. Fétis wrote the preface. Fielden[36] felt there was a refreshing liberal-mindedness about Fétis' writing and about the way he faced the new technical problems arising during the transition to the romantic period. For example, he saw no reason why the thumb could not be used on the black keys when necessary although the older writers felt it "threw the hand out of position."[37] Fétis pleaded for a broader outlook on technique and for an abandoning of narrow methodism:

It is necessary to make an important observation in order to obviate any objections which may be offered by the partisans of particular systems; the artists above alluded to, the virtuosi of their schools, and many others, have acquired a just celebrity by different means. The habit of considering the art under one aspect has, however, convinced them in general, of the exclusive excellence of the peculiar method which they have adopted, and has inspired them with very little esteem for those methods which differ more or less from their own. They forget that the fact that men follow methods other than theirs, or modifications of them, is sufficient proof that those

139

other methods are of much more importance than they have been led to imagine, being simply the result of observations made on different objects of the art with different ends in view. . . . A new method for the piano developing an absolute system which would be infallibly the case with one written by an artist devoted to the peculiar principles which have produced his own style, would only put into circulation certain particular ideas on the art of performing on the instrument without any advance towards the amalgamating and writing of all the elements of art, under the most general point of view. To embrace all that is useful in the various methods up to the present day; to give, on every point, the opinions and principles of the most celebrated masters; to analyse them, and apply them with discretion, are the only means of producing results of *general* utility; the only means of substituting reason for prejudice.[38]

But reason and prejudice would still have to exist along side each other for a good many years to come. Fortunately, however, there would be a Chopin opposite a Kalkbrenner and a Deppe contemporary with a Lebert and a Stark.

Notes

[1] Adolph Kullak, *The Aesthetics of Pianoforte-Playing,* p. 42.

[2] Maria Levinskaya, *The Levinskaya System of Pianoforte Technique and Tone-Colour through Mental and Muscular Control,* p. 30.

[3] Cited from Daniel Gottlob Türk, *Klavierschule oder Anweisung zum Klavierspielen für Lehrer und Lernende, mit kritischen Anmerkungen von Daniel Gottlob Türk. Musikdirektor bender Universität zu Hull (Clavier Method of Instruction regarding Clavier Playing for Teacher and Student with Critical Observations),* by Levinskaya, *ibid.,* p. 31.

[4] *Ibid.*

[5] Cited in Fritz Rothschild, *Musical Performance in the Times of Mozart and Beethoven,* p. 67.

[6] *Grove's Dictionary of Music and Musicians,* 5th ed., II, p. 826.

[7] Jan Ladislav Dussek, *Instructions on the Art of Playing the Pianoforte or Harpsichord,* p. 28.

[8] *Grove's Dictionary,* 5th ed., II, p. 827.

[9] Ludwig Spohr, *Ludwig Spohr's Autobiography,* pp. 98-99.

[10] Johann Bernhard Logier, *An Explanation and Description of the Royal Patent Chiroplast or Hand-Director,* pp.16-21.

[11] *Ibid.*, p. 24.

[12] W. Nixon, *A Guide to Instruction on the Piano-Forte designed for the Use of Both Parents and Pupils in a Series of Short Essays, dedicated to the Young Ladies of the Musical Seminary, Cincinnati,* p. 52.

[13] *Ibid.*

[14] *Ibid.*, p. 50.

[15] *Quarterly Musical Magazine and Review,* i, 111, cited in *Grove's Dictionary,* II, p. 264.

[16] J.B. Logier, *An Authentic Account,* cited in *Grove's Dictionary,* 2nd ed., II, p. 264.

[17] Carl Czerny, *Complete Theoretical and Practical Piano Forte School,* Opus 500, III, p. 129.

[18] Carl Engel, *The Pianist's Hand-book, a Guide for the Right Comprehension and Performance of Our Best Pianoforte Music,* p. 4.

[19] Cited in Kullak, *Aesthetics of Pianoforte Playing,* p. 57.

[20] Charles Hallé, *Life and Letters of Sir Charles Hallé being an autobiography (1819-1860) with correspondence and diaries,* pp. 213-14.

[21] *Grove's Dictionary,* 5th ed., IV, p. 692.

[22] Oscar Bie, *A History of the Pianoforte and Pianoforte Players,* p. 190.

[23] Cited by Kullak, *Aesthetics of Pianoforte Playing,* pp. 69-70.

[24] Friedrich Wilhelm Kalkbrenner, *Méthode pour apprendre le Piano à l'aide du Guide-Mains,* Op. 108 (*Method for Teaching Piano with the Help of the Hand-guide*), preface, translation by Clarence B. Hale.

[25] Vernon Loggins, *Where the Word Ends, The Life of Louis Moreau Gottschalk,* pp. 54-55.

[26] William Murdoch, *Chopin: His Life,* p. 115.

[27] Loggins, *Where the Word Ends,* p. 58.

[28] Alexander Wheelock Thayer, *The Life of Ludwig van Beethoven,* II, p. 381.

[29] *Recent Music and Musicians As Described in the Diaries and Correspondence of Ignaz Moscheles,* p. 164.

[30] W.F. Pecher, "The Emotional Legacy of the Classical School: Reminiscences of the Teaching of Moscheles," *The International Library of Music,* III, pp. 28-30.

[31] Robert Schumann, *On Music and Musicians,* p. 221.

[32] *Ibid.*

[33] Moscheles, *Diaries,* pp. 196-97.

[34] *Ibid.*, p. 250.

[35] *Ibid.*, pp. 256-57.

[36] Thomas Fielden, "The History of the Evolution of Pianoforte Technique," *Proceedings of the Royal Music Association*, Session 59, January 17, 1933, p. 49.

[37] *Ibid.*

[38] Cited in Fielden, *ibid.*, pp. 49-50.

9.   The Lyricism of Chopin

When Frédéric François Chopin (1810-1849) first came to Paris in 1831, the influence and popularity of Kalkbrenner was very great. Liszt and Thalberg had not as yet eclipsed his fame. Even Chopin, already the fully developed pianist at twenty-one, approached the forty-seven-year-old vainglorious man with considerable awe and surprising admiration. Letters of introduction which he brought with him, together with his unforgettable keyboard touch, quickly gave him access to the inner circle of the best musicians in Paris. These included Paër, Rossini, Cherubini, and, of course, Kalkbrenner, who was quick to realize the enormous potential of the young Polish pianist. Chopin related their first meeting in a letter of December 12, 1831, to his good friend from boyhood days, Titus Woyciechowski:

Thanks to Paër who is Court Conductor I got to know Rossini, Cherubini, etc., Baillot, etc. He also introduced me to Kalkbrenner. Just imagine how curious I was to hear Herz, Liszt, Hiller and the rest — they are all nobodies compared with Kalkbrenner. I confess I have played as well as Herz, but I long to play like Kalkbrenner. If Paganini is perfection itself, Kalkbrenner is his equal but in quite a different field. It is impossible to describe his *calm,* his enchanting touch, his incomparable evenness and the mastery which he reveals in every note—he is a giant who tramples underfoot the Herzes, Czernys and of course me!

What happens? On being introduced to Kalkbrenner he invites me to play something. Willy nilly, not having heard him beforehand but knowing how Herz plays, I sit down at the piano, having put aside every shred of conceit. I played my E minor Concerto which the Rhinelanders — the Lindpainters, Bergs, Stunzes — and all Bavaria could not praise highly enough. I surprised M. Kalkbrenner, who at once questioned me as to whether I was a pupil of Field, for he found that I have the style of Cramer and the touch of Field. I was terribly pleased to hear that—and even more pleased when Kalkbrenner took his seat at the piano to show off to me but got lost and had to stop. But you should have heard how he took the repeat—I never imagined anything like it. From that time we have been seeing each other daily, either at his house or mine, and now that he has got to know me well he proposes that I should become his pupil for three years and he will make of me something very, very . . . !¹

Chopin's earlier letter to his family regarding his association with Kalkbrenner had received an immediate reaction in Warsaw. At first they felt flattered that so great a man as Kalkbrenner would think so highly of Frédéric and desire him as a student. But there must also have been something of a feeling of apprehension because the following day, after receiving Chopin's letter from Paris, they went to talk with Joseph Elsner (1769-1854), Chopin's highly regarded former Warsaw Conservatory teacher. Elsner immediately had misgivings. Frédéric's sister Louise wrote his reaction on November 27, 1831:

. . . As soon as he heard your letter he expressed dissatisfaction with Kalkbrenner's proposition, crying, "Ah, jealousy already! Three years!" and shaking his head — although I talked to him (I was amazed that his immediate opinion was contrary to mine) and pointed out Kalkbrenner's merits and his love of art, and repeatedly quoted those sentences of yours showing that he was completely disinterested, etc. It was no good. Elsner continued to exclaim and said he would write to you himself, adding, "I know Fryderyk; he is a good lad, and has no vanity or desire to push himself forward: he is easily influenced. I'll write to him and tell him how I see the matter." And indeed this morning he brought his letter, which I am enclosing, and continued to discuss the business with us. We, judging in the simplicity of our hearts, could never have believed that Kalkbrenner was anything but a completely honourable man. But Elsner does not quite believe it and observed today: "They've recognized genius in Fryderyk and are already scared that he will outstrip them, so they want to keep their hands on him for three years in order to hold back something of that which Nature herself might push forward. Mme. Szymanowska [a famous pianist] is supposed to have said of Kalkbrenner: 'He is a scoundrel,' and so he is trying to speculate on Fryderyk's talent—to claim at least that he is his pupil. But in spite of all his love of art his real aim is to cramp his genius."

Elsner says he can't understand what sort of "solid foundation" Kalkbrenner demands, and he goes on to say, "If he possesses this 'foundation' himself, well, as far as technique is concerned, you can acquire and assimilate it too, if you want to, without having to sign on as a pupil for three years." For Elsner does not want you to imitate anyone, and he expressed a correct opinion when he said: "All imitation is as nothing compared with originality; once you imitate you will cease to be original. Although you may still be young your ideas may be superior to those of more experienced writers. You have inborn genius, and your compositions are fresher and better: you have the style of playing of Field, although you took lessons from Zywny—so what does it all prove?" Besides, Mr. Elsner doesn't wish to see you merely as a concert-giver, a composer for piano and a famous executant—that is the easy way and is far less significant than writing operas. He wants to see you in the role Nature intended and fitted you for. Your place must be with Rossini, Mozart, etc. Your genius should not cling to the piano and to concert-giving; *operas* must make you immortal. . . .

What infuriated Elsner immensely was what he called Kalkbrenner's audacity and arrogance in asking for a pencil to cross out a certain passage [in the E minor Concerto] when he had merely glanced at the score, never having heard the complete effect of the concerto with orchestra. He says that if Kalkbrenner had offered you some advice, as for instance, to try to write a shorter first movement [*Allegro*] in another concerto—*that* would have been different. But to instruct you to strike out what was written, *that* he cannot forgive. . . .[2]

Both Elsner and Chopin's father sent letters along with Louise's — expressing bafflement as to why such a long period of apprenticeship under Kalkbrenner was necessary. Elsner sensibly remarked:

One cannot advise a pupil to devote too much attention to a single method or manner or national taste, etc. What is true and beautiful must not be imitated but experienced according to its own individual and superior laws. No one man and no one nation must be taken as the unsurpassable, perfect model. Only eternal and invisible Nature can be *that,* and she contains it within herself. Men and nations can only offer us examples, more or less successful, to profit by. A final word: Those things by which an artist, always taking advantage of everything which surrounds and instructs him, arouses the admiration of his contemporaries must come from himself, thanks to the perfect cultivation of his powers. . . .[3]

On December 14, Chopin replied to Elsner's letter. He sought to allay his fears:

> ... In my view, so far as making a name in the musical world is concerned, he is a lucky man who can be both composer and executant at the same time. I am already known here and there in Germany as a pianist; a few musical papers have mentioned my concertos and have expressed the hope that I shall shortly be seen taking my place among the leading exponents of my instrument — which is as good as saying: Work hard, lad, and we'll make a gentleman out of you. Today I have before me a unique opportunity of realising the promise that is within me: why should I not profit by it? In Germany there is no one I would take piano lessons from, for although a few people there felt that I still lacked something, I could not then see in my own eye the beam which today prevents me from aiming higher. Three years is a lot — far too long, as Kalkbrenner himself admitted after observing me more closely. *That* should prove to you that a real virtuoso with a well-deserved reputation does not know the meaning of jealousy. However, I would even agree to three years' work if I could thereby make a great step forward in my plan for the future. I am firmly convinced that I shall not be an imitation of Kalkbrenner: *he* has not the power to extinguish my perhaps too audacious but noble wish and intention to create for myself a new world. And if I do work it will be in order to stand more firmly on my own feet. It was easier for Ries, since he was known as a pianist, to achieve fame in Berlin and Frankfort with his opera *The Robber's Bride;* and Spohr too was long known as a violinist before he wrote his *Jessonda* and *Faust*. I am sure you will not refuse me your blessing when you know on what basis and with what enterprise I shall proceed.[4]

Fortunately, Chopin did not succumb to Kalkbrenner's influence, but went his own way in developing his unique and remarkable gifts in performance and composition.

Let us at this point trace Chopin's rapid rise to a place of such high esteem in Paris at the age of twenty-one. He was born on the outskirts of Warsaw to a Frenchman, Nicolas Chopin, who had settled in Poland and married Justyna Krzyzanowska. Frédéric was the second of four children, all of the others girls. Never of robust health, he early showed a strong gift for music and soon came to the public's attention. First mention of him appeared in the Warsaw *Review* of January 1818. The writer told of a polonaise which he had written at the age of eight. Then he added that Frédéric

... is a real musical genius. He is the son of Nicolas Chopin, professor of French language and literature at the Warsaw lyceum. He not only performs the most difficult pieces on the piano with the greatest ease and extraordinary taste, but is also the composer of several dances and variations that fill experts with amazement, particularly in view of the author's youth. If this boy had been born in Germany or France, his fame would probably by now have spread to all nations. May the present notice remind the reader that geniuses are born in our country also and that they are not widely known only because of the lack of public notice.[5]

Frédéric's first teacher was a Czech, Adalbert Zywny (1756-1842), whom Liszt called "a passionate disciple of Sebastian Bach who during many years directed the boy's studies in accordance with strictly classical models."[6] He early showed rare gifts in composition and improvisation. From 1824, Chopin studied with the second and only other major music teacher he was to have. His name was Josef Elsner, a man of far-reaching influence in Polish music. Born in Silesia and trained in Austria and Germany, he had come to Warsaw as the musical director of the National Symphony. In 1821 Elsner was named director of the newly founded Warsaw Conservatory, a post he held until it was forced to close because of the Revolution against Russia in 1831. He was described in 1841 in the *Neue Zeitschrift für Musik* as a teacher who

... does not endeavour, as other professors too often do, to turn out all his pupils from the same mold as that in which he was cast himself. This was not Elsner's way. At a time when everybody in Warsaw thought Chopin was going astray in bad, anti-musical ways, and ought to hold fast to Himmel and Hummel, or else he would do no good, the skillful Elsner had already clearly understood what a germ of poetry there was in this pale young dreamer, he had felt long before that he had before him the founder of a new school of piano music.[7]

By 1825 Chopin had already written his first work, to be published shortly thereafter, the Rondo in C Minor, Op. 1. The same year he was well established as a public performer, appearing twice in benefit concerts.

Op. 2, the Variations in B Flat Major for piano and orchestra on the duet *Là ci darem la mano* from Mozart's *Don Giovanni*, was written towards the end of 1827. This was the music that was to introduce Chopin to Schumann. In 1831 Schumann described it fully in the *Allgemeine musikalische Zeitung* in the celebrated ar-

147

ticle containing the words, "Hats off, gentlemen — a genius."[8] Also in 1827 his sister Emilia died of tuberculosis, a disease to which the Chopin family seemed peculiarly susceptible. Emilia's death was the first of many personal tragedies which were to enlarge the melancholia residing deep within Frédéric's sensitive nature. But his was also a personality that could show gaiety, clever wit and satire, and a great magnetic personal charm that would soon draw the elite of Paris into his inner circle. As a mimic he was unexcelled: his imitations of the mannerisms and appearances of the popular pianists of the day would have family and friends doubled with laughter.

During the summer of 1828 a two-week trip to Berlin began to widen his musical horizons. He heard a number of operas including Weber's *Freischütz*. He thought though that some of the female singers reminded him of the Warsaw "screech owls!"[9] But Handel's *Ode for St. Cecilia's Day*, he said, "comes close to the ideal I have formed of great music."[10] He then returned to complete his final year at the conservatory. It was during this year that Paganini had come to Warsaw, an event that greatly moved Chopin, as no doubt had Hummel's appearances during the previous year. In July of 1829, restless to see more of the musical world, he went to Vienna with friends for nearly two months. While there he presented two concerts during which he performed his Variations, Op. 2 and was welcomed as a true artist. The *Wiener Theaterzeitung* on August 20, 1829, remarked that

[Chopin] surprised people, because they discovered in him not only a fine, but a really very eminent talent; on account of the originality of his playing and compositions one might almost attribute to him already some genius, at least, in so far as unconventional forms and pronounced individuality are concerned. His playing, like his compositions — of which we heard on this occasion only variations — has a certain character of modesty which seems to indicate that to shine is not the aim of this young man, although his execution conquered difficulties the overcoming of which even here, in the home of pianoforte virtuosos, could not fail to cause astonishment; nay, with almost ironical *naiveté* he takes it into his head to entertain a large audience with music as music. And lo, he succeeded in this. The unprejudiced public rewarded him with lavish applause. His touch, although neat and sure, has little of that brilliance by which our virtuosos announce themselves as such in the first bars; he emphasised but little, like one conversing in a company of clever people, not with

148

that rhetorical *aplomb* which is considered by virtuosos as indispensable. He plays very quietly, without the daring *élan* which generally at once distinguishes the artist from the amateur. Nevertheless, our fine-feeling and acute-judging public recognized at once in this youth, who is a stranger and as yet unknown to fame, a true artist; and this evening afforded the unprejudiced observer the pleasing spectacle of a public which, considered as a moral person, showed itself a true connoisseur and a virtuoso in the comprehension and appreciation of an artistic performance which, in no wise grandiose, was nevertheless gratifying.[11]

The *Allgemeine musikalische Zeitung* was also perceptive in describing him as "a master of the first rank, with his exquisite delicacy of touch, indescribable finger dexterity, and the deep feeling shown by his command of shading."[12] After the second concert the *Wiener Theaterzeitung* on September 1, 1829 added:

He is a young man who goes his own way, and knows how to please in this way, although his style of playing and writing differs greatly from that of other virtuosos; and, indeed chiefly in this, that the desire to make good music predominates noticeably in his case over the desire to please.[13]

Chopin's intensely musical nature, his incredible control of an infinite number of subtle dynamic shadings and rhythmic nuances always had a stronger appeal for the musically discerning than for the populace. But still his friends told him that "people were jumping on the benches."[14] While in Vienna he also spent time at Czerny's home playing duets, as well as gaining the respect of such musicians as Ignaz Schuppanzigh (the fat, genial violinist and conductor of the imperial opera and companion of Beethoven, who labeled him "Lord Falstaff").

Chopin then was to return to Warsaw for another full year during which time he presented three concerts and wrote his two piano concertos. After one of these appearances, the *Correspondent's Gazette* remarked:

As a performer he surpassed even Hummel in tenderness of feeling and refinement of taste. If he did not equal Hummel in technique and evenness of tempo, he is unequaled by others in these qualities. As a composer he has assumed a distinguished place among the foremost music writers, and Hummel himself would not disown his adagio and rondo.[15]

By and large the press was not intelligent enough to appreciate him fully. There was very little more that Warsaw could offer him, and he knew that his musical future lay to the west. Carrying the premonition that he would never see his beloved Poland again, he left for Vienna on November 1, 1830. The Vienna which he now found was not the same one that had given him his successes the year before; Europe was in political turmoil and Poland was in the midst of it. Years before, Poland had been partitioned and both Russia and Austria had shared in the conquest. The Poles had become restless under the Russian occupation long before Chopin said his final farewell in Warsaw. Shortly after Chopin's arrival in Vienna, violence erupted and civil war broke out. The Viennese sympathy was with the Russians. And their musical inclinations were increasingly toward the waltzes of Johann Strauss and company. Little of Beethoven was heard; living in Vienna in 1830, one would have found it hard to believe that Beethoven had died there just three years before. But the faithful Czerny was still there. Chopin wrote to his family on December 1:

I have been to see Czerny, who was as polite as ever, and asked, "Have you been studying diligently?" He has arranged another Overture for eight pianos and sixteen players, and seems very happy about it.

Except Czerny, I have seen none of the pianists this time.[16]

Soon Chopin found that he had a rival pianist to contend with by the name of Sigismond Thalberg (1812-1871). Younger than Chopin and favoring a style designed to please the public, he already was much more widely known throughout Europe. His specialty, which he had adopted from the harpist Parish-Alvars, was his singing melody line divided between the two hands in the middle of the keyboard. This he combined with embellishing figurations and full chords which dashed up and down the keyboard on either side. So overpowering were his effects that his audience thought he surely must have three hands to cover so much ground! Chopin himself was moved to write one of his Warsaw friends, Jan Matuszynski, on December 26, 1830:

Thalberg plays famously, but he is not my man. He is younger than I, pleases the ladies very much, makes pot-pourris on *La Muette* [*Masaniello*], plays the *forte* and *piano* with the pedal, but not with the hand, takes tenths as easily as I do octaves, and wears studs with diamonds. Moscheles does not at all astonish him; therefore it is no wonder that only the *tuttis* of my concerto have pleased him. He, too, writes concertos.[17]

It was a time of intense despair for Chopin. He received no

sense of fulfillment in Vienna. His heart was with his family and friends in his native Poland. He wished to return home and contribute what he could to the revolution, but was physically unable to do so. Finally Chopin decided to seek a new life in Paris, in the land of his father's birth and among a people more sympathetic to the Poles. After overcoming passport difficulties, he left Vienna late in July of 1831—proceeding to Paris by way of Salzburg, Munich, and Stuttgart. He found a Paris caught up in political turmoil of its own, but one which included sympathetic demonstrations for the battered Polish peoples. And he found a Paris for which he felt a kindred spirit. He wrote to Titus on December 12, 1831: "Paris is whatever you care to make of it. You can enjoy yourself, get bored, laugh, cry, do anything you like, and no one takes any notice because thousands here are doing exactly the same—everyone goes his own way."[18] And the news from home was looking up: his family and friends were safe. The move from Vienna to Paris was a fortunate one. His circle soon included not only Kalkbrenner and the other musicians, but men like Hugo, Balzac, and Delacroix. Then there were friends in the large Polish community. Chopin now began a life of creative activity and one which contained a limited number of performances, a schedule of teaching, and many evenings in the company of his friends and French society.

Wierzynski has made the interesting observation that Chopin, in all of the eighteen years which he spent in Paris, appeared in only four concerts in which he was the principal performer.[19] He also played in public on a limited basis a mere fifteen other occasions. There was a shyness in his nature which could not easily be subjected to the critical gaze of a disinterested public. He came to dislike public performance intensely. Liszt records Chopin's confession to him:

> I am not fitted to give concerts, the public frightens me, I feel suffocated by its panting breath, paralyzed by its curious glance, mute before those unknown faces; but you are destined for it, for when you do not win the public you are able to overwhelm it.[20]

The records of Chopin's Parisian appearances during his first few years there — and more playing was done then than thereafter—are very revealing. His debut in Paris came off on January 15, 1832. The audience was made up largely of musicians and a great many of the Polish aristocracy. Chopin performed his own F Minor Concerto and the Variations for Piano and Orchestra on

Là ci darem la mano. Also included were instrumental and vocal selections and, perhaps as a gesture to Kalkbrenner, Kalkbrenner's Grand Polonaise with Introduction and March for Six Pianos performed by Chopin, Kalkbrenner, Stamaty, Hiller, Osborne, and Sowinski. Both Liszt and Mendelssohn were in attendance at the Pleyel Salon where it was held. Mendelssohn was seen to clap vigorously. Liszt later wrote of this event: "The endlessly renewed applause did not seem sufficiently to express our enchantment at the demonstration of this talent, which disclosed a new level in the expression of poetic feeling and such felicitous innovations in artistic form."[21]

Fétis, the founder and critic of the *Revue musicale,* gave his own views on March 3, 1832:

Here is a young man who is true to his natural impressions and follows no model. Even though he has not brought about a complete reform of piano music, he has at least partially achieved something that has long been sought after in vain, namely, an abundance of original ideas, of a kind not encountered anywhere else. . . .[22]

What a delightful, yet bewildering, experience it must have been for the conservative Fétis and his friends for the first time to have heard the unique pianism of Chopin. Chopin's fellow countryman, Antoni Orlowski, could hardly contain himself. He wrote home that "our dear Frycek gave a concert that earned him great reputation and a bit of money. He killed all the local pianists. All Paris is stunned."[23]

In the next few months successive appearances firmly established his position as a leading Parisian pianist. There is even record of his having performed a movement of Bach's Concerto for Three Claviers in December of 1833 with Ferdinand Hiller[24] (1811-1885) and Franz Liszt. But success did not turn his head. He wrote to a boyhood friend, Dominik Dziewanowski:

I move in the highest society — among ambassadors, princes, and ministers; and I don't know how I got there, for I did not thrust myself forward at all. But for me this is at present an absolute necessity, for thence comes, as it were, good taste. You are at once credited with more talent if you are heard at a *soirée* of the English or Austrian Ambassador's. . . .[25]

So there were still the realities of life and a living to earn. Chopin never realized great financial returns from his compositions. He was in demand as a teacher and he received twenty francs

152

for an hour lesson. But in his social status, the clothing and refinements he dearly loved cost considerably. Physical strength nearly always was a great problem for him and there was continually the intense longing for his family and his homeland. As he settled into his life in Paris, he began to envision more clearly his own unique role as composer and pianist.

His days in Paris were broken up by short trips, particularly to Germany and England. In May of 1834, Chopin went with Hiller to attend the Rhenish Music Festival at Aix-la-Chapelle where they found Mendelssohn. Mendelssohn greatly respected Chopin, although with his strong classical bent could not fully appreciate him. He wrote to his mother:

> . . . In the first tier was seated a man with a moustache, reading the score; and when, after the rehearsal, he went downstairs, and I was coming up, we met in the passage, and who should stumble right into my arms but Ferdinand Hiller, who almost hugged me to death for joy! He had come from Paris to hear the oratorio, and Chopin had left his scholars in the lurch and come with him, and thus we met again. I had now my full share of delight in the Musical Festival, for we three lived together, and got a private box in the theatre where the oratorio is performed, and of course next morning we betook ourselves to the piano where I had the greatest enjoyment. They have both improved much in execution, and, as a pianist, Chopin is now one of the very first of all. He produces new effects, like Paganini on his violin, and accomplishes wonderful passages, such as no one could formerly have thought practicable. Hiller, too, is an admirable player — vigorous, and yet playful. Both, however, rather toil in the Parisian spasmodic and impassioned style, too often losing sight of time and sobriety and of true music; I, again, do so perhaps too little; thus we all three mutually learn something and improve each other, while I feel rather like a schoolmaster and they a little like *mirliflors* or *incroyables*.[26]

Then during the following summer, his parents having journeyed to Carlsbad for a short visit, Frédéric went to join them for a joyous reunion. In the months before, friendship with the Wodzinska family had been revived, through correspondence and also through the son Anton's move to Paris. Chopin became greatly interested in the daughter Maria. At the time of his Carlsbad visit, she and her family were in nearby Dresden on their return journey to Poland. Chopin was invited to see them. It was a happy time for Chopin and his love for Maria quickly deepened.

On his way back from Dresden to Paris, Chopin stopped at Heidelberg for his historic meeting with Robert Schumann, Clara Wieck, and her father Friedrich. Friedrich was a difficult person, as Clara and Robert well knew, and he was skeptical of Chopin. Unfortunately Chopin delayed his call at the Wieck house until the very end of his Heidelberg stay—having spent most of his time with Mendelssohn. Wieck felt quite rebuffed. But during the course of the visit, the playing by both Chopin and the sixteen-year-old Clara warmed the atmosphere considerably and all parted on very hospitable terms. Chopin had asked Clara to play two of his etudes and Robert's recently completed Sonata in F Sharp Major. He was deeply impressed by her performance as were the hosts to Frédéric's playing. The Davidsbündler had truly gathered and the Philistines had been slain; Schumann was shortly to put the following words in Eusebius' mouth: "Chopin came. Florestan rushed to meet him. I saw them walking arm and arm, but it was as though they were floating on clouds, not walking."[27]

The total impact of the visit on Mendelssohn was quite overwhelming and he soon wrote his sister Fanny on October 6, 1835:

> The day after I accompanied the Hensels to Delitsch Chopin came; he intended only to remain one day, so we spent this entirely together in music. I cannot deny, dear Fanny, that I have lately found that you by no means do him justice in your judgment of his talents; perhaps he was not in a humour for playing when you heard him, which may not unfrequently be the case with him. But his playing has enchanted me afresh, and I am persuaded that if you, and my Father also, had heard some of his better pieces, as he played them to me, you would say the same. There is something thoroughly original in his pianoforte playing, and at the same time so masterly, that he may be called a most perfect virtuoso; and as every style of perfection is welcome and acceptable, that day was most agreeable to me, although so entirely different from the previous ones with you, — the Hensels.
>
> It was so pleasant for me to be once more with a thorough musician, and not with those half virtuosos and half classics, who would gladly combine *les honneurs de la vertu et les plaisirs du vice,* but with one who has his perfect and well-defined phase; and however far asunder we may be in our different spheres, still I can get on famously with such a person; but not with those half-and-half people.[28]

Returning to Paris in the fall of 1835, he found a pianistic battle shaping up between Thalberg and Liszt and their followers.

Although he did not let himself become involved, he nevertheless did assist Liszt in one of his triumphal recitals in April of the following year. The two of them performed Liszt's Grande Valse at the close of the program which earlier had featured some of Chopin's Etudes. But with the successes also came the trials: the previous November Chopin had become very seriously ill and had shown early indications of the tuberculosis which was soon to begin its ravaging of his body. However, recovery seemed complete. The summer of 1836 was similar to the previous one with visits to the Wodzinska family in Marienbad and with his musical friends in Leipzig. He left Marienbad secretly engaged to Maria. On his return to Paris he found a cooling on the part of the Wodzinska family. Perhaps there was a feeling that their noble status was too far above Chopin's lowly origins. Perhaps it was Maria's immaturity. Chopin was never sure; nevertheless he was plainly jilted. It was a crucial, agonizing time for him.

Liszt, of course, was in Paris—in company with the Countess Marie d'Agoult. Through them, Chopin had been introduced to Aurore Dudevant, estranged wife of Casimir Dudevant, mother of two small children, and a writer of some note whose *nom de plume* was George Sand. In the revolutionary spirit of the time, she defied convention—wearing trousers, smoking cigars, and generally creating quite a masculine appearance. Chopin's reaction at first was one of revulsion; but as he knew her better, he felt drawn to her.

Throughout the summer of 1837 he still awaited some encouraging word from Maria Wodzinska or her mother. He did not leave Paris except to go to England for a few weeks in company with the French piano manufacturer, Camille Pleyel. Chopin's health was not good. He wanted the visit kept secret so as not to tax his strength. But when he was invited to play after a dinner given by Broadwood, the beauty of his playing immediately identified him to the guests present—even though he had only been introduced as Monsieur Fritz. A review of this appearance was published in the *Musical World:*

> Were he not the most retiring and unambitious of all living musicians, he would before this time have been celebrated as the inventor of a new style, or school, of pianoforte composition. During his short visit to the metropolis last season, but few had the high gratification of hearing his extemporaneous performance. Those who experienced this will not readily lose its remembrance. He is, perhaps, *par éminence,* the most delightful of pianists in the drawing-room. The animation of his

style is so subdued, its tenderness so refined, its melancholy so gentle, its niceties so studied and systematic, the *tout-ensemble* so perfect, and evidently the result of an accurate judgment and most finished taste, that when exhibited in the large concert-room, or the thronged saloon, it fails to impress itself on the mass.[29]

By fall Chopin's hopes for Maria had completely vanished. He turned to George Sand; by the following year their friendship had developed into a relationship which would last for the next ten years. Much of this time was spent at her family home at Nohant. There was also the celebrated journey to Majorca that further deteriorated Chopin's health. Chopin still gave an occasional recital. Liszt reported on such an event for the *Gazette musicale* on May 2, 1841:

Last Monday, at eight o'clock in the evening, M. Pleyel's rooms were brilliantly lighted up; numerous carriages brought incessantly to the foot of a staircase covered with carpet and perfumed with flowers the most elegant women, the most fashionable young men, the most celebrated artists, the richest financiers, the most illustrious noblemen; a whole *élite* of society, a whole aristocracy of birth, fortune, talent, and beauty.

A grand piano was open on a platform; people crowded round, eager for the seats nearest it; they prepared to listen, they composed themselves, they said to themselves that they must not lose a chord, a note, an intention, a thought of him who was going to seat himself there. And people were right in being thus eager, attentive, and religiously moved, because he for whom they waited, whom they wished to hear, admire, and applaud, was not only a clever virtuoso, a pianist expert in the art of making notes [*de faire des notes*], not only an artist of great renown, he was all this and more than all this, he was Chopin. . . .

In Monday's concert Chopin had chosen in preference those of his works which swerve more from the classical forms. He played neither concerto, nor sonata, nor fantasia, nor variations, but preludes, studies, nocturnes, and mazurkas. Addressing himself to a society rather than to a public, he could show himself with impunity as he is, an elegiac poet, profound, chaste, and dreamy. He did not need either to astonish or to overwhelm, he sought for delicate sympathy rather than for noisy enthusiasm. Let us say at once that he had no reason to complain of want of sympathy. From the first chords there was established a close communication between him and his audience. Two studies and a ballade were encored, and had it not been for the fear of adding to the already great fatigue which betrayed itself on his pale face, people would have asked for a repetition of pieces of the programme one by one. . . .[30]

In many ways George Sand was the dominating spirit in Frédéric's life and unresolvable conflicts developed as her children by her marriage to Dudevant grew older. In fairness to her, it must be pointed out that she did provide him with much of the loving care he needed to carry on his composing and teaching during his long, losing battle with tuberculosis—a tragic condition which was present throughout their entire relationship. The final break between them, after which he rarely composed again, came in 1847, two years before his death.

Broken in spirit and almost completely in body, he nonetheless tried to show that he could get along without her. He was persuaded by Pleyel and others to present a public recital on February 16, 1848. This event turned out to be his farewell Paris appearance. Lacking strength, yet playing surprisingly well, he presented a masterful program, characterized by the most exquisite Chopin subtleties and shading.

The critic from the *Gazette musicale* wrote in glowing words on November 20:

A concert by the Ariel of pianists is a thing too rare to be given, like other concerts, by opening both wings of the doors to whomsoever wishes to enter. For this one a list had been drawn up: everyone inscribed thereon his name; but everyone was not sure of obtaining the precious ticket; patronage was required to be admitted into the holy of holies, to obtain the favour of depositing one's offering, and yet this offering amounted to a louis; but who has not a louis to spare when Chopin may be heard?

The outcome of all this naturally was that the fine flower of the aristocracy of the most distinguished women, the most elegant toilettes, filled on Wednesday Pleyel's rooms. There was also the aristocracy of artists and amateurs, happy to seize in his flight this musical sylph who had promised to let himself once more and for a few hours be approached, seen, and heard.

The sylph kept his word, and with what success, what enthusiasm! It is easier to tell you of the reception he got, the transport he excited, than to describe, analyse, divulge, the mysteries of an execution which has nothing analogous in our terrestrial regions. If we had in our power the pen which traced the delicate marvels of Queen Mab, not bigger than an agate that glitters on the finger of an alderman, of her tiny chariot, of her diaphanous team, only then should we succeed in giving an idea of a purely ideal talent into which matter enters hardly at all. Only Chopin can make Chopin understood: all those who were present at the *séance* of Wednesday are convinced of this as well as we.

The programme announced first a trio of Mozart, which Chopin, Alard, and Franchomme executed in such a manner that one despairs of ever hearing it again so well performed. Then Chopin played studies, preludes, mazurkas, waltzes; he performed afterwards his beautiful sonata with Franchomme. Do not ask us how all these masterpieces small and great were rendered. We said at first we would not attempt to reproduce these thousands and thousands of *nuances* of an exceptional genius having in his service an organisation of the same kind. We shall only say that the charm did not cease to act a single instant on the audience and that it still lasted after the concert was ended.[31]

He had planned to give a second program, but the Revolution of 1848 made it impossible and also deprived him of his living. With the aid of his student from Scotland, Jane Stirling, he left for England and Scotland in April and did not return to Paris until November 24. It turned out to be an ill-advised undertaking. The travelling, the climate, the entertaining and performing that were forced upon him brought him to his lowest ebb. He still had to teach and play in order to support himself. In July he wrote to his friend Grzymala regarding an appearance he had made at Lord Falmouth's house in London:

I don't know whether I made 100 guineas. . . . The season here is finished. I don't know how my plans will turn out. I have not much savings in my pocket, and don't know what I shall do. I may go to Scotland. My Scottish ladies are kind and lovable, but sometimes they bore me horribly. . . . My health varies from hour to hour; but often in the mornings it seems as if I must cough my life out. I'm depressed in spirit, but my head gets muddled; I even avoid solitude, so as not to think, for I must not be ill long here, and want to avoid getting feverish.[32]

He did go on to Scotland, giving concerts in Glasgow and Edinburgh, and in Manchester en route. The review in the *Manchester Guardian* appeared on August 30:

Chopin appears to be about thirty years of age. He is very spare in frame, and there is an almost painful air of feebleness in his appearance and gait. This vanishes when he seats himself at the instrument, in which he seems for the time perfectly absorbed. Chopin's music and his style of performance partake of the same leading characteristics — refinement rather than vigor, subtle elaboration rather than simple comprehensiveness in composition, an elegant, rapid touch rather than a firm, nervous grasp of the instrument. But his compositions and his playing appeared to be the perfection of chamber music — fit to be associated with the most refined instrumental quartets and quartet-playing — but wanting breadth and obviousness of design and executive power to be effective in a large concert hall.[33]

It was surprising that he could perform at all. When he got to Scotland, he did not help his condition by staying at nearly a dozen different locations within a two-month period. His correspondence to Grzymala during this time was full of despair. He wrote on October 1, 1848:

If I don't write you jeremiads, it is not because you won't comfort me, for you are the only man who knows everything about me; but once I begin, there will be no end to them, and it is always the same thing. I am inaccurate in saying "the same," because with regard to the future everything goes from bad to worse with me. I feel weaker, I can't compose anything, not only because I have no desire but also because of physical obstacles, for each week I am tossed on a different tree limb. And what am I to do? Moreover, this saves me a little money for the winter. I have plenty of invitations and I cannot even go where I should like to—for instance, to the Duchess of Argyll or Lady Belhaven—because the season is too advanced for me to travel in my condition. All morning, up till two o'clock, I am fit for nothing. Then when I dress, everything bothers me, and I gasp like this until dinner, after which one must sit for two hours with the men at table, and look at them talking and listen to them drinking. Bored to death (thinking of not the same things as they think of, despite all kind courtesies and French remarks at that table), I go to the drawing room, where I need all my courage to revive myself somewhat, for then they are usually eager to hear me. Then my good Daniel carries me upstairs to my bedroom (which, as you know, is always on the upper floor here), undresses me, puts me down, leaves a candle, and I am allowed to breathe and dream until morning, when the same thing

159

begins all over again. And as soon as I get accustomed to one place, I must go to some other place, for my Scottish ladies leave me no peace; either they come to fetch me or they drive me to visit their families (*nota bene,* I always insist on being personally and very much invited). They will stifle me by their kindness, and I won't stop them from doing this out of politeness.[34]

Finally Chopin came back to London in November and made his last public appearance on the 16th at a benefit ball for Polish exiles. And thence back to his friends and beloved Paris. He lingered on for some months, composing a few fragments, in company with friends and his sister Louise. His struggle ceased on October 17, 1849, after living, as Jules Janin has commented, "ten miraculous years with a breath ready to fly away."[35]

This résumé of Chopin's life and performance career points up the integration of Chopin the intensely human, suffering man with the musician and unrivalled keyboard poet. Here was a man whose performance style and technique were completely dedicated to the most genuine musical ideals. Chopin the performer perfectly interpreted Chopin the composer in a most original manner. and there was not the faintest suspicion of technique for technique's sake. Is it any wonder that the impact was so overwhelming to truth seeking listeners of that day whose ears had become jaded to the musical superficialities of Herz, Kalkbrenner, and even Thalberg?   In Chopin we have a profound, influential chapter in early modern pianism. He set both a musical and a technical ideal for years to come. Perhaps it took a lifetime of suffering to accomplish it fully.

The many first-hand observations by those who heard Chopin play and the comments from his many biographers make it fairly easy to construct a clear picture of his keyboard style. Mendelssohn called him the perfect virtuoso. His technical dexterity was complete; his physical coordination and freedom were of the highest quality. The touch was smooth and even, perfectly articulated with the greatest of refinement and elegance, somewhat in the Hummel tradition. There was a true natural feeling that could express a wide range of emotion. Often it was tinged with Chopin's melancholy spirit. His control over the most subtle shades of dynamics probably has never been surpassed. His meagre physical means made it imperative for him to exploit the pianissimo range of the piano. In his younger days when he had greater physical strength, he did not hesitate to make use of a solid forte sound, but he never "thumped." He oftentimes would prefer to understate an idea. He was most conscious of a legato, cantabile melody line and took great pains to teach it. He strongly advocated that the pupil study both singing and Italian opera. His pupil, Mathias, described Chopin's method of teaching as "absolutely of the old *legato* school, of the school of Clementi and Cramer."[36] Mathias spoke also of his great variety of touch.

And always there was a certain spontaneity and improvisatory character to his performance that emanated from a very supple body and a thorough understanding of rubato. The Chopin rubato has been thoroughly discussed by his contemporaries. Liszt described it to one of his pupils: "Look at these trees! The wind plays in the leaves, stirs up life among them, the tree remains the same, that is Chopinesque rubato."[37]

Madame Dubois, one of Chopin's students, said that Chopin directed that the left hand should conduct and maintain a strict beat.[38] And he was supposed to have told another pupil, the Polish pianist, Karol Mikuli (1821-1897):

> While the singing hand, either irresolutely lingering or as in passionate speech eagerly anticipating with a certain impatient vehemence, freed the truth of the musical expression from all rhythmical fetters, the other, the accompanying hand, continued to play strictly in time.[39]

In the Mazurkas, which Chopin felt his Polish students could best express rhythmically, he took considerable liberties. One day Charles Hallé confronted Chopin with the observation that he had actually played them in 4/4 time rather than 3/4 time. At first he denied it; but, when Hallé then counted as Chopin played, he admitted it — laughingly commenting that it was a nationalistic trait.[40]

He would never plead guilty to erratic timing in his playing. A Madame Elise Peruzzi, whose father was the Russian consul-general to the United States, heard Chopin play frequently in private gatherings in Paris about 1838. She described his playing and his reaction to such criticism:

> When I knew him he was a sufferer and would only occasionally play in public, and then place his piano in the middle of Pleyel's room whilst his admirers were around the piano. His specialty was extreme delicacy, and his *pianissimo* extraordinary. Every little note was like a bell, so clear. His fingers seemed to be without any bones; but he would bring out certain effects by great elasticity. He got very angry at being accused of not keeping time; calling his left hand his

maître de chapelle and allowing his right to wander about *ad libitum.*[41]

Notable advances in piano technique for which he is responsible stem directly from his individual style of writing. His Nocturnes, the style of which Chopin received from John Field, emphasize strongly the validity of a singing piano technique. Numerous of his Etudes call for the extension of the hand to the interval of at least a tenth or more. Chopin's hand, not large but possessing spatulate fingers, could open up to a startling degree. Stephen Heller said that it seemed to cover a third of the keyboard and looked like the mouth of a serpent about to swallow a whole rabbit.[42] His student, Adolph Gutmann (1819-1882) said he was so flexible of body that he could place his legs over his shoulders like a clown.[43] In these same Etudes Chopin thoroughly explored the technical demands of the instrument—to a greater extent than any before him. Yet the technique is absolutely subservient to the music. In comparing the technical demands made by both Chopin and Liszt, Arthur Rubinstein pointed out

> . . . that even the most difficult figurations of Chopin belong to creative music. Liszt cultivated technical preciosity; the difficulties he contrived were a camouflage, and he exploited them for greater effect. Chopin was interested only in the musical idea, and the difficulties of his works are logically inherent in his thought. . . . I can play a pyrotechnical Liszt sonata, requiring forty minutes for its performance, and get up from the piano without feeling tired, while even the shortest etude of Chopin compels me to an intense expenditure of effort.[44]

Chopin's works call for radical changes in the areas of fingering and pedaling; he did not hesitate to make them in his own playing. Particularly in the Nocturnes and the other lyric pieces he was the master poet of the pedal. He was most particular in teaching it and reiterated frequently: "The correct employment of it remains a study for life."[45] Antoine François Marmontel in his *Les Pianistes Célèbres* asserted that "No pianist before him has employed the pedals alternately or simultaneously with so much tact and ability,. . . in making constantly use of the pedal he obtained *des harmonies ravissantes, des bruissements mélodiques qui étonnaient et charmaient.*"[46]

His use of the thumb on the black keys and the passing of certain fingers over others, considered radical in his day, are absolutely essential in his music. Hipkins, who heard Chopin in London in 1848, noticed that he adopted "the easiest fingering, although it might be against the rules, that came to him. He changed fingers upon a key as often as an organ-player."[47] Mikuli described his fingering in greater detail:

> In the notation of fingering, especially of that peculiar to himself, Chopin was not sparing. Here pianoforte-playing owes him great innovations which, on account of their expedience, were soon adopted, notwithstanding the horror with which authorities like Kalkbrenner at first regarded them. Thus, for instance, Chopin used without hesitation the thumb on the black keys, passed it even under the little finger (it is true, with a distinct inward bend of the wrist), if this could facilitate the execution and give it more repose and evenness. With one and the same finger he took often two consecutive keys (and this not only in gliding down from a black to the next white key) without the least interruption of the sequence being noticeable. The passing over each other of the longer fingers without the aid of the thumb (see *Etude, No. 2, Op. 10*) he frequently made use of, and not only in passages where the thumb stationary on a key made this unavoidably necessary. The fingering of the chromatic thirds based on this (as he marked it in *Etude, No. 5, Op. 25*) affords in a much higher degree than that customary before him the possibility of the most beautiful *legato* in the quickest *tempo* and with a perfectly quiet hand.[48]

From every indication we have, Chopin must have been a superb teacher. It has always therefore been something of a mystery why he never developed one truly outstanding pianist while Liszt had so many. Part of the reason may lie in the differences in the nature and popular appeal of the two men. Liszt, with his sometimes flamboyant technique and his man of the world magnetism, exhibited during his extensive European tours, was of course more universally known and appreciated. The retiring, frail Chopin was little seen by the general public and could never fully identify with it. Then, too, Liszt's teaching career was a much longer one and came largely after Chopin, when the popularity of the piano had increased considerably. A large share of Chopin's students was comprised of female aristocracy possessing varying degrees of talent. His most promising student was Karl Filtsch, who came to him from Transylvania at the age of eleven. He was so extraordinary that Liszt remarked after hearing him perform at a salon gathering: "If this youngster begins a concert tour, I'll close my shop."[49] But even here misfortune followed Chopin. Young Karl died in 1845 when only fifteen.

His students admired him greatly, respecting him for his

perfectionism and disciplined teaching, shown even through his many periods of infirmity. Most of his teaching was done in the afternoons until about four or five o'clock. He could show both anger and great patience in turn. Friederike Müller, later Madame Streicher, recalled her study in about 1840:

Feeble, pale, coughing much, he often took opium drops on sugar and gum-water, rubbed his forehead with eau de Cologne, and nevertheless he taught with a patience, perseverance and zeal which were admirable. His lessons always lasted a full hour, generally he was so kind as to make them longer .... One morning he played from memory fourteen Preludes and Fugues of Bach's.[50]

Mikuli stressed the other side of the picture:

To be sure, Chopin made great demands on the talent and diligence of the pupil. Consequently, there were often *des leçons orageuses,* as it was called in the school idiom, and many a beautiful eye left the high altar of the Cité d'Orléans, Rue St. Lazare, bedewed with tears, without, on that account, ever bearing the dearly beloved master the least grudge. For was not the severity which was not easily satisfied with anything, the feverish vehemence with which the master wished to raise his disciples to his own stand-point, the ceaseless repetition of a passage till it was understood, a guarantee that he had at heart the progress of the pupil? A holy artistic zeal burnt in him then, every word from his lips was incentive and inspiring. Single lessons often lasted literally for hours at a stretch, till exhaustion overcame master and pupil.[51]

The student would sit at a large Pleyel grand piano with Chopin alongside at an upright instument of the same make. Liszt described Chopin's preference of instruments:

While Chopin was strong and healthy, as during the first years of his residence in Paris, he used to play on an Érard piano; but after his friend Camille Pleyel had made him a present of one of his splendid instruments, remarkable for their metallic ring and very light touch, he would play on no other maker's.

If he was engaged for a *soirée* at the house of one of his Polish or French friends, he would often send his own instrument, if there did not happen to be a Pleyel in the house.

Chopin was very partial to Pleyel's pianos, particularly on account of their silvery and somewhat veiled sonority, and of the easy touch which permitted him to draw from them sounds which one might have believed to belong to those harmonicas of which romantic Germany has kept the monopoly, and which her ancient masters constructed so ingeniously, marrying crystal to water.[52]

Chopin himself remarked: "When I am indisposed, I play on one of Erard's pianos and there I easily find a ready-made tone. But when I feel in the right mood and strong enough to find my own tone for myself, I must have one of Pleyel's pianos."[53]

In his approach to the keyboard, Chopin did not begin with the key of C. He felt that a more natural position of the hand was to be found if the thumb and fingers were to be placed on the keys E, F#, G#, A#, B. The white key technique had best be left until last. Madame Dubois said that

> Chopin made his pupils begin with the B major scale, very slowly without stiffness. Suppleness was his great object. He repeated, without ceasing, during the lesson: "Easily, easily" (*facilement, facilement*). Stiffness exasperated him . . . . He feared above all the *abrutissement* of the pupils. One day he heard me say that I practised six hours a day. He became quite angry, and forbade me to practise more than three hours. This was also the advice of Hummel in his pianoforte school.[54]

Of all his students, Mikuli has left us the most complete summary of Chopin's teaching procedure. In his preface to his edition of Chopin's works, he stated:

> What concerned Chopin most at the commencement of his instruction was to free the pupil from every stiffness and convulsive, cramped movement of the hand, and to give him thus the first condition of a beautiful style of playing, *souplesse* (suppleness), and with it independence of the fingers. He taught indefatigably that the exercises in question were no mere mechanical ones, but called for the intelligence and the whole will of the pupil, on which account twenty and even forty thoughtless repetitions (up to this time the arcanum of so many schools) do no good at all, still less the practising during which, according to Kalkbrenner's advice, one may occupy one's self simultaneously with some kind of reading. . . .
>
> Chopin treated very thoroughly the different kinds of touch, especially the full-toned [*tonvolle*] *legato*. As gymnastic helps he recommended the bending inward and outward of the wrist, the repeated touch from the wrist, the extending of the fingers, but all this with the earnest warning against over-

fatigue. He made his pupils play the scales with a full tone, as connectedly as possible, very slowly and only gradually advancing to a quicker *tempo* and with metronomic evenness. The passing of the thumb under the other fingers and the passing of the latter over the former was to be facilitated by a corresponding turning inward of the hand. The scales with many black keys (B, F sharp, and D flat) were first studied, and last, as the most difficult, C major. In the same sequence he took up Clementi's *Préludes et Exercices,* a work which for its utility he esteemed very highly. According to Chopin the evenness of the scales (also of the *arpeggios*) not merely depended on the utmost equal strengthening of all fingers by means of five-finger exercises and on a thumb entirely free at the passing under and over, but rather on a lateral movement (with the elbow hanging quite down and always easy) of the hand, not by jerks, but continuously and evenly flowing, which he tried to illustrate by the *glissando* over the keyboard. Of studies he gave after this a selection of Cramer's *Études,* Clementi's *Gradus ad Parnassum,* Moscheles' style-studies for the higher development (which were very sympathetic to him), and J.S. Bach's suites and some fugues from *Das wohltemperierte Clavier.* In a certain way Field's and his own nocturnes numbered likewise with the studies, for in them the pupil was—partly by the apprehension of his explanations, partly by observation and imitation . . . to learn to know, love, and execute the beautiful smooth [*gebundene*] vocal tone and the *legato.* With double notes and chords he demanded most strictly simultaneous striking, breaking was only allowed when it was indicated by the composer himself; shakes, which he generally began with the auxiliary note, had not so much to be played quick as with great evenness: the conclusion of the shake quietly and without precipitation. For the turn (*gruppetto*) and the appoggiatura he recommended the great Italian singers as models. Although he made his pupils play octaves from the wrist, they must not thereby lose in fulness of tone.[55]

The consensus among Chopin's students seems to be that in addition to the composers listed above, Chopin also taught Hummel, some Beethoven, Moscheles, Schubert, Weber, Mendelssohn, and a limited amount of Liszt. Only Mikuli mentions Mozart, an oddity since Mozart was a particular favorite of Chopin. The music of Schumann he almost entirely ignored—he never did reciprocate wholeheartedly Schumann's feeling for him. His fondness for Bach is indicated by his statement to Lenz: "When I am about to give a concert, I close my doors for a time and play Bach.''[56]

In his last year Chopin began work on a proposed method book, a project which unfortunately he was unable to complete. Alfred Cortot, who acquired the fragmentary Chopin manuscript in 1936, described its disappointing quality:

It consists of nothing more than a dozen sheets varying in size and quality, from cheap note paper to music paper ruled à l'italienne, that Chopin always used, written in very bad French. The pages are not numbered, and there is no logical sequence of ideas. It is little more than a puzzle made up of the most commonplace clichés on the teaching of the elements of music.

Why such an elementary work should contain so many crossings-out, alterations, and words written one on top of the other to the point of illegibility is hard to understand. So far as one is able to judge from these notes carelessly strung together, Chopin's intentions fall far short of the high ambitions Liszt attributed to him.[57]

Two short passages, from the section of the manuscript which Cortot quotes, follow:

Having some idea of notation, key signatures, and the mechanism of the piano, the next step is to sit down in front of the keyboard, so as to be able to reach either end, without leaning sideways. Placing our right foot on the pedal, without bringing the dampers into play, we find the position of the hand by placing our fingers on the notes E, F sharp, G sharp, A sharp, B.

The long fingers will be found to be on the black keys with the short fingers on the white. In order to obtain equality of leverage, the fingers on the black keys must be kept in line. The same applies to the fingers on the white keys. The resultant move will be found to follow the natural formation of the hand.

The hand should remain supple and the wrist and forearm round themselves into a curve making for ease of movement that would be unobtainable if the fingers were outstretched. It is useless to begin to learn scales with that in C major. While it is the easiest to read, it is the most difficult for the hands, since it contains no purchase points. We shall begin with one that places the long fingers comfortably over the black keys—B major for example. . . .

Since each finger is formed differently, it is far better to develop their special characteristics rather than attempt to destroy their individuality. The strength of each finger is relative to its shape. The extremities of the hand are formed by the thumb, which is its strongest member, and by the little finger. While the third finger has a greater freedom as a point of support, the second finger . . ., the fourth finger is bound to the third by the same tendon like a Siamese twin and is the weakest. One can try with all one's might to separate them, but this is impossible and, thank heavens, useless. There are as many different sounds as there are fingers. Everything hangs on knowing how to finger correctly. Hummel is the most knowledgeable person on this subject. It is important to make use of the shape of the fingers and no less so to employ the rest of the hand, wrist, forearm, and arm. To attempt to play entirely from the wrist, as Kalkbrenner advocates, is incorrect.[58]

From this material we can clearly see that Chopin is not in sympathy with the repetitious, mechanical finger training advocated by Kalkbrenner and his school. Chopin's arm working in conjunction with a supple wrist helps to fortify the weaker fingers. Careful fingering can also assist. Just a short time before in Scotland in all his misery, Chopin still could quip that all he had left was a big nose and an undeveloped fourth finger.[59] Technique was never a dry mechanical process for him. Happily Chopin never could separate it from a cantabile approach. The musical pianist had to sing and with his singing there must be the most natural phrasing. If he failed in this regard, Mikuli quoted Chopin often repeating

... that it struck him as if some one were reciting, in a language not understood by the speaker, a speech carefully learned by rote, in the course of which the speaker not only neglected the natural quantity of the syllables, but even stopped in the middle of words. The pseudo-musician, he said, shows in a similar way, by his wrong phrasing, that music is not his mother-tongue, but something foreign and incomprehensible to him, and must, like the aforesaid speaker, quite renounce the idea of making any effect upon his hearers by his delivery.[60]

Notes

[1] Arthur Hedley, ed., *Selected Correspondence of Fryderyk Chopin,* abridged from Fryderyk Chopin's correspondence, collected and anno-

tated by Bronislaw Edward Sydow, pp. 98-99.

[2] *Ibid.*, pp. 95-96.

[3] *Ibid.*, p. 97.

[4] *Ibid.*, pp. 103-04.

[5] Casimir Wierzynski, *The Life and Death of Chopin*, p. 30.

[6] William Murdoch, *Chopin, His Life*, p. 17.

[7] Henri Bidou, *Chopin*, pp. 10-11.

[8] Robert Schumann, *On Music and Musicians*, p. 126.

[9] Wierzynski, *Life and Death of Chopin*, p. 72.

[10] *Ibid.*

[11] Frederick Niecks, *Frederick Chopin as a Man and Musician*, I, pp. 99-100.

[12] Murdoch, *Chopin, His Life*, p. 57.

[13] Wierzynski, *Life and Death of Chopin*, p. 84.

[14] *Ibid.*, p. 99.

[15] *Ibid.*

[16] Moritz Karasowski, *Frederic Chopin, His Life and Letters*, p. 174.

[17] Niecks, *Chopin . . . Man and Musician*, I, p. 181.

[18] *Ibid.*, pp. 97-98.

[19] Wierzynski, *Life and Death of Chopin*, p. 162.

[20] Franz Liszt, *Life of Chopin*, p. 84.

[21] Wierzynski, *Life and Death of Chopin*, p. 163.

[22] *Ibid.*, p. 164.

[23] *Ibid.*, p. 163.

[24] Hiller had come to Paris in 1828 after having studied under Hummel at Weimar. He was a serious pianist who performed Bach and Beethoven frequently during his appearances in Paris.

[25] Niecks, *Chopin . . . Man and Musician*, I, p. 252.

[26] Paul and Dr. Carl Mendelssohn-Bartholdy, eds., *Letters of Felix Mendelssohn-Bartholdy from 1833 to 1847*, pp. 34-35.

[27] Cited in Wierzynski, *Life and Death of Chopin*, p. 209.

[28] Mendelssohn, *Letters*, p. 80.

[29] Niecks, *Chopin . . . Man and Musician*, I, p. 312.

[30] *Ibid.*, II, pp. 90-91.

[31] *Ibid.*, II, pp. 206-07.

[32] Murdoch, *Chopin, His Life*, p. 352.

[33] Wierzynski, *Life and Death of Chopin*, p. 387.

[34] *Ibid.,* p. 390.

[35] James Huneker, *Chopin, the Man and His Music,* p. 75.

[36] Niecks, *Chopin . . . Man and Musician,* II, p. 181.

[37] *Ibid.,* II, p. 101.

[38] *Ibid.,* II, pp. 101-02.

[39] *Ibid.,* II, p. 102.

[40] *Ibid.*

[41] *Ibid.,* II, p. 339.

[42] *Ibid.,* II, p. 96.

[43] *Ibid.*

[44] Foreword by Artur Rubinstein to Wierzynski, *The Life and Death of Chopin,* p. xi.

[45] Niecks, *Chopin . . . Man and Musician,* II, p. 341.

[46] Cited in *ibid.,* II, p. 99.

[47] Edith J. Hipkins, *How Chopin Played,* p. 5.

[48] Niecks, *Chopin . . . Man and Musician,* II, p. 186.

[49] Cited in Wierzynski, *Life and Death of Chopin,* p. 314.

[50] Murdoch, *Chopin, His Life,* p. 278.

[51] Niecks, *Chopin . . . Man and Musician,* II, p. 183.

[52] *Ibid.,* II, p. 105.

[53] *Ibid.*

[54] *Ibid.,* II, pp. 182-84.

[55] *Ibid.,* II, pp. 183-85.

[56] Hipkins, *How Chopin Played,* p. 7.

[57] Alfred Cortot, *In Search of Chopin,* pp. 36-37.

[58] *Ibid.,* pp. 43-45.

[59] Murdoch, *Chopin, His Life,* p. 359.

[60] Karol (Carl) Mikuli, Introduction to the *Complete Works for the Pianoforte by Frederic Chopin.*

10.   Liszt and Virtuoso Technique

The greatest of all nineteenth century pianists, Franz Liszt, was born in Raiding, Hungary, in 1811, just a year after Chopin. His father, Adam Liszt, was a land steward in the employ of Prince Esterhazy. Adam loved music, played both the violin and the guitar, and gave Franz his first piano lessons. The boy presented his first recital at the age of nine in nearby Oedenburg. Subsequent appearances resulted in royal financial backing in 1821 for further study in Vienna under Salieri and Czerny. (Czerny's recollections of young Franz are recorded in an earlier chapter.) Here he remained for two years during which time he met both Beethoven and Schubert.

Seeing his son continue his phenomenal progress, Adam Liszt decided to take him on tour to Paris and London. In Paris he begged Cherubini to take the twelve-year-old Franz as a student at the Conservatoire of which he was director. A regulation forbidding foreign students made this an impossibility, but private study was arranged under Reicha and Paër. Franz played with outstanding success both in public concerts and elite salons. Then father and son proceeded to England in 1824 where the boy performed before George IV. Two visits followed in 1825 and 1827. Adam Liszt became ill on the third visit and died shortly thereafter. Franz, now sixteen, settled in Paris with his mother where he gave piano lessons for their support. It was a difficult period of soul searching. Plagued by serious illness, he spent many hours in the study of religion, philosophy, and literature. As his health improved, he worked diligently at the keyboard—regularly practicing, as he recalled later, at least ten hours a day. By 1829 he had several pieces published — including a fantasia in the popular style of the day.

The year 1831 was an eventful one for Liszt, who was now twenty. During that brief span he was to meet Berlioz, Paganini, and Chopin. Each was to leave a lasting mark upon him apart from the prevailing salon influence he had previously encountered. Berlioz' impressive orchestral writing led Liszt to complete a piano arrangement of the *Symphonie Fantastique* in 1833. The tremendous impact of the twenty-four Caprices by Paganini inspired him to begin work on his own transcriptions of some of them—the Paganini Etudes. These in turn were stepping stones to the *Transcendental* Etudes—all highwater marks in piano etude literature of the nineteenth century. Paganini's technical wizardry on the violin also served as a strong motivating force in the development of Liszt's piano technical equipment. And Chopin's creative output and pianistic style were to have a great refining influence on Liszt, particularly in directing him to the best and most serious of the piano literature. By 1832 Liszt had mastered all of the Beethoven sonatas; but when he programmed them, he dared not give the composer's name because Beethoven was considered dull during the years immediately following his death. Schumann and Weber were great favorites. Liszt was more influential than any other pianist in the first half of the nineteenth century in getting the best piano literature before the general public. He was the first to play complete programs by himself and the first to perform from memory.

Liszt was very well received during his early years in Paris. Emotions ran strong among his listeners. His own highly charged temperament had as much to do with this as had his unprecedented technical accomplishments. One startling account is found in the description by an Englishman, Henry Reeves, of a Liszt recital in Paris in 1835 when the pianist was only twenty-four:

> Liszt had already played a great fantasia of his own, and Beethoven's 27th Sonata. After this latter piece he gasped with emotion as I took his hand and thanked him for the divine energy he had shed forth. At last I managed to pierce the crowd, and I sat in the orchestra before the Duchesse de Ranzan's box, talking to Her Grace and to Madame de Circourt who was there. My chair was on the same board as the piano when the final piece began. It was a duet for two instruments, beginning with Mendelssohn's *Chants sans Paroles* and proceeding to a work of his own.
> We had already passed that delicious chime of the Song written in a Gondola, and the gay tendrils of sound in another lighter piece, which always reminded me of an Italian vine. As the closing strains began I saw Liszt's countenance assume that agony of expression, mingled with radiant smiles of joy,

which I never saw in any other human face except in the paintings of Our Saviour by some of the early masters; his hands rushed over the keys, the floor on which I sat shook like a wire, and the whole audience was wrapped with sound, when the hand and frame of the artist gave way. He fainted in the arms of the friend who was turning over the pages for him, and we bore him out in a strong fit of hysterics. The effect of this scene was really dreadful. The whole room sat breathless with fear, till Hiller came forward and announced that Liszt was already restored to consciousness and was comparatively well again. As I handed Madame de Circourt to her carriage we both trembled like poplar leaves, and I tremble scarcely less as I write this. [1]

Shortly after this episode, Liszt went to Geneva, Switzerland for eighteen months with the Countess Marie d'Agoult. During his absence, the virtuoso Austrian pianist, Sigismond Thalberg, came to Paris in November of 1835. His performances aroused great enthusiasm. The periodical, *Le Ménestrel,* on March 13, 1836, expressed the universal acclaim he received: "Thalberg is not only the first pianist in the world, but he is also a most distinguished composer." [2] This pupil of Hummel and Kalkbrenner dazzled his public with salon transcriptions. Niecks thought that Thalberg's secret of success could be attributed as well to "the aristocratic nature of his artistic personality, in which elegance and calm self-possession reigned supreme." [3]

Here is Sir Charles Hallé's first-hand account of Thalberg's playing and technique:

Totally unlike in style to either Chopin or Liszt, he was admirable and unimpeachable in his own way. His performances were wonderfully finished and accurate, giving the impression that a wrong note was an impossibility. His tone was round and beautiful, the clearness of his passage-playing crystal-like, and he had brought to the utmost perfection the method, identified with his name, of making a melody stand out distinctly through a maze of brilliant passages. He did not appeal to the emotions, except those of wonder, for his playing was statuesque; cold, but beautiful, and so masterly that it was said of him, with reason, he would play with the same care and finish if roused out of the deepest sleep in the middle of the night. He created a great sensation in Paris, and became the idol of the public, principally, perhaps, because it was felt that he could be imitated, even successfully, which with Chopin and Liszt was out of the question. [4]

William Mason, who later observed his technique in both Europe and America, thought that he did not use enough free arm action. He felt that his

> . . . octave-playing was not altogether elastic and free from rigidity, for in long-continued and rapid octave passages a close observer would have noticed a contraction of his facial muscles and a compression of the lips, which would have been avoided under the conditions of properly devitalized upper-arm muscles and loose wrists. [5]

On a concert tour to America some time after his Parisian encounter with Liszt, Thalberg had stayed for an extended period in the home of Mason's brother in West Orange, New Jersey. Mason was fascinated by the prolonged opportunity for studying Thalberg's practice procedures:

> His daily exercises included scales and arpeggio passages played at various rates of speed and with different degrees of dynamic force. These were always put into rhythmic form, and the measure, sometimes in triple and sometimes in quadruple time in many varieties, were invariably indicated by means of accentuation. Dynamic effects, such as crescendos and diminuendos, also received due attention. In short, as it seems to me, he made it a point—as well in the cultivation and development of physical technic as in his public performances—to play musically at all times.
> Thalberg's technic seemed to be confined mainly to the finger, hand, wrist, and lower arm muscles, but these he used in such a deft manner as to draw from his instrument the loveliest tones. He was altogether opposed to the high-raised finger of some of the modern schools, and in his work entitled *"L'Art du Chant appliqué au Piano"* he cautions students against this habit. [6]

Thalberg was always famous for his beautiful singing tone. In this work, *The Art of Singing on the Pianoforte,* Op. 70, a selection of his opera transcriptions, Thalberg included a preface which contains his ideas on technique and tone:

> Broad, lofty, dramatic songs must be sung with a full chest; much is therefore expected of the instrument, from which the greatest possible volume of tone must be drawn, though never by roughly striking the keys, but rather by catching them closely and deftly, and pressing them down with power, decision, and warmth. For simple, tender, and graceful melo-

dies one should knead the keys, so to speak, pressing and working them as with a boneless hand and fingers of velvet; in such strains the keys should be felt rather than struck.—To those occupying themselves seriously with the pianoforte we can give no better advice, than to learn, study, and thoroughly test the beautiful art of singing. To this end no opportunity should be missed of hearing great artists, whatever their instrument may be, and great singers in particular. As a possible encouragement for young artists we will add, that we ourselves studied singing during five years under the direction of one of the most celebrated teachers of the Italian School. [7]

When Liszt in Geneva heard reports of Thalberg's conquest of Paris, his curiosity got the better of him. He interrupted his extended Swiss visit to return to Paris in March of 1836—only to find that Thalberg had departed the day before. He then stayed long enough to perform at two private soirées at Pleyel's and Érard's. Liszt had worked feverishly while in Switzerland and astounded his listeners with his vast improvement. The enthusiasm of his followers was rekindled and musical Paris now found itself in two camps—each believing it had found the true school of piano playing.

Liszt left Switzerland permanently in December, 1836, and almost immediately performed at an orchestral concert in Paris. Hallé reported:

Such marvels of executive skill and power I could never have imagined. He was a giant, and Rubinstein spoke the truth when, at a time when his own triumphs were greatest, he said that in comparison with Liszt all other pianists were children. Chopin carried you with him into a dreamland, in which you would have liked to dwell for ever; Liszt was all sunshine and dazzling splendour, subjugating his hearers with a power that none could withstand. For him there were no difficulties of execution, the most incredible seeming child's play under his fingers. One of the transcendent merits of his playing was the crystal-like clearness which never failed for a moment even in the most complicated and, to anybody else, impossible passages; it was as if he had photographed them in their minutest detail upon the ear of his listener. The power he drew from his instrument was such as I have never heard since, but never harsh, never suggesting "thumping." [8]

At an orchestral concert conducted by Berlioz, the *Marche au Supplice*, that most gorgeously instrumented piece, was performed, at the conclusion of which Liszt sat down and played his own arrangement, for the piano alone, of the same movement, with an effect even surpassing that of the full orchestra, and creating an indescribable furore. The feat had been duly announced in the programme beforehand, a proof of his indomitable courage! [9]

Thalberg did not return to Paris until the following March. By then the city was in an uproar trying to determine who was the greater. Liszt's chief protagonist was Berlioz, supported by Chopin, while Thalberg was championed by the critic Fétis. Thalberg played first at the Conservatoire to four hundred people. They heard his fantasias on *God Save the King* and on *Mosé*. Liszt countered by appearing before nearly four thousand at the opera house with more worthy repertoire: the *Concertstück* by Weber and Beethoven's *Hammerklavier* Sonata. But he was not without a fantasia—his own based on the *Niobe* of Pacini. Shortly thereafter each appeared on the same benefit program presenting their previously performed fantasias. The public verdict was clearly in favor of Liszt. The controversy had entered the newspapers and even Liszt could not contain himself.

Although Liszt expressed his respect for Thalberg the performer, there seems to be a bit of hypocrisy on his part in condemning Thalberg's superficial works while he himself was playing fantasias that were not always much better. Liszt's nature was full of paradoxes. He performed and fully appreciated the best of the literature, including Bach. He wrote many works of a high order and was the champion of worthy new composers such as Wagner. Yet considerable trivia flowed from his own pen. He savored his role as a performer in a manner that bordered on grandiloquence, but he also devoted countless hours to his students without any thought of remuneration. There was the deeply religious, aesthetic side of his nature that finally culminated in monastic vows, but throughout most of his life he remained the person who still needed his father's parting words to him as a youth: "Je crains pour toi les femmes." [10]

A short time after his Parisian successes, Liszt and Madame d'Agoult travelled to Italy where he gave a number of performances. In 1839 they reached the first parting of their ways which did not become final until five years later: she back to Paris with the children and he to the summit years of his performance career. The period from 1839 to 1847 was Liszt's time of greatest virtuosity and public acclaim. And by now Liszt, the composer of unparalleled *Transcendental* Etudes, [11] was worthy of being performed by Liszt, the unrivaled pianist. Sitwell has written:

If Liszt, as a virtuoso, was incomparable in the music of other men, he was no less remarkable when playing his own compositions. There was, indeed, no other pianist of the time who was capable of executing them. This was because they combined fresh principles and systems of construction with new scales of ornament; they required new gradations of tone; they called for a flashing, scintillating rapidity and a power of endurance that none of the old order of executants possessed. In fact, his own piano pieces were the most sensational part of his programmes. [12]

Liszt arrived in Vienna in the middle of November, 1839 for a series of recitals which he had volunteered to give in order to raise funds for the construction of a Beethoven memorial monument at Bonn. Everywhere he was feted. In public he performed such works as the *Hexameron* Variations, his transcriptions of the Beethoven *Pastoral* Symphony and the *William Tell* Overture, a Beethoven concerto, and selections from his own *Transcendental* Etudes and the *Années de Pèlerinage*. In private he favored select listeners with Chopin, Schumann, Bach, Scarlatti, other worthy literature and with many more of his transcriptions: from Schubert, Italian opera, Hungarian folk melodies, etc. Thence to Hungary where he was presented a jewelled sabre and letters of nobility and ushered home from a recital with a torchlight procession. Then it was back to Vienna, to Leipzig, London, Berlin, Moscow, St. Petersburg, Spain, Portugal, and elsewhere throughout Europe during the ensuing years.

The programs were always presented in the grand manner. In England Salaman recalled:

At these recitals, Liszt after performing a piece set down in his programme, would leave the platform, and, descending into the body of the room, where the benches were so arranged as to allow free locomotion, would move about among his auditors and converse with his friends, with the gracious condescension of a prince, until he felt disposed to return to the piano. [13]

In Berlin where he presented twenty-one recitals in a two month period, ladies collected his cigar butts and poured his coffee dregs into little vials they had brought with them. His pictures were everywhere. And with his purse fattened, Liszt dressed in the most princely manner. His first concert in St. Petersburg on his triumphant Russian tour in 1842 is detailed in the third person by the critic Stassov who was then a student of twenty:

> Liszt also wore a white cravat, and over it the Order of the Golden Spur given him by Pius IX (Mozart had been given the same order by Clement XIV, in 1770). He was further adorned by various other orders suspended by chains from the lapels of his dress-coat. But that which struck the Russians most was the great mane of fair hair reaching almost to his shoulders. Outside the priesthood, no Russian would have ventured on such a style of hairdressing. Such dishevelment had been sternly discountenanced since the time of Peter the Great.
>
> My friend Stassov was not favourably impressed at first sight. Liszt was very thin, stooped a great deal, and though I had read much about his famous Florentine profile and his likeness to Dante, I did not find his face beautiful. I was not pleased with his mania for dressing himself with Orders, and afterwards I was as little prepossessed by his somewhat affected demeanour to those who came in contact with him.
>
> There were three thousand people in the audience, Glinka among them. Liszt mounted the platform, and pulling his doeskin gloves from his shapely white hands, tossed them carelessly on the floor. Then, after acknowledging the thunderous applause, such as had not been heard in Russia for over a century, he seated himself at the piano. There was a silence as though the whole hall had been turned to stone, and Liszt, without any prelude, began the opening bars of the overture to *William Tell.* Curiosity, speculation, criticism, all were forgotten in the wonderful enchantment of his performance.
>
> His Fantasia on *Don Juan,* his arrangement of Beethoven's *Adelaide,* the *Erl-King* of Schubert, and his own *Galop Chromatique* followed upon this. After the concert, Serov and I were like madmen. We scarcely exchanged a word, but hurried home, each to write down his impressions, dreams and raptures. But we both vowed to keep this anniversary sacred for ever, and never, whilst life lasted, to forget a single instant of it. [14]

Even Schumann himself wrote in similar superlative terms when he heard him two years earlier:

> Still exhausted by a series of six concerts which he gave in Prague during an eight-days' stay there, Liszt arrived last Saturday [March 14, 1840] in Dresden. Perhaps he was never more eagerly expected anywhere than in the capital where pianoforte music and its performance are prized above all. On

Monday he gave a concert; the hall presented a brilliant spectacle, filled with the most distinguished society, including several members of the royal family. All eyes were fixed on the door through which the artist was to enter. Many portraits of him were in circulation, and that by Kriehuber, who has most correctly rendered his Jovian profile, is excellent; but the youthful Jupiter himself, of course, interests us to quite a different degree. A great deal has been said about the prosaic nature of our present times, the stuffy atmosphere of courts and capitals, of railroad civilization, etc.; but let the right man appear, and we listen reverently to his every manifestation. How much more to this artist, whose miraculous performances were famous even twenty years ago; whose name we have been accustomed to hear mentioned with the very important—before whom, as before Paganini, all parties bowed and for a moment appeared to be reconciled. Indeed the whole audience excitedly acclaimed him at his entrance; whereupon he began to play. I had heard him before; but it is one thing when the artist is playing before a public, and another, when he is playing before a small group—even the artist himself changes. The beautiful illuminated hall, the glow of candlelight, the handsomely dressed audience—all this tends to elevate the frame of mind of the giver as well as that of the receiver. And now the daemon began to stir in him; first he played with the public as if to try it, then gave it something more profound, until he had enmeshed every member of the audience with his art and did with them as he willed. With the exception of Paganini no artist to a like degree possesses this power of subjecting the public, of lifting it, sustaining it, and letting it fall again. . . . Within a few seconds tenderness, boldness, exquisiteness, wildness succeed one another; the instrument glows and flashes under the master's hands. All this has already been described a hundred times, and the Viennese, especially, have tried to catch the eagle in every way—through pursuits, snares, pitchforks, and poems. But he must be heard—and also seen; for if Liszt played behind the screen, a great deal of poetry would be lost.

From beginning to end he alone played and accompanied. Just as Mendelssohn is said to have once had the idea to compose an entire concert with overture, vocal pieces, and other appurtenances (one may safely publish this idea for the general benefit!), so does Liszt nearly always give his concerts unassisted. Only Madame Schroeder-Devrient—almost the only artist capable of asserting herself in such company—toward the close of the concert performed Schubert's *Erlking* and some of his smaller songs together with Liszt. [15]

In 1844 Liszt began to spend a quarter of each year in Weimar as the conductor and musical director at the court of the Grand Duke Karl-Alexander. His last public concerts for which he received remuneration were in Russia in 1847 after which he settled permanently in Weimar until 1861. [16] The Princess Carolyne von Sayn-Wittgenstein came from Poland to join him and the Villa Altenburg soon became one of the musical capitals of Europe. By this time he had become financially independent and never again accepted pay for any musical service. He still continued to lead an active life composing, conducting, and teaching. In 1861 Liszt went to Rome and four years later became an abbé in the Roman Catholic Church, but after 1869 he continued to spend a portion of each year in Weimar. In 1886, at the close of his life, he made a final tour to France and England.

Liszt's contribution to the historical development of piano technique is immense. His manner of playing is directly related to Chopin's free, elegant, yet natural technique. But he expands the dimensions. Where Chopin was limited by lack of physical strength and inhibited by the public's critical, impersonal gaze, Liszt knows no such boundaries. The dynamic range is increased to its musical limits, and the arms and body also know no restrictions. He freed piano technique completely from the fetters of the quiet hand, stiff finger school. His superb bodily mechanism, controlled by a near perfect coordination is utilized fully to serve musical objectives. When there is added the Liszt personality and stage manner, the ideal nineteenth century romantic pianist emerges. Liszt cares little for technical analysis; he achieves his transcendent musical interpretations without becoming so preoccupied. His teaching in his maturity dwells almost entirely on the aesthetic side of performance. But the theorists, as well as the many aspiring pianists of the day, are greatly intrigued by what they see and hear. Liszt becomes the model of the best of piano technique. Probably no other pianist's influence has been so great.

Liszt's reputation as a great teacher stems principally from his Weimar years. But during his youth when he was living in Paris and still not far removed from the Czerny influence, he taught privately. These early lessons show a real concern with technical detail. There exists a very interesting record of a series of lessons which Liszt, at the age of twenty, gave in 1832 to Valérie Boissier, daughter of a distinguished family from Geneva that also had a Paris home. Her mother, Mme. Auguste Boissier, took notes and recorded them in a book, *Liszt as Pedagogue*.

This early teaching, while based on Czerny and even recommending the Kalkbrenner Hand-guide, is unmistakably Liszt. The

180

description of a number of the lessons follows:

The first lesson was devoted to posture, hand position, and two etudes by Bertini. Liszt wants the body held straight, with the head bent slightly backward rather than forward. There must be nothing suggestive of tension in the way the hands are held, but they can move with grace when the musical text warrants it. However, one must never play from the arms and the shoulders. He insists very much on these points.

Liszt sat at the piano and gave Valérie a few examples of how to interpret the Bertini etudes. It was a revelation. I would say that he possesses all different touches imaginable. His fingers are long, his hands narrow and slender. He does not hold his fingers curved because he says this position creates dryness and he has a horror of that. Neither does he hold the hands completely flat, but his are so limber and pliable that they maintain no definite fixed position. They contact the keys in all manners and forms. At one moment he interrupted Valérie: "Do not be so stiff, so rigid," he said. "Allow yourself a certain abandon, a certain 'give' here and there. And when the *fortissimo* comes, please listen to the quality of your tone. It is too hard and brittle.

Liszt started this lesson with an emphasis on the importance of octave study. Valérie had prepared the etude by J. C. Kessler dealing with this particular phase of technique, but he was not satisfied: "You must give more time to octave practice. Your hands are rather weak. In order to strengthen them I want you to drill your wrists every day, striking octaves on the same note while lifting the hand high. Start slowly. Hand and wrist must remain relaxed without the slightest contraction or 'cramping up.' Then get faster gradually but with no excess."

To prevent the forearm from moving Liszt recommended the Chiroplaste invented by Logier and perfected by Kalkbrenner. "Later on you will go through major and minor scales not only in plain octaves but also in broken octaves," he continued. "Repeated chords of four notes and five notes in diminished sevenths will soon increase the power of your fingers and hands."

Then he had Valérie play the elementary exercise: do—re—me—fa—sol—fa—me—re—do, striking each note six, eight, or twelve times while holding down the notes not involved. Valerie had trouble holding them down and occasionally released the third or fourth fingers. Liszt then asked her to play the exercise as fast as she could and without holding down any keys. "Can you hear how uneven it is? You need much work here. Somehow your fingers are entangled. They must be freed."

He sat down and demonstrated. The speed he can reach in the octaves, the pearl-like quality he obtains in running scales, the shadings he projects onto everything are amazing. Even in such difficult positions as B-flat and F-sharp minor his playing is astonishingly easy. And my surprise was even greater when he said that while working on his technique he reads in order not to be bored.

This afternoon Liszt explained to Valérie how he proceeds in assimilating a new piece. First of all he makes a thorough examination of the music and plays it slowly a few times in order to eliminate any possible reading mistakes. The second time he pays stricter attention to the values, the rests, the tempi. Still another time he concentrates on the dynamics, the *fortes, pianos, crescendos, sforzandos,* all the shadings indicated by the composer. Since composers are often careless in their markings, he said one must evaluate these markings and make whatever changes that seem advisable. . . .

Liszt once more laid emphasis on daily work on five fingers and dynamics. He does not want purposeless mechanical study, he requires that one's soul should always search for expression; all the shadings which form the true palette of musical coloring are ready in his hands to utmost perfection with no necessity of particular study at the moment when he summons them up. He also recommended practicing each hand separately. According to him it is the surest way to acquire perfect smoothness.

For this lesson Liszt was not in a good mood—sharp, hypercritical, faultfinding, impossible to satisfy. We had a glimpse of what a temperamental artist can be. There was dryness in his soul. I could have cried, for to me it was as if we were losing a friend. To us he was like a stranger and nothing more. He is a capricious and changeable young man who usually shows elevation, spirit, and idealism in his soul. Having been used to praise, adulation, and glamour from an early age he expects it. But since present conditions deprive him momentarily of such successes, I am sure he feels somewhat bitter. When we arrived he said he was not good for anything and he certainly kept his word. He gave the lesson because he had to, he never seemed to get interested, he split hairs over trifles of fingerings. The whole lesson was not worth ten minutes of his usual ones, and I admired the zeal, application, and sweetness of my dear little Valérie as she took great pains to please him without receiving any word of encouragement. Naturally I was incensed and I would have liked to tell him frankly how I felt. Perhaps we have spoiled him; young men are generally conceited and he, so superior to all others, may not be exempt from this weakness.

Today's lesson was altogether admirable. Liszt was full of genius, eloquence, sparkling with wit. He embodies intelligence and enlightenment. He further explained his system of technical study, which is at the same time broad-minded and simple.

Concerning touch, he does not want pressure from the fingertips near the nails but from the "palm" of the finger because this little cushion is soft and resilient, which helps to give the tone a lovely mellowness.

One must play from the wrist, using what is called "la main morte" (dead hand) without interference from the arm, the hand falling onto the keys in a motion of total elasticity. Again and again, he requires an impeccable evenness in scale playing. His sensitive ears perceive the tiniest unequality. All tones must be rich and full. "The fourth finger is naturally weak and sometimes also the third," he says, "so we must listen attentively and correct them with great care." He considers staccato and legato as accessories which of course have to be studied. But all figures and formulas used in music, whatever they may be, can be reduced to a few basic patterns which are the key to everything.

"Have patience with yourself," Liszt said. "Your future is ahead of you. Rome was not built in one day."

The highlight today was a little lecture Liszt gave us on the importance of self-analysis: "I had been playing the piano for years and had concertized with great public acclaim. I thought I was marvelous. Then one day as I realized that I failed to express the feelings and emotions which oppressed me, I decided to make a thorough analysis of myself. This proved to me that I did not know how to play a trill properly and that neither my octaves nor certain aspects of my chord playing were satisfactory. I set to work and soon my whole approach was radically changed."

Again he urged Valérie to do some "déchiffrage" — sight-reading — every day and try to look at the text as a whole, not in small details. He himself sight-reads all the time, which probably accounts for his phenomenal knowledge of the musical repertoire, recent or old.

As we left, he told me to watch and see that Valérie does not neglect her octave practice, for once octaves are conquered, one can confidently face any difficulties that may occur. He told Valérie to work every day and for two hours on scales in staccato octaves detached with energy, lifting up the hand quickly on each octave so as to acquire a free and flexible strength; then repeated chords, accelerating them with continued flexibility up to *fortissimo;* then the scales in broken octaves beginning with C major followed by its relative A minor, F major and its relative D minor, and so on.

Liszt thinks it unwise to have beginners take up scales too soon. They might develop wrong habits by doing so. It is wiser to leave them on five finger exercises for some time as preparation. Even in these the tone at first may be thin, tinny, constricted. It must be improved before the passing under of the thumb is considered. He was pleased with Valérie's playing of easier scales but not so with the E-flat minor. "When you think you are practicing very slowly . . . slow down some more," he said. "You spoil everything if you want to cut corners. Nature itself works quietly. Do likewise. Take it easy. If conducted wisely, your efforts will be crowned with success. If you hurry, they will be wasted and you will fail."

As to such mannerisms as the high raising or low diving of hands and arms, motions of the body, and other gesticulations, he considers them theatrical and unworthy of genuine artists. The same applies to exaggerated contrasts and sentimentality. Liszt's own expression is always simple because it is not motivated by a desire to show off at the expense of good taste. He does not play for others but for himself. He depicts his own feelings, he expresses his own soul, and it is probably the best way to reach that of his listeners. [17]

In the final lesson with her he suggested some daily exercises for both hands which he said "must be practiced in all keys up the chromatic ladder by half tones, then reversed in coming down from the top in the same way." Mme. Boissier quoted them: [18]

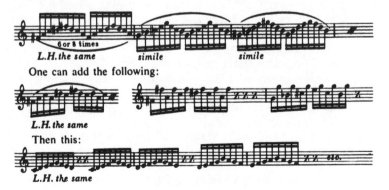

When Liszt advised Valérie to work slowly, perhaps he was thinking of his own early practice. Many years later William Mason was to recall a statement made by Liszt to his students in the mid 1850s:

In early years I was not patient enough to "make haste slowly"—thoroughly to develop in an orderly, logical and progressive way. I was impatient for immediate results, and took short cuts, so to speak, and jumped through sheer force of will to the goal of my ambition. I wish now that I had progressed by logical steps instead of by leaps. It is true that I have been successful, but I do not advise you to follow my way, for you lack my personality. [19]

At the conclusion of Valérie's lessons, Mme. Boissier was convinced that the youthful Liszt was perfection personified. She wrote:

Liszt's talent is the most complete, the most accomplished, the most perfect imaginable. Admirable fingers, superior organization of the mind, a fiery soul, lofty spirit, he has everything and, above all, goodness and elevation in his heart. [20]

Liszt's major teaching career, which covered many years following the abandoning of his concert life and his settling in Weimar, contrasted greatly from the type of instruction which he gave during his days in Paris. He was still concerned enough about technique to have written twelve volumes of Technical Exercises between 1869 and 1879 which were published posthumously in 1886 by Alexander Winterberger. These emphasized all manner of technical problems. In every phase of technique, he was thoroughly progressive. In fingering, he advocated the thumb frequently passing over the fingers as well as under. He gave technical advice when he felt the need to do so. But as a rule he would only work with those pianists whose technique was already advanced and well formed. No doubt many of his students went on teaching technical approaches which they had learned earlier and may in some ways have been in contradiction to Liszt's own manner of performance. For example: he used a higher seat than many of his students later did and most pianists had before him. [21] This position permitted the forearm to slant downward toward the hand and allow for greater power in arm playing. Fielden also observed that his students d'Albert, Reisenauer, and Klindworth taught finger training by "stiff up and down movement, the wrist in the same way, and the arm hardly at all." [22] Liszt's greatest contribution was in the

185

musical inspiration and insight which he imparted to those who came to him.

One of his earliest Weimar students was the young American William Mason (1829-1908), the third son of the famous hymn writer, Lowell Mason. He went to Europe in 1849 at the age of fourteen and remained for five years. His study with Liszt began in 1853. His recollections about the man himself and his instructional procedures are of more than passing interest. Mason wrote in *Memories of a Musical Life:*

> As I remember his hands, his fingers were lean and thin, but they did not impress me as being very long, and he did not have such a remarkable stretch on the keyboard as one might imagine. He was always neatly dressed, generally appearing in a long frock-coat, until he became the Abbé Liszt, after which he wore the distinctive black gown. His general manner and his face were most expressive of his feelings, and his features lighted up when he spoke. His smile was simply charming. His face was peculiar. One could hardly call it handsome, yet there was in it a subtle something that was most attractive, and his whole manner had a fascination which it is impossible to describe. [23]

Mason was impressed by Liszt's teaching approach:

> What I had heard in regard to Liszt's method of teaching proved to be absolutely correct. He never taught in the ordinary sense of the word. During the entire time that I was with him I did not see him give a regular lesson in the pedagogical sense. He would notify us to come up to the Altenburg. For instance, he would say to me, "Tell the boys to come up to-night at half-past six or seven." We would go there, and he would call on us to play. I remember very well the first time I played to him after I had been accepted as a pupil. I began with the "Ballade" of Chopin in A flat major; then I played a fugue by Handel in E minor.
>
> After I was well started he began to get excited. He made audible suggestions, inciting me to put more enthusiasm into my playing, and occasionally he would push me gently off the chair and sit down at the piano and play a phrase or two himself by way of illustration. He gradually got me worked up to such a pitch of enthusiasm that I put all the grit that was in me into my playing.
>
> I found at this first lesson that he was very fond of strong accents in order to mark off periods and phrases, and he talked so much about strong accentuation that one might have supposed that he would abuse it, but he never did. When

he wrote to me later about my own piano method, he expressed the strongest approval of the exercises on accentuation.

While I was playing to him for the first time, he said on one of the occasions when he pushed me from the chair: "Don't play it that way. Play it like this." Evidently I had been playing ahead in a steady, uniform way. He sat down, and gave the same phrases with an accentuated, elastic movement, which let in a flood of light upon me. From that one experience I learned to bring out the same effect, where it was appropriate, in almost every piece that I played. It eradicated much that was mechanical, stilted, and unmusical in my playing, and developed an elasticity of touch which has lasted all my life, and which I have always tried to impart to my pupils. [24]

Glorying in Liszt's very musical emphasis, Mason also recorded remarks which Liszt made to one of Mason's friends a few years later (1858): "What I like about So-and-so is that he is not a mere 'finger virtuoso': he does not worship the keyboard of the pianoforte; it is not his patron saint, but simply the altar before which he pays homage to the idea of the tone-composer." [25]

During Liszt's early days at Weimar his class was small. Mason said there were only two other students at the time—Dionys Pruckner and Karl Klindworth, as well as a former student, Joachim Raff, who served as his private secretary and was frequently in attendance at the classes. Over the years the number increased and Weimar became a mecca for aspiring concert pianists. Amy Fay, who studied with him in 1873, said that Liszt told her that "people fly in his face by dozens." [26] He willingly worked with the many who showed merit and promise—never taking any remuneration. But he had a way of putting the less worthy in their place. Otis Boise (1844-1912), an American composer who had taken one of his compositions to him for criticism on several occasions, recounts an incident:

One day a rather assertive young lady called with an introductory card and said she had come to ask the master's advice. She claimed to desire his verdict as to whether she should dedicate herself to music, but obviously wanted and expected an invitation to join his class. Liszt was blind to her charms, although she was a sightly creature, and he was displeased with her manner. He did not respond promptly and the situation became painful for me as a spectator, for she evidently did not feel more than could and did pass away in a momentary blush. She renewed the attack with, "Will you permit me to play for you?" He having reservedly signified his willingness to hear, she began the F major etude (No. 8) of Chopin, Opus 10. Her lackadaisical playing was startling, if anything so mild could be, when contrasted with her appearance and manner. It lacked every quality that could have made it adequate to her chosen task. Liszt could endure but a half-dozen measures and then shouted "No! No!" rushed to the piano, nudged her off the chair, and seating himself gave vent to his feelings in the most impetuous performance of this piece that I have ever heard. It relieved the master and did no violence to Chopin. As he turned from the piano, he said, "It should be something like that. Now go home, forget your dawdling, and come again later if you see fit." [27]

Arthur Friedheim (1859-1932), who studied with Liszt as late as the 1880s, observed the same reaction by Liszt to the unworthy student:

To be sure he expected technique, a very fine technique, of any student who approached him. He would show considerable indignation if anyone presumed to come to him insufficiently trained. To such hapless students he displayed scant consideration. There were numerous conservatories, he would tell them, where they could get the grounding they needed. He was no professor of piano. Not even from those whom he admitted to his lessons would he endure haphazard, slovenly playing. "Wash your dirty linen at home!" he would admonish such performers. [28]

It is also interesting to note that Friedheim mentioned several pianofortes in Liszt's salon including one given to him by Steinway & Sons. Amy Fay also spoke of a new Steinway grand in 1873. [29] Recent improvements in the Steinway must have excited him considerably because in 1884 he wrote to New York: "When Mr. Steinway gets here, I shall have a piano shop talk with him, about the new construction of his grands."[30] Liszt also favored the Érard and Bösendorfer instruments. By this period—the 1870s and 1880s —the grand pianos were much like the large, solid, full-bodied tonal instruments of our present day. Grove points out that the individual key resistance on the Broadwood had increased considerably from 1817 to 1877: Lowest C from 2-5/8 ounces to 4, Middle C from 2-3/8 to 3-1/8, and Highest C from 1-3/4 to 2-3/8. [31] This proved to be too much resistance because shortly after the end of the nineteenth century the amounts of resistance were returned nearly to the original figures.

Friedheim in his reminiscences recorded in *Life and Liszt* gave a complete account of the classes he attended:

The Master seldom bothered with explanations to pupils who seemed slow to understand. In such cases he would address his remarks to the class in general, sometimes with delightful innuendo and sly sarcasm. There might be as many as thirty or forty students and "recording hearers"—auditors—at these gatherings. The legitimate pupils, who were rarely told beforehand what to play, would bring music of their own selection and lay it on the pianos. Liszt would enter, give a general greeting and shake hands with only two or three. Occasionally he went over to some especially attractive bit of femininity and kissed her on the cheek. It became the custom for such fortunate young ladies not to wash, for some day after, the spot the Master's lips had touched!

After these ceremonies, Liszt would look over the music lying about and make choice of the things he wished to hear, according to his mood. Only two compositions were rejected regularly, Chopin's B-flat minor Scherzo, which he called the "Governess Scherzo" because "every Governess plays it well," and his own Second Hungarian Rhapsody. Both works were heard too much, he said. Everything else by Chopin found permanent favor with Liszt, and particularly the Preludes . . . .

Liszt's system of instruction, if it could always be called that, followed no classifiable method. He was severely academic at times, and again astonishingly complacent. When he was in a strict mood, he would speak in short, sharp, authoritative sentences of the work under discussion, its relation to other music by the same composer, and to the work of his predecessors and contemporaries. He would draw attention to the structure and proportions of the opus and point out its leading moments of eloquence and climax. If a phrase was unsatisfactory in tone or expression, if the attack and execution of a passage did not please him, he would have the pupil repeat three or four times until the desired effect was gained. On occasions of marked stupidity or incompetence he was subject to fierce flashes of temper and would sometimes send the offender out of the room in tears. But this happened very rarely.

Those who had the right to desire explicit information, and knew how to ask for it, could always have Liszt explain the intricacies and subtleties of pedalling and even get him to suggest useful fingerings. But this he did oftener in his small classes in Rome than before the larger groups in Weimar . . . .

189

Having invented the class system of teaching, Liszt believed in it implicitly, on the ground that the teacher does not have to play the same piece over and over for different pupils and repeat endlessly his suggestions for fingerings, phrasings, pedalling and the like; that if the pupil who is only a listener knows the work that is being played he has the same advantage of the performer, and if he does not know it, he becomes better prepared to study it later. It was also Liszt's opinion that even the best teacher has his good and his off days and the class system enables everyone to profit from the good days. Its best aspect is, of course, the chance the pupils have to play for critical listeners and so rid themselves of nervousness and gain confidence. [32]

The Englishwoman Bettina Walker visited Liszt's summer classes in Weimar. Her narrative description of the first session she attended captures the atmosphere of these gatherings. It shows Liszt in the role which he greatly loved and played to the hilt:

When we entered the villa all the rooms through which we passed were arranged as if for a *fête*, and beautifully decorated with flowers—a prominent object in the ante-room being a life-size bust of Liszt crowned with laurel. The two ladies, on hearing that I was a 'Lisztianerin' (the Weimar appellation for Liszt's followers), received me with great cordiality, showed me to a seat in the room where Liszt would be most of the time, and introduced me to all those near me. It was then about a quarter to four, and all who had access to these reunions were now assembled and waiting for Liszt, who both at these and the reunions held at his own house never appeared till all had arrived. It was, indeed, considered a great breach of etiquette to come in after he was in the room, instead of being there to await his arrival, as at the approach of royalty.

A minute or two after four the hum of voices suddenly ceased. 'Der Meister kommit!' was whispered from one to the other; and when Liszt immediately afterward entered the room, everyone stood up, and all the younger people went towards him and kissed his hand. He looked as if he enjoyed all this homage, and his face lighted up as he glanced kindly at the eager faces which, from the moment he appeared, seemed to have no eyes but for him. Indeed, from the moment he came in, we were all listening to try and catch whatever he might please to say to those nearest to him. He did not play; but his expressive face showed the most cordial interest in all that was going on. Siloti, the distinguished young Russian pianist—a pupil of Nicolas Rubinstein (brother of Antoine)—

190

played a Tausig-Berlioz piece with great *bravura:* Herr Reisenauer and Fräulein Emma Koch played some duets at sight; there was some singing, some violin-playing by a very clever little boy of eleven, and then a small slight girl sat down and charmed me by the ease and beautiful clearness with which she played one of Liszt's *Rhapsodies hongroises.* As she concluded this, Liszt came over to the piano; and as she curtsied to him he kissed her on the forehead, his custom when the playing of a lady found favor with him.

'Who is she, and with whom has she studied?' I asked of a lady who was sitting beside me.

'She is my daughter,' was the reply, 'and the only pupil of his Excellency Herr von Henselt, of St. Petersburg.'

I cannot remember all that was played that afternoon, for, like those around me, I was far more occupied in watching the Meister's movements and trying to catch his words, than in either listening to the music or getting into talk with my neighbours. After about two hours and a half—during which time there had been one or two short pauses, when cake and wine and lemonade were handed around—Liszt rose to depart, and, as was the case when he came in, all the guests present rose, and remained standing until he had left the room. When he was gone I was conscious of a sensation which I am sure was shared by pretty nearly everyone in the room, whether they were quite aware of the feeling or not. Everything seemed to have become all at once flat and dull and uninteresting; conversation languished; it was as if a shadow had fallen on a landscape, and that which a moment before, when illumined by the sun, was a mass of warm and glowing colours, was now all gray, monotonous, and chill. [33]

The most colorful word picture we have of study under Liszt is contained in the correspondence of the American pianist, Amy Fay (1844-1928). In 1873 Liszt was reigning as the master supreme. She characterized him as the benevolent monarch to whom you sit down to play when he extends his royal scepter. She said: "You lay your notes on the table, so he can see that you *want* to play, and sit down. He takes a turn up and down the room, looks at the music, and if the piece interests him, he will call upon you. We bring the same piece to him but once, and but once play it through." [34]

The following excerpts from Miss Fay's letters are included because of the realistic manner in which Liszt is revealed:

May 1, 1873
Liszt is the most interesting and striking looking man imaginable. Tall and slight, with deep-set eyes, shaggy eye-

brows, and long iron-gray hair, which he wears parted in the middle. His mouth turns up at the corners, which gives him a most crafty and Mephistophelean expression when he smiles, and his whole appearance and manner have a sort of Jesuitical elegance and ease. His hands are very narrow, with long and slender fingers that look as if they had twice as many joints as other people's. They are so flexible and supple that it makes you nervous to look at them. [35]

May 21, 1873

Never was there such a delightful teacher! and he is the first sympathetic one I've had. You feel so *free* with him, and he develops the very spirit of music in you. He doesn't keep nagging at you all the time, but he leaves you your own conception. Now and then he will make a criticism, or play a passage, and with a few words give you enough to think of all the rest of your life. There is a delicate *point* to everything he says, as subtle as he is himself. He doesn't tell you anything about the technique. That you must work out for yourself . . . There is such a vividness about everything he plays that it does not seem as if it were mere music you were listening to, but it is as if he had called up a real, living *form,* and you saw it breathing before your face and eyes. It gives *me* almost a ghostly feeling to hear him, and it seems as if the air were peopled with spirits. Oh, he is a perfect wizard! It is as interesting to see him as it is to hear him, for his face changes with every modulation of the piece, and he looks exactly as he is playing. He has one element that is most captivating, and that is, a sort of delicate and fitful mirth that keeps peering out at you here and there! It is most peculiar, and when he plays that way, the most bewitching little expression comes over his face. It seems as if a little spirit of joy were playing hide and go seek with you. [36]

June 6, 1873

However, all playing sounds barren by the side of Liszt, for *his* is the living, breathing impersonation of poetry, passion, grace, wit, coquetry, daring, tenderness and every other fascinating attribute that you can think of! I'm ready to hang myself half the time when I've been to him. Oh, he is the most phenomenal being in every respect! All that you've heard of him would never give you an idea of him. In short, he represents the whole scale of human emotion. He is a many-sided prism, and reflects back the light in all colours, no matter how you look at him. His pupils *adore* him, as in fact everybody else does, but it is impossible to do otherwise with a person whose genius flashes out of him all the time so, and whose character is so winning. . . . [37]

July 24, 1873

... Perhaps, after all, the secret of Liszt's fascination is this power of intense and wild emotion that you feel he possesses, together with the most perfect control over it. [38]

With an influence and winsome personality only half as attractive as that which Amy Fay presented, Franz Liszt was bound to attract a large share of the great young pianists of his time. The list of his pupils is a distinguished one. Carl Tausig (1841-1871) was Liszt's favorite: "He will be the inheritor of my playing." [39] This Chopin devotee, who abhorred a "spectakel" at the piano, had a most promising, but short-lived, career. His *Daily Exercises* are of technical value and still available today. Eugene d'Albert (1830-1894), the much married husband of Teresa Carreño, in his youth foresook his native England for Germany where he became a great Beethoven specialist. Then there was the dictatorial German super-patriot, Hans von Bülow (1830-1894), who was inclined to be cold and over-scholarly in his interpretation. Others include Moriz Rosenthal (1862-1946), the superb virtuoso; Emil Sauer (1862-1942); Alexander Siloti (1863-1945), the teacher of Rachmaninoff; Stephan Thoman (1862-1940), whose students included Dohnányi and Bartók; Moritz Moszkowski (1845-1925); and the refined Chopin editor, Rafael Joseffy (1853-1915), who also wrote an exhaustive exercise book entitled *School of Advanced Piano Playing*. The list could go on almost ad infinitum.

Perhaps a summary of the greatest piano personality of the entire nineteenth century can best be given by the virtuoso himself as he envisioned his role. Liszt wrote:

> The virtuoso is not a mason who, chisel in hand, faithfully and conscientiously whittles stone after the design of an architect. He is not a passive tool reproducing feeling and thought and adding nothing of himself. He is not the more or less experienced reader of works which have no margins for his notes, which allow for no paragraphing between the lines. Spiritedly-written musical works are in reality, for the virtuoso, only the tragic and moving *mise-en-scène* for feelings. He is called upon to make emotion speak, and weep, and sing, and sigh—to bring it to life in his consciousness. He creates as the composer himself created, for he himself must live the passions he will call to light in all their brilliance. He breathes life into the lethargic body, infuses it with fire, enlivens it with the pulse of grace and charm. He changes the earthy form into a living being, penetrating it with the spark which Prometheus snatched from Jupiter's flesh. He must send the form he has

193

created soaring into transparent ether: he must arm it with a thousand winged weapons; he must call up scent and blossom, and breathe the breath of life. [40]

Notes

[1] Sacheverell Sitwell, *Liszt*, p. 30.

[2] Frederick Niecks, *Frederick Chopin, As a Man and Musician*, I, p. 296.

[3] *Ibid.*

[4] Charles Hallé, *Life and Letters of Sir Charles Hallé being an autobiography (1819-1860) with correspondence and diaries*, pp. 39-40.

[5] William Mason, *Memories of a Musical Life*, p. 211.

[6] *Ibid.*, p. 212.

[7] Cited in Adolph Kullak, *The Aesthetics of Pianoforte-Playing*, p. 90.

[8] Hallé, *Life and Letters*, pp. 37-38.

[9] Cited in Sitwell, *Liszt*, p. 41.

[10] Sitwell, *Liszt*, p. 14.

[11] The only other composer who came close to matching Liszt in the creation of immense, bravura etudes was Alkan (Charles-Henri Valentin Morhange) (1813-1888), sometimes called the "Berlioz of the piano." Creator of over one hundred works in many forms and a friend of Chopin, he led a bizarre, secluded life which ended when a bookcase, from the top of which he was trying to reach a Hebrew religious volume, fell on and crushed him.

[12] Sitwell, *Liszt*, p. 53.

[13] Cited in Sitwell, *ibid.*, p. 98.

[14] Cited in Sitwell, *ibid.*, p. 105.

[15] Robert Schumann, *On Music and Musicians*, pp. 155-56.

[16] In the wake of such displays of virtuosity as those by Liszt and Thalberg, others tried to match them in their own fashion. Henry C. Lahee, *Famous Pianists of Today and Yesterday*, p. 112, tells of an organist, towards the middle of the nineteenth century, "who undertook, for a wager, to play one million notes on the piano in less than twelve hours. He succeeded in doing this at the average rate of about 125,000 notes an hour. The actual time consumed in the playing was eight hours and twenty minutes which, with the periods of rest which he allowed himself, amounted to a few minutes less than the twelve hours."

[17] Madame Auguste Boissier, "Liszt as Pedagogue," translated by Maurice Dumesnil in *The Piano Teacher*, Vol. 3, No. 5, May-June, 1961, pp. 12-14 and Vol. 3, No. 6, July-August, 1961, pp. 14-15.

[18] *Ibid.*, p. 15.

[19] Mason, *Memories*, p. 114.

194

[20] Boissier, *Liszt as Pedagogue,* Vol. 3, No. 6, July-August, 1961, p. 15.

[21] *Grove's Dictionary of Music and Musicians,* 5th ed., VI, p. 748.

[22] Thomas Fielden, *The History of the Evolution of Pianoforte Technique,* p. 48.

[23] Mason, *Memories,* p. 102.

[24] *Ibid.,* pp. 97-100.

[25] *Ibid.,* p. 116.

[26] Amy Fay, *Music-Study in Germany, from The Home Correspondence of Amy Fay,* p. 210.

[27] Otis Boise, "An American Composer Visits Liszt," *The Musical Quarterly,* Vol. XLIII, No. 3, July, 1957, p. 323.

[28] Arthur Friedheim, *Life and Liszt, The Recollections of a Concert Pianist,* p. 52.

[29] Fay, *Music-Study in Germany,* p. 263.

[30] Theodore E. Steinway, *People and Pianos, A Century of Service to Music,* p. 50.

[31] *Grove's Dictionary,* 5th ed., VI, 748.

[32] Friedheim, *Life and Liszt,* pp. 47-48, 51.

[33] Bettina Walker, *My Musical Experiences,* pp. 90-92.

[34] Fay, *Music-Study in Germany,* pp. 219-20.

[35] *Ibid.,* pp. 205-06.

[36] *Ibid.,* pp. 213-14.

[37] *Ibid.,* pp. 222-23.

[38] *Ibid.,* pp. 242-43.

[39] *Ibid.,* p. 250.

[40] Friedheim, *Life and Liszt,* p. 52.

11.   The Schumann Circle

Two of Chopin's and Liszt's greatest contemporaries were Felix Mendelssohn and Robert Schumann, both outstanding composers and pianists. If we also consider Schumann's wife, Clara, and her father, Friedrich Wieck, we have a group of pianists which might be termed "the Schumann circle." Serious musicians of the highest integrity, they stood united against the salon type piano music so common in their day. The pianism they exhibited is worthy of comparison with Chopin and Liszt and constitutes a proud chapter in nineteenth century piano technique history.

Mendelssohn (1809-1847), born into a closely knit Jewish-Christian family of means, ranks among the greatest of all child prodigies at the piano. His older sister, Fanny, was an excellent pianist as well. Although he performed with some degree of regularity throughout his life, Mendelssohn finally chose joint careers of composer, conductor, and music benefactor. He was the conductor of the famous Gewandhaus concerts in Leipzig from 1835. He also founded the highly respected Leipzig Conservatory in 1843 and persuaded such musicians as Moscheles, Niels Gade, and the violinist Ferdinand David to join its faculty. A great lover of Bach, he was instrumental in performing the *St. Matthew Passion* in Berlin where it was received with enthusiasm and resulted in a revival of interest in the works of Bach. Beloved in Germany, Mendelssohn was also greatly appreciated in England and conducted many orchestral performances there.

His early childhood days were spent in Berlin where he studied under Ludwig Berger and Karl Friedrich Zelter. Felix as a youth was a particular favorite of the aging poet-philosopher Johann Wolfgang von Goethe. With Zelter, he paid his first visit to Goethe at Weimar at the age of twelve. The eccentric Zelter cautioned the group who were to hear him:

I have come beforehand, gentlemen, to ask a favour of you.

197

You are going to meet a twelve-year-old boy, my pupil. His ability as a pianist will astonish you, and his talent for composition will in all probability astonish you still more. Now the boy has a peculiar character. The fawning of amateurs does not affect him; but he listens eagerly to the opinions of musicians and takes everything at face value, for the young sprout is naturally too inexperienced to distinguish between well-meant encouragement and merited appreciation. Therefore, gentlemen, if you are prompted to sing his praises, which I both hope and fear, please do so moderato, without too much noisy instrumentation, and in C major, the most colourless of the keys. Hitherto I've preserved him from vanity and overestimation of himself, those damnable enemies of all artistic progress. [1]

After this unwarranted admonition to the musicians present, Goethe, likewise advised, entered immediately preceded by Felix who "came prancing in, a thriving, perfectly beautiful boy of decidedly southern type, slender and agile. Thick black curly hair flowed down to the nape of his neck; spirit and animation sparkled in his eyes." [2] Felix played so wholeheartedly that he became flushed in the face, but only received brief comments such as "Good!" or "Bravo!" and a parting word from Goethe on this first meeting: "The faces of these gentlemen plainly declare that your production has pleased them. Now go down into the garden, where you are awaited, and cool off, for you look as if you were on fire." [3] After he had left the room, Goethe, who had also heard Mozart as a child of nine in 1763, exclaimed to Zelter: "What this little man is capable of in improvisation and sightreading is simply prodigious. I would not have thought it possible at such an age." [4] The musicians present readily concurred and observed that he

... was producing more independent ideas than Mozart at the same age, for the latter had turned out nothing but adroit imitations of his models. From this it seemed likely that in this boy the world had been blessed with a second Mozart; it seemed all the more certain since the child radiated health and since all the outer circumstances of his life were so favourable to him ... [5]

In subsequent performances before Goethe and his coterie in Weimar, Felix improvised and performed Mozart, Beethoven, Cramer, Bach, Hummel and the like with great success. Ludwig Rellstab, who was present at one of these triumphs, describes his reaction to an improvisation on a trivial melody that Zelter had suggested to Felix:

198

Felix first repeated the song, and without reflection—taking the triplet figure *unisono* in both hands, brought his fingers into the track of the main figure, so to speak . . . But then he plunged without more ado into the wildest allegro. The gentle melody was transformed into a surging figure which he took first in the bass, then in the soprano voice, developing it with lovely contrasts—in short, created a torrential fantasia that poured out like liquid fire—Hummel's manner of dealing with such tasks must have been most in his mind. The whole company was thunderstruck; the boy's small hands worked into the masses of tone, mastered the most difficult combinations; the passages rumbled and dropped like so many pearls, flew by in ethereal whispers; a stream of harmonies flowed forth; surprising contrapuntal phrases were built up among them—only the banal melody was rather neglected and scarcely had a voice in this brilliant parliament of musical tones. [6]

These remarkable creative powers were quickly channeled into the production of enduring masterpieces. In five short years from these boyhood experiences, Mendelssohn had already composed his *A Midsummer Night's Dream.* Throughout his adult life he maintained his powers as a great pianist. Clara Schumann, at least at one point, thought him to be the best of his day—surpassing Thalberg. She wrote to Robert: "He played so consummately and with such fire that for a few minutes I really could not restrain my tears. When all is said and done, he remains for me the dearest pianist of all . . . " [7] Ferdinand Hiller also was greatly moved by what he heard in Mendelssohn's performance:

He played the piano as a lark soars, because it was his nature. He possessed great adroitness, sureness, strength, fluency, a soft full tone . . . but when he played one forgot these qualities; one overlooked even the more spiritual gifts which are called ardour, inspiration, soulfulness, intelligence. When he sat at the piano music poured out of him with the richness of an inborn genius—he was a centaur and the piano his steed . . . [8]

Mendelssohn's performance and technical ability revealed some of the gentleness, sensitivity, and refinement of Chopin as well as much of the brilliance and excitement of Liszt. The scholarly Mendelssohn continued to play until near the end of his days. In 1832 he was the first pianist to play publicly two of Beethoven's sonatas: the *Waldstein* and the Sonata *quasi una Fantasia,* Op. 27, No. 2. His last public performance took place in Lon don in April of 1847 when he played the Beethoven G Major Concerto at a Philharmonic concert.

In January of 1846, three years after he founded the Leipzig Conservatory, Mendelssohn began active teaching duties there, with two classes in piano and one in composition. One of his English students at that time, William Smyth Rockstro, later discussed Mendelssohn's role as a teacher:

Members of the upper classes for the study of the pianoforte and composition met regularly, for instruction, on Wednesday and Saturday afternoons, each lesson lasting two hours. The first pianoforte piece selected for study was Hummel's Septet in D Minor: and we well remember the look of blank dismay depicted upon more than one excitable countenance, as each pupil in his turn after playing the first chord, and receiving an instantaneous reproof for its want of sonority, was invited to resign his seat in favour of an equally unfortunate successor. Mendelssohn's own manner of playing grand chords, both in *forte* and *piano* passages, was peculiarly impressive; and now, when all present had tried, and failed, he himself sat down to the instrument, and explained the causes of his dissatisfaction with such microscopic minuteness, and clearness of expression, that the lesson was simply priceless. He never gave a learner the chance of mistaking his meaning; and though the vehemence with which he sometimes expressed it made timid pupils desperately afraid of him, he was so perfectly just, so sternly impartial in awarding praise, on the one hand, and blame on the other, that consternation soon gave place to confidence, and confidence to boundless affection. Carelessness infuriated him. Irreverence for the composer he could never forgive. *"Es steht nicht da!"* ("It is not there!") he almost shrieked one day to a pupil who had added a note to a certain chord. To another, who had scrambled through a difficult passage, he cried, with withering contempt, *"So spielen die Katzen!"* ("So play the cats!"). But, where he saw an earnest desire to do justice to the work in hand, he would give direction after direction, with a lucidity which we have never heard equalled. He never left a piece until he was satisfied that the majority of the class understood it thoroughly. Hummel's Septet formed the chief part of each lesson, until the 25th of February. After that it was relieved, occasionally, by one of Chopin's studies, or a Fugue from the *Wohltemperierte Klavier.* But it was not until the 21st of March that it was finally set aside, to make room for Weber's *Concert-Stück,* the master's reading of which was superb. He would make each pupil play a portion

200

of this great work in his own way, comment upon its delivery with the most frankness, and, if he thought the player deserved encouragement, would himself supply the orchestral passages on a second piano-forte. But he never played through the piece which formed the subject of the lesson in a connected form. On a few rare occasions—we can only remember two or three—he invited the whole class to his house; and, on one of these happy days, he played an entire Sonata—but not that which the members of the class were studying. And the reason of his reticence was obvious. He wishes his pupils to understand the principles by which he himself was guided in his interpretation of the works of the great masters, and at the same time to discourage servile imitation of his own rendering of any individual composition. In fact, with regard to special forms of expression, one of his most frequently reiterated maxims was, "If you want to play with true feeling, you must listen to good singers. You will learn far more from them than from any players you are likely to meet with."

Upon questions of simple technique he rarely touched, except—as in the case of our first precious lesson upon the chord of D minor—with regard to the rendering of certain special passages. But the members of his pianoforte classes were expected to study these matters, on other days of the week, under Herren Plaidy, or Wenzel, professors of high repute, who had made the training of the fingers and wrist their specialty. It would be impossible to over-estimate the value of this arrangement, which provided for the acquirement of a pure touch, and facile execution, on the one hand, while on the other it left Mendelssohn free to direct the undivided attention of his pupils to the higher branches of art. [9]

Robert Schumann (1810-1856), like Mendelssohn, early showed promise of becoming a first-rank pianist. His father died when he was sixteen and his mother urged him to prepare for a stable career as a lawyer. For a time he was a law student—first at the University of Leipzig and then at Heidelberg. On July 30, 1830 from Heidelberg he wrote to his mother that "My *whole life* has been a twenty years' struggle between poetry and prose, or, if you like to call it so, Music and Law." [10] Just a few months earlier on November 6, 1829, in a letter to Friedrich Wieck, he revealed his dedication to piano study:

Without over-estimating my own abilities, I feel modestly conscious of my superiority over all the other Heidelberg pianists. You have no idea how carelessly and roughly they play, and of the noisiness, slap-dash, and terrible feebleness of their

201

style. They have no notion of cultivating "touch," and of bringing a fine tone out of the instrument; and as to regular practice, finger-exercises, and scales, they don't seem ever to have heard of anything of the kind. The other day one of them played me the A minor Concerto [Hummel]. He performed it very correctly and without mistakes, keeping a sort of rhythmical march-time, and I could conscientiously praise him. But when I played it to him, he had to admit, that though his rendering was quite as correct as mine, yet somehow I made the whole thing *sound* different; and then how in the world did I get such a *violin-like* tone, etc.? I looked at him with a smile, put Herz's finger-exercises before him, and told him to play one every day for a week, and then come and try the Concerto again. This he did, and in due time came back enchanted and delighted, and called me his good genius, because my advice had helped him so much. And he actually did play the Concerto ten times better. [11]

The study of law was clearly so distasteful to Schumann that finally on August 6, 1830 Wieck wrote to Schumann's mother, Johanna, in an attempt to gain her consent to Robert's entering into a trial period of study under him. A mother could hardly fail to be moved by such a rosy future as was promised her son:

I herewith promise that your son Robert, with his talent and imagination, shall in three years' time be turned by me into one of the greatest now living pianists, more spirited and warm than Moscheles and more grandiose than Hummel. For proof I cite my own eleven-year-old daughter [Clara], whom I am just beginning to present to the world. [12]

That turned the trick and very shortly thereafter Robert, a youth of twenty, went back to Leipzig to study with Wieck and also to reside in his home.

He also took up the study of composition under Heinrich Dorn; his earliest important works date from this time. Dorn seems to have terminated the relationship abruptly in April of 1832, evidently because of Schumann's undisciplined ways and unconventional style. He wrote to Dorn: "But my whole nature seems to rebel against any instigation from the outer world, and I feel as if my ideas ought to come to me quite independently, to be then worked out and put in the proper place." [13] He began to show as much promise in composition as at the piano. On June 14, 1832, he sent his mother the good news that "Everybody tells me that my *Papillons* are pretty universally popular," and also that "Clara and Wieck are very fond of me." [14] Then he mentioned that

202

. . . Edward will have told you of the singular accident I have met with. This is why I am going to Dresden next Monday with Wieck. Although I go partly by the advice of my doctor, and partly for the sake of the change, I shall still have to work a good deal. [15]

What Schumann had foolishly done was to devise an apparatus intended to strengthen and help gain independence for the fourth finger on his right hand; but instead of benefit, serious injury resulted. For a time he had hopes that the damaged finger would heal. He told his mother on August 9:

My whole house has been turned into a doctor's shop. I really got quite uneasy about my hand, but carefully avoided asking a surgeon, because I was so afraid he would say the damage was irretrievable. I had begun to make all sorts of plans for the future, had almost resolved to study theology (not jurisprudence), and peopled an imaginary parsonage with real people, yourself and others. At last I went to Professor Kuhl, and asked him to tell me on his honour whether my hand would get well. After shaking his head a good deal, he said, "Yes, but not for some time, not for about six months." When I once heard the word, a weight was taken off my heart, and I readily promised to do all he required. It was quite enough, namely to take *Thierbäder* (Translator's note: To bathe the affected part in the blood of a fresh-killed ox, or to envelop the body entirely in the skin of the animal. This treatment was greatly recommended by the ancients, and seems to have come into use again early in this century.)—let Schurig describe them to you—to bathe my hand in warm brandy-and-water all day long, to put on a herb poultice at night, and to play the piano as little as possible. The remedies are not exactly pleasant ones, and I very much fear that some of the nature of the ox may pass into mine; but on the whole they appear to be very beneficial. And I feel so much strength and spirit in every limb, that I really feel inclined to give some one a good thrashing! [16]

But the finger did not get better and Schumann mentions also trying electrical treatments and homeopathy. It was a time of real disappointment, but by March of 1834 he tried to reassure his mother: "Do not worry yourself about my finger! I can compose without it; and I should hardly be happier as a travelling virtuoso." [17] But as late as December 29, 1838 he confided to Clara:

It sometimes makes me unhappy that I have got a disabled hand, especially now that I am here [Vienna]. And I must tell you that it keeps getting worse. I often complain bitterly, and exclaim, "Good heavens! why should this have befallen me?" It would have been such a great advantage to me just now to have had the use of my hands; I am so full of real genuine music that it is like the breath of my nostrils, and as it is I can barely manage to pick it out, and my fingers stumble over one another. It is very dreadful, and has often caused me much pain.

Well, after all, you are my right hand, and mind you take care of yourself, so that nothing happens to you. What happy hours you will give me by your art! [18]

The inevitable result was that Schumann was forced to devote himself more fully to composition and that Clara did, so to speak, carry on his career as a pianist and make known his works throughout Europe. Their path to marriage in 1840 was a difficult one. Her father, Friedrich Wieck, had steadily opposed it, perhaps partially because of the unstable emotional nature which Robert seemed to have inherited. But it was a happy marriage and Schumann grew steadily as a great composer. In 1843 he taught at the Leipzig Conservatory and in 1853 became municipal director of music at Düsseldorf. As a teacher he was not successful. Carl Reinecke (1824-1910), who succeeded Mendelssohn as director of the Leipzig Conservatory, had this to say about his role as a piano instructor:

Since he was very reticent by nature he had but little to say in the piano lessons which were assigned to him . . . It once happened that a pupil played Mendelssohn's Capriccio in B Minor for him without his making a single interruption. When she ended he remarked genially, "You must hear that from Clara sometime," and with that the lesson was over. But as soon as he had a pen in his hand there flowed from its point the most thoughtful maxims and apothegms. [19]

This ability to express himself freely with the written word developed early. In 1831 by the time he was twenty-one and studying piano under Wieck his first important music article had appeared in the *Allgemeine musikalische Zeitung*. This famous presentation of Chopin was also the first to introduce the members of Schumann's Davidsbündler, whose avowed purpose was to slay the unworthy musical Philistines. Although the names of certain members of David's cohort represented a number of Schumann's colleagues, others existed only in Schumann's romantic dual nature—particularly the dreamy, introverted Eusebius who often engaged in conversation with the more fiery, temperamental

Florestan. The article on Chopin's Opus 2 begins with Schumann describing their meeting:

Eusebius came in quietly the other day. You know the ironic smile on his pale face with which he seeks to create suspense. I was sitting at the piano with Florestan. Florestan is, as you know, one of those rare musical minds which anticipate, as it were, that which is new and extraordinary. Today, however, he was surprised. With the words, "Hats off, gentlemen—a genius!" Eusebius laid a piece of music on the piano rack. [20]

Frequently it was Master Raro who would moderate their discussions. Hugo Riemann speculated that he represented the integrated viewpoint of Clara and Robert: the united ClaRA-RObert.[21]

Schumann had had difficulty getting the reactionary *Allgemeine musikalische Zeitung* to accept his material and by 1834, together with his friends, had formed his own organ, *Neue Zeitschrift für Musik*. He continued as its guiding force for the following ten-year period. Schumann described its founding:

In Leipzig toward the end of 1833 a few musicians, mostly young men, met as though by accident every evening. What brought them together chiefly was their pleasure in each other's company; also their desire to discuss the art which was the meat and drink of life to them, music. The musical situation in Germany at the moment was anything but inspiring. Rossini reigned in the opera-houses, and nothing was to be heard on the pianoforte save Herz and Huenten. Yet merely a few years had passed since Beethoven, C.M. von Weber, and Franz Schubert had lived among us.

It is true that Mendelssohn's star was rising and wondrous tales were told of a Pole named Chopin. But neither of these composers had as yet begun to exert his future far-reaching influence. So on a day the following idea came to these musical young hot-heads. "Let us not be mere spectators! Let us lend a hand ourselves for the glory of things! Let us bring the poetry of our art into honor once again!" Thus the first pages of a new musical journal saw the light. [22]

In its pages, the writings of Schumann stand revealed as some of the best literary musical criticism of all time. We find such illuminating thoughts as these:

The older I grow, the more convinced I am that the piano expresses itself mainly in the following three styles: (1) richness of sound and varied harmony progressions (made use of by Beethoven and Franz Schubert); (2) pedal effect (as with

Field); (3) volubility (Czerny, Herz, and others). In the first category we find the expansive players; in the second, the fanciful ones; and in the third, those distinguished by their pearly technique. Manysided, cultured composer-performers like Hummel, Moscheles, and finally, Chopin, combine all three, and are consequently the most beloved by players; those writers and performers who neglect to study any of these fall into the background. [23]

The public has lately begun to weary of virtuosos and, as we have frequently remarked, we have too. The virtuosos themselves seem to feel this, if we may judge from a recently awakened fancy among them for emigrating to America; and many of their enemies secretly hope they will remain over there; for, taken all in all, modern virtuosity has benefited art very little. [24]

Schumann was master of the aphorism. A goodly number of these, of great value to pianists, were appended to his *Album for the Young,* Op. 68 under the title "House-Rules and Maxims for Young Musicians." A sampling of these can be appropriately listed here:

You must practice scales and other finger exercises industriously. There are people, however, who think they may achieve great ends by doing this; up to an advanced age, for many hours daily, they practice mechanical exercises. That is as reasonable as trying to recite the alphabet faster and faster every day. Find a better use for your time. [25]

"Dumb keyboards" have been invented; practice on them for a while in order to see that they are worthless. Dumb people cannot teach us to speak. [26]

Always play as though a master were present. [27]

If you have finished your daily musical work and feel tired, do not force yourself to labor further. It is better to rest than to practice without joy or freshness. [28]

Do not seek to attain mere technical proficiency—the so-called *bravura.* Try to produce with each composition the effect at which the composer aimed. No one should attempt more; anything further is mere caricature. [29]

As you grow older, converse more frequently with scores than with virtuosos. [30]

Industriously practice the fugues of good masters; above all, those of J. S. Bach. Let *The Well-Tempered Clavichord* be your daily meat. Then you will certainly become an able musician. [31]

Rest from your musical studies by industriously reading the

poets. Often take exercise out in the open. [32]

Lose no opportunity of practicing on the organ; there is no instrument which takes a swifter revenge on anything unclear or sloppy in composition and playing. [33]

Regularly sing in choruses, especially the middle voices. This will make you musical.

What do we mean by being musical? You are not so when, with eyes painfully fixed on the notes, you struggle through a piece; you are not so when you stop short and find it impossible for you to proceed because someone has turned over two pages at once. But you are musical when, in playing a new piece, you almost foresee what is coming; when you play an old one by heart; in short, when you have taken music not only into your fingers, but into your heart and head.

How may one become musical in this sense? Dear child, the principal requisites, a fine ear and a swift power of comprehension, come, like all things, from above. But this foundation may and must be improved and enlarged. You cannot do this by shutting yourself up all day like a hermit, practicing mechanical exercises, but by a vital, many-sided musical activity; especially by familiarizing yourself with chorus and orchestra work. [34]

Never miss an opportunity of hearing a good opera. [35]

At another time Schumann had the extrovert Florestan give his opinion on the importance of public performance from memory:

Whether out of daring or charlatanism, it is always a proof of uncommon musical powers. Wherefore the prompter's box, wherefore fettered feet, when the head has wings? Do we not know that a chord played from notes—no matter how freely— is never half so free as one played from the imagination? We are all alike; and I, because a German and therefore wedded to tradition—I also would be astonished, had I seen the actor or dancer produce his or her written part in public in order to perform it with more assurance; and yet, I, too, am like the Philistine, who, upon seeing a virtuoso quietly continue to play after the score had fallen from the desk, cried out in hot excitement, "Look, look, that is indeed art! He knows it by heart!" [36]

A study of Schumann's wife Clara as pianist should be preceded by a brief consideration of the role of her father, Friedrich Wieck (1785-1873), in the development of piano technique. His most influential students were Robert and Clara and Hans von

207

Bülow. That he was sought after as a fine teacher is evident from the fact that Mendelssohn tried unsuccessfully to secure his services for the Leipzig Conservatory. A methodical German individualist, he was also a serious, sensitive musician whose technical thought even in his earlier teaching days was considerably ahead of his time. Wieck had started as a teacher advocating Logier's method, but soon gave that up for his own ideas, consisting of "the application of the greatest care, sense and intelligence possible to the teaching of technique and expression." [37] A severe critic of the stiff, high-finger Stuttgart school, he presented views on touch and relaxation that were considerably more penetrating than his predecessors and that place him among the earliest forerunners of modern technical thought. In the introduction to his Piano Studies, a collection of forty-five short drills still worthy of use on the intermediate level, he stated that they are "mit Hineinlegen in die Tasten zu spielen" (to be played with the fingers bedding the keys)—with a pressure rather than a percussive stroke. [38]

In his book, *Piano and Song* (1853), Wieck bemoaned the fact that "We also have much better aids in instruction books, etudes, and suitable piano pieces; but still we find everywhere 'jingling' and 'piano-banging,' as you express it, and yet no piano-playing." He also stressed the importance of "bringing out a fine legato tone with loose and quiet fingers and a yielding, movable wrist, without the assistance of the arm." [39] It would seem that what he really wanted is the subtle, quiet assistance of the pressure and weight of the arm, with a touch which is carefully prepared and not percussive. Later he discussed relaxation in detail:

> This is the place for me to explain myself more fully with regard to playing with a loose wrist, in order that I shall not be misunderstood. The tones which are produced with a loose wrist are always more tender and more attractive, have a fuller sound, and permit more delicate shading than the sharp tones, without body, which are thrown or fired off or tapped out with unendurable rigidity by the aid of the arm and forearm. A superior technique can with few exceptions be more quickly and favorably acquired in this way than when the elbows are required to contribute their power. I do not, however, censure the performance of many *virtuosos,* who execute rapid octave passages with a stiff wrist; they often do it with great precision, in the most rapid *tempo,* forcibly and effectively. It must, after all, depend upon individual peculiarities whether the pupil can learn better and more quickly to play such passages thus or with a loose wrist. The present style

of bravoura playing for *virtuosos* cannot dispense with facility in octave passages; it is a necessary part of it.

I will now consider the use of loose and independent fingers, in playing generally; i.e., in that of more advanced pupils who have already acquired the necessary elementary knowledge. The fingers must be set upon the keys with a certain decision, firmness, quickness, and vigor, and must obtain a command over the key-board; otherwise, the result is only a tame, colorless, uncertain, immature style of playing, in which no fine *portamento,* no poignant *staccato,* or sprightly accentuation can be produced. Every thoughtful teacher, striving for the best result, must, however, take care that this shall only be acquired gradually, and must teach it with a constant regard to individual peculiarities, and not at the expense of beauty of performance, and of a tender, agreeable touch. [40]

Wieck took great pride in his high musical standards and his thorough, exacting technical approach, especially as exemplified in the performance career of his daughter Clara—his most outstanding pupil. He was a vigorous, influential teacher even in his old age. Amy Fay recalled a visit in 1872 to the Wieck household, at the invitation of Clara's sister Marie Wieck—also a pianist with a touch Miss Fay described as perfect. [41] Wieck was then about eighty-seven and still able to reveal his eccentric dignity:

I was in high glee at that proposal, for I was very anxious to see the famous Wieck, the trainer of so many generations of musicians. Fräulein Wieck appointed Saturday evening, and we accordingly went. B. had instructed us how to act, for the old man is quite a character, and has to be dealt with after his own fashion. She said we must walk in (having first laid off our things) as if we had been members of the family all our lives, and say, "Good-evening, Papa Wieck,"—(everybody calls him Papa). Then we were to seat ourselves, and if we had some knitting or sewing with us it would be well. At any rate we must have the apparent intention of spending several hours, for nothing provokes him so as to have people come in simply to call. "What!" he will say, "do you expect to know a celebrated man like me in half an hour?" then (very sarcastically), "perhaps you want my autograph!" He hates to give his autograph. . . .

He *lives* entirely in music, and has a class of girls whom he instructs every evening for nothing. Five of these young girls were there. He is very deaf, but strange to say, he is as sensitive as ever to every musical sound, and the same is the case with Clara Schumann. Fräulein Wieck then opened the ball.

209

She is about forty, I should think, and a stout, phlegmatic-looking woman. However, she played superbly, and her touch is one of the most delicious possible. After hearing her, one is not surprised that the Wiecks think nobody can teach touch but themselves. She began with a nocturne by Chopin, in F major. I forgot to say that the old Herr sits in his chair with the air of being on a throne, and announces beforehand each piece that is to be played, following it with some comment: e.g., "This nocturne I allowed my daughter Clara to play in Berlin forty years ago, and afterward the principal newspaper in criticising her performance, remarked: 'This young girl seems to have much talent; it is only a pity that she is in the hands of a father whose head seems stuck full of queer new-fangled notions,'—so new was Chopin to the public at that time." That is the way he goes on. . . .

The old Herr then said, "Now we'll have something else;" and got up and went to the piano, and called the young girls. He made three of them sing, one after the other, and they sang very charmingly indeed. One of them he made improvise a *cadenza,* and a second sang the alto to it without accompaniment. He was very proud of that. He exercises his pupils in all sorts of ways, trains them to sing any given tone, and "to skip up and down the ladder," as they call the scale. [42]

From these observations, one can readily surmise what a disciplinarian Friedrich Wieck must have been in training his daughter Clara (1819-1896) many years before. As a girl of eight, she wrote in her diary:

My father, who has long vainly hoped for a change of mood on my part, remarked today that I am still idle, negligent, unmethodical, self-willed, etc., especially in piano playing and practicing. . . . He tore the copy [a set of variations by Hünten] to pieces before my eyes, and from today will not give me another lesson, and I may only play scales, Cramer's etudes, and Czerny's studies on the trill. [43]

He must have expected the impossible from the small child. Nevertheless, she applied herself diligently to developing her outstanding talent. By the time she was nine she had made her first public appearance and was playing concertos by Hummel and Mozart by memory with very favorable reaction from the public. Her first Gewandhaus recital was presented on November 8, 1830. Performances followed throughout Germany and in Paris. In the meantime Robert Schumann had come into the Wieck household and into Clara's life. A few months after Schumann had reviewed

Chopin's Variations on *Là ci darem,* Op. 2, Clara was performing them in Leipzig in July of 1832. From the same year, with the presentation of the G Minor Concerto by Moscheles, dates a long series of orchestral appearances at the Gewandhaus concerts. When Chopin heard her on his private visit to Leipzig in 1836, he remarked that she was the only woman in Germany who could play his music. [44]

By that date Clara and Robert had already made it known to Wieck that they wished to marry. He steadily opposed them, even to the point of taking court action. But they persevered and were finally married in 1840. Especially interested in presenting Robert's piano compositions to the public, she travelled and performed as much as family responsibilities permitted—there were eight children to think about as well as Robert's declining health. After his death in 1856, she played extensively, establishing her reputation as one of Europe's greatest pianists. She and Schumann's pieces were especially well received in England. She joined the faculty of the Hoch Conservatory in Frankfurt in 1878. Her performance career continued into the late 1880s. Performing the Mozart D Minor Concerto and using her own cadenzas, she celebrated her Diamond Jubilee on October 20, 1888—sixty years before the public. [45]

Clara Schumann was surely one of the most scholarly pianists of the nineteenth century and a true classicist at heart. She was dedicated to presenting the best serious literature, ranging from Bach and Scarlatti to Chopin, Mendelssohn, and Brahms, and she deplored the Liszt personality cult. One of her students, Franklin Taylor, left a fine characterization of her playing:

> As an artist, Mme. Schumann's place was indubitably in the very first rank, indeed she may perhaps be considered to stand higher than any of her contemporaries, if not as regards the possession of natural or acquired gifts, yet in the use she made of them. Her playing was characterised by an entire absence of personal display, a keen perception of the composer's meaning, and an unfailing power of setting it forth in perfectly intelligible form. These qualities would lead one to pronounce her one of the most intellectual of players, were it not that that term has come to imply a certain coldness or want of feeling, which was never perceived in her playing. But just such a use of the intellectual powers as serves the purposes of true art, ensuring perfect accuracy in all respects, no liberties being taken with the text, even when playing from memory, and above all securing an interpretation of the composer's work which is at once intelligible to the listener—this

211

certainly formed an essential element of her playing, and it is worth while insisting on this, since the absence of that strict accuracy and perspicuity is too often mistaken for evidence of deep emotional intention. With all this, however, Mme. Schumann's playing evinced great warmth of feeling, and a true poet's appreciation of absolute beauty, so that nothing ever sounded harsh or ugly in her hands; indeed it may fairly be said that after hearing her play a fine work (she never played what is not good), one always became aware that it contained beauties undiscovered before. This was, no doubt, partly due to the peculiarly beautiful quality of the tone she produced, which was rich and vigorous without the slightest harshness, and was obtained, even in the loudest passages, by pressure with her fingers rather than by percussion. Indeed, her playing was particularly free from violent movement of any kind; in passages, the fingers were kept close to the keys and squeezed instead of striking them, while chords were grasped from the wrist rather than struck from the elbow. She founded her *technique* upon the principle laid down by her father, F. Wieck, who was also her instructor, that "the touch (i.e., the blow of the finger upon the key) should never be audible, but only the musical sound," an axiom the truth of which there is some danger of overlooking, in the endeavour to compass the extreme difficulties of certain kinds of modern pianoforte music. [46]

As early as the age of nineteen Clara was compared very favorably with Liszt, Thalberg, and Adolf von Henselt (1814-1889) in an article published on April 27, 1838 in the *Neue Zeitschrift für Musik*. Henselt was the German who settled in Russia in the 1830s. Chopin, because of illness, was no longer actively giving concerts. The article went to great length to compare the various attributes which they possessed. Liszt embodied impassioned performance; Thalberg, refined sensualism in expression; Clara, irrepressible enthusiasm; Henselt, Germanic lyricism. Liszt's playing was diabolical; Thalberg's, fascinating; Clara's, ennobling; Henselt's, exciting. [47] One might argue with some of the judgments of the author, but certainly not with the fact that here was a woman pianist to be reckoned with. As late as 1869 when Clara was fifty, Amy Fay was enchanted by her playing when she heard her in Berlin:

I heard Clara Schumann on Sunday, and on Tuesday evening, also. She is a most wonderful artist. In the first concert she played a quartette by Schumann, and you can imagine how lovely it was under the treatment of Clara Schumann for the piano, Joachim for the first violin, De Ahna for the second, and Müller for the 'cello. It was perfect, and I was in raptures. Madame Schumann's selection for the two concerts was a very wide one, and gave a full exhibition of her powers in every kind of music. The *Impromptu* by Schumann, op. 90, was exquisite. It was full of passion and very difficult. The second of the *Songs without Words,* by Mendelssohn, was the most fairy-like performance. It is one of those things that must be tossed off with the greatest grace and smoothness, and it requires the most beautiful and delicate technique. She played it to perfection. The terrific Scherzo by Chopin she did splendidly, but she kept the great octave passages in the bass a little too subordinate, I thought, and did not give it quite boldly enough for my taste, though it was extremely artistic. Clara Schumann's playing is very objective. She seems to throw herself into the music, instead of letting the music take possession of her. She gives you the most exquisite pleasure with every note she touches, and has a wonderful conception and variety in playing, but she seldom whirls you off your feet.

At the second concert she was even better than at the first, if that is possible. She seemed full of fire, and when she played Bach, she ought to have been crowned with diamonds! Such *noble* playing I have never heard. In fact you are all the time impressed with the nobility and breadth of her style, and the comprehensiveness of her treatment, and oh, if you *could* hear her *scales!* In short, there is nothing more to be desired in her playing, and she has every quality of a great artist. Many people say that Tausig is far better, but I cannot believe it. . . . I send you Madame Schumann's photograph which is exactly like her. She is a large, very German-looking woman, with dark hair and superb neck and arms. At the last concert she was dressed in black velvet, low body and short sleeves, and when she struck powerful chords, those large white arms came down with a certain splendor. [48]

After Amy Fay had studied in Europe for four years she became more critical of Clara's playing. She observed its methodical, more prosaic side. Perhaps by then Amy was somewhat prejudiced by her days in the Lisztian circle. Liszt and Clara lost no love on each other. Amy Fay wrote again from Berlin on November 7, 1873:

Clara Schumann is entirely a classic player. Beethoven's sonatas, and Bach, too, she plays splendidly; but she doesn't seem to me to have any *finesse,* or much poetry in her playing. There's nothing subtle in her conception. She has a great deal of fire, and her whole style is grand, finished, perfectly rounded off, solid and satisfactory—what the Germans call *gediegen.* She is a *healthy* artist to listen to, but there is nothing of the analytic, no Balzac or Hawthorne about her. Beethoven's Variations in C minor are, perhaps, the best performance I ever heard from her, and they are immensely difficult, too; I thought she did them better than Bülow, in spite of Bülow's being such a great Beethovenite. I think she repeats the same pieces a good deal, possibly because she finds the modern fashion of playing everything without notes very trying. I've even heard that she cries over the necessity of doing it; and certainly it is a foolish thing to make a point of, with so very great an artist as Clara Schumann.—If people could *only* be allowed to have their own individuality! [49]

Another facet of Clara's personality may be seen in the reminiscenses left by one of her daughters, Eugenie, of piano lessons which Eugenie had with her mother:

I remember my first lesson most distinctly. It began, like all the subsequent ones, with scales and arpeggios, and the first Study from Czerny's School of Velocity followed. I played a page of it, then my mother said, "That is all right so far, but don't you think chords sound much nicer like this?" She played the first eight bars from the wrist with all the notes of equal strength, forte, yet exquisitely mellow in tone, never stiffening the wrist for an instant, and knitting the chords rhythmically together so that the simple piece suddenly took on life and character. It was a revelation to me; my feeling for beauty of touch and rhythm was stirred into life from that moment.

The study was followed by the Bach fugue in E minor from Vol. 1 of the *Wohltemperierte Klavier.* I learnt strict legato and subtle shading of rhythm in this. My mother took endless trouble with the first few bars; but when these had been mastered, the fugue became easy, and I soon learnt to play it well enough to make it a pleasure to myself.

Beethoven formed the nucleus of every lesson. . . .

"And now we must work at some of Papa's music," she said . . . "and I would like to start you with the *Jugend Album.*" So we took each of these little gems one by one in their proper order, and I remember every word the beloved teacher said about them. These pieces would teach me rhythm and characterisation; underlying ideas I might supply myself. "Whatever your father did, saw, read, would at once shape itself into music. When he read poetry, resting on the sofa after dinner, it turned into songs. When he saw you children at play, little pieces of music grew out of your games. While he was writing down the *Humoresque,* some acrobats came along and performed in front of our house; imperceptibly the music they made stole into the composition. He was always quite unconscious of these inspirations; it would be foolish to think that he had used them intentionally as an incentive. He invented their titles after they were finished. These are quite characteristic, and might help in the interpretation, but they are not necessary." [50]

One other composer-pianist should be included in the present chapter because of his close connection with the Schumann circle. Johannes Brahms (1833-1897) became an intimate acquaintance of the Schumanns in the early 1850s and was a tower of strength to Clara during the years of Robert's final illness. Brahms' humble beginnings were in Hamburg where his father finally rose to the position of double bass player in the Stadttheater and the Philharmonic Orchestra. His formal lessons began at the age of seven with Otto F. W. Cossel, a sound teacher and pupil of Eduard Marxsen. He was brought up on the standard fare of Czerny, Clementi, etc., and sometimes Bach. By the time he was ten he was playing so well that a concert agent who heard him wanted to take him on a tour of America, an offer wisely declined. Composition came as easily as did the piano. Later he was to tell his friend Widmann that, "My finest songs would come to me early in the morning, while I was cleaning my boots" and "I had invented myself a stave before I knew that such a thing had long been in existence." [51]

At ten, Cossel sent him to his own teacher, Marxsen (1806-1887), a thoroughly fine person and ardent admirer of Bach and Beethoven. Brahms' first serious recital came in September of 1848 when he was fifteen and included both a Bach fugue and the *Waldstein* Sonata. Appreciating his great potential, Marxsen commented at the time of Mendelssohn's death: "A great master of the musical art has gone hence, but an even greater one will bloom for us in Brahms." [52] During these early years, Brahms was helping to support himself by playing in dance halls at night, giving piano lessons, and composing and transcribing music during the days under the pen names of G. W. Marks and Karl Würth. His first real break was when the Hungarian violinist, Eduard Remenyi, came to Hamburg as a political refugee. Together they set out on tour in April, 1853 and Brahms' musical genius soon became apparent. Marxsen later wrote:

Brahms' memory is so amazing that it never occurred to him to take any music with him on his concert tours. When he started out into the world on his first tour, as a young man of twenty, the works of Beethoven and Bach, besides a large number of modern concert-pieces by Thalberg, Liszt, Mendelssohn, and others, were indelibly impressed upon his mind. [53]

His transposition feats are well known: such as the time in Göttingen when he transposed the Kreutzer Violin Sonata from A to B flat because of the low-pitched piano. It was the great violinist Joseph Joachim who heard him do this and shortly thereafter, during a visit to Hanover, gave him and Remenyi a letter of introduction to Liszt. Joachim also insisted that he call on Schumann. After Brahms' death Joachim recalled his reaction to the first visit in Joachim's home in Hanover:

Never in the whole of my artistic career have I been overcome by a more joyful astonishment than when my fellow-countryman's almost shy-looking fair-haired accompanist played, with a noble, uplifted expression, the movements of his sonata, of an originality and power which nobody would have suspected. It affected me like a revelation when I then heard the song *O versenk' dein Leid* for the first time. Add to this his piano-playing, so tender, so imaginative, so free, and so full of fire, that it held me absolutely spell-bound. [54]

In June of 1853 Brahms went with Remenyi to Weimar for a six week period. Here he became well acquainted with Liszt, who recognized the greatness in Brahms' early piano sonatas and the Scherzo in E flat minor. But Brahms, with his low German background, his blunt honesty, and the strong strain of classicism which ran through him, simply could not identify with the more sophisticated Lisztian circle—and especially with its advocacy of a neo-German style of composition which Brahms did not feel was truly German. Brahms respected Liszt's piano playing, but he did not care for his works. Leaving the Altenburg in Weimar, he paid a return visit to Joachim with whom he began a lifelong association and friendship.

Then on September 30 of the same year, he first called on the Schumanns, then living in Düsseldorf. This meeting was crucial in Brahms' life. Schumann was completely enchanted by the young Brahms. After he had played only a short time, he stopped him with the remark: "Clara must hear this." When Clara had entered the room, Schumann told her: "Here, dear Clara, you shall hear music such as you have never heard before." The visit stretched into weeks. Schumann wrote Joachim in his florid literary manner, likening Brahms to a "young eagle, who has descended upon us from the Alps so suddenly and unexpectedly" and to a "splendid river, which, like the Niagara, shows itself at its finest when it rushes roaring from on high with a rainbow playing on its waters, with butterflies fluttering round it on the bank, and accompanied by the song of nightingales." He also told Joachim that "Johannes is the true apostle, and he too will write Revelations, the secret of which many Pharisees will still be unable to unravel even centuries later." [55]

Brahms was the last bright spot in Schumann's troubled closing years. Schumann's first significant writing heralded the appearance of Chopin; his final article, which had a profound effect upon the musical world, was entitled *Neue Bahnen* ("New Paths") and presented the twenty-year-old Brahms. It appeared in Leipzig on October 23, 1853 in the *Neue Zeitschrift für Musik* as follows:

YEARS HAVE PASSED—almost as many as I once devoted to the editing of these pages—ten indeed, since I have made myself heard in this place so rich in memories. Despite intense productive work I often felt impelled to continue. Many new and significant talents have arisen; a new power in music seems to announce itself; the intimation has been proved true by many aspiring artists of the last years, even though their work may be known only in comparatively limited circles. To me, who followed the progress of these chosen ones with the greatest sympathy, it seemed that under these circumstances there inevitably must appear a musician called to give expression to his times in ideal fashion; a musician who would reveal his mastery not in a gradual evolution, but like Athene would spring fully armed from Zeus's head. And such a one *has* appeared; a young man over whose cradle Graces and Heroes have stood watch. His name is *Johannes Brahms,* and he comes from Hamburg, where he has been working in quiet obscurity, though instructed in the most difficult statutes of his art by an excellent and enthusiastically devoted teacher. A well-known and honored master recently recommended him to me. Even outwardly he bore the marks proclaiming: "This is a chosen one." Sitting at the piano he began to disclose wonderful regions to us. We were drawn into even more enchanting spheres. Besides, he is a player of genius who can make of the piano an orchestra of lamenting and loudly jubilant voices. There were sonatas, veiled symphonies rather; songs the poetry of which would be understood even without words, although a profound vocal melody runs through them all; single piano pieces, some of them turbulent in spirit while graceful in form; again sonatas for violin and piano, string quartets, every work so different from the others that it seemed to stream from its own individual source. And then it was as though, rushing like a torrent, they were all united by him into a single waterfall the cascades of which were overarched by a peaceful rainbow, while butterflies played about its borders and the voices of nightingales obliged. [56]

After Schumann's mental condition had deteriorated to the point where he attempted suicide by throwing himself into the Rhine on February 27, 1854, Brahms hurried to Düsseldorf to be with Clara. Their friendship deepened during the trying months ahead. Clara wrote to a friend: "Brahms is my dearest, truest support; since the beginning of Robert's illness he has never left me, but has gone through everything with me and shared my sufferings." [57] Theirs was a lifelong friendship fortified by their common musical ideals and distaste for Liszt. Even after Brahms settled in Vienna in 1863, he still frequently came to visit her and she was a staunch advocate of his music and frequently presented it on her concert tours.

Performing more adequately in his youth than in later life, Brahms, like Beethoven, was more composer than pianist. And he played in the creative, individualistic manner of a composer—not always with the greatest finesse or virtuosity, especially as his practice became less regular. Later, it seems, his appearances were more in chamber groups. But in his twenties, Brahms' playing was compelling. Schumann spoke of his "piano-playing of genius, which turned the piano into an orchestra of wailing and exultant voices;" [58] and Walter Hubbe, who heard him frequently then in Hamburg, said:

He does not play like a consummately trained, highly intelligent musician making other people's works his own (like, for instance, Hans von Bülow), but rather like one who is himself creating, who interprets the composer's works as an equal, not merely reproducing them, but rendering them as if they gushed forth directly and powerfully from his heart. [59]

When Joachim first heard him he was greatly impressed by "an intense fire, and what I might almost call a fateful energy and inevitable precision of rhythm which proclaim the predestined artist." [60]

Brahms' piano students were few, but their writings have left us with considerable insight into his playing and instruction methods. The Englishwoman Florence May came to know him through Clara Schumann, with whom she had studied in London in 1871 on one of Clara's visits there. Her study with him in the early 1870s, when Brahms was about forty, left her with rhapsodical praise:

> Brahms united in himself each and every quality that might be supposed to exist in an absolutely ideal teacher of the pianoforte, without having a single modifying drawback . . . He was strict and absolute; he was gentle and patient and encouraging; he was not only clear, he was light itself. [61]

Gustav Jenner's personality and achievement under Brahms must have called forth a different side of Brahms' nature. At least Jenner seemed to see him primarily as a stern disciplinarian whose philosophy was to put students through a strict contrapuntal and technical routine with no words of praise in order to prove the students' true worth. [62] Perhaps Brahms was more gentle with his feminine pupils!

But he still gave them technique to work on. Florence May tells us:

> Remembering what Frau Schumann had said of his ability to assist me with my technique, I told him, before beginning my first lesson, of my mechanical difficulties, and asked him to help me. He answered, "Yes, that must come first," and, after hearing me play through a study from Clementi's "Gradus ad Parnassum," he immediately set to work to loosen and equalise my fingers. Beginning that very day, he gradually put me through an entire course of technical training, showing me how I should best work, for the attainment of my end, at scales, arpeggi, trills, double notes, and octaves.
>
> He not only showed me how to practise; he made me, at first, practise to him during a good part of my lessons, whilst he sat watching my fingers; telling me what was wrong in my way of moving them, indicating, by a movement of his own hand, a better position for mine, absorbing himself entirely, for the time being, in the object of helping me.
>
> He did not believe in the utility for me of the daily practice of the ordinary five finger exercises, preferring to form exercises from any piece or study upon which I might be engaged. He had a great habit of turning a difficult passage round and making me practise it, not as written, but with other accents and in various figures, with the result that when I again tried it as it stood the difficulties had always considerably diminished, and often entirely disappeared. [63]

She also mentions that a considerable portion of her lesson periods were devoted to the study of Bach—to the *Well-Tempered Clavier* and the *English Suites*. As her technique developed, he devoted more and more time "to the spirit of the music":

... His phrasing, as he taught it to me, was, it need hardly be said, of the broadest, whilst he was rigorous in exacting attention to the smallest details. These he sometimes treated as a delicate embroidery that filled up and decorated the broad outline of the phrase, with the large sweep of which nothing was ever allowed to interfere. Light and shade, also, were so managed as to help to bring out its continuity. Be it, however, most emphatically declared that he never theorised on these points; he merely tried his utmost to make me understand and play my pieces as he himself understood and felt them.

He would make me repeat over and over again, ten or twelve times if necessary, part of a movement of Bach, till he had satisfied himself that I was beginning to realise his wish for particular effects of tone or phrasing or feeling. [64]

Frequently at the close of her lessons, Brahms would perform many of the Bach Preludes and Fugues for her. She was particularly struck by the emotional, poetic qualities of his Bach playing. On his playing in general, Florence May commented:

At this time of his life Brahms' playing was stimulating to an extraordinary degree, and so *apart* as to be quite unforgettable. It was not the playing of a virtuoso, though he had a large amount of virtuosity (to put it moderately) at his command. He never aimed at mere effect, but seemed to plunge into the innermost meaning of whatever music he happened to be interpreting, exhibiting all its details, and expressing its very depths. Not being in regular practice, he would sometimes strike wrong notes—and there was already a hardness, arising from the same cause, in his playing chords; but he was fully aware of his failings, and warned me not to imitate them. [65]

She also summed up Brahms' views on the relationship of technique to musical expression:

Brahms, in fact, recognised no such thing as what is sometimes called "neat playing" of the compositions either of Bach, Scarlatti, or Mozart. Neatness and equality of finger were imperatively demanded by him, and in their utmost nicety and perfection, but as a preparation, not as an end. Varying and sensitive expression was to him as the breath of life, necessary to the true interpretation of any work of genius, and he did not hesitate to avail himself of such resources of the modern pianoforte as he felt helped to impart it; no matter in what particular century his composer may have lived, or what may have been the peculiar excellencies and limitations of the instruments of his day.

Whatever the music I might be studying, however, he would never allow any kind of "expression made easy." He particularly disliked chords to be spread unless marked so by the composer for the sake of a special effect. "No arpège," he used invariably to say if I unconsciously gave way to the habit, or yielded to the temptation of softening a chord by its means. He made very much of the well-known effect of two notes slurred together, whether in a loud or soft tone, and I know from his insistence to me on this point that the mark has a special significance in his music. [66]

Another of Brahms' students during the same period was Clara Schumann's daughter, Eugenie. Her recollection of Brahms' playing is graphic:

To hear Brahms play his own works was, if not always satisfying, at any rate in the highest degree interesting. He brought out the themes very emphatically, with a tendency, which was characteristic of his playing, towards slightly irregular accentuation; everything in the nature of an accompaniment he merely sketched in, in such a way as to give rise to remarkable effects of light and shade. If he was playing an impassioned piece, it was as though a stormwind were driving through clouds, spreading devastation with heedless recklessness. On such occasions one felt how inadequate the instrument was for him. From the point of piano technique his playing could never be satisfactory; in general he confined himself in later years to playing his own things, and in these he did not trouble about technical perfection. [67]

Eugenie, when she was seventy-seven, also wrote an account of Brahms' technical approach when she studied with him as a young woman of about twenty-two. This account follows:

In the spring of 1872 my mother told me that she was going to ask Brahms to give me lessons during the summer. She thought that the stimulating influence of a fresh teacher might incite me to a more eager pursuit of my studies. I felt very unhappy; Mamma could not be satisfied with my progress, and I thought that I had done my best. There was no one for whom I would have worked rather than for her. Now Brahms really did come twice a week. He entered the room

221

punctually to the minute, and he was always kind, always patient, and adapted his teaching to my capabilities and the stage of my progress in quite a wonderful way. Also he took a great deal of trouble in the training of my fingers. He had thought about such training and about technique in general much more than my mother, who had surmounted all technical difficulties at an age when one is not yet conscious of them. He made me play a great many exercises, scales and arpeggios as a matter of course, and he gave special attention to the training of the thumb, which as many will remember, was given a very prominent part in his own playing. When the thumb had to begin a passage, he flung it on the key with the other fingers clenched. As he kept his wrist loose at the same time, the tone remained full and round even in a fortissimo. Considerable time was daily given to the following exercises on the passing-under of the thumb:—Also to be played in triplets.

I had to take the note on which the thumb was used, quite lightly—so to speak, on the wing—and accentuate the first of every four notes strongly. Then I had to play the same exercise in triplets, with strong accents on the first note of every triplet. When I could play the exercises faultlessly in keys without the black notes, I played them, always beginning with the thumb, in C sharp, F sharp, A flat, E flat, and D flat.

Then followed the common chords with inversions through three or four octaves, also in groups of four notes and in triplets, beginning with the accent on the first note. When I had played this about ten times, I changed the accent to the second, then to the third note of each group, so that all the fingers were exercised equally. I practised these arpeggios alternately as triplets and groups of six, and had to distinguish clearly between the groups of twice three and three times two notes.

Brahms made me practise shakes also in triplets. In all exercises he made me play the non-accentuated notes very lightly. I practised the chromatic scale with the first and third, first and fourth, and first and fifth fingers, and he often made me repeat the two consecutive notes where the thumb was

223

passed under. They were all, in fact, quite simple exercises; but carefully executed, first slowly, then more rapidly, and at last prestissimo. I found them extremely helpful for the strengthening, suppleness, and control of the fingers. I also played some of the difficult exercises published later as 'Fifty-one Exercises for Pianoforte by Brahms,' in which he did not include the easier and musically less valuable ones.

With regard to studies Brahms said: play easy ones, but play them as rapidly as possible. He thought very highly of Clementi's 'Gradus ad Parnassum,' and made me play a great number of these.

In the study of Bach's works Brahms laid the greatest stress on rhythm, and gave me directions which, like seeds, took root and continued their growth throughout my musical life. They greatly increased my perception of the subtleties of rhythmic movement. He made it one of the principal rules that in constantly recurring figures the accents should always be the same, and that they should be stressed not so much by strong attack as by greater pressure on the accentuated and more lightness of the non-accentuated notes.

The melodic notes of figures he made me play legatissimo; the harmonic, however, e.g. the notes of broken chords, quite lightly. He never wrote purely rhythmic accents in above the notes, as he held them to be an integral part of the figure; but accents specially intended, or not self-evident, he marked, to make them quite clear, and pencilled phrasing in with slurs. But I was never allowed to interpret a passage thus phrased by lifting and fresh attack of the hands; only by rhythmic emphasis and nuance.

Brahms gave much attention to syncopations. They had to be given their full value, and where they produced dissonances with the other parts he made me listen to the syncopated in relation to each one of the dissonant notes. He made the suspensions equally interesting to me; I could never play them emphatically enough to please him. Of all the works which I studied with Brahms I enjoyed the French Suites most; it was pure joy to work at them in this way, and he made me see things which I had hitherto passed without noticing, and of which I never again lost sight.

In any work by Bach, Brahms would occasionally permit an emphatic lifting of the notes (portamento), but never staccato. "You must not play Bach staccato," he said to me. "But Mamma sometimes uses a staccato in Bach," I demurred. Then he replied, "Your mother's youth goes back to a time when it was the fashion to use staccatos in Bach, and she has retained them in a few cases."

224

Brahms did not give me many directions with regard to the interpretation of the Suites; he confined himself to explanations of their rhythm and the simplest rules for nuances. "Play away, play away," he would call out from time to time in a quick movement.

In the course of the summer I studied with him three French Suites, several Preludes and Fugues from the second book of the *Wohltemperierte Klavier*, some pieces by Scarlatti, an almost unknown Sonata by Mozart in F major, Variations on a theme in F major by Beethoven (each of which was in a different key), his 32 Variations in C minor, Variations in B flat (Impromptu) by Schubert, some of Mendelssohn's Songs without Words, and Chopin's Nocturnes. If I remember rightly, nothing of my father's. I must confess to my disgrace that I enjoyed of all these things only the Suites, the C minor Variations, and the Songs without Words; all the others I hated. I had revelled in my father's G minor Sonata the previous winter, and now I was expected to play all these queer, unexciting pieces. I have often wondered why Brahms made just this selection? Perhaps he wanted me to form my own judgment on things which I had never heard my mother play, in which I had no tradition to go upon, and thought it would be good for me to become more independent, more self-reliant.

I thought it natural that my mother should devote time and strength to me, and it made me happy. But I never got over the fact that I strummed to Brahms for a whole long summer, and, though in later years he often kindly urged me to play to him again, I could never bring myself to do so. But the seed which he sowed fell upon good soil and bore fruit in the course of years, and when I began to teach I recognized how much I owed to him. I only wish I had told him this. [68]

Notes

[1] Heinrich Eduard Jacob, *Felix Mendelssohn and His Times*, p. 33, citing J.C. Lobe, *Der Gartenlaube*, Christmas Issue, 1866.

[2] *Ibid.*, pp. 33-34.

[3] *Ibid.*, p. 34.

[4] *Ibid.*

[5] *Ibid.*

[6] *Ibid.*, p. 36, citing Ludwig Rellstab, *Aus Meinen Leben*.

[7] *Ibid.*, p. 188, citing B. Litzmann, *Clara Schumann*.

[8] *Ibid.*, pp. 271-72, citing Ferdinand Hiller, *Felix Mendelssohn-Bartholdy*.

[9] W.S. Rockstro, *Felix Mendelssohn-Bartholdy,* pp. 105-108.

[10] *Early Letters of Robert Schumann* originally published by his wife. p. 113.

[11] *Ibid.,* p. 78.

[12] Bertita Harding, *Concerto, the Glowing Story of Clara Schumann,* p. 23.

[13] *Schumann Letters,* p. 162.

[14] *Ibid.,* p. 176.

[15] *Ibid.*

[16] *Ibid.,* pp. 179-80.

[17] *Ibid.,* p. 222.

[18] *Ibid.,* p. 284.

[19] Carl Reinecke, "Mendelssohn and Schumann: Personal Recollections of Them as Teachers," *The Etude,* XXVII, No. 12, December, 1909, p. 803.

[20] Robert Schumann, *On Music and Musicians,* p. 126.

[21] *Ibid.,* p. 17.

[22] *Ibid.,* p. 25, written in 1854 as a preface for the complete edition of his collected articles, 1834-44.

[23] *Ibid.,* pp. 82-83.

[24] *Ibid.,* p. 81.

[25] *Ibid.,* p. 30.

[26] *Ibid.*

[27] *Ibid.,* p. 31.

[28] *Ibid.,* p. 32.

[29] *Ibid.*

[30] *Ibid.,* p. 33.

[31] *Ibid.*

[32] *Ibid.*

[33] *Ibid.,* p. 34.

[34] *Ibid.,* pp. 34-35.

[35] *Ibid.,* p. 35.

[36] *Ibid.,* p. 51.

[37] *Grove's Dictionary of Music and Musicians,* 5th ed., IX, p. 286.

[38] Maria Levinskaya, *The Levinskaya System of Pianoforte Technique and Tone-Colour through Mental and Muscular Control,* p. 41.

[39] Friedrich Wieck, *Piano and Song, How to Teach, How to Learn, and How to Form a Judgment of Musical Performances,* p. 27.

⁴⁰ *Ibid.*, pp. 148-49.

⁴¹ Amy Fay, *Music-Study in Germany, from The Home Correspondence of Amy Fay,* p. 163.

⁴² *Ibid.*, pp. 164-166.

⁴³ Florence May, *The Girlhood of Clara Schumann,* pp. 24-25.

⁴⁴ *Grove's Dictionary,* 5th ed., VII, p. 600.

⁴⁵ Julia Smith, *Master Pianist, The Career and Teaching of Carl Friedberg,* p. 15.

⁴⁶ *Grove's Dictionary,* 2nd ed., IV, p. 344.

⁴⁷ Harding, *Concerto, . . .* Clara Schumann, pp. 62-63, citing the *Neue Zeitschrift für Music,* April 27, 1838.

⁴⁸ Fay, *Music-Study in Germany,* pp. 25-26.

⁴⁹ *Ibid.*, p. 274.

⁵⁰ Eugenie Schumann, *The Schumanns and Johannes Brahms,* pp. 97-98.

⁵¹ Walter Niemann, *Brahms,* p. 11.

⁵² *Ibid.*, p. 21.

⁵³ *Ibid.*, p. 29.

⁵⁴ *Ibid.*, p. 31.

⁵⁵ *Ibid.*, pp. 40-41.

⁵⁶ Robert Schumann, *On Music and Musicians,* pp. 252-54.

⁵⁷ Niemann, *Brahms,* p. 78.

⁵⁸ *Ibid.*, p. 191.

⁵⁹ *Ibid.*

⁶⁰ *Ibid.*, p. 31.

⁶¹ Florence May, *The Life of Johannes Brahms,* I, p. 9.

⁶² Niemann, *Brahms,* pp. 196-97.

⁶³ May, *Life of Brahms,* I, pp. 10-11.

⁶⁴ *Ibid.*, I, p. 12.

⁶⁵ Niemann, *Brahms,* p. 192.

⁶⁶ May, *Life of Brahms,* I, pp. 18-19.

⁶⁷ Cited in Niemann, *Brahms,* pp. 192-93.

⁶⁸ Eugenie Schumann, *The Schumanns and Brahms,* pp. 141-47.

12.

The Beginnings of Modern Technical Methods

The great performers and teachers from the harpsichord-clavichord and the early piano periods favored a close finger technique and minimal use of the arms and body. Such a state was highly desirable, and even necessary, on the early instruments with their easy actions and limited tonal powers. An autonomous independence in all the fingers, could largely meet the demands of both music and instruments. Yet a premium was placed upon a condition of freedom, of suppleness and elasticity, of smoothness and fluency. Men like Couperin and Rameau, J.S. Bach and his son Carl Philipp Emanuel, Mozart, and even Hummel and Czerny undoubtedly did not give a second thought to the validity of the modest, natural usage of the arm when needed.

It is therefore unfortunate that, as the piano in the early nineteenth century began gradually to augment its power and correspondingly increase the heaviness of its touch, its technique did not also evolve naturally to meet the new demands placed upon it. The great natural performers, such as Beethoven, Chopin, Mendelssohn, Liszt, Anton Rubinstein, and even Clara Schumann, with their transcendental keyboard abilities instinctively kept pace and became the prime examples of enlightened piano technique. But many of the descendants of the finger school, a legitimate group during the baroque and early classic days, resisted the new technique. They became more and more entrenched in their "finger dancing," as Beethoven termed it, as the century wore on. They fed upon the technical systems of Hummel, Kalkbrenner, Czerny and company, not without some merit if taken in moderation, but too conducive to the development of a high finger action, excessive fixations in the joints, and a superficial musical

229

expression. Little thought was given to efficient muscular coordination.

By mid-century many of the European conservatories, particularly the German ones epitomized by the Lebert-Stark school at Stuttgart, were teaching this reactionary percussive, stiff arm technique. It is difficult to understand how so many of the instructors of the period could be so blinded to the physical and musical evils of their system and so little influenced by the freedom and abandon of a Liszt or Rubinstein performance or the more subtle arm pressure touch exhibited in Clara Schumann's playing. But perhaps there are obvious reasons when one considers, as Charles J. Haake pointed out, that

> . . . percussion touch was, as an entity, of more definite substance and form than a vague pressure playing, and method will always thrive on that that can be definitely projected and prescribed. Also, the touch was easily developed: when more force was required, as to play sixths or octaves, the hand moved at the wrist as a hinge; for bravura effects the elbow became the hinge, whereby we had a complete hinge method that used the arm to the elbow, but did not recognize the free arm as a fundamental condition for a good technic. [1]

Once this system was well established on the conservatory level, it became a thriving business proposition and tended to perpetuate itself.

Sigismund Lebert (1822-1884), who had studied with Tomaschek and Dionys Weber in Prague, and Ludwig Stark (1831-1884), educated in Munich, both Germans, were the principal founders of the Royal Conservatory at Stuttgart in the mid-1850s. It was several years in developing and assumed its official title in 1865. Lebert and Stark's *Grosse Klavierschule (Grand Theoretical and Practical Piano School for Systematic Instruction in all Branches of Piano Playing from the First Elements to the Highest Perfection)* in four volumes appeared first in 1856. The method advances by degrees—thirty-three *Artistic Etudes* by Liszt, Brahms, Moscheles, Theodor Kullak, and others comprise the final volume. It was so universally adopted and so well promoted that, when the fifth edition appeared about 1870, no less than nineteen written endorsements appeared in the introduction to the elementary book. Among these were commendations by Liszt, Marmontel of the Paris Conservatoire, Hiller from the Cologne Conservatory, and Moscheles from the Leipzig Conservatory. Liszt stated that "It educates real artists, not parisitical dabblers." [2] In their opening remarks, Lebert and Stark emphasized learning the classic literature from the Clementi sonatinas to the more difficult works of Beethoven and Bach, and the Chopin and Liszt Etudes. And technique, at least theoretically, was not separated from musicianship. They wrote:

By the term correct *technique* we mean the right formation of tone, that is, the ability to elicit from the instrument a beautiful, rich tone, whether forte or piano. . . . Besides the correct *touch,* however, which produces this artistic tone, and upon which alone depends the power to give it at pleasure any degree of power from *ff* to *pp,* an artistic technique also requires a melodious *legato,* together with its opposite, the *staccato,* and finally as much *execution* as is required for the faultless rendering of a work. [3]

But practice suggestions seemed to counteract such commendable goals:

At first, play every piece slowly and forte throughout; in the beginning observe only the principal shadings, the *legato* and *staccato* in their different forms, and not until the piece can be executed without a mistake notice the lesser signs of expression. By a study of this kind a firm style of playing will be obtained. [4]

With such mechanical directions, a "firm," rigid technique naturally developed. The basic technical instructions of the Lebert-Stark method—with its typical emphasis on outward position and movement—are herewith quoted.

POSITION OF THE ARM: The arm must hang down from the shoulder in a light and easy manner; the elbow must not be turned outward, but must point downward, in such a manner, that there is a distance of about one inch between the arm and the body. The piano-stool must be placed so that the elbow, wrist and hand form as nearly as possible a straight line. The arm must form a straight line with the hand, because, if it is held higher, we are apt to play with it, while, on the contrary, it should always be perfectly quiet. If the arm be held too low, the hand has not full control of its power.

Though we wish that the pupil should not acquire *technique* mechanically, but understandingly, and, therefore, advise the use of mechanical apparatus only in extreme cases, yet for the first technical exercises we consider the HAND—GUIDE of great use. When attached to the piano, it must be on a level with the white keys, and so far from the piano that

231

the wrist can rest upon it. By this we best fulfill the first requirement for legato playing, that is, a quiet position of the arm. All this refers to the arms, and not to the hand and wrist.

If the hand moves from the middle of the key-board in either direction, the fore-arm only must move it, while the elbow and upper arm should remain as near to the body as possible.

POSITION OF THE HAND: The hand must always be held, as it were, suspended above the keys, and in such a position that the fingers, after being rounded without bending in or stretching out, strike the MIDDLE of key with the tip, but never with the nail of the finger. The hand should be a little inclined towards the thumb, and in such a manner that the fingers strike from the same height, because only in such a position can they move independently and be made independent of each other. The thumb must be placed on the key only up to the root of the nail, lest the other fingers come in contact with the black keys.

MECHANISM OF THE PIANO: The mechanism of the piano, whose most important principle rests upon the rapid rising of the hammer from a fixed point, and the equally rapid falling back into its first position, requires a corresponding counter-action on the part of the hand. All the fingers must, on an average, be held firmly about one inch over the keys (this, of course, depends upon the size of the hand), strike rapidly and perpendicularly and just as rapidly return to their first position. This is the normal touch; its modifications (nearer or quite near the keys), as they will be required by the different character of pieces, can only be learned by personal instruction.[5]

Five-finger exercises are introduced, to be practiced at a *mezzo forte* level. A warning is given, but for most students it must have fallen on deaf ears:

If at the commencement the touch be too powerful, there is danger of its becoming hard. Care should, therefore, be taken in the beginning, that the tone be formed by the most rapid fall of the finger possible and without the least pressure. The strength will develop of itself with the gradual development of the independence and elasticity of the finger-joints. [6]

With the advocacy of a high finger action with a forte level of sound, pursued with German tenacity and soon labeled "Lebert's Touch," the finger school of technique became an overpowering reality. Maria Levinskaya described its dubious achievements:

From such teaching [the Lebert-Stark method] little more

232

than a parody on correct finger work could arise, the essence of which was endless finger grinding, striking with force, stiffening the wrist, producing a jar of the hand, the tone getting sharp and hard, without any possibility of the true binding or any mellow sound connection. [7]

Pianists went all out in their efforts to strengthen the fingers both at the keyboard and away from it. Kalkbrenner's Hand-guide was not the last appliance for the pianist's development. The Digitorium, invented by Myer Marks, was a six-inch square box equipped with five keys (in the small versions) which were regulated by strong springs. Three models provided three different degrees of resistance—the medium touch provided twelve ounces. Attached to the sides of the box were devices for supporting the wrist and for stretching the fingers. Toward the close of the nineteenth century an American invention by J. Brotherhood, the Technician, modeled itself after the Digitorium, but also allowed for strengthening the lifting finger. About the same time, A.K. Virgil's Tekniklavier came on the scene. It will be discussed in a later chapter. Throughout all of this time silent keyboards with standard resistance were employed.

Gymnastic exercises for the strengthening of the fingers without the aid of gadgetry were introduced as early as 1818 by A.E. Mueller and have continued to be used down to the present day. The first English collection appeared in 1874: *Gymnastics for the Fingers and Wrist* by E. Ward Jackson. Some of his exercises made use of cork cylinders held between the fingers and others with the finger tips resting on a notched stick. Gát said that Jackson had lectured on gymnastics in Budapest as early as 1864. [8] Other English proponents included Leffler Arnim (*Wrist and Finger Gymnastics*), Thomas Fielden, and Ridley Prentice. *Hand Gymnastics* by Prentice (1842-1895), who studied at the Royal Academy of Music under Walter Macfarren and later taught at the Guildhall School of Music in London, has had wide acceptance and is included in the Novello music primer series. Prentice organized his thirty-four exercises into six groupings or lessons with gymnastics for arm, wrist, hand, fingers and thumb included in each section. He emphasized the importance of deep breathing exercises for the pianist. Prentice's objective in the use of gymnastics was to strengthen and balance opposing sets of muscles. He wrote:

Now, it will be readily admitted that the keyboard has no pretensions to be a gymnastic apparatus suitable for this scientific training; it was not invented for any such purpose.

233

The player's hand and arm remain practically always in the same position [he seems to reflect the finger school's thinking], subject of course to innumerable slight changes, which do not however affect the argument. The set of muscles exercised is always the same. Here is at once a source of weakness. All motions of the limbs, all positions of the limbs, even in a state of rest, are the result of a balance between two opposing sets of muscles. If one set is strengthened unduly, the other set becomes too weak for its work, and gives way. In the great majority of cases where weakness is due to excessive practice it shows itself at the back of the hand and just above the wrist. . . . It is easy to perceive the vital importance to a pianist of an equal development of each set of muscles. [9]

Around the late 1880s the American W. Macdonald Smith wrote a pamphlet, *From Brain to Keyboard,* including gymnastics. Breithaupt mentioned similar German writing during the first decade of the twentieth century by Krizek, Gorter, and Schnee. Hungarian theorist József Gát, in *The Technique of Piano Playing* (1965), built a strong case for the use of gymnastics and included a number of them in his book. He also told of a work published in Budapest in 1897 by Anna Lukacs-Schuk entitled *Reform of Piano Teaching.* In it she relates how her grandfather, a medical doctor, had invented a series of hand gymnastics for her so that it would not be necessary to practice etudes for six hours a day. They improved her technique so much that Liszt, with whom she was studying, had his less-developed students work on hand gymnastics during the 1886-1887 season. [10] He told her:

In this way we will give striking proof of the supremacy of this new method, because I am convinced that less-developed pupils, taught by the new method, will soon surpass even the best pupils having been taught according to the old one. For now, we will keep the whole thing in secret and we will present it to the public only on the basis of facts and sure results because this is the only way to convince the stubbornness of the people of the old school, opposed to every innovation. [11]

Liszt's final verdict was not recorded. In recent years, Otto Ortmann has also admitted the validity of gymnastics. It would be interesting to experiment with modern isometrics to determine how much they would develop the piano playing muscles.

But let us return to the nineteenth century where equal finger development was unrealistically encouraged—notwithstanding inequities in the hand's natural structure. Charles Hanon (1820-1900), the French pianist who composed *Le Pianiste Virtuoso,* encouraged all who would faithfully practice his exercises with the fond hope that "If all five fingers of the hand were absolutely equally well trained, they would be ready to execute anything written for the instrument, and the only question remaining would be that of fingering, which would be readily solved." [12] Disillusion and frustration were the lot of the average conservatory student. The fingers, held in a sharply bent, "cropped" position with the bridge of the hand quite level with the wrist, were lifted high in unceasing vigorous repetition. As fingers tried to take over much of

The Correct Position of the Hand and Fingers

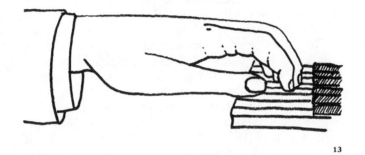

13

the work of the arms in the more sonorous literature of the romantic period, fatigue came quickly along with tension and rigidity in the wrists and arms. C.A. Ehrenfechter, the English disciple of Deppe, observed that "Several young students at Stuttgart lost the use of the third finger through overstraining it." [14] Since forte finger development came first, these newly acquired tensions were carried over into later practice of chords and octaves where the arms did participate. Such a cold mechanical approach was bound to destroy or, at the least, inhibit free musical expression. After four years in Europe, Amy Fay appraised the conservatory situation in 1873 and came to the conclusion that "The grand thing is to have each of your five fingers go 'dum dum' an equal number of times." Then she pinpointed Stuttgart as the place to go "to get the machine in working order." [15] When she arrived in Europe and began her study under Ehlert at Tausig's Conservatory in Berlin, she quickly received this same kind of indoctrination:

You have no idea how hard they make Cramer's Studies here. Ehlert makes me play them tremendously *forte,* and as fast as I can go. My hand gets so tired that it is ready to break,

235

and then I say that I cannot go on. "But you *must* go on," he will say. It is the same with the scales. It seems to me that I play them so loud that I make the welkin ring, and he will say, "But you play always *piano*." And with all this rapidity he does not allow a note to be missed, and if you happen to strike a wrong one he looks so shocked that you feel ready to sink into the floor. [16]

Existing alongside the finger extremists, and at times even among them, were the early proponents of a more complete technique. They took into account the advancing instrument and its musical capabilities and physical demands. The first major pioneer teacher of an effective system combining both arm and finger technique was Ludwig Deppe (1828-1890). Others in company with Deppe who will be given brief prior consideration here are William Mason, Adolph Bernhard Marx, and Adolph Kullak. They were preceded by a lineage of pianists that could be loosely grouped into a so-called pressure school pointing in the direction of weight playing. Among this number, which acknowledged the legitimacy of an arm pressure touch, were previously discussed performers such as Hummel, Adam, Kalkbrenner, de Kontski, Thalberg, Wieck, and Clara Schumann.

William Mason (1829-1908) seems to have been the first original thinker in America in the area of piano technique. He gave his debut recital in Boston in 1846 where he studied with an obscure pianist by the name of Henry Schmidt. In his autobiography, Mason detailed a type of finger touch taught to him by Schmidt, which he felt greatly reduced fatigue and promoted endurance. Later he came to the conclusion that it was quite similar to J.S. Bach's finger touch as described by Forkel. Here is Mason's explanation:

> The touch is accomplished by quickly but quietly drawing the finger-tips inward toward the palm of the hand, or, in other words, slightly and partly closing the finger-points as they touch the keys while playing. This action of the fingers secures the cooperation of many more muscles of the finger, wrist, hand, and forearm than could be accomplished by the merely "up-and-down" finger touch. It is difficult to describe in detail without an instrument at hand for illustration. If correctly performed, however, the tones produced are very clear and well defined, and of a beautifully musical quality. The simile of "a string of pearls" of precisely similar size and shape has often been used in describing their fluency and clearness of outline. A too rapid withdrawal of the finger-tips

236

would result in a short and crisp staccato. While this extreme staccato is also desirable and frequently used, it is not the kind of effect here desired, namely, a clear, clean delivery of the tones which in no wise disturb the legato effect.

Of course it requires the cultivation and skill to secure just the right degree of finger-motion to preserve the legato and at the same time the slight separation of each tone. Therefore the fingers must not be drawn so quickly as to produce a separation or staccato effect, but in just the right degree to avoid impairing the legato or binding effect. For the sake of convenience in description I have named this touch the "elastic finger-touch," and through its influence a clear and crisp effect is attained. . . . While it has relation solely to finger action as distinguished from the action of the wrist and arm, it cannot be accomplished properly without bringing into action the flexor and extensor muscles, principally of the forearm from wrist to elbow.

Through the medium of this touch pianissimo effects are possible which no other mechanism can reach, for passages of the most extreme delicacy and softness still retain the quality of vitality and clearness of outline. [17]

This is analytical writing foreshadowing the work of the great twentieth century theorists. Mason was intrigued by the role of the upper arms and shoulders and began to make observations on his own. When Leopold de Meyer (1816-1883), Austrian virtuoso and former student of Czerny, came to the United States on tour in 1847-48, Mason thoroughly analyzed his style:

It was from a careful study of the manner of his playing that I first acquired the habit of fully devitalized upper-arm muscles in pianoforte-playing. The loveliness and charming musical beauty of his tones, the product of these conditions, greatly excited my admiration and fascinated me. I never missed an opportunity of hearing him play, and closely watched his movements, and particularly the motions of hand, arm, and shoulder. I was incessantly at the pianoforte trying to produce the same delightful tone quality by imitating his manner and style.

My continued perserverance was rewarded with success, for the result was a habit of devitalized muscular action in such degree that I could practically play all day without a feeling of fatigue. The constant alternation between devitalization and reconstruction keeps the muscles always fresh for their work and enables the player to rest while playing. The force is so distributed that each and every muscle has ample opportunity to rest while yet in a state of activity. Furthermore the tones resulting from this touch are sonorous and full of energy and life. An idea of my own which was persistently carried into action aided materially in bringing about the desired result. This was to allow the arms to hang limp by my side, either in a sitting or standing posture, and then to shake them vigorously with the utmost possible looseness and devitalization. This device was in after years recommended to my pupils, and those who persistently followed it up and persevered for a while gained great advantage from it, and eventually acquired a state of habitual muscular elasticity and flexibility. [18]

When Mason went to Europe shortly thereafter he encountered the typical finger and wrist action teaching. Before he went to Liszt, he studied under Dreyschock and reacted in this manner:

At the time of which I write (1849-1850) very little seems to have been known [in Europe] of the important influence of the upper-arm muscles and their very efficient agency, when properly employed in the production of tone-quality and volume by means of increased relaxation, elasticity, and springiness in their movements.

I received considerably over one hundred lessons from Dreyschock, and with slow and rapid scale and arpeggio practice his instruction had special reference to limber and flexible wrists, his distinguishing feature being his wonderful octave-playing. Beyond the wrists, however, the other arm muscles received practically little or no attention, and the fact is that during my whole stay abroad none of my teachers or their pupils, with many of whom I was intimately associated, seemed to know anything about the importance of the upper-arm muscles, the practical knowledge of which I had acquired through the playing of Leopold de Meyer. . . . In the Tomaschek method, as taught and practised by Dreyschock, the direction to the pupil was simply to keep the wrists loose. To be sure, this could not be altogether accomplished without some degree of arm-limberness, but no specific directions were given for cultivating the latter. [19]

After study under Liszt, Mason returned to America in 1854 and settled in New York City where he was a vital influence on the musical scene for fifty years — teaching, performing, and promoting musical events. He and Theodore Thomas were among those who began chamber music concerts during the year of Mason's arrival. From the very beginning of his piano teaching in New York, he laid considerable emphasis on accentual treatment of technical practice. He related an anecdote as to how this first came about:

In 1855 I accepted as pupils some four or five young ladies who were being educated at a fashionable boarding-school in New York. One of these girls was very bright and intelligent but without special musical talent. She was extremely averse to application in study, and the problem for me was to invent some way by which mental concentration could be compelled, for from the moment she sat down to the piano to practise she was constantly looking at the clock to see if her practice-hour was up. After a little study I found that in playing a scale up one octave and back, without intermission, in 9/8 time, there are necessarily nine repetitions of the scale before the initial tone falls again on the first part of the measure. . . . Such an exercise is called a rhythmus, and the repetitions compel mental concentration just as surely as the addition of a column of figures does. I found that if the compass was extended four octaves . . . [two octaves on either side of middle C], the nine repetitions of the scale would require from three to four minutes if played at a moderate rate of speed. I saw at once that a state of mental concentration could not be avoided by the pupil, and that in this exercise lay a basic principle. I gave the exercise to my pupil. The result was that when the next lesson-hour came around and I asked her how she found the new exercise, she exclaimed: "How do I like it? Why, you have played a pretty trick on me! It took me nearly an hour to accomplish it; but I like it. Why did you not give it to me before?" "Because," I said, "I invented it simply in order to compel your attention to your work." Following up the principle of grouping the tones, I applied the rhythmic process not only to all sorts of scale passages but included in the treatment arpeggios, broken chords, octaves, and in fact all passages idiomatic of the pianoforte. The work of amplification was readily accomplished, and the result was a complete method in which for the first time, so far as I am aware, scientific rhythmic treatment was elaborated. This "Accentual Treatment of Exercises," as I called the system, was first published in the Mason & Hoadley Method, New York, 1867. [20]

After expanding these concepts for some years in his teaching, Mason in 1889 finally published another more important method book entitled *Touch and Technic; or, The Technic of Artistic Touch by Means of the Two-Finger Exercise,* a work widely used in America for many years. He credited Liszt with the original idea that the two-finger drill, going up and down either the diatonic or chromatic scales in two note phrase groups (CD DE EF FG etc.) using adjacent fingertips (12 12 12 etc., then 23 23 23 etc. and finally 34 and 45), was the basic form of technical practice. Similar suggestions go back to C.P.E. Bach, who considered the trill the foundation exercise. Liszt's revelation to Mason came about as the result of a conversation with Mason's fellow students at Weimar:

One day the boys were discussing the subject of mechanical technic and wishing for some little *"multum in parvo"* exercise, which should be so comprehensive and far-reaching in its results as to do away with a multiplicity of exercises, and acting like magic, accomplish the whole thing *instanter* and thus obviate the necessity of slow plodding. They finally referred the matter to Liszt, and his reply was that inasmuch as all pianoforte pieces consisted of scale, arpeggio, chord, and octave passages, the practice of these could never be wholly dispensed with; but, he continued, "of all exercises of which I have knowledge, for stimulating, strengthening, and limbering the fingers, this simple little exercise is the most effective." He went to the piano and played the two-finger exercise . . . "You know," he continued, "that I have given up my concerts and public playing, but when occasionally I do play in private for my friends and feel the need of preparation, I practice this exercise solely and for two or three hours uninterruptedly. As a result I regain my full technic without practice of anything else, either exercise or piece." [21]

In *Touch and Technic,* Vol. I, the two-finger exercises, to be transposed into all of the keys, are applied first to the diatonic major scale and following that to the diatonic broken thirds, diatonic double thirds, chromatic scale, black key pattern, diminished seventh chord, diatonic sixths, and finally octaves. Also included are exercises for two, three, and four fingers using trills, mordents and inverted mordents. Two basic accents are used: those with the first note of the two-note phrase group always accented and those with the second note receiving the emphasis.

Mason presented a description of various types of finger, hand, and arm actions to be used in the practice of these two-finger exercises. His ideas on relaxation and appropriate muscular contraction with its timing to the point of tone anticipated the work of Matthay and Ortmann. And in opposition to Breithaupt and his followers, Mason maintained a more independent, articulate finger action without denying simultaneous arm participation. Although he called for an overly high finger action in slow practice, he was concerned about avoiding the stiffening of wrist and arm.

He named three types of finger touch: the Clinging Legato, the Finger Elastic, and the Plain Legato, and suggested that the first two be practiced in alternation in the two-note phrase groups. Mason's descriptions of these touches is given in the following quotes from *Touch and Technic:*

The clinging legato is by reason of its nature a foundation touch and "built upon a rock," so to speak. This expression, "built upon a rock," is not intended to convey any idea of rigidity, hardness, or stiffness in the touch, but, distinctly differing from that, it signifies stability, strength, repose. If applied in the right way the result will be a tone which is full, warm, and pervasive. The finger falls upon the key with decision, but free from rigidity—settles down upon it with a sense of having come to stay. This steady, continued, though never rigid pressure is transferred at exactly the proper time to another key through the agency of another finger. In this way the tones are bound together, and, as it were, melt into each other, as expressed by the *legato,* signifying to bind. Each key must be held with moderate pressure and without rigidity throughout the full time-value of the tones as indicated by the notes, but not one instant longer. [22]

The elastic touch, also a fundamental form, is the direct antithesis of the clinging legato, inasmuch as in its performance the finger takes the key while "on the wing," so to speak; that is, the finger strikes and sweeps the key while in the act of flexion, or in pulling toward and closing up to the hand. . . . The tone produced by this touch has a buoyancy, lightness, and flexibility which is enlivening and exhilarating. The tones float and rebound, as it were, and are not dull, colorless, or monotonous. [23]

The legato, called also *plain* legato, is the standard and staple touch for ordinary and general use. It closely resembles the clinging legato, but in the latter touch the pressure always exceeds the natural power of the fingers, drawing somewhat from the arm, whereas in the plain legato this is not the case, but the required strength comes from the fingers alone. The clinging legato is especially adapted to the bringing or pressing out of a full and sonorous tone in the performance of melodies. . . . The legato is applicable to the accompaniments of melodies as well as to all varieties of scale and arpeggio passages.

In the clinging legato and elastic touches the exertion is considerable, being such as is proper in earnest and somewhat impassioned playing only. In order to counteract the

Two finger exercises. Diatonic Scale.

Exercise № 1. First slow form. *The clinging legato touch.* See Sections 14 & 15

For the sake of abbreviation the exercises which follow are written out on the right hand part of the staff.
The left hand plays uniformly one octave below the right, beginning on c of the small octave. Fingering above the notes for the right hand and below for the left.

№ 2. Second slow form. *Rhythm I. Clinging legato touch and Elastic touch in alternation.*

See Secs. 16 & 17

№ 3. Second slow form. *Rhythm II.* See Secs. 16 & 17

To avoid crowding the plates the application of the other three pairs of fingers is here omitted, but on no account must they be neglected in practice. See Sec. 10.

№ 4. First moderato form. *Rhythm I.* See Secs. 18 & 19

Caution. Be careful to give the rests their entire value in both exercises, Nos. 4 and 5.

№ 5. First moderato form. *Rhythm II.* See Secs. 18 & 19

№ 6. Second moderato form. *Rhythm I.* See Secs. 18 & 19

№ 7. Second moderato form. *Rhythm II.* See Secs. 18 & 19

242

MATERIAL.

No. 8. First fast form. *Rhythm I. Acc. of 8*   Secs. 18 & 19.

No. 9. First fast form. *Rhythm II. Acc. of 8*   Secs. 18 & 19.

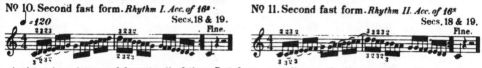

Practise all of these and the following forms a part of the time with the Mild Staccato touch exclusively. See Sec. 15, and the outline cut at the end of that Section. Do not neglect the Legato touch.

No. 10. Second fast form. *Rhythm I. Acc. of 16*   Secs. 18 & 19.

No. 11. Second fast form. *Rhythm II. Acc. of 16*   Secs. 18 & 19.

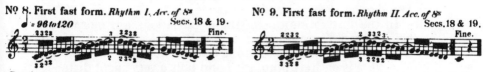

Apply various degrees of force to all of these Fast forms, as well as to the Moderato forms. Play many times in succession forte; then many times mezzo; afterwards piano, and finally pianissimo, as delicately as consistent with clearness, accuracy and precision.

No. 12. Third fast form. *Rhythm I. Acc. of 12*   Secs. 18 & 19.

Another very useful way of practising is to make a well-graded, and continous crescendo throughout the ascending passage and a corresponding diminuendo in descending. Do not hurry the time while making the crescendo. Give equal attention to the Legato, and to the Mild Staccato touches.

Play rapidly, lightly and delicately; also with uniform distinctness and elasticity of touch, but with an unmistakable accent on the first part of each measure.

No. 13. Third fast form. *Rhythm II. Acc. of 12*   Secs. 18 & 19.

No. 14. Triple measure.   **No. 15. Compound double measure.**   **No. 16. Compound triple measure.**

Triple measure combines both Rhythms I and II. Likewise Compound double, and Compound triple measure.

William Mason, *Touch and Technic*, I, pp. 21, 22.

243

one-sided influence which would result from the exclusive use of this method of practice, the light and fast forms will be found to be of very great importance.

In the fast forms the rhythmic pulsations are more than twice as rapid as in the forms already given, and each pair of tones is played as if constituting a single word of two syllables. The wrist is entirely limp, the hand falls a very slight distance upon the first tone of every alternate pair, and the second or every fourth tone is played with the least possible finger motion, with a slight drawing inward of the point of the finger on leaving the key. The value of this exercise does not turn upon the amplitude or intensity of the motions, but upon their clearness, quickness, flexibility, and lightness.

The fingers, instead of being raised high, as in the slow forms, must be held close to the keys in order to favor rapidity of motion, for there is not time for superfluous motion in a degree of speed which is hardly exceeded by the quickness of thought. [24]

Mason's teaching of the hand touch cautioned against the typical rigid and isolated condition of the arm so prevalent in his day:

In the free-hand touch the hand moves upon the wrist with extreme pliancy, the finger delivering the force to the keys. Contrary to the usual teaching of elementary books of technic, the impulse which comes to expression through the hand motion has its origin further back in the arm, and can never be correctly or effectively expressed by a motion entirely localized in the hand. If, for example, the hand be laid in the lap, and while the forearm remains entirely quiet the hand be moved upward and downward, we have the type of hand touch which is often taught as the correct method of playing chords and octaves. This peculiar touch doubtless contributes in some degree to facile wrist motion, but it is not in accordance with the mechanism of artists in playing chords and octaves. The true touch . . . has its origin further back in the arm. [25]

In analyzing arm participation, he dealt with the roles of specific muscles such as the biceps and the triceps:

The highest service which the proper use of the triceps [extensor muscle at the back of the upper arm] renders is in the capacity of a guide, for its influence quickly "leavens the whole lump" of the muscular system; it penetrates, pervades, and vitalizes the entire action, and accomplishes more in bulk and in detail in the development of a *temperamental* touch than is possible in any other way. Under its influence the

244

feeling of restraint, common to most players at a certain stage, is quickly counteracted and overcome, and a sense of suppleness, ease, and repose takes its place. Playing ceases to be a labor and becomes a source of joy. The relaxed and limber condition of the muscles affords a sense of exhilaration, and the whole muscular movement is characterized by a freedom of action which is suggestive of the flight of a bird.

As applied to the "Clinging Legato" touch, the triceps is exceedingly useful when that touch, as is commonly the case, draws upon the arm for the elastic quality; also in all forms of the up-arm touch and generally in all cantabile passages where the tone is produced without preliminary raising of the fingers; also in all tones produced by a springing motion in a direction backward from the keys, the finger-points having at the moment of beginning the touch been in actual contact with the keys.

It is the neglect of this entire class of touches (of the arm) which renders the technic developed solely by finger-falls so dry, inoperative, and unsatisfactory as concerns character. It is desirable that the pupil should become familiar with this element in touch very early in the course of instruction. [26]

The exercise below is one which Mason suggests for a relaxed arm, making use of a free swinging arm and hand:

[27]

The impulse for every group of notes should be from the upper arm. That he saw the relationship between relaxation and contraction is evident from his further instruction:

In accenting the first tone of each group there will necessarily be a slight muscular contraction in the tip of the finger which falls upon the key. Muscular relaxation instantaneously follows, and is again succeeded by muscular reconstruction in time for the next group. In the same manner, play the fast two-finger exercises. [28]

A novel study from *Touch and Technic,* Vol. IV, illustrates Mason's concern for developing a highly refined tonal control through the use of the arm touch. This little pedal study makes use of only one finger and demands the careful differentiation of melody and accompaniment and the delicate control of crescendos and diminuendos:

29

Mason's nephew, Daniel Gregory Mason, remembered particularly his musicianship as revealed in his tone and touch at the keyboard:

His own piano playing was in itself an unforgettable musical experience. His rich and at the same time discriminating sensuous feeling voiced itself in the most exquisite piano touch I have ever heard. His way of bringing out the tone by pressing rather than striking the keys made the whole tissue of his melodies literally "sing." All the ornamental work was done with a delicious evenness and lightness that perfectly subordinated it to the more sonorous voices (in such things for instance as the Chopin etudes, preludes, and nocturnes). Never have I heard him bring a harsh or hard tone from the piano. Of course the style of the piano music of his prime was more ornamental than we like today, and his playing naturally had much of the "string of pearls" quality—but was ever string so smooth, were ever pearls more lustrous and opalescent!"

Nor was the beauty of his playing merely the sensuous beauty of the touch; he was too good a musician to neglect the higher beauty of proportionate light and shade. To hear him play his little One-finger Study was an illumination of piano art. The one finger with which it was played was far subtler than the "melodious fore-finger" so delightfully championed in Stevenson's letters. It had to create and carry, by its varying touches, three separate tonal lines, on three distinct planes: the singing melody in the foreground, the hardly less singing bass slightly behind it, and in the background the more neutral accompanying tones. How exquisitely he guarded the clarity of each of the three lines, yet merged them all in harmony together! I can see him yet, as he would sit at his Steinway grand with his rather rounded shoulders and his air of complete relaxation, his head bent to listen and his usually prominent eyes veiled in concentration, producing with his short unerring finger the deliciously adjusted sonorities. [30]

In Germany, the works of Adolph Marx (1795-1866) were written a few years prior to Mason's first method book of 1867. Marx, who studied with Türk (who in turn had worked under J.S. Bach's pupil Homilius), was both composer and musical scholar. Like Schumann, he began his career as a lawyer and later founded a musical journal, the *Berliner Allgemeine musikalische Zeitung*. His views on piano technique are incidentally included within such aesthetic and analytical volumes as *The Music of the Nineteenth Century* (1855), *Interpretation of Beethoven* (1863), and a preface to *A Selection from Sebastian Bach's Compositions*. To Marx, a piano virtuoso's technique is meaningless if it does not exist to portray the deep inner meaning of the music itself. Marx also felt that a superficial finger equality is inadequate for the projection of an expressive melody line. He spoke of a weighted tone when he wrote:

> In significant melodies there are decisive single moments in which single notes have to be brought out like outstanding lights (Lichtpunkte). Here the opposition to co-operation and equality of the fingers becomes a necessity. Each finger must be "individualized" to be able to transfer through its own nervous energy a different expression to each sound. . . .
> In polyphony although the principal voice should stand out and the accompanying one made subordinate to it, nevertheless, the due amount of weight must not be allowed to be sacrificed. [31]

A fusion of musical feeling and appropriate technical means is a necessity. Marx explained:

> . . . each finger must be able to seize the emotional tone by itself, with the requisite degree of tenderness in accentuation, of individualization, or of melting into the next tone—must, as it were, have a soul and independent life of its own, to conduct through its nerve the soul of the player to the key. For

as the pianoforte is inferior to bowed and wind instruments in melodic power, as regards the blending of tones and their gradation in volume, much more may be achieved than one usually hears or believes, if the key be touched gently and caressingly, not dabbed at or struck; if the finger lay hold of it with intelligence, so to speak; if even extreme power be not expressed in rough blows, but issue from the native power of the musical conception. The key must be felt, not pushed or struck, it must be seized with feeling, as one presses a friend's hand only with sympathy—both in moments of mightiest and of tenderest agitation—otherwise the poetry of Bach and Beethoven can never attain full utterance. [32]

Marx's sensitive musical insight was passed along to two of his pupils, Ludwig Deppe and Adolph Kullak (1823-1862), both fine, gifted musicians. Kullak was a music critic who also taught for a period at his brother's conservatory in Berlin, founded in 1855 as the Neue Akademie der Tonkunst. Theodor Kullak (1818-1882), thorough and conscientious, was considered by Liszt to be one of the best of the conservatory piano teachers, along with Carl Reinecke (1824-1910) from the Leipzig Conservatory. Theodor Kullak was a rather dry technician and is remembered for his *School of Octave Playing.* Adolph Kullak was the author of *The Art of Touch* (1855), *The Musically Beautiful* (1858), and *The Aesthetics of Piano Playing* (1860), all of which deserve to be better known. He, too, advocated both finger and arm activity as the music demanded. In legato passage work he felt there was need of a quiet hand with independent finger action for these reasons given in *The Art of Touch,* which he dedicated to Franz Liszt:

Firstly, because the piano, thanks to the shortness of its tone, depends mostly on passage work.

Secondly, because nothing is for the pianist of greater importance than legato passage playing, and everything else is built on this foundation.

Thirdly, that the pianist's efficiency should be judged by his legato.

And lastly, that the lack of it in early training always shows itself afterwards. [33]

But in the same volume he also saw the need of more than pure fingers in portato-like passages:

. . . the lifting of the fingers is done with the help of the hand, and when more intense expression is required then even the help of the whole arm is brought into play. . . . In majestic parts this will automatically transform itself into a swinging elevation (Emporheben) of the arm. . . . Often the whole power of the arm is required to influence the tone production, supported by the wrist and fingers. [34]

In his emphasis on melody playing, secured through forearm participation and a flexible wrist, Adolph Kullak echoed his teacher Marx's sentiments in these selected passages from *The Aesthetics of Piano Playing,* an exhaustive work:

. . . But in the singing touch the pressure takes the front rank in the mechanical action. Formerly the down-stroke was the characteristic feature; now it is the downward pressure. The hammer-stroke on the string was then produced by a stroke; now it is caused by a firm, short, close pressure on the key. The falling finger has a dashing, striking effect; a pressing finger has, firstly, in its feeling a more intimate relation to the key, and secondly, the predominance of pressure takes something of its hard, rough peculiarity from the stroke of the hammer. One can say, that a *part* at least of the sharp and thin-toned principle of percussion is obviated thereby.

The finger-tip, as the point chiefly engaged, requires long practice to gain the necessary strength; for the exertion of the finger is here a very peculiar one. In less motion greater strength must be manifested; the tone must be louder, while the outward activity of the finger is restricted. Just as expression is a matter of hidden psychic feeling, the technique of melody, too, resides mainly in the nerve-power of the fingers. Hence the advice of idealistic teachers: "One should press the key as one grasps the hand of a friend, with warmth, with feeling. . . . " [35]

The same wrist movements may be applied with brilliant success to that singing tone, produced by pressure, in which a legato is effected by different fingers. To begin with, all the scales should be practiced with the normal fingering, and raising the wrist for each touch, lowering it again, of course, while the tone is holding. Next, practice with the movements reversed, sinking for the touch and rising during the hold. Further, study the scale of C-major, for example, with a drop of the wrist on *c,* a rise at *d,* a drop at *e,* and so on. Let it be the aim of study, that each finger shall be practiced both with the rise and the drop in all positions on the keys; and that perfect lightness of wrist-play will be attained, which not only insures the best binding touch of the finger in the legato, but is also retroactively of essential benefit to the style of hand-technique previously discussed. The treatment of the melody-note demands full freedom from all constraint of form, which is unattainable with a rigid wrist. Study all varieties here mentioned, choose from these according to the individuality of the passage, and add new features whenever it may appear needful. Throughout, pressure without stroke is a *conditio sine qua non*. A cooperation of the lifting and sinking of the back of the hand with the forms of striking-technique is likewise useful under certain circumstances; but more so for the reason, that the mechanical practice should, on principle, include all forms. [36]

As long as the fingers execute a pearling legato, the cooperation of the arm is not allowable. Should it take place, the evenness and independence of the finger-strokes would be lost. It is, however, a different matter with separate long-sustained series of singing tones or accents not gliding on in unbroken flow. Here the weight of the arm aids the pressure of the fingers and augments the singing tone. This occurs most often with singing notes in the modern style, where they are to penetrate through a full figurate accompaniment, and are held long. The gesture unconsciously follows the impulse of the thought. As already remarked in speaking of melody, expression is outwardly symbolized in the feeling of pressure. Moreover, the wrist unconsciously rises higher while holding the important note, and together with the arm presses down on the finger-tip.—Externally and internally a co-operation of the whole nervous playing apparatus is involved, which exercises a delicate influence on the production of tone. A series of tones thus played will be distinguished by softness, fulness, and melting melody.—But not only singing notes in the modern sense call for this treatment, but all notes of deep, soulful expression, and a simply figurated chorale by Bach will often afford ample opportunity for the same.—In fugue-playing it is, of course, still more frequently employed.

Such is the influence of the arm on the finger-stroke, the chief agent. Its working, though sensible, was still invisible. [37]

Following this discussion, Kullak went on to describe the more visible movements of the forearm and the full arm.

We come now to the central figure of this chapter. Although he wrote very little compared to Kullak, Ludwig Deppe is better known. The literary efforts of his pupils have propagated his teachings. Amy Fay came to him in Berlin in December of 1873 following study with Liszt, Tausig, and Theodor Kullak; she was so impressed by what he had to offer her technically that she wrote home on January 2, 1874:

Ah, if I had only studied with Deppe before I went to

Weimar! When I was there I didn't play half as often to Liszt as I might have done, kind and encouraging as he always was to me, for I always felt I wasn't *worthy* to be *his* pupil! But if I had known Deppe four years ago, what might I not have been now? After I took my first lesson of Deppe this thought made me perfectly wretched. I felt so dreadfully that I cried and cried. When I woke up in the morning I began to cry again. I was so afflicted that at last my landlady, who is very kind and sympathetic, asked me what ailed me. I told her I felt so dreadfully to think I had met the person I ought to have met four years ago, at the last minute, so.—"On the contrary, you ought to rejoice that you have met him *at all*," said she. "Many persons go through life without ever meeting the person they wish to, or they don't know him when they do." [38]

She had observed Kapellmeister Deppe a number of times at orchestral concerts. At least at that time, he was better known as a conductor than as a piano teacher. In fact, he applied the relevant principles of violin playing to piano technique. Before settling in Berlin, Deppe had studied with Marx in Hamburg and also conducted there.

Their first meeting took place at a musical party and it was another American pianist, William Sherwood (1854-1911), who introduced her. After also studying with Liszt, Kullak, and Deppe, he returned to the United States in 1876 to become one of America's foremost pianists. In 1897, he founded the Sherwood Music School in Chicago.

After hearing her play, Deppe told Amy Fay, as she relates,

. . . that my difficulties were principally mechanical ones— that I had conception and style, but that my execution was uneven and hurried, my wrist stiff, the third and fourth fingers (in German, the fourth and fifth) very weak, the tone not full and round enough, that I did not know how to use the pedal, and finally, that I was too nervous and flurried. [39]

He made her lay aside the program she had been planning to give in Berlin under Kullak's auspices, return to basic exercises in order to work out his technical principles, and practice only slowly for some months. She observed at once that he was against high finger lifting because

. . . it makes a *knick* in the muscle, and you get all the strength simply from the finger, whereas, when you lift the finger moderately high, the muscle from the whole arm comes to bear upon it. Lifting the finger so very high, and striking with force, stiffens the wrist, and produces a slight jar in the

251

hand which cuts off the singing quality of the tone, like closing the mouth suddenly in singing. It produces the effect of a blow upon the key, and the tone is more a sharp, quick tone; whereas, by letting the finger just fall—it is fuller, less loud, but more penetrating. [40]

He also emphasized that a higher finger action interferes with a perfect legato.

With the technical teachings of Ludwig Deppe we come to the true beginnings of the modern era of piano technique. In 1885, Deppe had published in the *Deutsche Musiker-Zeitung* an article entitled *Armleiden des Klavierspielers* ("Ailments of the Arm among Pianists"). In it he bemoaned the low level of musical performance and the lack of teaching which helped the student avoid strains and tensions. He also stated that he was planning to publish a large volume of piano studies including, not only finger exercises, but also those for "strengthening the shoulder and arm muscles." [41] He made similar comment to Amy Fay as far back as 1873:

At the first conversation I had with Deppe in Berlin, he told me that it was his object to establish a school of Piano-playing, and surprised me very much by saying that up to the present day, no school of Piano-playing has existed. What he meant to say was, that in Piano-playing no particular way of doing anything had ever been decided upon, and recognized as the true method, as has been the case in singing, and in playing the Violin. . . . But when it comes to the Piano, there are no fixed laws, and each teacher goes his own way. Now there is no reason why there should not be a logically developed system for forming a fine Piano *technique,* which, if rightly followed out will enable the player to obtain the results he aims at. This Deppe claims to have done, and fourteen years of constant teachings of his ideas has only increased their value in my opinion, and I wish that all teachers would examine them. [42]

Unfortunately Deppe died before his study material with its accompanying technical explanations was formalized and published. However, in this his only presentation which reached print, Deppe attempted to show ways in which his individual approach to teaching differed from the mediocre teaching he observed about him. Most of Deppe's short essay is reproduced herewith:

In my opinion the principal reason for the frequently occurring arm strain in pianists is the seat at the instrument being too high.

252

The pianist should sit so that the forearm from the elbow to the wrist will be slightly raised—in this way the hand will remain free from any oppressive influence of the elbow and the horizontal scale movements can be easily accomplished.

In response to this statement, most pianists will immediately raise the question: "How then, when one is sitting so low, can fullness of tone be brought out. One cannot properly strike the keys in this manner."

But this is precisely the point where my teaching method begins. Primarily it was the desire for artistic results that led me to this conclusion. However, I was overjoyed to discover that there were physical benefits as well. In all of my years of teaching I have only encountered one case of overstraining the hand and that was definitely caused by negligence to maintain a proper seat level combined with continuous, forced practicing.

My tone production does not develop through striking, but solely through the weight of the hand, through simple movements of lifting and falling, with quiet, relaxed fingers. The tone produced in this manner is not only more refined, but also more intense in character, resulting in a more penetrating sound than the one which is struck. The former tone does not come about through more or less forced, nerve-irritating muscle action; it forms itself much more in complete repose, without any inner or outer excitement—so to speak—"with conscious unconsciousness."

Even a player of moderate talent, if he has made this discipline of mind and hands his own, will be capable of accomplishments which earlier had seemed impossible to him.

The lower seat undoubtedly is to be preferred for one's physical well-being, since in effect it forces one to sit erect. Thereby nervous tension is averted. I would like to mention that a number of women students who were bothered with this condition found that it disappeared after lessons with me. These same students, until they came to me, had used a high seat. With the low seat, the entire body posture is freer and more attractive. For very industrious, energetic people a high seat can be especially harmful, particularly if, besides practicing the piano, they spend much time at a desk. The great majority of people who just play the piano for their enjoyment, it is true, run less of a risk.

Besides a few finger exercises, I also at the same time suggest exercises for strengthening the shoulder and arm muscles. In my previously mentioned major work on piano playing, these exercises are of course specifically presented with consideration of the anatomy of the torso.

Finally it should be mentioned that the seat which I have recommended will eliminate the unsightly, frequently seen external mannerisms—I mean the meaningless movements with the hands and certainly the motions of the elbows reminding one of the shoemaker's workshop.

The low seat, by the way, by no means requires an abnormally low chair; on the contrary, the matter can be corrected at once by elevating the legs of the piano just a few centimeters. [43]

Apart from this material which opposes the finger-hitting and tensions of the Lebert-Stark school and advocates free, relaxed tonal production, we must study Deppe's contributions through the summaries and observations of his followers. These included Amy Fay, Hermann Klose, C.A. Ehrenfechter, and Elisabeth Caland who said that he had shown her certain materials for his unpublished method book. What they have to say reveals, if imperfectly, a figure of genuine musical stature, one who is very much concerned about sensitive tone production while realizing that the whole body in all its complexity must be involved in an adequate technical system. That he was first a highly respected operatic and orchestral conductor and second a piano teacher no doubt aided him in gaining a much deeper insight than many a conservatory recluse had. From his vantage point on the podium, he was able to observe the technique of leading pianists who came to Berlin and draw his own conclusions. Deppe had a keen, analytical mind. He was also a musical idealist with the profoundest respect for Mozart and the classics.

Before accepting Amy Fay, he wanted her to observe the playing of one of his best students, an assistant—Fräulein Steiniger. In her technique, Amy observed:

There was a wonderful vitality, elasticity and *snap* to her chords which impressed me very much, and a unity of effect about her whole performance of any composition which I don't remember to have heard from the pupils of other masters. The position of the hand was exquisite, and all difficulties seemed to melt away like snow or to be surmounted with the greatest ease. I saw at a glance that Deppe is a magnificent teacher, and I believe that he has originated a school of his own. [44]

He seemed to generate such enthusiasm in his teaching that to her his "shabby little room" seemed like a "little Temple of Music." [45] She later summarized his teaching approach:

In my study with Kullak when I had any special difficulties,

254

he only said, "Practice always, Fräulein. *Time* will do it for you some day. Hold your hand any way that is easiest for you. You can do it in *this* way—or in *this* way"—showing me different positions of the hand in playing the troublesome passage—"or you can play it with the *back* of the hand if that will help you any!" But Deppe, instead of saying, "Oh, you'll get this after years of practice," shows me how to conquer the difficulty *now*. He takes a piece, and while he plays it with the most wonderful *fineness* of conception, he cold-bloodedly dissects the mechanical elements of it, separates them, and tells you how to use your hand so as to grasp them one after the other. In short, he makes the technique and the conception *identical,* as of course they ought to be, but I never had any other master who trained his pupils to attempt it.

Deppe also hears me play, I think, in the true way, and as Liszt used to do: that is, he never interrupts me in a piece, but lets me go through it from beginning to end, and *then* he picks out the places he has noted, and corrects or suggests. These suggestions are always something which are not simply for that piece alone, but which add to your whole artistic experience—a *principle,* so to speak. So, without meaning any disparagement to the splendid masters to whom I owe all my previous musical culture, I cannot help feeling that I have at last got into the hands not of a mere piano virtuoso, however great, but, rather, of a profound musical *savant*—a man who himself, has made such a study of the piano, that probably all pianists except Liszt might learn something from him. [46]

And when she watched him conduct, she wrote:

I love to see Deppe direct the orchestra when Steiniger plays a concerto of Mozart. His clear blue eyes dance in his head and look so sunny, and he stands so light on his feet that it seems as if he would dance off himself on the tips of his toes, with his baton in his hand! He is the incarnation of Mozart, just as Liszt and Joachim are of Beethoven, and Tausig was of Chopin. He has a marvellously delicate musical organization, and an instinct how things ought to be played which amounts to second sight. [47]

Deppe in his teaching placed strong emphasis upon the fundamental importance of proper functioning upper arm and shoulder muscles, something of which the early piano methods were scarcely aware. These muscles were not only involved in the exercising of free falling arm weight, but also in holding back that weight when the situation warranted it. Furthermore they were to

255

function in total harmony with the muscles of finger, hand, and forearm—these smaller muscles which had been so overworked by the high finger school and had been made to assume much of the upper arm's rightful activity. None were to engage in isolated activity. Elisabeth Caland (1862-1929) in her book, *Die Deppesche Lehre des Klavierspiels (Artistic Piano Playing as Taught by Ludwig Deppe),* called this condition "muscular synergy" (co-operation), the keystone of the arch in the Deppe approach. She used a quotation from *Esthétique du Mouvement* by Paul Souriau (1852-1926) to describe the total process:

> When we have to make an exertion of strength, *muscular synergy* is requisite in order to avoid fatigue. Not only do we spare ourselves, in this way, a painful sensation of strained effort, but we actually develop more of real energy. Force is not transmitted to the muscles, but is engendered by them; and, each of them having but a limited amount of energy at its disposal, it follows that, if we wish to put into any movement every available atom of energy, then we must obtain the concurrent working of the greatest possible number of muscular fibers. In order that these diverse muscular actions shall not counteract one another, it is indispensable that they be fashioned under the law of a common rhythm, and this is what we understand by *muscular synergy.* In executing any movement which is somewhat complicated the muscles do not work simutaneously, but act one after the other; and the effi-cacy of the result depends on the perfection of the rhythm which is bestowed upon this series of partial efforts. It is necessary that these be combined in such a way that each muscle shall come into action at the most favorable moment. The habit of this rhythm once formed, it appears to us a per-fectly natural proceeding; at first it is, of course, not so easy. When we have to make an unaccustomed movement, we soon realize that we must first find out a certain method by which to shape that movement. [48]

Deppe felt that in most keyboard playing too much inanimate weight and muscular activity were focused in the fingers and the hand. Not enough use was made of the upper arm and the back and shoulder muscles in controlling the arm weight. In order to achieve a light, refined touch, he recommended a very low seat which shifted the center of gravity of the arm to the elbow. Amy Fay said that she cut two inches off of the legs of her piano chair. In most playing, and particularly in passage work, he continually emphasized his rule that "Your elbow must be *lead* and your wrist a *feather."* [49] This "feather-light" hand was to be carried about and supported by the arm, with much of that support centered in the large upper arm and shoulder muscles. In order to strengthen and develop these largely neglected muscles, Deppe recommended physical activity away from the keyboard, such as on the horizontal bars. Elisabeth Caland had to exercise with dumb-bells and even carried one about during her daily walks. She recalled that when Deppe greeted her at the lesson that "his first act was always to grasp my hand in greeting; to meet his requirements,it had to be 'light as a feather,' so that he could guide it in any direction he pleased, and yet never have the sensation of sustaining any weight whatsoever." [50]

She suggested two basic exercises to develop this condition wherein the arm was carrying the hand:

... First raise the arm, very slowly ... [until high above the head with wrist slightly raised], *but do not elevate the shoulder in the slightest degree.* After retaining the arm for a moment in this position, let it sink, *still slowly,* till the finger-tips touch the keys, so lightly that they are not depressed. *During the whole course of this exercise, concentrate the entire attention on the action of the muscles of the back and shoulder, in order to gain a vivid and conscious perception of the truth that these muscles do work conjointly in the task of carrying and sustaining the arm.* Unless this simple exercise be performed with thoughtfulness and deliberation, it will be quite fruitless, for then the sensation which proves the co-operative working of the muscles under consideration will not be experienced....

Raise the arm ... [about six inches above the keyboard with wrist higher than the passive hand]; then, by a *conscious use of the back and shoulder muscles,* describe slow, circular movements with the entire arm, moving it freely in the shoulder socket, and allowing the hand to hang loosely from the wrist. Though the hand is, necessarily, sustained by the wrist, the wrist by the forearm, and that in turn, by the upper arm, yet in none of these members should there be any exertion of *independent* activity. The arm must be in a state of complete rest and passivity, and simply allow itself to be *guided as a whole* through the prescribed motions. Given these conditions, the hand will surely prove "as light as a feather." Since this exercise—which is not specially fatiguing —does not demand the use of a piano, it will be found profitable to practice it in front of a mirror, and obtain thereby a profile view of the movements. One may test the perfection of this exercise by watchful attention to the bend of the elbow; for, from first to last, the angle between upper arm and forearm must remain absolutely unaltered; in actual piano practice this angle, of course, undergoes constant change of dimensions. [51]

Deppe quickly applied this condition to basic exercises at the keyboard. The arm was slowly lowered to the keyboard with the tips of the fingers very lightly touching the keys—with the arm still supporting the hand. The wrist remained slightly higher than the back of the hand with the elbow hanging freely at the side. The fingers were well rounded. A distinguishing feature of Deppe's position was that "the line *formed by the fifth finger, the outside of the hand, and the fore-arm should* be a straight one." [52] In other words the hand is turned slightly inward at the wrist. The hand may turn on the third finger, which acts as a pivot until the straight line position is achieved. The knuckles of the fourth and fifth fingers are higher than the second and third so that the hand is gently tilted downward towards the thumb. Elisabeth Caland cited three immediate advantages achieved by this position:

(1) Owing to the straight line running through the hand and arm, the muscular connection between the two becomes of the most direct and positive kind. When the hand is allowed to *turn out at the wrist*, this *"rapport"* is summarily broken at that point, and the fourth and fifth fingers—no longer lying parallel with the keys, but stretched diagonally across them—suffer a proportionate loss of freedom and of power.

(2) The very important muscles which lie along the *under* or (or inner) side of the forearm are now brought into exactly that position which is most favorable to their free and unhampered cooperation with the muscles of the upper arm; hence follows a notable increase in their strength and efficiency.

(3) Through the agency of this hand-position the fingers are effectually aided in attaining to *complete independence,* and *equality* of power. [53]

The first basic exercises used by Deppe, with the arm still supporting the hand, were described by both Amy Fay and Elisabeth Caland. Amy Fay published them in her version in Chicago in 1890. Miss Caland's description of them is quoted here:

Now we come to the few finger exercises which Deppe prescribed and which he always prefaced by a command to concentrate the whole attention on the movement to be performed, the player making, as it were, a mental map of the entire route from brain to finger tips.

First place the hand upon the keyboard in the manner of the preliminary exercise, and with the fingers on the same keys [white keys]. Then raise the fifth finger a very little from its key *(the other fingers remaining poised lightly on their respective keys)*, but be careful not to raise it too high, else there will result a "crack" in the muscles, and, according to Deppe, there will be a consequent interruption of the connection between hand and arm. By a direct effort of the will maintain the finger in its elevated position for a moment; then, by a single, quick, decisive movement bring it on to the key below. The finger should not be thrown on the key, nor should the tone be the result of a push or a blow thereon; on the contrary, the movement should be so direct, so rapid, *so devoid of all outward appearance of effort,* as to give the impression that the finger has simply been allowed to fall of its own weight upon the key. Deppe always said, "Do not strike; let the fingers fall"; and he used this expression in order that his pupils might have their attention effectually directed to the importance of the *apparent* unpremeditation which underlies artistic tone-production. . . .

After the fifth finger has gone through several careful repetitions of the above exercise—each time returning to its exact original position—execute the same movement with the other fingers, each in its turn, meanwhile maintaining the most complete tranquillity in the hand itself and in the unemployed fingers. Each separate finger, quite unaffected by the task which its neighbor has to perform, must carry out with perfect independence the commands transmitted to it from the brain. In this manner one may, by watchful observation, obtain an exact idea of the extent to which his fingers actually work under the *conscious* direction of the will. At first the effort to maintain the hand in the strict Deppean position will occasion a certain amount of trembling in hand, arm, and finger; but, after a short time of practice has brought the fingers under better domination, this feeling of tension will disappear. Still further practice will so "educate" the hand—to use Deppe's word—that the fingers will learn to yield instant obedience to the will, and a tranquil pose of the hand and of the unemployed fingers will become habitual with the player.

At this point one is ready to proceed to the binding together of two consecutive tones, beginning with the fifth finger as before, and listening with keen attention to make sure that each tone, as it dies away, is really carried over to the next one, in pure legato style. The *liaison* should be so perfect that, in expressive German parlance, "no air is perceptible between the tones," and to this end it is essential that the ear be trained to possess a fine critical faculty.

The next step is to use two fingers simultaneously—under precisely the same conditions as at first—in producing the thirds B—D; B—D; A—C; A—C; G—B; G—B, etc., thus preparing the hand for binding together, as smoothly as if they were single tones, the thirds B—D, A—C; A—C, G—B, etc. The left hand goes through the same exercises, three octaves lower on the keyboard, except that the fifth finger, instead of the thumb, rests on the key G. It will be found that the effect of the work performed is, in a measure, communicated from one hand to the other, with beneficial result; and, since the hands go through the same exercises, under identical conditions, it follows that they are finally brought under absolutely equal control. These exercises—the only ones which Deppe prescribed—form the daily bread of a Deppean pupil, and even a very advanced player will prove that they constitute, when practiced with deliberation and accuracy, an unrivaled means of discipline for hands and fingers.*

*Allow me to emphasize the fact that, from first to last, the hand and arm find no point of support on the keyboard. Therein these exercises differ radically, therefore, from various similar ones in which certain keys are held down by one or more fingers during the performance of the exercise. (E.S.S.—translator). [54]

Utmost concentration on tonal control, extreme sensitivity in the finger tip, and conscious guidance of each physical movement and position during slow practice was insisted upon by Deppe. He objected most strenuously to any fast practice until every "detail of phrasing and execution can be subjected to strong and perpetual control, and the movement forms characteristic of each particular composition firmly impressed on the memory." [55] With enough of this kind of practice the control became a spontaneous, instinctive thing. The sensitive type of finger action he encouraged reminded Elisabeth Caland, like Mason, of Forkel's description of Bach's technique. To encourage this delicate finger tip feeling and at the same time strengthen the muscles in the palm of the hand, Deppe advocated an exercise in which a small rubber ball was held in the hand and gently squeezed by the finger. The touch resulting from these simple exercises suggested to Amy Fay the kind of sound she had heard in Liszt's playing:

Don't you remember my saying that Liszt had such an

extraordinary way of playing a melody? That it did not seem to be so loud and cut-out as most artists make it, and yet it was so penetrating? Well, dear, *there* was the secret of it! *"Spielen Sie mit dem Gewicht* (Play with *weight*)," Deppe will say. "Don't strike, but let the fingers *fall*. At first the tone will be nearly inaudible, but with practice it will gain every day in power."—After Deppe had directed my attention to it, I remembered that I had never seen Liszt lift up his fingers so fearfully high as the other schools and especially the Stuttgart one, make such a point of doing. That is where Mehlig misses it, and is what makes her playing so sharp and cornered at times. When you lift the fingers so high you cannot bind the tones so perfectly together. There is always a break. Deppe makes me listen to every tone, and carry it over to the next one, and not let any one finger get an undue prominence over the other—a thing that is immensely difficult to do—so I have given up all pieces for the present and just devote myself to playing these little exercises right. [56]

Following such drills, practice progressed to scales, arpeggios, etude passages, chords, octaves, etc. In scale playing, Deppe cautioned against turning the thumb under and insisted upon a fine legato where "The binding of tones should be in the hand itself." [57] Rather, the upper arm controlled lateral movement at the keyboard. The supple wrist continued to maintain its straight line and there was no reaching out in the hand for the next key. Caland explained the process:

Each finger is conducted to a point *exactly over the key which it is to depress,* and thus, as no finger need ever forestall the progressive movement of hand and arm by an independent stretching out toward its key, it follows that the harmony of the *ensemble* is never disturbed. And so, while the fingers take the first three keys, the hand is carried, by a lateral and progressive movement of the wrist, so far to the right that the passing under of the thumb, as it sinks on F, is barely perceptible to the eye: as for the second, third, fourth, and fifth fingers, they have but to take the keys over which they naturally find themselves. The third finger, it will be remembered, serves, by virtue of its position, as a regulator for the straight line which one must always imagine as running through hand and forearm. [58]

Amy Fay further illuminated this type of scale execution with its oblique motion by recounting her learning of the E major scale under Deppe's direct supervision:

He always begins with the one in E major as the most useful to practice. His principle in playing the scale is *not* to turn the thumb under! but to turn a little on each finger end, pressing it firmly down on the key, and screwing it round, as it were, on a pivot, till the next finger is brought over its own key. In this way he prepares for the thumb, which is kept free from the hand and slightly curved.—He told me to play the scale of E major slowly with the right hand, which I did. He curved his hand round mine, and told me as long as I play right, his hand would not interfere with mine. I played up one octave, and then I wished to go on by placing my first finger on F sharp. To do that I naturally turned my hand outward, so as to make the step from my thumb on E to F sharp with the first, but it came bang up against Deppe's hand like a sort of blockade. "Go on," said Deppe. "I can't, when you keep your hand right in the way," said I. "My hand isn't in the way," said he, "but *your* hand is out of position."

So I started again. This time I reflected, and when I got my third finger on D sharp, I kept my hand slanting from left to right, but I prepared for the turning under of the thumb, and for getting my first finger on F sharp, by turning my wrist sharply out. That brought my thumb down on the note and prepared me instantly for the next step. In fact, my wrist carried my finger right on to the sharp without any change in the position of the hand, thus giving the most perfect legato in the world, and I continued the whole scale in the same manner. Just try it once, and you'll see how ingenious it is—only one must be careful not to throw out the elbow in turning out the wrist. As in the ascending scale one has to turn the thumb under twice in every octave, Deppe's way of playing avoids twice throwing the hand out of position as one does by the old way of playing straight alone, and the smoothness and rapidity of the scale must be much greater. The direction of the hand in running passages is always a little oblique.

Don't you remember my telling you that Liszt has an inconceivable lightness, swiftness and smoothness of execution? When Deppe was explaining this to me, I suddenly remembered that when he was playing scales or passages, his fingers seemed to lie across the keys in a slanting sort of way, and to execute these rapid passages almost without any perceptible motion. Well, dear *there* it was again! As Liszt is a great experimentalist, he probably does all these things by instinct, and without reasoning it out, but that is why nobody else's playing sounds like his. Some of his scholars had most dazzling techniques, and I used to rack my brains to find out how it was, that no matter how perfectly anybody else played, the minute Liszt sat down and played the same thing, the previous playing seemed rough in comparison. I'm sure Deppe is the only master in the world who has thought that out; though, as he says himself, it is the egg of Columbus—"when you know it!"[59]

When it came to practicing chords, he believed in letting the necessary weight rest in the fingers. He applied the term "controlled free-fall" to dropping an individual finger or the whole arm in chord playing. He felt that the descending movement should be so artfully controlled that the arm seemed to fall naturally and solely by its own weight. Amy Fay quoted Deppe directly regarding chord playing:

He says that the principle of the scale and of the chord are directly opposite. "In playing the scale you must gather your hand into a nut-shell, as it were, and play on the finger tips. In taking the chord, on the contrary, you must spread the hands as if you were going to ask a blessing." This is particularly the case with a wide interval. He told me if I ever heard Rubinstein play again to observe how he strikes his chords. "Nothing cramped about *him!* He spreads his hands as if he were going to take in the universe, and takes them up with the greatest freedom and *abandon!*" Deppe has the greatest admiration for Rubinstein's *tone*, which he says is unequaled. . . .[60]

Deppe was greatly concerned about the aesthetic element in physical movement at the piano and its relationship to beauty of performance. He coined an expression which he used frequently: "When it *looks* pretty, then it is right." [61] Elisabeth Caland said that nothing bothered him more than observing a pianist lacking in good tone production or beautiful movement:

The fusion of these two things—*i.e.,* beauty of movement and beauty of tone—was to him a law of primary importance in the art of music. In other words, he claimed that all movements on the keyboard could be shaped in such wise that beauty of tone would be the natural consequence of beauty of movement. For if, in the acts of ordinary life, a graceful movement produces a pleasing result, with how much greater force and significance will this law apply to piano playing—a manifestation of art which justly holds so high and aesthetic a place! [62]

It was his desire that this movement, which involved the full arm, should always be curvilinear and as simple, direct, and purposeful as possible. It should have a continuous quality to it which contributes an unbroken rhythm to the phrase line and fosters a perfect natural unity in the overall interpretation. Always this bodily movement should have a graceful, spontaneous quality about it that finally conceals the careful, conscious preparation that goes into it; each movement should truly be a natural outgrowth of the music itself. It was Deppe's desire that even the simplest piece should be performed "with such artistic grace and finish as to turn it into a masterpiece." At first there were sure to be "doubled" or superfluous movements in the learning process just as there might be in learning such skills as skating and swimming. [63] But with intelligent practice these could be eliminated so as "to reap a maximum of result from a minimum of effort." [64]

Elisabeth Caland describes the nature of the Deppean movement:

> . . . this movement is a continuous one, beginning with the first note of a piece, and ending only when the last tone has been sounded: therefore it is unsurpassed as a means whereby a composition may be rendered in most compact and perfect form; for, since all meaningless and superfluous motions are avoided, the movement adapts itself with the utmost nicety to the varying demands of the music. Even when a rest occurs, the movement is not interrupted, for the hand, when lifted from the keyboard, is carried to the keys next to be played in a curve, the magnitude of which is accurately proportioned to the duration of the rest. So unbroken is the rhythm of the composition, through the use of this simple means, that, as Deppe said, "the very rests become music." And so this curved and continuous movement, always reflective in its character, forms, as it were, a connecting thread, running through and uniting the ideas of the entire piece. [65]

Caland finds justification for the curved movement in playing by quoting Johann Gottfried von Herder (1744-1803):

> "A cycle unites all tones and successions of tones by an indissoluble bond, in such a way that, with one tone, we have all the others, and we are given not only one melody, but the whole series of melodies which a certain definite scale can produce. And just as a beautiful form is never born from the straight line and the square alone (although these constitute the basis of accuracy in art as well as in geometry), so harmony—which is to tone what geometry is to forms—can never give rise to the ever-changing melody of passion unless each sentiment has its curve, its climax, its aim, and its measure. The multitude of lines lying between the straight line and the circle are all lines of beauty, and, in music, these lines are melodic curves, each having its own path, distinct from that of

any other, but all united by one eternal law, *the law of the tone-circle.*" [66]

The practical outworking of this principle of movement is described by Caland in this extensive quotation:

When Deppe uttered the axiom, "a flat pose of the hand *sounds* flat"—*i.e.,* lifeless or wooden—he meant thereby to emphasize the importance of making *every* movement a curved one, for it is only by an awkward and angular movement that one can lay the hand "flat" upon the keys, and the inevitable consequence thereof is a hard, unmusical tone. But the placing of the hand, with wrist well raised, upon the keys, is the beginning of a curvilinear movement; this is continued in the pliant, downward-and-outward motion with which the wrist returns the hand to the normal position; and it finds further expression as the wrist rises again, with an equally flexible, yet controlled, movement, and thus prepares the hand for a new descending curve. In this manner the hand describes, at each successive displacement, a curve which joins itself to the one next following; *thus the movement becomes an uninterrupted one, because the hand is meanwhile carried over the keys by the same continuous movement that enchains the separate curves.*

When this combination movement of wrist, hand, and arm has been made one's own, then will come of itself a clear perception of the fact that this "simple movement" lends itself with equal readiness to the performance of runs, thirds, sixths, arpeggios, chords, octaves, trills, and staccato passages—though naturally, in the execution of such varying forms, different muscles will be brought into play and will exert a degree of force proportionate to the demands of the passage to be played. The player should always endeavor to create for himself a *mental picture* of a composition, in which these various arpeggios and runs, chords and octaves figure as entwining ropes of pearls; he should follow in imagination the curving lines formed by the execution of such passages, and have a vivid consciousness of the fact that by his two hands these invisible threads are to be ceaselessly interwoven.

Progressions of thirds and sixths are played with the hand and wrist in the position so often described, special pains being taken to insure *infinite lightness in hand and wrist*—a condition absolutely essential to smooth and rapid progression of the fingers. Given this condition, if the fingers are also thoroughly alive to their task, and are *carried* over the keys to be played, then the tones will be bound with such perfection that, to use Deppe's phrase, "there will not be room between them for the tiniest grain of sand."

265

The same conditions obtain for the execution of arpeggios and broken chords. As usual, the hand returns to regulation position during the playing of the first three notes, thus beginning that curved movement, the characteristic form of which is never absent (during *preparatory practice,* be it said) from the mental consciousness of the player. During an ascending arpeggio or broken chord—embodying the first half of the circular movement—the hand is managed precisely as in a scale, the only difference being that greater intervals now separate the tones. And so, by the elastic outward movement of the wrist, governed as before by upper arm and shoulder, the hand is conducted over the keys in a slightly oblique position, which reduces the passage of the thumb to a point almost of imperceptibility. At the same time, by means of the mentally-controlled expansion and contraction of hand and fingers, the individual tones, drawn from the instrument by the sensitive finger tips, will sound conscious and alive *(bewusst and beseelt)*. In the descending arpeggio (second half of the circular movement) the wrist must now maintain a restraining influence on the hand, for, according to Deppe, "if the hand, under such circumstances turns to the left at the wrist in order to facilitate the passage of the third and fourth fingers, then their respective tones will be produced by means of a detached stroke or blow of the finger—a heterogeneous, mechanical, and utterly superfluous action, which will materially impede the harmonious progression of the melodic thought."* (*Klose: Die Deppe'sche Lehre, page 13.) He held the opinion that any anticipatory movement on the part of the hand, forearm, or finger—any *isolated* activity of these members—was certain to cause a variation in the normal hand position, and to derange, more or less, by consequence, the entire playing apparatus. Under such circumstances the fingers and the upper arm are no longer "en rapport," for the communication between them has been interrupted by some independent, arbitrary movement, to right or left, of a finger, the hand, or the forearm. This erroneous movement, however, should by no means be confounded with that indispensable and elastic lateral movement of the wrist which is directed and controlled by upper arm and shoulder. In the latter case, the *hand will always be found in the correct position*—that is, with a straight line running through hand and forearm—simply because correct hand position and perfect wrist movement are both dependent upon the same cause—namely, the operation of upper arm muscles, ably supported by those of back and shoulder. [67]

When applied to sequential single note passages of perhaps a

266

fifth in overall span or in the following exercise designed by Deppe for "concentration of tone-producing power in the palm of the hand,"

68

there must be a continuous alternating contraction and expansion motion in the hand. When the Deppean position is involved, it makes the hand appear as if it were

... *"caressing"* the keys—so sweet, so tender, yet so full of nervous energy, are the tones produced when curvilinear movements are employed.

A rule of great importance in this connection concerns the management of the wrist: it "should revolve (*sich drehen*) as if on a pivot." This movement, apparently so natural and spontaneous, is in reality of the utmost importance, seeing that it insures a continually curved carriage of the hand. Through the same influence the fingers take the keys in easy, elastic curves, melting and blending into one another; and thus is imparted the lovely legato quality which lends such charm to the playing of a finished Deppean scholar. [69]

Ehrenfechter cautioned that this elastic, flexible condition in the wrist should not be taken to mean there is no strength in the wrist. Its condition should be like that found in the lion: ". . . its paws look as flabby as a piece of wash-leather, yet, let him just gently pat you on the shoulder, and you will be surprised to find what strength there is in such a paw." [70]

Deppe prepared the way for the weight school of piano playing which was to appear shortly and unfortunately, with its excesses, was to repudiate his teachings to a large degree. But seen in perspective from the present day, Deppe is remarkable in that he anticipated many of the views of the modern-day theorists. Certainly he put appropriate emphasis on the vital role of the arm in the total development of piano technique. He realized, too, that weight is a fluid quality that needs to be manipulated in a controlled manner, that it seldom is used with complete relaxation, and that consciously or unconsciously it should not be relegated to the static, useless role it played in the high finger school. But he retained the best of the finger technique: a close finger action with a desirable

267

degree of hand and arm fixation. Fortunately, too, Deppe was such a fine, aesthetically minded musician that he clothed technique in artistic garb. Beauty and grace of movement in playing, he felt, had to be present for technique to function fully and objectively in achieving its only valid goal, beautiful and meaningful interpretation in the performance of the great classics.

Notes

[1] Charles J. Haake, "Modern Piano Technic—How New Is It?", Music Teachers National Association *Proceedings,* 16th series, 1921, p.74.

[2] Sigismund Lebert and Ludwig Stark, *Gross Klavierschule* (*Grand Theoretical and Practical Piano School*), I, p. iii.

[3] *Ibid.,* p. xii.

[4] *Ibid.,* p. xiv.

[5] *Ibid.,* p. xxi.

[6] *Ibid.,* p. 1.

[7] Maria Levinskaya, *The Levinskaya System of Pianoforte Technique and Tone-Colour through Mental and Muscular Control,* p. 58.

[8] Józef Gát, *The Technique of Piano Playing,* 2nd ed., completely rewritten by the author, p. 249.

[9] Ridley Prentice, *Hand Gymnastics for the Scientific Development of the Muscles Used in Pianoforte Playing,* p. 11.

[10] Gát, *Technique of Piano Playing,* p. 249.

[11] *Ibid.*

[12] Charles Hanon, *The Virtuoso Pianist,* preface.

[13] H.R. Palmer, *Palmer's Piano Primer,* p. 88.

[14] C.A. Ehrenfechter, *Technical Study in the Art of Pianoforte-playing (Deppe's Principles),* p. 34.

[15] Amy Fay, *Music-Study in Germany, from the Home Correspondence of Amy Fay,* pp. 266-267.

[16] *Ibid.,* pp. 21-22.

[17] William Mason, *Memories of a Musical Life,* pp. 17-18.

[18] *Ibid.,* pp. 19-21.

[19] *Ibid.,* pp. 68-70.

[20] *Ibid.,* pp. 191-93.

[21] William Mason, *Touch and Technic; For Artistic Piano Playing,* Op. 44, I, p. 4.

[22] *Ibid.,* p. 8.

[23] *Ibid.*, p. 51.

[24] *Ibid.*, p. 10.

[25] *Ibid.*, p. 16.

[26] *Ibid.*, pp. 14-15.

[27] *Ibid.*, p. 16.

[28] *Ibid.*

[29] *Ibid.*, IV, p. 18.

[30] Daniel Gregory Mason, *Music in My Times and Other Reminiscences*, pp. 50-51.

[31] Cited in Levinskaya, *The Levinskaya System*, pp. 46-47.

[32] Adolph Kullak, *The Aesthetics of Pianoforte-Playing*, p. 85.

[33] Cited in Levinskaya, *The Levinskaya System*, p. 32.

[34] *Ibid.*, pp. 32-33.

[35] Kullak, *Aesthetics of Pianoforte-Playing*, p. 150.

[36] *Ibid.*, pp. 154-55.

[37] *Ibid.*, pp. 190-91.

[38] Fay, *Music-Study in Germany*, p. 302.

[39] *Ibid.*, p. 287.

[40] *Ibid.*, p. 288.

[41] Ludwig Deppe, "Armleiden des Klavierspielers," reprinted in *Neue Zeitschrift für Music*, Volume 70, p. 315. Translation by Helmut Ziefle.

[42] Amy Fay, *The Deppe Finger Exercises for Rapidly Developing an Artistic Touch in Piano Forte Playing*, preface.

[43] Ludwig Deppe, "Armleiden des Klavierspielers," p. 315.

[44] Fay, *Music-Study in Germany*, pp. 294-95.

[45] *Ibid.*, p. 313.

[46] *Ibid.*, pp. 318-20.

[47] *Ibid.*, pp. 324-25.

[48] Elisabeth Caland, *Artistic Piano Playing as taught by Ludwig Deppe*, p. 24.

[49] Fay, *Music-Study in Germany*, p. 293.

[50] Caland, *Artistic Piano Playing*, p. 20.

[51] *Ibid.*, pp. 21-22.

[52] *Ibid.*, p. 26.

[53] *Ibid.*, pp. 27-28.

[54] *Ibid.*, pp. 29-30.

[55] *Ibid.*, p. 54.

[56] Fay, *Music-Study in Germany,* pp. 288-89.

[57] Caland, *Artistic Piano Playing,* p. 35.

[58] *Ibid.*

[59] Fay, *Music-Study in Germany,* pp. 290-91.

[60] *Ibid.*, p. 300.

[61] Caland, *Artistic Piano Playing,* p. 17.

[62] *Ibid.*, p. 19.

[63] *Ibid.*, p. 18.

[64] *Ibid.*, p. 19.

[65] *Ibid.*, pp. 33-34.

[66] *Ibid.*, p. 34.

[67] *Ibid.*, pp. 41-44.

[68] *Ibid.*, p. 50.

[69] *Ibid.*, pp. 51-52.

[70] Ehrenfechter, *The Art of Pianoforte-Playing,* pp. 23-24.

13.

The Leschetizky Influence

About the time that Deppe in Berlin was teaching the principles of arm involvement in piano technique, another famous piano teacher, Theodor Leschetizky (1830-1915), had come to Vienna where he began developing many world famous pianists. Leschetizky eventually rivaled Liszt in his total output of products for the concert world. This roster reads like a Who's Who in music: Paderewski, Schnabel, Hambourg, Friedman, Essipov, Brailowsky, Moisewitsch, and many others. Like Chopin, Leschetizky was Polish by birth. Moving with his family to Vienna, he became a pupil of Czerny at the age of eleven. He developed rapidly and began his long career as a teacher at the age of fourteen—much as Czerny had.

The pianists he heard in Vienna in his youth had a considerable influence upon his development. At first he was duly impressed by the dazzling superficial quality of their technique and their high regard for "the perfect finger." [1] Then about 1850 there appeared an unknown Bohemian pianist by the name of Julius Schulhoff, who had been an intimate of Chopin in Paris and had absorbed something of his style of playing. Schulhoff's simple manner and the way in which he was able to make the piano "sing" greatly impressed him. Here was a higher goal for Leschetizky than all the virtuosity he had previously heard. Leschetizky described the experience:

Under his hands the piano seemed like another instrument. Seated in a corner, my heart overflowed with indescribable emotions as I listened. Not a note escaped me. I began to foresee a new style of playing. That melody standing out in bold relief, that wonderful sonority—all this must be due to a new and entirely different touch. And that cantabile, a legato such as I had not dreamed possible on the piano, a human voice rising above the sustaining harmonies! I could hear the

271

shepherd sing, and see him. Then a strange thing happened. He had finished and had awakened no response. There was no enthusiasm! They were all so accustomed to brilliant technical display that the pure beauty of the interpretation was not appreciated. . . . Dessauer, coming toward me, a slight sneer of disapproval on his face, asked me what I thought of it. Still very much moved, I answered: "It is the playing of the future. . . ." Schulhoff's playing was a revelation to me. From that day I tried to find that touch. I thought of it constantly, and studied the five fingers diligently to learn the method of production. I practiced incessantly, sometimes even on the table-top, striving to attain firm finger-tips and a light wrist, which I felt to be the means to my end. I kept that beautiful sound well in my mind, and it made the driest work interesting. I played only exercises, abandoning all kinds of pieces, and when my mother advised me to go back to them, I only answered: "Oh, no! it is not ready—I shall not leave it for three months." In the meantime, Schulhoff had conquered Vienna. Heard in a large hall, his playing produced the proper effect. [2]

Annette Hullah later spoke of the impact of this moving experience:

The change in him was to be of farther reaching influence than he dreamt of at the time, for it filtered through him to his pupils and created in them the germ of what developed later into the famous Leschetizky School. Schulhoff's visit marked an epoch in Leschetizky's life. [3]

In his early twenties, Leschetizky went to Russia where he established himself as a fine pianist and teacher. He taught Anton Rubinstein's pupils while Rubinstein was on tour. In 1862 he became head of the piano department of the St. Petersburg Conservatory where Rubinstein was director. Ever after, Rubinstein's playing was a great inspiration to Leschetizky in his teaching. Concert tours also took him to England several times. Finally in 1878 he settled down in Vienna and devoted the rest of his life to teaching, even though he was a very fine performer.

During the course of his long fruitful career, according to Artur Schnabel, his pupils numbered nearly 1,800. [4] They came from everywhere, attracted in part, at least, by the reputation of his most famous student, Ignace Paderewski (1860-1941). But more than that, there was magnetism in the Leschetizky personality. For him, music making was a vital experience, as urgent and important as life itself. He spared no pains in communicating these feelings to his students. Sometimes it was through a kindness and generosity which entered into their personal lives; at other times it was achieved through a volatile temper and unrelenting idealism. He told Ethel Newcomb:

> Be ideal, think ideally. We can all afford to cultivate that quality. . . . Whether it makes you happier or not, it is worth the trouble to try to live ideally. If you think yourself a poor specimen, you will probably always remain one, or most likely become one, but if you think of yourself as having the possibilities of greatness in you, there is a chance for you. [5]

Much has been written regarding the character of Leschetizky's teaching. But the famed "Leschetizky method" is not easily defined. Like Liszt, he was more concerned about matters of musicianship and interpretation than the technical means. He deplored much of the teaching that went on in his name, particularly by students who had worked under him for only a short time. They still managed to perpetuate their own peculiarities and inartistic styles of playing, often by exaggerating one technical point. Leschetizky avowed that he had no special method. In exasperation he once declared:

> I *have* no method and I *will have* no method. Go to concerts and be sharpwitted, and if you are observing you will learn tremendously from the ways that are successful and also from those that are not. Adopt with your pupils the ways that succeed with them, and get away as far as possible from the idea of a method. Write over your music-room the motto: "NO METHOD!" [6]

Later he had second thoughts: "If I had a method it would be based upon the mental delineation of a chord." [7] Ethel Newcomb explained what he meant:

> Many times he would ask the pupil to make a list of all the chords, as well as of groups of notes, to make a picture of them in his mind's eye, and to study the picture, at the same time shaping the hand according to the picture, before touching the keys. He called this the "physiognomy of the hand" . . .
> . . . His principle was that one should not strike a note or a chord without thinking of, and visualizing, or sometimes even saying, the next one. [8]

Probably more than anything else his secret was his ability to get his pupils to project musical values in their playing, to listen to themselves, and to apply intense concentration to their work. Paderewski summed it all up:

273

The method of Leschetizky is very simple. His pupils learn to evoke a fine tone from the instrument and to make music and not noise. There are principles, you will agree, that are to be uniformly inculcated in every pupil—that is, breadth, softness of touch and precision in rhythm. For the rest every individual is treated according to his talent. In one word—it is the method of methods. [9]

Leschetizky remarked: "I study for hours when I am walking alone in the night. I look far down the street and imagine a beautiful voice, and I learn that far-away pp quality—that means attention." [10] For him "the best study could be done away from the piano. . . . Listening to the inward singing of a phrase was of far more value than playing it a dozen times." [11] He had come to appreciate a fine melody line from the singing of his first wife, Mme. Anne de Friedebourg, whom he had married in Russia. (His three later wives were all former students, including Annette Essipov, one of the greatest of nineteenth century women pianists.) He felt that muscular relaxation in piano playing was like deep breathing to a singer. He told Ethel Newcomb:

. . . what deep breaths Rubinstein used to take at the beginning of long phrases, and also what repose he had and what dramatic pauses. "There is more rhythm between the notes than in the notes themselves." He reminded me that Liszt used to say this. "Paula Szalit is the only one who ever asked me to tell how Rubinstein breathed. No one else ever seemed interested to know." [12]

To Frank Merrick he said: "I advise you very often to stop and listen when you are practising, and then you will find out a great deal for yourself." [13]

Annette Hullah recalled that he felt that four or, at the most, five hours a day of concentrated practice was sufficient. He told Ossip Gabrilowitsch two or three. [14] Miss Hullah wrote:

Concentrated thought is the basis of his principles, the corner-stone of his method. Without it nothing of any permanent value can be obtained, either in art or anything else. No amount of mechanical finger-work can take its place; and the player who repeats the same passage, wearily expectant that he will accomplish it in process of time, is a lost soul on a hopeless quest. Leschetizky enumerates the essential qualities of good work as follows: First, an absolutely clear comprehension of the principal points to be studied in the music on hand; a clear perception of where the difficulties lie, and of the way in which to conquer them; the mental realizations of these 3 facts *before* they are carried out by the hands.

"Decide exactly *what* it is you want to do in the first place," he impresses on every one; "then *how* you will do it; then play it. Stop and think if you played it in the way you meant to do; then only, if sure of this, go ahead. Without concentration, remember, you can do nothing. The brain must guide the fingers, not the fingers the brain." [15]

Perhaps the most individualistic and discerning of the Leschetizky students was Artur Schnabel (1882-1951). The great classicist and Beethoven authority auditioned for him at the age of nine. (He said Leschetizky was always late and that he had waited two hours for the initial appointment.) He studied first with Annette Essipov for a year and from time to time with five or six other assistants who had varying approaches to music. He then played regularly in all of Leschetizky's classes until he was sixteen. [16] He was more critical in his judgment than the other Leschetizky pupils and revealed the basic conflict between the classic pianist and the romanticist with his natural inclination toward virtuosity:

What I learned from Leschetizky himself, I am unable to say, to estimate, to appreciate. He succeeded in releasing all the vitality and *élan* and sense of beauty a student had in his nature, and would not tolerate any deviation or violation of what he felt to be truthfulness of expression. As you see, all this devotion, seriousness, care and honesty is compatible with the virtuoso type represented by him. Why we, today, have in general a less flattering opinion of the virtuoso is a problem I recommend you to think about, again and again.

Leschetizky's limitations showed in his comparative indifference to, or even dislike of, the kind of music in which the "personal" becomes just an ingredient of the universal. He had, for instance, not much use, or love, or curiosity, for the second half of Beethoven's production. The more glory the music itself emanates, the less it leaves for the performer. It was such transcending music which he seemed to evade, by instinct. . . . [17]

He saw music as a, so to say, public function. For him it was not music itself which gave to the musician, who took. For him the musician, as a person, was the giver, and he who listened took. . . . When Leschetizky . . . denied that I should ever be a pianist but said that I was from the beginning apparently, a musician, he meant perhaps to indicate that my type "takes" from music. . . . I was one of a handful who never had to study Hungarian rhapsodies by Liszt. I was quite pleased with his choice for me. He did not always like me. He was very strict with me, and sometimes even hard, but yet he absolutely respected what he believed to be my musical disposition. [18]

Nothing is more revealing of Leschetizky's romantic nature than his reaction to the *Well-Tempered Clavier:* "Go ahead and play it if it interests you, but why waste time on it when there is all of Beethoven, Schumann, Chopin, Liszt, and Brahms to master?" [19] From Czerny, Leschetizky learned much about Beethoven's manner of freely interpreting his own sonatas. With this Leschetizky was fully in accord. But one wonders about the strong aversion to Bach. Czerny can hardly be blamed. Leschetizky described the nature of his study with him:

I played a great deal of Bach under him, some compositions by Alkan, some by Thalberg, and above all, those of Beethoven. Czerny taught that Beethoven should be rendered with freedom of delivery and depth of feeling. A pedantic, inelastic interpretation of the master made him wild. He allowed me to play Chopin just as I pleased, and though he appreciated the great Polish writer, he sometimes said his compositions were sweetish. Again he would become enthusiastic and say that they were "famose Musik". Chopin's works were compared to sweetened water, flavored with paprika. Czerny did not fully recognize the value of the late Beethoven Sonatas; Mendelssohn he understood. I remember studying the "Songs without Words" almost as soon as they appeared. [20]

Leschetizky was ever aware of moving an audience emotionally. His preference for the romantic literature may be one reason why so many of his students were so successful in their public appearances.

He counseled Ethel Newcomb about audience communication:

"I have yet to discover whether you can ever put freedom and sureness together. I want you to know that you can," he went on, in almost pathetic tones, "for accuracy without expression isn't worth that," snapping his fingers.

"Our lessons from now on must have a different character entirely. You must play your pieces too freely for a while, and learn sureness from a different angle. Don't be afraid to express yourself. One player you may like to hear; the other, who knows far more perhaps, you do not care a bit for. Why is it? Your audience does not know either. They only know that there is something they like with the one; with the other they are more apt to say they never liked the piano anyway, and your audience longs to be pleased, and your uneducated audiences are also hard to please. They want emotion and expression more than technique. Educated audiences will give you credit for all kinds of things that the other audiences will not, and how every one loves beautiful tones and stirring rhythms!" [21]

Each student's interpretation of a piece was fashioned to the student's personality. Benno Moisewitsch (1890-1963) remarked that Leschetizky never taught two pupils the same piece in the same way, that there was a sense of urgency about his music making:

Whatever he did was intensely felt and shaped to that ideal: he made us think of the shape of the phrase, of the paragraph, of the composition. Each of the phrases in the dissecting process would be different and separately perfect. Put together, there was a sublime and unpredictable continuity of feeling about the piece as it took shape in one's newly minted interpretation. [22]

Leschetizky's individualistic approach was also applied to the presentation of technique. It is difficult to determine how thoroughly he had formulated a technical system; he never did leave an adequate account of any kind. One scrap of evidence might be Eleanor Spencer's description of his hand position. She said that his hand often lay quite flat upon the keyboard and that the first joints of the fingers had been curved so firmly for so long that they stayed that way even "if he only passes his fingers through his hair!" [23] But he told Annette Hullah:

I have no technical method, there are certain ways of producing certain effects, and I have found those which succeed best; but I have no iron rules. How is it possible one should have them? One pupil needs this, another that; the hand of each differs; the brain of each differs. There can be no rule. I am a doctor to whom my pupils come as patients to be cured of their musical ailments, and the remedy must vary in each case. There is but one part of my teaching that may be called a 'Method,' if you like; and that is the way in which I teach my pupils to learn a piece of music. This is invariably the same for all, whether artist or little child; it is the way Mme. Essipoff studies, the way *we* study—and *we* have much talent. [24]

Edwin Hughes (1884-1965) said that, during all of the years he was associated with him as a student and later as one of the *Vor-*

277

bereiters or assistant teachers, he could hardly remember "his having spoken a dozen words to me on the subject." [25] Hughes did secure an interview with him for *The Etude* (April 1909) and quoted Leschetizky directly:

Of course, in the beginning I have a method. A knowledge of correct hand position and of the many different qualities of touch which I use and which give a never-ending variety to the tone must be learned before one can go very far. The fingers must have acquired an unyielding firmness and the wrist, at the same time, an easy pliability in order to avoid hardness of tone. Besides this, there are the rules for singing, which apply to melody playing on the piano to just as great an extent as to melody singing in the voice.

The natural accents must be properly placed and long notes must receive an extra pressure in order to overcome the difficulty of sustaining tones on the pianoforte. All these things a good preparatory teacher can give as well as I, and for this reason I require my pupils to go first to an assistant, to the saving of both their time and money. Of course, the assistants are responsible to me.

After pupils have once gotten this foundation they branch off in every direction; each has his peculiarities and no one method will answer for all any more; the teaching must become individual. The enforcement of strict rules cannot then be insisted upon. It is just as in law. Not everyone who kills his fellow-man is hanged or guillotined or electrocuted. [26]

All seem to have gone through elementary five finger exercises. Then scales, arpeggios, chords, and octave work followed. "Next came the study of tone production in various forms," as Bertha Fiering related, "a good quality invariably being the result of a free condition of the arm combined with strength of fingers and hand." [27] And a liberal dosage of Czerny etudes was a must for every student. To Leschetizky they were more pianistic in style than those by Clementi, Cramer, and Kullak. The latter group always placed

. . . obstacles in the way in their etudes. All at once there comes a clumsy point in a passage which gives you the same sort of feeling as when you get your walking-stick caught in between your legs.

In Czerny, however, one has a clear road; there are no complications in the figures. [28]

Schnabel described his childhood study of Czerny under Leschetizky's wife, Annette Essipov:

She used to put a coin on my hand, a silver coin almost as big as a silver dollar (a gulden) and if I played one Czerny study without dropping it, she gave it to me as a present. I think that was sweet of her. In the meantime, I have changed my way of handling the piano so radically that now if I were to play only a few tones the coin would drop. I don't think that the "static" hand is a recommendable technique for the expression of music. For very young beginners, however, it might, temporarily, be the only method . . . .[29]

I don't believe in finger playing. The fingers are like the legs of a horse—if its body won't move, there wouldn't be any progress, it would always remain on the same spot. [30]

Strangely enough Schnabel seemed to overlook the fact that Malwine Brée in her method book quoted Leschetizky with similar imagery as saying that the pianist should "yield to the movements of the arms as far as necessary, as the rider yields to the movements of his horse." [31] Perhaps he did use more pliable arm movement than many of his students.

If we are to believe the account of an anonymous Leschetizky student in the February, 1899 issue of *The Musician*, Leschetizky must have heard of the theories of arm relaxation discussed by Mason and Deppe:

Leschetizky teaches his pupils to save their bodies fatigue by devitalizing the muscles not called into play. Let anyone support the extended arm of another, and then at a given word allow the arm to drop. If it falls to the side instantly and quite limp, it is said to be devitalized, but many people find difficulty in letting the arm go entirely in this way with all their muscles relaxed. [32]

In spite of the fact that Leschetizky objected strenuously to being the author of a method, he himself was responsible for perpetuating the idea. One day he informed Ethel Newcomb:

Frau Brée is writing a book—a book about my (long pause)—about my method. One has to call it something, if one must write a book at all about the way to study. It is the most difficult thing to write about; and most books are worse than useless. But hers will be good—as good as a book can be; but method—well, method depends on the person you have before you. [33]

This technical volume appeared in 1902 under the title, *The Groundwork of the Leschetizky Method, issued with his approval by his assistant Malwine Brée.* Inside appears his personal endorsement over his signature:

279

Honored Madam: My best thanks for the dedication of your book, which I of course accept most gladly. As you know, I am from principle no friend of theoretical Piano-Methods; but your excellent work, which I have carefully examined, is such a brilliant exposition of my personal views, that I subscribe, word for word, to everything you advance therein. Your "Groundwork of the Leschetizky Method" leads with a practised hand along the same path on which, for many years, you have won such striking success as my assistant by teaching in accord with my intention. Moreover, the tone of your work is not monotonously didactic, but enlivened by clever conceits and humor.

Approving the illustrations of my hand as genuine and lifelike, I declare your book to be the sole authorized publication explanatory of my method, and wish it all success and popularity. [34]

Forty-seven plates of Leschetizky's hand positions are shown—most of them with vertical fingers.

Two months later he wrote a testimonial for a second book by another of his assistants, Marie Prentner. It was entitled *The Modern Pianist, Being my Experiences in the Technic and Execution of Pianoforte Playing according to the Principles of Prof. Theo. Leschetizky.* The volume, which bears certain similarities to the Bree method, however did not receive the same full endorsement. So we must assume that, if there is a Leschetizky technical method, it is contained in the pages of Mme. Brée's book.

The Groundwork of the Leschetizky Method, covering nearly one hundred pages and twenty-eight sections, contains both verbal text and exercise material (pure technique as well as excerpts from pieces). The familiar forms of technique are presented as well as topics relating to performance and practice. Sections of the text are quoted in the following paragraphs:

I

ATTITUDE AT THE PIANO

Here one remark by Leschetizky: "Sit at the piano unconstrained and erect, like a good horseman on his horse, and yield to the movements of the arms as far as necessary, as the rider yields to the movements of his horse." Sit at such a distance from the keyboard that when the arms are easily bent the finger-tips may rest on the keys without effort, and the feet reach the pedals comfortably. The elbows should be held neither too close to the sides nor too far away; moreover, they should be on a level with the keys, or be held but very little higher. Too low a seat, in particular, necessitates (in accord with the laws of leverage) greater exertion on the player's part, so that he is compelled, when playing forcible chords, to raise his shoulders, which has no very graceful look.

Many—even eminent—pianists lay too little stress on a graceful attitude while playing. They seem to think: "If only the ear be satisfied." That is not enough. The listener's ear should first be seduced through the eye, and thus be rendered more impressionable.

The pianist must renounce the so-called aristocratic hand, slender and gracefully formed, with well-kept nails. A thoroughly trained "piano-hand" becomes broader, supple in the wrist, and muscular, with broad finger-tips. The nails, too, must be kept short, for the springy pad of the finger-tip yields a mellower tone than the inelastic nail.

The hand should assume a decidedly vaulted form for, apart from the unpleasing, amateurish impression made by playing with flat hands and fingers, the only way to get strength into the fingers is to hold the hand rounded upward. The wrist must be held somewhat lower than the knuckles, and the fingers so curved that the tip-joints fall vertically on the keys, which are touched by the tips of the fingers only. The thumb forms the sole exception, as it strikes the key not with the tip, but the edge; it is held away from the hand, with the tip-joint bent.

III

WRIST-EXERCISE

As soon as the posture of the hand is quite under control, press rather firmly on the five white keys and lower and raise the wrist slowly and repeatedly, taking care (1) that the hand remains rounded upward, (2) that the fingers retain their position, (3) that on raising the wrist it does not rise higher than its original position, and (4) that the upper arm does not follow the wrist-motion.

Repeat this exercise for only a few days, and with the hands in alternation.

IV

SOME GENERAL RULES

The following fundamental rules are very important even for the finger-exercises; they should, therefore, be learned at the very beginning.

(1) It is best to play all finger-exercises at first only with a light touch; after two or three days one may try to get more tone, always endeavoring to play evenly (with equal strength of tone) with all the fingers. This is accomplished by an unequal exertion of pressure on the keys in conformity with the unequal length and muscular strength of the fingers. Strongest of all is the thumb; then comes the 3d finger, followed in order of strength by the 5th, 2d, and finally, as the weakest, the 4th. But in this case we do not observe the ordinary educational rule, and treat the weakling with indulgence; we must, on the contrary, exert the strongest pressure on it, to remedy its inequality. The dynamometer for the exertion of force at any given time is the ear. One must *hear* whether the tones finally sound equal in force. After some practice the fingers will accustom themselves to the necessary degree of pressure.

(3) Without interrupting practice, lower and raise the hand frequently while playing, as described in Section III. By so doing one prevents the hand from growing stiff.

(4) When the finger is raised from the key, it must not change its form, but remain curved. Bending the raised finger inward, or stretching it out stiff and straight, does not look well, and is a waste of strength at the expense of tone and velocity.

(5) Always keep a watchful eye on the finger-tip, and strike the key exactly with the tip; for that is the only way to bring out a full, strong tone.

(6) Let us remark, in advance, that in playing a melody *forte*, or for strong accents, the black keys are struck, not with rounded, but with outstretched fingers. The fingers thus touch a wider key-surface and are less apt to slide off.[35]

XIV

STYLES OF TOUCH

When a strong, full tone is to be brought out *legato* in a *cantilena*, the strength of the fingers does not suffice, but must be reinforced by wrist-pressure in the following way: Touch the key lightly and force the finger to press it down deep (without losing contact with it) by means of a swift upward movement of the wrist; at this instant, wrist and finger-joints must be firm. The same effect may also be obtained by a rapid down-stroke of the wrist. Immediately after striking the tone, the wrist must return to its normal position, while the finger holds the key lightly. Practise this singing tone on five tones.[36]

XVI

CHORDS

The principle of playing chords is to press, not to strike them. The tones of a chord struck from on high sound hard, and do not carry well. Therefore, press the chords down in the following manner: The hand is arched as far as the stretch permits; the fingers are curved; the finger-tips and wrist remain firm during the stroke, which, as described in detail in Section XIV (*legato* in a *cantilena*), is effected by a wrist-movement upward or downward. In a slow succession of chords, either wrist-movement may be utilized; in a rapid succession, only the upward movement. For playing chords *forte* or *fortissimo* the wrist-movement must be greater and more vehement, for *piano* chords less extended and slower.

In order that chord-playing may not tire one too soon, it is indispensable not to hold the chords with a stiff wrist after striking them. Relax the wrist instantly after the stroke; then it will be unnecessary to expend more strength than is requisite simply to hold the keys down. Thus the hand rests, and can better resist fatigue.

To make sure of striking a chord clean, it must be prepared before taken. To prepare, place the fingers on their respective keys, as if to take the measure of the chord; now, try to take its measure away from the keys, in the air, and keep on until the correct stretch is learned. By dint of practice, the hand finally learns to prepare the chord rightly at sight of the notes—to recognize its physiognomy, as it were. This is of peculiar value in taking the chord-leaps in modern virtuoso-pieces. [37]

XXVII

MOVEMENTS OF THE HAND AND ARM

Pianists of fiery temperament often execute acrobatic marvels with their uplifted hands, as if to show the audience that they have risen superior to all earthly trammels, and make a mere play of difficulties. These are fancy tricks not wholly devoid of piquancy, and may be viewed with indulgence when accompanying virtuoso performance. In contrast to these are the necessary movements of the wrist, which serve to facilitate the execution of phrases, to support the rhythm, or to rest the hand after the tension of *forte*-playing by relaxation of the joint; there are, besides, the motions of the arms, which are thrown upward by an involuntary reflex movement after striking vigorously. None of these movements should be destitute of freedom and grace. [38]

Obviously this material was no advance in the piano technique field. Deppe and Mason accomplished far more in promoting a meaningful piano technique. There is even more to learn from the Czerny and Hummel method books. What we find is the tightly curved hand position, vertical fingers with unprepared percussive action, the low wrist—all remarkably similar to the Stuttgart finger school and its antecedents. Diligent repetition is stressed to achieve strength, accuracy and speed. It is true that the necessity of preparing tones is seen in the references to pressing the chords and using wrist pressure in the cantilena legato touch. Free movement in the wrist and relaxation of the hand are encouraged, but the work of the fingers and hand is stressed far more than that of the arm. Arm weight is not mentioned. And nowhere is there any real explanation of what the muscular coordination should be, a fault Brée has in common with all the early methods. Schultz has pointed out, "Different muscular co-ordinations and different types of movement may show exactly the same outward appearance and yet be radically different in the musical effect which they produce. Concerning these factors of co-ordination and movement-type, Mme. Brée remains completely silent." [39]

Furthermore Mme. Brée's text is full of vagaries and erroneous statements. For example, the tightly curved finger is not the best one for gaining strength; a flatter finger, which has to exert itself more, is. And the finger tip is not the only way to bring out a full, strong tone. By raising and lowering the hand, one does not necessarily prevent the hand (she probably means the wrist) from growing stiff.

No doubt Leschetizky's personal technique transcended Malwine Brée's explanations, yet he put his stamp of approval on her quite inconsequential book. He seemed not to have been greatly aware of nor concerned about the work of Matthay or Breithaupt and the relaxation-weight school which was contemporary with him. Too often the impression of the Leschetizky method that came down through many of his students was the one which Josef Hofmann had received, "I have not studied Leschetizky, but I think that he believes in a very low position of the hand and a sort of super-energetic tension of the tendons of the arms and hands."[40]

But Leschetizky's vital emphasis on tone and an intensely live musical expression surely established him as one of the finest inspirational teachers of piano although, like Liszt, he added little of significance to the physical technique literature. A few of his teaching aphorisms may shed more light on the reasons for his phenomenal success with his students:

To make an effective *accelerando* you must glide into rapidity as steadily as a train increases its speed when steaming out of a station.

Teach yourself to make a *rallentando* evenly by watching the drops of water cease as you turn off a tap.

A player with an unbalanced rhythm reminds me of an intoxicated man who cannot walk straight.

Your fingers are like capering horses, spirited and willing, but ignorant of where to go without a guide. Put on your bridle and curb them in till they learn to obey you, or they will not serve you well.

If you are going to play a scale, place your hand in readiness on the keyboard in the same position as you would if you were going to write a letter—or to take a pinch of snuff.

The bystander ought to know by the attitude of your hand what chord you are going to play *before* you play it, for each chord has its own physiognomy.

If you play wrong notes, either you do not know *where* the note is or *what* the note is.

If your wrists are weak, go and roll the grass in the garden.

If you want to develop strength and sensitiveness in the tips of your fingers, use them in every-day life. For instance, when you go out for a walk, hold your umbrella with the tips instead of in the palm of your hand. [41]

Notes

[1] Annette Hullah, *Theodor Leschetizky*, p. 5.

[2] Countesse Angèle Potocka, *Theodore Leschetizky, An Intimate Study of the Man and the Musician*, pp. 89-91.

[3] Hullah, *Leschetizky*, p. 6.

[4] Artur Schnabel, *My Life and Music*, p. 124.

[5] Ethel Newcomb, *Leschetizky as I Knew Him*, p. 194.

[6] *Ibid.*, p. 107.

[7] *Ibid.*, p. 127.

[8] *Ibid.*, pp. 127-28, 132.

[9] *Musical Courier*, February 15, 1893, Vol. XXVI, No. 7, p. 11.

[10] Newcomb, *Leschetizky as I Knew Him*, p. 194.

[11] *Ibid.*, p. 19.

[12] *Ibid.*, p. 40.

[13] Frank Merrick, *Practising the Piano*, p. 1.

[14] *Musical Courier*, December 27, 1930, Vol. CI, No. 26, p. 6.

[15] Hullah, *Leschetizky*, pp. 49-50.

[16] Schnabel, *My Life and Music*, p. 10.

[17] *Ibid.*, p. 26.

[18] *Ibid.*, p. 124.

[19] Harold C. Schonberg, *The Great Pianists, from Mozart to the Present*, p. 277.

[20] Potocka, *Leschetizky, An Intimate Study*, pp. 51-52.

[21] Newcomb, *Leschetizky as I Knew Him*, pp. 31-32.

[22] Quoted in *London Sunday Telegram*, reprinted in *Piano Teacher*, January-February, 1963, p. 3.

[23] Harriette Brower, *Piano Mastery*, p. 150.

[24] Hullah, *Leschetizky*, pp. 41-42.

[25] Brower, *Piano Mastery*, p. 127.

[26] Edwin Hughes, "Theodor Leschetizky on Modern Pianoforte Study", *The Etude*, April, 1909, p. 227.

[27] Brower, *Piano Mastery*, p. 54.

[28] *The Etude*, p. 227.

[29] Schnabel, *My Life and Music*, p. 11.

[30] *Ibid.*, p. 137.

[31] Malwine Brée, *The Groundwork of the Leschetizky Method issued with his approval by his assistant Malwine Brée*, p. 1.

[32] Schonberg, *Great Pianists*, p. 279.

[33] Newcomb, *Leschetizky as I Knew Him*, pp. 54-55.

[34] Bree, *Groundwork of Leschetizky Method*, p. iv.

[35] *Ibid.*, pp. 1-5.

[36] *Ibid.*, p. 29.

[37] *Ibid.*, pp. 33-34.

[38] *Ibid.*, p. 78.

[39] Arnold Schultz, *The Riddle of the Pianist's Finger and Its Relationship to a Touch-Scheme*, p. 234.

[40] Josef Hofmann, *Piano Playing with Piano Questions Answered by Josef Hofmann*, p. 145.

[41] Hullah, *Leschetizky*, p. 63.

14.   Russian Nationalism

While Liszt and Leschetizky were presiding over their in-
formal conservatories in Weimar and Vienna, other formally
organized ones were flourishing in the music centers throughout
Europe. The piano had fully come into its own and students of
every nationality were diligently pursuing careers as performing
pianists and teachers. The prototype of all conservatories was
founded in Paris in 1795: the Conservatoire de Musique. The first
quarter of the nineteenth century saw others come into existence in
Milan, Naples, Prague, Brussels, Florence, Vienna, London and
The Hague. In 1843 Mendelssohn founded the Leipzig Conservatory, and Anton Rubinstein the St. Petersburg Conservatory in
1862. Nationalistic traits began to be evident and definite schools
of piano playing to emerge. Leschetizky observed these differences.
His student, Annette Hullah, summarized his impressions:

From the English he expects good musicians, good workers,
and bad executants; doing by work what the Slav does by instinct; their heads serving them better than their hearts.

The Americans he finds more spontaneous. Accustomed to
keep all their faculties in readiness for the unexpected, their
perceptions are quick, and they possess considerable technical facility. They study perhaps more for the sake of being
up to date than for the love of music.

The Russians stand first in Leschetizky's opinion. United to
a prodigious technique, they have passion, dramatic power,
elemental force, and extraordinary vitality. Turbulent
natures, difficult to keep within bounds, but making wonderful players when they have the patience to endure to the
end.

The Pole, less strong and rugged than the Russian, leans
more to the poetical side of music. Originality is to be found
in all he does; refinement, an exquisite tenderness, and instinctive rhythm.

The French he compares to birds of passage, flying lightly up in the clouds, unconscious of what lies below. They are dainty, crisp, clear-cut in their playing, and they phrase well.

The Germans he respects for their earnestness, their patient devotion to detail, their orderliness, and intense and humble love of their art. But their outlook is a little grey.

The gentle Swedes, in whom he finds much talent, are more sympathetic to him; and the Italian he loves, because he *is* Italian—though he cannot, as a rule, play the piano in the very least. [1]

How they all may have varied in their physical approach to the piano is not so clearly defined. The stereotyped technique of the Stuttgart school may well have been indicative of the methodical, meticulous aspects of the German character, and an Anton Rubinstein technique more likely to develop among the characteristically more passionate Slavic peoples. Although cultural makeup will surely be reflected to a considerable degree in interpretation at the keyboard, an ethnic cataloging of different types of technique is impossible. Schnabel was quick to underscore this point:

I cannot accept that there is anything specifically Russian about playing with straight and flat fingers. I lived for thirty years in Germany and even so I would not be able to say what the "German technique" is. For in Germany all kinds of piano techniques were taught—flat or round fingers, stretched out or drawn in, elbows fixed or waving, glued to the hips or far out, like a washerwoman's. Some put the tip of their nose on the keys, others looked at the ceiling. Which one was the "German technique"? . . . There is only one good technique, whether you ride a bicycle or swim or whatever else you do, and that is to attain a maximum of achievement with a minimum of effort. That applies to all physical activity. [2]

The development of piano technique among the Germans has thus far occupied a considerable portion of this study. It was not until the second half of the nineteenth century that a school of Russian pianists began to achieve international recognition. And when the Russians finally came into their own, they all but took over the piano scene. Western European pianistic influence in Russia first began to be felt when John Field, pupil of Clementi, settled in St. Petersburg in 1803. He became well-known as both performer and teacher.

Then Adolph von Henselt (1814-1889), a German who had studied with Hummel, came to Russia in 1838 and began an influential forty-year teaching career. In St. Petersburg he was the official imperial court pianist and teacher of the royal children. As musical inspector of the imperially endowed, elite girls' boarding schools, he supervised the training of the music teachers and personally administered student examinations. He had much to do with laying the foundation of a significant school of Russian pianists. Rachmaninoff's grandfather was one of his students. Dannreuther called Henselt the link between the styles of Hummel and Liszt: "With Hummel's strictly *legato* touch, quiet hands and strong fingers, Henselt produced effects of rich sonority something like those which Liszt got with the aid of the wrist and pedals." [3] A specialty of his was to play widespread chords and arpeggio patterns with his enormous reach and without the assistance of the pedal. Indefatigable in his practice habits, he was a sensitive, serious pianist, highly regarded by his contemporaries. Liszt said that no one could imitate Henselt's wonderful touch. [4]

Bettina Walker, who studied with Henselt at the very close of his life, was ecstatic over what she heard:

To speak of this wonderful touch, so as to convey any idea of what it was like to those who have never heard him—now, alas! will never hear him—is, I feel, a hopeless, an almost absurd task; and yet I shall try by just one or two imperfect metaphors to give some idea of it, however faint and dim.

Henselt's touch suggested a shelling—a peeling off of every particle of fibrous or barky rind; the unveiling of a fine, inner, crystalline, and yet most sensitive and most vitally elastic pith. With this, it suggested a dipping deep, deep down into a sea of tone, and bringing up thence a pearl of flawless beauty and purity; something, too, there was of the exhalation of an essence—so concentrated, so intense, that the whole being of the man seemed to have passed for the moment into his finger-tips, from which the sound seemed to well out, just as some sweet yet pungent odour from the chalice of some rare flower. [5]

She was also greatly impressed by the flexibility in his playing. Hearing that he once told a pupil "to imagine that he was sinking his fingers into warm wax," Miss Walker became curious:

On my repeating this to Henselt, he said he had not spoken of warm wax. "But I believe I have," he said, "told pupils to think that they are going to sink their fingers in dough." This is but one instance of Henselt's abhorrence of anything inelastic. "An ass," he said once, "can give the notes a knock like that!" And another time, when a pupil had come down with too hard an emphasis, he exclaimed in anger, "You just come in there with the tramp of a trooper!" [6]

Henselt said that his only method was "a simple and thorough carrying out of those fundamental and absolutely incontrovertible principles of true art which all musicians and all teachers are bound to know and follow, and which are contained in every sound pianoforte school." [7] His Etudes, Opuses 2 and 5, have great musical as well as technical value.

It will be recalled that Liszt's concert tours took him to Russia as did Leschetizky's. Leschetizky stayed to teach before moving on to Vienna. But the first giant among pianists to spring from the Russian soil was Anton Rubinstein (1829-1894), who was born in the southwestern frontier of Bessarabia. When he was five, his family moved to Moscow where he continued his early study with his mother. At the age of eight, he began five years of instruction under Alexandre Villoing (1804-1878), the son of a Frenchman who had come to Russia during the 1789 Revolution. At this time the outstanding piano teacher in Moscow, Villoing had had his early training under John Field's student, Dubuc. In 1840 Villoing took young Rubinstein to Paris ostensibly for further training at the Conservatoire. Cherubini, the director, would not even consent to hear the young foreign-born pianist and Villoing, still holding a strong paternal interest in him, had no desire to press the matter. Anton remained in Paris for a year under Villoing's tutelage. He became well-known as a performer and received considerable encouragement from both Chopin and Liszt. Liszt, whose grandiose style Anton was quick to imitate, feared the boy was being exploited and urged Villoing to take him to Germany for more serious music study, particularly in counterpoint. En route through the Netherlands, so many performance opportunities developed that Villoing dropped the idea and instead embarked upon a concert tour lasting over eighteen months.

Rubinstein was enthusiastically received throughout Europe, England, and Scandinavia, returning to Russia in 1843. The following year Anton's mother took him and his brother Nicholas to Berlin; later Nicholas also had a brilliant career as a pianist, and was the guiding force at the Moscow Conservatory. At Mendelssohn's suggestion, Nicholas studied piano with Kullak and, along with his brother Anton, theory with Siegfried Dehn. Anton had already begun his long career as a prolific composer, but temperamentally he was not fitted to a rigid discipline of polyphonic study under Dehn. When in 1846 word was received of his father's death, his family returned to Moscow while Anton went to Vienna. There he did not receive the encouragement from Liszt he thought he would in resuming his concert career. Things went from bad to worse. His days of childhood triumph were over. Eventually he returned to Russia and settled in St. Petersburg in 1849 to begin a period of teaching and intense self-development. In 1854 he set out once more for Western Europe on the beginning of his long, successful adult career, one which closely rivaled Liszt's in its greatness.

Von Bülow called Rubinstein the "Michelangelo of Music."[8] There was a grandeur, a loftiness, an intensely passionate, spontaneous quality in his playing that even Liszt could scarcely match. The elements of the Russian musical character were all present: warm emotional projection, drive, abandon, and sincerity. He was called the "Russian bear" and his appearance and manner greatly resembled Beethoven's. Sitwell summarized his stage appearance:

> He is described as coming on to the platform with his curious, shambling walk, looking like an old animal. He had something animal about his downcast, shaggy head and the shape of his limbs and back. He was like a bear led along on a chain; so awkward were his legs, with their appearance of being jointed the wrong way, that he was even compared by some witnesses to an elephant. This curious impression that he gave continued until he touched the piano. Then, everything altered. His head was held high in the air, and he assumed a magnificent leonine presence. As soon as his fingers touched the notes, the transition came over his whole personality. His first attack was famous and unforgettable.[9]

Probably no great pianist missed more notes and yet so profoundly moved his listeners. Rachmaninoff recalled a recital in which he forgot while playing Balakireff's *Islamey*. He improvised for about four minutes and finally returned to play the concluding section correctly. This irritated him so that the next selection was played "with the greatest exactness, but, strange to say, it lost the wonderful charm of the interpretation of the piece in which his memory had failed him."[10] Rachmaninoff felt that "for every possible mistake he may have made, he gave, in return, ideas and musical tone pictures that would have made up for a million mistakes. When Rubinstein was over-exact his playing lost something of its wonderful charm."[11]

Josef Lhevinne attributed many of Rubinstein's inaccuracies to "a fat, pudgy hand, with fingers so broad at the finger-tips that he often had difficulty in not striking two notes at one time."[12]

Rubinstein himself said that he did not have hands, but paws. [13] His fleshy finger tips, Lhevinne felt, had much to do with "his glorious tone." [14] Like Chopin and Liszt, Rubinstein's playing and his physical technique were a great inspiration to and exerted a powerful influence upon the important teachers and theorists of the day—such as Leschetizky, Deppe, Breithaupt, and Matthay. In spite of his sometimes erratic, impetuous manner, Rubinstein's technique had certain ideal qualities about it. Through his teacher Villoing, with his Clementi-Field musical ancestry, he received encouragement for developing a fine finger technique and tonal sensitivity. And temperamentally Rubinstein naturally adopted Liszt's free use of full arm movement. Lhevinne observed how he "employed the weight of his body and shoulders." He said that "Rubinstein could be heard over the entire orchestra playing fortissimo. The piano seemed to peal out gloriously as the king of the entire orchestra; but there was never any suggestion of noise, no disagreeable pounding." [15]

Although Thalberg and Herz preceded him, Rubinstein was the first truly great European pianist to play in America. During the 1872–1873 season from September to May, he made no less than 215 appearances throughout the land—in New York, Boston, Montreal, Detroit, Cleveland, Chicago, New Orleans, and many other cities. He gave unstintingly; his manager, Grau, wrote:

> The moment he arrived in his hotel room, Rubinstein would begin to practice. He never slighted a single audience, no matter how small, by neglect or carelessness. He studied and worked, studied and worked continuously. How his constitution stood the immense strain is remarkable. Yet there was never a complaint. His was the most lovable disposition imaginable. [16]

Rubinstein's most lasting effect was felt in Russia where he exerted profound influence in music education circles. From 1862–1867 he was the first director of the newly formed St. Petersburg Conservatory which had both Leschetizky and Dreyschock on its piano faculty. In 1866 his brother Nicholas had become the director of the newly formed Moscow Conservatory. By the time Anton returned to St. Petersburg in 1887 to resume its directorship for a brief four-year period, these conservatories were already playing a major role in the development of a Russian school of first-rank pianists and teachers. These included Safonov, Zverev, Siloti, Gabrilowitsch, Josef and Rosina Lhevinne, Rachmaninoff, Blumenfeld, and Annette Essipov—Leschetizky's second wife, who taught Prokofiev and Isabelle Vengerova. Mme. Vengerova was also a Leschetizky pupil and later taught at the St. Petersburg Conservatory before joining the Curtis Institute of Music in Philadelphia in 1924. [17] There she taught with distinction and developed pupils of the stature of Samuel Barber, Lukas Foss, Jacob Lateiner, Gary Graffman, and Leonard Bernstein. Contemporary descendants of the Russian School, related directly or indirectly, are such great pianists as Vladimir Horowitz, Artur Rubinstein, Heinrich Neuhaus and Neuhaus' students, Sviatoslav Richter and Emil Gilels—the latter now an artist-teacher at the Moscow Conservatory. Neuhaus (1888–1964) has had an immense impact on Russian study. His invaluable book, *The Art of Piano Playing,* was translated into English in 1973.

Rubinstein returned to the St. Petersburg Conservatory a conquering hero. Throughout the 1885–1886 concert season he had presented in the major European cities a monumental series of historical recitals, seven lengthy programs covering a large part of the literature. Many times the following morning, he would repeat the program of the previous evening, without charge, for the benefit of the students. In Berlin alone he gave seventeen recitals. He climaxed the season by presenting the series in both Moscow and St. Petersburg. Even the most severe critics were won over by his mature art. Eduard Hanslick, hearing him in this crowning achievement, was moved to write:

> Young virtuosi must beware of imitating the excesses of Rubinstein's playing, rather learning from him to play with expression, keeping strict watch over the tempo. . . . The merits of Rubinstein's playing are found principally in his elemental powers, and from this source spring also many of his faults. With years, his playing has become more equal. The bewitching beauty of his tones, the power and delicacy of his touch have now reached their climax. One seldom finds in contemporary pianists that genuine, spontaneous inward fervor which in the heat of passion dares all things, even to indiscretion, rather than pause to reason and reflect. Where reflection is absent, there may be heard the overwhelming voice of the passions and the heartstrings echoing in response. Rubinstein's temperament is of such compelling force that exhausted Europe yields submissive to his will. [18]

The twelve-year-old student of Zverev at the Moscow Conservatory, Sergei Rachmaninoff (1873–1943), also heard him and later wrote:

> It was not so much Rubinstein's magnificent technique that held one spellbound as the profound, spiritually refined

293

musicianship, which spoke from every note and bar he played, and singled him out as the most original and unequaled pianist in the world. Naturally I never missed a note, and I remember how deeply I was affected by his rendering of the *Appassionata* or Chopin's *Sonata in B Minor.*

Once he repeated the whole finale of the *Sonata in B Minor,* perhaps because he had not succeeded in the short crescendo at the end as he would have wished. One listened entranced, and could have heard the passage over and over again, so unique was the beauty of the tone which his magic touch drew from the keys. I have never heard the virtuoso piece *Islamey,* by Balakirev, as Rubinstein played it, and his interpretation of Schumann's little fantasy, *The Bird as Prophet,* was inimitable in poetic refinement; to describe the diminuendo of the pianissimo at the end as the "fluttering away of the little bird" would be hopelessly inadequate. Inimitable, too, was the soul-stirring imagery in the *Kreisleriana,* the last (G minor) passage of which I have never heard anyone play in the same manner. One of Rubinstein's great secrets was his use of the pedal. He himself has very happily expressed his ideas on the subject when he said, "The pedal is the soul of the piano." No pianist should ever forget this. [19]

From September 1889 to May 1890, Rubinstein gave a weekly historical lecture series at the conservatory in which he discussed as well as performed the great milestones of piano literature he had presented so triumphantly on tour. His audiences included such musical greats as Glazounov, Rimsky-Korsakov, Gabrilowitsch, and Leopold Auer. Throughout these latter years at the conservatory he furthered his influence by teaching a class of advanced piano students. He paid little attention to a theory of touch, calling himself a practical musician. [20] If a student wanted theoretical instruction he should go to Leschetizky; in turn Leschetizky told his students to observe Rubinstein's tone, his pedaling, his breathing and relaxation. [21] Sometimes, in order to get the type of touch he desired, he would stroke the back of the student's hand in the appropriate manner. His Scottish pupil, Lillian Macarthur, said that in order to gain the effect Rubinstein wanted, she achieved it more by willing the tone rather than by touching the key in any particular way. [22] This vague approach worked for some and not for others. His temper was a powerful motivating factor in his students just as Villoing's had been in the young Rubinstein. He complained one day: "Why are my pupils afraid of me? All I do is stamp on their feet and scream at them. They should not fear a little screaming." [23] He expected intensive work habits from each one. He informed one boy that Field had practiced a passage three thousand times. Each time the boy hesitated, Rubinstein screamed at him, "3000 times!" [24]

Although he had much earlier taken a fatherly interest in Teresa Carreño's career, the only non-conservatory student he ever had was Josef Hofmann. These lessons took place during two winters in the early 1890s after Rubinstein had retired from the conservatory and was residing temporarily near Dresden. Hofmann told about his teaching method: his refusal to demonstrate at the piano, his indirect approach through the use of imagery, his refusal to allow liberties with the text, his insistence on mood projection. In playing an identical phrase repetition (as in a sequence), Hofmann was advised: "In fine weather you may play it as you did, but when it rains play it differently." [25]

Although Rubinstein had often played with considerable liberty himself, he admonished his student: "When you are as old as I am now you may do as I do—if you can." [26] He also told him:

Before your fingers touch the keys you must begin the piece mentally—that is, you must have settled in your mind the tempo, the manner of touch, and above all, the attack of the first notes, before your actual playing begins. And bye-the-bye, what is the character of this piece? Is it dramatic, tragic, lyric, romantic, humorous, heroic, sublime, mystic—what? [27]

Hofmann further described the nature of his instruction:

He would stand at my side, and whenever he wanted a special stress laid upon a certain note his powerful fingers would press upon my left shoulder with such force that I would stab the keys till the piano fairly screamed for me. When this did not have the effect he was after he would simply press his whole hand upon mine, flattening it out and spreading it like butter all over the keys, black and white ones, creating a frightful cacophony. Then he would say, almost with anger, "But cleaner, cleaner, cleaner," as if the discord had been of my doing.

Once I asked him for the fingering of a rather complex passage. "Play it with your nose," he replied, "but make it sound well!" This remark puzzled me, and there I sat and wondered what he meant. As I understand it now he meant: Help yourself! The Lord helps those who help themselves!

As I said before, Rubinstein never played for me the works I had to study. He explained, analysed, elucidated everything that he wanted me to know; but, this done, he left me to my own judgment, for only then, he would explain, would my achievement be my own and incontestable property. I learned from Rubinstein in this way the valuable truth that the conception of tone-pictures obtained through the playing of another gives us only transient impressions; they come and go, while the self-created conception will last and remain our own. [28]

Later Hofmann wrote how he evaluated Rubinstein in relation to Liszt. He said:

As a virtuoso I think Liszt stood above Rubinstein, for his playing must have possessed amazing, dazzling qualities. Rubinstein excelled by his sincerity, by his demoniacal, heaven-storming power of great impassionedness, qualities which with Liszt had passed through the sieve of a superior education and—if you understand how I mean that term— gentlemanly elegance. He was, in the highest meaning of the word, a man of the world; Rubinstein, a world-stormer, with a sovereign disregard for conventionality and for Mrs. Grundy. The principal difference lay in the characters of the two. As musicians, with regard to their natural endowments and ability, they were probably of the same gigantic calibre, such as we would seek in vain at the present time. [29]

One of the finest piano teachers the St. Petersburg Conservatory produced was Rubinstein's close friend, Vassily Ilyitch Safonov (1852–1918). He had studied there with Leschetizky and Brassin, a pupil of Moscheles. Safonov taught at the St. Petersburg Conservatory from 1881 to 1885 and moved on to join the faculty of the Moscow Conservatory in 1885. He was its director from 1889 to 1905 where his distinguished pupils included Alexander Scriabin and Josef and Rosina Lhevinne. In 1915, he wrote a short technical treatise entitled *New Formula for the Piano Teacher and Piano Student.* This twenty-eight page booklet, which contains exercises in five-finger patterns, double notes, rhythmic scales, and chords, has a fourfold objective: finger independence, evenness in touch, dexterity, and tonal beauty. Safonov's definition of independence is "the faculty of combining each finger of the right hand with each finger of the left, and vice versa, *ad libitum.*" As an example, a simple five-finger pattern might be practiced with the following combination of fingerings between the hands:

Ex.2.

30

An exhaustive series of formulae is provided. He cautioned against mechanical repetition: "Vividness of tone is the only condition of fruitful study." [31] In connection with double note studies, Safonov stated:

Legatissimo is another important feature of these exercises, therefore the sound must never be produced by hitting the keys, but by an elastic fall on them from the root of the fingers, so that the weight of the arm is felt in the finger-tips, without the slightest stiffness of the wrist. [32]

His suggestion on chord playing shows the Rubinstein influence:

Unless a special effect of roughness is intended, a chord must never be prepared in a stiff position, for then the sound becomes hard and wooden. The chord must, so to speak, be hidden in the closed hand, which opens, in falling from above for the necessary position, just at the moment of striking the keyboard. This means that the chord must be ready in the thought of the player before the hand opens. This was the secret of the incomparable beauty of sound in the chords of Anton Rubinstein, whose playing the author of this book had the good fortune to watch closely for many years. [33]

Here is invaluable material coming from a master piano teacher who for a time was conductor of the Moscow Philharmonic and later of the New York Philharmonic. Safonov directed without baton and often made use of his conducting techniques in guiding his piano students into feeling a musical line or interpretative detail. Maria Levinskaya studied for five years with Safonov at the Moscow Conservatory and observed that "his teaching tended towards extreme smoothness and pliability. He was continually reminding students of the circular turn of the elbow and shoulder at the end of scales and arpeggios for their return journey." She also felt that he was "a connecting link between active finger technique and weight methods." [34]

Later Mme. Levinskaya herself worked at perfecting a system to incorporate the best features of the old finger methods and the weight school exemplified by Breithaupt. In 1930 she published a volume entitled, *The Levinskaya System of Pianoforte Technique and Tone-Colour through Mental and Muscular Control*. In it she devotes a chapter to making a discerning comparative survey of various historical approaches to piano technique. In two interesting charts, included here, she depicts the advantages and disadvantages of the conflicting methods and outlines the advantages of her own amalgamation. [35]

297

OLD FINGER METHODS   MODERN WEIGHT METHODS

Their advantages and possible disadvantages   **Their advantages and possible disadvantages**

HARD TOUCH

STRENGTH AND BRILLIANCY IN

STIFFNESS

ff PASSAGES

INDEPENDENT FINGER ARTICULATION AND WRIST ACTION

CLEARNESS AND DELICACY IN

CRAMP

pp PASSAGES

HITTING AND BEATING THE KEYS

EXAGGERATED ARM MOVEMENTS

BEAUTIFUL

TONE

LACK OF SUSTAINED LEGATO

WEIGHT RELAXATION ROTATION AND NON-BEDDING OF THE KEYS

IN

LYRIC

BLURRED PASSAGE WORK LACKING IN STEEL-LIKE BRILLIANCY AND CRISPNESS

MELODY

LACK OF DEPTH AND INTENSITY OF TONE

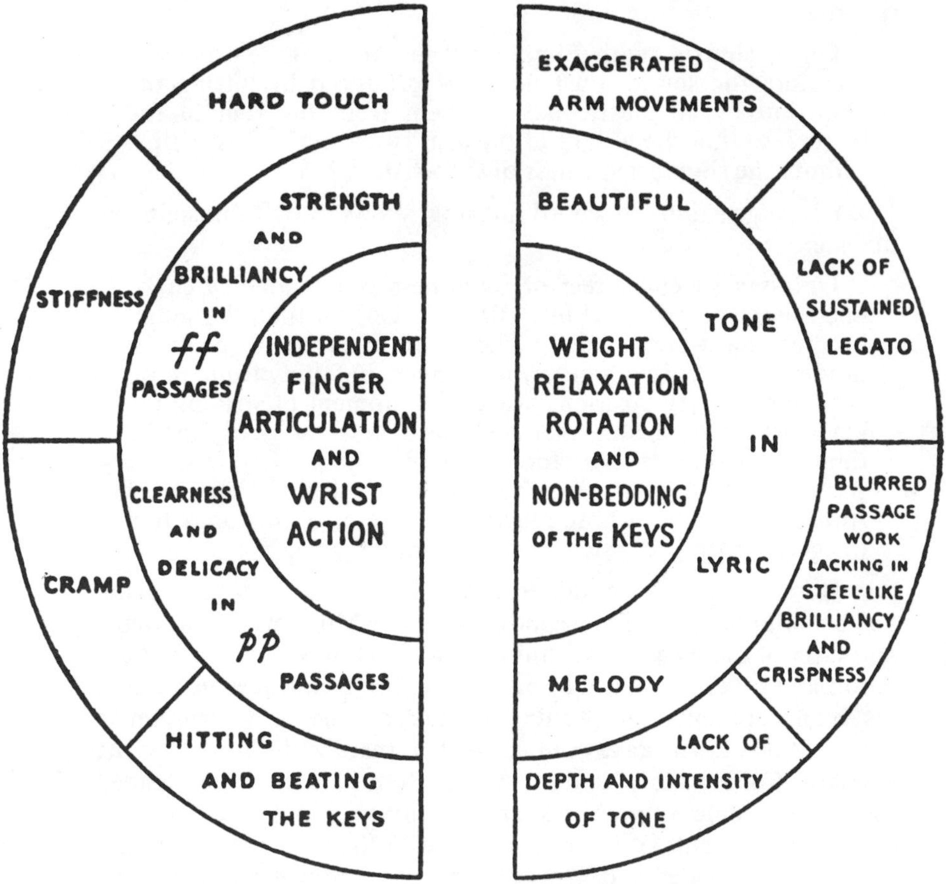

FIG. 1.—DESCRIPTION OF THE DIAGRAM

THE SEMI-CIRCLES are intended to represent the two halves (the old and the new) of the complete Art of Piano Playing.

INSET—The leading principles on which each is based.

INNER BAND—The outstanding qualities of each.

OUTER BAND—The frequent failings through lack of scientific knowledge.

298

THE LEVINSKAYA SYSTEM

Incorporating the best of the old and the new, and introducing new features.

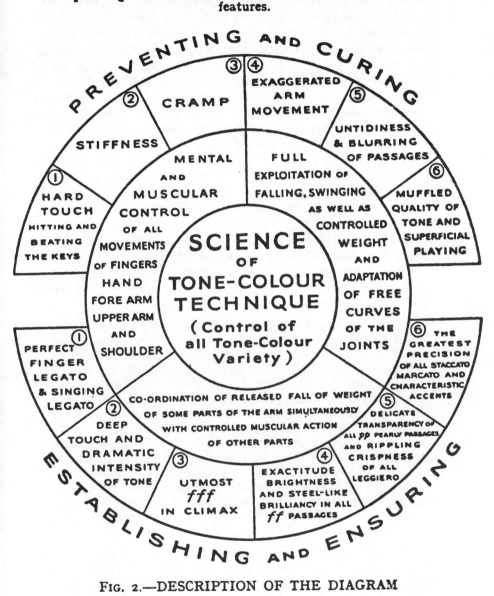

FIG. 2.—DESCRIPTION OF THE DIAGRAM

THE COMPLETE CIRCLE embodies the art and science of pianoforte playing as a whole as presented in the LEVINSKAYA SYSTEM.

INSET—Its rock-bottom basis—aesthetic discrimination of any tone colour through which vista the whole art of pianoforte playing is analysed and synthesised.

INNER BAND—The leading principles on which the system is based.

OUTER BAND—The upper half shows faults eliminated, the lower half shows the artistic qualities acquired.

Safonov's greatest pupil was Josef Lhevinne (1874–1944), who studied with him from the age of four. When he was fourteen, he was selected to play the Beethoven *Emperor* Concerto at the Moscow Conservatory under Anton Rubinstein. After graduating from the conservatory, where he won the gold medal in piano playing and the Rubinstein Prize awarded annually in Berlin, he married his fellow student, Rosina. Besides concertizing, sometimes with his wife as a two-piano team, he taught at the School of the Imperial Russian Musical Society in Tiflis and then the Moscow Conservatory before coming to the United States to present more than one hundred concerts during 1906–1907. The Lhevinnes then settled in Berlin. They returned permanently to the United States immediately after World War I where both became members of the piano faculty of the Juilliard School of Music in New York City. Josef's pupils included Abram Chasins, Adele Marcus, Sascha Gorodnitzski, and Josef Raieff; and Rosina's: Tong Il Han, John Browning, and Van Cliburn.

Few pianists have ever performed with the great refinement, poetic feeling, and perfectionism revealed in Lhevinne's playing. Chasins described the effect that it had on him:

> In the old days I faithfully attended the annual recitals of Josef Lhevinne. They were easy to enjoy. Every piano-lover could revel in his fabulous technical equipment and ravishing tonal palette. His style was refinement itself; his sounds glittered and flowed. Even so, we looked for more in those palmy days: for intellectual profundity; for new concepts and meanings; for an imaginative transfiguration of the music we knew backward and forward.
>
> Well! The other day I replayed the LP disc of Lhevinne issued by Victor in 1955. I felt like an utter fool. At first I was humiliated to remember that I had once dared to sit in critical judgment of Lhevinne's art and to regard it as incomplete. Then I realized what had happened to me and my standards—how I had unconsciously been seduced and persuaded to yield to contemporary criteria of piano mastery. [36]

Madame Lhevinne's performance career, while her husband was alive, had almost entirely been limited to their two-piano appearances. Since 1955, when she performed at Aspen, she has played concertos occasionally. At the invitation of Leonard Bernstein, she made her solo orchestral debut with the New York Philharmonic at Lincoln Center in the Chopin E Minor Concerto in January, 1963, at the age of eighty-two, with remarkable success.

Josef Lhevinne's writings are of great value to present-day students. In 1917 an article on piano study in Russia appeared in James Francis Cooke's book, *Great Pianists on Piano Playing*. He wrote that the folk song and the classics were a vital part of Russian home life and that a great love for music was fostered in the children from the earliest age. Lhevinne said that at the age of five he could already sing some of the Schumann and Beethoven songs. When a musical talent was evident, the whole family united to develop it to its fullest extent. The materials which the teachers gave their students were most carefully graded. Thorough study on each level had to be achieved before the child was permitted to go on to the next, and great care was taken that the advancement was not too rapid.

Lhevinne went on to tell how the Russian pianist achieved his famous technique. Without being permitted to lose sight of musical values, the technical training was exceedingly solid and thorough. He stated:

. . . They build not upon sands, but upon rock. For instance, in the conservatory examinations the student is examined first upon technic. If he fails to pass the technical examination he is not even asked to perform his pieces. Lack of proficiency in technic is taken as an indication of a lack of the right preparation and study, just as the lack of the ability to speak simple phrases correctly would be taken as a lack of preparation in the case of an actor.

Particular attention is given to the mechanical side of technic, the exercises, scales and arpeggios. American readers should understand that the full course at the leading Russian conservatories is one of about eight or nine years. During the first five years, the pupil is supposed to be building the base upon which must rest the more advanced work of the artist. The last three or four years at the conservatory are given over to the study of master works. Only pupils who manifest great talent are permitted to remain during the last year. During the first five years the backbone of the daily work in all Russian schools is scales and arpeggios. All technic reverts to these simple materials and the student is made to understand this from his very entrance to the conservatory. As the time goes on the scales and arpeggios become more difficult, more varied, more rapid, but they are never omitted from the daily work. The pupil who attempted complicated pieces without this preliminary technical drill would be laughed at in Russia. I have been amazed to find pupils coming from America who have been able to play a few pieces fairly well, but who wonder why they find it difficult to extend their musical sphere when the whole trouble lies in an almost total absence of regular daily technical work systematically pursued through several years.

Of course, there must be other technical material in addition to scales, but the highest technic, broadly speaking, may be traced back to scales and arpeggios. The practice of scales and arpeggios need never be mechanical or uninteresting. This depends upon the attitude of mind in which the teacher places the pupil. In fact, the teacher is largely responsible if the pupil finds scale practice dry or tiresome. It is because the pupil has not been given enough to think about in scale playing, not enough to look out for in nuance, evenness, touch, rhythm, etc. etc. [37]

Rachmaninoff, in the same volume, reinforces Lhevinne's description of conservatory technical development. [38] He tells of the very important part that the Hanon studies played during the first fives years of study. At the fifth year examination, the student was required to play selected ones in any key at certain metronomic speeds. He also said that scales were tested as fast as 120 with eight notes per beat. The Tausig, Czerny, and Henselt studies were used with advanced students. Rachmaninoff felt that the beauty of the Henselt Etudes qualified them to be placed in the same class as the Chopin Etudes.

A series of personal conferences with Lhevinne appeared in *The Etude* and shortly afterward was compiled and published in 1924 under the title, *Basic Principles of Pianoforte Playing*. Lhevinne's approach is strictly empirical and non-scientific. But the observations are those of a very sensitive musician and the practical advice, often clothed in imagery, is invaluable to the student. Like Rubinstein and all of the Russian school, the emphasis is on thinking moods into the fingers and arms. A beautiful singing tone must first be conceived mentally. Then the "richness and singing quality of the tone depends very largely (1) upon the amount of key surface covered with the well-cushioned part of the finger and (2) upon the natural 'spring' which accompanies the loose wrist." [39] Lhevinne describes how a legato singing touch may be achieved:

The cultivation of a singing touch should be a part of the daily work of every student who has passed the first few grades of elementary study, if indeed it may not be introduced earlier with students of more mature intelligence. All sorts of exercises will be devised by the skillful teacher. One of the simplest is to take the simple scale like this [G major one octave scale in whole notes].

Poise the hand about two inches above the keys. Hold the hand in normal position as you would upon the piano keyboard (not with the fingers drooping down toward the keys). Now let the hand fall a little with the first joint of the second finger, the wrist still held very flexible so that the weight of the descending hand and arm carries the key down to key bottom, quite without any sensation of a blow. It is the blow or the bump, which is ruinous to good tone. The piano is not a typewriter to be thumped upon so that a sharp, clear type impression will be made. Rather imagine that you are actually playing upon the wires, ringing them with soft felt covered hammers and not with hard metal bars.

As the hand descends for this swinging touch, the finger is curved normally; it is not held straight. As the finger touches the key-surface, it feels as though it were grasping the key, not striking or hitting it. There is a vast difference of sensation here. Always feel as though you had hold of the keys, not that you are merely delivering a blow to it. Do not think of the ivory surface of the keyboard as you would of a table. That idea is entirely wrong. Those who play the piano as though they were strumming on a table will never get the innate principle of a good tone.

Again when the hand descends, as large a surface of the finger tip as feasible engages the key; and the wrist is so loose that it normally sinks below the level of the keyboard. Observe your hand sensations very carefully. The tone is produced in the downward swing of the hand. If it were possible to take one of the exaggeratedly slow moving pictures of this touch, there would be no spot, no place, no movement where the movement seemed to stop on the way down. If there were such a place it would produce a bump. The tone seems to ring out beautiful and clear. The key is touched "on the wing," as it were, in the downward passage. All this concerns only the first note of the melody or phrase. The other notes, if the melody is to be played legato, must be taken with fingers quite near the keys, raising or dropping the wrist according to the design of the melody.

The student who values a good tone will have the patience to practice all his scales, in both hands, one finger at a time, until this principle becomes automatic, until it is just as natural as free and easy walking. He will find that his playing becomes more graceful, more pleasurable, more satisfying to his sense of tonal beauty and to his hearers. But he has to listen! [40]

Lhevinne also concerned himself with the matter of achieving a fine, delicate touch and emphasized three conditions that must be present: (1) the upper arm and forearm must have a feeling of extreme lightness—as though "they are floating in the air" and "with entire absence of nervous tension or stiffening," (2) delicacy is meaningless without depth of tone—every key must touch bottom, (3) the raised fingers must stay very close to the surface of the keys. [41] Then in achieving a fine, agreeable sound in chord playing, he recommended playing

> . . . with the wrists loose, employing the fleshy parts of the fingers and feeling that the weight and power are communicated to the keyboard from the shoulder. This beautiful composition [Military Polonaise] is often ruined by banging, whereas it may be delivered with a lovely tone and rich singing quality. [42]

In an article appearing in *The Musician* for July 1932, Lhevinne amplified the relationship between tone and physical technique:

> One of the most important, as well as one of the most practical things to be acquired by the pianist, is a knowledge of the principle of relaxation and how to apply it to touch and tone. But when one speaks of relaxation one meets with many obstacles, so little is the correct use of relaxation understood. Everything that "flops" is called by this name, when it may be very wide of the mark, and mean nothing at all. The whole world has gone mad over the idea of relaxation, without knowing what it means, or how it should be applied to piano playing.
>
> There must be hand-firmness, or there is no power, exactness, or control. There must be finger-firmness also, or there is no accuracy, and consequently no good tone.
>
> Then, you may ask, where does relaxation come in? In the wrist and arm principally, though the secret of its use and application is to use it in the right place, and not in other places where it would prevent the production of firm, elastic, vibrant tone. That kind of a tone is not produced by flabby, relaxed fingers. We must have firmness and relaxation at one and the same time, but not in the same place. There must generally be resistance in the fingers, no matter how loose wrists and arms may be.
>
> This seeming contradiction of terms is one of the difficulties of touch and tone production, and the subject should be early understood. We can recall some pianists now before the public who are so excessively relaxed that there is much to be desired in the way of accuracy and clearness in their playing.

There are others who go to the other extreme and are stiff and tense, thereby producing a hard, metallic tone. The golden mean would be a just mingling of the two principles.

In regard to position of hand and fingers, I would say, that as a fundamental principle the hand should be arched. Just how much this is to be done depends on the formation of the hand. The fingers can either be played on their tips or on the ball, with high or low wrist. All these things affect in some degree the quality of the tone. Rounded fingers, played on the tips, produce a more or less brilliant tone. Fingers played more upon the ball produce a more velvety quality. For some effects fingers are held quite close to the keys and scarcely raised at all. This is the opposite of the well raised foundation touch, with distinct finger action.

These two touches, namely: high finger action with well rounded fingers, and low action with flatter fingers, are produced in entirely opposite fashion, and naturally effect the tone, although we may say the instrument producing this is mechanical. We know of a certainty that if we strike a quick blow on the key, we get a sharp, brilliant tone; if we caress the key with extended or flat fingers, we evoke a sweet mellow tone. We also know that an artistic use of the pedal will greatly modify the quality of tone.

In regard to playing with weight—which always requires some relaxation, in the right place of course, I would say there should be some conscious weight, as well for pianissimo as for fortissimo. For without weight the tone sounds thin and dry. Just as a voice without resonance has little carrying power, so a touch without weight has no tone quality. Thus to learn how to graduate this use of weight and adapt its use to various effects is a great study. No one can tell the player exactly how to do this; he must find it out for himself, through feeling and experiment. It comes after one is thoroughly grounded in the fundamentals, not before. [43]

Rosina Lhevinne's teaching approach is individual and typically Russian. Winthrop Sargeant noted that

... in the tradition of Anton Rubinstein, she always starts out by getting the student to project the appropriate mood, and to do so with beautiful piano tone as well as adequate technique. "You imagine the sound you wish to produce, and then you produce it," she tells her students over and over. This is not as simple as one might think. Mood is something that must be felt by the individual performer, but merely to feel it is not sufficient. The mood must also be conveyed clearly to the auditor, and it is surprising how few fledgling pianists are able to hear themselves as others hear them. The conscious control of the varying nuances of a composition—of the ebb and flow of phrases and climaxes—to the point where the audience is made clearly aware of them is something that demands great objectivity as well as feeling. [44]

And, like Rubinstein, she never would play for a student nor encourage his listening to a master's recording of a work during the time he is actually studying—for fear of the student's turning into a mimic and sacrificing his own individuality.

Vladimir Horowitz (1904–   ) voiced the identical views in an interview with Jan Holcman. He went on to summarize his own approach to technique and practice as reported by Holcman:

He does not believe in so-called mechanical practicing, but he does take great care to practice with utmost accuracy and control, listening constantly to make sure that everything is properly measured, the "dose" precise. How close his technical and musical aims have been fused may be deduced from his own explanation about the fifth fingers, those real recalcitrants for pianists interested in tonal color. When he was twenty-eight, he already knew that "from the moment one feels that the finger must *sing*, it becomes strong." This approach of Horowitz follows the older traditions and reflects trends of the Russian school—that is, leads to the *expressive* treatment of technique, to "singing" scales instead of metronomic monotony. He says "technique is a temperament and a skill," and he emphasizes: "That means to have the right idea of what to do and the adequate capacity to carry it out."

His own habits have changed little since he described them some years ago: "It is not necessary to repeat the work all the way through. A piece can be practiced 100 times and when it is taken to the stage it can sound simply like practicing the 101st time—it is not fresh. In my work I play a new large-form composition all the way through to obtain an overall viewpoint of its meaning and structure" (horizontal view, the late Prof. Igumnov of Moscow would have said). "Then I do not play it all through again until it is ready for public performance." Before it is ready, Horowitz works at sections, passages, details "one movement today, another tomorrow." He advocates arduous, concentrated labor, though never mechanical. He believes the essential task for a teacher is to show a student how to form his own thoughts and to face, soberly, his strong points and limitations. "To strive for perfection" is one of his mottoes and to do so without being in-

spired by false ambitions or expectations of quick and superficial rewards. Rather to strive because of an inner obligation
which every true artist must feel. [45]

The above statement does not imply that Horowitz does not
engage in pure technical practice. [46] In 1966 he told Abram
Chasins how he rebuilt his technique after his temporary
retirement, begun in March, 1953. Chasins wrote:

For one full year, that sabbatical year, Horowitz never even
touched his piano. Much of that time he accepted no social invitations and invited no one to his home. Rachmaninoff, his
great idol, had once urged him to go for long walks. "If you
don't walk," he had said, "your fingers will not run."

Once he was back at the keyboard, the slow resurrection
began. "I learned something important about retirement," he
recalls. "You must immediately impose new disciplines upon
yourself. Becoming free as a bird after a lifetime of routine
can make you feel awfully lost. At first I just moped around.
Then I realized I had to work out new daily schedules for
myself—so much time for study, for rest, for reflection, for
exercise. . . . Soon my days had a new rhythm, a new serenity.
Every day I start with what I call calisthenics, exercises that I
invent myself. Each day a new set, which I play very, very
slowly. When I practice the standard literature that I have
played before, I practice section by section, and I never move
from one to the other until I am satisfied. Each week I devote
at least two to three hours of my practice time to music I have
never seen or played before." [47]

One product of the St. Petersburg Conservatory who chose to
live in Russia throughout his lifetime was Sergei Prokofiev (1891–
1953). Anti-romantic in his approach to both piano music and
technique even as a young student, he proved to be a trial for Mme.
Essipov with his inclination to explore the sharp, percussive
capabilities of the piano. She wrote regarding his examination at
the conservatory in the spring of 1910: "Has assimilated little of my
method. Very talented but rather unpolished." [48] Reinhold Glière
also encountered similar problems of technical conformity in
Prokofiev's earliest study with him:

He played the piano with great ease and confidence,
although his technique left much to be desired. He played
carelessly and he did not hold his hands properly on the
keyboard. His long fingers seemed very clumsy. Sometimes he
managed rather difficult passages with comparative facility
but at other times he could not play a simple scale or an ordinary arpeggio.

307

I did not know much about pianoforte playing in those years, but I could see that Seryozha's chief trouble was the incorrect hand position. Technically his playing was careless and inaccurate, his phrasing was poor and he paid little attention to detail. Sitting beside him while he played scales, etudes and pieces I tried to help him to overcome these defects. I must say that he was rather obstinate and did not always take my advice in the matter of finger technique. And sometimes he would ask me, not altogether innocently, to play him some difficult passage in an etude or sonata, much to my discomfiture.

At such moments I truly regretted that I had not mastered pianoforte technique myself. (I had had only a few years of obligatory pianoforte study at the Kiev Conservatoire.) I must confess that I have been conscious of this gap in my musical education all my life. I am not envious by nature, but when I see a composer who is at the same time a good pianist I cannot help envying him. True, I studied the violin under such fine tutors as Sevčik and Grzhimal; I have played a good deal in quartets and in orchestras as well, all of which of course has been of much value to me as a composer. But for a composer the violin cannot substitute the piano.

That is why I did my best to help Seryozha in his piano studies and greatly regretted the inadequacy of my own pianistic knowledge.

Seryozha was very fortunate to have been enrolled in the class of such an outstanding pianist and tutor as Annette Essipov. I know that she had quite some difficulty in correcting his hand position, and in the first years many sharp conflicts arose between the distinguished pedagogue and her young pupil. Once, in a fit of anger, Essipov declared, "Either you will place your hands properly on the keyboard, or leave my class!" Prokofiev told me this himself much later. [49]

But the Essipov years were not without lasting benefit. Prokofiev's Russian biographer, Israel Nestyev, felt that

Prokofiev's brilliantly individual style of playing, with its clean-cut finger technique, steel-like touch, and exceptional freedom of wrist movement bore the stamp of the Essipov-Leschetizky school. Prokofiev became one of the greatest Russian virtuosos, and in his best works he enriched piano literature by altogether new means of expression. [50]

The Prokofiev piano works, among the greatest and most significant of the twentieth century with their driving sarcastic rhythms, and both percussive and intensively lyrical qualities, helped to formulate decisively the complete piano technique. Every physical resource had to be employed. That Prokofiev's own mature physical technique was just that is evident from Dmitri Kabalevsky's remembrance of Prokofiev playing his own Third Sonata:

It is hard to describe the impression Prokofiev made on us that evening. I think I shall not be mistaken if I say that that first performance of his gave many of us an entirely new understanding of his music, very different from that gained from the performance of other musicians, who tended to emphasize the elemental quality of the music, the dynamic contrasts and the mechanical elements. The music sounded far richer, far more subtle when Prokofiev played it. Everything he played sounded full-blooded and healthy, both spiritually and physically, everything was colourful, dynamic but without the slightest exaggeration, the slightest crudity let alone coarseness. In short, nothing "Scythian." And what was most important, everything was illumined by the light of sincerity, poetry and human warmth. Moreover, the whole performance was distinguished by a quiet reserve, a total absence of any external pianistic effects that conveyed an impression of a great spiritual calm. With his extraordinary pianistic talents, Prokofiev revealed that rich lyrical feeling in his music which we had failed to notice until then. This was a joyous and unexpected discovery for us. [51]

Kabalevsky also revealed more about Prokofiev in describing another incident:

Once in 1937, when I was staying at the Hotel Europe in Leningrad, I heard some familiar sounds on the piano coming from the next room. At first I could not make out what it was, but after a while I recognized passages from Prokofiev's Third Concerto. What puzzled me was that they were being played so slowly, each figure being repeated over and over again with such persistence that it was hard to recognize the music at once. This painstaking work was continued on the following day as well. On the third day I bumped into Prokofiev in the lift. It turned out that it was he who occupied the room next to mine. I naturally could not refrain from asking him why he was doing such a careful "Conservatoire" job on a piece he had played so brilliantly for so many years in nearly all the concert halls in the world. "The Third Concerto is not the Fifth which nobody ever plays and which very few people know," he replied. "Every dog knows the Third Concerto and so every single passage has to be perfect." The next day he gave a concert in the Large Hall of the Philharmony and played the concerto with his usual brilliance.[52]

Piano study in Russia today does not differ greatly from the days of Lhevinne, Rachmaninoff, and Prokofiev. Outstanding talent is quickly recognized and carefully nourished. Students preparing for conservatory study on the college level still receive thorough technical and musical preparation on the elementary and secondary levels. Jan Holcman stated that there are over five hundred schools alone for the beginner.[53] Prof. A.A. Nikolaev, prorector at the Moscow Conservatory recently wrote:

> We do not have a special technical program of examinations since any pianist or student of piano entering the conservatory is extremely well prepared in piano technique which he receives in any middle-educational institution prior to entering the conservatory. In our program of examinations, we include compositions bringing out a vast technical ability of a young musician. Frequently students perform etudes by Chopin, Liszt, Rachmaninoff, Scriabin, Debussy and other contemporary composers.[54]

Not only in the development of young artists, but in the special conservatory classes for the education of coach-accompanists and children's music teachers is the study demanding and the standard of excellence very high. An official *Syllabus of Special Classes in Piano for Music Schools* published by the Soviet Ministry of Culture in Moscow in 1960 outlines the goals to be achieved. The teachers of these classes (the instruction is actually given in private lessons) are first exhorted to tend to the intellectual and social development of their students so that they may become "true patriotic sons of the fatherland."[55] Musical emphasis includes development of an appreciation for folk music and the classics from Russia and other nations, of sight reading and analytical abilities, and of interpretative and practice skills. Great stress is placed upon learning to work independently on pieces: "The ability to perform and to project an independent interpretation of a composition on the basis of careful and thoughtful study of the text must be developed."[56] Once or twice a year this work is evaluated by the teachers in the presence of his fellow students. Every student must also appear in public performances or exams at least three times a year.

Technical development is equally stressed. The syllabus states:

> The teacher must in every way encourage the student to work on the perfection of his technique. The development of technique in the broad sense of the word is brought about by

all compositions which the student masters; the development of technique in the narrow sense of the word (velocity, agility, evenness) is achieved by systematic work on etudes, scales, and exercises. When working on technique it is imperative to give exact, individual assignments and to supervise their execution regularly. Never must work on technique lead to a piling up of a great number of exercises and their mechanical execution. Here, not only the quantity but the quality of the work, the constant refinement of the performance are important.[57]

Yearly technical requirements are similar to those followed in most American universities and schools of music:

First Year Course.—Major, minor and chromatic scales in octaves in parallel and contrary motion, scales in thirds, sixths and tenths in parallel motion. Broken chords, arpeggios and chords in major and minor with inversions. Dominant seventh chords with inversions, diminished seventh chords.
Second Year Course.—Same scales as in first year, at faster speed. Arpeggios starting on same note (eleven chords) in parallel motion, starting on all white keys. Some scales in double thirds.
Third Year Course.—Major and some (harmonic) minor scales in double thirds, in parallel motion. Chromatic (minor) double scales.[58]

Russia has had its own great—such as Anton Rubinstein, Safonov, and Essipov—who have left a strong imprint on Russian piano technique. But the Russians have also been quick to absorb the best of Western influence. Holcman recently completed an exhaustive study of the present condition of Russian piano playing. He wrote in the *Saturday Review:*

Onto the Russian root and stem have been grafted selected shoots from Western keyboard art that further strengthened modern Soviet methodology. Thus the Soviets adapted ideas from Busoni, Hofmann, Leschetizki, and Breithaupt—who otherwise were open to reserved Soviet criticism.

Current Western trends also keenly interest the Russian musical scholar. While the West generally remains aloof from Soviet piano methods, the Soviets closely follow the West at the keyboard, at times giving the impression that New York is closer to Moscow than Moscow to New York. Every significant bit of material from the West finds its way to the library of the Soviet conservatory. There it is carefully studied by experts with the view of assimilating useful ideas. For instance, all notable 78s (of which a school like the Juilliard

311

owns relatively few) are collected and copied at the Moscow Conservatory, where students and artists may listen to duplicates. It is no accident that on his American tour, Ashkenazy feverishly shopped for Rachmaninoffs, or that Goldenweisser conducted correspondence with Landowska, who gave him some stimulating suggestions for his second Beethoven edition.[59]

Notes

[1] Annette Hullah, *Theodor Leschetizky*, pp. 72-73.

[2] Artur Schnabel, *My Life and Music*, pp. 195-96.

[3] *Grove's Dictionary of Music and Musicians*, 5th ed., IV, 244.

[4] Bettina Walker, *My Musical Experiences*, p. 164.

[5] *Ibid.*, pp. 164-65.

[6] *Ibid.*, pp. 222-23.

[7] Maria Levinskaya, *The Levinskaya System of Pianoforte Technique and Tone-Colour through Mental and Muscular Control*, p. 35.

[8] Henry C. Lahee, *Famous Pianists of Today and Yesterday*, p. 151.

[9] Sacheverell Sitwell, *Liszt*, p. 290.

[10] James Francis Cooke, *Great Pianists on Piano Playing*, pp. 218-19.

[11] *Ibid.*, p. 218.

[12] Josef Lhevinne, *Basic Principles in Pianoforte Playing*, p. 16.

[13] Catherine Drinker Bowen, *"Free Artist"; the Story of Anton and Nicholas Rubinstein*, pp. 335-36.

[14] Lhevinne, *Basic Principles*, p. 16.

[15] *Ibid.*, p. 31.

[16] Bowen, *"Free Artist,"* p. 239.

[17] Isabelle Vengerova (1877–1956) taught at the St. Petersburg Conservatory from 1906 until coming to the United States in 1923. In an unpublished article by Soviet pianist and music scholar Vitaly Neuman, based upon his research in the Vengerova musical archives preserved in Leningrad and translated by Nicolas Slonimsky, we get an interesting description of Mme. Vengerova's pedagogical emphasis, and by inference, the Russian teaching of her day. The great industry of the Russian pianist is evident in one of her early letters to her mother: "Music takes up eleven hours of my day, and I sometimes feel very tired. I have 45 students, of whom 20 are at the Conservatory, and 25 are private." Neuman writes:

The pedagogical talent of Isabelle Vengerova was developed in all its brilliance during her professorship at the St. Petersburg Con-

312

servatory. Her influence on her students was profound. She creatively elaborated the pedagogical principles of her own teachers Leschetizky and Annette Essipov, but introduced also her individual characteristics. The position of the hands, which Vengerova regarded as most important in piano technique, was characterized by the following: (1) The elbows to be kept away from the torso, (2) The wrists to be held with complete freedom, (3) The fingers to maintain a curved position, with strength and precision. Vengerova paid particular attention to the necessity of quick removal of a finger from the key immediately after it is struck, and instantly shifted to the position above the next key to be played. Vengerova devoted much effort to the digital technique, and also gave instruction for the coordination of the movements of the fingers with the motions of the forearm, which she regarded as imperative in order to attain a variety and richness of instrumental sonority.

Jacob Lateiner, who studied with her at the Curtis Institute during his teens, has summarized a number of her concerns: a singing sound and a fine legato, a hand that was molded to the keys for very even playing, the need of playing deeply into the keys with strong fingers, a flexible wrist which all of her students incorporated into their technique. Before working with her, each one had to go through a period of intensive technical drill.

[18] Bowen, *"Free Artist,"* p. 290.

[19] *Ibid.,* pp. 291-92.

[20] *Ibid.,* p. 344.

[21] *Ibid.,* p. 336.

[22] *Ibid.,*

[23] *Ibid.,* p. 335.

[24] *Ibid.,* p. 338.

[25] Josef Hofmann, *Piano Playing with Piano Questions Answered by Josef Hofmann,* p. 58.

[26] *Ibid.,* p. 60.

[27] *Ibid.,* pp. 60-61.

[28] *Ibid.,* pp. 61-64.

[29] *Ibid.,* p. 159.

[30] Vassili Safonoff, *New Formula for the Piano Teacher and Piano Student,* p. 5.

[31] *Ibid.,* p. 19.

[32] *Ibid.,* p. 15.

[33] *Ibid.,* p. 25.

[34] Levinskaya, *The Levinskaya System,* p. 42.

[35] *Ibid.*, ff. p. 72.

[36] Abram Chasins, *Speaking of Pianists*, p. 155.

[37] Cooke, *Great Pianists on Piano Playing*, pp. 176-177.

[38] *Ibid.*, pp. 210-11.

[39] Lhevinne, *Basic Principles*, p. 26.

[40] *Ibid.*, pp. 22-23.

[41] *Ibid.*, pp. 26-28.

[42] *Ibid.*, p. 32.

[43] Josef Lhevinne, "Good Tone Is Born in the Player's Mind," transcribed by Harriette Brower, *The Musician*, July, 1923, Vol. 28, p. 7.

[44] Winthrop Sargeant, "The Leaves of a Tree," *The New Yorker*. January 12, 1963, Vol. XXXVIII, No. 47, p. 52.

[45] Jan Holcman, "An Interview with Horowitz," *Saturday Review of Literature*, Vol. XLIII, No. 18 (April 30, 1960), p. 60.

[46] As early as 1932 Horowitz granted an extensive interview to Florence Leonard of *The Etude* in which he spoke regarding many of his views on technique.

[47] Abram Chasins, "The Return of Horowitz," *The Saturday Evening Post*, October 22, 1966, pp. 102-103.

[48] Israel V. Nestyev, *Prokofiev*, p. 39.

[49] Prokofiev, S., *Autobiography, Articles, Reminiscences*, pp. 146-47.

[50] Israel V. Nestyev, *Prokofiev*, p. 40.

[51] Prokofiev, S., *Autobiography, Articles, Reminiscences*, p. 204.

[52] *Ibid.*, p. 208.

[53] Jan Holcman, "Keyboard Left to Right," *Saturday Review*, July 25, 1959, Vol. 42, p. 33.

[54] Letter to author dated May 26, 1967, translated by Mrs. Carl Swenson.

[55] "Syllabus of Special Classes in Piano for Music Schools," reprinted in *The Journal of Research in Music Education*, Fall, 1964, XII, No. 3, p. 199.

[56] *Ibid.*, p. 203.

[57] *Ibid.*, p. 200.

[58] *Ibid.*, p. 207.

[59] Holcman, "Keyboard Left to Right," p. 33.

15.

The French School

Turning from the German and Russian schools to France, we find that the oldest of modern music schools, the Conservatoire Nationale de Paris, produced numerous fine pianists. Few approached the greatest of the German and Russian performers; as Leschetizky observed, French pianists, by and large, did not possess great emotional intensity, but flew "lightly up in the clouds" reflecting the suave, sophisticated Parisian culture. The earliest conservatoire teachers of importance were Louis Adam, followed by Friedrich Kalkbrenner and Pierre Zimmerman (1785-1853). Kalkbrenner's refined, somewhat superficial, *carezzando* finger touch was passed along to later generations. Antoine de Kontsky (1817-1899), the Polish pupil of John Field who spent part of his life in Paris, described in his *Indispensable du Pianiste* this *carezzando* touch where the key is stroked by the finger from about the middle to the front edge.[1] The key is thus very gently depressed.

Chopin, whose polish and refinement surely outshone the best of the French, revealed far greater substance in his playing and did not truly reflect the prevailing French provincialism. His influence spread far beyond the French borders. Kalkbrenner and his fellow student at the conservatoire, Zimmerman (he took first prize in piano in 1800 and Kalkbrenner, second), are the grandfathers of the French school. Its supple technique was largely finger and hand, descending from the classical refinement of the Couperin-Rameau harpsichord touch. There was none of the super-energetic keyboard digging of the Stuttgarters. The touch was sensitive, it stayed close to the keys, and it did not press deeply. It also was fluent, deft, immaculate like a fine etching. Therefore the tone was likely to be of smaller dimensions—shallow, pale, transparent. Behind it was an unruffled emotional spirit which highly valued such aesthetic graces as elegant, calculated proportions and subtle phrasing.

315

From Kalkbrenner descended Stamaty, whose pupils included Gottschalk and Saint-Saëns; Saint-Saëns taught Gabriel Fauré (1845-1924). It was Fauré, with perhaps the greatest lyric gift of any modern French composer, who created such exquisite preludes, barcarolles, impromptus, nocturnes, mazurkas, and songs without words. They represent the essence of a refined French keyboard technique. Marguerite Long (1874-1966) expressed the concern that none of this be lost in the performance of Fauré:

> We are presently witnessing an evolution in pianistic technique which, in the employment of certain percussive works, runs the risk of compromising the qualities required for articulation in Fauré: the depth of sound in the suppleness of the attacks, the even lightness of the fingers (that famous gliding over the keyboard), the rapid, winged action which characterizes the technique of Fauré—reflecting that of Chopin.[2]

Another Kalkbrenner student, also a Chopin pupil, was Georges Mathias (1826-1910). Under him worked Raoul Pugno (1852-1914) and Isidor Philipp (1863-1953), the great technician and master teacher who taught at the American Conservatory at Fontainebleau. It is Guiomar Novaes (1896-   ), Philipp's former student, who epitomizes the best of French pianism, although at least in the interpretation of Debussy and Ravel, paradoxically the name of the German, Walter Gieseking (1895-1956), must also be included. A Brazilian by birth, Novaes entered the conservatoire at fourteen, impressing everyone by her enormous natural ability and ease of execution. Throughout her career she combined French grace and beauty with integrity and interpretative maturity.

Moritz Moszkowski (1854-1925), the Polish pupil of Kullak and Liszt, had come to Paris to retire and was a member of Novaes' audition jury in 1909, with Debussy and Fauré. Moszkowski was the composer of such valuable study material as the Etudes in Double Notes, Op. 64, and the *Études de Virtuosité*, Op. 72. In 1910 he wrote for *The Etude* magazine regarding study at the conservatoire and the competitive nature of the entrance examinations which continue to be very selective to the present day:

> Since I have been a member of this jury for a long time, and for the most part have had the duty of hearing the trial performances of young women pianists, I can testify with good conscience that the tasks of both the examined and the examiners are extremely exacting. The first are required to possess no small degree of virtuosity, and must therefore be

prepared with a selection of pieces and ballades by Chopin, etudes by Liszt, difficult sonatas by Beethoven, extended fugues by Bach, etc., etc.; while the latter must possess strong powers of memory to keep in mind the merits and defects of each individual performance, as well as no less strength of nervous resistance to be able to withstand such a long-drawn-out musical enjoyment. The contingent of ladies playing the piano is always the largest; in the last few years we have always had in the neighborhood of 250 pianists to examine, which has taken three days from early in the morning until evening. . . .

Since there are but three piano classes for women, and each class may consist of but twelve pupils, there is room for only thirty-six in all. Of these an average of ten leave each year, therefore no more than this number can be admitted. If one will but consider that of the 240 who fail at least 200 weep, and their respective fathers and mothers, uncles and aunts scold, it will be readily understood why the members of the jury always seek to beat a hasty retreat from the precincts of the Conservatory.[3]

In Zimmerman's early class were Antoine Marmontel (1816-1898), Alkan (1813-1888), Ambroise Thomas (1811-1896), and César Franck (1822-1890). Zimmerman's mantle fell on Marmontel in 1848 and from him emanated many of France's most distinguished musicians: Georges Bizet (1838-1875), Claude Debussy (1862-1918), Vincent d'Indy (1851-1931), Francis Planté (1839-1934), Louis Diémer (1843-1919), and Marguerite Long (1874-1966). Marmontel observed the pianistic great of his day and in 1878 wrote a book entitled *Les Pianistes célèbres*. His other writings were *L'Art classique et moderne du piano* (1876) and *Histoire du piano et de ses origines* (1885). Camille Bellaigue, critic of *La Revue des Deux Mondes* and former pupil of Marmontel, described his venerable appearance and manner in his later years:

Marmontel was a bald headed little man with a grey, pointed beard, with grey fingers too, stunted as if they had been worn down in the practice of his art. . . . He was the patriarch of the piano. Perhaps he had at one time been a virtuoso; he was now not even a pianist. At any rate none of us had ever heard him play. The most he would sometimes do, and even this was difficult for him, was to play a run, illustrate a fingering, or the value or accent of a note, but it was done so clumsily that he himself was the first to smile. But how he made up for this shortcoming in his lessons! In everything he did he showed impeccable style. He loved music, and he loved us too for what we meant in music for him, this old master surrounded by his apprentices. Sometimes he would grasp his long beard with his two hands, pulling at it as if to lengthen it still more. His eyes half closed, he would utter deep sighs, muttering to himself, 'Oh mon Dieu! Oh mon Dieu!' It seemed as if he were calling on the heavens to witness our blunders and the suffering we were causing him, though he tried his best to conceal it. With the slightest sign of intelligence on our part, on the other hand, his face would invariably light up.[4]

Diémer became one of the greatest of all French pianists, performed many French works such as the *Variations Symphoniques* by Franck for the first time, and succeeded to Marmontel's chair at the conservatoire in 1888. He likewise produced many of the great: Édouard Risler (1873-1929), Marcel Dupré (1886-1971), E. Robert Schmitz (1889-1949), author of *The Capture of Inspiration*, Robert Casadesus (1899-1973), and Alfred Cortot (1877-1962).

Cortot, Philipp, and Marguerite Long exemplify the best in twentieth century French piano teaching. Marguerite Long took over Diémer's post in 1920 and was a dominant force in advancing French pianism and in making known worthy French music. Philipp joined the conservatoire faculty in 1893 and Cortot in 1907, but neither limited his activity to that institution exclusively. In 1941 Philipp came to reside in America. In 1919 Cortot helped to form the École Normale de Musique. The most important modern French pianist-musician-intellectual, he conducted Wagner in Germany and was also the pianist in the Casals-Thibaud Trio. The virility and profundity of his pianism were due in part to the German influence, but he did not neglect his native music nor the works of Chopin, which he edited with extensive commentary.

His lasting contribution to piano technique is his formidable volume, *Rational Principles of Pianoforte Technique,* which appeared in 1928. In the foreword, Cortot objects to the overwhelming amount of technical materials of a contradictory nature from the past, but feels that in more recent teachings ". . . the mechanical and long-repeated practice of a difficult passage has been replaced by the reasoned study of the difficulty contained therein, reduced to its elementary principle."[5] Cortot brought the powers of his penetrating intellect to bear on the gamut of technical material. The practice formulae he developed are concise, comprehensive, and entirely relevant to the standard concert literature. They are divided into five basic chapters[6] covering finger training, thumb passage in relation to scales and arpeggios, double note and polyphonic mastery, the problem of extensions, and wrist and chordal techniques.

Within each chapter are three sub-groupings: Series A, B, and C. There is also an introductory chapter entitled *Daily Keyboard Gymnastics* written with a view to obtaining ". . . the reasoned loosening of all the pianist's muscular apparatus . . . fingers, hand, wrist and even forearm."[7] For long range development, Cortot advocates an hour a day of practice in his book; fifteen minutes given to the warm-up gymnastic exercises then forty-five minutes to one of the chapter series.[8] Series IA will be practiced for twelve successive days. On the first day all of the drills will be played in the keys of C major and C minor, the second day, C# or D♭ major and C# minor, and thence chromatically through all the keys. In other words, thirty-six practice days are needed to complete each chapter. As the practice progresses, much of the material can be varied in ways other than simple key transposition. A Transferable Table is included giving chromatic, harmonic, and rhythmic variants. At the back of the volume, Cortot presents an extensive listing of repertory in which he grades individual pieces by difficulty and also gives the technical chapter numbers to which they are related. For systematic and thorough technical development, the Cortot method book, thoroughly annotated, is among the best and merits serious consideration.

Already in the 1890s, Philipp was writing widely accepted exercise material based on the idea of transposition. His *Exercises for Independence of the Fingers* gives extensive short study patterns based entirely on the diminished seventh chord—each to be drilled at all twelve points within the octave. Realizing the dangers of tension development, he cautions: "Practice slowly, with a very supple arm, and strong finger action, depressing each key to the bottom with a full, round, even tone."[9] Philipp also wrote a *Complete School of Technic for the Pianoforte* in which the typical exhortations for imaginative practice are included: varied touches, dynamics and rhythmic patterns with careful attention to relaxation.

Marguerite Long has been characterized as the *grande dame* of twentieth century French music. Her performance career covered a seventy-year period; during that time she knew Fauré, Debussy, and Ravel, and received directly from them interpretative suggestions regarding many of their works. In 1965 she told Henry Kamm:

Having studied their works with the composers [Fauré, Debussy, and Ravel] gives me an obligation no one else has. I am the only one who knows, from Debussy, how Debussy wanted his piano works played. My task has been to serve the great composers who chose me as their interpreter by passing on to others how their music sounded to them.[10]

Several generations of French and non-French students came under her influence at the Paris Conservatoire. Among the most illustrious of the French have been Jean Doyen, Samson Françoise, Philippe Entremont, Jeanne-Marie Darré, and Nicole Henriot.

Long's piano method, entitled *Le Piano,* is a major work. It is widely used outside of as well as within France—notably so in the Soviet Union. The volume, which contains much significant exercise material in the various areas of piano technique, is begun with a long essay. Here we find the distillation of a rich and wonderful life experience in piano performance and technique. No one has a greater right or knows better how to summarize the French technique than Marguerite Long herself. She felt that there are personality differences manifest among the great French pianists; yet all of them identify with a common French style and technique, characterized by such attributes as gracefulness, elegance, clarity, moderation, and suppleness. Although French performance is not noted for great power, she believed it is unsurpassed in "depth of inner feeling."[11] There is the concern that every note be delivered "in the manner of an orator or of a singer."[12]

With clarity and enunciation an integral part of the French style, finger training is vital to Marguerite Long. She felt finger activity to be so much at the heart of fine technique that "it is not our mind which moves our fingers, but our fingers and their almost conscious movements which set our mind in motion."[13] There should be a rigorous program of both exercises and etudes, the best of which are those by Czerny. All five fingers should be thoroughly trained for vigor, elasticity, firmness, and independence so that each can overcome common obstacles. She believed that the "held note" exercises in *Le Piano* produce evenness in finger technique and the five-finger exercises, which can be varied in an unlimited number of ways, result in the fingers gaining "the ease of articulation and the rapidity of reflexes"[14] which give technical security.

While one should develop all of the body involved in piano playing, there is nothing more important to strive for than finger articulation. She stated that "this is an elementary truth"[15] and should be pursued as diligently as a runner and a dancer work to develop their legs for strength and flexibility. Such calisthenics as scales, purposely delayed in their presentation in *Le Piano,* should be practiced daily "by the experienced performer for limbering the muscles."[16]

With finger training comes advice on fingering. Awkward fingering interferes with gracefulness in the hand, without which beauty of tone and phrasing are impossible. She commented, "Ugly to the eye, ugly to the ear."[17] Long also felt that a composer's own given fingerings should be followed with the greatest respect. He knows, as part of the creative process, which hand position will achieve the best musical results. In the case of Ravel, she had to admit that he was right, after experimentation on her own.

She seems to have been apprehensive of much of the weight-relaxation thought of the Breithauptian era:

> Today the terms "to relax" and "to let go" are overused terms which I condemn. These are not proper terms because they are contrary to the action of playing the piano.
> If one has fingers, he does not need "to let go." To be supple is enough. There is no need to use a special term.[18]

The overall implications of technical training are beautifully summarized in *Le Piano.* Technique, of course, includes the mastery of all that is physical; but it goes far beyond that. A refined hand, having arrived at the "sensitive stage of its 'mission' when 'bending before each emotion' as Liszt required,"[19] senses musical shape in the work being performed. In a larger sense, technique is the accomplishment of all that makes for beauty in interpretation.

The whole process of developing technique is laborious and can be very discouraging. Marguerite Long recalled Liszt's advice for patience with oneself. In practicing the exercises, she suggested that there must always be the ideal of beauty set before the student. She encouragingly stated that "This austere and laborious novitiate is to prepare for a true priesthood" and further advised meditation on an aphorism by Dunoyer de Segonzac, a noted French painter, "One spends his entire lifetime building his house."[20]

Then follow practical suggestions for technical drill,[21] such as omitting pedal, playing with depth of tone but avoiding undue fatigue, emphasizing energetic finger lift and release, encouraging freedom throughout the arm and shoulder, and working regularly from one tempo to a slightly faster one but always including slow drill.

Without a doubt, the twentieth century Frenchman who most influenced modern technique was Claude Debussy. He went to Marmontel at the conservatoire in 1872 at the age of ten. After a year Marmontel reported, "A charming child . . . a true artistic temperament; much can be expected from him." By the time he was twelve, he was playing the Bach Chromatic Fantasy and Fugue and the Chopin F Major Ballade well enough that a newspaper critic saw promise of his becoming "a virtuoso of the first order."[22] But Debussy's development was by no means a conventional one. He began to prefer sight reading arrangements of the Mozart and Haydn string quartets and Marmontel would be surprised to observe him improvising original chord and arpeggio sequential patterns before launching into his assigned pieces. There is also a record of a highly romanticized and personalized performance of the F minor Prelude from Book II of the *Well-Tempered Clavier* which Marmontel seemed not to have been offended by, but which had an adverse effect on the elderly conservatoire director, Ambroise Thomas. Lockspeiser was intrigued by the colorful picture it must have presented:

> The vision indeed is choice of the future composer of the *Preludes* and the marvellous *Etudes,* a swarthy, uncouth, fourteen-year-old lad, astonishing these established masters with a novel view of Bach, the bald-headed Marmontel, with long pointed beard, looking on approvingly while the remote Ambroise Thomas, with deep-set eyes and flowing hair, his overcoat slung over his shoulders, had the appearance of a ghostly, extinct Verdi.[23]

Debussy objected more and more to the discipline demanded by classic literature, and showed the impulsive side of his nature. His classmate, Maurice Emmanuel, said that his playing of Beethoven was on the heavy side, and Gabriel Pierné, while admitting his inner sensitivity, complained that ". . . he literally charged at the keyboard and overdid every effect. He appeared to be in a rage with the instrument, ill-treating it with impulsive gestures and puffing noisily during the difficult passages."[24] When he was fourteen in 1877, he won the second prize for his performance of the Schumann G minor Sonata. This was to be his greatest accomplishment in performance and from then on he began to abandon the idea of a pianist's career for that of a composer.

But as he opened new paths as an impressionistic composer, the piano became a major vehicle for him. His sensitive, sensuous nature created most unusual sonorities and textures—nothing so original and unique had been heard on the piano since Chopin. His treatment of keyboard touch and pedal was at opposite poles from his youthful, whimsical, and percussive approach to the classics.

Much later when Leon Vallas heard Debussy, he called him "an original virtuoso, remarkable for the mellowness of his touch. He made one forget that the piano has hammers—an effect which he used to request his interpreters to aim at—and he achieved particularly characteristic effects of timbres by the combined use of both pedals."[25]

Others said that his playing was mostly pianissimo and at times almost inaudible, dimmed, and veiled. In refinement of tonal control, his technique, and for that matter his entire style, was thoroughly French. He reveled in the delicate mingling of sounds and overtones. He prized very highly a concert grand that contained a special installation invented by Blüthner—an extra string was strung above each of the standard ones. These in no way were touched by the hammers, but simply vibrated sympathetically and thus increased the richness of the sonority. In public performance he always desired the lid of the piano to remain closed, literally *drowning* the tone.

No one was better qualified to list the qualities of the pianist Debussy than Marguerite Long:

> Debussy was an incomparable pianist. How could you forget the suppleness, the caress, the depth of his touch! As he glided with such a penetrating softness over the keyboard, he kept close to it and obtained from it tones of an extraordinarily expressive power. *There* we find the secret, the pianistic *enigma* of his music. *There* resides the *special* Debussy technique: this softness in the continuous pressure, and the color he obtained with this touch on the soft dynamic level alone. He played almost always in half tints, but with a full and intense sonority without any harshness in the attack, like Chopin. . . . The scale of his nuances went from *pianississimo* to *forte* without ever arriving at immoderate sonorities and without the subtlety of the harmonies ever being lost.[26]

Debussy could not tolerate his impressionism carried to the point of unpleasant blur. Dumesnil said that he was irritated at hearing the term "impressionism" because he felt that he was a musical descendant of the eighteenth century harpsichordists and shared their concern for perfection and logic.[27] He did not like to write out pedal indications since they would vary so from room to room and from one piano to the next. Late in life, he recalled what Madame Maute de Fleurville, a pupil of Chopin, had told him years before about pedaling: "Chopin wanted his pupils to study

323

without using the pedal and only to use it sparingly when performing. It was this use of the pedal as a kind of breathing that I noticed in Liszt when I heard him in Rome."[28]

And when it came to fingering, Debussy again did not like to be pinned down to rules. He stated:

To impose a fingering cannot logically adapt itself to the different formations of the hand. The absence of fingerings is an excellent exercise, it suppresses the spirit of contradiction which prompts us to prefer not to use the author's fingering, and verifies these everlasting words: "One is never better served than by one's self."[29]

Maurice Dumesnil, who in his student days played for Debussy many of the composer's own works for his advice and criticism, recalled the true Debussy touch:

I noticed that at times the position of his fingers, particularly in soft chord passages, was almost flat. He seemed to caress the keys by rubbing them gently downward in an oblique motion instead of pushing them down in a straight line.[30]

He also told Dumesnil: "Play with more sensitiveness in the finger tips. Play chords as if the keys were being attracted to your finger tips, and rose to your hand as to a magnet."[31]

Marguerite Long stated that the Debussy pianist "must feel the sound at the tips of his *fingers*; he must keep softness in strength and strength in softness."[32]

The movement of the arm with a flat finger and yielding wrist is the best way to control a Debussy pianissimo. But Debussy was afraid of too much relaxation: "In *pianissimo* chords, for instance, the fingers must have a certain firmness so that notes will sound together. But it must be the firmness of rubber, without any stiffness whatsoever."[33]

But not all of Debussy is extreme delicacy. He advised his students to play such brilliant works as the suite *Pour le Piano, L'Isle Joyeuse,* and the *Études pour les Octaves* with considerable bravura. His Etudes are some of the most significant since those by Chopin and Liszt.

There exists a physical description of Debussy, the man and the composer, by E. Robert Schmitz, who worked closely with him for a seven year period from 1908 to 1915. The following excerpt from "A Plea for the Real Debussy" throws a fascinating sidelight on why Debussy pianism, and French piano technique in general, developed as it did:

Debussy was not a careless, sensual pagan, drifting wherever the wind of inspiration might blow him. He did not "toss off" his pieces as a diamond cutter might chip off a fleck of diamond dust. He did not sit down at the piano, close his eyes, and compose a confused jumble of notes. Rather, he was a typical Frenchman of the *bourgeois* class—neat, precise, with a beautifully ordered mind and a habit of thinking clearly about everything he did.

Everything about him had to be well ordered and perfect. His house, surrounded by a garden, off the beaten path of the Square du Bois du Boulogne, was always quiet and smooth running. He seldom entertained. It seemed almost as though he felt that a great many visitors would have disturbed the or-dered serenity of his home, so necessary to his creative life. His study, the "sacred room of the house," was typical of its master. It was not a large or a cluttered room, such as one is accustomed to associate with a busy composer. Everything in it was carefully selected and refined. In spite of the fact that he was a man of wide reading, the books in his study did not number more than a hundred or so, and these were only authors that Debussy had chosen as his particular favorites— Rossetti, Maeterlinck, François Villon in an old edition, Mallarmé. There was a small upright piano, in one corner between the light high windows, a desk on which there were several small carved wooden animals, a bowl of beautiful goldfish. The colors of the room were subdued, the furnish-ings practical. Only a few precious prints and watercolors adorned the walls.

Debussy was very particular about everything in this room. He could not work properly if a picture hung crooked or one of the small wooden animals on the desk were turned the wrong way. Perhaps best illustrative of this trait is an incident now recalled. I was one day accompanying Miss Maggie Teyte, the soprano, at the piano for a rehearsal. Debussy was standing near the instrument. Again and again he stopped us, saying, "No, no, it is not right." Although we were used to endless interruptions and corrections whenever Debussy rehearsed a piece, it seemed that he was exceptionally restless that morning. At last he stopped us for a long time and stood there in silence. We waited for him to give us the signal to start again; but, instead, he stooped down and picked up a pin—a single straight pin—which was lying on the carpet, put it into a little box and stuck the box in his pocket. Then, with a relieved expression on his face, he motioned to us to go on. All was right again.

Debussy was as particular in his habits of work as he was in these peculiarities of his personal life. He wrote very slowly, and he never released anything to the publisher until he was sure of every note. The *Passepied* to the "Suite Bergamasque" he refused to release for months, just because the last four measures were not exactly right. This in spite of the fact that he had promised it to his publisher long before.

Time and again I have seen him look at a page of music, his head a little to one side, knowing something was wrong. He would not know just what. Then suddenly the idea, the remedy, would come to him. He would lean forward, his face lit up, and change—a single note. In my possession there are original editions of his preludes, which, even though they were published, he still insisted upon correcting. In tiny handwriting, meticulous, in lavender ink, the corrections run all over those pages—illustrative of Debussy's restless desire for perfection.[34]

Debussy's contemporary, Maurice Ravel (1875-1937) also exerted a major influence on French piano playing, and indeed upon Debussy himself. It was Ravel's *Jeux d'Eau* (1901), with its colorful, daring harmonies and cascading, pearling displays of impressionistic virtuosity which far outshone in originality *Pour le Piano* by Debussy, written the same year. It markedly affected the Debussy style. Pierre Lalo, writing in the Sunday edition of *Le Temps* for March 19, 1907, observed that the Ravel masterwork offered "the first example of a special technique in the art of writing for the piano and of a new virtuosity."[35] This was virile music, still displaying the elegant finger technique and polish of the French school, but in the tradition of and even going beyond the Chopin Etudes and the Liszt *Transcendental* Etudes. Ravel said that *Jeux d'Eau* "should be played in the way you play Liszt."[36] Then with the Ravel suite, *Gaspard de la Nuit* (1908), French music could now offer some of the most difficult, yet playable, scores ever written. The Debussy-Ravel specialist Walter Gieseking felt that Ravel's writing is "the most pianistic ever written, making the most perfect and universal use of the resources of the modern piano."[37]

Like Debussy, Ravel had no intention to achieve his full potential as a great pianist. Both can be heard, nonetheless, to very good effect playing several of their own compositions on the recent long-playing record reproductions made from the Welte piano rolls. Henri Gil-Marchex, a French pianist who knew Ravel well, described his finger technique as descending from the clavecinists, particularly Scarlatti, and being strongly influenced by Chopin.[38] Gil-Marchex further stated:

Ravel never studied the piano and therefore he had to be satisfied with being only a moderately good pianist whose

326

hands, as Weber once put it, played the despot over his musical creative process. He sat astonishingly low at the keyboard, which perhaps explains the fact that he never used octave runs. His long, lithe fingers, and narrow, elongated hand set on an exceedingly supple wrist resembled those of a conjurer. His thumb turned with amazing ease under the palm of his hand, which enabled him to reach back easily to a large number of notes.[39]

Even at the age of sixteen, Ravel's urge to improvise and create at the piano was greater than his desire to practice exercises or the standard literature. When he was studying in Charles de Bériot's class in Paris in 1891, Bériot admonished Ravel: "It is criminal of you to be always last in the class when you could be first."[40] Ricardo Vines described his practice problems at this time:

In order to conquer his dislike of practising the piano, his mother conceived the idea of giving him six sous for every hour's work—the wages of a household in those days. The scheme would have worked with anyone else but Ravel, and if he had not had a balcony and so many reasons—Place Pigalle!—for running out every five minutes under the pretense or excuse that there had been an accident, a passing fire-engine, a street row or a bird which had flown into a neighboring trap—and then he had music itself—and all those hitherto unthought of resolutions, those voluptuous dissonances, those polyphonic games which were able to give so much more relish than tiring five-finger exercises, and all those problems, fascinating and hazardous, which occupied Ravel's imagination so much more than the sporting interest of working the fourth finger.[41]

Notes

[1] Adolph Kullak, *Aesthetics of Piano Playing*, p. 79.

[2] Marguerite Long, *Au piano avec Gabriel Fauré*, p. 109, translation by William A. Henning.

[3] Moritz Moszkowski, "Methods and Customs of the Paris Conservatoire," *The Etude*, Vol. XXVIII, No. 2 (February, 1910), p. 81.

[4] Edward Lockspeiser, quoting Camille Bellaigue, *Debussy: His Life and Mind*, Vol. I, p. 26.

[5] Alfred Cortot, *Rational Principles of Pianoforte Playing*, p. 1.

[6] *Ibid.*

[7] *Ibid.*, p. 2.

[8] *Ibid.*

[9]Isidor Philipp, *Exercises for Independence of the Fingers*, Part I, p. 2.

[10]Henry Kamm, "The Grande Dame of French Music," *The New York Times*, Sunday, January 31, 1965, Section X, p. 11.

[11]Marguerite Long, *Le Piano*, p. II, translation by William A. Henning.

[12]*Ibid.*, p. VI.

[13]*Ibid.*, p. III.

[14]*Ibid.*, p. V.

[15]*Ibid.*, p. VI.

[16]*Ibid.*, p. VII.

[17]*Ibid.*, p. XIII.

[18]Long, *Au piano avec Gabriel Fauré*, p. 103.

[19]Long, *Le Piano*, pp. IX, X.

[20]*Ibid.*, p. XXI.

[21]*Ibid.*, p. 2.

[22]Lockspeiser, *Debussy: His Life and Mind*, p. 26.

[23]*Ibid.*, p. 29.

[24]*Ibid.*, p. 30.

[25]Oscar Thompson, *Debussy, Man and Artist*, p. 250.

[26]Marguerite Long, *Au piano avec Claude Debussy*, pp. 36-37, translated by William A. Henning.

[27]Maurice Dumesnil, "Coaching with Debussy," *The Piano Teacher* September-October, 1962, Vol. 5, No. 1, p. 12.

[28]Lockspeiser, *Debussy: His Life and Mind*, Vol. I. p. 22.

[29]Maurice Dumesnil, *How to Play and Teach Debussy*, p. 3.

[30]Dumesnil, *"Coaching,"* p. 11.

[31]Dumesnil, *How to Play. . .* , p. 9.

[32]Long, *Au piano avec Claude Debussy*, p. 41.

[33]Dumesnil, *"Coaching,"* p. 13.

[34]E. Robert Schmitz, "A Plea for the Real Debussy," a conference secured by Lucille Fletcher, *The Etude*, December, 1937, Vol. 55, p. 781.

[35]Victor I. Seroff, *Maurice Ravel*, p. 106.

[36]*Ibid.*, p. 66.

[37]Rollo H. Myers, *Ravel, Life and Works.* p. 153.

[38]*Ibid.*

[39]Frank Onren, *Maurice Ravel*, pp. 45-46.

[40]Madeleine Goss, *Bolero, The Life of Maurice Ravel*, p. 33.

[41]Norman Demuth, *Ravel*, p. 4.

16.   Breithaupt and Weight Technique

After Deppe's death in 1890, a continuous stream of publications on piano technique with an emphasis on physiology, especially on the functions of the arm, came from the press. In the years after the turn of the century, it became virtually a torrent—particularly in Germany. Besides the Deppe pupils, there were Eugen Tetzel, Alexander Ritschl, Paul Stoye, Tony Bandmann, Friedrich Adolf Steinhausen, and the most influential of them all, Rudolf Maria Breithaupt (1873-1945). Outside of Germany, there were Tobias Matthay and William Townsend in England and Marie Jaell in France, while in Vienna the assistants of Leschetizky were busy writing. In much of this literature, particularly during the first decade of the twentieth century, the trend was completely away from the old high finger school with its exceedingly energetic action and resulting tensions. For Breithaupt and his followers it was almost entirely arm activity, free falling weight, and super-relaxation. Weight and relaxation became a passion, a cult, the very atmosphere pianists breathed. Ethel Leginska, Leschetizky's pupil, reflected the spirit of the age when she wrote:

> I fancy if Clara Schumann, for instance, could return and play to us, or even Liszt himself, we should not find their playing suited to this age at all. Some of us yet remember the hand position Mme. Schumann had, the lack of freedom in fingers and arms. It was not the fashion of her time to play with the relaxed freedom, with the breadth and depth of style which we demand of artists today. . . . Stiffness seems to me the most reprehensible thing in piano playing, as well as the most common fault with all kinds of players. When people come to play for me, that is the thing I see first in them, the stiffness. While living in Berlin, I saw much of Mme. Teresa Carreño, and she feels the same as I do about relaxation, not only at the keyboard, but when sitting, moving about or walking. She has thought along this line so constantly, that

329

sometimes, if carrying something in hand, she will inadvertently let it drop, without realizing it—from sheer force of the habit of relaxation.[1]

Teresa Carreño (1853-1917), the Venezuelan pianist who studied under Gottschalk in America, later with Matthias in Paris, and on occasion with Anton Rubinstein, had a long and influential career. As a child she played at the White House for Abraham Lincoln and many years later she was to perform there again for Woodrow Wilson. Possessing a great natural freedom in her technique and being immensely gifted (she said that anything she had ever performed she was able to play in every key), she became one of the leading inspirations for the weight theorists. Like so many others, she heartily endorsed relaxation, albeit adding the qualifying adjective "controlled":

The secret of power lies in relaxation; or I might say, power *is* relaxation. This word, however, is apt to be misunderstood. You tell pupils to relax, and if they do not understand how and when they get nowhere. Relaxation does not mean to flop all over the piano; it means, rather, to loosen just where it is needed and nowhere else. . . . This quality of my playing must have impressed Breithaupt, for, as you perhaps know, it was after he heard me play that he wrote his famous book on "Weight Touch," which is dedicated to me. . . . Many artists and musicians have told me I have a special quality of tone; if this is true I am convinced this quality is the result of controlled relaxation.[2]

Breithaupt, who had studied at the Leipzig Conservatory and later taught at Stern's Conservatory in Berlin, fully acknowledged his debt to her. In 1911 he wrote that

The present writer's first suggestions of weight were received from Teresa Carreño and her "School," but especially from the highly-gifted technic of the artist herself. The weight-feeling had become second nature to her. She had "taught and rolled" the weight long before the subject was systematized in my writings, which made the attempt at a complete, unified representation.[3]

He also received inspiration from a good many more: Liszt, d'Albert, Anton Rubinstein, Hofmann, Godowsky, Harold Bauer, and Artur Schnabel—to name a few whom he said made more or less use of the principles which he advanced. It is unfortunate that among this number Leopold Godowsky (1870-1938) did not write the most influential book typifying the "weight era" in piano

330

playing, rather than Breithaupt. It would have been the product of a far greater musical and intellectual mind. Godowsky, of Polish-Russian extraction, spent many years in Berlin and in America. No pianist of his time possessed greater technical or interpretative powers. His natural reticence made it somewhat difficult for him to communicate with the general public, but to his fellow musicians he was known as a "pianist's pianist." Breithaupt should have learned far more from him than he did. Godowsky's technical teachings, as embodied in a number of music periodicals of the era, are sensible, balanced, and thoroughly tested by his own stupendous technique. Godowsky's paraphrases on the Chopin Etudes, including some exclusively for the left hand, are completely suited to the instrument and far exceed the technical demands made on it even by Liszt.

Godowsky taught principles of arm participation, weight and relaxation as early as 1892. In 1923 he recounted how he had discovered them in about 1891. He was planning an extended concert tour and had to learn a very large selection of pieces. He wrote:

Relaxed weight! What an important role it plays in modern pianism! My own discovery of this great principle was a revelation to me. It came about in this wise.

At one time in my career I was anxious to enlarge my répertoire as much as possible, and was practising a great deal, sometimes twelve or fourteen hours—practically all day. At the end of the day, after a couple of hours' rest, I would sit down to the piano in the evening and play awhile. I began to notice that, in spite of the fact that I was weary, I played very easily; it was no effort for me, only pleasure. Why should playing after a hard day's work seem easy, when the next morning, at a time when I should be feeling fresh, the same things did not seem easy; on the contrary, were more fatiguing. I pondered this state of things for some little time, till I came to the conclusion that, owing to weariness, I let my arms hang down with their own weight, and made no effort to hold them up. In short I was playing with relaxed arm weight, and playing with this condition did not tire me at all—not in the least. I developed this principle for myself in many ways, and found it of the greatest benefit. Many other pianists use this principle of course, but few are able to explain it. Rubinstein certainly exemplified relaxed weight. He had such heavy large hands and arms he did not try to hold them up any more than was absolutely necessary. Yet he was unable to explain the principle.[4]

Godowsky had a great fear of crystallizing his thought into a method—it might soon be ossified and ready to bury. He realized that there was more to piano playing than just weight and relaxation. In an article entitled "The Best Method Is Eclectic," he said:

Unfortunately every opinion announced by any innovator immediately leads to all sorts of fallacious statements, contradictions and misunderstandings, by those who jump at conclusions without comprehending the fundamental principles. People inferred that I proposed to do away with all other phases of mechanical training. This is by no means the case. I believe firmly in five-finger exercises, scales and arpeggios, practiced through raising the fingers high through staccato effects and even through pressure. *My Miniatures* for piano (four hands) are built on the five finger position. All these things add to one's efficiency in mechanism, when one comprehends the general principles of weight and relaxation. That is, the principles of Deppe, Kullak, Erlich, Mason, Lebert and Stark, and others, do not become less valuable, but all become a part of a great preparatory mosaic which is embraced in weight and relaxation.[5]

Godowsky's overview of technique is clearly set forth in his summation:

Technique is something entirely different from virtuosity. It embraces everything that makes for artistic piano playing—good fingering, phrasing, pedaling, dynamics, agogics, time and rhythm—in a word, the art of musical expression distinct from the mechanics. Some critics think they are abusing me when they call me a technician but they don't know that they couldn't pay me a higher compliment. I consider it an insult to be called a virtuoso. Any fool can learn the mechanics of piano playing. . . .

Weight, relaxation and economy of motion are the foundation stones of technique or interpretation and mechanism in piano playing. Ninety per cent of my playing is based on the weight principle and I taught it scientifically as early as 1892. The keyboard was made to rest—to lean on, and you must feel that the hands are formed of rubber and adjust them carefully to the keys. But, above all else, you sacrifice everything for beauty of tone. The great difficulty in piano playing in general lies in giving the listener a complete mental and aural picture or impression of a composition as a whole at one hearing with the many details of nuancing, dynamics, agogics, pedaling, etc., all carefully worked out. The only way I can explain some of the things pianists, who I feel must know better, do, is that they do not listen attentively enough to their own playing or they would hear what they do and correct it. You must emphasize everything clearly, like a good actor so the listener will also get what you are trying to express and play in a sort of imaginative, subconscious way to yourself.[6]

It would be interesting to have a specific account of Breithaupt's reaction to Godowsky's performance. We do, however, have such a record involving the great Beethoven specialist, Artur Schnabel:

The first book I saw on piano-playing problems was one written by a Mr. Breithaupt in Berlin, in 1904. He was critic for a musical monthly, a very interesting, original, fascinating man. In those first years in Berlin I saw him very often and he would always have me play for him alone. I did not see why. Years later he published, with far-reaching effect, a book on piano playing. In the private seances on which he so toughly insisted, I had served him, as I know now, as one of his guinea-pigs. Once, also before the book was out, he came to the artists' room after a concert and announced with excitement and jubilance: "Schnabel, you play with shoulder-participation." I and people around me thought he was crazy. What did he mean? He had come to the concert only to watch and, as he hoped, to establish that I played with shoulder-participation. I had never speculated how much shoulder-participation is required, how much "fall," "weight," wrist-rolling, what elbow angles—and endlessly on. . . .[7]

Although Schnabel may never have contemplated such things, Breithaupt surely had. Writing in *The Musician*, he thought that ". . . perhaps even Father Bach may have had some idea of weight"[8] and so had Beethoven. Then he neatly fit Liszt into his own technical system as well, itemizing his playing point by point:

1. Played with complete relaxation of muscles and joints (therefore not with the stiff finger-lifting or the "cock's step").
2. Used to the fullest extent the massive weight of the whole arm, and its parts. Unlike all the other players of his day (Thalberg and others) he played from the shoulder. Hence the grandeur and force of his style.
3. Made use of all the functions in the most skilful way and with the greatest ease. Especially he exploited to the last limits the swing, the fore-arm rolling, and the fore-arm extension.
4. Played with perfectly loose "slung" fingers, and easily dancing or "dropping" hand.

333

Liszt played—and this is important—with long extended fingers, and passive fall of the hand, not with curved, high-cocked, stiff, striking fingers, and active over-tension of the hand. On the contrary, he shook his hands from his arms, with an easy, loose swing. At all events he did not hold the members firmly, for he wished to avoid all stiffening of the muscles, all friction in the joints.[9]

Breithaupt did admit that it was "that much-despised Hofkapellmeister Deppe who had the first theoretical notion of how a great genius plays. He came upon the idea of letting the arm fall from the shoulder through correct observation of Rubinstein's playing."[10] But Breithaupt felt that the fixation of the joints and the pronation of the hand which he had observed in Deppe and his students were objectionable. He did not lose sight of the fact that an enthusiastic Deppe pupil for twelve years and author of a number of texts on piano technique, Tony Bandmann, had withdrawn and joined with him and his close associate Steinhausen. But he added that Dr. Steinhausen had erroneously stated that Miss Bandmann was "the discoverer of the weight."[11] This was not true: she had first heard the word used by Ferruccio Busoni in Weimar.

Breithaupt consulted the physiologist-pianist Steinhausen (1859-1910), whose major work was entitled *Die physiologischen Fehler und die Umgestaltung der Klavier-technik (Physiological Defects and the Reform of Pianoforte Technique)*. Breithaupt explained their association in the following account in which he takes full credit for the entire weight movement:

The following points were new and quite unknown to any "method," namely, the idea of power from "throw," mass, and velocity; the participation of the shoulder and the whole arm in most of our playing-movements; the rotary action of the fore-arm which I suggested in 1903, in *Die Musik,* and which, two years later, was scientifically established by Dr. Steinhausen. (In the preceding statements a careful distinction must be made between the discovery or detection of a motion and the explanation or demonstration of it. It is the merit of the present writer to have pointed out first the fore-arm roll; but Steinhausen was the first to explain and demonstrate it.) Especially was the relaxation, as taught by Steinhausen and myself *entirely new.* Steinhausen supported the idea of weight-playing through his brilliant and destructive criticism of the finger-methods. In its essentials this was correct, though too far-reaching in its form. He set forth the ideas of "passive hanging" and "passive weighting" (in contradistinction to the active finger-tension and pressure), established the idea of relaxation, and indicated especially the value of passive movement. From me arose the whole psychology of the subject, the fundamental ideas of teaching the movements, and their practical significance, as well as the whole explanation of modern dynamics. Entirely unknown before my writing appeared was the fore-arm extension, explained in the English translation of my "school," which helped to make the passive hand motion and gave thereby the secret of the vibrato in the octave technic.[12]

The first major theoretical work by Breithaupt, published in 1905 and entitled *Die natürliche Klaviertechnik (The Natural Piano Technic)*, Volume I, was followed about two years later by Volume II, *Die Grundlagen der Klaviertechnik (School of Weight-Touch)*. Between 1916 and 1921 he published in five volumes his *Praktische Übungen (Practical Studies)*, which did not add significantly to the earlier writings. In the preface to the *School of Weight-Touch*, which soon became popular in both French and English, he first offered the standard apology regarding method and then went on to describe his objectives:

> In publishing this volume, I am merely fulfilling a promise, made in the first volume of my work entitled: "Natural Piano-Technic." Myself an opponent of all so-called "methods," I undertook the present work very unwillingly, knowing from practical experience how difficult it is to formulate these apparently simple fundamental principles of technic without the aid of practical demonstrations. Besides, am I not adding one more to the already stupendous number of Methods? The Fundamental Principles of weight-produced touch having, however, been laid down theoretically, it became more and more necessary to develop those principles in a gradual manner from practical experience for practical use. Also, yielding to the repeatedly expressed wish to have the substance of my work divested of its scientific encumbrance and reduced to its simplest form, in order to render the ideas clear to all, and the *"new theories"* universal, I have now condensed the work to the present volume, which contains all that is essential and important for the elementary development of a natural manner of playing.
>
> I would here oppose the wrong idea that my object is to upset all that has existed heretofore, and to explain music by "psycho-physiology." Our aim is to do away with wrong ideas and to trace back to their real and natural sources the action of our playing members and the effect produced by them.

335

What we purpose to teach is in itself nothing new: we would disencumber the body and thus assist the playing members in their action, and teach them to play. Our young musicians shall no longer be tormented unnecessarily with five-finger-exercises, their little hands lamed, stiffened and ruined by performing impossible stretches and exaggerated extensions.[13]

A view of Breithaupt's personal teaching procedures may help to place his *School of Weight-Touch* and its objectives in a revealing setting. His enthusiastic American pupil, Florence Leonard, described what it was like to go to him. Selections from "How Breithaupt Teaches" follow:

Rudolph Maria Breithaupt, the brilliant author of *Natural Piano Technic,* and the foremost teacher of the modern ideas of weight-playing, is an indefatigable worker. So the student who comes for the first lesson of the day, whether in the suburb of Berlin, or in the charming village of the Harz mountains where Breithaupt makes his summer home, the first comer of the day is apt to pause before entering the music room, to listen a moment to Breithaupt's practising. "A teacher should play in the early hours of every day. That is the only way to preserve freshness of nerves and keep out of a rut. I play till eleven o'clock every morning." The listener is struck with the brilliancy, smoothness, and depth of the changing tone, the swiftness of the runs, the extraordinary technic in octaves and chords. Every sort of technic is covered, though some varieties are passed through briefly, in these morning improvisations. "I take the figures and drive them through all the keys." "It is laziness that makes us seek out the white keys."

On entering the student is met with a hearty greeting, one of genuine courtesy and friendliness. Indeed it would be difficult to imagine Breithaupt teaching without the undercurrent of friendly interest. In appearance he is taller, rather pale, with the profile of a musician, the brow of a thinker, eyes which indicate imagination and kindliness. His handshake must not be taken as a test of cordiality. For hands, to a player, are a most precious possession, and since "all the actions of the hand in daily life, grasping, lifting, carrying, and the like, are active (the opposite of actions useful in playing) and fatigue the hand," Breithaupt avoids these actions of the muscles, and gives the most relaxed of handshakes. One notices, too, that all his movements are relaxed. If, by chance, in illustrating a point, his hand once falls on the arm or shoulder of his interlocutor, at the next approach, it falls only on thin air,—it has been avoided,—for of all heavy hands it seems the heaviest. "My friends always draw back when I begin to gesture," he says, laughing. "They are afraid of my arm."

The student takes his place before a Steinweg piano, Breithaupt sitting at the right, between the two pianos. But the lid of the Steinweg is closed, and the music rack stands on the closed lid—alas, for the player whose tone is small to begin with! For he must learn to make it large and sonorous in his fortissimos, lid or no lid. (He learns later, that when he particularly deserves it, or on state occasions, the lid is lifted.)

Our student is a player of some confidence, however, for he has already pleased audiences in some of the smaller German cities, since his graduation from a well-known conservatory, over a year before. So he boldly attacks his Beethoven sonata, hoping that he will at least get approval for his smooth runs, and be given some suggestions for more velocity and brilliancy, and some help on his octaves. But he plays only half a page, and then, without hearing any comment on his performance, he is plunged into a sea of new ideas. First of all, he finds that he sits too stiffly; his shoulder is stiff, his elbow is stiff, his wrist is too firm; his carefully trained "high hand" is stiff, although he thought that his fingers were "relaxed at the knuckle." Even his neck is stiff.

He is shown how to relax the wrist after a certain fashion, and his first thought is of instant rebellion, for this motion is rank heresy toward all the best teaching he ever heard of. But he decides to wait and see what the result is. (He wrote later to a friend, "I have burned all my bridges, but I'm thankful that I have.") Then his arm is swung, pushed and pulled over his keys, his hand is pushed into the required looseness, while Breithaupt adjures him, "let go," "let the hand fly," "pump," "roll," "loose, loose," "don't press," and gives examples at the keys for him to imitate, describing the motion desired, illustrating also perhaps, by anecdote.

Thus Breithaupt, with inexhaustible ingenuity, tries in two ways to communicate the new idea, by giving the word which shall suggest the motion to the mind, and at the same time (because so many of us are slaves to former habits of thought, and do not take in the meaning of the word) he produces in the arm the motion which shall excite the necessary physical consciousness in joints and muscles. Finally, the pupil becomes aware of the motion and can make it at will, but the process must continue until he does master it, whether it takes two lessons or twenty. So, as the first lesson proceeds, he realizes that Breithaupt's first object is to establish a perfectly free, natural set of movements, movements which are to the purpose, and waste no energy. (Breithaupt would be a great acquisition to a corps of the modern students of efficiency. He regards every movement which comes to his attention, from this point of view, whether it is the mowing of a lawn or the punching of tickets at a train.) . . .[14]

After this glimpse of Breithaupt at work in his studio, let us examine his *School of Weight-Touch*. It is divided into two parts: "The Elementary Forms of Weight-Touch" (eight chapters) and "Forms Applied" (four chapters). In the very first chapter, he concerns himself, as so many have before him, with posture and hand position. In the beginning of piano study, he prefers a low seat as he wants to make "the joints supple, of maintaining relaxation of the muscles of the arm, of accustoming the arm itself to assume and retain a position of passive suspension and of developing the shoulder-muscles."[15] This early quotation is indicative of the errors and vague, involved language which permeate much of the text. Obviously, a low seat will mean the hands will have to be held in a higher position at the keyboard, thus increasing the possibility of tension in the muscles of the arms and shoulders. But later on, he says that one's sitting height may be adjusted in accordance with one's physical proportions.

The same is true for hand position:

There is no hard and fast rule to determine one special way of holding the arms, hands and fingers to suit all cases and answer all purposes. All so-called *normal* positions are to be rejected. In the beginning one thing is required for weight-technic, i.e. for the transmission, support, and balance of the weight of the arm: a *firm, steady hand-bridge,* on which the arm *rests* like the superstructure of a bridge on its arches and pillars.[16]

Then later, the hand *"must suit itself to the musical or technical forms."* But at the outset Breithaupt wants a position which he variously describes as "arch-set hand," "umbrella-hand," "ball-shaped hand," and the shape of a "claw." Although these analogies surely suggest tension, he does not want this position to be "considered as a rigid hand-pose," but one that is "merely intended to assist in developing an energetically rounded form of the hand supported on a firmly set fingers and knuckles."[17] He is very much against the old school with its

. . . *full-cock setting* of the fingers . . . when viewed from

338

the stand-point of free weight-produced touch, for we no longer need such exaggerated tension of the fingers; besides, the bending-in of the fingers would destroy the bridge and hand-arch, and thus, from the outset, render transmission of weight impossible.[18] [See illustrations of various hand positions on pages 340-1.]

The latter statement must be contradicted: such weight transfer may not be desirable, but it is not impossible.

Once the student has achieved the desired beginning hand position, Breithaupt is then concerned about having the fingers experience the sensation of supporting the full weight of the arm. In a wordy and inaccurate statement (he fails to see that arm weight cannot vary in quality from one person to the next) he says:

> The full utilization of the massive weight of the arm (which differs as to quantity and quality with each individual), when combined with the elastic muscular tension of the whole physical apparatus set in motion (shoulder, upper- and fore-arm, hand, fingers), constitutes the fundamental elements of piano-technic. The essential condition of its employment is a clear conception of the various degrees of energy needed—the mental control of the heavy, loose, freely oscillating arm, or *realisation of weight.*
>
> In order to perceive this and put it to practical use, so that it shall be "felt" and "lodged" in the finger-tips, lay the arm, with all its muscles relaxed, at full length and flat upon a table, . . . arch the hand to form the bridge, . . . and, raising the upper- and fore-arm, transfer the weight to the hand and to the firmly set fingers. . . . The arm, hanging loose and inactive in the shoulder-joint, is *"supported"* by the hand or by the fingers (passive bearing, in contrast to active bearing of the arm by the shoulder-muscles—light arm).
>
> After supporting the arm a while, let it fall again on to the table. . . . Repeat this movement, until the weight is realised in the finger-tips, i.e. until the actual consciousness of weight is awakened.[19]

With the fingers still supporting weight on the table top or on weighing scales, he next suggests an exercise whereby "The arm thus set swinging in its three principal joints (shoulder, elbow and wrist), may very appropriately be compared to a rope, the transmission of its movements producing a succession of continuous undulations." What is achieved? "This movement and the suspension of the relaxed arm constitute the most elementary forms of *releasing the weight.*"[20] Nowhere does Breithaupt seem to be aware of the fal-

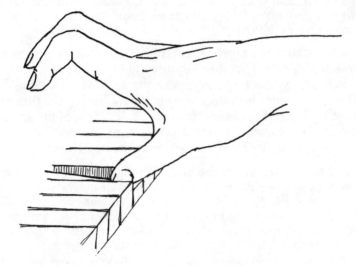

Over-tension of the fingers with stiffened knuckle-joints and wrist as taught by the old schools and methods: wrong.

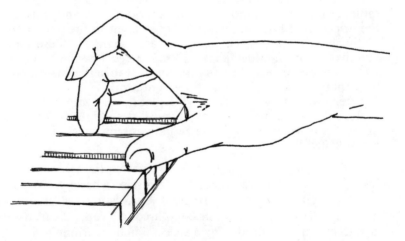

"Cocked-gun" pose with absolutely stiffened knuckle-joint: wrong.

340

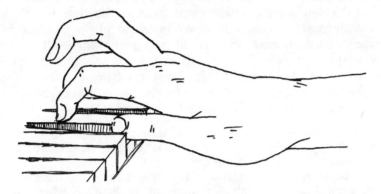

Finger raised, old method, with low-set hand and stiffened wrist:
radically wrong.

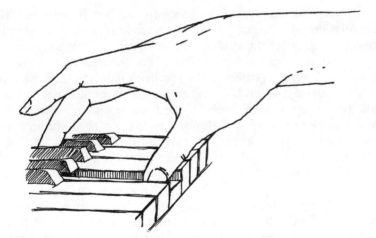

Natural curve of the extended fingers lightly thrown forward, the wrist
being held high or low: good pose.

lacy that just by undulating the arm a relaxed arm condition will automatically be assured; sets of antagonistic muscles may remain contracted with excess contraction by one set creating movement.

At the conclusion of chapter one, he concerns himself with the various degrees of weight involved in piano playing—from full release through gradual withdrawal to a point where all is held back at the shoulder. He emphasizes that one should distinguish between three definite classifications: the two extremes thus described and a confusing third (number one in his organization) which is really not true weight at all but muscular force:

1. The hand weighted to the utmost, i.e. the greatest amount of pressure together with full muscular power and the whole weight bearing on the keys.
2. Suspension or removal of the weight resulting from the withdrawal of the point of support of the arm, as when the arm is raised from off the table and held, borne by the muscles of the shoulder (active carriage) up in the air, a form of muscular action which takes place even during the shortest pause or rest in playing.
3. The arm weighted "for playing," i.e. the weight of the relaxed arm, or the normal pressure of the bulk of the arm suspended passively or reposing with its full weight, all its muscles completely relaxed.[21]

The second chapter of Breithaupt's method is entitled "The Transmission of Weight." The first section is concerned with weight testing. After the student is able to release arm weight away from the piano, the teacher is advised to "bear the full-weighted arm of the pupil (supported on the teacher's hand) to the keyboard, and set it upon the middle-finger placed perpendicular upon a black key."[22] If the arm "holds," the teacher may remove his own support and let the student balance the weight with the hand firmly set and the wrist quite high. This exercise should be practiced with the second, fourth, and fifth fingers. Breithaupt says that the resulting "bending-in of the first joint is no absolutely objectionable feature, provided the middle joint is sufficiently firm. Liszt and Chopin almost constantly played with a more or less flat touch and with the first joints bent in, as the case required and as the execution suited the fingers."[23] The broken nail joint is something most teachers have always tried to avoid—with good reason, yet Breithaupt here unconsciously hints at a very desirable and useful finger coordination that Schultz later was to explain fully:

The first exercises at the keyboard are to be practiced from bedded key to bedded key *without sounding* them, the fingers weighing heavily and with their full breadth on the keys (somewhat after the gait of plantigrades). The sensation must recall that felt in walking over a moor, the ground giving at every step. The noiseless bedding of the keys and the careful shifting of the weight exact a concentration of mind, which in its turn facilitates and intensifies the realization of weight. The fingers must not be raised, they merely take turns in carrying and transmitting the weight, passing, as it were, the load from one high, curved knuckle to the other.[24]

The second division in the chapter is taken up with "Releasing the Weight"—that is, removing weight from the key-bed and transferring it to the shoulder. The following silent exercises are recommended:

Exercise: Bring the weight of the arm to bear upon each of the fingers separately, including the thumb, firmly set on the bedded key; then suddenly carry the weight by allowing the finger to rise with the key (the key bearing the finger up). . . .
This exercise: *fall of the weight—relaxation—rising with the key,* must be repeated, until the alternate charging and discharging of the arm, can be performed perfectly and with ease, i.e. without any contraction or muscular resistance, at a moment's notice.
Having succeeded in this, leave the (finger) hand on the key and let the *descent be followed by instant relaxation.* The best way to do this is to relax the arch-set hand and slacken all its muscles: the hand, becoming soft and pliable, rests with only as much pressure on the key as is required to keep it down and sustain the tone. . . .
Preliminary exercise: Place the hand upon any interval of a sixth or octave, without sounding it, arm and hand relaxed, oscillating, in natural rise and fall (flexion—tension), up and down, the fingers bedding the keys without further pressure. Every movement must be supple, perfectly free from muscular contraction or stiffness, every joint, muscle and sinew of the limb being relaxed. The arm should oscillate naturally in the wrist-joint. Notice the perfect spring in the fetlock-joints which gives that elegant grace to the step of a thorough-bred horse, or a stag or a deer.[25]

Although this material is not without merit, again it is clouded by statements that are not completely valid nor clear. It is impossible for an oscillating arm to have "every joint, muscle and sinew of the limb" fully relaxed nor every movement "perfectly free

343

from muscular contraction." You cannot have movement without muscular exertion and fixation. Breithaupt goes as far to the left as the stiff finger school went to the right—at least in his description.

Then the silent exercises are to be played with sound. At the end of the chapter he lists a number of repeated note studies that are to be executed with gradually increasing or decreasing degrees of intensity. These, he says, are of utmost importance: *"The mastery of weight-technic, the study of its natural dynamic gradations, with perfect alternation between normal muscular action and muscular relaxation, forms the secret of all technic."*[26] Here we can discern a half truth and point out a fallacy apparent throughout all of Breithaupt's method. "Weight-technic" does not accurately and truthfully describe it. It is more muscular action and contraction than weight—it cannot be otherwise. As Schultz pointed out, his system should have been named the *School of Arm-Touch,* but it would not have been nearly so popular, since the word "weight" cast a magic spell over Breithaupt's era.[27]

The introductory chapters of the *School of Weight-Touch* were limited entirely to the single tone. In chapters three, four, five, and eight, he presents what he considers to be the four primary actions of piano playing: (1) The longitudinal oscillation of the arm; (2) the extension of the fore-arm; (3) the rolling of the fore-arm; and (4) the free oscillation of the fingers.

In order to achieve the longitudinal oscillation of the arm, Breithaupt has the student first practise a "Stützschwung" (supported swing) exercise:

> Set the weighted arm, supported by the middle-finger upon the middle C. . . . Count sharply and with marked precision: 1—2—3—4, discharging the arm with lightning rapidity on 4, swing it off the key, dropping it with its full weight upon the next key D, and so on, *always on the third finger.*[28]

Then each finger (the thumb excepted) is to drill in the same manner throughout every major scale. After that he explains that

> The arm—one suspended mass—must descend with the swing of a massive iron hammer, this being the *martellato form of the non-legato touch. . . .It is the sudden, unexpected, unconscious descent that begets what we may call the "brazen rhythmic tread"* of the physical organs set in free motion.[29]

The student is not to worry about wrong notes. He does not say how any kind of rhythm can be discerned. Double notes are also to be practiced in this manner.

344

From these unmusical sounds, the Breithaupt pianist progresses to lateral transference (shifting) with a deep-fall and high-fall action which is at the heart of longitudinal oscillation. Stepwise motion with the use of successive fingers is now employed, but the fingers are not to be raised nor leave the keys. The down and up motions of the arm, particularly apparent at the wrist, are to produce the tones. "Low-fall" and "high-fall," terms vital to Breithaupt's system, he describes as follows:

"High-fall," characterised by the projection of the weight of the arm from below upward, in which the hand and arm, passing from the low position, below the key-board, to the high position, execute a sort of recoil. . . . .

S: shoulder. E: elbow. H: wrist.

High-Fall

S: shoulder. E: elbow. H: wrist.

Low-Fall

In the low-fall the hand is straightened out (balancing posture), in the high-fall it is curved (curved position), suspended passively. The movements in the high-fall are merely the inversion of those in the low-fall.[31]

Breithaupt is not accurate here either. The movements in the misnamed "High-fall" cannot be the inversion of those in the "Low-fall." Gravity works downward and not upward and makes for two entirely different types of action. Nor is any recoil involved in the "High-fall"—it is a separate, independent action.

Three, four, and five-finger roulades are to be practiced ascending, then descending—first with "Low-fall" and then "High-fall." Broken chords, double notes, thirds, sixths, octaves, chords follow. And for the time being, Breithaupt is not concerned "whether the finger falls upon the very tip or on the more fleshy, softer part of that joint. The chief object is to retain the arch-set pose of the hand, and that the weight remain in the *knuckle-joints* of the fingers."[32] He also states categorically that "The so-called wrist-stroke must be abolished" and *"All spreading of the fingers, all grasping, binding with finger-pressure is prohibited."*[33]

Breithaupt's second major action, extension of the forearm, he defines as:

> . . . *the jerked extension of the fore-arm,* proceeding from shoulder and upper-arm and *producing a passive extension of the hand.* The extension of the fore-arm is equivalent to a stretching-out in the elbow-joint. The important object of this action is in the first place to remove the habitual stiffness and limber the elbow-joint. The constant practice in jerking the fore-arm forward tends to stretch the elbow-joint and render it flexible, thus counteracting the static fixation produced by our daily grasping and bending actions and gradually paralyzing the same.
>
> In the second place—and this is the *experimentum crucis—an absolute relaxation of the wrist-joint is a certain consequence* of the action. The action of the fore-arm, in straightening-out, resembles the motion of the piston-rod on an engine.[34]

Here again he shows his fear of fixation and his unrealistic approach to relaxation. It is as though the ordinary movements of daily life are bound to stiffen us and are completely apart from those involved in piano playing. And this "jerked extension," so poorly named and making no use of weight at all, is so important that it "accompanies almost every action" and "occurs in the

346

longitudinal swing of the arm and in the movement accompanying the simple fall (drop) of the hand."[35]

Then when this forearm extension is combined with a rapid alternate rise and fall, he comes up with an action called extension-vibrato:

> The alternation in rise and fall (of the arm, of the weight) is already imperceptible, scarcely more than a slight vertical oscillation of the hand, a vibration which must be executed as gently and in as rippling a manner as possible, so that in fact the hand is at last supported, as it were, by the keys, rising and falling with them, i.e. abandoning itself entirely to the repeating-action of the instrument. This vibratory action, performed by the lightest possible touch . . . of the oscillating member in its descent, is quite sufficient for the performance of any musical passages of the kind taken at any normal speed.
>
> The extension-vibrato, i.e. the *extension of fore-arm and hand worked up to a vibrato, is the action producing the octave-execution of the virtuoso, the so-called "lightning octaves" with the greatest velocity in the fastest tempo.*
>
> *This is the key to the passive action and absolute relaxation in wrist-vibrato, a key which we are the first to discover.*[36]

It is difficult to understand what he actually means by this last statement or how the full arm can vibrate so rapidly, evidently as fast or faster than the smaller hand-vibrato.

Breithaupt's third important action or touch form, and probably the one for which he is best known, is "Rollung," the German word which his translator, John Bernhoff, says has no exact English equivalent. He renders it "Rolling of the Fore-Arm" with the sub-title "Lateral Rolling of the Weight." The chapter is divided into two sections: the first considers the "Absolute Rolling Motion" and the second the more complex "Combined Rotary Motions." At the outset, Breithaupt describes "Rollung" as "rotary or rolling action, emanating from the rotary joints of the elbow" and with "the fore-arm turning naturally on its own axis, the hand *passively* following the movement."[37] He adds that

> . . . the outward twisting of the fore-arm together with the hand, showing the palm turned upwards, is called *"supination"* (outward rotation), the corresponding term for the reversed position, i.e. of the hand turned inwards, being *"pronation"* (inward rotation). The motion of the hand in boring with a gimlet, a corkscrew would be counted under

347

"outward rotation or supination"; whereas unscrewing a corkscrew, etc. would come under the list of movements headed "inward rotation, pronation."[38]

Breithaupt says this is the commonest form of action employed in forearm tremolo-like patterns of broken thirds, sixths, octaves, chords, trills, etc. and then also in five-finger exercises, scales, arpeggios, and various figurations. A caution is given that the thumb must remain *"relaxed* and *passive"* throughout: much of the fatigue and cramp that players experience is induced by "the incessant exaggerated straightening action of a thumb generally stiff to begin with" and also because the figures "are rapped out with the fingers rising and falling." Before practicing at the keyboard where the interval of a sixth is first introduced, the action is to be practiced in the air "with the arm suspended free and hanging heavy from the shoulder, . . . the evolutions being gradually accelerated to the utmost possible speed." Breithaupt fails to point out that, as the speed increases movement cannot be confined to the forearm alone; the upper-arm becomes involved. He did realize however that "the greater the diameter or the axis on which the hand rocks, the easier and more perfect will be the motion; the smaller the diameter, the more difficult will it be to distribute the weight."[39] But then he added:

> It follows that the *shake* is chiefly the result of the rocking motion of the fore-arm and *not* of the rise and fall of alternate fingers, which, so far, do not participate actively in the motion required by the various forms of the *"tremolo."* They merely support the weight and must accordingly be held as naturally as possible. Later on, in the free action of the fingers . . . they participate slightly in the attack, being raised but very little. Some virtuosi perform the shake with an almost imperceptible rise of the fingers, apparently, simply by a rocking motion of the fore-arm.[40]

Here once again Breithaupt's thinking was confused. One wonders if he really did try to execute a trill with pure rotary action. It is impossible to do so except at a very slow rate of speed, too slow, in fact, to be called a trill. A shake is chiefly the result of finger action: the rapid rotation of the arm weight mass, which also involves overcoming inertia continuously, is not only exceedingly inefficient but is practically an impossibility, even when combined with a limited finger action. Tremolos on the larger intervals with pure rotary action of course are desirable touch forms. Breithaupt advises practicing with various levels of the wrist: high, level, low

348

and with slight lateral adjustments. But he considers the abducted form of the hand in the Lebert-Stark method and the adducted Deppean hand as being too extreme. And "away with the rigid 'normal positions and postures,' " such as are found in the Lesche-tizky-Brée School.[41]

In the second part of the fifth chapter, Breithaupt deals first with "Rotary motion combined with extension of the fore-arm." Practice begins with five-finger roulades, stepwise, then by skip in broken chords. He describes a series of movements, using the five white keys from C to G:

1. The fall of the arm upon the thumb: C^2.
2. The transmission by rotation of the weight from the thumb to the other fingers: 2-3-4-5: D^2-E^2-F^2-G^2 (from key-bed to key-bed, without raising the fingers).
3. A short, jerked extension of the fore-arm towards the 5th finger.
4. The light rise and swing of the arm or of the hand on to the 5th finger preparatory to its again falling on to the thumb: D^2, etc.

The transmission of the weight from one finger to another by means of five successive attacks, . . . now becomes one single rotary action. Instead of executing 5 swinging and falling movements or 5 rises and 5 falls, *one* rotation (as if driving a gimlet) of the fore-arm in the elbow-joint suffices to cause the weight of hand and arm to bear, or rock upon the *five* participating fingers, or upon the five keys.

The fingers themselves do not take any essential, active part, for the time being. . . . The simple rotation of the fore-arm in one single rotary action renders the other actions superfluous.[42]

Then the "Rollung" action is applied to scale activity. An octave scale consists of nothing more than a three note and a five note roulade. They are

. . . instantly joined one with the other by rotation of the fore-arm, each time a passage requiring a "passing-under" or a "passing-over" of the fingers occurs. This means: *doing away with the old style passing-under of the thumb, as also with the passing-over of fingers 3 and 4 (and 2 and 5) and with all nonsensical* special studies. A lateral shifting or removal of the hand *without* rotation or extension of the fore-arm, as taught by the old school-methods, is *inadmissable*.[43]

Breithaupt develops the whole procedure at considerable length, utilizing various exercises and excerpts from standard classics including what he calls "Extended Scales (Passage-work and Arpeggi)." It would be a real boon to piano technique if all passage work could be performed in this almost glissando-like fashion. But thoughtful analysis will show that Breithaupt's scheme is an impractical one. If no finger action is used in playing a stepwise five note roulade, all keys must be played while the fore-arm rotates in a mere 3/8 inch arc, the distance of key depression. And this must be done very quickly; experimentation will show that at even a moderate rate of rotation no sound can be achieved at all. Intensity control is completely at the mercy of the speed of rotation; and furthermore no gradations of volume within a figure are possible at all. Finger action is inevitable. And the joining of the scale roulades by this same motion cannot be achieved as quickly as he would indicate, surely not in the time that elapses between two adjacent notes within one of the roulades.

Before concluding his presentation of "Rollung", Breithaupt briefly considers the possibility of combining rotary motion of both fore- and upper-arms. He says that in this situation

> ... the arm describes a very arched curve, backwards, like a sower casting seed, or a mower's backward movement of the right hand. This back curve of the arm is essential, especially in very rapid passages, to secure a purling, liquid flow and elegance of form, and affords the most natural solution of many a difficult passage, etc. Physiologically this form of movement is nothing more than a combination of upper and fore-arm-rolling.[44]

But he fails to see, as Arnold Schultz has shown, that "the upper-arm movement is properly to be considered an *alternative* rather than an aid to movement in the radio-ulnar joints. There can be no point in voluntarily combining two movements each of which causes the forearm to rotate."[45]

Inserted before the chapter on his fourth principal action, "Free Oscillation of the Fingers," are two short chapters on legato and staccato. Obviously, Breithaupt attributes legato to the "Rollung" action. He writes:

> Viewed physiologically, *legato* is the result of fore- and upper-arm rolling combined. The connecting of the various tones of a consecutive series proceeds, properly speaking, from the rolling of the fore-arm. The natural transfer of the weight from key to key, the finger-tips remaining constantly and closely in contact with the same,—produces of itself a natural "legato." And yet the legato thus obtained rather con-

350

stitutes a rapid non-legato, a relative legato.[46]

But how can a legato not be a legato? He continues:

A strict connecting—absolute legato, necessitates a further movement: the inward or outward rolling of the upper-arm, i.e. the rolling of upper or fore-arm combined with the extension (straightening-out) of upper and fore-arm. . . .

The arm, as it were, rolls the weight, or its own weight, before it, thus suggesting the handle of a roller (the hand), rolling or unrolling, as it is pushed or drawn. The arm pushes a scale (downwards) and draws it out (ascending). This rolling and unrolling or gliding of the hand by means of rotary action of the fore- and upper-arm, constitutes the fundamental principle in connecting a series of tones. Real *legato*, a legato aesthetically and technically perfect, depends upon the equality and the purling, smooth flow of the series of tones to be played, and is obtained with the aid of the movement in question, i.e. by the rotary action of upper- and fore-arm, combined with the extension of upper- and fore-arm. We must reject the idea of connecting the tones by independent finger-action consisting in pressure and over-stretching— which is wrong.

Mechanical practice in changing keys, entailing that nervous watching for the correct moment at which to release one key and strike the next, is a thing of the past, involving superfluous and useless labour. All conscious pressing with the fingers, holding down the keys, all spreading, seizing, clutching exerted by digital power, with the object of connecting two tones, exhausts energy, strength, wastes time, and is therefore *wrong*. In reality, neither hand nor fingers connect tones, this connecting is effected by a uniform, steady and sure gliding of the arm over the key-board. *This fact must constantly be borne in mind.* Provided the playing member or members be uniformly weighted, such weight being equally distributed in the rotary action, the change of key and finger must follow as a natural result. The weight being balanced, rolls from key-bed to key-bed, the sound continuing as long as the key is weighted. The only thing to be guarded against, here as in legato playing, is the too early releasing of the weight.[47]

It should be emphasized again that pure rotation, except under the most limited circumstances, is unable to depress or release the keys, let alone connect them. And if the rotation were marked enough to lift the fingers from the keys, each finger must be released before the next finger plays.

351

Breithaupt's solution for staccato playing, which he calls "The Natural Rebound of the Weight" (Arm or Hand), is as unconvincing as that for legato. Once again the arm is the only solution which he can perceive—it need only bounce. He explains:

> When an elastic body falls to the ground, it rebounds, i.e. it is thrown back in the reverse direction, until the power of impulsion (throw, shock or fall) is exhausted. This faculty of rebounding it is that distinguishes elastic bodies (India rubber ball, glass globe) from solid bodies. . . . If we let the compact mass of the arm (arm, hands, fingers) descend, with a free swing upon the key-board, and rebound naturally, we obtain a tonal effect corresponding to a sharp and short *martellato* sound. The greater the precision and rapidity of the fall, the greater will be the precision and rapidity of the rebound, and the sharper and shorter will be the effect of the tone produced. The *drop-staccato* is a *non-legato*, shortened both as regards attack and duration of sound.
>
> Hence, that tonal effect which we call *staccato*, is, mechanically speaking, nothing more nor less than the rebound of the striking mass. . . . But in ordinary staccato, with the natural rebound of the whole arm, as one mass, released, neither hand nor finger participates actively in the movement: *With this fact falls the old-style wrist-technic.* . . . Staccato is not the result of wrist-action, but of the whole arm oscillating in its three principal joints.[48]

The main fallacy in his argument is that the arm and hand are not elastic bodies like an India rubber ball. All we need to do to test his theory is to drop the weight of the arm on the keyboard—the arm stays right there. A quick flexor contraction with the speed of a reflex action may be employed to simulate a bouncing arm. But this is a different matter entirely. And to this day, the old-style wrist-staccato still stands. A vibrato hand staccato with the forearm serving as a base is faster than the movement of the whole arm.

Breithaupt completes his technical foundation with the presentation of "Action IV. Free Oscillation of the Fingers." Here he finally discusses the role of the fingers in his system of "natural technique." Up to this point they have been limited to passive support of the weight. But, once the student can do this and then train the arm and hand to fall and roll on relaxed fingers, "the fingers may participate in the general oscillation of the organs of percussion. They should now be thrown lightly forwards and allowed to co-oscillate in their knuckle-joints."[49] An exercise to illustrate this action follows:

Exercise: Set the weighted arm with raised hand on the middle finger: E^2. With the arm in repose, count sharply: "one",—"two"; at "one" swing the relaxed 2nd finger lightly forward, and at "two" let it descend upon D^2, instantly and simultaneously transferring to it the whole weight from the 3rd finger: This is the transfer of weight by means of free oscillation of the finger and descent of the arm. Do the same with the 1st, 4th and 5th fingers and finally with the thumb, practising the usual three, four and five-finger exercises on the before-named principles, i.e.: thumb on C^2, swing of the 2nd finger and instantaneous descent of the brachial weight on to D^2, rise of 3rd finger and instantaneous descent of the weight of arm and hand on to the 3rd finger on to E^2, rise of 4th finger and descent on to F^2, rise of 5th finger and descent of weight on to G^2, and so on.[50]

He stresses that "The rise of the finger must resemble a light 'soaring', upward swing, a sudden tilting, an elastic jerk, the motion of the fingers themselves resembling that of arrows darted from the string of a bow." The fingers should never rise more than an inch above the keys. They will be at their greatest height when they are straightened out to their full length. Nor should they be trained from a strictly curved position because this paralyzes them and "prevents their free co-oscillation."[51] The excesses of the Stuttgart finger school are still vividly in his mind:

Any active tension of the fingers in the shape of the cock of a gun or pistol which still haunts the minds of master and pupil, is *prohibited, as infringing the law of friction,* for, besides the loss of time, waste of energy and the wrong and pernicious muscular exertion which results, the realization of the most important feature of the whole movement is rendered impossible, viz. the free, loose swing of the fingers and the unimpeded descent of the weighted brachial mass. The tension must only be a *momentary* one, like that of the bowstring.

The swing of the fingers (tension—flexion) must in no way impede the flexibility or action of wrist or elbow-joint, *i.e.* it must not in the least interfere with their relaxation; *therefore* the joint or member must not be stiffened or cramped.[52]

Even so, Breithaupt advocates unprepared finger strokes, as the finger school had. He seemingly cannot conceive of the legitimacy of a close finger action with minimal fixation at the wrist. He feels that the old reactionary finger school is all that there is of pure finger technique, and that it is anathema. Weight is the panacea and it must jog along in company with any finger movement. It matters not that it may be a cumbersome thing, nor that too much relaxation will serve no useful purpose, and actually interfere with efficient piano technique. Breithaupt summarizes his thinking on finger technique in the following manner:

> We have to choose between: Finger-action *without* weight, which is altogether wrong, as it tires the fingers, and Finger-action *with* weight, which is the only correct action.
>
> To what extent *active* muscular tension shall participate, depends upon the technical requirements and difficulties of the composition, and must be decided by the individuality of the player who knows what he is capable of doing.
>
> What must be discarded, as absolutely wrong, is: excessive tension and faulty manner of holding the arms and hands, stiffening of the joints, exaggerated extension of the fingers, obstinate and continual drilling of each finger separately, resulting in a complete or partial stiffening of the wrist or elbow-joint, which while it unnecessarily wastes muscular energy, impedes the free, natural oscillation of the arm by preventing its utilizing its natural weight. He that commands a loose arm and can *"play with weight-touch"*, may use the fingers as much as he likes and whenever he feels they are required—no matter where. As long as the fingers participate in the oscillation of the whole arm and hand, they may do anything; but the moment they perform their movements without participation of arm and hand, *everything is wrong*. Finger-action, finally, becomes a question of dynamics, or aesthetics.
>
> The question is, however, a very important one. Finger-action *without* weight, i.e. the old style, produces a thin, wooden, sharp, dry tone, very different from that of weight-produced touch, which embellishes the tone rendering it full, sonorous and round, enabling the artist to put expression and power into his playing, never dreamt of by the old school.[53]

Part II of Breithaupt's *School of Weight-Touch* is an elaboration of his above discussed views on various aspects of piano playing. He discusses polyphonic and figural playing, dynamics, aesthetics, touch and style, rhythm ("The root of all rhythmic difficulty will be found in stiffness of the body"), fingering ("Weight-produced touch renders any set-down special fingering superfluous"),[54] and practice procedures. In a final attack on the finger energists, Breithaupt states:

Conformably to the laws of a normal and natural technic, we must abolish:

1. All mechanical finger-exercises, the sole purpose of which is "precision," "detaching" and equalizing" the fingers (as all these are acquired by employment of weight),—more especially the unnatural exercises with "set fingers" and changing-fingers, and all special exercises, such as passing the thumb under, octave-studies, etc.
2. All scales and exercises, the sole object of which is to develop "velocity", independence, equality and other illusionary ideas.
3. All purely acrobatic or gymnastical exercises intended to develop extraordinary muscular power or exaggerated "looseness" and "flexibility" and all mechanical practice on dumb pianos and "machines" (Virgil, Jackson, etc.).
4. All monotonous, interminable, useless repetition of one and the same musical figure.

Velocity, i.e. rapidity, is the product of two factors: muscular relaxation and lightning activity. It is attained simultaneously with the acquisition of loosened, *i.e.* limp, joints (more especially of the shoulder and the rotary ariculation of the elbow), of a free, loosely oscillating arm, hand and fingers performing the shortest and least movement.[55]

Strangely enough in his concluding chapter, almost as a post-script, Breithaupt dwells at length on "fixation:"

All that which corresponds to the idea of immobility, of *"fixation"*, and which practically only belongs to the artistic education of the professional pianist properly speaking, has been omitted from this "School" which demonstrates rather the general, natural aids to free action. Contrary to other methods, we start from the principle that we must begin by developing looseness, flexibility and suppleness in the physical organism, before attempting to strengthen and fix the muscles and joints. Experience teaches us that he who can let go, when and wherever he will, can hold fast when and wherever he will,—not the other way about. This fact points exactly the way we have to take. . . .

To make it more clear, we will add that by "fixation" we simply mean a slight, momentary fixing or a light holding, setting of the joints and muscles of arm and hand, or finger, justified by aesthetic reasons, for artistic or technical purposes.

Fixation practically means: to set arm, hand, fingers in a rigid (fixed) pose, all fixed together for a definite purpose, in a certain part of the keyboard; for instance, in a *pp* chord or particularly delicate legato or portato passage. This, naturally, requires a particular muscular tension. Prolonged immobilizations, however, such as we encounter in virtuosity, constitute exceptions which do not come into account. Is it advisable to teach such things methodically? That is the great question of dispute. According to the author's practical experience and personal feelings in the matter, such technical peculiarities should be left to the artistic impulse of the individual, as they present themselves. In passages calling for a certain effect, a gifted individual will, of his own accord and unconsciously, exert a certain muscular tension as required by the part or situation. . . .

. . . If free descent of the weight be the object of natural technic, its retention is that of "artistic" technic. The weight lends the tone its fullness, its consistency, its volume just as the spontaneous "attack" with the whole arm as a mass, lends power and grandeur to the playing, imbuing rhythm with that ponderous brazen tread as of elemental powers. The retained action, the delicate touch, glide and rise, such as we observe in the rhythmic flight of a hovering butterfly—is what lends grace. And nothing but a perfect mastery over both these great complexities of form, the free *and* the fixed styles *will lead* to a perfect equilibrium of the forces, and thus to that perfect harmony between technical and artistic reproduction which nothing material can clog or blemish. The highest degree of tonal precision, light, floating rhythm, perfect equality and uniformity in the melodic outlines can only be attained by will-power with an organism at its disposal not only loosened and ever ready for action, but also possessing that precision and spring which alone secures equality and uniformity of muscular power. To play "fixed" is perhaps the same as to play "with concentrated attention"; it is midway between relaxation and rigidity, and produces the sensation of a fine, constant muscular tension, holding the balance between absolute independence (relaxation) and retention (active stiffening) of the joints. . . .[56]

Are we to infer that this technique which admits a limited role for fixation (which is always more or less present in the most relaxed technique) is reserved only for the artist pianist? Are most pianists, who never reach that level, destined forever only to roll their arms about the keyboard and strive for a hyper-relaxation that becomes an end in itself? Obviously in his fear of the old school and in his efforts to combat the evils inherent in it, he moved to the other extreme in his teaching emphasis. In spite of his vague, pretentious, and sometimes incoherent language and his failure to perceive vital technical truths, Breithaupt became a powerful influence on the piano pedagogical scene. He did benefit his followers by encouraging more arm participation. This, of course, resulted in a greater sonority with less effort and a more easily obtained freedom.

Nevertheless, he also provided them with about as unbalanced a technique as the finger school possessed. By delegating so much exaggerated activity to the full arm and at least implying that it can move about as quickly as the smaller levers, by denying his students the independent activity of fingers and hand with prepared attacks and the necessary degree of fixation in hand and arm, he endowed them with great problems in velocity, intensity control, and legato. Relaxation became an obsession and percussive, clumsy, insensitive playing too often the rule. Any technique which does not permit the full, legitimate participation of all of the playing levers does not have the right to label itself *The Natural Piano Technique,* as Breithaupt's did. Fixation was a minor concern in Breithaupt's teaching. His image today is still one of weight and relaxation, of rolling arms and subordinate fingers, such as he communicated to Maria Levinskaya when she interviewed him after completing study in her native Russia:

> After having received my diploma at the then Imperial Moscow Conservatoire, under Safonoff, I came to Berlin with the intention of finding a music teacher for "finishing lessons!" I paid a visit, amongst others, to Mr. Breithaupt, who at our first interview, whilst developing his theories, approached the piano and showed a few passages. I am sure he will forgive me when I say that on hearing his version of correct passage playing it was so far removed from my own ideal that at once I decided to study with Godowsky. It is only now [1930], in the light of my analysis of Breithaupt's theories in print, that I can fully understand why such an impression was inevitable, for in playing he evidently tried to follow his own precepts, and avoid all precise finger articulation. Possibly he was never actually a master of it, for having once realised the sense of control it creates, it seems too great a sacrifice even for the purpose of proving one's theories to voluntarily renounce so wonderful an asset.[57]

Notes

[1] Harriette Brower, *Piano Mastery*, p. 47.

[2] *Ibid.*, p. 161.

[3] Rudolph M. Breithaupt, "The Idea of Weight-Playing—its Value and Practical Application," *The Musician*, Vol. 16, No. 1, January, 1911, p. 12.

[4] Harriette Brower, "Where Technique and Mechanics Differ," *The Musician*, September, 1923, Vol. 28, p. 9.

[5] Leopold Godowsky, "The Best Method Is Eclectic," *The Etude*, November 1933, Vol. 51, p. 784.

[6] J.G. Hinderer, "We Attend Godowsky's Master Class," *The Musician*, Vol. 38, July, 1933, p. 3.

[7] Artur Schnabel, *My Life and Music*, p. 161.

[8] Breithaupt, "The Idea of Weight Playing," p. 12.

[9] *Ibid.*

[10] *Ibid.*

[11] *Ibid.*

[12] *Ibid.*

[13] Rudolph M. Breithaupt, *Natural Piano-Technic, School of Weight-Touch*, II, p. 5.

[14] Florence Leonard, "How Breithaupt Teaches," *The Musician*, Vol. XX, No. 4, April, 1915, p. 225.

[15] Breithaupt, *Natural Piano-Technic*, II, p. 7.

[16] *Ibid.*, p. 8.

[17] *Ibid.*

[18] *Ibid.*, p. 10.

[19] *Ibid.*, pp. 11-12.

[20] *Ibid.*, p. 12.

[21] *Ibid.*

[22] *Ibid.*, p. 14.

[23] *Ibid.*, p. 15.

[24] *Ibid.*, p. 16.

[25] *Ibid.*, pp. 16-17.

[26] *Ibid.*, p. 18.

[27] Arnold Schultz, *The Riddle of the Pianist's Finger and Its Relationship to a Touch-Scheme*, p. 289.

[28] Breithaupt, *Natural Piano-Technic,* II, p. 19.

[29] *Ibid.*

[30] *Ibid.,* p. 21.

[31] *Ibid.,* p. 20.

[32] *Ibid.,* p. 21.

[33] *Ibid.,* p. 24.

[34] *Ibid.,* p. 25.

[35] *Ibid.,* p. 26.

[36] *Ibid.,* p. 28.

[37] *Ibid.,* p. 32.

[38] *Ibid.*

[39] *Ibid.,* pp. 32-34.

[40] *Ibid.*

[41] *Ibid.,* p. 36.

[42] *Ibid.,* p. 34.

[43] *Ibid.,* p. 37.

[44] *Ibid.,* p. 48.

[45] Schultz, *The Riddle,* p. 281.

[46] Breithaupt, *Natural Piano-Technic,* II, p. 49.

[47] *Ibid.,* pp. 49-50.

[48] *Ibid.,* p. 52.

[49] *Ibid.,* p. 54.

[50] *Ibid.*

[51] *Ibid.,* pp. 54-55.

[52] *Ibid.*

[53] *Ibid.,* p. 56.

[54] *Ibid.,* pp. 88-89.

[55] *Ibid.,* p. 98.

[56] *Ibid.,* pp. 99-100.

[57] Maria Levinskaya, *The Levinskaya System of Pianoforte Technique and Tone-Colour through Mental and Muscular Control,* p. 56.

17.

The English School: Matthay;
His Pupils and Colleagues

Piano instruction in England at the close of the eighteenth century was greatly influenced by the foreign-born musicians Muzio Clementi, Johann Baptist Cramer, and, unfortunately, the master promoter Johann Bernhard Logier. All had come to England in their early years (Clementi at the age of fourteen from Italy and Cramer at two and Logier at ten from Germany). They all had absorbed much of the prevailing musical culture; still they were not native Englishmen. The continental influence became even stronger in the nineteenth century and was particularly evident in the eclectic teaching of pianists in the conservatories in London.

The English were not far behind the French in establishing schools of music. The Royal Academy of Music was first proposed at a meeting at the Thatched House Tavern in London in July of 1822. The school was opened in March of the following year; the first piano lesson was given by Cipriani Potter to one Kellow Pye. Potter (1792-1871), a scholarly pianist who had first acquainted the English with several Beethoven concertos, had studied piano for five years with Wölffl. Through his counterpoint instruction with Thomas Atwood (1765-1838), Potter could trace his musical lineage back to Mozart. Atwood, a founder of the London Philharmonic Society in 1813, had been a favorite pupil of Mozart and later was an ardent supporter of Mendelssohn. Mendelssohn, who performed and conducted frequently in Britain between 1829 and 1847 with outstanding success, did more than any other person to establish an ideal for English pianism during the nineteenth century. His refined, classical style appealed greatly to the methodical English temperament. The German-born pianist Charles Hallé (1818-1895), in his youth a student of Kalkbrenner and friend of Chopin, followed Mendelssohn to England. He settled there permanently in 1848 and succeeded to Mendelssohn's popularity. In 1880 when Tobias Matthay, the greatest of English piano teachers, began to teach at the Royal Academy of Music, his wife Jessie (daughter of the famous Scottish folk singer, David Kennedy) later recalled,

> England was playing the pianoforte very placidly under the high priesthood of Charles Hallé. Hallé's art was a definite one, tending to a cold perfection, which in itself was of great service to the musical England of his time, for Society pianists had been wallowing in a cheap, shallow, perfunctory sentimentality.[1]

In 1882 the Academy's counterpart, the Royal College of Music, was founded by Edward VII (then Prince of Wales), with Sir George Grove (1820-1900) of dictionary fame serving as its first director. Its earliest piano faculty included such continentally trained musicians as Franklin Taylor (1843-1919), student of Plaidy, Moscheles, and Clara Schumann; and Arabella Goddard (1836-1922), who at six years of age was a pupil of Kalkbrenner and later studied with Thalberg. As early as 1857, she played the late Beethoven Sonatas for her fellow Englishmen. Then there was the Austrian pianist Ernst Pauer (1826-1905), whose mother belonged to the Streicher piano manufacturing family. In the 1860s Pauer presented historical piano recitals in London; by 1870 he had revived interest in the harpsichord.

Long before the establishment of the Royal College of Music, the Royal Academy of Music had been holding examinations in performance and theory on various levels of advancement throughout the United Kingdom. In 1889 the two schools joined forces in administering these, not only at home, but to thousands throughout the Empire. The Associated Board of the Royal Schools of Music was formally organized in 1932 for this purpose. It also became involved in publishing editions of music to be used in these examinations: the editions of Bach and Beethoven by the scholarly pianist-musicologist, Donald F. Tovey (1875-1940), are notable examples of this activity. Tovey was greatly influenced and helped by the teaching and advice of Ludwig Deppe, although he never studied formally with him.

It was in such a musical environment that Britain's major contributors to technical thought emerged. Even before Breithaupt refuted the old finger school, it should be noted that William Townsend in Scotland had delivered a telling blow. His excellent treatise of one hundred pages, entitled *Balance of Arm in Piano*

Technique, was published in London in the 1890s. It is evident that he recognized the entire technical problem more accurately than Breithaupt, and was able to express himself more succinctly than Matthay. At the outset he was impressed that the writers on technique he had knowledge of insisted on a percussive action as a means of developing strength and independence in the fingers and equality of sound. But he felt that if muscular strength needs to be increased, it is better to achieve it through the employment of hand-gymnastics away from the keyboard. In finger action, the fingers must be "kept in constant contact with the keys."[2] Striking makes it impossible to test key resistance and to control tonal intensity; the velocity of the finger is "broken when it meets the key, being retarded by the sudden shock caused by the resistance of the latter."[3] Then, too, the noise of the blow of the finger spoils the tone quality. Furthermore he believed the keys should be handled as true levers:

Now the keys of the piano, in their nature as levers, differ in no wise from the pedals of the same instrument, or from the keys and pedals of the organ. In these cases the levers are put there for the purpose of lifting or moving something. But the pianist in using his pedals, would not raise the sole of his foot and bring it down with a stroke, any more than the organist would strike his keys from a distance, or stamp on his pedals. These levers are used in conformity with the laws of mechanics when they are touched before being pushed down by finger or foot. Why then should the use of those levers by means of which the piano is played be regulated by a different law? Why should the piano-keys be struck, while the organ-keys and the pedals of both organ and piano are pushed? It can surely not be that the fact of the piano being an instrument whose tone is produced by percussion—by the stroke of a hammer on a wire—has led the player to imagine that the key must also be struck—that because there is a hammer at one end of the lever it is necessary to have a hammer at the other end.[4]

Townsend pointed out that the old technicians thought the only way to achieve true finger independence was by lifting the fingers high. Actually just the opposite result is achieved: the playing and nonplaying fingers, wrist, and arm ("many movements of the fingers are made by means of muscles lying in the arm"[5]) are all tied together in tension and stiffness:

The appearance of independence which the finger presents when raised, is therefore a snare. Its height above the others,

363

and its isolation from them, give it this appearance. But it has been seen that that kind of independence is a false one. Some manner of action must therefore be found, which, while causing any finger to move will simultaneously allow the other parts of the hand to remain quiescent.[6]

He clearly defined the problem of independence in this way:

A true estimate of the nature of the keys cannot be formed unless the fact of their independence of one another be taken into consideration. No key can influence its neighbours. It controls its own hammer and damper, and no other. But this quality or property of independence entitles the keys to expect or demand a similar—or as nearly as possible similar—independence in the fingers which play upon them. And the fingers, regarded as playing agents, are, by nature, very unindependent of each other. they are a too united family. Unfortunately, their Unity is not Strength, but weakness: seeing that no single finger in its untrained state, when called upon to transmit force to the keys, can do so without distributing some of that force to the other fingers of the same hand, thus itself losing strength, and also setting up uncalled-for motion in these other fingers. The problem therefore will be to find some method of training the hand, which, from the beginning, will not only encourage but compel independence in the fingers.[7]

Obviously Townsend favored individual key treatment, an area in which Breithaupt fell short. What was Townsend's solution to the evils of the old percussion school? To achieve the greatest possible independence, he would not only reduce excessive movement in the lever—the finger—but give careful attention to the muscular condition of the finger's base—the hand and arm:

True independence, cultivated to its highest point, gives the hand and arm a constant appearance of naturalness and grace, convincing the onlooker of a feeling of comfort in the player. . . . . each piano-key is absolutely independent in its action, and to match this quality in the keys, a similar—or as nearly as possible similar—independence in the fingers ought to be expected from the player. The training of the hand therefore, must, from the beginning of study be based upon the idea that movement in any finger which causes simultaneous movement in any other finger is not independent enough. Every finger-movement—to be a really independent one—must be made without occasioning the movement of any other part of the hand. The strictest inhibition of all other movements becomes then as important a matter as is the movement itself. But this inhibition is impossible as long as the weight of the hand and arm is incorrectly used, or, in other words, as long as the hand and arm are not balanced. . . . The student must therefore first bring his hand and arm back to nature's state of ease and freedom, in which the muscles possess a yielding and elastic consistency. Then only can true independence among the fingers be attained.[8]

We come now to the central point of Townsend's book: the balance of the arm in piano technique. The weight of the arm should be supported or released with the greatest care; muscular control should be kept at its most delicate minimum—just enough to support the amount of tone desired. If a finger is raised above the key, the balance is destroyed because of the resulting tension. The fingers are only free to move independently if the balance of the arm is correctly adjusted. This leads to another benefit:

There is a quality in the key's resistance besides its weight which only the balanced arm and hand of the pianist can adequately test. This is that subtle and undefinable feeling which is sent through the fingers by the peculiar type of mechanism in the particular piano played upon.[9]

Undoubtedly he was working in the direction of the clearly defined solutions of coordination and sensitivity of touch which Ortmann and Schultz were later to achieve. Although he fell short of analyzing it in adequate detail, the muscular control of the base was of vital importance to Townsend: ". . . if balanced arm-weight [the gist of the text implies knowing when to support it as well as release it] is not constantly in use during playing, the result is loss of tone-quality, of correct leverage, of independence of finger-action, of physical comfort and of naturalness of demeanour."[10] The sensation of a finely balanced arm (it seems closely akin to the sensation of an arm with minimal muscular fixation), he says is hard to describe. But his description is meaningful, even though he fails to warn that arm movement in itself does not necessarily mean that the antagonistic muscles are properly coordinated with minimal contraction:

The balanced state is that in which, when the fingers are resting on anything—in the present case the keyboard—the whole limb from shoulder to finger-tips is at any moment ready and willing to swing: up, down, sideways, or circularly, at the wrist; or sideways at the elbows; and the problem to be solved by the student is, how to practise and at the same time preserve this condition of balance as a constant bodily habit.[11]

There follows a series of exercises at the piano for the purpose of developing fine muscular co-ordination in the arms and hands. The first series is concerned with "balance without hold" (the arm glides up and down the keyboard with the wrist sometimes undulating, the fingers resting lightly but surely on the surface of the keys, none of which are depressed) and the second with "balance with hold" (with a single key depressed silently, the arm delivers the smallest degree of weight needed to keep it down):

> Let him [the student] then, while keeping the key down . . . move his wrist up and down, that is vertically, trying to preserve a perfect balance in the arm, and watching closely the held-down key. If the latter shows the least sign of quivering, as if it were going to move upwards, the Balance of arm is incorrect.[12]

After this, the fingers push the keys down by "Impulse" with close attention given to the sensation of key resistance, to the timing of the "push" which "must stop at the instant of tone-creation and give place to the hold,"[13] and to "elasticity at the wrist."[14] Much of this explanation bears a distinct resemblance to Matthay's system of "Staccato-and-Legato resting" and "Added-impetus," but Matthay seemingly never acknowledged Townsend's influence. With the practice of finger exercises, true independence is kept uppermost in Townsend's mind:

> When any single finger or simultaneous combination of fingers is being drilled, it is possible to inhibit motion in every other part of the hand. The inhibition of all unnecessary and uncalled-for movement—commonly known as independence of finger—is however quite impossible unless the student first reduces his arm to a state of Balance. This balance of arm brings with it stillness without stiffness—repose without rigidity.[15]

The fingers are to be pushed down individually with a minimal degree of fixation and a careful balance in the arm. Townsend also gives exercises and instructions for controlling arm weight in its "fall" to the keys:

> The best fall is that which produces tone with the least noise of the contact of finger and key, and with the most immediate "give" at the wrist. This elastic motion is indispensable. The student will find it a safe rule to remember—that, the more noisily the key-and-finger-contact is made the less elastic will be his wrist, and the poorer consequently will be the tone produced.

It will be best for him to be content with the production at first of only a quiet tone. When he is thoroughly familiar with the action, he may proceed to try the fall in conjunction with the production of a bigger tone.[16]

Besides Townsend, another Englishman, who deserves more than passing mention because of his unique musical stature, was actively engaged in solving his own personal problems in piano technique at about this same time—the 1890s. His name was Harold Bauer (1873-1951). His early training was almost entirely in violin, although he played the piano well enough to perform on both at a public London recital in 1885. His only piano lessons were with a musician aunt. On the advice of Paderewski, for whom he had auditioned, Bauer went to Paris in 1892 to study with the violinist Gorski, who thought he had more ability as a pianist and hired him as an accompanist. At the same time Paderewski, residing in Paris while engaged in enlarging his concert repertoire, asked him to play on a second piano the orchestral reductions of several concertos which he was rehearsing. Bauer commented:

I learned a great deal by being in the presence of this great master; when he had finished this rehearsing with me it was my custom to ask for his help in dealing with certain problems of the piano which I naturally looked upon as a secondary instrument. Paderewski was good enough to try to get me engagements as a violinist, but there were too many young violinists of brilliant talent in Paris at that time.[17]

In 1894 Bauer went to Russia on tour as accompanist for the singer Louise Nikita. He had expected to assist her by playing violin solo groups during her intermissions, but was forced to turn to the piano instead because of his difficulty in securing accompanists. On his return to France the following year, Bauer was faced with the unusual dilemma of embarking upon the career of a concert pianist with no formal technical training whatsoever! His account of how he started on the road to pianistic immortality, while achieving an enlightened technique as he went, is one of the most refreshing anecdotes in piano technique literature:

When I reached Paris and saw old friends and again made efforts to start playing the violin, I was laughed at because I had admitted that I had been playing the piano in public for several months. I received invitations to play with singers and instrumentalists; and finally some of my friends thought I had made sufficient progress to guarantee the expenses of a piano recital. How was I going to make people believe that I was

367

worthy of playing the piano in public when I had no technique! ...

I had become a pianist in spite of myself, yet I had no technique and I did not know how to acquire it. In the midst of this perplexity, I went one day to a private house to see a young woman dance. I paid no attention at that time to her name. She went through a lot of gestures and posing to the strains of classical music familiar to me. It was unusual. I had never seen anything like it before. I noticed that she was using gestures that seemed to illustrate all the dynamic variations of the musical phrase. Her movements fascinated me with their beauty and rhythm. Every sound seemed to be translated into terms of motion and, as I watched her carefully, the idea crept into my mind that this process might—conceivably—be something like a reversible one. I said to myself that as long as a loud tone apparently brought forth a vigorous gesture and a soft tone a delicate gesture, why, in playing the piano, should not a vigorous gesture bring forth a loud tone and a delicate gesture a soft tone? The fact that this was precisely what had always taken place did not occur to me. It seemed to me that I had made a great discovery and, looking at the dancer, I imagined that if I could get my hands to make on a reduced scale certain motions that she was making with her whole body, I might perhaps acquire some of those fine gradations of tone which, to me, represented the most important qualities of piano playing. At any rate, I was desperate and I determined to try. I started by making angular and ridiculous gestures at the piano in a way no human being had ever done before. Any other pianist seeing me practise might have doubted my sanity. I persisted, however. There was the preconceived idea of a certain kind of tone and it was necessary to find the gesture that could produce it.

This eluded me as a rule, but once in a while tone and gesture seemed to belong together, quite unmistakably, and at such moments a ray of hope seemed to indicate that I was on the right track. Right, that is to say, *for me,* at that time, because my main idea was that if I could give an expressive sound to my performance next Saturday night, when I hoped to earn fifty francs, the audience might tolerate, to some extent at least, my lack of fluency and mechanical skill. This way of practising, first dictated by necessity, later on became a habit of both mind and muscle, from which I never subsequently departed.

Thirty years later I gave a recital in Los Angeles at which my old friend, Eugene Ysaye, was present. He came to see me in the artists' room after the concert with a lady who was a perfect stranger to me. He said, "Of course you know Isadora." I said, "Isadora who?" He said, "Isadora Duncan." I said I did not know the lady but should like very much to meet her. He presented me to her. I said, "Miss Duncan, I must tell you the story of my life because you are certainly unaware that you have had greater influence on it than anyone else."[18]

Overshadowing Townsend and Bauer stands Tobias Matthay (1858-1945). His parents, both of German birth, had migrated to England before their marriage. His father had become resident master at Clapham Grammar School where his special interest was in languages, in particular French and German literature. Tobias Matthay early studied piano with Edwin Hirst, a pupil of Moscheles. At fourteen he entered the Royal Academy of Music as a scholarship student in composition under William Sterndale Bennett (1816-1875), a protégé of Cipriani Potter and principal of the Academy from 1866. Later Matthay worked under Arthur Sullivan and Ebenezer Prout. Matthay's early aspirations were more in composition than in piano: he showed considerable promise by winning the Charles Read Prize in composition for a quartet for piano and strings and by having an orchestral tone poem, *Country Life,* performed at a Covent Garden promenade concert in 1880.

Matthay's piano study at the Academy was with a colleague of Sterndale Bennett, William Dorrell, from whom he received his introduction to Bach's *Well-Tempered Clavier.* A staid Englishman, Dorrell thereafter presented him with more recent fare, prefacing it with the statement: "Now, I am going to give you something modern—but I don't know that I ought to, as it is so revolutionary."[19] This radical work turned out to be the Mendelssohn D Minor Concerto. Matthay found piano study at the Academy prosaic and superficial, with little intense preparation in either interpretation or technique. In both these areas he soon was to make unique and enduring contributions—he shed the continental influence so apparent in his predecessors.

Matthay taught piano from his mid-teens; in 1880 he was named assistant professor of piano at the Royal Academy of Music. Until 1894 he presented regular public piano recitals in London and throughout much of his life he continued to compose. But after his appointment to the Academy, these activities were subordinated to his career as a piano teacher and theorist. His apprentice teaching years were spent largely with untalented students, but were far from wasted. During this time, his intense intellectual curiosity focused itself upon the basic problems of piano playing and the evils which were evident in the English teaching of the period, so strongly influenced by the German finger school. Like Breithaupt in Germany, Matthay was deeply impressed by the great pianists who came to London during this period. He heard Liszt who, after a forty-five years' absence, returned in 1886 for a farewell appearance. Then there were Hans von Bülow and Anton Rubinstein. After observing them, he experimented with his own playing and teaching and soon arrived at the principles of which he became so thoroughly convinced. Later he was to tell Harriette Brower:

> I made a study of *Rubinstein's* playing, for I found he played a great deal better than I did. So I discovered many things in listening to him, which he perhaps could not have explained to me. These facts are incontrovertible and I have brought many of my colleagues to see the truth of them. More than this, I have brought many even of my older colleagues who had a life-time of wrong mental habits to impede them, to realize the truth of my teachings.[20]

Not only Rubinstein's playing, but his piano had a great influence on Matthay. Jessie Matthay wrote how this came about:

> . . . Naturally after hearing Rubinstein he had to attempt the C Major staccato study. He had been playing it on a piano with little key-surface resistance.
>
> On now changing for a season to the Érard piano (which had been Rubinstein's instrument), he was told by the manager: "Ah, you will find it much easier to play this Etude on the Érard." However, Matthay found to his surprise, when he began practising on the Érard, that the new action, so far from helping him, entirely baulked him, and that the C Major went from bad to worse!
>
> The fact is that in those days, practically the full weight of the Érard action was left against the player, and was not disguised (as it usually is to-day) by leaden weights inserted in the fronts of the keys. Obviously, Matthay had been indulging in *key-hitting;* and when this full key resistance was met it caused him to miss sounding the notes! He therefore had to readjust his technical notions until he could successfully cope with this heavy surface resistance.
>
> The Érard, in fact, taught him the valuable lesson that hit-

ting was useless, and that the key had to be taken hold of when met. Thus arose one of his most important teachings; that one must adjust oneself for every note to the resistance experienced after reaching the key. Thus the law of ATTENTION TO KEY RESISTANCE.

After that there was much experimenting with other pianos. Von Bülow with his *Bechstein* captured his interest and attention and completely satisfied his ear with its wealth of tone colour.[21]

Even prior to this, in the early eighties, he had experimented with strengthening his fingers by installing a set of strong springs in the action of his old upright piano. The springs could be regulated so as to change the key resistance. On this very hard action he practiced fast and brilliant passages. Later he marvelled that he had avoided physical damage.

By the 1890s Matthay was working with more serious, talented students who won prizes and scholarships at the Academy. Strangely enough his first serious pupil was his own sister Dora, eleven years his junior. While he perfected his teaching techniques, he also was busy writing. By 1897 Matthay had accumulated a voluminous draft of his thoughts on technique. This material was published in 1903 as his first and most significant work, *The Act of Touch*—one year before Breithaupt's *The Natural Piano Technic*.

Initial contact with this formidable work is likely to be a rather bewildering experience because of its involved sentence structure, its unending supply of footnotes, and its repetitious nature. One can hardly be blamed for reacting initially as did the reviewer in the *New York Tribune* on September 28, 1904:

> Of economy, either in time, words, paper or printing ink, Mr. Matthay has no conception. He writes a book to tell what he is going to say in a book which follows; supplements that with a book promulgating what he has written; amplifies all this in another volume of appendices. The result is so bewildering that the reader is not likely to carry away much more than this: that to play on the pianoforte one must press upon a lever called a key sufficiently hard to cause the hammer to hit the string. Of course there is much more in the book, and many things that have pedagogical value; but it is laborious to dig them out of Professor Matthay's verbal tumulus.[22]

Much later one of Matthay's colleagues, Ambrose Coviello, tried to help his readers along by writing a little volume entitled *What Matthay Meant, His Musical and Technical Teachings*

Clearly Explained and Self-Indexed. Notwithstanding all of this, with careful study of *The Act of Touch* we get a picture of Matthay, the tireless English schoolmaster completely devoted to his mission in life, getting across to his students and the general pianistic public his version of musical and technical truth. With his generous use of summaries and recapitulations it is not too difficult to comprehend his teachings. Two years later in 1905, the summary material from *The Act of Touch,* together with two supplementary chapters, was published for schoolroom use under the title, *First Principles of Pianoforte Playing.* His basic principles were subsequently simplified in separate monographs: *The Child's First Steps in Pianoforte-Playing* (1912) and *The Nine Steps towards Finger Individualization through Forearm Rotation* (1923).

The Act of Touch is grouped basically into four divisions: Part I: "Introductory—General Aspects of the Problems of Pianoforte Playing"; Part II: "Key-Treatment from its Instrumental Aspect"; Part III: "Key-Treatment from its Muscular Aspect"; Part IV: "On Position." In the introductory section, Matthay shows his concern with interrelating the elements of fine piano playing. He writes regarding the intellectual and emotional perception and artistic judgment of musical shapes as well as the physical execution involved in communicating these perceptions to the listener. All of this involves careful attention to the laws controlling key treatment as an important means of developing the art of tone production. He was very much against the old empiric, haphazard way of practicing where many senseless repetitions finally become the means of developing physical technique or of stumbling into a musically expressive performance. The intelligent, discriminating musician is continually concerned with relating the most minute detail to overall shapes and concepts. Matthay, the superlative musician, wrote:

> "Shape," in performance, therefore eventually resolves itself into RHYTHM, both in its narrowest, and in its widest sense. The constituent *atoms* (the single sounds) must, each one, have its definite place in the scheme of the Whole, if that is to be satisfactory. To enable us to succeed in this, the work as a Whole must constantly be kept in mind,—while yet, for the sake of it, carefully placing each and every note at the precise *time-spot* thus dictated; and not only that, but at the exact tone-amount—and more important still—at the exact tone-*quality* thus demanded. Unless this be accomplished, the resulting music-picture can neither be homogeneous, nor per-

372

fectly harmonious, nor *just* in its outlines; while the expression of the *emotional*-import underlying these mere shapes (popularly mal-termed "sound") obviously remains quite impossible.[23]

In spite of his diffuse and at times ambiguous expositions, Matthay was a master teacher and had a great gift for analyzing and organizing his subject material. The following chart summarized for him the rational approach to performance:

The Act of INTELLIGENCE *In Playing,*
implies:

Attention Inwards—	*Attention Outwards—*
to enable us to obey Music :	to enable us to obey the Key :
This implies use of our Musical-Imagination so that by perceiving Musical-Emotion and Musical-Shape, we shall be able to judge the	This implies Attention *Muscularly and Aurally,* to enable us to
TIME-SPOT *and* TONE-KIND *due for each note.*	*Feel* key-resistance before and during [descent, and to *Hear* the completion of key-descent.

Or finally, to put the case as a positive direction :

I : *We must try to SEE the Emotion, and the Musical-material ;—*
—the latter being the material-shapes of Time (rhythm) and Tone, through which the former is exhibited ;
and II : *We must try to OBTAIN this mentally-pictured Music from the Keys ;*
—by employing our knowledge of the requirements of Key-treatment, and our muscular-adaptations to these.

The latter moreover involves, that we must give :
a) *Muscular-Attention* to the key-Resistances, and [key-descent.
b) *Aural-Attention* to the beginning of each sound—the consummation of

24

The facsimile reproduction of Matthay's summary to Part I of *The Act of Touch* on page 374 gives insight into the entire structure of the Matthay system.

In Part II, which deals with the instrumental aspect of key-treatment, Matthay analyzes the piano in its most vital constituent parts. He discusses the behavior of the strings from an acoustical point of view. He also dwells on the importance of treating the key as a lever manipulated by the application and interaction of weight and muscular force or energy. In the following recapitulation of Part II he gives his theory of tone quality as well as certain basic directions for key control, a number of which are similar to Townsend's principal points:

SUMMARY OF PART I.

THE ACT OF PLAYING

—Is accomplished by the union of *two quite distinct acts:*—

I:

CONCEPTION,

—the Perception of Musical Sense.

—and—.

II:

EXECUTION;

—the Communication of such perception to others.

The power of perceiving musical sense, depends on the degree of our

MUSICIANSHIP.

Musicianship, the power of understanding Music, has two sides:—

The power of communicating musical sense, depends on the extent of our

EXECUTIVE-ATTAINMENTS.

Executantship, the power of expressing that which one perceives, has two sides:—

(a):

The EMOTIONAL SIDE;

Emotional Musical-ability, or *Musical-Feeling*, permits us to perceive: the *Emotional Import* of Music.

It permits us to perceive, and enjoy, the sensuously Beautiful in Music; and its parallelism to Human emotion.

and

(b):

The INTELLECTUAL SIDE;

Intellectual Musical-ability, or *Musical-Reasoning*, permits us to perceive: the *Musical-Shapes* employed to convey such emotion.

It permits us to perceive, and enjoy, the perfections shown in the musical structure: workmanship—in its largest and smallest manifestations.

It enables us to perceive Rhythmical structure:—the facts of Climax, or Crisis, in its large swings of form, and in its smaller ones of the Phrase and its subdivisions—down to its component Ideas.

(a):

ARTISTIC-JUDGMENT;

Artistic-Judgment, embraces: Knowledge of, and Taste in the application of the instrumental effects, through which it is alone possible to translate such sense as one can perceive musically.

It also embraces *pulsational* sensibility; a sensibility that should be keen enough to feel the continuance of Pulse, even when its reiterations are temporarily suspended,—as in "*Rubato.*"

and

(b):

The ART OF TONE-PRODUCTION;

This implies, *Ability* to obtain from the instrument, every possible kind of tone: of any Quantity, Quality, Duration; and at any Speed of succession. It embraces Agility, and Colouring.

Adeptness in the Art of Tone-making has two separate aspects:—

(aa):

INSTRUMENTAL-KNOWLEDGE;
—*Consciousness of what are the requirements of the Key.*

and

(bb):

MUSCULAR-HABIT.
—*Muscular-ability, to fulfil these requirements, correctly formed and rapidly retained.*

Muscular-Habit, implies two distinct things :—

(aaa):

Muscular-Determination;

The power to provide the requisite Muscular Activities, and *Inactivities.*

(bbb):

Muscular-Application.

The power to apply these to the Requirements of the Key, as to Time and Degree.

Training is hence required in both the departments, Conception and Execution, and in all the subsidiary aspects of these.
Moreover, such Training can only bear fruit, provided ATTENTION is consciously or unconsciously given during the Act of Playing.
This Act of ATTENTION or VOLITION in performance, although apparently but one flash of consciousness, must nevertheless comprise

FOUR COMPONENTS:—

MUSICAL attention.—*Inwards* :—

(I):

As to TIME;

—*WHERE each note should begin;*

—An Attention, Judgment, and consequent Volition originating from our Musical Feeling and Intelligence, provided we insist on these faculties determining the proper mission of each Note.—*as Part of a WHOLE*

(II):

As to TONE;

—*HOW each note should sound.*

PHYSICAL attention.—*Outwards* :—

(III):

As to RESISTANCE,

Experienced from each KEY;

—Attention and Judgment by means of: the MUSCULAR-SENSE.

(IV):

As to PLACE, in KEY-DESCENT;

WHERE each Sound BEGINS; •

—Attention and Judgment, by means of : the AURAL-SENSE.

The Result to be obtained by such perfect act of Attention and Volition is : that the **PLACING** (both as to Time and as to Tone) of each and every note, will be *directly prompted* by our Musical Feeling and Intelligence.
The result moreover is : that the Muscular-Conditions, necessary to consummate this "*Placing,*" will be Started, and "Aimed"—*i.e.*, ceased :—
Firstly, by our Muscular-sensation—of the key's resistance before and during descent :
Secondly, by our Aural-Sensation—of the commencement of tone, arising from the completion of each Key-movement.

The supreme necessity for an unbroken continuity of Attention and Judgment in both these particulars, becomes self-evident, when the real problems of Tone-production itself are considered, as they will be, in Parts II. and III.

26

a): The Pianoforte Key is a machine to facilitate the production of Speed in the String. It is a compound-lever, akin in principle to the See-saw.

b): It follows, that Tone-production can only be effected by giving Motion to the Key; since this forms our only means of conveying motion to the String.

c): Energy brought to bear upon the Key *ceases* to create Tone, the moment that the place in Key-descent is reached, where the hammer's motion culminates, and causes Sound to *begin*.

d): The act itself of Tone-production can hence never take longer than it does in the most extreme *Staccatissimo*.

e): The Ear apprises us of the moment more quickly than can any other of our senses; hence we must *listen* for the beginning of sound, if we would have Accuracy in tone-production.

f): The greater the tonal speed we induce during each individual key-descent, the greater is the tone-*quantity*.

g): The more *gradually* this key-speed is attained, the more beautiful is the Tone-*character*,—the fuller, more "sympathetic," singing and carrying is its quality, and the finer the control.

h): The more *sudden* the key-depression, the harsher is the resulting Tone-quality; it may be more "brilliant," but it will be less effective in carrying power.

i): The *softest* possible sound is obtained, when *Weight* is brought upon the key until a point is reached where the key's opposition (or resistance) to movement is just overcome—and it consequently slips down with the most gentle movement compatible with its hammer reaching the string.

j): Such amount of Weight, allowed to remain resting upon the key, *beyond* the moment that the latter's full depression is reached, forms the effect of *tenuto*. The duration of such Tenuto is determined by the duration of such Resting.

k): The effect of legato is induced by *transferring* such continuously resting light Weight from key to key; such Transference being unbroken for each Musical Phrase.

l): Weight of less amount than this, *insufficient* therefore to cause key-depression, may be left resting on the keys without causing either Tenuto or Legato.

It is such *lightness* in resting, that forms the Basis of all staccato effects, provided it is combined with an accurately-aimed Promptness in the *cessation* of the Energy that causes key-*descent*; for the keys are in this case left free to *rebound* the moment that Tone-production is completed.

m): Such combination (of light Resting and accurate Ceasing of the act of key-depression) also forms the secret of all great Agility in playing.

n): It is futile to *squeeze* the key upon its bed with the object of inducing Tone; since sound, if produced at all, is given off *before* the key reaches its full depression.

o): It is almost as futile to attempt to obtain good tone by *knocking* the key; since the concussion here caused at the key-surface forms *waste* of Energy intended to create tone, and thus engenders *inaccuracy* in the tonal-result,—the actual tone obtained not corresponding to the tone intended.

p): We find (also vide Part III) that instead of squeezing the key-bed, or hitting the key-top, that correct Tone-production demands:—that the finger be brought comparatively gently into contact with the key-board surface, so that the Energy requisite to move the key may be there estimated by our sense of key-resistance. As the key-resistance varies with each change in Tone-shading, this will lead to the requisite *muscular-conditions* being almost automatically prompted into existence,—in accurate response therefore to the dictates of our musical-consciousness as to Time, Tone-amount, Tone-quality, and Duration.[25]

The matter of tone quality at the piano—whether or not an individual tone produced by different pianists at exactly the same intensity level can vary qualitatively—has been a matter of intense concern to pianists. Throughout the nineteenth century and well into the twentieth, especially during the golden era of the great romantic pianists, it was firmly believed that the mystical touch of a Chopin, a Rubinstein, or a Liszt could produce a beauty of tone unmatched by ordinary mortal pianists.

In attempting to explain their secret and formulate an adequate theory of tone production, Matthay turned to the investigations into the nature of musical sound conducted by the German physicist, Hermann L. F. Helmholtz (1821-1894). Helmholtz's monumental study, *On the Sensations of Tone*—still a work of the first magnitude in the field of acoustics—had first appeared in German in 1862, written while he was a professor at the University of Heidelberg. An English translation by Alexander J. Ellis appeared as early as 1885. Helmholtz established through careful laboratory investigation that the material composition of the piano's hammers and the length of time they remained in contact with the strings were among the most important determinants of the nature of the resulting tone quality. He wrote:

376

If the string is struck with a sharp-edged metallic hammer which rebounds instantly, only the one single point struck is directly set in motion. Immediately after the blow the remainder of the string is at rest. It does not move until a wave of deflection rises, and runs backwards and forwards over the string. This limitation of the original motion to a single point produces the most abrupt discontinuities, and a corresponding long series of upper partial tones, having intensities, in most cases equalling or even surpassing that of the prime. When the hammer is soft and elastic, the motion has time to spread before the hammer rebounds. When thus struck the point of the string in contact with such a hammer is not set in motion with a jerk, but increases gradually and continuously in velocity during the contact. The discontinuity of the motion is consequently much less, diminishing as the softness of the hammer increases, and the force of the higher upper partial tones is correspondingly decreased.[26]

Helmholtz tabulated a chart of his findings. For ease in comparison he assumed 100 to be the intensity of the prime tone:

Theoretical Intensity of the Partial Tones of Strings

		Striking point at 1/7 of the length of the string				
		Struck by a hammer which touches the string for				
Number of the Partial Tone	Excited by Plucking	3/7 c''	3/10 g'	3/14 C_1-c' of the periodic time of the prime tone	3/20	Struck by a perfect hard Hammer
1	100	100	100	100	100	100
2	81.2	99.7	189.4	249	285.7	324.7
3	56.1	8.9	107.9	242.9	357.0	504.9
4	31.6	2.3	17.3	118.9	259.8	504.9
5	13	1.2	0	26.1	108.4	324.7
6	2.8	0.01	0.5	1.3	18.8	100.0
7	0	0	0	0	0	0

27

From this study, it is easy for us to conclude that the more forcibly the hammer is struck (with resulting greater tonal intensity), the shorter will be the duration of time that the hammer is in contact with the string. Therefore, the louder one plays, the greater will be the intensity of the upper partials or overtones, and the more brilliant or harsh will be the quality of the sound. Thus tone quality will vary with intensity and length of time the hammer is in contact with the string. Unfortunately Helmholtz did not carry his investigation further to determine if a piano hammer could be activated in different ways, at the same exact tonal intensity level, so

377

as to achieve different tone qualities—different combinations and intensities of fundamental or prime tone and overtones or partials.

Nevertheless, accepting Helmholtz's valid research and attempting to build upon it, Matthay began theorizing. He came to the non-scientific conclusion that tone quality could be varied in separate tones of identical intensity level produced by the same hammer, a view that shortly would be refuted. As stated in the recapitulation to Part II of *The Act of Touch,* he felt that, if the desired key speed necessary for a certain level of sound were achieved gradually, the hammer would be driven with greater momentum and control against the string, that it would remain in contact with the string for a longer duration, and that the resulting tone would thus be more "sympathetic." He reasoned:

> It is certainly conceivable, that the greater the momentum of the hammer, when it finally reaches the string, the *longer* will it then *"remain lying"* upon the latter,—the more will the string-surface be driven into it,—the flatter will the hammer in consequence become,—and the "less acute" will then be the angle subtended by the string in its initial push-off;—thus bringing the process into accord with Helmholtz's teaching, as to the difference in attack that causes the string to move off in comparatively *pure* (fundamental) sound rather than in harmonics of the harsher kind.[28]

This opinion became such an integral part of his system that when confronted as late as 1931 by the results of the William Braid White experiments conducted for the American Steel Institute, which showed that quality differences of tone can only go hand-in-hand with quantity differences, Matthay hedged and objected: "Yet there is a fly in the ointment! . . . the experiments here are not at all convincing or final. Evidently the artists who experimented did play more harshly as they played louder; the records of the harmonics prove that."[29] But it is to Matthay's credit that he was concerned with controlling key speed through the use of prepared key attacks and relating both to the most desirable musical ends, regardless of his views on hammer momentum. There is no question that his students played with tonal sensitivity. He strenuously opposed finger action that involved key hitting as well as pressing too deeply into the keys—"key-bed squeezing." In the appendix to Part II, he lists his arguments against key hitting:

> a): *It is mechanically thoroughly wrong and ineffective;* since the key is but a tool, intervening between finger-tip and

string, for the purpose of setting the *latter* into motion. To knock the key-lever, forms as absurdly great a misapplication in the use of this tool, and forms as wasteful and disadvantageous an application of muscular-energy, as would be the case, were we to hit the handle of a tennis-racket, hammer, oar, or cue, or to stamp upon a cycle-pedal, instead of using those tools properly.

b): *We cannot estimate* the weight of the tool itself, nor the amount of energy required to move it at any particular grade of speed, or increase of speed during its movement, if we hit the end of the lever we are using,—whether this be that of the Piano-key, or any other of the just-mentioned tools; and it follows that we cannot direct such tool with any accuracy, and that we cannot therefore obtain any intended subtle result.

c): *Loss of energy,* and consequent paucity of tone, and inaccuracy in expression result from the *concussions arising at the key-surface.* Such concussions swallow up Energy intended to produce tone;—molecular-vibrations of the key-surface and finger-surface taking the place of the desired movement of the key itself.

d): *We are debarred from gradually obtaining momentum* in the whole mass of the key-lever and hammer; since the hammer instantly quits its seat on the hopper, when the key is really struck,—with the consequence, that sympathetic (or beautiful) quality of tone is impossible of attainment.

e): *A tendency toward percussion at the string-surface* supervenes, in place of the intended movement of the whole body of the string; which again implies loss of power, and loss of tone-beauty.

f): *Unreliability in the case of rapid reiterations* of the same note. This is due to the fact that the key will "wobble" if the finger-tip rapidly quits its surface. As the key in question may not have fully come to rest before its depression is again required, this induces uncertainty in enunciation, often amounting even to non-repetition of the note.

g): *Impossibility of availing ourselves of the repetition-device:* We can only make use of this refinement of touch,—which gives us the option of very rapidly reiterating a note at its softest, the so-called "Be-bung,"—provided we retain the finger-tip on the key in question, and keep the latter depressed almost (though not quite) to its fullest extent.

h): *Unnecessary muscular fatigue;* due to the improper application of energy as before-described.

i): *Risk of overworking the muscles,* and inflaming the ten-

379

dons; owing to the incessant jarring, arising from the blows against the key-surface.

j): *Finally,* it debars us from truly *using,* directing or "aiming" the key into sound. For if we hit at the key, we are compelled to think of the surface-concussion as the thing aimed at; whereas, as the sound does not appear until the key is almost fully depressed, it is to that point—the sound-beginning—that our muscular-effort should be directed. The result being again, loss of power and beauty of tone, and besides that, inaccuracy and haziness in RHYTHM.

It is however difficult to decide whether such "Key-striking" is the most fell disease, or whether there is not a worse one still—in the shape of KEY-BED SQUEEZING![30]

In Part III, entitled "Key-Treatment from its Muscular Aspect" and overlapping much of the material from Part II, we get to the heart of the Matthay system. We find an exhaustive treatment of his subject matter. Perhaps the best way to approach it initially is through one of his own summaries:

§12. We can only gauge key-resistance, by physically feeling it through the muscular-sense, before and during Key-depression.

§13. The act of *Attention* during performances is dual, since it implies attention musically and attention instrumentally. We must listen inwardly and outwardly, so that we hear what should be, and so that we also hear the actual result; and we must meanwhile constantly *feel* the giving-way point of the keys, so that we can gauge the necessary efforts.

§14. Since the key must be reached so carefully, the contact should never be in the form of an actual blow, unless accuracy as to notes and expression do not matter.

§15. The act of Touch is consequently a Duplex process—excepting in the case of *ppp-* Tenuto or Legato:—

It consists of the two acts (a) of Resting, and (b) of Adding Energy to the key to move it.

§16. The act of Resting (which is continuous during each phrase) may either occur (a) at surface-level of key-board, or (b) at bottom-level of key-board.

This slight difference in Resting-weight constitutes the difference in Basis between Staccato and Tenuto, or Legato.

§17. The first (or lighter) form of Resting does not assist key-depression. The second (or heavier) form does;—being slightly heavier, it suffices to overbalance the key into deflection.

Both forms of Resting serve to tell us where the keys are, and their resistance.

§18. The absolute *pp* is obtained by employing this second form of the Resting, unassisted by any Added-impetus.

§19. The Added-impetus (Energy momentarily applied to the key during descent) is meanwhile required in all touches (except in *ppp*-Ten. or Leg.) to induce the requisite tone-amount and quality.

§20. This Added-impetus must absolutely cease to exist at the moment that sound-emission begins,—in Legato as well as in Staccato.

§21. The Added-impetus can be muscularly provided in the following three forms of Touch-construction or formation:

1st Species: Finger-exertion alone, with passive hand and self-supported arm.

2d Species: Hand-exertion behind the finger, with self-supported arm.

3d Species: Momentary lapse in arm-support, behind the hand and finger exertions.

§22. The Muscular-components which provide the Act of Touch are therefore: (a) Finger-exertion, (b) Hand-exertion, and (c) Arm-weight.

§23. The sensations of correct touch are hence always UP-WARDS—upwards by reaction from the key, against knuckle and wrist.

This, because we can only positively *feel* the actions of the finger and hand, and not the operation of arm-weight, since the latter is derived from *lapse* in muscular-exertion.

§24. Movement during key-descent depends on which of these three components is slightly in excess of the other two at the moment. The resulting distinctions of movement are termed: Finger-touch, Hand-touch and Arm-touch.

§25. The third Species is available in either of two Subgenera: either as "Weight-touch" or as "Muscular-touch." This, because the combination of the three touch-components may, in this Species, be *started* either (a) by Weight-release—that of the arm, or (b) by Exertion—that of the finger and hand.

The first makes for roundness of tone; the second for brilliance and even hardness.

§26. Hardness or harshness is bound to ensue if we apply arm down-force to any appreciable extent, and when we apply our efforts *too far down in key-descent.*

§27. We should therefore be careful always to play "only to the sound."

§28. Quality of tone is moreover influenced by the two diverse Attitudes of the finger and upper-arm, respectively termed, the "Clinging" and the "Thrusting."

The first helps towards sympathetic (and carrying) tone, the second towards brilliant (and short) tone.

§29. It is the condition of the upper-arm (or elbow) that determines in which of these two ways the finger shall act.

§30. Most of the finger's work must be done by the Knuckle-phalanx; this applies equally in clinging and in thrusting attitude.

§31. To obtain the most sympathetic effect, we must provide key-descent through the co-operation of the clinging attitude with the third species, in the latter's weight-initiated form.

§32. Arm-weight, when employed in the Added-impetus, must automatically cease its operation—in response to the accurately-timed cessation of the up-bearing stress at the wrist-joint.

§33. The transfer of the Resting weight should likewise be an automatic process, occasioned by the accurately-timed cessation of the supporting duty of the finger last used.

§34. Perfect freedom is imperative in all the movement and muscular actions employed in playing,—freedom from contrary-exertion.

§35. Rotary-freedom of the fore-arm must be insisted upon, as well as horizontal and vertical freedom of the wrist-joint. Rotary actions are required for every note.

Lack of rotary-freedom, especially, is one of the most common faults, since the here continually required adjustments mostly remain invisible.[31]

Like Breithaupt, Matthay put great emphasis on both weight and relaxation. The evils of the old German school of finger technique were still so fresh in mind that as late as 1932 when his last major work, *The Visible and Invisible in Pianoforte Technique* (a final summation of his technical beliefs), was published, he wrote in rather heated fashion:

To be told to render such and such a bodily-hinge immobile, or set, or "fixed" or "anchored," can only lead to *stiffness,* and general technical incapacity. The term "Fixation" should therefore be strictly banished from the Pianist's vocabulary.[32]

There is the almost unreasoning fear that fixation will inevitably lead to undesirable tension. The employment of weight is so important that he felt that "Touch, in a word, resolves itself ultimately into an act of levering more or less weight upon the key during descent."[33] Matthay welcomed the efforts of Steinhausen

382

and Breithaupt to combat the old Stuttgart school of key hitting and key bed squeezing, but he thought that they went much too far in their use of weight. In 1911 in *Some Commentaries on the Teaching of Pianoforte Technique,* he stated:

And when, after a time, some better ideas began to dawn upon the minds of a few rare teachers [including Breithaupt and Matthay,] such as a vague notion of "Weight" for instance, such ideas, even though on the right path, often led to the most disastrous results. The full weight of the arm was, for instance, allowed to be carried from key to key, thus actually laming and often permanently disabling many of the talented but unfortunate aspirants who worked only too well on the "systems" evolved from such half-truths. . . . He [Steinhausen] starts by denying the possibility of Quality-variations . . . and while he does good work in insisting (as I did in the earlier work [*The Act of Touch*]) on Arm-weight and Forearm Rotation, he makes the grave blunder of concluding that *all* touch is a sort of cross between Touch by Arm-weight and Arm-force, and is always more or less "arm-throw" whatever the passage! Moreover, he also, like Breithaupt, fails to see that full Weight must never be applied except *during* the act itself of tone-production, if Music and limbs are to be safe.[34]

Matthay became even more impatient with Breithaupt when in *The Visible and Invisible in Piano Technique* he objected:

You cannot realize that each and every tone in a *musical* passage must have a *separate* musical and technical entity, and at the same time believe in the "full weight of the arm" (Breithaupt's "Schwere Tastenbelastung") carried from key-*bed* to key-*bed*—to the utter destruction of Music-sense, and risk to limb and Piano! The claimant to this proposed wizardry complains of having suffered from "cramp"; and is not "cramp" (or Neuritis) so often induced precisely by such fallacious and clumsy *full-weight-carrying* process?[35]

Matthay advanced the development of piano technique greatly by stressing time and time again that technique is far more than a study of outward posture or position and movements to be drilled incessantly.

Malwine Brée's presentation of the Leschetizky method, he said, fails to cope with the invisible muscular coordinations:

For instance, in a work published last year [1902], purporting to teach Technique, and which is avowedly the "only authorised publication of the teachings" of LESCHETIZ-

KY—the justly-renowned Artist-teacher, we fail to find any description of the true causes and explanations of correct Technique. Instead, the little advice given relatively to tone-production, relies almost exclusively on Position and on Movement, and on the practice of carefully-planned Methods of Note-practice,—on exercises, the practice of which does not, however, in the least ensure that the learner will happen to discover for himself HOW he should use the key or his own muscles, i.e.—what key-treatment and muscular-habit should be, in any of its manifold aspects![36]

Fully appreciating the enduring contribution of Ludwig Deppe, Matthy was still similarly critical of Elisabeth Caland's presentation:

We find the same fallacy—of relying mostly on the phenomena of Position and Movement—exhibited by those who profess to teach the methods of another of the last century's really great teachers—LUDWIG DEPPE, who indeed was probably the most advanced of all the well known nineteenth-century teachers. He, for instance, clearly recognised the necessity for the free wrist, and its source, the "carried" arm; also he instructed in touch by weight-release, although he perhaps hardly recognised that the released weight of the arm was the cause. *(Vide "Die Deppeschs Lehre des Klavierspiels,"* E. CALAND.) On reading this little work one clearly perceives that Deppe himself must have been able to obtain the true "sympathetic" touch-quality, and that he stimulated his pupils to do likewise. His idea of the "arm-carried hand" lapsing "upon the key," being indeed within reach of that full realisation of the real facts of the case, which, after all, seems to have eluded him. And this, in spite of what was truly a monumental striving after Truth in the matter; especially when we take into consideration the state of absolute ignorance of first principles—and disbelief in there being any—in which he found the musical world.[37]

In working out his own system of touch in Part III of *The Act of Touch,* Matthay advances far beyond the position and movement explanations found in many of the early methods. But even he does not have an easy time defining the role of weight, visible or invisible, in a well coordinated technique. Weight, he says, is basic to all Resting, of which there are two types depending on the nature of the music: Legato or Tenuto, with the finger at the bottom of the key, and Staccato, where the finger is resting lightly on the

384

raised key surface. Coexistent, yet separate, is each split-second tone-producing Added-impetus ("which is directed to, but which *ceases* with the consummation of each and every key-depression, and which is therefore discontinuous"[38]). In Legato- or Tenuto-resting, Matthay states that "we must *rest continuously* on the key-board, with sufficient weight to compel the implicated fingers to retain their keys depressed."[39] Then he adds: "This necessary weight is obtained by relaxing the *whole* arm from the shoulder, relaxing it sufficiently but no more, than will just over-balance the key into descent. . . . Such legato-compelling weight must in this case be *transferred* from finger to finger."[40]

Then in Staccato-resting, as a key is released, the weight is withdrawn so judiciously that "the key *will rebound,* and will even take up with it the super-incumbent finger and hand, provided the latter lie on it in a perfectly loose and inactive condition the moment they have *completed* their necessary action."[41]

At a slow tempo it is possible to retrieve enough weight between Added-impetuses to return continually to a condition of Legato-resting and then transfer this minimal weight from key to key in a legato manner. Arm action is almost inevitably involved. But at faster tempos, where finger and hand actions are called into play, this is surely an impossibility. At a fast tempo, to attempt to transfer this minimal resting arm weight in a legato manner, as Matthay requested, will result in pure and complete weight transfer, something which he was very much against and which he took Breithaupt severely to task for encouraging. Separate key-treatment with individual intensity gradations is then no longer attainable. To attempt these gradations at a fast tempo will result in the arm being displaced and the legato destroyed. What Matthay probably wanted was a condition similar to Townsend's balanced arm. In fast passages, a feeling of gentle resting, either on the depressed key or on the upper key surface, may be interpreted as lightly released weight when in actuality it is a buoyant, very mildly fixated arm condition.

Matthay also ran into difficulties in working out the role of weight in connection with his very important three main principles or Species of Muscular-combination or Touch-formation. Regarding his First Species, he particularized:

> The Arm gently supported by its own muscles, floats over the key-board; while the hand, inactive, merely lies lightly on the keys at surface level. Work of key-depression is consequently here entirely relegated to the Finger, without aid

385

either from Hand or Arm. Tone, limited to the "brilliant" type, can also be but small in quantity; while Finger-movement is alone available. Permits, on the other hand, the attainment of the extremest grades of Agility or Velocity conceivable—provided we strictly adhere to the law of accurate *cessation* of work at the moment of sound-emission and provided we do really enact this first form of muscular combination,—finger-use only, combined with a passive hand, and absence of all arm-weight or force.[42]

Every moving lever, whether it be finger, hand, or arm, must react against the base to which it is attached. This base must be stabilized in some manner—by weight resting upon the playing lever, by downward muscular exertion, or by fixation (simultaneous contraction) of the antagonistic muscles which control the base. If it is not, the base itself will be displaced, seriously hampering velocity and legato at the faster tempos. Taking Matthay at face value, we must accept his "loose-lying hand" as the base stabilized by weight. At a fast tempo, even a very slight degree of finger exertion, not to mention the many varying exertions necessary for the intensity control of individual notes, will overcome the small amount of weight of the hand, move the hand upward, and seriously interfere with key control and velocity. It fits Schultz's description of a finger touch involving the hand fixated at the wrist with the slightest possible degree of contraction of the antagonistic muscles. In this case the fingers are propelled only by the small muscles of the hand—thus eliminating any tension at the wrist resulting from contraction of the long finger tendons. Released weight surely plays no role at all in Matthay's First Species.

Matthay's middle Second Species is meant for moderate velocity and moderate tonal intensity of which there are considerable amounts in most piano playing. This obviously important form, which employs only muscular exertions of both finger and hand, is the only one in which he in reality does not call for the application of weight. But again taking Matthay's description literally ("The arm is in this case to be supported by its own muscles gently, elastically, and certainly not stiffly, so that the arm as it were floats along the key-board, and thus *carries* the loosely lying hand and fingers towards the desired notes, which, being reached, are then depressed by the combined action of Hand and Finger."),[43] we seem to have no real base at all for the finger and hand movements to react against if the arm is in such a light, buoyant state with only the lifting arm muscles contracting. With only the inertia of the self-supported base to resist the upward reaction from the playing movements (and that felt, unfortunately, only as the base is driven upward), Matthay admitted that the degree of resistance would be small and "the quantity of tone also is far more limited than in the previously-described combination [Third Species]."[44] It would surely seem that Matthay's students used a mildly fixated arm to support the action of the long finger tendons involved in this touch form.

The Third Species is the one in which weight plays its leading role and to which Matthay assigned a great amount of versatility. He described various aspects of its function:

> . . . We may, in producing any of the varieties of this Species, optionally employ *movements* either of the Arm, the Hand, or the Finger; *i.e.,* this Species may optionally take the form either of Arm-touch, Hand-touch ("Wrist-action") or Finger-touch . . .
> While this form of muscular-combination is therefore only available, when the speed required does not exceed a comparatively slow gait, it is nevertheless the only form that will allow us to obtain the *full* measure of good tone permitted us by our particular physical endowment; for this combination alone will permit us to utilise the whole weight of the relaxed arm and shoulder as recoil-breaker (or Basis) for the operations of the finger and hand against the key during its descent.
> While Species III thus offers us the opportunity of obtaining the fullest tone-amounts, this combination may with equal facility be employed for the production of *lesser* tone-amounts, down to the least. For we can supply this combination (of Arm-release with activity of Finger and Hand) in a measure so slight—it can be minimised to such an extent—that the total effect upon the key need not exceed the amount necessary just to over-balance it into descent; thus forming the true *pp* by 'Weight-touch," provided we are careful to eliminate all Finger and Hand Initiative.[45]

It was obvious to Matthay that, if weight is to be withdrawn after its individualized application to each key, the species is basically suitable only for the slower tempos. He realized the serious drawback encountered in the weight-transfer touch: successive tones will be reduced *"more or less* to a dead level of tone and duration. . . . All that is possible with Weight-transfer touch are *gradual* inflections of tone and duration—swirls of crescendos and diminuendos, and *gradual* changes in the degree of legato

387

and staccato."[46] He stated that its usefulness is primarily limited to soft passages that are accompaniment-like in character and do not need individual tonal inflections, such as those encountered in the Chopin *Aeolian Harp* Etude.

Finally Matthay pointed out that in actual performance these different species *"gradually merge one into the other.* No rigid, separating distinctions should consciously be made between them when we have actually learnt to play—except for some special point of practice."[47] Any attempt to separate them will lead to artificiality. We should observe that "the three primary colours are only rarely employed in a pure and unmixed state."[48] In his own teaching, Matthay said that he rarely referred to these various touch forms by name. He preferred to use terms which referred "to the bare physical *facts* themselves."[49]

Another integral part of the Matthay system, closely related to his ideas on both touch and tone quality, was his teaching on finger position and action. For Matthay there were two basic opposing finger attitudes: the Bent-Finger or Thrusting attitude associated with the muscularly initiated touches primarily and the Flat-Finger or Clinging attitude used with the weight touches. He described them in this manner:

> In the *first,* or "hammer-touch" variety, which we will term the BENT-FINGER attitude, or "Thrusting attitude," a greatly curved or bent position (like the hammer of an old-fashioned percussion-gun) is assumed by the finger when it is raised as a preliminary to the act of tone-production. The finger in this case un-bends (or un-curves) slightly, in descending towards and with the key; the nail-joint however, remaining vertical throughout. The Elbow has to take the brunt of the slightly backward tendency of the recoil that arises in this form of touch from the thrusting action of the finger against the key. The Upper-arm must therefore here be supported with a forward *tendency* (but not movement) towards the key-board, so that this forward-tendency at the Elbow may serve to counteract the recoil-thrust of the finger experienced at the knuckle and elbow.
>
> In the *second,* or "clinging" variety of touch, which we will term the FLAT-FINGER attitude (or "Clinging-attitude") a far less curved position is assumed by the finger as a preliminary, and it may indeed be almost unbent or "flat." Exertion is in this case almost entirely restricted to the *under*-tendons of the whole finger. The key is moreover reached (and

moved down) with but little change from this flatter or straighter position, and its involved muscular-attitude. As the *clinging* action of the finger in this instance tends to drag the Elbow towards the key-board, this tendency must be counter-balanced by allowing a sufficient lapse to intervene in the supporting-muscles of the Upper-arm. Such release of the upper-arm tends to drag the elbow away from the key-board and thus balances the pull of the finger; whilst the additional weight thus set free, materially helps to drag the key down.

The first kind of finger-attitude (with its correlated upper-arm conditions) is exceedingly less *elastic* than the second.

When the most sympathetic quality of tone is required, we must therefore choose this second (flatter) attitude—with its elastic Knuckle and Wrist, and consequent furthering of *gradual* key-descent, and must employ this in conjunction with Weight-touch,—touch initiated by lapse in arm-support.[50]

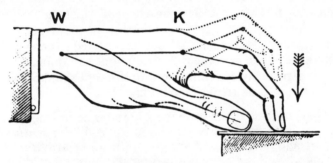

The Thrusting (Bent) Finger-attitude.

The position is with depressed key; the dotted lines exhibit the index-finger fully raised.

W is the Wrist, K the Knuckle.

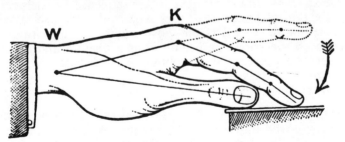

The Clinging (Flat) Finger-attitude.

The position is with depressed key; the dotted lines exhibit the index-finger fully raised.

[51]

389

Such a correlation between the lapsed arm and the clinging touch and also between the supported arm and the thrusting attitude is certainly possible, but does not always necessarily follow. There is even some question as to whether Matthay always held to only these two pronounced finger attitudes. One of his students, Rodney Hoare, said that Matthay played with a natural hand position, somewhat of a compromise between the bent and flat-finger attitudes.[52] Hoare thought that he did not publicly advocate this because it was too radical a change from the past and would not receive a fair evaluation. Still, it is interesting to note in *The Act of Touch* that by the time Matthay works through his three species with finger, hand, and arm touches, with weight and muscular initiations, with bent and flat finger attitudes, and with staccato and legato or tenuto resting, he comes up with forty-two different varieties of touch.

Perhaps the best known of the Matthay teachings is that concerned with forearm rotation, an element which he in later years termed "perhaps the most important of all pianistically, physiologically, and pedagogically."[53] But he objected to carrying weight-transference to the extreme that Breithaupt had done. And he also similarly vigorously dissented from Breithaupt's and Steinhausen's "Rollung" or "Side-stroke" technique:

> They, in fact, make so grave a blunder as to teach that the forearm rotation is to be employed to "roll" the *continuously* resting and *fully* released Weight of the *whole* arm from finger to finger! Nothing more misleading and harmful could well be conceived. Like so many others, they have only gone by "the look of the thing," and have quite failed to grasp that these same rotary exertions can quite well be applied without in the least showing any *movement* in consequence of such rotary application of force. Also, they seem quite to have failed to realize that the very first and most vital law of all technique is, that each tone must be produced as a distinct and separate muscular act (except in the solitary and rare case of "passing-on" touch) if there is to be any ease as regards Agility, or any *accuracy* musically.[54]

Matthay's forearm rotation is of two varieties—the visible and the invisible, the latter receiving the greater stress in his writing and teaching. When the visible was overstressed and he felt that he was misrepresented in his presentation, his temper quickly rose to the boiling point, as illustrated by this heated comment in *The Visible and Invisible in Piano Technique*:

In spite of all that I have written and lectured on this very point, I am still persistently and stupidly misrepresented as dealing solely with rotatory MOVEMENTS—movements which had already been recognized and approved "for occasional use" in tremolos, etc., half a century ago! Whereas, throughout, I am referring to rotatory actions or stresses, inactions and reactions, mostly unaccompanied by any movements whatsoever.[55]

His first statement on Fore-arm Rotation is found early in Part III of *The Act of Touch*. He gives the reason for its employment:

Constant changes in the state of the fore-arm's rotary Release and rotary Support are imperative, if the fingers at opposite sides of the hand are to be equally "strong"; i.e., if the little finger and the thumb are to have equal successive apportionments of weight (or resistance) to act against, when one of these fingers is applied against the key. Weight must be *released* rotarily towards the little-finger side of the hand, when the little finger is required to work effectively against its key;—a rotary lapse of the fore-arm, that must be precisely reversed, when we wish forcibly to employ the thumb. In the same way, we have rotarily to support the thumb-side of the hand, when we wish to employ a finger at the opposite side of the hand alone; and we must reverse the process, when the little-finger side of the hand has to be held off the key-board.[56]

We discover rotation exercises almost immediately in his most elementary method materials, *The Child's First Steps in Piano-Playing* and *The Nine Steps towards "Finger Individualization,"* where the hand, in a clenched fist position at the keyboard, is used first to release arm weight by playing on the broad fifth finger side of the hand with the thumb pointing upward. This, of course, is the normal position of the hand as it is brought to the keyboard from its resting place hanging at the side. Then individual notes on the black keys and notes a third apart are soon executed by a back-and-forth rocking motion of the hand. Numerous rotation exercises are also included in his most important technical work designed for use at the piano, the famous *Muscular Relaxation Studies* (1912) which covers all phases of his system.

Rotation is so all important that Matthay in *The Visible and Invisible in Piano Technique* says that forearm rotatory help must be provided for every single note, regardless of the touch form employed: ". . .without its application your hand would stand upright on the keyboard (with the thumb up)."[57] He goes so far as to define finger passage work in terms of forearm rotation: *"Individually applied FOREARM rotation impulses TRANSMITTED to the keyboard by the OBEDIENT exertion of the finger and hand for each note."*[58] He hastened to add that the actual rotatory movements are optional. During slow practice they are certainly harmless and may even be beneficial. But in fast practice "they may become a hindrance, and even impossible, and finger-*movements* must here be substituted—but do not in the meantime lose the benefit of the INVISIBLE rotational help given individually for each note."[59] Certainly nothing seems more impractical and cumbersome than to try to move the larger forearm unit about rotatively with a separate, individualized exertion for each note in a rapid finger passage.

Matthay's very lengthy Part III in *The Act of Touch* is closed by a brief section, "On Position." In it he states that the "correct muscular Actions and Inactions" will necessarily be followed by "correct position of limb and body."[60] But just assuming a correct Position will not guarantee the necessary muscular co-ordinations. He emphasizes:

> It is necessary to insist on this point, since a degree of importance has been generally attached to Position that is absurdly out of all proportion to its real significance. The fallacy has been, to perceive in Position the CAUSE of good technique; whereas we must now recognize it in its true aspect—and let it arise, mostly, as a RESULT of the correct muscular and mechanical conditions being fulfilled at their easiest.[61]

Since Position is not all-important, minor posture variations from the mean are surely allowable and sometimes a necessity. Then follows a presentation of many of the specific conditions of Position encountered in correct piano playing, including these eleven main points:

a): Sufficient distance between shoulder and key, with the seat sufficiently removed from the instrument to admit of this.

b): The distinction between the two kinds of finger-movement, with the finger sufficiently bent before its descent, in thrusting touch.

c): Avoidance of the depressed knuckle.

d): Lateral adjustment of the hand and wrist to each particular passage; the hand being turned inwards for single-notes scales and arpeggi, and turned in the direction travelled, during double-notes passages.

392

e): Above all things, one should insist (a) that each finger is in position, and *feels* each key, *before* the act of key-depression proper is commenced; and (b), that the position in key-descent is aimed for, where key-depression culminates in sound-beginning;—so that each key-propulsion is aimed to culminate at the very moment that the hammer reaches the string.

Subsidiary Points of importance are:—

f): Not to allow the hand to slope towards the fifth finger—unless apparently so during the movement of Rotation-touch.

g): To keep the thumb well away from the hand,—with the nail-phalanx in line with its key.

h): Not as a rule to allow the fingers to reach the keys near the outside edge of the key-board.

j): The slight re-adjustments of wrist-height, in passages with the thumb alternately on black and white keys.

k): In Hand-touch, and Arm-touch, the assumption of the depressed position of the fingers relatively to the hands, *before* the down-movement of the hand or arm.

l): Attention to the two alternative return-movements of the finger in *thrusting* or *clinging* Finger-staccato respectively.[62]

The contribution which Matthay made to piano technique literature is a very significant one. We observe a keen musical mind at work—constantly stressing the importance of listening. Sensitive listening throughout is coupled with sensitivity in the touch. Matthay knew the physical sensations of fine piano playing. He did not fully succeed in analyzing and explaining them; some of his solutions are unworkable. But his technical thought, with its penetrating desire to get to the invisible conditions of good muscular co-ordination and relaxation, was an advance over any before him. He encouraged the use of the arm; and his ideas on weight are less objectionable than those of Breithaupt. He was against the continuous release of weight and was for individualized key treatment. This included the individualized use of the fingers, although the old style finger hitting appalled him. There must be sensitivity to key resistance as well as sensitivity in the finger and arm coordinations.

Tobias Matthay wrote prolifically. His books are concerned primarily with technique with the exception of one published in 1912, *Musical Interpretation.* But Matthay was a solid musician and in each volume technique is continually viewed as a means to a musical objective. He once remarked in a lecture that his first

American student had exclaimed to him after his first few lessons: "Well, I came here to learn Technique, but I find you are teaching me Music!"[63] Like Godowsky, he objected strenuously to the idea that there was a Method of playing. He felt that the "Matthay Method of Playing" conjured up visions of fads and fetishes: "sunk-in knuckles, low wrists, absurdly raised and hitting fingers." He freely admitted that "there is, however, indeed a Matthay Method of Teaching," which "implies that the true causes of all good and all bad playing are disclosed and made plain to everyone—everyone imbued with a desire to know the true fundamentals of Pianoforte Playing."[64]

With his unbounded enthusiasm and unselfish dedication to his students, Matthay was probably even more successful in his teaching than in his writing. The greatest of his students, Myra Hess, told of how he inspired his students:

When teaching, examining, lecturing, or attending a concert of one of his students, he is oblivious of his own presence in his absorbing interest in what is going on. Only those of us, who are familiar with the sight of his hat and coat hanging in the artists' room, can know the inspiration of his presence, and the encouragement of his words of counsel. As a student I sometimes felt it was going a little too far to be told, when shivering on the brink, to enjoy myself on the platform, but those words, "Enjoy yourself, enjoy the music," have ever stayed in my mind and have, I know, helped many others to face an audience in a spirit of musical spontaneity.[65]

Another of his students, Denise Lassimonne, felt that his true greatness lay

. . . in his teaching of the INTERPRETATION of Music and not in the Technical approach to piano playing as one is led to believe. . . But his conception of the word "Technique" takes on another meaning in that it reveals to us the impossibility of separating technique from Music . . . which union forms a perfect marriage *never* to be dissolved.[66]

Of his works, *Musical Interpretation, its Laws and Principles, and their Application in Teaching and Performing* stands near the top of the list. The sections on "The Nature of Musical Attention and of Musical Shape" and "The Element of Rubato" are particularly valuable. Matthay's comments on timing, on rhythmic progression and movement, and on proportion are of the highest order. Note the following:

As I have before insisted upon, during performance it is

394

really impossible *definitely* to guide any note, unless we do thus think of its Time-spot: the precise place in Time where the sound is musically due to begin, and where the key's motion is therefore due to *finish* its act of tone-production. The most striking and most definite thing about a note is the fact of its transition from nonexistence to existence—the moment of transition from Silence to Sound; for this is an absolutely definite point of demarcation at the Piano, as definite as the surface (or beginning) of a piece of wood or stone.

We cannot, therefore, definitely think a note in playing unless we thus *think* the time-place of its *beginning*—the beginning of the sound. Moreover, we must try to realise, that this law has a far deeper significance even than this. The fact is we cannot experience any act of consciousness, we cannot direct our minds and think about or realise anything definitely, without just such an act of *timing*—a timing of our consciousness. The act of bringing or directing our thought or attention upon anything is therefore a *rhythmical process;* Thought and Rhythm are inseparable. Again, we see the reason why in the absence of Rhythm there can only be Nothingness—emptiness, non-being. . . .

In painting or drawing the *movement is upon the canvas,* and this in a double sense; for there is, first, an actual *movement* of the painter's brush or pencil in the act of making the picture; and secondly, an actual *movement* again, in viewing the picture—an actual movement *of our eyeballs* in following its lines, or at least a suggestion of such movement.

In Music the distinction is, that the movement is upon a *time-surface,* as it were—instead of upon a canvas. . . .

This idea of *motion* in Music, continuous Movement, we must make clear to anyone and everyone, even to a child at his very first lesson in Music.[67]

As early as 1905, Matthay had gathered such a devoted group of students and experienced teachers about him at the Royal Academy of Music that the Tobias Matthay Pianoforte School was formed in London with its own separate facilities. Matthay served in both schools until 1925 when he resigned from the academy, a member of its faculty for fifty-three years. His own school continued to grow and flourished right into the years of World War II. In 1939, there were 500 students and forty teachers. Many of England's finest musicians have been Matthay trained or associated: Myra Hess, Harriet Cohen, Harold Craxton, Cuthbert Whitemore, Felix Swinstead, Denise Lassimonne, Lilias Mackinnon, Irene Scharer, and Rae Robertson. Eileen Joyce came from

Australia and many also journeyed from the United States and other lands. Matthay's reputation grew internationally and his American Summer School Lectures were particularly popular. These were held at Matthay's hilltop rural estate, High Marley, located in Sussex Downs. In 1925 his American pupils founded the American Matthay Association with the express purpose of teaching his principles in the United States.

One of his early American students, Bruce Simonds, had first gone to Paris in 1919 to study piano, but had not found a satisfactory teacher. In the spring of the following year he heard of Matthay. Within a few months he went to England—determined to study with him. He related that

> ... in midsummer I found myself in London. The Matthay School was closed, the concerts over. The School building itself was a modest building, not a marble palace. I wrote to Matthay and received a cordial reply inviting me to come to Haslemere and play for him. "You might get one of my books and read it," he added. I found "The Act of Touch" and was somewhat bewildered, having never had the idea that it was necessary to know anything about the piano in order to play it. On the 12th of August (I noted the date) I emerged from the train at Haslemere and hired a cab to take me to the house. I remember noticing every turn of the road, every fork with frenzied attention, for I knew that my slender purse would certainly compel me to walk back. We went on and on through the enchanting Surrey lanes, up and up, around hairpin curves, and just as I had reconciled myself to being hopelessly lost, we arrived at High Marley. I was ushered into a large sunny music room and had just time to see vaguely a wide expanse of beautiful country through one of the windows, when there was the man himself. Tall and somewhat stooped, dressed in an un-American costume which included tweeds and gaiters, with grey hair falling away from a domed forehead, he was looking at me with keen eyes partially hidden behind very thick spectacles. He seemed a vigorous, open-air sort of person, as his ruddy complexion indicated: the stoop suggested the scholar, but nothing about him seemed eccentric or consciously aesthetic. He asked me if I were acquainted with his ideas, and when I mentioned the recently-acquired "Act of Touch" he groaned, "Oh, *that!* My *first* book!" In a few moments, I had embarked on the *Prelude, Chorale et Fugue* by César Franck, and instead of stopping me at the very first note, he was listening patiently with that sympathetic attitude which somehow never degenerated into

undiscriminating encouragement. At the end, he did not prescribe a regimen of exercises, but among other things made the remark that I was forcing my tone. This aroused my curiosity. I had never made a study of tone, but flattered myself that mine was not half bad. Then he took me out on the terrace, and introduced me to Mrs. Matthay, whose expression of alertness and kindliness I can vividly recall at this moment. Where was I to live? How long should I stay in England? I felt not merely at home, but rather as if I had returned to some familiar place.[68]

This benevolent spirit was even evident at times in the concert hall. Public recitals were frequently held at the Matthay School in London. *The Daily Telegraph* on February 7, 1931, described one of these occasions when "Uncle Tobs," as he was affectionately called by his pupils, presided:

The Conway Hall; eight o'clock; the audience conversing in a state of incurious expectancy. They become silent as a bent and venerably kind figure in a brown velvet jacket makes his way to the front of the stage. He calls a name. In the auditorium a small girl with a chubby face framed in ringlets rises. She makes her way on to the platform.

Our master of ceremonies sees that she is comfortably seated. Yes; her toes can just touch the pedals. He pats her encouragingly on the shoulder, and retires to a seat in the stalls. And then Miss Eight-Year-Old plays—in this case one of the master's own pieces—with perfect aplomb and a really remarkable control of tone, colour, and dexterity of finger and wrist.

There is, of course, immaturity, but no crudity. Our artist in the bud ends a brilliant cadential passage, forgets to bow, but as she returns to the front of the house does not forget to go up and kiss Mr. Tobias Matthay, who is, of course, the gentleman in brown velvet. And then everyone applauds more. After which Mr. Matthay introduces the next performer. And so the programme goes on.

The other pupils playing at this Tobias Matthay School concert are older. Some have reached the stage when they may at any time shine in the glory of a recital in the West-end. And if providence has not given them all an equal talent, Mr. Tobias Matthay and his system have at least taught them all that the piano has not an irremediably hard heart.[69]

Ambrose Coviello once inquired of Matthay the secret of his successful teaching. He replied: "I have often been asked that, and I think the answer is 'Through making "duds" play well.' "[70]

397

Coviello also told of the experience of a friend who called on Matthay. Arriving early, he waited in a room below his studio. For over an hour he sat and listened to the opening two measures of the Brahms Scherzo in E flat minor repeated incessantly. Finally Matthay appeared, remarking only, "I could not leave her until we had got those two bars right." Caviello added: *"He could not leave a fault uncorrected."* [71]

It is safe to say that after Matthay, the English pianistic world would never be quite the same; all later English writers on technique were conditioned by him in one way or another. James Ching remarked: "It is a matter of common knowledge that, for at least twenty-five years (from say 1910 to 1935) nearly all the most promising English students of the piano gravitated at some stage of their student life, towards the Matthay School." [72] The pedagogical materials of Lilias Mackinnon, Hetty Bolton, and Joan Last are quite Matthay oriented. Victor Booth's *We Piano Teachers* (1947) and Gerald d'Abreu's *Playing the Piano with Confidence* (1965) are possible exceptions. But such theorists as Coviello, Thomas Fielden, and Ching have been more or less critical of the Matthay dogma. And two influential piano educators of the present day, Frank Merrick (1886-   ) and Sidney Harrison (1903-   ), other than in their references to rotary movement, show very little of the Matthay influence in their recent works. Merrick, a Leschetizky student, wrote *Practicing the Piano* (1958), a book containing many suggestions useful in the development of both technique and literature. Harrison's *Piano Technique* (1953), in its emphasis on graceful arm movement and its relationship to phrase-line proportioning, shows something of a kinship with the Caland volume on Deppe and Abby Whiteside's *Indispensables of Piano Playing*. Harrison writes:

> Since melodies are seldom banged out very loudly the fingers could apply enough power to produce the necessary tone. And they could operate from a self-supported arm or from one that exerted a slight pressure on the key bed. In practice, however, we find that the subtle shades of gradation that constitute good cantabile playing are better judged by arm action. Furthermore, arm action tends to turn a legato into a legatissimo, and this is an important factor in persuading the ear that the tone of the piano is beautiful. Still further, the arm, in making a slow approach to a note, sometimes delays it a little. The note "speaks" a little late, and this also can produce an effect of tenderness. [73]

... In the conduct of the arm, the good student will find again and again that the arm movement is at its best when it seems almost to be conducting the music. In some cases, of course, the rhythm of the arm is not in a simple or obvious relationship with the rhythm of the music. But most of the time it is. Most of the time the arm swings from beat to beat and from accent to accent with something of the impulse that governs the baton of a conductor.[74]

Coviello, the self-styled interpreter of Matthay, largely agreed with him, but objected to the confusion of his many touch forms. And while accepting Ortmann's investigations into tone quality, he still felt that Matthay's theory of tone production did gain very desirable tonal results. Coviello also held certain reservations regarding Matthay's presentation of rotation, rubato, and the inclusion of Resting as an integral part of the act of touch.

Thomas Fielden (1883-) is one of the major English writers on technique. His book *The Science of Pianoforte Technique,* published in 1927, has been widely accepted. After study at the Royal College of Music and at Oxford, he worked under Breithaupt for a time—but he was as critical of Breithaupt as of Matthay, his colleague. In 1953 he became director of the new Rhodesian Academy of Music in Bulawayo, Rhodesia. Discussing their differences in method in his opening chapter, he nonetheless emphasized the unity of Matthay's and Breithaupt's achievement: "The foundation stone of the discoveries of the two masters was the use of the weight in the production of tone, and the use of relaxation both in producing that tone and in avoiding stiffness in the hands and arms."[75] And he also underscored the unity of their shortcomings:

... it is necessary to point out that neither of these men, Matthay less than Breithaupt, sufficiently emphasized the necessity for scientific knowledge of physiology, and the relations and coordinations of muscular actions; nor did they insist enough on a knowledge of the laws of mechanics, as far as the application of the laws of leverage was concerned . . . .[76]

Their methods are now suffering from the complete volte-face which they caused in the hitherto accepted theories of technique, since, having abolished the old system of finger-training and meticulous attention to detailed *finger* work, the playing of their pupils necessarily lost in clearness and often in crispness, on account of the loss of the faculty of swift muscular contraction. Nevertheless, the wonderful results they have achieved are sufficient criterion of the value of their theories, and many of the best modern pianists are numbered among their pupils. At the same time, the fact must not be lost sight of that the great performers are not great solely on account of the method of their tuition: often they are so in spite of it; we must judge a method by its results on the ordinary pupil, and these modern methods do not always come triumphantly through that test. The great performers are, as already stated, physical geniuses, laws unto themselves: the great methods are the result of continuous observation of their work: and we are arriving at a stage where it is being realized that these methods are based on purely natural movements, akin to the movements that take place in ordinary active life, in walking, running, cricket, tennis, or any other form of natural physical effort. A knowledge of muscular processes is desirable, and a deep study of the marvellous mechanism of the hands and arms: and the goal should be the mental and nervous control of all the movements of which these wonderful implements are capable.[77]

Fielden included in his work an analysis of the arm and finger muscles used in piano playing, a series of gymnastic exercises for strengthening these muscles, and also a discussion of leverage as related to the act of touch. Then speaking of controlled contraction and fixation, he wrote:

Stiffness in playing arises from too much contraction beforehand—nervous tension and fear of weakness at the critical moment: too much relaxation before this moment, on the other hand, leads either to flabbiness or to hard, thumping tone. True suppleness lies in securing the full contraction at the right moment, neither before nor after: this constitutes *perfect timing*. Finally, at the point of contact the muscles are not in relaxation at all, as advocated by the devotees of relaxation: on the contrary, they are in contraction, but resilient, preparatory, if necessary, for relaxation, but most frequently using their resilience to carry the arm to its next movement.[78]

It is this power of controlled fixation and contraction which gives authority and definiteness to a performer's interpretation, since it must carry with it the exercise of sustained will-power, and it is this power which the great players constantly use, connoting, as it does, masterful vitality and *verve*.[79]

Yet in the implementation of his theory of fixation, Fielden attempted to incorporate certain features from the weight school,

400

with a freely moving arm and arm weight performing a vital role in the functioning of the base or "anchorage."

The mere contraction of the finger is not enough to depress the key with sufficient speed and weight to produce good tone, and the secret of producing good tone is dependent on the accurate timing of the entry of the arm-weight into the action.[80]

In all swift passages for the fingers, where strength is required, the anchorage, whether of forearm or whole arm, may be maintained practically in a permanent though flexible state of fixation, capable of being eased (or broken) and shifted *en bloc* by the undulatory movement of the wrist—but sufficiently controlled to prevent any involuntary upward jerking of the arm above alluded to. The fingers should still fulfil their own function as fingers, moving unimpeded from their own anchorage, and should therefore be capable of swift and clear articulation: the vital factor is that, as each finger takes up the reinforcement of the arm on contact, the succeeding finger should be swinging freely and unimpeded from its own anchorage in the hand preparatory to performing its own work in its turn. . . . In all swift playing this swinging of the anchorage of the arm must be held in what may be called flexible fixation so as to allow of the free movement of the fingers, especially in repetition action.[81]

James Ching opposes Matthay even more than does Fielden. A portion of Ching's early study at the Royal Academy of Music had been with Matthay, but later he came to disagree with him almost completely. Writing a year after Matthay's death in 1945, Ching acknowledged his indebtedness and his esteem for him. But nonetheless he was moved to say that

. . . there came a time when I had finally to decide whether I should try to suppress and repress my loyalties to what I had come to believe to be the truth about technical theories and keep at least an outward and visible loyalty to Mr. Matthay, or whether to publish my own ideas and damn the consequences.[82]

Ching became a well-known English pianist—appearing on the Promenade Concerts and also at the Edinburgh Festival. In 1945 he founded the James Ching Pianoforte School in London and promoted with considerable success the James Ching Method of piano playing. His writings have included *Piano Technique: Foundation Principles* (1934), *Piano Playing, a Practical Method* (subtitled: *A rationale of the psychological and practical problems of pianoforte playing and teaching in the form of twenty-five lectures*

401

originally given in London in the years 1944-1945) (1946), and *The Amateur Pianist's Companion* (1965). Prior to 1939, he had worked with certain university physiological professors and thus claimed that his method was the first really scientific one. Matters of muscular co-ordination had long been a concern of his. Ching wrote from personal experience how he had solved his own technical problem:

> When I went up to Oxford as an undergraduate and started to play the piano seriously (after a break of many years) I developed that most frightening of all pianistic afflictions, the complaint commonly known as "pianist's cramp." You may think that a strange symptom from one whose earlier training had actually been with the founder of the relaxation school. However, I naturally took my troubles to Mr. Matthay, who did his best to rid me of them. He was not successful. The cramp persisted. I wandered round Europe. But none of the eminent teachers I visited was able to solve the problem. . . .
> And then a most exciting thing happened. One day, some time after I had started the research which forms the basis of these lectures, I was working out the theoretical physiological mechanics of finger touch in conjunction with the method of continuous hand and arm pressure. Without any idea of the wider (and very personal) implications I realised that, when the method of continuous finger pressure was being used there was no mechanical necessity for any contraction in the raising muscle of the hand. (I should add that previous investigation had shown the necessity for considerable and continuous tension in this muscle in connection with finger touch operating in conjunction with the self-supported arm). And then, suddenly and in a flash, I realised that the region of my cramp pain coincided with the position, in the forearm, of the raising muscle of the hand. I experimented for a few days with the method of continuous pressure, taking great care that the hand raising muscle was continuously relaxed in the way in which my theoretical investigation had shown to be possible. My cramp disappeared in a few weeks and I have never had even a trace of it from that day to this. Moreover, I have never yet had a case of cramp in a student which failed to clear up equally quickly.[83]

Here was a radical disagreement with Matthay who had made much of a base stabilized by weight. Such a pressure base, Ching felt, achieved all the desired results:

> The method of continuous hand and arm pressure provides the most satisfactory method of ensuring efficient basic

stabilisation. It is also the most efficient method for producing *legato* or *legatissimo* effects. It is thus the most satisfactory method in respect of tone control as well as for the production of those full, resonant qualitative effects which are themselves a by-product of *legato* or *legatissimo* effects.[84]

Such an approach may minimize the tension brought about by high finger lift, but it also brings with it some of the problems associated with a weighted base: legato, velocity, and intensity control. But, for Ching, weight was anathema. In one of his lectures he exhorted his listeners:

Ladies and Gentlemen, can we not now, once and for all, make a real effort to eliminate the whole concept of weight from the theory of piano technique, a concept which has hung like a millstone (and a very heavy one at that) round the necks (or should I say the fingers, hands and arms) of pianists since the beginning of the century.[85]

Ching questioned whether it was really possible within the split second instant of key depression to sense the degree of key resistance and then make the necessary force adjustment for the desired tonal intensity level. He doubted too if "the force of each touch movement must cease instantaneously and completely at the moment of the production of tone."[86]

The Ching Method, as simplified in the *Amateur Pianist's Companion*, has three principal concerns in its technical application: utilizing certain definite correct postures, making the correct specified movements, and controlling the conditions of tension and relaxation in the bodily joints associated with piano playing. Ching lists seven correct standard and three variable postures, and four principal and four auxiliary movements. The joints are categorized as those of movement, transmission, and stabilization. Conditions of tension permissible at the different joints under varying conditions are considered and tabulated in numerous charts, which seem artificial and contrived.

Ching is also one of the first of the writers on piano technique to emphasize strongly the psychological aspects of piano playing. In fact one of his lectures in *Piano Playing* is entitled "Freudian Psychology and the Pianistic Art."

It is evident from these chapters, concerned primarily with Matthay and Breithaupt, that, while the entire weight and relaxation school was surely not without merit, it contained numerous weaknesses and fell short in providing the solution to a satisfactory complete piano technique. But the stage was prepared for a more significant development.

Notes

[1]Jessie Henderson Matthay, *The Life and Works of Tobias Matthay,* p. 16.

[2]William Townsend, *Balance of Arm in Piano Technique,* p. 63.

[3]*Ibid.,* p. 19.

[4]*Ibid.,* p. 8.

[5]*Ibid.,* p. 12.

[6]*Ibid.,* p. 26.

[7]*Ibid.,* pp. 20-23.

[8]*Ibid.,* pp. 38-39.

[9]*Ibid.,* p. 28.

[10]*Ibid.,* p. 42.

[11]*Ibid.,* p. 43.

[12]*Ibid.,* p. 50.

[13]*Ibid.,* p. 57.

[14]*Ibid.,* p. 59.

[15]*Ibid.,* p. 74.

[16]*Ibid.,* p. 68.

[17]Harold Bauer, "Self Portrait of the Artist as a Young Man," *Musical Quarterly,* Vol. XXIX, No. 2, April 1943, p. 158.

[18]*Ibid.,* pp. 163-65.

[19]Jessie Matthay, *Life and Works of Tobias Matthay,* p. 11.

[20]Harriette Brower, *Piano Mastery,* p. 87.

[21]Jessie Matthay, *Life and Works of Tobias Matthay,* p. 17.

[22]*Ibid.,* p. 38.

[23]Tobias Matthay, *The Act of Touch in all its Diversity, An Analysis and Synthesis of Pianoforte Tone-Production,* pp. 13-14.

[24]*Ibid.,* p. 34.

[25]*Ibid.,* pp. 89-90.

[26]Hermann L.F. Helmholtz, *On the Sensations of Tone as a Physiological Basis for the Theory of Music,* p. 75.

[27]*Ibid.,* p. 79.

[28]Matthay, *Act of Touch,* p. 95.

[29]Tobias Matthay, *The Visible and Invisible in Pianoforte Technique,* p. 137.

[30]Matthay, *The Act of Touch*, pp. 98-99.

[31]*Ibid.*, pp. 317-19.

[32]Matthay, *The Visible*, p. 25.

[33]Matthay, *The Act of Touch*, p. 103.

[34]Tobias Matthay, *Some Commentaries on the Teaching of Pianoforte Technique*, pp. 45-47.

[35]Matthay, *The Visible*, p. 166.

[36]Matthay, *Act of Touch*, pp. 324-25.

[37]*Ibid.*, p. 326.

[38]*Ibid.*, p. 114.

[39]*Ibid.*, p. 112.

[40]*Ibid.*, pp. 112-13.

[41]*Ibid.*, p. 111.

[42]*Ibid.*, p. 106.

[43]*Ibid.*, pp. 220-21.

[44]*Ibid.*, p. 221.

[45]*Ibid.*, pp. 217-19.

[46]Matthay, *The Visible*, p. 91.

[47]Matthay, *Some Commentaries*, p. 14.

[48]*Ibid.*

[49]Matthay, *The Visible*, p. 117.

[50]Matthay, *The Act of Touch*, pp. 109-10.

[51]*Ibid.*, p. 151.

[52]Rodney Hoare, "What Matthay Meant," *Piano Teacher*, March-April, 1962, p. 3.

[53]Matthay, *The Visible*, p. 49.

[54]Matthay, *Some Commentaries*, pp. 1-2.

[55]Matthay, *The Visible*, p. 50.

[56]Matthay, *The Act of Touch*, pp. 117-18.

[57]Matthay, *The Visible*, p. 30.

[58]*Ibid.*, p. 64.

[59]*Ibid.*

[60]Matthay, *The Act of Touch*, p. 273.

[61]*Ibid.*, p. 274.

[62]*Ibid.*, pp. 314-15.

[63]Jessie Matthay, *Life and Works*, p. 97.

[64]*Ibid.*

[65]*Ibid.,* p. 106.

[66]Denise Lassimonne, "Tobias Matthay, 1858-1945," *The Piano Quarterly,* No. 36, Summer 1961, p. 17.

[67]Tobias Matthay, *Musical Interpretation, Its Laws and Principles, and Their Application in Teaching and Performing,* pp. 30-34.

[68]Jessie Matthay, *Life and Works,* pp. 99-100.

[69]*Ibid.,* p. 81.

[70]Ambrose Coviello, *What Matthay Meant, His Musical and Technical Teachings Clearly Explained and Self-Indexed,* p. 10.

[71]*Ibid.,* p. 13.

[72]James Ching, *Piano Playing, A Practical Method,* p. 358.

[73]Sidney Harrison, *Piano Technique,* p. 15.

[74]*Ibid.,* pp. 19-20.

[75]Thomas Fielden, *The Science of Pianoforte Technique,* p. 5.

[76]*Ibid.,* p. 8.

[77]*Ibid.,* p. 10.

[78]*Ibid.,* p. 66.

[79]*Ibid.,* p. 86.

[80]*Ibid.,* pp. 98-99.

[81]*Ibid.,* pp. 126-127.

[82]Ching, *Piano Playing,* p. vii.

[83]*Ibid.,* pp. 270-71.

[84]*Ibid.,* p. 282.

[85]*Ibid.,* p. 164.

[86]*Ibid.,* p. 53.

18.   Ortmann: Piano Technique Comes of Age

Americans Gottschalk, Mason, Sherwood, and Amy Fay, who went to Europe for study along with hundreds of other aspiring pianists during the nineteenth century, have been considered in previous chapters. Mason's four-volume technical work, *Touch and Technic* (1889), was extensively used in the United States for many years. Amy Fay's letters, published under the title *Music Study in Germany* (1881), are still widely read today. After returning from Germany, she taught the Deppean principles in Chicago for many years. Her best known pupil, Almon Kincaid Virgil, came to her from Peoria about 1880 as she later related, ". . . for the express purpose of learning from me all about Deppe's method, and I taught it to him in the most exact and careful manner."[1]

He then moved to New York where shortly he published his *Foundation Exercises in Pianoforte Playing* (1889). Amy Fay said that it was, in truth, ". . . a new presentation of Deppe, point for point."[2] She berated him for not giving Deppe his deserved credit:

> Where did Mr. Virgil get his ideas of turning out the hand from the wrist, of holding the tip end joints of the fingers, which he calls the "third phalanx," perpendicular to the key? Of stretching from thumb, of avoiding throwing out the elbow, of attacking from above, of sinking with the wrist in chords and octaves, of holding the hand high on the outside, of lifting the fingers and holding them in the air, which he calls "stroke position"? Of all these things, and many more, nobody ever spoke before Deppe.[3]

Virgil's wife, Antha Minerva, gained more influence than her husband when in 1902 she became the author and founder of *The Virgil Method*. She was also director of the Virgil Piano School located in New York City. The Virgil books rivaled in importance those by Mason; they were surely helped along in their popularity by their advocacy of the use of the Tekniklavier, an instrument

407

which would have delighted both Logier and Kalkbrenner. Invented by A.K. Virgil himself, a seven-octave model looked much like a present-day spinet piano. It was equipped with a dual clicking action to indicate legato. The action of each key could also be regulated so as to offer resistance of from two to twenty ounces to the finger. But with no musical sound available, this sense of key resistance could not relate to tone production. Even so, William Mason endorsed the benefits of the Tekniklavier.

Its functioning was described by Mrs. Virgil in *The Virgil Method:*

> The Tekniklavier is an improved instrument for piano practice, having *an action* similar to that of the piano and a touch identical *with it.*
>
> It is constructed for the sole purpose of enabling the piano student to acquire correct, easy, graceful and accurate playing motions, and relation of motions not only in technic but in pieces. Right and wrong movements and motions are so clearly defined that every intelligent person, young or old, may quickly discern the difference. Good judgment and common sense cannot fail to appreciate the Tekniklavier, for it is surely apparent to every one that an hour's practice making perfectly correct motions is bound to carry the student further in his musical progress than twenty hours of practice with wrong motions and wrong conditions of the muscles and nerves. It has been thoroughly demonstrated that its use hastens progress, develops intellectual, mechanical and rhythmical ability, and materially shortens the course of study. Hence its use is true economy in every sense of the word.
>
> Clicks.
>
> It is provided with clicks both at the down and up action of a key.
>
> By a clever device, these clicks are so arranged as to be used separately or together, and may be brought into action or disconnected by simply turning a lever, the down click lever being at the right hand end of the keyboard and the up click at the left.
>
> The Purpose of the Down Click.
>
> The down click establishes the fingers in the habit of *"taking" keys* with a perfectly quick dropping of the fingers, as the click will not respond to a slow movement of the key. Consequently, if the finger action is slow, the key action will necessarily be slow, and the result will be either *no click* or one almost inaudible.

408

In short, the *down click* indicates clearly to the player the accuracy and quickness of *down motions.*

A slow finger action is equally faulty at the piano, and will result in giving either no sound, or else a light and imperfect one.

The Purpose of the Up Click.

The up click establishes the fingers in the habit of *"leaving" keys* promptly with a quick up motion, thus preventing the slovenly and unmusical overlapping of tones which is so prevalent among piano players. On the Tekniklavier the result of a slow up motion will be *no* click. On the piano the result will be overlapping, blurred tones, and a lack of velocity in brilliant passages requiring rapid execution; and, in trill work unsteadiness and uneven tones.

The Down and Up Clicks Used Together.

A most important object is gained by the united use of the down and up clicks, viz.: the obtaining of the proper finger action and correct relation of finger and key movements necessarily employed in legato and the different kinds of staccato touch.

Legato Touch.

The two clicks sounding *simultaneously* in passing from key to key, proves that the keys have been "taken" and "left" with a perfectly quick down and up motion, and that a key was "taken" and a key "left" at identically the same instant, thus producing what is termed a perfect legato touch.

On the piano, the result would be in passing from key to key tones perfectly connected, without the least *blurring.*

The two clicks sounding *separately* in passing from key to key indicates that the keys have been "taken" and "left" with a perfectly quick motion, but that one key was "left" *after* the other was down, or else *before* the other was down. Both of these relations of key movements are *wrong* for legato touch. On the piano the result would be either overlapping tones, which means *blurring,* or a disconnection of tones. *Either result* is *not only undesirable,* but *absolutely* bad.[4]

Piano study in America by this time was receiving encouragement from many other quarters. The late 1860s had seen the formation of such pioneer music schools as the Oberlin and Cincinnati Conservatories, the New England Conservatory in Boston, the Chicago Musical College, and the Peabody Conservatory in Baltimore. In 1885 the National Conservatory was founded in New York City, as was the Institute of Musical Art, led by Frank

Damrosch, in 1905. Fifteen years later, through the legacy of Augustus D. Juilliard, the Juilliard Foundation was established and in 1924 the Juilliard Graduate School came into existence. Two years later the Institute became a part of the Juilliard organization. Finally in 1946 the two were amalgamated into a single school, the Juilliard School of Music. Now located in Lincoln Center, and housing departments of drama and dance, the school has shortened its name to the Juilliard School. Through a gift by George Eastman, the Eastman School of Music was formed in 1919 in Rochester, New York, with Howard Hanson as director. In 1924 the Curtis Institute of Music was founded in Philadelphia through the endowment of Mrs. Edward Bok. Shortly thereafter Josef Hofmann became its head.

Prior to World War I, it was considered more desirable to study piano in Europe for the greatest teachers were still there: Leschetizky, Breithaupt, Matthay, and all of their artist pupils—as well as those from the Russian and French schools. But after the war there was a great migration of continental pianistic talent to America. New York City rapidly became the musical capital of the world. Artist teachers like Rosina and Josef Lhevinne, Alexander Siloti, James Friskin, Carl Friedberg, and Ernest Hutcheson were found at Juilliard, and Josef Hofmann, Isabelle Vengerova, and Rudolph Serkin at the Curtis Institute. Other schools similarly profited.

Piano students in America in the early years of the twentieth century could also find much discussion of technique in the leading musical publications of the day. Theodore Presser founded *The Etude* magazine in 1883 and remained its editor until 1907. *The Musician* was begun in 1895 with Thomas Tapper guiding it until 1905. A few years later the more scholarly *Musical Quarterly* was established by Rudolph E. Schirmer with O.G. Sonneck as its first editor. *The Etude* and *The Musician* were filled with interviews with and articles by the great European piano teachers. Books written by Americans also expanded European teachings, with those by Harriette Brower and James Francis Cooke, successor to Presser as editor of *The Etude,* the most popular. Other writers included W. S. B. Matthews, Clarence G. Hamilton, Clayton Johns, Mac-Donald Smith, Marie Unschuld, and Howard Wells. Few did much original thinking. Wells is probably typical; he commented in his preface to *Ears, Brain and Fingers* that

> The writer wishes to make grateful acknowledgment to Prof. Theodore Leschetizky for many of the ideas and

410

exercises used in this book. He makes no claim that it is a "Leschetizky Method" feeling as he does that the so-called "Leschetizky Method" cannot be embodied in any book, because it is Leschetizky himself.[5]

Making a complete break with such subjective, unoriginal writing which preceded him, America's most important writer on piano technique, Otto Rudolph Ortmann (1889-   ), engaged in his monumental research and published his most important works during the 1920s. In 1925, *The Physical Basis of Piano Touch and Tone* appeared. It was followed four years later by possibly the most valuable source book on piano technique ever written, *The Physiological Mechanics of Piano Technique.* The latter book, appearing first in England during the Depression years, was further hampered in its circulation when the original plates were destroyed in a German bombing raid on London during World War II. Its influence in recent years has been increased considerably by its republication in the United States in 1962.

Ortmann was born in Baltimore and educated at the Peabody Conservatory where he studied piano with Ludwig Breitner, George Boyle, and Max Landow—all foreign-born and -trained concert pianists. Boyle had been a student of Busoni. Ortmann also took a teacher training course under Ernest Hutcheson. After graduating from Peabody in 1917 and serving on its faculty, Ortmann in 1928 became its director, a position he held until 1942. He was chairman of the music department at Goucher College from 1943 until his retirement in 1958. Throughout his professional career, he taught piano extensively. While at the Peabody Conservatory, Ortmann was responsible for organizing its famous research department in 1925 which was devoted, as he stated ". . . . to scientific investigation of musical talent, instrumental and vocal problems and their effects on music pedagogy."[6] He has also written of his early training and experience and of how he was led into his research activity:

> . . . I do not now recall any fixed methodology, although, ramifications of the Leschetizky method were discussed, as were "Liszt Technique," "Paderewski Technique" and the techniques of other "schools." In my earliest training the weight approach was emphasized and it was probably the limitation of this approach and the divergence of opinion, among teachers themselves, as to details of technique which led me to an experimental approach to the problem. Naturally, I had read Matthay's books carefully.

411

Moreover, I became aware of the marked difference between my own technical achievements and those of well known concert pianists. This, in turn, led to an investigation of the whys and wherefores of individual technical variations. The explanations given me were so often the subjective expression of the player himself that the underlying physiological facts were unintelligible, nor was there agreement among the pupils even of any one teacher. This subjective approach indicated, in my mind, the need for an objective experimental investigation. And thus began the laboratory work. Later on, as Director, the general work at the Conservatory convinced me that similar research was needed in practically all phases of music education and, I organized the first Research Department at the Peabody, with specialists undertaking specific problems. So far as I have been able to learn, this was the first undertaking of this nature at a Conservatory in this country and, if the reports that have reached me are dependable, the distinction applies also to European Conservatories.[7]

Ortmann's laboratory contained extensive apparatus, some of which he had invented himself. In 1967 he expressed the wish that he could have had, "at that time [the 1920s], the scientific equipment which is now at hand. It would have saved many hours of labor and many headaches."[8] While in charge of the Peabody laboratory, Ortmann had complete control over problem formulation and experimental procedures. He further qualified himself for this important work by taking special courses at Johns Hopkins University and working individually with doctor friends who were anatomists and physiologists at several hospitals and medical schools. He also received advice from engineers at the United States Bureau of Standards and at Western Electric. The scholarly character of Ortmann's work was further enhanced by his status as cofounder of the American Musicological Society.

The classic *Physiological Mechanics of Piano Technique* was a radical departure from every work on technique which had gone before it. Ortmann approached every aspect of the subject with the objective attitude of the dedicated scientist: no *a priori* reasoning, no preconceived notions as to how the piano should be played. Nowhere is there any attempt to twist the data to fit his own personal biases. He went to the pertinent scientific fields: physiology and anatomy, physics and acoustics. All of the vital material was thoroughly studied and presented. William Newman has pointed out that not until the "writings of the Americans Otto Ortmann and Arnold Schultz has there been enough understanding of allied

412

sciences like acoustics and anatomy to permit of scientific conclusions."[9]

Ortmann spent many hours in the laboratory observing the different aspects of piano playing about which theorists of the past had only drawn subjective, superficial conclusions. The laboratory records of piano playing were made chiefly by Peabody Conservatory faculty members recognized in this country and abroad as concert pianists of distinction. The investigator simply reported the test results as he observed them and pointed out the laws necessary for consistent, accomplished playing.

Such a seemingly unconventional approach was bound to raise the criticism, particularly among emotionally dominated pianists, that this was much too cold, impersonal, and mechanical a procedure. It was quite likely, too, that pet theories might be destroyed. Furthermore, some argued that such a detailed introspection of one's playing would dehumanize an interpretation and remove its spontaneity and warmth. Ortmann felt the criticism that such an approach robs music of its emotional and artistic values was not justified, since he planned the two books in question as the first and second volumes of a three-volume series, the third volume to be devoted to the psychological and emotional aspects of piano playing. He is a thorough musician as well as a scientist, uncompromising in his view of the truth. Throughout his study, musical objectives are continually kept in mind and practical observations permeate his work. The history of the humanities is replete with the names of men of great artistic achievement who were also seekers of scientific understanding. Pianists for too long a time have approached their study in an unintellectual and even anti-intellectual manner. If the serious student's technique is to develop fully, it must be built upon a sensitivity to all the known facts. Ortmann is the student's first source.

The pianist's body, in order to function at maximum efficiency, must be in accord with the principles of physics and physiology. *The Physiological Mechanics of Piano Technique* supplies this information to a remarkable degree. The mastery of the book's scientific vocabulary and precise, albeit sometimes complex logic is not too difficult a matter for the pianist willing to make the effort. Not only will it enable him to understand more fully the nature of the great concert pianists' technical achievements, but it will surely be beneficial to his own technique.

The Physiological Mechanics of Piano Technique examines those subjects of major concern to both Breithaupt and Matthay.

413

In his exhaustive study, Ortmann organized his material into three broad categories: "The Physiological Organism," "General Aspects of Physiological Movement," and "The Touch-Forms of Piano Technique."

In Part One, before discussing the skeletal, muscular, neural, and circulatory systems, the fundamental principles involved in playing the piano are set forth. There is only one basic concern in piano technique: "the variations of forces produced at the key-surface by the player. The present study is concerned with the manner in which these force-variations are produced."[10] Looking at the human organism from a purely mechanical point of view, he defined certain properties of matter and laws of mechanical action as a basis for his investigation.

The depressing of a key, resulting in the sounding of a note is, mechanically speaking, work. Of the various work-producing apparatus, levers are most important to his analysis of the mechanics of piano playing, since fingers, hands, arms, and their respective joints are considered an interconnected system of levers of the third class. Following are the principal classifications of levers:

Class 1: Fulcrum between Power and Resistance (Ex.: see-saw)

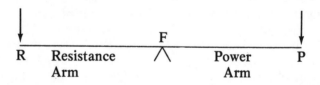

Class 2: Resistance between Power and Fulcrum (Ex.: nut-cracker or wheel barrow)

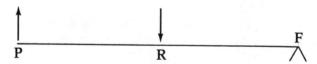

Class 3: Power between Fulcrum and Resistance (Ex.: draw-bridge)

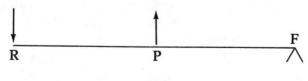

Discussed are the ways in which levers behave when acted upon by forces at various points (the variation of the ratio of the power arm PF to the resistance arm RF) and from different directions. For example, for Class 3 levers the power is always applied between the fulcrum and the resistance; for a given movement of P to some P′, R must move through a greater distance in the same amount of time. With Class 3 levers, this "speed" is greater than that generated by the same power with a Class 2 lever. But a Class 2 lever can overcome greater resistance with the same amount of power than can a Class 3 lever. In other words, if the same power is applied to the lever at different points, variations in both speed and the capacity for overcoming resistance will be observed point to point. Moreover, the angle at which the force is applied to the lever will show this same kind of result. In the figure below it can be seen that, when power is applied at right angles to the lever (direction 1), there is a power advantage, but a comparatively small movement of the resistance arm RF from R to R′. However, when the direction of power application (direction 5) is very close to the line of the lever itself (as with the pianist's muscles), there is a loss of force but a great gain in speed from R to R″. In summary: "Combinations of these power points, and direction relationships can produce any gradation of force-effects."[11]

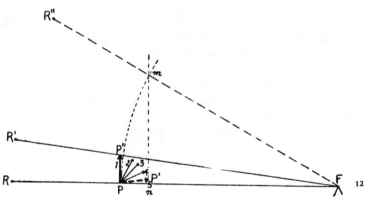

Then considered are the results generated by a number of levers working in concert. The resultant movement may appear simple, but this "composition of forces shows why the visual aspect of movement is not a safe guide to the muscular causes of the movement, since this may result from a few or many components."[13] This, of course, points up the enormous complexity of coordination and relaxation in piano playing.

415

The skeletal system determines posture and provides the levers basic to playing. Ortmann thoroughly described the various joints important to the pianists: their names and classifications and the movement patterns, simple and complex, permitted the bones or levers. A typical joint permits movement through a prescribed arc in a single plane, with the joint acting as the focus of the arc. He precisely indicated the range of movement in degrees. Knowing the capabilities of each joint, the pianist should realize that, for physiological ease and endurance, motion should largely be confined to the mid-range of each arc.

This is physiological textbook material, but the data Ortmann selects can enrich the student's understanding of the physiological equipment he uses in playing, thereby contributing to a more complete and correct approach to the piano. For example, he cleared up a false assumption regarding elbow movement. The radio-ulnar joint is very close to, but entirely separate from, the elbow joint itself. Too often they are thought to be one and the same. The former involves the articulation of two forearm bones that join together near the elbow in a modified ball-and-socket joint, permitting rotation in an arc of 150° to 170° between supination (palm of the hand up) and pronation (palm down). The elbow joint is strictly a hinge joint capable only of flexion (bending) and extension (straightening) with the hand confined to a single plane. In another example is discussed the value of "stretch exercises." The pianist is limited by the basic skeletal span of the hand, but massage may help relax the ligaments and muscles and thus permit greater freedom in the joints.

The potentialities of joint coordination are limitless. Every point can be reached within the entire sphere of movement for the pianist, limited only by the reach of his extended arm. Although movement may be confined to a single joint, it is also true that

> . . . any keyboard movement of considerable range involves a constantly changing coordination of movement among the various joints concerned. It is never made in precisely that same way for any two positions of the arm. What to the eye is a simple continuous movement, may be finished by muscular action radically different from that by which the movement was begun.[14]

Ortmann also addressed himself to the muscles that supply the energy needed to activate the levers of piano playing. The complexities of coordination present in movement at the bone joints will of necessity be reflected in muscular coordination. The simplest movement involves more than one muscle; and one muscle may activate more than a single joint and assist in varied movements. Moreover, the greater the distance or forcefulness of movement, the greater the involvement or "spread" of muscle participation. This is not always easily observed. Even the visual simplicity of certain straight-line movements by the hand belies the necessity of harmonious interaction of the entire arm musculature.

Other cases of visual illusion may be cited. Absence of motion is no guarantee of muscular inactivity: the opposite sets of antagonistic muscles may be contracting against each other with equal force, rendering movement impossible. Movements that seem to be equal and opposite may involve unequal opposing muscular activity. Gravity necessitates more muscular contraction for an upward movement than a downward one. Also, a supination movement of the forearm involves muscles more powerful than the opposing ones directing pronation. The difference is clearly evident when these movements are applied to the turning of a screwdriver.

The high finger school could have saved itself much frustration, and even physical harm in some cases, had it possessed a more profound knowledge of the musculature of the hand and arm. The inherent weakness of the fourth finger, and also its inability to lift as high as its neighbors, is caused by the tendonous interconnections with the fingers on either side. The figure on page 418 clearly illustrates the lack of independence in fourth finger action.[15] It is futile to expect even the most highly developed finger technique to achieve full equality for the fourth finger.

Proper handling of work loads by the muscles and problems of fatigue and relaxation are interrelated concerns. In proportion to the work demanded of it, a muscle will show a graded response of contraction on its own part, or it will enlist the cooperative support of related muscles. Ortmann stated "that a muscle does its best work with relatively light loads, although some investigators have found maximum efficiency at half the maximum load."[16] The muscle or musculature should be big and powerful enough for the task delegated to it. An overload will result in undesirable tension. This in turn leads to loss of sensitivity to key resistance and poor judgment of tone quality.

Muscular activity should not be carried out beyond moderate fatigue. Short rest periods in practice are advised to eliminate fatigue, the chemical process resulting in the accumulation of waste products such as lactic acid and carbon dioxide in the muscles. Undesirable muscular tension across a joint occurs when there is

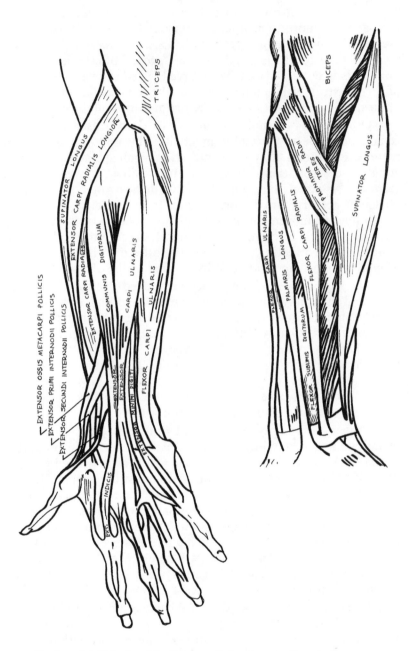

The Superficial Muscles of the Forearm: C, dorsal aspect; D, ventral aspect.
Modified after Gray.

418

more contraction than is needed to overcome a specified resistance in the keys. Other examples of muscular incoordination too often present in piano playing are hypo-relaxation (with sets of antagonistic muscles, one set relaxes at a slower rate than the other contracts—with resultant tension) and hyper-relaxation (one set relaxes at a faster rate than the other contracts). Too much relaxation can be as detrimental in keyboard performance as too little. There should be a harmonious blending of relaxation and contraction. The basic muscular condition the performer brings to the piano is never one of complete relaxation: healthy muscle-tone does not permit a single completely relaxed joint in the entire body.

Toward the end of the book nearly forty pages are devoted to analyzing physical differences and their effects. He studies variations in arm weight and size, in muscular structure and strength, and other significant factors. A complete chapter is taken up with the hand with consideration given to the problem of "double-jointedness."

Ortmann makes brief mention of the neural and circulatory systems. Both are highly integrative in their structure and permeate the entire skeletal-muscular complex. Every muscle cell is stimulated by nerve impulses and nourished by the blood stream. The brain is the center of volitional control; the connecting spinal cord with its intricate circuitry of nerve fibers, is responsible primarily for the body's acquired reflex patterns. There is no substitute in piano practice for the careful, conscious repetition of a movement in order that there may be complete reliability when the movement later comes under reflex action control. Since an adequate blood supply is necessary for the playing members, the condition of the circulatory system is of vital importance and does cause differences in technical proficiency among pianists. Adequate warm-up time before a lesson or recital is essential.

In Part Two, Ortmann studies in great detail the nature of physical movement at the keyboard. Like Matthay, both visible and invisible characteristics concern him. Many times they are interrelated and cannot be analyzed separately. Outward manifestations are seen in the various patterns of physical movement that make up both good and bad playing. The less visible forces at work involve the basic problems of muscular exertion and coordination, relaxation, weight application, action and reaction, activity and passivity, isolation and fixation. These Ortmann studied in the

419

laboratory in their variable degrees of speed, force, dynamic intensity, and range of movement. Data gathered by use of precision instruments led to conclusions more physiologically accurate and detailed than would normally be possible from purely personal observation.

In one experiment, a crescendo was to be made during the execution of a diatonic octave progression. A light was attached to the hand and the pattern of movement photographed. Two of the players insisted that the hand had not progressively lifted higher from the keyboard as the crescendo developed with each successive octave, that there was only greater force applied while the height of arm lift remained constant throughout the passage. But Ortmann observed that

> . . . the photographs of both movements showed the usual increase in amplitude. I cite this to prove again the danger of relying upon the opinion of even first-rate pianists in an analysis of movement. Introspection usually alters the physiological response and the normal speed of movement we are considering is too great to be analyzed by the unaided eye. The graphic method alone is here dependable.[17]

The miracle remedies of the Breithaupt era, relaxation and weight transfer, are given a chapter apiece by Ortmann. His laboratory experiments show the fallacies they contain. He used a mechanical arm to demonstrate that pure arm weight does not play the dominant role in piano playing as is often thought. With the arm suspended in various positions, he recorded weight measurements at the finger tip, wrist, elbow and shoulder. It was found that the position allowing the greatest amount of weight application to the keyboard was the one universally rejected by pianists: high wrists and the upper arm extending forward at a slight descending angle. The position most popular with pianists, trunk slightly forward with shoulder over the elbow, transfers the smallest amount of weight to the finger tip. Ortmann concluded that "The advantage of the forward position is in other phases, and its universal adoption by pianists proves that free arm weight is probably never used in actual playing but is replaced by a muscular contraction added to gravity."[18]

Using several types of dynamographs he recorded fluctuations in weight transfer: a rise in the line on the recording paper indicated a weight increase and a fall of the line a weight decrease. It was impossible to use weight technique in passages made up of rapid movement repetition, but a certain amount could be transferred if the fingers were taken in sequence and not soon repeated. A percussive touch was found to be detrimental to weight transfer—continuous finger tip contact with the key was interrupted. Ortmann discovered that, in the transfer of arm weight with a legato touch, a very slow tempo and a very soft dynamic level had to be maintained; therefore, this arm action is greatly limited. Furthermore, in the most used position, as stated above, very little of the total arm weight ever reaches the finger—less than one-fourth. If more weight is to be transferred, the arms must be extended and the joints fixated. Then he pointed out a contradiction:

> Moreover, the fixation of all intervening joints is diametrically opposed to the whole doctrine of weight-transfer, which demands a relaxed arm as a necessary physiological condition of this transfer. Exactly the opposite is true: weight-transfer demands fixation of joints, not relaxation.[19]

Ortmann concentrated specifically upon Breithaupt's *Rollbewegung* technique. This is the touch where the arm weight is to be rolled from one key to the next, much like a wheel with the weight carried from spoke to spoke. He calls this concept an illusion which goes against the principles of mechanics of movement. In tests with the dynamograph, if the arm was relaxed, over ninety percent of the weight was withdrawn when the arm was raised in preparation for the next downward movement. For there to be a continuous transfer of full arm weight from finger tip to finger tip, it would be necessary that the muscles antagonistic to arm lift also be contracted. The result is immediately undesirable:

> But simultaneous contraction of antagonistic groups [of muscles] always results in a hyper-tension, a stiffness, and consequently any arm-lift with sustained key-pressure in excess of that of the freely ascending arm, is, pianistically, an incoordinated movement. It is not arm-weight that is transferred, but a force resulting from muscular contraction opposed to arm-lift.[20]

His analysis of visible physical movement at the keyboard reinforces the Deppe-Caland teaching regarding the importance of graceful, curvilinear movement. The constant change in direction inherent in all piano playing, with inertia and momentum continually to be reckoned with, makes curvilinear movement desirable. The awkwardness of angular bodily movement is obvious.

Where fast repetitive movement is necessary, Ortmann noticed the tendency of all players he studied to avoid an unchanging position of the base. This they accomplished, he observed,

> . . . by shifting some other part of the arm than the part directly engaged in tone-production. This attempt, not always entirely successful, was so general that some physiological necessity must have prompted it. The necessity is probably muscular fatigue. . . . By adding a slow movement of larger muscles to the rapidly repeated movement, the player changes the movement from one of absolute repetition to one of relative repetition. With this he eliminates muscular repetition and consequently, in the case of rapid movements, reduces the danger of early fatigue.[21]

A full chapter is devoted to the principle that "forces acting on any point at rest are equal and opposite."[22] Any force moving down into the key is opposed at the point of resistance by an upward acting force, at both key contact and of greater degree, when the key bed is reached. Matthay gave much space in his writings to this principle of action and reaction. In a series of Ortmann tests in which aluminum levers were attached to various parts of finger, hand, and arm, and time-line readings of motion were recorded and magnified three times, the slightest degree of downward resistance encountered in the key showed noticeable upward movement at hand knuckle, wrist, or elbow. This reaction movement, but not the force, can largely be eliminated by appropriate fixation in the joint affected. In other tests, it was found that a similar lateral reaction was present in finger action.

The player's control of muscular contraction is continually involved with these reacting forces. Even during the non-resistance phase of a percussive movement, muscular contraction will be experienced before key contact, as the result of the imagined tonal image. Ortmann stated that:

> What actually happens is that the player images the key-resistance, and hence prepares the speed of muscular contraction, the necessary fixation of the joints, before the key is reached. Through experience and talent, this image can function very accurately, and upon its accuracy depends the question of whether or not the player will get the desired tonal result. Insufficient fixation or an excess thereof, is to be classed as incoordinated movement, because, from the standpoint of interaction, a coordinated movement is one in which action and reaction are equal and opposite.[23]

A discussion of action and reaction must lead to a consideration of two opposite types of movement: *active* movement, caused by muscular contraction resulting from neural stimuli, and *passive* movement, resulting from the external application of a force outside the body. The differences in muscular coordination resulting from similar active and passive movements should be a matter of real concern to the piano teacher. Ortmann showed through laboratory experiment that when the teacher moves the student's finger or arm through a desired path, the muscles responsible for a similar active movement do not contract and therefore are not being trained. The physical appearance of the muscle in both passive and active movement may be similar (for example, the biceps muscle will bulge in either case), but coordination can not be determined by a movement's appearance, only by its mechanical nature. If the student's muscle is to be trained properly, the teacher should introduce resistance in opposition to the desired movement. If more finger lift is wanted, the teacher should press against the finger; if more finger drop is desired, press up against the finger descending. But care must be taken to distinguish between positive and negative movement—there is danger, for example, of placing too much emphasis on training the negative upward lift of the finger or arm. One should note that a movement such as controlled arm drop may have both active and passive elements present in it at the same time. Indeed, gravity is a vital factor in all muscular movement and coordination.

Ortmann gets to the heart of good piano technique in his lengthy discussion of coordination and incoordination. The elements of keyboard movement are four: weight, distance, time, and aim. If a keyboard movement is well coordinated, it must meet the demands of each of these with as little waste of physiological energy as possible. Needed is "just that degree of muscular relaxation that will transmit the desired force to the desired point in the proper time."[24] Either too much or too little relaxation can lead to incoordination. For example, the joints of finger and hand must be rigid enough to support the weight of the arm resting on the keys. But, on the other hand, there should be no greater degree of joint fixation than is necessary to withstand key impact. A condition often found in students is the "stiff wrist" caused by too high a finger lift; the tendons in the fingers pass over the wrist and create undue tension there, whenever contracted.

Most of Ortmann's investigation of muscular coordination is concerned with how this coordination is affected by varying degrees of speed, force, and range of movement. Muscular reaction and coordination change greatly with differences in speed. The timing and the intensity of the contraction, and the contraction's location within the range of movement at a slow speed are not at all like those at a fast speed. In a slow movement there is less of an inertia problem at the beginning of the movement, but more effects from gravity and other factors such as joint resistance, and there is less force involved. Muscular contraction need not be as intense, but it will be more prolonged than during a fast movement. The contraction needed to stop a movement may come almost at the very end of the slow movement; while in a rapid one the contraction will have to come earlier and will need a stronger action.

In rapid movements, overcoming inertia and checking momentum are of vital concern. Ortmann found that a quick getaway, an initial muscular contraction strong enough to overcome the inertia and to achieve the desired speed of movement immediately, needed about half the expenditure of the sustained energy necessary for a movement which gradually accelerated to the desired speed. This initial whiplike action is followed by enough muscular relaxation to cause the arm to move as a free body through part of its range. In a fast movement the maximum muscular contraction will be achieved a little before the point of key resistance—in fact some relaxation may already have set in at this point.

Ortmann attached a pneumatic tambour* to the arm and later to the wrist to measure the degree and duration of muscular tension during both arm and finger movements in slow and fast speeds at the keyboard.[25] In one rapid arm movement, the contraction of the muscles observed (the pectoralis major) occurred sixteen one-hundredths of a second before key-depression. By the time the key was touched, muscular relaxation had already begun to set in. The graph of a slow arm movement showed a less intense but earlier arm contraction and one which gradually relaxed. The same type of muscular reaction in fast arm movement was observed also in tests of finger movement. Here the time elapsing was only two-

---

*This tambour consisted of a shallow disc covered with a thin rubber membrane, to the center of which was attached a writing instrument capable of graphing changes of air pressure. Called a tambour, it was inserted at one end of a rubber tube while within the other end was located a piston device to be held against the muscle tested. As the muscle contracted, the piston communicated the timing and degree of contraction to the air within the tightly sealed tube. The sensitive membrane then recorded these fluctuations of air pressure.

to three-fiftieths of a second between maximum finger flexor contraction and key contact.

Ortmann summarized:

> Time-relationship between muscular contraction and duration of stroke may, therefore, be considered a basic element of coordination. . . . Muscular contraction does not parallel the range of movement as speed increases. The faster the movement, the more does the muscular contraction approach an initial maximal "twitch" [a simple, fleeting contraction] followed by relaxation.[26]

Force variations are directly related to speed variations; with an increase in speed there will come an increase in force. This of necessity will cause a change in the muscular coordination. Muscles do their best work in their middle ranges of action; before maximum contraction can be reached other muscles will assist in supplying the additional force, and the necessary joint fixation. This muscular spread will always be towards the larger muscles. But further assistance in withstanding the added force is also provided by the bone structure itself—the bones in the hand and arm tend to line up in a straight line with the bone ends pressing against each other. The body is acting at the best mechanical advantage and thus in a coordinated manner.

There is also a shift in muscular activity in accordance with the particular range of movement. The finger extensor, when it has fully extended the finger, will bend the wrist back if the contraction continues, since the tendon involved also passes over the wrist. A muscle has more than one function. And along a range of movement certain functions may be prevented by the contraction of the appropriate antagonistic muscles. Where simple flexion at the elbow without supination is wanted, the antagonistic pronating muscles act as an inhibiting factor. This is a good example of a well coordinated movement which is not a relaxed movement as well.

Ortmann also examined the effect on muscular coordination of a moving object, such as the finger encountering external resistance. When the finger strikes the key and reaches the key bed with a certain amount of force in a coordinated movement, there is a corresponding reaction or relaxation in the antagonistic muscles. The greater the force applied to the key, the greater the amount of slack in the antagonistic muscles. When the key is released, the lifting muscles must contract, and expend energy until all of the slack is taken up. With continued contraction, upward movement will take place. Ortmann said that, "Since coordination means the

425

muscular response doing a required amount of work in a given time with the least waste of energy, the state of contraction of a muscle is independent of the mere position of the skeletal parts it moves."[27]

If the same movement can be made by both a large or a small muscle, it must be determined which provides the better coordination. Ortmann laid down the principle that rapid movements and small range movements naturally belong to the smaller muscles and joints; movements of power and those of wide range are better handled by the larger muscles and joints. In the latter case, the larger mass cannot move rapidly in various directions in a coordinate manner because of the problems of inertia and momentum involved. Where rapidly repeated movements or a quick change of direction are necessary, the small levers of finger and hand should be used.

Conservation of energy being essential in a coordinated movement, it is vital that no more time be consumed in muscular contraction than is absolutely necessary. Piano playing is alternation between rapid contraction and relaxation. Ortmann wrote:

> The ratio between the time of contraction and relaxation is one measure of coordinated movement. In fact, I am inclined to believe that the readiness with which relaxation sets in between movements, be they movements of fingers, hand, or arm, is a fair index of kinesthetic talent as applied to the piano.[28]

He further states:

> The relaxation following tone-production has frequently, but erroneously, been supposed to exist during tone-production as well, and has given rise to a pedagogy of tone-production that robs the player's style of much force, velocity, and brilliance. A coordinated movement, considered in its time phase, is one in which the muscular contraction is of as short duration as possible in view of the desired effect. . . . The contraction of the muscle should take place a moment before or upon the introduction of the resistance which the muscle has to overcome. It should cease not later than removal of the resistance.[29]

Ortmann finally pointed out that reflex action is involved in coordination, that a movement should not be taught by calling attention to the muscles taking part. With proper resistance present, proper contraction will normally follow.

The terms *coordination* and *incoordination* are not confined to one chapter, but weave their way throughout the entire Ortmann study. Ortmann's place in technical history would be secure if it

426

rested only upon his many definitions of coordination and incoordination deduced from his laboratory experiments. After examining the basic principles of physical piano technique in Part Two, he turned to their application in specific forms of keyboard technique. Most of this material is found in Part Three and coordination is the touchstone used throughout. Ortmann gave his careful attention to vertical and lateral arm movement, finger action, scales, arpeggios, staccato, tremolo, and miscellaneous movements.

Three kinds of vertical arm movement are described: free arm-drop, modified or controlled arm-descent, and forced downstroke. The free arm-drop has no use in piano technique other than as a limited practice measure to heighten the sense of relaxation. Tests were run to determine the effects of arm-descent, under varying conditions of tonal intensity, tempo, and percussion, upon muscular coordination. In every case muscular contraction was found to be a necessary part of tone production. Ortmann wrote that "In the time and force relationships between the arm-stroke and the muscular contraction necessary to offset key-resistance and hammer-impact, we have the true physiological basis of coordinated movement."[30] Contraction should occur at just the right time to overcome key resistance and be of as short duration as possible. In a coordinated movement the contraction is so brief that the relaxationists thought that relaxation was present during tone production.

Ortmann used a pantograph method to record lateral arm movements on paper and also a photographic procedure with a tiny ophthalmoscopic bulb attached to the player's hand. He found that the curves of movement are asymmetrical in character and that asymmetry is present throughout all phases of piano technique. In the rapid leap of an octave, the hand should be highest toward the end of the lateral movement. Such a curve-form allows for the best muscular coordination, maximum force advantage, and economy of movement. An increase in dynamics showed an increase in the amplitude of the lateral curve. And when speed was present with increased intensity, accuracy became much more of a problem. Rapid playing must always be accompanied by relatively light playing, but the preceding practice of such a passage should be slow and forte. The path of a well coordinated slow lateral movement varies greatly from that of a rapid one. The slow lateral movement remains close to the keyboard surface and then has a separate lift at the end of the lateral movement.

In the chapter on finger action, Ortmann states that finger

strokes can only vary in direction and in intensity. He does not make the in-depth study of finger muscular coordination that Schultz later made; but flat finger, curved finger, and elliptical finger strokes are examined and compared. Practical advice is included. Fingers can be strengthened more by exercising them in a flat position because of the mechanical disadvantage at which they work. The broken nail joint so common among children with weak fingers can be overcome more effectively by also working from a flat finger position rather than by asking for more finger curve. Ortmann suggests introducing resistance to the muscle's contraction. The flat finger should be placed on a black key. As it presses firmly against the key, the finger tip should glide or be stroked towards the palm of the hand.[31]

Children beginning to learn finger action should not be taught an excessively high finger lift because the fingers work at a mechanical disadvantage in the extreme range of the finger stroke. The wrist, of course, will also stiffen; such an action will result in a percussive touch. Ortmann states that a well-coordinated finger touch will have the unused fingers maintaining close proximity to the key surfaces. He conducted extensive experiments showing the problems in touch and tone that arise from a percussive touch. The results are included in both *The Physiological Mechanics of Piano Technique* and in *The Physical Basis of Piano Touch and Tone*.

Ortmann also discussed isolation in relation to finger action. Isolation limits movement to only one joint. If the finger is the playing lever and the fulcrum the hand knuckle, the hand and arm together provide the base. Except for the softest levels of tone production by the fingers, there must be some fixation of the wrist joint by the simultaneous contraction of the transverse antagonistic muscles. Isolated finger movements result. In a fine coordination the degree of contraction will nicely balance and counteract the upward force of reaction of the finger impact upon the key bed. With finger action of more intensity, elbow fixation will occur. Ortmann, throughout his entire study, effectively demonstrated that at every point of tone there must be appropriate muscular contraction. He strenuously opposes the hyper-fixations of the high finger school, but also opposes the fallacy of Breithaupt's relaxation theory. At the same time Ortmann seems reluctant to espouse the resulting "practical" isolation which must inevitably follow in many individual movements at the piano.[32] The fulcrum must have a solid base or the lever—the moving finger, hand, or arm—will encounter serious musical problems. Theoretically, there is no such thing as

428

absolute isolation. The base will always show a slight tremor; there will always be "sympathetic movement" of a minute nature visible in the unplaying fingers regardless of the degree of fixation. And muscular activity can never be wholly confined to a single set of muscles. Yet for all practical purposes, simple movement can and must frequently be confined to one joint and to one set of muscles in well-coordinated piano playing.

In scale and arpeggio playing, Ortmann defined most decisively the nature of well-coordinated movement. The pictures he took graphically show the asymmetrical nature of ascending and descending lines in the same hand. The ascending right hand scale is a series of angles and the descending one a series of curves. The difficulty with the thumb is not passing it under the hand—and he found that it did in the normal rapid scales—but playing the key while under the hand. The thumb-under flexion action is a natural movement present from infancy where it is associated with the grasping reflex. The student should be able to make the thumb tip touch the base of the fifth finger as a means of easily learning the thumb-under movement.

The coordination and curve for a slow scale are different than for a rapid one: separate movements as opposed to a continuous, unified movement. A certain amount of arm movement and shift cannot be avoided. Ortmann wrote: "A rapid scale is played with a continuous arm-shift, which is accomplished by a partial passing-under of the thumb."[33]

This free arm movement is even more apparent in the arpeggio, which is never played completely legato. In his test pictures, Ortmann found the path of arm movement to be spiral-like with movement in three planes: lateral-horizontal, forward-horizontal, and vertical. The passing-under of the thumb is merely part of the arm-shift. Exercises which teach it with a quiet hand are not relevant. He felt that free arm movement should be encouraged in slow practice. The slow practice should approximate the actual fast coordination. Ortmann also emphasized the importance of developing strong fingers particularly for arpeggio work because of the abducted (spread) position they continually must maintain.

Ortmann's tests established the limited amount of weight that can be transferred with a rotary action in tremolo passages. Recording with a dynamograph, he found that it was "quite impossible to keep the needle of the instrument at a fixed level, regardless of the speed at which the tremolo is played."[34] In the legitimate use of the forearm tremolo in the wider spans such as the octave, he observed that even here a certain amount of finger action is employed with movement at several joints. In trills a coordinated technique will use finger action alone unless added power is needed. But the addition of forearm activity brings with it problems in inertia and momentum resulting in clumsiness and loss of speed. Lack of strength in the fingers is a cause of arm tension which sometimes develops in trill playing.

Ortmann devotes much space to the true nature of staccato and the physical means for producing it. In the first place, the shortest staccato note is not as short as one might believe it to be. An important limiting factor is the natural rate of key ascent—a finger may rise much more quickly than its key. In tests, he found that it took between two- and three-fiftieths of a second. In a practical situation it is usually longer. Ortmann added: "The tone produced is longer than the finger-key contact and the extreme *staccatissimo* effects are an auditory illusion resulting from the brevity of the kinesthetic and visual sensations. The tone is not as short as we imagine it is."[35]

A suggested pedagogy for hand staccato again illustrates the practical, along with the immense theoretical value of his inquiry: arch the hand, holding the fingers close to each other; depress the fingers with the small muscles of the palm of the hand, since they do not extend back across the wrist into the forearm; the third finger, followed by the other fingers individually, should play repeated staccato notes with the thumb pressed against it below the nail joint; then practice thirds with the second and fourth fingers; finally, practice with first and fifth fingers, starting with the smallest possible intervals, even the third, and gradually increasing to the octave distance. Such a study procedure will insure maximum freedom at the wrist.

A simple staccato test measures accurately the talent and training of the student: tapping as rapidly as possible for a given period of time. A dynamograph recorded the force variations through the amplitude of the stylus fluctuations. The untalented student showed a large degree of tension and misdirected energy. The line fluctuations were wide and wild and showed the fewest number of taps. An average good student showed a regularity of pattern with moderate height and speed to the movement. The line graph of the very talented student indicated that the tapping was done with the lightest of touches and with the wrist slowly un-

dulating through many small hand movements. The stylus fluctuations were small and close together with wave-like crests appearing in each group of ten or twelve taps. Here again is shown the
presence of muscular spread in a well-coordinated technique.

The vibrato touch, frequently used in rapid and usually forte
staccato passages, is the only instance in which the muscles are in a
truly elastic condition. The antagonistic muscles contract simultaneously but the stronger contraction of one set creates the playing
movement. Vibrato movements are very small and tiring. Tests of a
hand vibrato confirmed that both extensor and flexor muscles were
in a continual state of contraction and fixation. While in this
condition,

> . . .the only stimulus is a plus pull on either side but not on
> both. Thus the number of neural stimuli needed is half of that
> needed for executing the movement in a relaxed manner. . . .
> When the additional contraction producing the movement
> ceases, the body moved returns [like a stretched rubber band]
> to its original position by virtue of a force already acting
> during the time of displacement.[36]

The experimenter also applied his photographic recording of
movement at the piano to other interesting areas. He tested the
comparative value of different types of fingering used in the same
sequential passage: the straight line fingering of the older school of
editors against fingering with more free-arm movement where the
thumb frequently uses the black key. In the latter, exactly the same
fingering was used in each pattern allowing ease of recall. But from
a physical point of view it was found to be inferior to the former
fingering because of the considerable amount of superfluous movement and the loss in accuracy of dynamic control resulting from the
hand shift. Ortmann did feel though that tones equally loud should
be played by the same fingers as much as possible when tempo and
hand position are favorable.

Observing the suppressed curves of some keyboard movement
patterns, Ortmann pointed out that pianists frequently would like
to move further in from the keyboard edge. He felt that the
scratches so apparent on conservatory piano fall-boards indicated
a hampering of free movement. One wonders why his
recommendation to piano manufacturers to drop the fall-board
back several inches has never been acted upon.

Movement photography also illustrated forcefully "the

431

effect of speed upon muscular coordination and the impossibility of transferring a movement learned slowly to the same passage played rapidly, without muscular readjustment."[37] But this does not mean that slow practice, from a psychological standpoint, has no value. It is absolutely necessary. This photography also showed that incoordinated movement is awkward, not so much in the large arm movements, but in the fine movements of finger and hand that occur in a complex pattern.[38] Furthermore, greater coordination skill is necessary in passages of speed and lightness than in ones of speed and force. More small muscles will be called into play. The performer who has great strength in these muscles will have a distinct advantage. And if a large muscle has to be used instead of a smaller one because of lack of strength, the student will have to contend with a slower moving mass and a greater inertia problem. Ortmann emphasized that "purely gymnastic training of the small muscles of the fingers, hand, and forearm, in order to increase their absolute strength, is, therefore, from a mechanical standpoint, highly desirable for piano technique."[39]

In *The Physiological Mechanics of Piano Technique* a chapter is devoted to the question of tone quality. Another chapter discusses the related subject of style. His articles on tone also appeared in *The Musical Quarterly, The Etude, The American Mercury*, and the *Music Teachers National Association Proceedings*. Furthermore, his earlier work, *The Physical Basis of Piano Touch and Tone*, is largely occupied with the subject. The validity of Ortmann's pioneer research was later reaffirmed by the experiments of William Braid White for the American Steel and Wire Company in 1930 and scientists at the University of Pennsylvania in 1934.

The effect of a pianist's touch in changing the quality of the piano tone is studied thoroughly in the 1924 volume. Ortmann himself later wrote: "After all, the chief reason for varying the standard touch-forms which we have been considering is the production of the desired tone-quality."[40] But exactly how does the manipulation of the piano key determine the character of the sound? It may be recalled that Matthay had taken exception to views "denying the possibility of quality-variations."[41] held by Breithaupt's associate F.A. Steinhausen—and similar to Ortmann's conclusions. Throughout the years tone and touch has been a lively topic.

Ortmann began his investigation by studying the effect of touch upon key depression speed. All that can be done to the key is to press it down approximately three-eighths of an inch. The fundamental properties of a moving body such as the finger, hand, or arm, which might be applied to the key surface, are mass, direction, and speed. These fundamentals, all variables, were tested in the laboratory. The key speed recording apparatus consisted of a piece of smoked glass mounted to the side of a key, and a tuning fork with a stylus attached, situated in such a manner as to trace its vibration pattern on the glass as the key was depressed. The most minute variation in speed of key descent registered as a variation in wave length on the smoked glass. The closer the time lines were together, the slower the key speed; the farther apart the markings, the faster the descent. Variations in speed within one key descent are accurately indicated. The rate of the tuning fork's vibration is constant. In all of Ortmann's tests a fork vibrating 256 times per second was used.

Obviously as greater force was applied, the faster the key moved and the louder the sound became. This is seen in Figure 1 where we have a record of movement of the key as produced first (a) by a finger touch, (b) a hand touch, (c) forearm, (d) full arm. All were non-percussive touches: before it depressed the key, the finger tip already was in contact with the key. Figure 2 shows movement patterns made with percussive touches. There is a record of

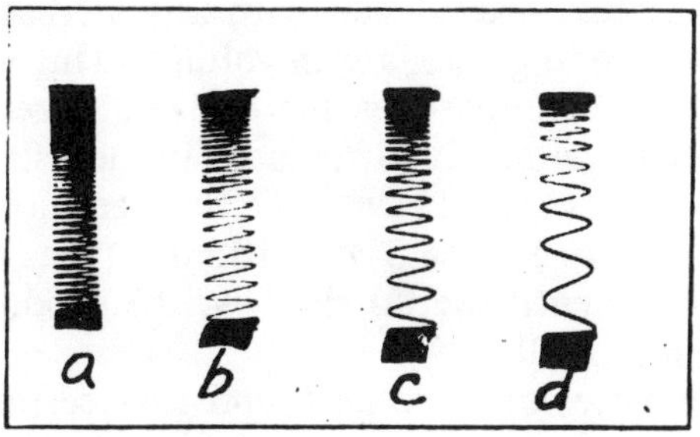

Figure 1

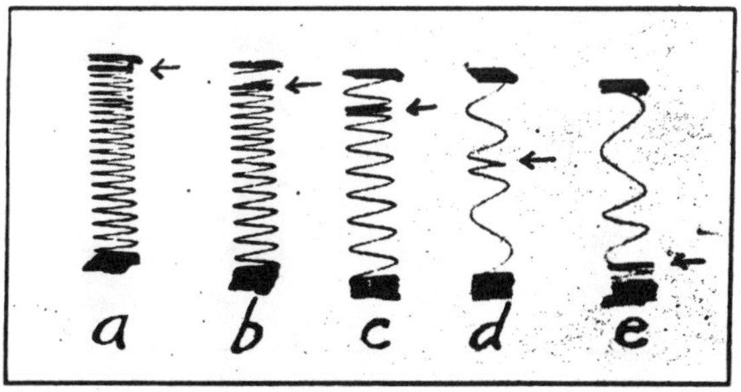

Figure 2

42

433

dynamic increase, but also a clear indication of change of key descent speed *within* the three-eighths of an inch distance travelled. The time lines show that the finger tip is momentarily retarded as it strikes the key. The key, uncontrolled, moves out in front of the finger. The finger catches up at the arrow points and then controls the key's descent for the rest of the movement. But the finger tip is never fully in control of the key's movement in a percussive touch—nor therefore of its dynamic intensity. In the non-percussive touch, Ortmann said that "the finger weights the key down throughout its descent, thus enabling us to gauge the resistance more accurately."[43]

Rigid and relaxed tone production patterns were also compared. It was found that a relaxed effort always resulted in slower key movement and a softer, somewhat more pleasant sound. Where intensity was exactly the same, there was no difference in key movement. A flat finger tended to press the key down more slowly than a bent finger, and also provided a softer, more agreeable sound. Wrist level did not materially affect key speed.

Ortmann asked experienced pianists to play what they felt to be different qualities of tone such as strident, brilliant, full, singing, round, dry, shallow, clear, velvety, bell-like, etc. He found that for each difference in quality there was a difference in key speed. Earlier he had proved that with any increase of key speed there is a corresponding increase in volume. This led him to conclude that "all these supposedly qualitative differences as applied to the single tone are merely differences in intensity."[44] The most unpleasant sounds were always at either end of the range of dynamic intensity. In Figure 3 are different types of tone quality that his subjects identified: (a) shallow, (b) good, (c) forced, (d) singing, (e) harsh, (f) full.

In another series of tests, he found that certain tone quality

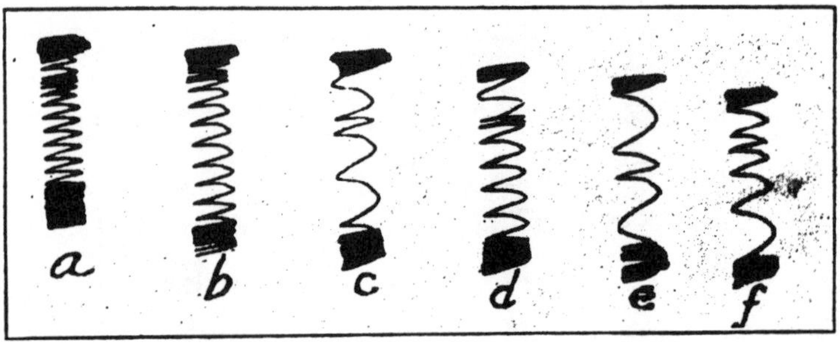

Figure 3   45

images were dependent upon and conditioned by the kinds of force variations transmitted to the keys. Aluminum recording levers were attached to the keys and the results transmitted to the smoked surface of a revolving drum. The resulting dynamographs recorded the force variation patterns. Two examples from the many which Ortmann provided may be cited. A sparkling tone, which is considered rather sharply percussive, showed a sudden, extremely brief increase of muscular force:

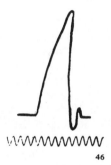
46

A velvety tone manifested a gradual pressure increase which was sustained and not intense. The touch was non-percussive:

47

The direction from which the force is applied to the key also affects key speed and the resulting dynamic levels. If eight ounces of force were applied from directly over the key, it would require sixteen ounces from a position deviating sixty degrees from the vertical.

Still another factor is natural key resistance. There is more in the bass register than in the treble—and especially the highest keys where the strings are not dampened. The further in on the keys one plays, the greater will be the key resistance and the greater the force needed.

Following his study of key movement, Ortmann devoted his attention to hammer movement, which is four times the speed of key movement. Here he arrived at similar conclusions in his research. Like the key, the hammer can only move a fixed distance in a fixed

435

plane. A change of hammer speed was the cause of every change in tone color. The velocity of the hammer at the instant it leaves the escapement is the sole direct influence on string vibration. From that point the hammer is no longer under key control—its speed *cannot* be increased and its manner of velocity achievement has no bearing at all upon hammer action against the string. It will always be percussive and be exactly the same at any one given speed. Ortmann rebutted certain erroneous views regarding hammer-string contact when he spoke of how

> . . . it is frequently stated that in percussive touches the hammer is jarred so badly that it "quivers" along its ascent and thus strikes the string differently than in non-percussive touches, thereby producing an ugly tone. If any such "quiver" existed it would be shown as irregularities along the hammer path, but. . . no such irregularities are found, the only difference being in the more abrupt beginning of the percussive stroke when compared with that of the non-percussive stroke. Many records made of hammer stroke show that the only factor directly responsible for string vibration is hammer velocity. Regardless of the touch used, the hammer-string impact is always sharply percussive; there can be no non-percussive attack of the string which corresponds to a non-percussive attack of the key. Any gradual setting into motion of the string by a correspondingly gradual increase of force by the player is a complete muscular and tonal illusion. The hammer records, therefore, verify the key movement records and prove that all the differences in tone quality, other than those determined by the noise elements, result from differences in hammer speed, hence mean differences in tonal intensity.[48]

Ortmann's conclusion that a change of hammer speed is the primary cause of every change in tone color seems to be amply borne out in the piano roll recordings of the great pianists made prior to his research in the 1920s. *Scientific American* explained that the amazingly refined recording instrument perfected by the Ampico Research Laboratory of the American Piano Company and employed to record such outstanding pianists as Josef Lhevinne, Rachmaninoff, and Rosenthal

> . . . measures accurately the length of time it takes the hammer to travel the last eighth of an inch before it strikes the string, and from this measurement the exact loudness of the tone produced can be easily calculated, 416 hundred-thousandths of a second being required to produce the softest

436

note and 51 hundred-thousandths for the loudest. About 60 times more energy therefore is expended in striking the loudest note than when producing a whispered pianissimo.[49]

John Farmer, who has been largely responsible for reviving interest in the Ampico piano rolls, adds that the instrument was so sensitive that it was "capable of measuring degrees of tone volume of one hundredth part of the minimum gradation detectable by the human ear."[50] That this means of reproduction, based to such a large extent upon duplicating hammer speed, was eminently successful is evident from the enthusiastic reactions of the performers themselves upon hearing the rolls played back to them on the reproducing Ampico piano. Listeners today can hear these same rolls activating a 1925 Grotrian-Steinweg grand piano fitted with an Ampico action—with resulting sound set down on high fidelity long playing discs. Denys Gueroult stated that in the twenties

> ... when the rolls were first issued, they were enthusiastically endorsed by the critics and the general public—and above all by the artists themselves—as absolutely faithful reproductions of the original performances. Concerts were given at which Cortot or Moiseiwitsch would perform a piece, and then the same work would be reproduced from the roll that the artist himself had made, so that direct comparison could be made. Rolls were played in which parts of the work had been left blank, and the live performer would fill in the missing bars. Responsible critics like Ernest Newman confessed themselves unable to tell when the man stopped and the machine took over. Testimonials in the most glowing terms poured in from every musician of note. Rachmaninov, Rosenthal, Godowsky, and Lhevinne all recorded and wrote eulogies on the result. Rosenthal called it "The only fully satisfying method of conveying my art to posterity"; Rachmaninov spoke of "Its absolute faithfulness;" Levitzki said that "It re-enacts the artist with unbelievable fidelity."[51]

It was the famous remark by Rachmaninoff spoken just after he had listened to the finished master rolls of his G minor Prelude and widely publicized—"Gentlemen, I have just heard myself play"[52]—that enabled Ampico to compete successfully with its already established and highly respected rivals, Welte & Son and the Aeolian Corporation.

"The Welte Legacy of Piano Treasures," a library of long-playing recordings based on piano rolls originally made between 1905 and 1920 by nearly all of the great pianists of that era, is now also available. Here too the Welte recording and reproducing system bears out the validity of the Ortmann studies in tone. Ben M. Hall, in the record notes, describes it "as a sort of monument to mechanical genius at the peak of its cog-wheeled, cammed and levered, pneumatic glory." He also details its operation:

The recording unit, connected to the Steinway in the *Musiksaal* (music hall), contained a roll of specially aged, thin paper, marked off into 100 parallel lines. Poised over each line was a little wheel of extremely soft rubber, with pointed edges. Each wheel was in contact with an ink supply, and in this much of the process it resembled a small offset printing press. Under the keyboard of the Steinway was a trough filled with mercury; attached to the underside of each key was a slim rod of carbon. As the key was depressed, the rod dipped into the mercury and an electrical contact was established between it and an electromagnet connected to the corresponding inked roller in the recording machine. The harder the pianist hit the key of the piano, the deeper the carbon rod would plunge into the mercury, and the stronger the current between the rod and the electromagnet would be. The harder the inked rubber wheel was pressed against the moving paper roll, the wider the mark it printed on the paper. The pianist's pedaling and speed of attack was captured in the same way.

After a selection had been finished, the paper roll was removed from the recording machine and run through a chemical bath to "fix" the colloidal graphite ink which had been printed on it by the rollers. This ink was electroconductive and when the roll was ready to play back, it was put into a master reproducing *Vorsetzer* which "read" the markings in almost the same way that a magnetic printing on bank checks is used in automated banking systems today. The *Vorsetzer* (it means "something set above or before" in German) however, made music as well as money.

Shortly after recording a selection, the artist returned to the *Musiksaal* and found the *Vorsetzer* "seated" at the piano where he had been playing. But nobody laughed when the Vorsetzer sat down at the piano. The results were astonishing. Extending along the front of the cabinet was a row of felt-tipped "fingers" (made the same length as a man's, from the wrist-pivot to the tips, in order to duplicate human touch), one for each of the piano's 88 notes; two more felt-slippered "feet" stood ready above the pedals. When the machine was turned on, the *Vorsetzer* re-created the ink markings into the pianist's own performance, with every pause, every shade of expression, every thundering chord. If the master roll was approved by the artist, it was then laboriously hand punched to translate the ink markings into performances in paper rolls which would have the same magical results when played on a standard *Vorsetzer* in a music lover's home.[53]

In returning to Ortmann's study, we can safely state that as far as touch is concerned in the production of a single isolated tone at the piano, the *one* and *only* direct physical control the pianist has over its quality is the speed of key descent and indirectly, the velocity of the hammer at the point of escapement. However, Ortmann forcefully emphasizes that still there are many complex factors affecting tone quality and the human personality's reaction to it. One of the most important of these is the non-musical sound which comes from the action of the instrument itself: the finger-key percussions, the hammer-string and key bed percussions, the numerous friction noises. They are all more substantial in amount than may be realized and vitally contribute to the composite tone quality—especially at the beginning of a sound. One need only block off a set of strings, then depress the related keys in order to evaluate the noise element. Other variables not under the pianist's management include the nature of the piano itself (the point at which the hammer strikes the string—between 1/7 and 1/9 of its length, the quality of the sounding board, etc.), the acoustics in the room, and the attendant problems of diffusion, reflection, interference, and resonance.

Also tone quality changes continuously as the sound dies away—the duration of the individual sounds which the pianist can control. But the greatest factor by far is the manner in which the pianist combines his individual tones. Ortmann is in full agreement with Harold Bauer when Bauer writes:

> I do not believe in a single beautiful tone on the piano. Tone on the piano can only be beautiful in the right place—that is, in relation to other tones. You or I, or the man in the street, who knows nothing about music, may each touch a piano key, and that key will sound the same, whoever moves it, from the nature of the instrument. A beautiful tone may result when two or more notes are played successively, through their *difference of intensity,* which gives variety. A straight, even tone is monotonous—a dead tone. Variety is life. We see this fact exemplified even in the speaking voice, if one speaks or reads in an even tone it is deadly monotonous. . . . Thus it is the *relation of tones* which results in a "beautiful tone" on the piano. . . . How can I play the piece twice exactly alike? I am a different man today from what I was yesterday, and shall be different tomorrow from what I am today. Each day

is a new world, a new life. Don't you see how impossible it is to give two performances of the piece which shall be identical in every particular?[54]

The pianist can change tonal quality with his unlimited ability to mix many or few sounds with an infinite number of degrees of loudness and sound duration. Various degrees of overlapping legato will also enrich tone quality. The employment of the different pedals on the piano will have the same effect. Ortmann explained the interaction:

> There are . . . certain physical phenomena beyond the direct influence of the player, the result of combinations of tones, which cannot be said to exist for the single tone. These are beats, summational tones, and differential tones. . . . It must be remembered that these new tonal elements are themselves possessed of only the three attributes, pitch, duration, and intensity, and that the intensity of beats and additional tones depends upon the intensity of each of the constituent tones. *Any change in tone-quality of any combination of tones is the result of a change in tone-quality of one or more of the constituent tones, which, in turn is the result of variations of intensity, pitch, or duration.*[55]

While stressing that there is no psychic quality in a pianist's finger which will mysticize a tone quality, Ortmann does not overlook the physiological and psychological sides of the listening experience. What the performer actually achieves at the keyboard and what the listener imagines he hears may differ greatly. All of the senses are involved in the listening process. Ortmann commented in *The American Mercury:*

> The auditor, since he does not experience the kinesthetic sensations of the player, cannot get the exact effect imagined by the player, except, perhaps, by the aid of the eye. Nor will the reactions of two auditors be the same. When such illusions are elaborated into the complex reactions to an entire composition or recital we have the beginning of an explanation of the curiously conflicting reports on the same performance: "Splendid! Best piano-playing I have heard!" "Rotten! So amateurish!"
>
> In music appreciation the eye is thus an important determinant. For doubters, especially if they are non-pianists, I suggest the following experiment: Attend a piano recital without knowing who is playing. See no printed programme. Listen throughout with closed eyes. Choose a seat in the rear of the hall. Let only unfamiliar compositions be played. Then

attempt to distinguish between relaxed and rigid tone production, flat and curved fingers, degrees of weight-transfer, religious and secular tone qualities,—or even between a Duo-Art and a Hutcheson.[56]*

Ortmann had intended to complete biological investigations in the area of piano technique, but never did. In 1967 he wrote:

I am very sorry that the Psychology of Piano Technique has never reached a satisfactory comprehensive level, for I am convinced that many of the apparent physical and physiological problems will find their explanations in the psychological field. My two books should be read and interpreted with this thought in mind. Years of experience in teaching have convinced me of this fact. At the present time my unpublished material is not available.[57]

Finally, Ortmann emphasized that the total quality of a person's playing, his own personal style is in a large measure determined by how dynamic and agogic variations, sound duration, and the noise elements are handled. The paths of physical movement at the keyboard will clearly reflect the control over these variables. Differences in style among different pianists playing the identical phrase of a piece will be indicated by correspondingly different lines of movement. In photographs Ortmann made, he found that "in no instance were the movements of two pianists exactly alike, and in every instance the variations were in keeping with the generally accepted version of the style of the particular performer."[58] The reader can profit greatly from studying the desirable movement characteristics of the best of the pianists whom Ortmann studied. In these cases there was always economy of movement. He also noticed basic movement curvilinearity "upon the path of which occur the finer movements of the hand or the fingers that actually produce the tones."[59] The regularity, the constancy in amplitude and manner of repetition in similar or identical patterns was very striking. The relationship between distance

*The Duo-Art reproducing piano was put on the market by the Aeolian Company in 1913 and its action was even installed in a number of Steinway pianos. Its piano rolls rivaled in sophistication of reproduction those by Ampico. The Duo-Art instrument, unmanned, actually appeared as soloist with the Philadelphia Orchestra with Stokowski conducting and the New York Symphony led by Damrosch. Ernest Hutcheson (1871-1951), the Australian concert pianist trained in Europe, came to America where he taught at the Peabody Conservatory and later became president of the Juilliard School of Music.

441

of lateral movement and intensity he formulated into a principle:

> Lateral movements of equal distance, other things equal, are conducive to tones of equal intensity, movements of unequal distances, to tones of unequal intensity. And, as a corollary: wide skips at moderate or great speed are associated with accent.[60]

In Ortmann, for the first time, we have a thorough study of the physiological organism and the various aspects of its movement at the keyboard based upon extensive laboratory experimentation adhering to sound scientific procedure. A solid body of technical truth is firmly established. Ortmann himself argued:

> Knowing the location of a muscle and its various angles of pull will readily prevent the assignment of impossible mechanical conditions; it will make possible correct muscular drill; it will aid in distinguishing normal muscular fatigue from the fatigue of incoordination; and it will economize in practice time and method.[61]

Throughout his research, the unity of the physical complex and the importance of each part operating in harmony with the whole are stressed. Physical coordination is related to musical objectives. It is affected by every change in tempo, intensity, and pitch. Practical conclusions must follow. For example, as previously stated, the muscular coordination of practice at a slow tempo is unlike that of performance at a fast tempo. And again, practice on a silent keyboard is useless in developing a fine applicable muscular coordination since this must base its adjustment upon a tonal image.

Another major accomplishment of Ortmann's work is its synthesis of the valid tenets from the conflicting historical schools of technical thought. Ortmann ruled out their excesses and found a meeting place on higher ground. He summarized:

> If the older school of pedagogy which insisted upon a rigid arm and quiet hand, erred on the side of too little movement, the modern relaxation school [Breithaupt *et al.*] errs equally on the side of too much movement. Wherever speed and change of direction are rapid, reduction in the inertia of the playing-mass to a minimum is mechanically desirable. And, conversely, wherever tone, tempo, and direction permit weight-transfer, the arm may advantageously be used, because it facilitates tone-control and reduces the undesirable elements of piano tone-quality—the impact noises—to a minimum.

442

In piano pedagogy, attention should be directed to both finger-action and arm-movement. Finger-action with quiet hand is just as necessary for the perfect execution of certain passages, as the addition of hand- and arm-movement to this action is necessary for other passages. The older school of pedagogy did not countenance the latter at all; the modern relaxation and weight schools have failed to give the non-weighted finger- and hand-technique its proper important place.[62]

Notes

[1]Amy Fay, "Deppe and His Piano Method," *Music*, Vol. 14, No. 6, October, 1898, pp. 578-88.

[2]*Ibid.*, p. 586.

[3]*Ibid.*, p. 588.

[4]Mrs. A.M. Virgil, *The Virgil Method of Piano Technique*, pp. 8-9.

[5]Howard Wells, *Ears, Brain, and Fingers*, preface.

[6]Letter to Arnold Schultz dated April 9, 1962.

[7]Letter to author dated September 9, 1967.

[8]*Ibid.*

[9]William S. Newman. "On the Special Problems of High-Speed Playing," *Clavier*, Vol. II, No. 3 (May-June 1963), p. 11.

[10]Otto Ortmann, *The Physiological Mechanics of Piano Technique*, p. 3.

[11]*Ibid.*, p. 7.

[12]*Ibid.*, p. 7.

[13]*Ibid.*, p. 12.

[14]*Ibid.*, p. 25.

[15]*Ibid.*, facing page 43.

[16]*Ibid.*, p. 55.

[17]*Ibid.*, p. 167.

[18]*Ibid.*, p. 130.

[19]*Ibid.*, p. 148.

[20]*Ibid.*, p. 181.

[21]*Ibid.*, p. 79.

[22]*Ibid.*, p. 82.

[23]*Ibid.*, p. 87.

[24]*Ibid.,* p. 100.

[25]*Ibid.,* p. 106.

[26]*Ibid.,* p. 112.

[27]*Ibid.,* p. 118.

[28]*Ibid.,* p. 120.

[29]*Ibid.,* pp. 120–21.

[30]*Ibid.,* p. 158.

[31]*Ibid.,* p. 225.

[32]*Ibid.,* p. 239.

[33]*Ibid.,* p. 259.

[34]*Ibid.,* p. 185.

[35]*Ibid.,* p. 197.

[36]*Ibid.,* p. 214.

[37]*Ibid.,* p. 283.

[38]*Ibid.,* p. 285.

[39]*Ibid.,* p. 289.

[40]*Ibid.,* p. 337.

[41]Tobias Matthay, *Some Commentaries on the Teaching of Pianoforte Technique,* p. 47.

[42]Otto Ortmann, "Tone Quality and the Pianist's Touch," *Music Teachers National Association Proceedings,* 1936, 31st Series, p. 128.

[43]Otto Ortmann, *The Physical Basis of Piano Touch and Tone,* p. 22.

[44]*Ibid.,* p. 26.

[45]Ortmann, "Tone Quality," p. 128.

[46]Ortmann, *The Physiological Mechanics,* p. 339.

[47]*Ibid.,* p. 340.

[48]Ortmann, "Tone Quality," p. 131.

[49]"Recording the Soul of Piano Playing," *Scientific American,* Vol. 137, No. 5, November, 1927, p. 422.

[50]John Farmer, "Josef Lhevinne on Ampico Piano Rolls," *The Juilliard Review Annual* 1966-1967, p. 28.

[51]Quoted in brochure accompanying the record series entitled *The Golden Age of Piano Virtuosi* and featuring Ampico Piano Rolls, issued by Argo Record Company, Limited, London, 1966.

[52]Farmer, "Josef Lhevinne," p. 27.

[53]Quoted in brochure accompanying the record series entitled *The Welte Legacy of Piano Treasures* and featuring Welte Piano Rolls, issued by Recorded Treasures, Inc., Hollywood, California, 1963.

[54]Harriette Brower, *Piano Mastery*, p. 97.

[55]Ortmann, *The Physical Basis*, pp. 135-36.

[56]Otto Ortmann, "Piano Technique in the Light of Experiment," *The American Mercury*, Vol. XII (Dec. 1927), p. 446.

[57]Letter to author dated September 9, 1967.

[58]Ortmann, *The Physiological Mechanics*, p. 368.

[59]*Ibid.*, p. 365.

[60]*Ibid.*, p. 367.

[61]*Ibid.*, p. 377.

[62]*Ibid.*, pp. 294, 296.

19. Contemporary Technical Thought

Otto Ortmann, through his research and his writings, laid a solid foundation upon which later piano technique could build. The first major theorist to become aware of this was Arnold Schultz (1903-1972). He quickly pointed out the significance of Ortmann's contribution and his indebtedness to the man in his own writing. Later he was moved to comment:

> In point of fact, I could not have written my book at all but for the fact that Ortmann had first written his . . . I am persuaded that the long backward look of the future will one day distinguish between the ante-Ortmann and the post-Ortmann eras.[1]

Schultz reminisced about his technical training and experimentation and the effect of the Ortmann encounter upon his own original thought:

> Despite the fact that my first serious training in piano technique was under the weight-and-relaxation dogma, I outwitted it and managed somehow to develop a considerable octave- and arm-technique during my high-school years. I was not, however, without pangs of conscience: I *knew* that my shoulder and elbow were fixed, sometimes very rigidly, during rapid octaves, but I found it impossible to forgo the musical effect in behalf of a theory that contradicted my deepest instincts. Similarly with finger-touches: although I practiced Hanon exercises an hour every day with full release of arm-weight, yet I played my Chopin etudes quite aware that I was tightening my wrist, my elbow, and my shoulder. Again, I did this not in the least defiantly, but with feelings of guilt and remorse—I felt I was somehow betraying my teachers even when the playing was going brilliantly and meeting with great public success. Apart from the technical training, I count myself fortunate in my teachers: Arthur Thompson (in the city where I was born, Winona, Minnesota) a teacher of subtle

musical conscience, a very able performer in his own right, and a pupil of Josef Lhevinne; Frederick Locke Lawrence at Carleton College, a fine musician and a warm and affectionate friend; finally, Gabriel Fenyves in Minneapolis, a Hungarian pianist of great ability and large experience who had worked with Bartók.

But if in private I felt myself to be breaking with the reigning ideas, I also in private, especially in my college days, began encountering variations in my finger-touches that distressed and baffled me. When passage-work came off with great speed, brilliance, and control, I was aware of muscular stress and strain centered in the palm of the hand; when it fell beneath this level, the palmar sensations were absent. I had no way of controlling them—before public performances I remember being virtually prayerful that they would appear. My first sharp *personal* interest in technical methods, accordingly, arose out of an effort to explain my finger-work—I had no problems about arm-technique.

I began with Matthay, but while he *described* the kind of piano-playing I was intent on, he brought me no closer to specific control than I had been before. My two years with Fenyves were pure Breithaupt, but this left me still further away from my goal. Moving to Chicago, I sought out exponents of the Matthay system, but I soon found that I knew more about what he had written than they did. Finally, I took what was for me the momentous decision of studying out the problem on my own without benefit of teachers.

I set out to understand the Authorities, and I submitted myself to them—after all, they had great and unquestioned reputations in the world. I submitted myself especially to Matthay—at one time I could almost have recited his "Act of Touch" from memory. His ruling dogma—and that of practically everyone else—was that the fixation of joints was absolutely impermissible. On such a first premise, of course, it was impossible to erect a consistent system of psychological mechanics, and I presently felt (though with great reluctance and dire misgiving—I was still a very young man) that Matthay and all the other authorities must be wrong about *something*. Unfortunately it didn't occur to me—I'm ashamed to confess it—that they were wrong about their very first premise of relaxation: like everyone else in my generation, I had been pretty thoroughly brain-washed. In the meantime, a number of years filled with an enormous amount of thinking and experiment had brought me no closer to an understanding of my palmar sensations than I had been before.

But help was on the way. At a gathering after a piano recital I played in southern Illinois, I picked up a current issue of the old *American Mercury* in my host's apartment and, casually thumbing its pages, came upon an announcement (not a review) of Otto Ortmann's *The Physiological Mechanics of Piano Technique.* Something about the announcement (I have forgotten exactly what—it may have been the very title) promised a new approach to the problem, and I could scarcely await my return to Chicago to get the book. I first had to order it. When it finally did get into my hands, I only had to turn over some of its pages and read only a few of Ortmann's calm, clear, unargumentative statements concerning verified *facts* of joint-fixation in good piano-playing to find that the whole relaxation dogma had suddenly gone up in smoke. Well, I hadn't altogether wasted the years I'd spent in my private cogitations about piano technique. I'd been up a great, great many bypaths of the problem, and once the relaxation dogma was gone, once I could accept fulcrummed movements proceeding from fixed bases, it took me no more than a half-hour to organize the mechanics of movements pretty much as I finally set them forth in the *Riddle.* In the meantime, of course, I still, in this half-hour of thinking, had no explanation of the palmar sensations that had been the main spur to my own inquiry. But I had been trying to explain them in terms of the mechanics of the movements (the almost exclusive concern of all theorists), and now that the mechanical problems had been set right for me by Ortmann, I realized that I must look elsewhere for the solution of my own problem. Then suddenly I knew that what I was concerned with were muscles, not mechanics, and that there had to be some special finger-muscles in the palm of the hand to account for the stresses and work that I had been feeling there. Not troubling with Ortmann further, I went down to the library at once, took a Grey's Anatomy off the shelf, and found the small muscles governing the first phalanges of the fingers exactly where I had inferred them to be. Ortmann of course considers these muscles, and I might have spared myself the journey had I settled down to read him at once. He happens not, of course, to have had any special concern with their co-ordination.

During all this time, of course, I hadn't had the faintest notion of writing a book about piano technique—I had only been trying to get things straight for myself. But after I had struggled with the pedagogics of small-muscle co-ordination, after I had seen the broken mid-joint stroke as the primary evidence of small-muscle dominance—a stroke plainly on

449

view in the playing of all concert pianists, and yet never acknowledged in piano-teaching (if anything, forbidden)—a publishing of what I'd found out seemed obligatory. I had an impulse, besides, to strengthen Ortmann's influence by writing in the field of reference he had created.[2]

Accepting the facts of joint fixation and the relative character of relaxation in fine piano playing, illustrated in Ortmann's research, Schultz went on to explore important aspects of technique with which Ortmann had not greatly concerned himself. Schultz's important contribution to the technical literature centers itself in two significant areas: (1) the clarification and evaluation of the various movement types used in all piano playing, and (2) a thoroughgoing study of the different muscular coordinations possible in finger technique. Such an analysis as the latter is unique in the entire literature and should be of great interest and importance to the piano student today. Schultz's thinking is embodied in *The Riddle of the Pianist's Finger*, a work which made its initial appearance in 1936, seven years after Ortmann's *The Physiological Mechanics of Piano Technique*. The two complement each other so well that they might be considered companion volumes.

Before defining the seven basic movement types, Schultz reviewed the playing units involved: the fingers, the hand, the forearm, and the full arm. When each unit is considered as a lever and capable of isolated movement (surely desirable for efficient piano playing), the matter of the base or fulcrum to which each is attached, and by which each is stabilized, must be of primary concern. The fingers play against the hand, the hand against the forearm, the forearm against the upper arm, and the full arm against the torso and even the entire body. In arriving at the movement types, both the type of force used to move the playing unit and the manner and degree of stabilization of the base must be considered.

Following is Schultz's organization of the basic movement types:

1. Weight movement—caused by weight alone.
2. Contra-weight movement—caused by muscular contraction with an unmoving base of weight.
3. Contra-pressure movement—caused by muscular contraction with an unmoving base of pressure.
4. Contra-fixation movement—caused by muscular contraction with an unmoving base of fixation.
5. Trans-weight movement—caused by muscular con-

450

traction with a moving base of weight.

6. Trans-pressure movement—caused by muscular contraction with a moving base of pressure.

7. Trans-fixation movement—caused by muscular contraction with a moving base of fixation.[3]

He considered a true weight movement to occur only when the lever falls unchecked or when its weight is partially retarded or opposed as it falls. All movement by muscular contraction, of necessity, is more or less influenced by the pull of gravity upon the playing unit, but this is of minor significance in the overall effect. If the base does not move vertically when the playing unit depresses its key or keys, we have a *contra-movement*—that is, the force stabilizing the base matches and offsets the upward reaction to the force which moves the playing unit. Where this downward movement of the playing unit is caused by muscular contraction, the muscles, which cross the fulcrum joint and connect the playing unit and the base, will pull equally on both. If the stabilizing force is overcome and the base moves upward, a *trans-movement* will result. Even when the playing unit moves downward by weight alone, the upward force of reaction will tend to dislodge the base. If the stabilizing force acting on the base is stronger than the force of the movement of the playing unit and the base moves downward, a larger playing unit is actually called into play.

The base may be stabilized in three different ways:

1. By weight—the pull of gravity upon the unsupported or partially supported base may be adjusted to match the force of the playing unit.

2. By pressure—the downward exertion of the muscles controlling the base will interact with the force of the playing unit.

3. By fixation—the antagonistic muscles that control movement in the base can control the strength of the base's stabilization.

In the first two, the base tends to bear down and rest directly on the playing unit. If the opposing forces are equal, no significant movement will be evident in the base. For each variation of tonal intensity caused by force variations in the playing unit, there must be a corresponding adjustment of the opposing force operating in the base or the base itself will be dislodged. Such is not the case where the base is set by fixation: the base is independent of the playing unit. In a series of contra-fixation movements, the strength of the fixation of the base may be maintained at a single level—strong enough to counter the reactions of the many minute force variations present.

451

All of the various movement types are evaluated for their effectiveness as touch forms. Musical criteria are always the measure: controlled key descents and the control of velocity, dynamic intensity, and legato. Schultz is continually concerned that all technical development contribute to musical performance.

Pure weight movement is only practical when the full arm is employed. Like Ortmann, Schultz pointed out that only a portion of its weight ever reaches the keyboard, the amount depending on the bodily posture. If the arm is forced down in any way, no true weight movement takes place. Key control is possible if the touch is prepared; if the arm starts from above the key, the speed of its movement must be increased when the finger tip touches the key. Legato can be achieved if there is a break at the wrist and, of course, there must be no independent finger movement. With a large moving lever, such as the arm, no great velocity is possible. The amount of speed is also determined by how quickly the shoulder muscles can retrieve the weight of the arm after each key depression. A large range of tonal intensity is possible when the weight or partial weight of the arm is employed.

Contra-weight movements are only practical where a small playing unit, such as the finger or the hand, is employed. The force of the muscular action can be balanced by the weight of the large base. The key descents are controlled since the touch must be prepared or the base will be displaced. Because in isolated movement the weight of the base must be continually adjusted, velocity and intensity control are greatly hampered.

Unlike pure weight movement where weight is released separately on each key descent, contra-weight movements can make use of weight transference, one of the touches which Breithaupt advocated. Schultz considered it "only rarely a legitimate touch-form in fine piano-playing."[4] In true weight transference there is a continuously released weight base. Two forms are possible: a complete transfer from key bed to key bed, or a graded transference from finger to finger. The first is slow and impractical. Contra-weight movements that employ the second form can achieve no real intensity variation except at a slow tempo and no velocity unless the fingers are used in a numerical sequence. In striving to achieve more velocity and intensity control, the student generally finds himself using trans-weight movement. He still falls short and also finds himself confronted with serious legato problems. Legato is one of the chief determinants of beautiful tone quality. The trans-movements tend to dislodge the base and make it move upward.

452

Weight transference can be almost entirely dismissed as a desirable touch form.

The pressure movements which Matthay termed "key-bed squeezing" were found to be even more undesirable than the contra- and trans-weight movements when measured in terms of legato, intensity, velocity, and key control. All that remains then are the fixation touches, and these the weight-relaxation school militantly opposed. Schultz summarized:

> The choice is definitely between the transference of weight or pressure, and acts against a fixated arm. Any general doctrine of relaxation must be on the side of the transference. The evils of weight-transference as just set forth are thus shown to be the evils of relaxation. And in the playing of those students whose attempts to follow the dictates of the relaxation doctrine have been at all successful, that is, who release weight continuously throughout a piece of passage-work, there are to be noted an insufficient velocity, an absence of subtle control over intensity, and a marked prevalence of trans-weight movements with, of course, the failure to produce a genuine legato.[5]

Schultz next explored the contra-fixation movements with the finger, hand, and arm considered in turn. In almost every way, when measured in musical terms, they are superior to the contra-weight and contra-pressure movements. Even the statement, "Contra-fixation movements of the arm are equal to weight-movements in the control of intensity which they afford,"[6] Schultz recently modified when he wrote:

> Were I to write the "Riddle" again, I should recommend levered arm-strokes practically to the total exclusion of pure weight-release. Where the arm is the playing unit, I think the former make for better key-control than the latter and that the exclusion of the latter makes for a greater consistency of style. Perhaps this would also be Ortmann's point of view today—perhaps both of us hesitated to break too rudely with a widely advocated touch-form of the past.[7]

The trans-movements, where the base is dislodged or moved upward after individual key descents of the playing units, Schultz believed to be the chief causes of technical inefficiency. These movements are always characterized by

> . . . first, the absence of control over tonal duration, expressed particularly in the absence of a pure legato; second, the absence of a refined control over tonal intensity; and,

453

third, the absence of the higher degrees of velocity—in other words, a fair catalogue of the results of poor technique.[8]

He did see a justification for the use of trans-fixation movements where considerable amounts of velocity and dynamic intensity are needed and particularly when a staccato touch is desired. When a trans-fixated base moves upward—when it is dislodged, it very quickly springs back to its original position by the strength of its fixation. The shift back and forth from contra- to trans-fixation movement is thus easily achieved. Muscular vibrato is nothing more than a rapid, intense form of this.

Another form of keyboard movement which both Schultz and Ortmann felt the weight-relaxation theorists overstressed is forearm rotation. Schultz believed that its easy and rapid execution in midair away from the keyboard has encouraged its popularity.[9] But when taken to the piano, the movement has very little ability by itself to achieve key depression. It must almost always be reinforced by weight or force from the arm and fingers. Schultz stressed too, much more than may be realized, that the movement is not confined to the radio-ulnar joint.[10] As more force and speed are needed, the full arm joins in the rotation or its rapid repetitive action, the vibrato. More energy is expended and, with the need to overcome the inertia of a larger playing unit, velocity is impeded. The rotary form is of legitimate, valuable usage in balancing weight on important fingers in chord playing and in the execution of tremolo figures when the distances are a fourth or a fifth or greater and the fingers are not close together.

In his significant study of the various possible finger coordinations, Schultz indicated that each of the finger phalanges is entitled to special consideration. He emphasized that "finger coordination is at once the most elusive and the most decisive factor of technical skill."[11]

The thumb has the least complex coordination to analyze. Only one possible muscular coordination in vertical movement is possible. Action is confined to the first phalanx in its joint near the wrist. In thumb-under movement, the flexor and extensor muscles act primarily upon the first phalanx.

A consideration of finger coordination must be based upon an understanding of the finger's musculature. Five sets of muscles are involved in finger action:

1. *Flexor profundis.* Its origin is in the ventral (under) side of the forearm and its insertion in the third (nail) phalanx.
2. *Flexor sublimis.* Its origin is also in the ventral side of the

454

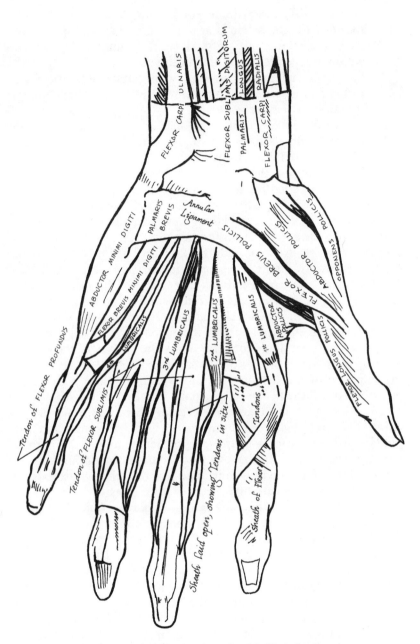

The Muscles of the Hand, palmar view. Modified after Gray.

455

forearm and its insertion in the second phalanx.
3. *Lumbricalis.* Its origin is at the base of the hand (palm) and its insertion in the first phalanx. It cannot be willed into action independently of the interossei.
4. *Interossei.* There are two sets, palmar and dorsal, similar in origin and insertion to the lumbricalis, but concerned mainly with lateral movement.
5. *Extensor communis.* Its origin is in the dorsal side of the forearm and its insertion in the nail phalanx. Its primary function is to lift the fingers.

Schultz grouped the two sets of flexors (they are never disassociated) and called them the long flexors. The lumbricalis and the interossei together are named the small finger muscles. He found that the three basic sets (long flexors, small muscles, and the extensor) are capable of seven fundamental finger coordinations.[12] Five criteria are used for judging their efficiency: degree of intensity, control of intensity, velocity, legato, and effect upon hand movements. Three coordinations are found to be impractical in achieving key depression and can immediately be discarded: *long flexors alone* (from a relatively flat finger position, the second and third phalanges, those closest to the finger tip, swing in the midjoint at a very poor angle for force along the surface of the key and towards the palm of the hand), *the extensor alone* (this is essentially the opposite of the *long flexors alone* coordination, with an impractical downward movement only possible when the finger begins its motion from an exaggeratedly bent position near the palm), and *small muscles plus extensor* (since the second and third phalanges begin from a nearly perpendicular angle, the outward and upward action of the extensor contributes nothing to key descent fully controlled by contracting of the small muscles). The remaining four have varying degrees of usefulness.

In the *long flexors plus the extensor* coordination, the two sets of muscles contract and pull on their tendons simultaneously, thereby stiffening the finger. The flexors then contract even more, moving the finger down into the key as a locked unit. The small muscles are easily bypassed in this coordination since the first phalanx is locked in with the second and third phalanges. The stronger flexor action renders that by the small muscles useless. This stiff finger coordination of the old school is called by Schultz the worst of all,[13] yet it is very common today. He suggested experiments[14] to show how even the relaxationists may use it in finger action and in supporting weight without realizing it. The ex-

456

periments also compare the *feeling* of relaxation with the *fact* of relaxation. Why is it so commonly used? Schultz said it must be because it is easier to lock all of the phalanges into a unit by the contractions of the antagonistic long tendons than to apply separate muscular pulls to each of the three phalanges.[15] While volume is easily achieved in this coordination, no fine sense of key resistance is possible or can be developed with it. In fact, the key seems to get in the way of the action. The higher levels of velocity are unattainable where the tendons of the long flexors are involved—a fact commonly overlooked. The long tendons extending across the palm of the hand cannot contract as the flexor muscles do. The "sag" in the palm of the hand from a quarter to half an inch (*more* than the depth of key-depression), create inertia problems, and thus slow down the finger action. Then too, tensions, which were so apparent in the old high finger school, develop at the wrist since the long flexors and extensor which pass across it must inevitably stiffen it as they simultaneously contract. When the fingers support hand movements with this stiff finger coordination, there also will be stiffening at the wrist and the hand movements will be greatly impeded.

A more desirable finger coordination is the *small muscles plus the long flexors.* Here each of the phalanges receives its own downward pull. The more natural position is with a fairly flat finger, but the position may not look unlike the stiff finger coordination. This again is testimony to Matthay's emphasis that muscular coordinations are invisible and cannot be judged from outward appearance. But it is likely in this coordination that the finger will not move as a locked unit. If the pull of the long flexors is greater, the mid-joint of the finger will tend to move up; if the small muscles dominate, the mid-joint may break or cave in. The intensity range is not as great as in the stiff finger coordination, but it is adequate for most finger work. And control over dynamic intensities is greatly improved since the muscles operate directly against the resistance of the keys and not against the opposing extensor. However, the fact that two sets of muscles are involved does hamper sensitivity. Velocity potential is increased; but, since the long flexors are still involved, there is some impending "sag." These same long flexors, contracting across the hand and wrist, will also set up some interference with hand movements.

A third available coordination is one involving the *small muscles alone.* In his excellent discussion, Schultz opened up a whole new technical dimension for today's pianists, most of whom are totally unaware of its existence and tremendous potential. Schultz has emphasized its presence in the technique of many of the great pianists. He has spoken of clearly viewing the broken joint of the fingers (a manifestation of the small muscle coordination) in the playing of Gieseking. Observers of Chopin's playing noticed a phenomenon in his finger technique that remarkably suggests this same broken mid-joint. William S. Newman at different times in his writing has called attention to Schultz's presentation and also has stressed the importance of applying the small muscle coordination to the light, rapid passage work found throughout Chopin's works.[16] Newman has called it "perhaps the most important of all advances in our understanding of high-speed techniques" and stresses that "every teacher has both a professional and personal obligation to study Schultz's valuable book."[17]

In this coordination the finger is propelled downward into the key solely by the small muscles pulling on the first phalanx. Schultz emphasized that there will be evident a slight extension of the finger as well as its downward movement. This is because the small muscles also have an insertion in the extensor tendon. As they contract there will be a slight upward pull on the second and third phalanges. The coordination may be employed from a rather flat finger or a decidedly bent position. Joint and key surface frictions are sufficient to hold the finger in the latter position and the long flexors need not be involved. The most marked outward visible manifestation of this coordination in the flat finger position is the broken mid-joint (a finger flattening or straightening out at the joint). A very slight break also occurs at the nail joint. When the coordination is employed in the bent finger position, these breaks in the joints will not obviously occur. The finger tip moves down quite perpendicularly; but, since there is also a slight degree of extension by the finger, a minute amount of forward friction will be felt at the key surface.

This touch restricts intensity of tone in the forte range. The small muscles are weak and their physiological endurance is also limited, but their use is of vital importance in piano technique. The finger tips descend perpendicularly into the keys, giving the coordination maximum efficiency. The finger is more sensitive to key resistance than in any of the other finger touches, and therefore capable of the most exacting control of dynamic intensity. This is the fastest of all finger coordinations—there is no displacement of tendons as found with the long flexors. Force is applied directly to the first phalanges. Also the small muscle coordination creates no tension in the wrist joint at all—the muscles only cross the hand-knuckle joint. The hand is at its freest.

Schultz was careful to present various pedagogical exercises which help the student to identify these various finger coordinations, since the outward appearance of both a desirable and an undesirable coordination may be remarkably similar. To gain something of the sensation of physical freedom that a small muscles coordination permits, he suggested the following: press a finger into the thigh without moving any of the finger joints. Then press again, but this time consciously break the mid-joint (the finger tip will move slightly forward). Now alternate between these two activities a number of times. Note the greater feeling of freedom evident on the ventral (under) side of the mid-joint when it is broken. Advance one step further: with the finger tip still pressing lightly into the thigh, but exerting no downward pressure whatsoever, let the fingers of the other hand gently break the mid-joint. The sensation of freedom on the ventral side of the mid-joint should be similar to that experienced when the small muscle coordination is in control at the keyboard.

After describing the sensations at both the mid-joint and at the hand knuckle in the small muscle coordination, and after giving suggestions for perfecting the touch, Schultz summarized the resulting sensations. He itemized seven of them:

1. Because of the absence of pull on the second and third phalanges the path of finger movement feels close to a vertical line.
2. Because of the fixed fulcrum the depression of each key feels definite, decisive, and controlled.
3. The keys feel heavy and the fingers exceedingly sensitive to their resistance. This is because the small muscles are relatively weak and because they apply themselves directly to the key-resistance.
4. The finger feels soft and pliable, and capable of great velocity. This is because muscular tension is virtually limited to the pull of the small muscles on the first phalanx.
5. The wrist feels light and ready. The absence of tension in the long finger tendons removes all sensation of heaviness and congestion.
6. The hand feels divorced from the arm. This is one of the most striking of all the sensations. The pull of the long tendons on the mass of the forearm having been eliminated, all work of key-depression goes on below the wrist-joint, the arm quietly standing guard, so to speak, over activity in which

459

it takes no part other than to provide a fulcrum. One theorist, who regards this separation between hand and arm as the most important determinant of velocity, supposes that it results from complete support of the arm at the shoulder. The problem, however, is scarcely so simple. As long as the finger tendons pull upon the arm, there obviously cannot be a feeling of separation between arm- and hand-activity.

7. Sensations of fatigue furnish the most convincing proof that the small muscles are performing the work of key-depression. Often these sensations amount to a sharp pain at the base of the hand where the lumbricales have their origins, often they are diffused over the whole palm, and sometimes they appear on the ventral side of the first phalanges. These locations vary not only from one student to another, but sometimes in the same student from day to day. Always, however, the sensations themselves are unmistakable. The fact that students without special training rarely feel fatigue at any of these points is evidence of the slight role which the small muscles ordinarily play when finger technique is left to unconscious adaptation. In each case in which I have induced the sensations, if only during the lesson hour, the student has exclaimed over a new capacity for velocity and key-control.[18]

Chopin and Gieseking had undoubtedly experienced the sensations of a fine *small muscle* coordination, as had Matthay and countless other sensitive musicians—even in the present day. Matthay tried to explain and systemize what he felt in his First Species touch, but fell short. It is with Schultz that we get the first adequate analysis of this remarkable coordination. He recently pointed out another evidence of its correct employment, writing:

I regret that as I wrote the book I had not yet perceived an easy way of checking up on the contraction of at least one of the small finger muscles, the interosseus operating the first phalanx of the second finger. It lies at the side of the metacarpus and attaches to the thumb and can be felt during an exertion of the second finger by the finger of the other hand. The difference in the amount of contraction between a broken mid-joint stroke and one in which it remains firm is rather dramatically on view (the testing fingers are pushed away by the contracting interosseus), and the view is a help in understanding and learning the coordination.[19]

Schultz listed yet a fourth possible finger coordination, one which modifies the stiff finger coordination to include the participation of the small muscles: *long flexors plus extensor plus small muscles*.[20] It has velocity limitations, and hampers activity in

460

the hand; thus it too should generally be avoided. Intensity control is fairly good, however. In this coordination the fixation caused by contraction of both the long flexors and the extensor is kept minimal and the key is then moved downward through small muscle contraction.

In delicate playing involving the small muscle coordination, the weight of the finger is so insignificant that the upward spring of the key is generally sufficient to raise the finger to the upper key surface level where it remains in a prepared touch until the next depression. But much of finger technique requires some activity on the part of the extensor. The extensor is used to work over the black keys and to pass the fingers over the thumb.

It needs to be understood clearly that the tendons which run to each of the fingers from the extensor are closely related. When one finger is pulled by the extensor, the others likewise feel a slight pull. (Ortmann frequently spoke of this interrelation and spread of muscular activity.) In order to keep the non-playing fingers from moving, the fingers are then very slightly fixated by an antagonistic contraction of the long flexors. This condition is prevalent throughout much of piano technique and does not constitute a specific finger coordination necessarily. But, when in this fourth workable finger coordination, it is present to a decidedly pronounced degree, it becomes an undesirable touch form. When the fixation is minimal, the undesirable features diminish greatly in degree.

Following the presentation of the various finger coordinations, Schultz considered the relative merits of the various finger positions. Basic to the discussion must be the realization that both good and bad coordinations may be similar in appearance and movement. A flat finger position must expend more energy for increases in intensity. It is advantageous for legato lines, especially for skips that occur in passage work or double notes and spread chords— there is greater finger spread. But too flat a finger increases tensions. A bent finger gives greater intensity with less energy output. Where detached-note touches are called for, it is particularly well adapted. It, too, is useful in the support of isolated chords. Wrist level is also an integral part of the whole problem. Generally it is well to strike a mean between the high and low positions. But modified extremes are both legitimate—the high supports force more efficiently, the low facilitates vertical finger articulation.

Like Ortmann, Schultz described the joints of the bones involved in piano playing and their characteristic movement patterns. Muscular activity was also studied. He pointed out that piano technique "must occupy itself with teaching correct movements and correct fixations rather than with the contraction of specific muscles."[21] His relaxation doctrine was based on Ortmann. In his last years he came more and more to feel that relaxation is as much a nervous as a muscular problem. He stated:

> Since writing the "Riddle," I have been working on problems of nervous as over against muscular co-ordination and hope to publish a book on the subject before I die.* Confusion between the two sets of problems has produced, I am convinced, much of the nonsense that has been written about piano technique. I regard the purveyors of this nonsense, to be sure, with much more sympathy than once I did, for they are intuitively right about many things that they were unable to define. The problems with which they sought to cope, moreover, were very formidable indeed. I see relaxation as first of all a nervous, not a muscular problem, and one of enormous importance. The theorists are to be respected for addressing themselves to the problem, and if they were confused about its nature, they merely repeated the confusion of the world at large. Unhappily, they brought their confusion to bear on a set of specific motor skills and I'm afraid there is no gainsaying the mischief that they wrought.[22]

Schultz enlarged on the psychological aspects of the relaxation problem in a footnote to his preface of Ortmann's treatise. He explained:

> My personal view is that though the weight-and-relaxation group said many incredibly foolish things, they were not, even so, fools. On the contrary, they were sensitive to problems that were at once very real, very difficult, and very important— problems in what I call nervous co-ordination—and their only mistake was to try to solve them in mechanico-muscular terms. The same mistake is being made today in areas far removed from piano-playing. Nervous strain, either sporadic or sustained, is something the piano-teacher almost constantly confronts in his students, and it is only natural that he should seek a way of treating it. The sudden release from strain certainly feels like a relaxation, but it is not a relaxation of muscles. One may feel an utter psychological relaxation without a hint of strain when his muscles are fixed in their maximal degree; and, *per contra,* one may feel strain—in-

*For thirty years Schultz worked in this area and recently completed *A Theory of Consciousness,* published posthumously in 1973.

deed, very great strain—in trying to relax his muscles.

Again, even the word "weight" can be given a psychological interpretation—if instead of reviving kinaesthetic sensations in memory during a movement, one feels them immediately with respect to the here-and-now muscular contraction, and if one is also in a state of nervous release, the sensations are of such a peculiarly thick and fleshy quality that they may easily be taken as a feeling of weight, this even though the movement they accompany takes place in a fixed joint. But these are matters that cannot be entered upon here. I only wish to say that the mere talk about weight and relaxation might conceivably have done some good if the student received it as a set of psychological meanings. But if he took it for what it actually said (and there must have been hundreds who did), then the doctrine was the sheerest mischief—the resultant physical inco-ordination could only have aggravated the nervous strain. Certainly this: real progress on the problem will never be made until the effort ceases to interpret nervous states in muscular terms.[23]

Schultz is not the only one who addressed himself to the psychological side of piano playing. Ortmann himself also did; but much remains to be done in investigating this area, even though piano teachers have long emphasized to students the importance of developing mental concentration and discipline in practice. Ferruccio Busoni, a classic example, remarked in 1910 that "Technique in the truer sense has its seat in the brain."[24]

But since the latter part of the nineteenth century, there has been a continuing serious attempt to understand more fully the mental and nervous processes as they are related to physical movement. European physiologists have led the way. Emil DuBois-Reymond (1818-1896) and Friedrich A. Steinhausen (1859-1910) both emphasized the importance of the central nervous system controlling the complex movements of piano playing. Gymnastics may strengthen the muscles for endurance, but can never develop the highest skills. In tests[25] in 1901, Oscar Raif determined the physiological limitations of individual finger action: the second and third fingers can make five or six movements per second; the other fingers only four or five. The ear can detect as many as twelve successive sounds per second—it is possible to play a trill that rapidly when more than one finger is involved. Here a highly refined nervous sytem orders a rapid succession of different finger movements. Others who have added to a rather sparse psychological-physiological literature adapted to the problems of piano playing include Willi Bardas *(Zur Psychologie der Klaviertechnik,* 1927)*,* Luigi Bonpensiere, and George Kochevitsky.

In 1953 Bonpensiere's *New Pathways to Piano Technique, A Study of the Relations between Man and the Body with Special Reference to Piano Playing* was published. In it he speaks of Ideo-Kinetics—"a transmutative process of the volitional motor acts through the diffraction of volition itself."[26] Rather extreme in bypassing all physical analysis, he envisions and strongly wills an act at the keyboard—"I imagine the act as if already performed—and lo! it is done. My hand did it, but I did not make any effort."[27] Later he advises one to "put down as a rule: *At every obstinate difficulty, stop playing and start thinking anew.*"[28] Ideo-Kinetics is further amplified by Bonpensiere in the following quotations:

> One can speak with authority about release only when the free flow of ideation finds immediate kinetic realization, without the least pre-occupation; when his hands, without the least mental push go about their business of scrupulous translation, just as though they were not his own hands (when they do not give him the least hint that they are any of his concern); when he feels sure that nothing can possibly go against this realization; when he feels not the slightest sense of fatigue; when he feels sure that finally he is at home in a world of sublimated laws, and when he is surprised at the past awkwardness of toil and its scope. Then he can speak with authority of having grasped the full meaning of release. Then, when his physiological practicing seems to be at the end of its resources, he can, by a deliberate act of ideation, declare his mental autonomy. . . .[29]
>
> Always keep in your mind . . . *Never think of your music in terms of execution (of what your hands and fingers should or are going to do) but in terms of interpretative rendering (what you would expect it to sound like if a performer from heaven were executing it for you).* This is the reason why you should never play for the sake of executing a passage. You play it only to see if your mental handling, refining, polishing and vitalizing has reshaped the passage to suit your taste. If not, take your hands off the keyboard and retouch it mentally with the carving and painting and repolishing tools of your mind until you are satisfied.[30]

This significant, philosophically oriented work deserves greater recognition. Bonpensiere's widow, Maria, stated that she and Georg Hoy, her co-worker in assembling the materials from her husband's notebooks for publication as *New Pathways to Piano Technique,* were the only persons to whom he conveyed his discoveries by word of mouth.³¹ Aldous Huxley wrote a glowing foreword to the book.

George Kochevitsky studied at the Leningrad and Moscow Conservatories and now teaches in New York City. In his *The Art of Piano Playing: A Scientific Approach* (1967), he briefly traced the historical theories of piano technique and then explored the structure and functions of the central nervous system and its involvement in piano playing. Sumner Goldenthal, M.D., in the foreword to the work, wrote of Kochevitsky's being influenced by Russian neurophysiologists and the Pavlovian school of reflexology, and then stated:

> While opinions from these sources are not completely shared by American neurophysiologists, it must be understood that the workings of the central nervous system are as yet far from being clearly outlined. Experimental results in all schools have a tendency to be conflicting. From this vast experimentation, however, scientists have drawn relatively firm conclusions on many aspects of voluntary motor activity, certainly to the point where the conclusions are applicable to musical performance.
>
> Mr. Kochevitsky has quite properly given a simplified explanation of the mechanism of the conditioned reflex and of the self-regulating processes involved in learning, the vast complexity of which would tend to obscure their application if rendered in even the approximate detail by which we now understand them.³²

In the Kochevitsky volume, practical suggestions are given for developing motor skills and velocity at the keyboard. The following is one practice routine which he suggests:

> Therefore, among several varieties of practice for finger articulation, the following is one of the best: first, fingers are prepared on the keys to be pressed. Each finger then presses with a light downward movement only, never leaving its key. (Thus the size of finger movement is equal to the depth of the key.) And playing proceeds very slowly, pianissimo, with the whole attention concentrated on fingertips. The downward movement of one finger must be synchronized with the movement of the preceding finger as it lets its key rise. At the slightest sensation of fatigue in the upper parts of the arm, this practicing should be stopped. (It is rather hard to hold the weight of the forearm without support.) By experimenting, the proper balance will be found, so that longer sections and eventually a whole study or piece can be played in this way. Such practicing is tiring to our central nervous system, as it

requires finest tonal control along with control over the accompanying sensations, and this is especially hard in pianissimo. But the consequence of such practicing is a feeling of strength in the fingers. This result would be surprising to the representatives of the old finger school. Of course it is not muscle, but nerve command over the fingers that is being strengthened![33]

After these digressions, we return to complete our summation of Schultz's contribution. In considering tone quality, Schultz was very conscious of the psychological reaction the listener undergoes. In June, 1967, he wrote:

Again, I followed Ortmann in my book in denying that there can be a difference in the quality of a piano tone independent of its intensity. I have no doubt at all that measured by an objective instrument the upper partials giving the tone its characteristic quality change only as the intensity changes. But today I would say we react to a sound also with our nervous systems, which are quite different affairs from objective instruments, and that different modes of nervous reaction cause us to hear different qualities of sound, and even by empathy the quality of sound that a given performer hears as he produces it. But if I say that the Hess sound was different from the Horowitz sound, I don't feel myself to be retreating from Ortmann's objective instruments into mysticism—I still wish to remain as rational as he in assessing the complicating factors that appear on the subjective pole of the hearing experience. But this is to hint at things rather than to say them, and to say them I should have to write a book that concerns many other things besides hearing—indeed, besides piano-playing.[34]

Besides backing Ortmann, in the chapter on tone quality in *The Riddle of the Pianist's Finger*, Schultz dwelt upon the great importance of mastering a fine legato and gaining the most refined intensity control. An unsatisfactory legato is not always detected and the effect it creates is easily construed as poor tone quality. He wrote:

The moment of union between two tones of different pitch constitutes a high aesthetic pleasure, an instinctive craving being satisfied when a given vibrational rate is merged with, or—to put it metaphorically—is born out of, another vibrational rate. The singer who failed to connect his tones would rob his audience of much of the pleasure they might otherwise have in the beauty of his tone.[35]

A series of intensity deviations in a phrase line can also be interpreted as poor tone quality. Percussive noises at the piano can be minimized by prepared key attacks and, especially where longer time durations are involved, holding the keys down for the full, exact length of time. Schultz placed a great premium upon such workmanship. In 1963 he wrote:

> The artists who are as constantly sensitive to the endings of their tones as to their beginnings, who in passage work are as intent upon the evenness of the hammer attack form for me a somewhat limited aristocracy of pianism—Horowitz, Schnabel, Kapell, Hess, Gieseking, and Glenn Gould are some names that come to mind.[36]

Finally, Schultz saw a strong interrelationship between his touch system and the development of a beautiful tone quality. The latter is best secured through controlled key descents, contra-fixation movements, and the predominant use of small muscles. Schultz constantly judged technical movements and coordinations by their ability to produce fine, musical performance—their control of tonal intensity, degree of intensity, sound duration, and velocity. At the end of *The Riddle of the Pianist's Finger* he added another—physiological ease. But he felt that this should always be the last to be considered. He pointed out[37] that the movement types which give the greatest endurance are those which also produce the poorest kind of piano work. This does not deny the employment of the largest playing unit compatible with the necessary velocity. In the following chart, Schultz has tabulated the contra- and trans-fixation movements (he also admitted arm weight movements), listing numerical sequences in which they favor velocity, intensity, and endurance.

Trans-fixation movement is only admissible where the gain in intensity does not cause the velocity level to drop below that possible by the use of the next largest playing unit. Wherever possible, endurance should be promoted and fatigue avoided. Tension should particularly be reduced as much as possible at the hand knuckle and mid-joint. Relying more on the small muscles and less on the long flexors and extensor, even in hand and arm movement, is one of the most effective means of diminishing and avoiding it. Fixations should always be kept at the lowest possible levels. Extreme fatigue should never be permitted. The student should look for frequent resting points in the music, withdraw force from the key bed where practicable, and be economical in the use of dynamic intensities.

TABLE I

Playing-Unit	Contra-fixation	Trans-fixation
Finger operated by small muscles alone......................	1	....
Finger operated by small muscles plus long flexors............	2	3
Finger stiffened and operated by long flexors.................	4	5
Hand..	6	7
Forearm plus upper-arm rotation...........................	8	9*
Whole arm..	10	11

INTENSITY

Playing-Unit	Trans-fixation	Contra-fixation
Whole arm...	1	2
Forearm plus upper-arm rotation...........................	3*	4
Hand...	5	6
Finger stiffened and operated by long flexors.................	7	8
Finger operated by small muscles plus long flexors............	9	10
Finger operated by small muscles alone......................	....	11

ENDURANCE

Playing-Unit	Weight	Trans-fixation	Contra-fixation
Whole arm..	1	2	—3
Forearm plus upper-arm rotation....................	....	4*	5
Hand...	....	6	7
Finger stiffened and operated by long flexors........	....	8	9
Finger operated by small muscles plus long flexors...	....	10	11
Finger operated by small muscles alone.............	....	....	12

*Forearm only.

38

Schultz devoted the final four chapters of *The Riddle of the Pianist's Finger* to thorough critical analyses of the works of Matthay, Breithaupt, Leschetizky, and Ortmann. Schultz himself said that his own method is "an amalgam of Matthay's formulations and Ortmann's research."[39] Explaining his reason for including these chapters, Schultz told the Music Teachers National Association Convention in December of 1936:

I have always believed that if all the piano methods could be brought together under one tent, a great deal of good might come of it. I could not, of course, collect all the methods. But I have collected three of the most influential ones, the Leschetizky, the Matthay, and the Breithaupt, and one rather less influential and more recent one, Mr. Ortmann's. My opinions of these works, stated very quickly, are: that Leschetizky did not tell enough, that he remained uncommitted on many elementary and essential aspects of the whole truth, but that errors in physiology and mechanics plunged him into absurdity; that Mr. Breithaupt tried to tell something that wasn't true, and told it very badly. Mr. Breithaupt, by the way, is the only writer on technique towards whom I feel a quite unreserved pianistic hostility. Finally, I included the critique of Mr. Ortmann's work with the main purpose of publicizing it more widely. The book is the classic of the field, and should be almost as much a part of the piano teacher's stock in trade as the instrument on which he teaches.

I should like to close this very partial survey of my book with a plea for greater interest in technical analysis. Technical treatises, cast as they are in scientific language, may often seem very difficult, but they are not invincibly difficult. I know of no class of people, moreover, more distinguished for self-discipline and persistence than are instrumentalists. I am convinced that if some of this discipline and persistence were transferred from the keyboard to an intellectual consideration of technical processes, a great deal of time could be saved, and the cause of first-rate pianism greatly advanced.[40]

Another strong voice on the contemporary American technical scene is that of Abby Whiteside (1881-1956). While possessing a high regard for Ortmann and his analytical research, she made her own observations outside of the science laboratory and throughout the world of nature—wherever physical skills were in evidence. She was a student of anatomy and body mechanics; she observed carefully the graceful, skilled movements of athletes in many fields:

469

dancers, jugglers, musicians (classical pianists and others, such as orchestra men, conductors, jazz pianists), and anyone else so engaged. She firmly believed and taught that a vital, all-encompassing rhythm (see definition, page 472) is the basic coordinating factor involved in building an effective technique. This rhythm must be the basis for musical continuity and beauty of interpretation. Such a rhythm will also express itself in physical continuity of movement and flow. Throughout her teaching career (Miss Whiteside's students included such outstanding musicians as Arthur Whittemore, Jack Lowe, Norman Lloyd, Morton Gould, Vincent Jones, Joseph Prostakoff—president of the Abby Whiteside Foundation, and many others), she applied such observations to the development of piano technique.

Abby Whiteside was a native of South Dakota where she received her music degree with highest honors at the University of South Dakota. Then after teaching at the University of Oregon, she went to Germany in 1908 and became a student of Rudolph Ganz. Later she returned to Portland, Oregon. From 1923 on, she taught privately in New York City with summer instruction frequently in other American cities, including Los Angeles, Dallas, Portland, Chicago, and San Francisco. Much of this teaching was sponsored by institutions like the Eastman School of Music, Mills College, the University of Chicago, and New York University.

Miss Whiteside's views on piano technique evolved through the years by experimentation in the studio and in her own practice at the piano. She considered an early work, published in 1929 and entitled *The Pianist's Mechanism, a Guide to the Production and Transmission of Power in Playing,* to be an outmoded, incomplete expression of her technical thought. Yet certain of the basic tenets expounded in her major book, *Indispensables of Piano Playing* (1955), are visible, at least in embryonic form, in the 1929 volume. In *The Pianist's Mechanism,* she wrote:

> The pianist's problem is to produce a phrase-line that has all the simplicity as well as the grace, balance and charm of the instruments whose tone is produced by a steadily flowing current of breath or the bow. Probably much of the struggle to find simplicity is due to the fact that a fluent finger-technique sufficed for the harpsichord and clavichord. The tradition is still present that if an independent finger-action is developed in Bach most of the difficulties in piano-playing will disappear. But consider the demands of those old instruments. A feather would almost suffice to depress the keys and the scale

of dynamics was very limited. In addition, the distance from one end of the keyboard to the other was appreciably shorter than on the keyboard of the piano, so that from the point of view of distance as well as of application of power, the forearm, used from the elbow, was quite equal to all demands. All that is changed in the modern piano, yet in great part we learn to play with the same material and in the same manner.

What would happen if we began with the requirements of our present-day instrument? Just this: at an early stage of his studies the talented student would secure with ease the speed and quality which would no longer be the exclusive acquirements of the so-called prodigy, who by good fortune had progressed in a straight line because his application of power was entirely right from the beginning. Only the right way is ever easy. The fluency of the boy who plays jazz from the beginning is an example. What he desired demanded chords and octaves all over the keyboard; so technique was acquired with the large muscles instead of with the small ones.

Is it reasonable to expect the master's consummate ease at the piano when the daily routine of practice never glimpses it? One might as well expect perfection in the technique of swimming from daily golf-playing. The mechanism used in daily practice at the piano is not much more nearly related to the actual perfection of the master, in many instances, than are those two sports.

The qualities of the piano that are undesirable for the student to imitate are heard far more frequently than the qualities which make the piano a beautiful medium of expression. That he may guard against wrong impressions, the common faults of much of the piano-playing he is exposed to are listed below:

A separate application of power is used for each tone. This interrupts the flow of the phrase, not in degree but in the same manner, as the sentence would be interrupted by taking a breath between each word. The power is relaxed and the intensity of the arm is changed after each motive. This ruins the dynamic line of the structure as a whole, and frequently is the cause of strain in fast playing.

The power drives too deep, below the level of the key-bed. This is a waste of energy and tends to break the phrase-line.

The small muscles in the hand and forearm are allowed to furnish part if not all of the energy for tone. The motive energy should always be furnished by the large muscles.

The hand and forearm take the control of placement, of finding the key. There should be lateral finger-spacing for

471

chord-formation in the hand, but the control of lateral progression of the playing mechanism belongs to the shoulder-joint.[41]

Joseph Prostakoff, Miss Whiteside's longtime associate, recalled:

Certainly there is at times some similarity between certain expressions in the two books, but they are related only superficially. What was always present, from 1931 to 1956 (the years during which I knew her and worked with her) was her concern with the upper arm and what it did. But, there really was a world of difference in her teaching over the years of the role it played; it was a process of endless refinement, as well as total alteration. At first (that is—when I first came to her) the wrist was not supposed to have any flexibility at all. The upper arm just about did everything, and the fact is that even then she was able to provide many students with a much more brilliant and unlabored technique. There was another stage where the torso was the initiator and pushed into the keyboard gently. Then, the torso pulled. Later on, it was the arms that pulled (the essential physical implementation of a rhythm). The torso responded to the emotional mood of the "basic rhythm," or "fundamental basic rhythm," or "fundamental rhythm," described the physical response by which the upper arm, in its reaction to the torso's activity, projected into sound the rhythm of form of the music.[42]

Abby Whiteside planned to present technical principles that had crystallized since the completion of *Indispensables of Piano Playing* in a study of the problems involved in the execution of the Chopin Etudes. She considered these pieces to be at the very heart of her teaching and of all successful piano performance. Recently Joseph Prostakoff and Sophia Rosoff have gathered together and edited her thought on the technical mastery of these etudes and other miscellaneous essays and comments in a volume entitled *Mastering the Chopin Etudes and Other Essays* (1969). A valuable foreword by the editors unifies and summarizes with great clarity the entire Whiteside approach to technique.

Essentially, she felt that the aural image of the music and a fundamental rhythm should completely control and define one's physical technique at the piano and also the musical elements of a fine interpretation. Such an approach would overcome the common evils of piano playing. In 1951 she wrote:

The music student should begin by playing by ear. He must

472

learn to read, quite obviously, but he should be an aural learner rather than a visual learner. Observe the ease and accuracy of pupils who have learned to play by ear. Their skill is never attained by those who learned the notes first and then built up a coordination that is dependent on the eye. Notes, after all, are merely symbols for sounds. The pupil who has learned music by the way it sounds hears the tone when he looks at the symbol. The movements that make this imagined tone audible are directed by his ear. They are as fluid, as efficient, as co-ordinated as his movements when playing without notes.[43]

Fine jazz pianists have naturally followed this plan and exhibit "a tune in their ears and a rhythm in their bodies and they let these two elements fuse by using nothing else as they learn their instrument."[44] No serious student can expect to achieve a beautiful performance and an adequate technique without following suit: he must *feel* the rhythm and he must *listen* to the sound he is producing—and he must let these guide his every movement.

A large portion of Whiteside's writing is concerned with emphasizing the importance of this all-encompassing rhythm and in describing the manner in which it manifests itself in physical activity at the keyboard. There is no true rhythm—it can never be developed—without physical activity. She said it "stems from the point of resistance to the application of power"[45] and can be clearly observed in the push-offs and gliding movements of the ice skater. Although none transferred this physical activity as effectively to the keyboard, without a doubt Miss Whiteside finds herself corroborated here by the teachings of influential figures in elementary music education, such as Émile Jacques-Dalcroze (1865-1950) and his disciple Carl Orff (1895-   ), Maria Montessori (1870-1952), Zoltan Kodály (1882-1967), and by the writers of present-day piano method books, including Bernice Frost, Faye Templeton Frisch, Frances Clark, and Robert Pace. They all advocate complete bodily physical activity in the child's rhythmic development. Too often these rhythmic physical manifestations are repressed or inhibited in the student's later technical study at the piano.

The great modern dance authority José Limón also stressed the basic importance of rhythm and the dance to the musician. He said, "I have always maintained that musicians are dancers, and that dancers can be good dancers only when they are also good musicians."[46] Emphasizing that the dance has been called "the matrix of the arts" and that from the beginning man has had "that supremely instinctual urge and capacity to dance," Limón under-

473

scored its universality in human experience and its presence in even the most profound music of J.S. Bach:

> Let me ... only point to that supremely choreographic composer, that incomparable dancer of the spirit, J.S. Bach. He dances not only in his French suites, and English suites, and partitas and sonatas for the various instruments, with their chaconnes, minuets, courantes, sarabandes, allemandes, gigues, and other dance forms, but he could not and did not exclude the dance from the cantatas and oratorios. Dance, as you know, is of all kinds and categories. There is a dance for every single human experience. What, may I ask, can we call the impassioned procreative act; what else but dance is the convulsion of birth; what is the perpetual delight of infancy and childhood but a dance; and what of the frenetic rituals of adolescence; and the sober solemnities of maturity, the weddings, academic processions, inaugurations, coronations, funerals; what are these but the dances with which we are conceived, are born, grow, live and die? All this is dance, both profane and sacred. Bach contains it in all his music, whether secular or religious. He was irrepressively a dancer. Embedded in the cantatas, the oratorios, among the chorales, the arias, and the recitatives, placed there with the most consummate mastery of drama and theater that compels you with the irresistible kinesthetic impetus which is dance.[47]

In Abby Whiteside's teaching an all-encompassing, long-line rhythm moves down through the music for the pianist outlining the phrases and pointing up the form. It gives a feeling of flow and continuity of movement and tends to interrelate each note to every other one. Without it, a sense of timing in performance and the "spacing between tones which produces a phrase that is breathtaking in its beauty"[48] are impossible. She observes that this fundamental rhythm is especially noticeable in an orchestral performance. The first-chair men can be spotted immediately "by their swaying bodies as well as by listening to their lilting phrases."[49] The powerful impact of rhythm is felt, too, by the concert pianist performing a concerto; he is swept along by the orchestra's rhythm and "his entire output is changed."[50] But left on his own the pianist does not have the benefit of the singer's breathing, the violinist's bow arm, or even the skater's balanced activity to force him into a long-line phrase procedure and a compelling rhythm in his body. He must use full arm and bodily participation in order to achieve such a rhythm.

474

But Miss Whiteside had a word of caution for every musician. Prostakoff wrote:

> There was a period in the early Thirties when she thought that a violinist or a singer might have less physical conflict in producing a long, sinuous, musical line. In the late Forties, I recall her saying that every musician, no matter what instrument he played, if he were trained to be notewise in tone production, managed to find some way of interrupting the physical flow of phrase-by-phrase performance.[51]

Accepting the axiom that piano tone can be varied only in loudness and time duration, Abby Whiteside said that, if the pianist's emotion during performance is not involved in the continuity of the upper arm's action, it will be directed to the vertical action of key hitting and a note wise performance will result. If the pulling action of the upper arm will be the channel for emotional satisfaction, a basic rhythm, directly affecting subtlety in timing and dynamics, will result. Such movement will never display undesirable mannerisms. She wrote: "Mannerisms which intensify a feeling for the phrase rhythm will regulate the intensity of feeling for dynamics. . . . Then it is that a fusion will take place between the rhythmic line and dynamics; and only then can performance reach the heights of emotional expression."[52]

The functions of the various members of the body involved in rhythmic movement are considered. The torso itself frequently must bounce and dance to the music. At other times it will serve as the fulcrum for activity by the arm. The upper arm or top arm, as Abby Whiteside terms it, is responsible most of all for a phrasewise rhythm. Because of the circular joint at the shoulder, it possesses a continuity of movement which easily spans a phrase-line. The upper arm while so engaged controls key drop, and supplies power for the most important tones "as it strides from one important tone of the phrase to another."[53] In between these tones it may act as a fulcrum for faster movements by the forearm. Throughout all this activity, it exerts a continuity of pull at the shoulder joint which coordinates all smaller movements. Miss Whiteside felt that "only when this pull of the top arm is actively involved in sharing the production of all tones can full speed and power be achieved without overburdening of small muscles."[54] The upper arm should also be in control of horizontal placement (key finding activity) at the keyboard as well as being the deter-

475

miner of the vertical level where energy is released in the production of tone.

The forearm, largely dominated by upper arm activity, has certain primary functions of its own. She stated that it is "the natural implement for a fast repeated action and its action is the central control for fast articulation. Its repeated action is always associated with the action of hands and fingers. That is, the hand and fingers operate inside its repeated action—while it is going on."[55] This alternating action between forearm and hand (which seems to bear some resemblance to Breithaupt's longitudinal oscillation) and rotary action, Miss Whiteside feels to be "the truly master mechanics for speed with brilliance in piano playing"[56] and should be given far greater attention than the development of an independent finger action.

Her great concern was that the fingers not assume functions not rightfully theirs. She said that incorrect use of fingers—reaching for any key with the fingers or using them primarily to supply hitting power—is at the heart of persistent technical difficulties. The fingers are merely the periphery of the playing mechanism; the center of the radius of activity, rather than the periphery, should largely control both horizontal and vertical activity at the piano. The fingers transmit, not initiate, the power. Miss Whiteside wrote: "In this matter of vertical distance, try everything first—before fingers. Then let the fingers come in as it were to extend to the activity of the larger levers. By no means let them usurp responsibility for the vertical keydrop."[57] Prostakoff has added:

> Incorrect use of fingers did not mean, especially, reaching for the key with the fingers, but any reaching for any key or using fingers primarily to supply hitting power. I can see where this might seem almost nonsensical. She taught that while the finger does do something, it was good teaching technique to stress that it was the upper arm which did 100% of the work; the forearm, hand, and fingers, were used to transmit the power of the upper arm.[58]

The burden of her message is that the old traditional finger teaching excluded adequate participation by every part of the body rightfully concerned with piano playing. Rhythmic phrase-line movement thus became an impossibility. In correcting the evil excesses of the older "finger-gymnasts," she virtually ruled out the legitimacy of all pure finger action and adopted an almost Breithauptian point of view. She did admit its possibility however: "Certainly a single trill can be played with fingers and beautifully played.

476

It is to be observed in use by many artists."[59] But nowhere did she give instruction for the development of specific muscular finger coordination. The feeling is that if the total body mechanism is functioning in a blended coordination, the fingers cannot help but function properly and do not need specific training. Her teaching on technique is well summarized in the following quotation:

> But *cooperation, not independence of action, by hand, fingers and forearm must be what is practiced—not individual controls*—if cooperation is believed in and desired, and is to be the *result of practice.* It is exactly this point which is basically unsound, in my opinion, in traditional training. Tradition believes in training levers for independent actions. The result is simply independent action—not cooperative actions. That is not nature's way of creating an expert coordination.[60]

Prostakoff wrote of the problems he found arising from individual finger training and insufficient cooperation:

> This is one of the primary points with which I have difficulty both with new students and with all the people with whom I correspond. It is so difficult—almost impossible—to accept such a concept when one hasn't *sensed* playing without really being aware of what fingers are chosen or that the fingers are doing anything at all, except being alert. Words, alone, are completely inadequate for transmitting this sensation. A person trained in the principle of finger development really finds it impossible to conceive of playing in such a manner. Here is something which is pertinent: Abby Whiteside said that nature provides a natural economy so that if fingers do the work the arm will not, if the arm does the work the fingers will not. The tendency of fingers to reach for the key and to do most of the work of striking it is so natural, even before finger training, that it is very difficult for a pianist to apply Abby Whiteside's theories at the keyboard, without supervision, or even to notice that the fingers are working more than necessary. The bulk of my work in the early stages of teaching a student consists of making him more aware of what he does physically, because without this there is no hope of changing any of his playing habits. This, really, is one of the hardest nuts to crack; I am inclined to think it is impossible to solve without some direct work with a student of Abby Whiteside. What happens at best is that the reading of the book stimulates a pianist to look for paths which are different from those he had used in the past. . . .
> . . . But, the essence of her teaching is that either there is a coordination which is dominated by the large lever (upper arm) and this coordination, to be completely expert, must

always operate (even in the softest playing), or this coordination is not efficient and operative when there is the slightest concern with independent action. The fact is, one of her favorite images was that if you had to remove a sliver from a child's eye you would not just use, say, the first and second fingers, or just the fingers. Both the arm, the entire body, for that matter, would be keyed up, alerted for the all-important delicate task. Again, note how a person moves when he is trying to enter a room without awakening someone who is asleep. . . .

. . . All our teaching [including his teaching associate, Sophia Rosoff] is predicated on the use of the small levers to *transmit* the physical activity of the upper arm into sound. This is operative whether the music is brilliant and loud, or the most delicate, wisplike adagio.

I would like to emphasize the importance of the last sentence, by saying that a good number of my own pupils are graduate musicians who in many cases have studied with well-known and even famous pianists. It is only by ridding them of the finger-training habits and substituting the coordination of a basic rhythm that I enable them to acquire a greater virtuosity than they ever possessed or even hoped to possess, and a much more subtle musical line.

This is not so much a personal boast as a statement concerning the effectiveness of this approach.[61]

The case which Abby Whiteside built in *Indispensables of Piano Playing* for total bodily involvement and interrelated action is a brilliant one and should be of great interest to the piano student. And the powerful roles of rhythm and the aural sense in guiding the technical development are also masterfully expounded. The tradition she spoke of was wrong in that it permitted excessive fixations and placed an undue burden upon the smaller playing levers. And no doubt it did not advocate sufficient cooperation among the members involved in tonal production. But it still must be considered, as Arnold Schultz and others might add, that an individual playing movement is most efficient in terms of control over velocity, tonal intensity, and legato when its lever, the finger, moves independently under its own muscular power against a fixed base that exerts no influence upon the lever. This surely does not preclude the base itself from engaging in long-line horizontal and even vertical movement to control keyboard placement, from feeling the rhythm or phrase-line development or even from becoming the playing lever itself in order to supply the extra power for the more important tones in the phrase line. There must be a

478

sense of full and appropriate cooperation among all of the members. With this last statement, Ortmann, Schultz, and Miss Whiteside would have agreed.

A list of contemporary writers on piano technique has to include the names of such Americans as Ernst Bacon, Guy Maier, William S. Newman, and Ruth Slenczynska. Bacon, born in Chicago in 1898 and educated at the University of Chicago, is composer-in-residence at Syracuse University where he has been active as conductor, pianist, and administrator. In addition to winning Pulitzer and Guggenheim awards in composition, he is the author of *Words on Music* (1960) and *Notes on the Piano* (1963). The latter work is divided into five sections: "The Performer," "Technically Speaking," "The Learner," "The Player and Writer," and "The Observer." Bacon writes from a strong empirical point of view. The book turns out to be a "Poor Richard's Almanac" for pianists. Note a portion of his introductory remarks:

> The piano is my point of departure. I go out from it into music, and then again return to the piano, laying on it the parental burdens of the art. The piano has stout legs, and will outlast many disparagements.
> Music is full of secrets. They may be shared by many, yet sparingly told. If you intend to do a great or beautiful thing, it is best you remain silent about it until it is done, for who but yourself could know what is involved? It is a good superstition to keep your plans under wraps, the more so the better they are. I intend to divulge no secrets, but will speak much of working habits, listening habits, playing habits; and hint at profitable devices for self-encouragement, even for advantageous self-deception, in the business of learning. . . .[62]

Bacon points out numerous practical solutions to technical problems. He emphasizes that pianists are, in a sense, dancers at the keyboard and must exhibit grace in all their movements. Of basic consideration to the pianist is the fact that

> The hand being wholly irregular, while the keyboard is precisely regular, the controlling of the latter by the former calls for the subtlest accommodation. *Weakness and strength must be equalized, or else utilized for unequal ends.* There is no object in attempting, as some of the older technicians did, a full equalization of the fingers in their innate strength (as, in particular, trying to make the fourth finger as strong as the third, or as free as the second).
> From the beginning, the hand should study how to achieve a balance between its members. It must move enough to help

the fingers, yet not so much as to impair their close tactility. The kind and degree of movement is determined, apart from the hand's accommodation, by the music—its tempo, its dynamics and its phrasings. By and large, the hand and the arm come into use in proportion as the musical pattern is open and extended.

It is the limp hand that feels its way best into the keyboard, extends and retracts most easily, tries the least, plays the softest, leaps the highest, looks the best, maintains a silent orientation with the least watching, and is capable of instantaneous resort to power.[63]

Guy Maier (1892-1956), after studying at the New England Conservatory and with Artur Schnabel privately, engaged in two-piano work with Lee Pattison. He was on the Juilliard faculty from 1933 to 1946, after which he went to the University of California in Los Angeles. He was best known for the workshops he conducted throughout the country and for the articles, many in question-and-answer form, which he wrote for a number of years for *The Etude*. Lois Maier made a selection of these and compiled them in *The Piano Teacher's Companion* (1963). Always writing in an engaging, sometimes humorous style, he did much to encourage high standards and to solve technical problems in an easily understood manner. Maier wrote, with his typical light touch:

> One item has, I think, been cleared up beyond all doubt; that is the matter of basic pianistic tone production. After you have examined "The Riddle of the Pianist's Finger," the scientific works of Ortmann, the interesting treatise by Levanskaya, the excellent book by Thomas Fielden, Matthay's volumes, and all the rest—if then you are still in your right mind, you come to the conclusion that there are a few simple, easily understood principles to work from.[64]

But Maier, whose teachings have been propagated by the Maier Musical Association, did not imply that touch can be achieved in a haphazard, unintellectual manner. He wrote:

> It burns me up to hear well known artists state that methods of tone production are not important, dismissing the whole subject with, "The way you play doesn't matter—the only thing that counts is the results." Oh yeah? And when the result is ugly, constricted and painful alike to pianists and auditor, what are you going to do about it? Where place the blame? What, pray, causes bad tone, insecurity, lack of speed and endurance, poor rhythm—but false tone production?

Call it quantitative instead of qualitative if you like, but don't blame it on anything but the pianist's approach to his instrument. There are good, sound ways of playing—but also poor, faulty ones. Artists with exceptional ears and pianists blessed with out-of-the-ordinary muscular response often produce excellent results in spite of faulty methods. Is that any reason why harmful methods of tone production should be foisted on the overwhelming majority of students who do not possess either natural facility or outstanding talent and who can learn to play well only if they are taught a logical, thoughtful, well coordinated approach? Indeed, most people do not find piano playing a cinch. Obviously, our Maker did not have piano playing exclusively in mind when he created us. Moreover, most of us have ordinary brains, ears, arms and fingers, and find that the processes of growth and maturity hinder rather than help the development of good piano playing. In other words, we need to be unremittingly on our guard against excessive muscular contraction, as well as mental inflexibility. Like you, we find that we cannot trust blind (or dumb) instinct in playing or teaching. And, as you put it, we crave to know what makes the wheels go 'round.

Unlike your experience I have yet to find a single student who became tense when clearly shown sound methods of tone production. On the contrary, the results invariably lead to decreased tenseness in playing as well as markedly increased concentration in practice.

Here are a few points to emphasize:

1. No tenseness before tone is made; instant release as soon as tone is heard.

2. Floating elbow; arm poised over piano like a gently moving paint brush.

3. Rotary forearm freedom resulting from this light elbow tip.

4. Contact with key top before making tone; swift, relaxed, lightly "flipping" preparation over each tone cluster to be played.

The "pure" touches are two, up and down. For up touch, hand and elbow are held quite low; tone is made by delicate upward and outward push of elbow (not by wrist or finger). Amount of tone, from *pp* to *ff*.

For down touch, hand and elbow are held high (finger tip touching key top always); tone is made by letting whole arm move into the key (wrist does not sink, sag or pull down before, during or after making the tone). Amount of tone for pure down touch, *pp* to *p* only.

Other touches are variations of these—the full arm

481

rebound, full arm dip, forearm rebound, "snapped" finger, quick percussive finger, rotary finger, and so on. Someday I'll take a whole page to try to clarify these for you, but I despair of doing it, for illustration and guidance "in the flesh" are indispensable.

And don't let anyone fool you by saying: "Bosh! What is the use of all that nonsense? The best it does is to make you feel better, but in reality the results are no different. . . ." Whereupon, you, with becoming modesty, will ask, "Oh, please, isn't that enough? If I feel so much better when I play, won't the improvement in my rhythm, phrasing, security, ease, smoothness, endurance, control, in fact, my whole attitude toward the piano, justify taking the pains? And wouldn't all that tend to improve the quality of my tone?"[65]

Without a doubt, the best introductory book that can be placed in the hands of the serious piano student, and especially a college piano major, is William S. Newman's *The Pianist's Problems* (1949). The material is arranged in four broad categories: musicianship, technique, practice, and performance. A later edition (1974) includes two chapters on methodology. Nine steps are carefully set down and then detailed for learning a new piece. Sight reading procedures are also outlined, with Newman (1912-) using Leonard Deutsch's *Guided Sight Reading* as his point of departure. Dr. Newman's summary of technique, built solidly on Ortmann and Schultz, is a most useful and lucid one. He is chairman of piano instruction and director of graduate musical studies at the University of North Carolina. Born in Cleveland, Newman studied piano with Arthur Loesser. Today he is one of the country's foremost piano pedagogical authorities and musicologists. His monumental three-volume *A History of the Sonata Idea* is a landmark in the literature.

In 1973 Ruth Slenczynska (1925-) celebrated the fortieth anniversary of her concertizing debut. Her first appearance as an eight-year-old was an impressive one. The chief critic from the New York Times, Olin Downes, characterized the young pianist as "the greatest piano genius since Mozart." Since then she has matured to become one of the world's great artists. Miss Slenczynska's own prodigious technique has been built, not only on understanding, but upon a tremendous sense of dedication and discipline. At present she is artist-in-residence at Southern Illinois University, Edwardsville. Her book, *Music at Your Fingertips,* is thorough, clear, down-to-earth in its suggestions of practice routines that build solid technical equipment and musicianship. She wrote:

A musician cannot give a good performance unless he can forget about his instrument. Technical mastery should not be considered an accomplishment in itself; it is the *sine qua non* of a virtuoso, the lowest rung of the ladder, the basic necessity, the starting point.[66]

Even when we practice scales the sound can be beautiful. We must never forget the infinite variety of tonal shading we are able to produce, the variations of touch, of which there are thousands.[67]

Numerous foreign technical treatises are also available today, largely in original German, Russian, French, and Italian editions. Following in the tradition of Liszt, the Hungarians Béla Bartók, Ernst von Dohnányi, and József Gát have made important technical contributions to pianists everywhere. Bartók (1881-1945), a brilliant performer in his own right, was not unlike Prokofiev in his contribution to contemporary piano literature and technique. The music is characterized by biting dissonance, driving rhythms, explosive accents, and frequent staccato or martellato touches. But it is not without romantic warmth in its frequent use of melodic lines based on the Slavic folk idiom. Because Bartók was a fine pianist, it is eminently playable. If ever a pianist needed full arm and bodily participation in his technique, it is in the music of Bartók, with its quick wide skips, many large chordal and octave passages, and détaché touches.

For a livelihood, it was necessary for Bartók to teach piano nearly all of his life. Erno Balogh, who for six years studied with him at the Academy in Budapest, described his manner of teaching:

The essence of his approach as a teacher was that he taught music first and piano second. Immaculate musicianship was the most important part of his guidance and influence. He clarified the structure of the compositions we played, the intentions of the composer, the basic elements of music and the fundamental knowledge of phrasing.

He had unlimited patience to explain details of phrasing, rhythm, touch, pedaling. He was unforgiving for the tiniest deviation or sloppiness in rhythm. He was most meticulous about rhythmical proportion, accent and the variety of touch.

Bartók insisted on first solving the musical problems and then the pianistic ones. In fact, he was not deeply interested in pianistic problems. He had a natural technique and although he was recognized in time as a virtuoso, virtuoso problems did not interest him.

All Bartók students naturally copied his playing style,

although it had a limited dynamic scale, was not effortless and did not exhibit *"Spielfreudigkeit"*, which is perhaps the most captivating element for the general audience. I refer to the type of playing in which neither the listener nor the player is conscious of details of execution, but the whole performance gives the impression of such spontaneity that the composition seems to be created right at that moment.[68]

Another outstanding Bartók exponent and former pupil, concert pianist Gyorgy Sandor, has written along somewhat similar lines:

It would be difficult to describe the piano teaching method of Bartók, because he had none. He was very active as a pedagogue, has written a number of "study" pieces (they all turned out to be masterpieces, too), has edited the entire W.T.C. by Bach, the Mozart Sonatas, a number of Beethoven Sonatas, etc., but as far as piano technique goes, he recommended "practicing". How? That was up to you. Just as well, since his own mechanical equipment was so much "sui generis", that he developed a technique that suited *him*. Needless to say that most of his pupils (and he had many, during the 28 or so years he was professor of piano at the Liszt Conservatory) had mimiqued knowingly or unknowingly his technique, but this usually turned out to be more or less a caricature of some of his mannerisms. This happens most of the time when people are under the influence of a strong individual, that Bartók certainly was.

Difficult passages had to be "practiced", that was all. However, he played most everything and showed *his* way, how he would play the piece . . . His only concern was the music itself. And there, of course, he had a lot to say. To use a crude analogy, I remember distinctly that listening to his interpretations of Bach, Beethoven, Mozart, Schumann, Liszt, Debussy et al, I had the feeling as if the wrappings, the covering of the works had been eliminated—one heard, sensed the piece as it ought to be, not the way one knew it before. The inner meaning, the structure and above all, the creative drives were everpresent, the music was fermenting. Nothing was stereotyped, according to formula, but individually shaped, molded in a most convincing manner. By the way, his technique was simply spectacular. . . .

In his polite, reserved manner, whenever I played a piece for him, he inevitably said "This is fine, Mr. Sandor", then sat down, played it through—and changed practically every note of the performance, for the better, of course . . . Only very seldom did he stop at the first statement.[69]

Bartók biographer Serge Moreux speaks of "a transcendent sense of phrasing" in his playing that may have for some lacked intuitive spontaneity. Bartók had a magnificent gift for expounding the form of a work in his playing. Moreux quoted Constantin Brailoiu as saying:

> He dismembered the musical argument piece by piece, laying its most tenuous articulations bare, like an X-ray which under the flesh illuminates the delicate details of the skeleton. Thus, in his hands, illuminated in depth, over-familiar masterpieces were born anew and as if heard for the first time, as if by some magic spell.[70]

When Bartók made his first public appearance at the Academy of Music in Budapest in 1901, the reviewer remarked about his "steely, well-developed technique" in the Liszt B Minor Sonata. He went on to say "In fact, he is *today* the only piano student at the Academy who may follow in Dohnányi's footsteps."[71] That he had early developed into a concert pianist of the first rank is evident from a letter which he himself wrote after a December 1903 appearance in the Bechstein-Saal in Berlin:

> The very significant Dec. 14 is over: my first real job of clearing accounts in the course of a concert. What I most feared—that my strength might not be equal to it—didn't happen; after the concert I was so little tired that I could have played another program from beginning to end. The Study for the Left Hand went splendidly; the greater part of the public were most impressed by this. The hall was quite 2/3 full. . . . Two 'celebrities' were in the audience, Godowsky and Busoni. The latter came to the artist's room after the third part, introduced himself, and congratulated me; he had already heard about me in Manchester, from Richter. My compositions, especially the Fantasy, pleased him very much. I heard the same about the others: he expressed admiration that I, who have such a fine left-hand technique—as he heard in the Study—still played the Chopin C-minor Etude so satisfyingly. . . After the 3rd and 4th parts there were encores (my own composition and the Juon Humoresque). . .[72]

Bartók's *Mikrokosmos* (1926-1937), 153 studies on an elementary to intermediate level of difficulty based to a large extent on the Hungarian folk music literature, is without a doubt the most important series of piano studies written in the modern era. In 1913 Bartók collaborated with Sándor Reschovsky to produce the *Bartók-Reschofsky Piano Method,* a valuable beginners book—but with little verbal technical explanation. Bartók's contribution was a set of eighteen elementary pieces entitled *The First Term at the Piano*.

Ernst von Dohnányi (1877-1960) studied at the Budapest Academy of Music, and from 1919 until 1945 was its director. He also led the Royal Conservatory of Music in Budapest. Displaced by World War II, he followed Bartók to America in 1949 where he taught at Florida State University. Dohnányi added significant works to the pianist's literature, including his *Essential Finger Exercises for Obtaining a Sure Piano Technique* (1929). In its preface, Dohnányi presented his philosophy of technical development:

> In music-schools tuition suffers mostly from far too much exercise material given for the purely technical development of the pupils, the many hours of daily practice spent on these not being in proportion to the results obtained. Musicality is hereby badly neglected and consequently shows many weak points. The fault lies on one side, that the pupils are not taught to practise properly, and on the other hand, that far too many studies and exercises are given from which only little value can be gained, whilst not enough time is left for the study of repertory pieces. A few show-pieces are usually repeated to excess, as they are needed for public production, whereby the teacher's reputation is generally more benefited than the pupil's progress. Correct sense of style can however, only be furthered by a sufficient knowledge of musical literature.
>
> Therefore, before all else the amount of studies ("Etudes") must be reduced and this can be done without harm if they are replaced by such exercises which, in lesser time, bring forth the same benefits. *Finger-exercises* are preferable to studies ("Etudes"), if only for the reason that they can be practised from memory, and consequently the whole attention can be concentrated on the proper execution, which is most important.
>
> The preparatory degrees are not considered here. Beginning with the middle stages, a judicious choice of studies by Cramer and Bertini suffices; later, a selection from Clementi's "Gradus" with the subservient exercises, is sufficient for obtaining a reliable technique. Everything else—even Czerny, is superfluous; it does not contain anything of essential importance which might not be acquired through finger-exercises, or by conscientious practising of appropriate passages of pieces. The Etudes by Chopin and Liszt belong of course to the category of concert-pieces, and play a role as important,

for higher and highest stages, as Bach's Two and Three Voiced Inventions in connection with Bertini and Cramer, and the Well-tempered Clavier with Clementi.

Thus, by diminishing the amount of studies ("Etudes"), time is won for repertory music, and this time can be utilised still better, if only *some* of the pieces ("concert-pieces") are practised up to finishing stage; concerning the larger number of pieces, the teacher should be satisfied as long as they are played by the pupil in a clear and efficient manner. In the long run the pupil will benefit by this.

A *wide* knowledge of musical literature can only be acquired by sight-reading. I cannot sufficiently recommend pupils to start early with sight-reading: piano- as well as chamber-music. I do not mean playing a piece once through, but to play it several times, so as to become well acquainted with it. It may be argued, that this must lead into superficial, untidy ("sloppy"), amateurish playing. The disadvantages of much sight-reading can be balanced by stricter demands put to the pupil, in regard to the performance of "concert-pieces", and to the execution of studies and exercises. Much sight-reading has however advantages, which are unfortunately not sufficiently considered. Independently of the great advantage of a wider knowledge of musical literature, thus acquired, the sense of style is improved, and it is also of use, in regard to technique, for the deftness and the surety of the fingers are increased.

The less time spent on purely technical studies, the more important it is to practise with full concentrated thought. It is absolutely useless to practise exercises in a thoughtless, mechanical manner, especially when the eyes are riveted on the music. When playing, even the simplest of finger exercises, the full attention must be fixed on the finger-work, each note must be played consciously, in short: *Not to practise merely with the fingers, but through the fingers with the brain.*[73]

József Gát (1913-1967) also taught piano in Budapest at the Royal Academy of Music in the studio where Bartók had instructed him. In 1958 Gát first published his *The Technique of Piano Playing* (*A Zongorajáték Technikója*). A second, greatly revised edition appeared in 1965. While the work is detailed and musical in its coverage of technical problems, it lacks the coherency and authenticity that a thorough knowledge of both Ortmann and Schultz might have brought. Gát does not seem to have been aware of either. Gát's basic terminology is somewhat difficult to grasp. Throughout

487

he made much of a direct and an indirect swing-stroke which he discussed in part in the following manner:

The factors of the swing-stroke

The swinging motion—to which we shall in the further course of this study apply the term "swing-stroke"—involves three factors:

1. A firm basis, 2. an elastic support, 3. an actively swinging unit for executing the swinging motion, subsequently referred to as "active unit."

1. A firm basis is attained by an appropriate position of the body; this involves a good music stool (or bench) and correct posture. (In some athletic sports a firm basis is of similar importance. The shot-putter, the discus-thrower or the boxer would be unable to give an adequate performance on loose, marshy ground, not to speak of an upholstered, springy mattress.)

2. In piano playing, the whole body functions as an elastic support. (Our body is always in an elastic state when working.) The rebound of the keys is unnoticeably absorbed by a series of elastic joints. . . .

Our whole body takes part in absorbing the rebound. It is therefore of great importance in piano playing to use the feet as a means of elastic support. Misinterpretation of this fact is at the root of the incorrect view that the feet play an *active* part in sounding a note.

3. In order to cause the hammer to strike, it is essential to execute an active swinging motion—the swing-stroke—starting from one of the joints. . . .

The two kinds of swing-stroke

The hammer can be brought into motion by the *direct* or *indirect* swing-stroke.

In the direct swing-stroke, the finger clings to the key, which is brought into motion as an elongation of the arm. The pianist has the sensation of practically grasping the key and by means of this hold playing directly with the key. (Many of the faults arising later could be prevented by making the children during the first months of their beginners' course play the clavichord instead of the piano. This method would not only eliminate the contrast between the fragile little fingers of the child and the clumsily functioning piano keys, but would once and for all show the beginner the right way of handling the key). This sensation of "grasping the key" is fully experienced only when playing from the shoulder joint.

488

The shoulder joint is, however, incapable of very fast movements for which we have to rely on the forearm or the fingers. Active work on the part of the fingers or the forearm, however, makes the direct swing-stroke inapplicable because the contact with the key becomes interrupted already at the beginning of the movement. The time-span of the contact will be abbreviated also by the fact that the fingers—in striving to display more energy—are forced to strike from a greater height. Thus—although the direct swing-stroke is the most perfect method of sounding the note—we have to apply (and even very often) the indirect swing-stroke also whenever our finger cannot "merge" with the key but strikes it.

In comparing the direct and indirect swing-strokes we may state the following:

Direct swing-stroke

1. The movement of the arm (active unit) accommodates itself to the movement of the key in order to keep the sensation of grasping and elongation.

2. The finger remains constantly in contact with the key.

3. The movement of the key is accelerated gradually, because it is in contact with the active unit from the very beginning of the movement.

Indirect swing-stroke

1. The finger or forearm (as active swinging unit) cannot accommodate itself to the fixed direction of the key's movement.

2. The finger has no contact with the key at the beginning of the movement.

3. The active swinging unit has already attained considerable speed at the moment of meeting the key. This will cause a sharp upper noise (on account of the inertia of the key). The collision will at the same time disturb the sureness of the strokes and therewith also the apportioning of the tone volume and the dynamic contours.

The most noteworthy drawback of the indirect swing-stroke is that the finger has no contact with the key at the beginning of the movement. Some methods try to eliminate this by restricting the active work of the fingers, which are made to touch the keys even when it is not their turn to strike. They thus give the impression of being able to execute a direct swing-stroke, too. As the finger is in contact with the key already at the beginning of the movement, the objections made under points 2 and 3 above are invalidated, but full accommodation to the direction of the key's rotation is impossible just

489

the same. In addition, we also loose the extra energy gained by the increased movement and muscular activity of the fingers. The result may be loss of velocity and inability to maintain the tempo due to the comparative weakness of the finger muscles. Moreover, we should not renounce the tone-colouring effects attained by raising the fingers to different levels.

Thus the use of the indirect swing-stroke proves to be unavoidable, but we have to find the means of bringing it as near as possible to the direct swing-stroke and of reducing its drawbacks to a minimum. For this purpose we should raise our fingers or arm only as much as is absolutely necessary for producing the desired tone colour. In addition, we should endeavour to make the active swinging unit accommodate itself as much as possible to the fixed rotation of the key; we should, therefore, slow down and brake its movement. This braking acquires special importance through the fact that to accomplish it more muscle work is required, necessitating more intense and resolute nerve impulses. The deeper the musical experiencing of the tones, the stronger the resulting nerve impulses will be, and thus appropriate braking is, in the last analysis, also a function of the musical concept.[74]

He also spoke much of "weight-effect" (not to be confused with the traditional meaning of "weight") and "the synthesizing process." He summarized them briefly in these italicized quotes:

The counterbalancing of the rebound of the key and the variation of the elasticity of the support in proportion to the force of the rebound complements the work of the active swinging unit and renders it more reliable. As the player has the sensation that this occurs with the aid of the weight of the arm or the body, respectively, it is called "weight-effect," or "weight-complement."[75]

The apportioning of the weight-effect—which means the alternating of the resistance by large musical units (e.g., a musical thought the size of a half-period)—is called the synthesizing process or in short: synthesizing.[76]

Included among the chapter headings are "On Finding Contact with the Instrument" (with a sub-section on "The Interrelation between Musical Imagination and Muscle Action"), "On the Naturalness of the Movements," "Slow Practicing of Fast Playing," "On the Role of the Various Joints," "Structure and Form of the Hand," and various forms of specific keyboard technique. An interesting selection of gymnastic exercises away from the keyboard is included. A fascinating feature is a series of photographs, scat-

490

tered throughout the book, of the hands of great pianists—from Chopin, Mendelssohn, and Liszt to those of the present day. Sequential, isolated frames from filmstrips of Annie Fischer, Sviatoslav Richter, and others playing passages from specific classical works are also shown, but their actual practical value is somewhat questionable.

Technical thought and assistance for the contemporary piano student is also available from numerous miscellaneous sources. In recent years, technical exercise collections by Carl Roeder, Ernest Hutcheson, Olga and Leon Conus, Geoffrey Tankard and Eric Harrison, Rudolph Ganz, and others have been widely used. Stimulating articles may also be found in present-day periodicals for pianists: *The American Music Teacher,* the official journal of the Music Teachers National Association; *The Piano Teacher,* founded in 1958 and absorbed in 1966 by *Clavier* (begun in 1962); the scholarly *Piano Quarterly,* which was started in 1952 by Mary Vivian Lee; and *Piano Guild Notes,* the publication of the influential National Guild of Piano Teachers, founded in 1929 by Dr. Irl Allison. Piano workshops and seminars have never been more numerous or widespread than today. Fine master teachers may also be found on college and university campuses and in private studios throughout the country.

A survey of contemporary technical thought cannot be complete without including some mention of the avant-garde and the experimental in piano music and with the instrument itself. Physical technique is inevitably affected. With the music of Ravel, Prokofiev, Bartók, Stravinsky, and such Americans as Copland, Barber, and Schuman, conventional technique, depressing as many keys as fingers can manipulate and involving as much full body strength and movement as can be summoned, has been pressed to its ultimate on the conventional piano, scarcely unchanged since Liszt's later years.

And yet composers have demanded more from the instrument. In his desire to have more keys played simultaneously than the hands can manage, Charles Ives in his *Concord* Sonata (1909-1915) had the pianist use a long piece of wood to depress the keys. This was only a forerunner to the work of the most important tone-cluster specialist, Henry Cowell (1897-1965). Cowell was brought up in California and on March 10, 1912 gave his first recital in which he performed *The Tides of Manaunaun,* a work which featured left arm tone-clusters covering an entire two-octave span. (See music and explanation, pages 492 and 493.) Other compo-

1. The Tides of Manaunaun

Story according to John Varian

Manaunaun was the god of motion, and long before the creation, he sent forth tremendous tides, which swept to and fro through the universe, and rhythmically moved the particles and materials of which the gods were later to make the suns and worlds.

For explanations and playing instructions
see inside back cover.

Henry Cowell
(1912)

492

Explanation of Symbols and Playing Instructions

The symbols 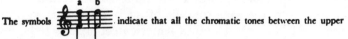 indicate that all the chromatic tones between the upper and lower tones given are to be played simultaneously.

Whole notes and half notes are written open, as in symbol "b"; notes of other time-values are written closed, as in symbol "a".

A sharp or flat above or below such a symbol indicates that only the black keys between the outer limits are to be played, while a natural in the same position indicates that only the white keys are to be played.

This rule is to be followed irrespective of key signatures, since the tones within such a cluster of tones are not affected by the key. Only the outer tones, the highest and the lowest, must conform to the key signature.

The tone clusters indicated by these symbols are to be played with the forearm, with the flat of the hand, or with the fist, depending upon the length of the cluster. All the tones should be played exactly together and the pianist must see to it that the outer limits of the clusters are absolutely precise, as written, and that each tone between the outer limits is actually sounded. In legato passages, the keys should be pressed down rather than struck, in order to obtain a smooth tone quality and a unified sound.

The forearm should not be stiff, but relaxed; in most cases, its weight is enough to produce the tones without the need for adding muscular effort. The arm should be held in a straight line along the keys, but if the arm of the pianist is too long, it must be partly dropped off the keys at an angle to give the proper length.

The symbols × and + indicate the use of the fist. When playing in this manner, the wrist should be relaxed, with the fist half-opened, not clenched tightly. The tone quality produced by the fists is different from that produced by the fingers.

If desired, the melody tones may be brought out with the knuckles of the little finger in the playing of clusters.

The symbols ♦, ♦, ♦, etc., represent a silent pressing down and holding down of the key in order that the open string may be subjected to sympathetic vibrations. Tone clusters to be played in the manner indicated by the above symbols will be written: , etc.

The use of the forearm, the flat hand, and the fist is introduced because the fingers alone are incapable of playing the many notes of the cluster, harmonies.

sitions followed which called for action by the flat hand and fist as well. Cowell's recitals in America and Europe, in the 1920s, aroused intense interest and stimulation wherever he went.

Harold Schonberg cited the coverage given one of his New York recitals by a sports writer. The headline shouted: KID KNABE VERSUS BATTLING COWELL.[77] It was the Knabe piano that took Cowell's blows. He nonetheless commanded the respect and won the sponsorship of such musicians as Bartók, Schnabel, and Janáček. The first American composer to be invited to Russia, Cowell was so well received that a number of works were published there about 1928—including *Tiger*, as percussive and heavily "note-clustered" as one could imagine.

But Cowell was not content just to strike the keys. He also went to the insides of the piano and played directly on the strings. *Aeolian Harp* (1923) is a hauntingly lovely and gentle miniature in which the keys involving certain chords and individual tones are silently depressed by the left hand so as to raise the dampers. The right hand then either sweeps across the strings in glissando fashion or plucks individual strings. In *The Banshee* (1925), not only are the strings plucked but the fingers are stroked along them longitudinally creating an eerie sound. Nicolas Slonimsky commented, "Everyone who has heard his weird glissandos, interpretative of the ghost of his Irish ancestors, 'The Banshee,' rendered directly on the piano strings, will admit that as a new orchestral color it is an undeniable acquisition."[78]

Cowell has also written many fine formally constructed works and his interest in the folk song has influenced such American composers as Aaron Copland and Roy Harris. His experimentation with the piano inspired others to follow after him—to name a few: Toshiro Mayuzumi, Alan Hovhaness, Lucia Diugoszewski, and John Cage. Cage is the most notable of those to tire of the conventional sound. An interviewer for *The New Yorker* magazine in 1945 described his exposure to Mr. Cage and his innovations:

Mr. Cage, who was wearing a black corduroy jacket, green corduroy trousers, a blue shirt, a rose sweater, and red socks, told us that he was teaching piano and composition in Seattle, his native town, eight years ago when the pioneering impulse seized him. "I wanted to explore the possibilities of rhythm," he said. "But naturally I had to develop a new set of sounds first. I had to have sounds that people had never heard before in music, so that the *sound* would call attention to the rhythm. Do you follow me?" We signalled to him to go on. His first move, he said, was to forget about his piano and organize a percussion orchestra composed of such inharmonious instruments as tom-toms, wooden blocks, bells, gongs, cymbals, anvils, and automobile-brake drums. The orchestra, while it lasted, occupied itself exclusively with rhythmic items composed by Mr. Cage. "However," Mr. Cage told us, "it was too unwieldy. I'd collected about three hundred different things that would make the kind of sounds I needed. You can see what a personal problem I had on my hands." He solved this problem by going back to his piano. "I remembered," he said, "that hot jazz pianists used to get new effects by placing sheets of paper between the piano strings. I started monkeying around with my piano strings." Mr. Cage ended up with what he named the prepared piano and an itch to come to New York, which he did two or three years ago. "People are more receptive to new ideas here than in Seattle," he said. "The New Music Society was very receptive to me."

Mr. Cage prepares his piano by inserting between its strings various objects—screws, pennies, splinters of wood, bits of felt or rubber, and practically any other small objects you can think of. This, as you might imagine, changes the sounds of the strings. Mr. Cage gets the particular sounds he requires by paying close attention not only to the kind of object but also to its size, weight, and longitudinal position on the strings. The possibilities are limitless and blood curdling. There are about two hundred and twenty-five strings on a piano, and each key, depending on the register, strikes from one to three strings. Nothing but prepared strings are played in Mr. Cage's compositions, and he prepares only a fraction of the strings. The most elaborate piano he has worked out so far has seventy-five prepared strings. No two of Mr. Cage's compositions (he has a repertoire of fifty) have the same preparation, his recent concert consisted of three compositions and required five different prepared pianos. "It's a kind of a bother," he said. "Sometimes it takes me three hours to prepare a piano for a complicated number—my 'The Perilous Night,' for instance." Mr. Cage is holding back some of his most effective sounds until after the war. "They're too frightening," he told us. "They sound too much like the scream of bombs, and planes, and rifle shots. It wouldn't be good taste to use them now. One of them even shocks me sometimes."[79]

Since that time, John Cage has added numerous works for prepared piano with bamboo slits, weather stripping, strips of rubber, nuts, bolts, screws, pennies, etc. In a 1943 four movement suite entitled *Amores,* the first and last parts of which are for prepared piano, Cage described in detail the preparation steps. (See the reproduced pages.) In his collection of *Sonatas and Interludes* (1960) he also includes an intricate preparation chart which is illustrated on page 499. Cage, Karlheinz Stockhausen, Pierre Boulez, and others have gone on to write numerous pieces involving indeterminacy of pitch and random succession. Choices are frequently left to chance or to the discretion of the performer himself. David Tudor is without a doubt the outstanding performer and champion of the avant-garde piano literature.

In recent years not only have unorthodox sounds and techniques been coaxed from the piano, but the instrument itself has been subjected to various forms of experimentation. As recently as 1965 Marguerite Long was championing Monique de la Bruchollerie's curved keyboard with the extremities brought within easier reach of the hands. The damper and soft pedals were converted to bars extending the entire span of the keyboard. Ten keys were also to be added at the top and five at the lower end of the keyboard. In addition the piano was to be fitted electronically with a push-button device whereby two to twelve keys could be activated simultaneously by pressing of a single key. An early forerunner of this model was the Chetsam curved keyboard which Rudolph Ganz had demonstrated in Berlin in 1912.

The quarter-toned piano invented by Ivan Wischnegradzky dates from the 1930s. LeRoy B. Campbell explained its construction:

> It is somewhat larger than the usual upright and has a larger sounding board. Of the three banks of keys, the upper and lower keyboards are tuned the same as the ordinary piano; while the middle keyboard is tuned one-quarter of a tone higher than the corresponding keys of the other keyboards. This upper keyboard, duplicating the lower, is needed for utility, because in playing on the middle keys in combination with the lower bank the hand was often unable to negotiate its key on the lower keyboard, yet it could easily reach the desired key on the upper keyboard.[80]

David Barnett constructed a three-tiered enharmonic pianoforte keyboard and demonstrated it at Town Hall in New York City in 1935. It was designed for the conventional semi-tonal system; all twelve tonalities are equivalent and playable with the same fingerings.

To Rue Shaw

AMORES

I
SOLO: PREPARED PIANO

By JOHN CAGE

I and IV

Prepared piano: Materials, acting as mutes, are placed between the strings pertaining to certain keys (18 keys in all). This is easily effected on a grand piano, but only with difficulty on an upright. The result obtained is a change in the acoustic characteristics of the strings affected.

Nine screws, eight bolts, two nuts and three strips of rubber are required.

In preparing the strings of the five following keys 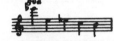 place between adja-

cent strings, in each case, a single screw. There being generally three pertinent strings for each of these keys (except in the case of the first E flat which has only two), one has the choice of placing the screw between the 1st and 2nd or between the second and third strings. The size and position of the screws, as indeed of all mutes, may be determined by experiment. If the screw is too small in diameter, an undesired metallic buzz will occur when the proper key is played. The screw must be large enough and so positioned on and between the strings as to produce a resonant sound, rich in harmonics.

In preparing the strings of the following two keys [music] somewhat smaller screws and 1 nut are

required for each set of strings. Choose nuts that are large enough to slide freely on the screw, yet small enough so that they do not slide off the screw-head end. Prepare each set of strings as follows: put a screw through a nut; then, place the screw with nut between two adjacent pertinent strings (e.g. 2nd and 3rd strings); finally, place second screw (without a nut) between the two remaining adjacent strings (e.g. 1st and 2nd strings). When the proper key is played, a resonant sound, as in the previous operation, will be produced, but, in addition, a metallic rattling sound occurs, due to the free movement of the loose nut on the screw, between the screw head and piano strings. Also, the nut, which is made to move by the vibrating strings, comes finally to rest on the strings, stopping their vibration and thereby shortening the duration of the sound.

In preparing the strings of the eight following keys [music] use bolts,

one for each set of pertinent strings. Otherwise the operation is similar to that described above for screws. Bolts are used in this lower register, rather than screws, because of their greater diameter, necessary in muting their longer strings to achieve the desired result: a sound resonant, rich in harmonics and free of any metallic buzzing.

The strings of three keys are prepared by placing in each case one end of a

strip of rubber (approximately 4" x 1" x ⅛") between two adjacent strings (e.g. 1st and 2nd), then the other end between the remaining adjacent strings (e.g. 2nd and 3rd), and, finally, pressing the rubber firmly down against and between the strings. The rubber may then be pushed into such a position along the strings that it will produce harmonics when the proper key is played. Because of the nature of the material, however, the sound produced is dull, thud-like, rather than rich. If rubber cannot be obtained, absorbent paper or cloth, folded several times, may be substituted.

It will be seen that the notation does not always agree with the actual duration of the sounds (e.g. 4th and fifth measures, page 1, rubber-muted "A"); the notation given facilitates phrase-reading.

The total desired result has been achieved if, on completion of the preparation, one may play the pertinent keys without sensing that he is playing a piano or even a "prepared piano." An instrument having convincingly its own special characteristics, not even suggesting those of a piano, must be the result.

TONE

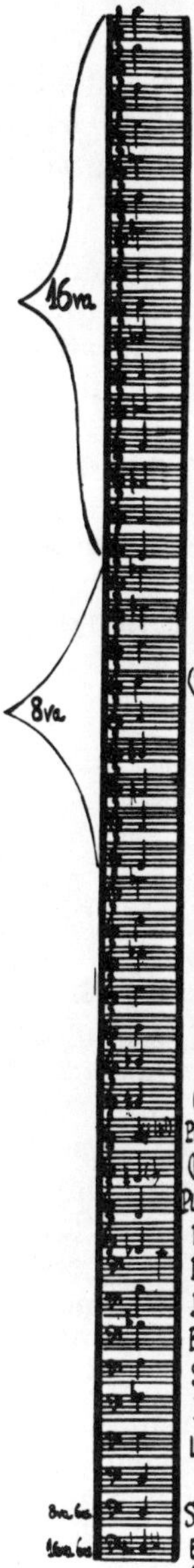

MATERIAL	STRINGS LEFT TO RIGHT	DISTANCE FROM DAMPER (INCHES)	MATERIAL	STRINGS LEFT TO RIGHT	DISTANCE FROM DAMPER (INCHES)	MATERIAL	STRINGS LEFT TO RIGHT	DISTANCE FROM DAMPER (INCHES)	TONE
			SCREW	2-3	1 3/4*				A
			MED. BOLT	2-3	1 7/8*				G
			SCREW	2-3	1 5/8*				F
			SCREW	2-3	1 15/16*				E
			SCREW	2-3	1 3/4*				E♭
			SM. BOLT	2-3	2*				D
			SCREW	2-3	1 9/16*				C♯
			FURNITURE BOLT	2-3	2 7/16*				C
			SCREW	2-3	2 1/2*				B
			SCREW	2-3	1 7/8*				B♭
			MED. BOLT	2-3	2 3/8*				A
			SCREW	2-3	2 1/4*				A♭
			SCREW	2-3	3 3/4*				G
			SCREW	2-3	2 15/16*				F♯
SCREW	1-2	3/4*	FURN. BOLT + 2 NUTS	2-3	2 1/8*	SCREW + 2 NUTS	2-3	3 1/4*	F
			SCREW	2-3	1 13/16*				E
			FURNITURE BOLT	2-3	1 7/8				E♭
			SCREW	2-3	1 15/16				C♯
			SCREW	2-3	1 1/16				C
(DAMPER TO BRIDGE = 4 1/16; ADJUST ACCORDINGLY)			MED. BOLT	2-3	3 3/4				B
			SCREW	2-3	4 5/16				A
RUBBER	1-2-3	4 1/2	FURNITURE BOLT	2-3	1 1/4				G♯
			SCREW	2-3	1 3/4				F♯
			SCREW	2-3	2 5/16				F
RUBBER	1-2-3	5 3/4							E
RUBBER	1-2-3	6 1/2	FURN. BOLT + NUT	2-3	6 7/8				E♭
			FURNITURE BOLT	2-3	2 9/16				D
RUBBER	1-2-3	3 5/8							D♭
			BOLT	2-3	7 1/8				C
			BOLT	2-3	2				B
SCREW	1-2	10	SCREW	2-3	1	RUBBER	1-2-3	8 1/4	B♭
(PLASTIC (see G))	1-2-3	2 5/16				RUBBER	1-2-3	4 1/2	G♯
PLASTIC (OVER 1 UNDER 2-3)	1-2-3	2 7/8				RUBBER	1-2-3	10 1/8	G
(PLASTIC (see D))	1-2-3	4 1/4				RUBBER	1-2-3	5 7/16	D♯
PLASTIC (OVER 1 - UNDER 2-3)	1-2-3	4 1/8				RUBBER	1-2-3	9 3/4	D
BOLT	1-2	15 1/2	BOLT	2-3	11/16	RUBBER	1-2-3	14 1/8	D♭
BOLT	1-2	14 1/2	BOLT	2-3	7/8	RUBBER	1-2-3	6 1/2	C
BOLT	1-2	14 3/4	BOLT	2-3	9/16	RUBBER	1-2-3	14	B
RUBBER	1-2-3	9 1/2	MED. BOLT	2-3	10 1/8				B♭
SCREW	1-2	5 7/8	LG. BOLT	2-3	5 3/8	SCREW + NUTS	1-2	1	A
BOLT	1-2	7 1/8	MED. BOLT	2-3	2 1/4	RUBBER	1-2-3	4 5/8 -	A♭
LONG BOLT	1-2	8 3/4	LG BOLT	2-3	3 1/4				G
			BOLT	2-3	11/16				D
SCREW + RUBBER	1-2	4 7/16							D
ERASER (OVER D UNDER C♯-E♭) AM. PENCIL CO. #386	1	6 3/4							D

*MEASURE FROM BRIDGE.

One of the most promising innovations is the double-keyboard piano, invented by the Swiss musician Emanuel Moór in 1921 and experimented with by Steinway, Bechstein, and Chickering. Godowsky, who performed on it, was greatly impressed with its potential. Liszt, a hundred years earlier, seems almost to have forecast its appearance. He wrote in the *Revue et Gazette Musicale* for February 11, 1838:

> The piano is more and more developing its adaptive potentialities. We strike chords which are only intended for the harp, long notes as on wind instruments as well as staccato ones, and runs which formerly were considered innate peculiarities of other instruments.
>
> The most recent advance in piano construction will no doubt make possible all tone contrasts which heretofore have been unattainable. The loud pedal on most pianos revealed the need of the extension of further possibilities. The expressive manuals of the organ will naturally lead to the creation of a piano with two or three keyboards, which will certainly conquer the musical world.[81]

Winifred Christie, Moór's wife and English virtuoso pianist, described the Moór double-keyboard piano's potential and operation in an interview with Laura Remick Copp in 1931:

A New Instrument is Born

"Emanuel Moór's interest in the two-piano keyboard is characteristic of the aspiring attitude which has marked his life. He has continually sought not only more beautiful and more simple means of expression but also more rational methods.

"He experimented on an old instrument in his own home. He made a model in his own workshop in Switzerland, demonstrating his ideas, which are to keep all of the good qualities and acquisitions of the piano of today and to add to them effects possessed by the clavecin but lost when the hammer piano came in. As M. Moór himself says, 'It seems hardly comprehensible why the piano, when it replaced the clavecin, gave up the rich effects of two keyboards and a coupling. In this respect the hammer-piano brought no improvement. In fact, it was rather a step backward, for the technic of the virtuoso. This elementary fact so inspired me that I busied myself with the development of pianos along constructive lines.'

With Orchestra

"After the numerous presentations in Paris, where the new

piano was heard with the Colonne and Paseloup orchestras, it was unanimously recognized that in comparison with it a single-manual piano sounded colorless and afforded little opportunity for expression of the musical thoughts of the masters, particularly those of the greatest creative musician of all times—Johann Sebastian Bach.

Bach's biographer, Wolfrum the Heidelberger, mentioned that Bach never composed for the hammer piano, as this instrument lacked the tone-color of his clavicembalo with its two manuals, coupler and register-stops. Bach never used the modern octave technic. His octaves were couplings, as on the organ, which in *forte* as well as *piano,* gave the performance an entirely different character from the laborious octave hammering.

Enriched Technical Resources

"Like the organ, on the cembalo all repetitions and sequences, which offer such pleasant variety on the different manuals, are easily executed, while on the piano, as we know it today, these changes in tone-color and expression cannot be produced without comparatively great effort. It can be assumed as common knowledge that Bach himself transcribed his own violin and piano compositions for the organ, the lute or orchestra."

Choice of Fingers

"One can always use his best fingers on this instrument instead of his worst." She proceeded to prove this by playing a passage from Schumann's *Carnaval. Traumeswirren,* another composition by Schumann, is a good example for the use of good fingers in both hands instead of poor ones; and this is a very tricky piece! In crossing hands, where ordinarily one must get his body into awkward and uncomfortable positions—detrimental oftentimes to the musical sound of the passage—this can be eliminated by playing the part for one hand on the upper keyboard. A good example is the D-flat concert study of Liszt, in which the hands cross continually for the high notes, which incidentally are the melody.

"The upper keyboard is an octave higher in pitch than is the lower, and one reaches very easily from one to the other, often playing on both at the same time with the same hand. This double keyboard obviates large stretches and makes it possible to play tenths and large intervals with perfect ease and smoothness. It entirely does away with big broken jumps.

Amplified Resources

"The coupling effect taken from the old clavecin is operated and made possible by a pedal, the middle one of the three, which affects the lower keyboard only; and such a passage as that in octaves in Beethoven's *Waldstein Sonata* can now be played *legato*, as the composer really intended it. No one could make this octave passage legato on the usual piano; but now it is easy and sounds as the composer wished it. Bass notes can now be held where this was formerly impossible, as in another *Fantasy-piece* by Schumann, *Des Abends (At Evening)*. Phrasing is greatly aided as is also clarity; and the remarkable effects of more resources as to overtones are quite overwhelming.

"These new possibilities are an aid to modern music as well as old. In Debussy's *Les Tièrces Alternées (Alternated Thirds)*, where the hands continually interlock, those thirds fairly scintillate when the part for one hand is taken on the upper keyboard, thus gaining perfect freedom. In *Jeu d'eau* and *Ondine* by Ravel there are passages where the hands are continually on top of each other.

The Voice of the Harpsichord

"In harpsichord music more color can be given to these old compositions, as in the *Italian Concerto,* for example, where it is necessary to differentiate between the solo and tutti passages; but the greatest triumph really is that it is now possible to play Bach Fugues with the same clearness as on the clavicembalo or organ, emphasizing certain tones, building contrasts and dynamics similar to those on an organ, and at the same time preserving the typical peculiarities of the piano.

"This invention makes the piano a polyphonic instrument and brings back to it the wealth of color which its predecessors possessed and which has been abandoned with the construction of the modern piano. This is an invention by a musician: for M. Moór is an organist and a pianist. He was also a pupil of Liszt. Casals plays many of his compositions, as do Ysaye, Thibaud and many other artists.

"The two-keyboard piano is the most significant innovation made in piano mechanism in one hundred and fifty years. In Germany it has been acclaimed unanimously by critics and public, when it has been demonstrated and played in special recitals in all of the principal cities."[82]

Whether any of these or other experimental pianos, or new electronic instruments such as the Moog synthesizer, will finally

502

supplant our conventional piano—in a way that the pianoforte replaced the harpsichord one-hundred-fifty years ago—cannot readily be ascertained. However, pianists will continue to be confronted with the problems and challenges of traditional piano technique for a long time to come.

Notes

[1] Otto Ortmann, *The Physiological Mechanics of Piano Technique,* introduction by Arnold Schultz, p. xxvi.

[2] Letter to the author from Arnold Schultz dated June 26, 1967.

[3] Arnold Schultz, *The Riddle of the Pianist's Finger and Its Relationship to a Touch-Scheme,* p. 34.

[4] *Ibid.,* p. 51.

[5] *Ibid.,* p.61.

[6] *Ibid.,* p. 81.
[7] Schultz letter.

[8] Schultz, *The Riddle,* p. 83.

[9] *Ibid.,* p. 183.
[10] *Ibid.,* p. 181.

[11] *Ibid.,* p. 102.

[12] *Ibid.,* p. 107.

[13] *Ibid.,* p. 108.

[14] *Ibid.,* pp. 109-110.

[15] *Ibid.,* p. 109.

[16] William S. Newman, "Styles and Touches in Chopin's Piano Music," *Handbook for Piano Teachers,* p. 94.

[17] William S. Newman, "On the Special Problems of High-Speed Playing," *Clavier,* Vol.II, No. 3 (May-June, 1963), p. 12.

[18] Schultz, *The Riddle,* pp. 157-58.
[19] Schultz letter.

[20] Schultz, *The Riddle,* p. 123.

[21] *Ibid.,* p. 13.

[22] Schultz letter.

[23] Ortmann, *The Physiological Mechanics,* introduction by Schultz, pp. xxii-xxiii.

[24] Ferruccio Busoni, *The Essence of Music and Other Papers,* p. 80.

²⁵George Kochevitsky, *The Art of Piano Playing: A Scientific Approach*, p. 12.

²⁶Luigi Bonpensiere, *New Pathways to Piano Technique*, p. 7.

²⁷*Ibid.*, p. 37.

²⁸*Ibid.*, p. 53.

²⁹*Ibid.*, pp. 13-14.

³⁰*Ibid.*, pp. 69-70.

³¹*Ibid.*, p. xiv.

³²Kochevitsky, *The Art of Piano Playing*, foreword by Sumner Goldenthal, M.D.

³³*Ibid.*, p. 25.

³⁴Schultz letter.

³⁵Schultz, *The Riddle*, p. 196.

³⁶Arnold Schultz, "Contest Standards—Are They Logical?" *The Piano Teacher*, Vol. 5, No. 5, May-June, 1963, p. 6.

³⁷Schultz, *The Riddle*, p. 210.

³⁸*Ibid.*, p. 207.

³⁹Letter to the author from Arnold Schultz dated June 10, 1964.

⁴⁰Arnold Schultz, "The Riddle of the Pianist's Finger," Music Teachers National Association *Proceedings*, 31st Series, 1936, pp. 142-43.

⁴¹Abby Whiteside, *The Pianist's Mechanism, A Guide to the Production and Transmission of Power in Playing*, pp. 7-8.

⁴²Letter to the author from Joseph Prostakoff dated February 18, 1968.

⁴³Abby Whiteside, "Successful Piano Teaching: The Physical Sensation Comes First," *Musical America*, December 15, 1951, Vol. LXXI, No. 16, p. 25.

⁴⁴Abby Whiteside, *Indispensables of Piano Playing*, p. 10.

⁴⁵*Ibid.*, p. 8.

⁴⁶José Limón, "Dancers are Musicians are Dancers." *The Juilliard Review Annual* 1966-1967, p. 5.

⁴⁷*Ibid.*

⁴⁸Whiteside, *Indispensables*, p. 11.

⁴⁹*Ibid.*, p. 10.

⁵⁰*Ibid.*, p. 13.

⁵¹Prostakoff letter.

⁵²Whiteside, *Indispensables*, p. 66.

⁵³*Ibid.*, p. 33.

[54]*Ibid.*

[55]*Ibid.*, p. 79.

[56]*Ibid.*, p. 39.

[57]*Ibid.*, p. 73.

[58]Prostakoff letter.

[59]Whiteside, *Indispensables,* p. 82.

[60]*Ibid.*, p. 107.

[61]Prostakoff letter.

[62]Ernst Bacon, *Notes on the Piano,* pp. 1-3.

[63]*Ibid.*, pp. 37-38.

[64]Guy Maier, *The Piano Teacher's Companion,* compiled and edited from his writings in *The Etude* by Lois Maier, p. 34.

[65]*Ibid.*, p. 36.

[66]Ruth Slenczynska, *Music at Your Fingertips,* p. 35.

[67]*Ibid.*, p. 23.

[68]Erno Balogh, "BARTÓK, The Teacher—As I Knew Him," *The Etude,* Vol. 74, January, 1956, p. 20.

[69]Letter to the author from Gyorgy Sandor dated March 1, 1970.

[70]Serge Moreux, *Béla Bartók,* p. 145.

[71]Halsey Stevens, *The Life and Music of Béla Bartók,* p. 15.

[72]*Bartók Béla levelei* (Letters collected in last two years). Edited by Jáns Demény, quoted in Halsey Stevens, *Life and Music of Bartok,* p. 20.

[73]Ernst von Dohnányi, *Essential Finger Exercises for Obtaining a Sure Piano Technique,* pp. 2-4.

[74]József Gát, *The Technique of Piano Playing,* 3rd edition, 1968, pp. 24-26.

[75]*Ibid.*, p. 27.

[76]*Ibid.*, p. 31.

[77]Harold C. Schonberg, "The Cluster Man," *The New York Times,* March 11, 1962, Section X, p. 11.

[78]Nicolas Slonimsky, "Henry Cowell," in *American Composers on American Music,* A Symposium edited by Henry Cowell. pp. 58-59.

[79]"Prepared Pianist," from *The Talk of the Town, The New Yorker,* February 24, 1945, Vol. 21, pp. 18-19.

[80]LeRoy B. Campbell, "Wischnegradzky's Quarter-Tone Piano," *The Musician,* Vol. 42, May, 1937, p. 93.

[81]Cited in "New Piano Effects Created by Double-Keyboard," *The Musician,* Vol. 35, August 1930, p. 7.

[82]Laura Remick Copp, "Should the Piano Have Two Keyboards?", An Interview with Winifred Christie, *The Etude,* Vol. 49, April, 1931, p. 240.

20. The Perspectives of an Enlightened Piano Technique

In the preceeding pages we have surveyed a significant portion of the most vital technical thought that has accompanied the piano's development. We saw first that piano technique in its historical beginnings was influenced by the models of enlightened harpsichord and clavichord technique, described in the writings of such men as Diruta, St. Lambert, François Couperin, Rameau, and Carl Philipp Emanuel Bach and exhibited in the superlative performance of clavier players of the stature of Domenico Scarlatti and Johann Sebastian Bach. Sebastian Bach's superb physical coordination, as recalled by Forkel, produced a highly refined finger technique perfectly adapted to both harpsichord and clavichord. It was then a very natural thing for Mozart, and later Hummel, to transfer a somewhat similar touch to the early Viennese piano. The latter possessed an easy key resistance, modest dynamic resources, and a clear, almost pizzicato sound.

But as the pianoforte began to find its own identity in the early English models, particularly those by Broadwood, its virtuosos broke away from this Viennese style. In Clementi, Cramer, and especially Beethoven, a well-defined bravura piano technique began to emerge. The greater key resistance, the expanding tonal and dynamic resources, as well as the more brilliant, chordal literature written for the instrument all called for greater bodily participation. At the same time the legato, cantabile resources of the piano were being developed. By 1850 Chopin and Liszt had, to a large extent, defined the piano's physical technique and its unique musical idiom. At that time the instrument was basically not unlike present-day sophisticated models.

Beethoven, Chopin, Liszt, Anton Rubinstein, and all the great natural performers who followed them accepted the mature piano on its own terms and molded their physical techniques to its

507

demands—just as J.S. Bach and Scarlatti had done with the harpsichord and clavichord, and Mozart and Hummel with the Viennese piano. While Hummel and Czerny put perhaps too much technical emphasis on finger equality and independence and suppression of arm movement, they still did not lose sight of the importance of a free, graceful approach to the keyboard nor the need of avoiding percussive, unmusical effects. This is evident in their writings, but the volumes of exercises and studies which they left contributed greatly to the development of a reactionary high finger school of pianists. These late descendants of the legitimate Viennese school refused to adapt to the technical demands of the modern grand piano. They seemingly blinded themselves to the natural beauties of a Chopin or Anton Rubinstein performance. By the end of the nineteenth century, the Stuttgart technique, with its finger hitting and excessive muscular fixations, was thoroughly entrenched in European conservatories.

Such an unnatural approach to piano technique, which fell short of attaining musical objectives and failed to utilize full bodily coordinations, had already begun to raise cries of alarm from discerning musicians from mid-century on. Teachers like William Mason, Adolph Kullak, and Ludwig Deppe analyzed and proclaimed the technical truths which Liszt and Rubinstein had empirically discovered. By the early years of the twentieth century, the short comings of the finger school had been fully exposed; but new evils and excesses had begun to take their place. Breithaupt and his contemporaries rightfully emphasized the need of more arm and bodily participation in piano technique, but in the process they threw out legitimate finger techniques and stressed erroneously conceived theories of weight and relaxation.

With Townsend and Matthay came solid progress in the direction of a well-balanced technical system. Matthay saw the need of studying the invisible as well as the visible conditions of fine piano playing, and he experienced the correct physical sensations; but his verbal explanations were sometimes confusing and too involved. Piano technique was not placed on a thoroughly rational basis until the work of Otto Ortmann had been accomplished. A technique with such a rationale will find itself in harmony with empirical and analytical truth from any period. The imbalances and errors of the past are not likely to be repeated. Arnold Schultz built solidly on both Matthay and Ortmann, gave wise counsel on how to use the various movement types most effectively, and scored a breakthrough in his analysis of finger coordination. Furthermore, he voiced an eloquent plea for integration of knowledge in the field. Many other contemporary pedagogues, including Whiteside, Bartók, Gát, Maier, Cowell, and others who may or may not have been mentioned in this study, have each contributed significantly to the technical literature.

In final summary, let us briefly enumerate some of the basic considerations that are vital to the formation of an enlightened piano technique, regardless of one's pedagogical ancestry.

The aesthetic imperative. A sound technique can never be divorced from musical objectives and careful listening. The better technical treatises of the past and present never lose sight of this fact. The importance of a beautiful tone—or, more accurately stated, of fine tonal balance—can never be overlooked. J.S. Bach and his son Philipp Emanuel, Türk, Mozart, Hummel, Chopin, Thalberg, Leschetizky, Josef Lhevinne, and others all emphasized a cantabile approach to piano playing. Imagery plays an important role in its development. Pianists should even sing vocally and, as Beethoven suggested, in a perplexing passage they should imagine the tonal coloring that a violinist or wind player might achieve.[1] Anton Rubinstein was strongly concerned about mood projection; so are Vladimir Horowitz and Rosina Lhevinne. In so doing, one's technical development is greatly influenced. It is also affected by a feeling for rhythmic proportions and for phrase-line flow and direction (Mozart: ". . . a passage which ought to flow like oil").[2] Fingering and pedal techniques are also inevitably involved. So is a keen understanding of the stylistic traits of the various periods.

Mental and psychological control. In recent years scientists and theorists have been absorbed in trying to understand the processes of the mind and nervous system used in achieving the complex coordinations necessary in fine piano playing. Even the listening process has strong psychological overtones and has been the object of serious study. Proper mental and nervous control can greatly affect such important areas of technique as accuracy, dexterity and fluency, relaxation and poise. The writings of Dubois-Reymond, Raif, Kochevitsky, Bonpensiere, and Schultz are worthwhile beginnings in the psychology of piano technique. The student can also improve his technical skills by developing strong habits of mental discipline and concentration. In practice, slow enough tempos should frequently prevail so that the depression of each key is preceded by the correct mental concept and adequate physical preparation. Time must also be allotted for a continuous judging process to take place. Frank Merrick has coined the term *delayed continuity,*[3] to describe such a procedure—working in short musical phrases and holding at the end of the phrase in order to judge the execution of the previous one and plan the next one. William S. Newman cautions that the student's motto should be, "Hesitate rather than err."[4] It must be remembered that one can strengthen inaccuracies and faulty concepts just as readily as the desirable traits—in fact more easily. Inadequate preparation, and lack of concentration, even for an instant, is a step in that direction. Recall that Leschetizky stated: "If I had a method it would be based upon the mental delineation of a chord."[5] Technique is initially mental; the conscious mind must train the sub-conscious mind.

An intellectual grasp of basic technical knowledge. Every student should acquire a working knowledge of the fundamentals of physics and physiology that directly influence piano technique. One's vocabulary may need to be expanded to include such terms as *rigidity, plasticity, elasticity, weight, mass, inertia, momentum, lever, fulcrum, base, force-variations, the geometrics of movement, coordination, fixation, isolation, action and reaction, activity and passivity,* and numerous others. A study of the means of activating a lever so as to depress the key most effectively and of stabilizing the lever's base is of vital importance. A rudimentary understanding of the musculature and the skeletal joints associated with piano playing will help the student to use them most efficiently and avoid working them beyond their limitations. Poor coordination and unnecessary fatigue will thus be avoided. A knowledge of the wide ranges of physical differences found in individuals will help the student to understand, accept, and adapt to his own limitations. Ortmann and Schultz are his best references in these areas.

Isolated movements. The four basic levers involved in piano playing are the finger (at times it will be more advantageous if its phalanges do not work as a single unit), the hand, the forearm, and the full arm. Frequently the movement of the torso itself may support the full arm. Since a smaller mass does not have as much inertia or momentum to contend with as does a larger one, it can move with greater velocity and agility. But it cannot supply the power that a larger mass can produce. Then, too, extremes in velocity and intensity are never compatible. These facts must all be kept in mind in the selection of the appropriate levers used in piano playing. How the individual lever is moved (by weight or muscular contraction) and how the base is stabilized (by weight, pressure, or fixation by the antagonistic muscles) or even displaced during the act of key depression, will have far-reaching effects upon the pianist's technical and musical achievement—upon the ability to control velocity, tonal intensity, speed of key descent, and physiological ease. The isolated movements of greatest concern in the history of piano technique are those made by the fingers. The development of a strong independent finger action became a passion and obsession with the Stuttgart school in the nineteenth century. This group of high finger enthusiasts failed to reckon with the fact that the third and fourth fingers, and in some individuals the fourth and fifth, are tied together with a common tendon. Chopin revealed his acceptance of finger inequality when he joked that all that remained for him was his large nose and his underdeveloped fourth finger.[6] The Stuttgart school did not assign enough work to the arms. Breithaupt and his followers erred in the opposite direction.

Coordinated movements. Isolated movement concerned with tone production is largely vertical in nature. But piano playing is also made up of horizontal and oblique motion. How to make a meaningful synthesis of all these many isolated movements made by the various levers is of primary concern to the sensitive pianist. Curvilinear, continuous movement, economically used, is more efficient than jerky, angular movement. It is musically more desirable as well. Deppe and his student, Elisabeth Caland, strongly stressed the relationship, even the fusion, of beauty of movement and beauty of tone: "... beauty of tone would be the natural consequence of beauty of movement."[7] Abby Whiteside worked along somewhat similar lines. The torso, and upper arm particularly, set up a fundamental, all-encompassing rhythm which outlines the phrase structure and helps to coordinate movement by the various levers. The principles that the center controls the periphery and that different playing levers may be simultaneously involved surely go back as far as Diruta at the end of the sixteenth century when he advised keyboard performers, "Let the arm guide the hand—this is the most important rule before all the others."[8] Without a doubt, the fingers will be at their best when the arm is functioning in such a manner and also providing accentual power; but a mastery of Schultz's small muscle finger coordination is vital too. Chopin's own exquisitely refined passage work must have instinctively made use of this coordination. The movement and coordination of the hand and arm is important as well in achieving velocity in passages that sweep up and down the keyboard—notes are grasped by patterns and clusters. The arm may

511

shift abruptly and unconventional fingerings may be in perfect order.

Muscular coordination. Coordinated movements are directly related to correct muscular coordinations. Such coordinations call for harmonious functioning of the various sets of antagonistic muscles and for muscular fixations graded to withstand the reactions of key impact and timed to the point of tone. Talented pianists instinctively set up a rhythm of contraction and relaxation, of muscular breathing that reduces fatigue to a minimum and promotes endurance, fluency, agility, and great flexibility. Rameau[9] considered this suppleness a most desirable technical trait, and Chopin[10] epitomized it. Leschetizky made a meaningful point when he stressed that the singer's deep breathing should have its counterpart in the pianist's muscular relaxation. And the pianist should actually engage in deep breathing like the singer. He observed, "What deep breaths Rubinstein used to take at the beginning of long phrases."[11] Elisabeth Caland's concern that the different muscles work in complete harmony prompted her to term the process for the pianist, *muscular synergy*,[12] after Souriau's treatise in which he wrote that "they be fashioned under the law of a common rhythm."[13] Abby Whiteside's teachings are closely related.

William Mason spoke of devitalized upper arm muscles, and Matthay's three species concern themselves with muscular coordination. Schultz's thorough analyses of various finger muscular coordinations carry the research even further. And in the laboratory experimentations of Otto Ortmann we have a complete picture of the pianist's ideal physical coordination. It is most important to realize that muscular coordination is greatly influenced by variations in velocity, force, and range of movement.

The kinesthetic sense. Nothing is more important in piano playing than the sense of touch—when it is considered that all of physical activity is finally focused in the finger tips as they contact the keys and drive them down to the key bed at varying rates of speed. The pianist must accurately sense key resistance and then completely control the entire downward movement of the key. A well-developed, cushioned feeling for key surface tension and resistance has been described by Arnold Schultz as a "fat kinesthetic." He advocated learning keyboard geography (individual chord and phrase patterns) through a "straight kinesthetic touch"—the feel of *hand* sensation alone.

Piano touches can be divided into two fundamental categories; prepared and unprepared—or non-percussive and percussive. A touch which originates from the surface of the key assures complete finger tip control over the speed of the key's descent. Ortmann showed that with a percussive or unprepared touch the key actually moves out in front of the finger for a portion of its descent—the finger is not in complete control. An exception occurs when the arm approaches the key with moderate speed, then accelerates its motion at the point where the finger tip first makes contact with the key surface, thereby controlling key descent. A slow arm movement with a flat finger (maximum finger cushion contact)—preferably with the tip already resting on the key surface—and with a flexible wrist action assures maximum key control and the softest possible degrees of pianissimo. This coordination is especially useful in projecting melody lines such as are found in the Chopin Nocturnes. Of course, not all percussive touches are always undesirable; but as a rule a high finger action is to be avoided.

Touch figures prominently in the historical literature. Diruta spoke about the keys being "gently depressed, never struck."[14] Bach's finger action, Forkel marveled, was so skillfully refined that he had so "small a motion of the fingers that it was hardly perceptible."[15] His fingers were placed on the keys—they never fell nor were thrown.[16] Couperin, as well, stressed the importance of "holding the fingers as close to the keys as possible."[17] It may be recalled that Schindler wrote of Beethoven's admonition, ". . . the fingers need not be raised more than is necessary. This is the only method by which the player can learn to *generate* tone, and as it were, to make the instrument sing."[18] Lhevinne phrased it in this way, "As the finger touches the key-surface, it feels as though it were grasping the key, not striking or hitting it."[19] Elisabeth Caland spoke of caressing the keys, and the French had a name for it, *carezzando*.[20] Kalkbrenner, de Kontsky, and Debussy all emphasized it. Friedrich Wieck and his daughter Clara Schumann were noted for their pressure touch. And no one hated "key-hitting" more than Matthay, while Townsend argued, "Why should the piano-keys be struck, while the organ-keys and the pedals of both organ and piano are pushed?"[21] Schultz was equally concerned with prepared touches—but also with exactness in treatment of damper fall, the exact duration of key depression. It may be added that exactness of pedal depression and treatment is just as important. From all these historical citations it becomes amply clear that scrupulous care must be given to the manner in which

513

the finger tip contacts the key.

Posture. The early literature of piano technique is largely made up of descriptions of correct physical positioning at the instrument and desirable external movements. The writers were concerned mostly with outward appearance. More enlightened modern technique is not so dogmatic about posture while performing at the piano. Differences of physical make-up and of personality and temperament will result in various natural approaches to the instrument. The invisible muscular coordinations are more important. Yet certain physical laws do operate to affect one's posture in a number of areas: the height of one's seat, the position of the torso, the angle at the elbow, the level of the wrist, the degree of finger curve. A high seat contributes power as does a high wrist; the more the fingers are curved, the more precise the finger articulation, etc. Matthay put his major stress on the unseen elements of fine piano technique; yet he devoted an important and extended section of his *Act of Touch* to posture. It still demands careful attention.

Means for specific technical development. How does one go about perfecting specific technical skills at the piano—developing endurance, velocity, dexterity, fluency, tonal control, a coordinated technique in a musicianly manner? Should there be endless hours of purely technical drill or should technical mastery be achieved largely through intelligent practice in the serious piano literature itself? The tenor of historical technical thought would seem to indicate a balance between the two. The most respected writers and musicians suggested simple basic exercises followed by scale and arpeggio patterns which, of course, are integral parts of the classic literature. Couperin wrote, "I have always given my pupils little finger-exercises to play, either passages, or strings of shakes or tremolos of different intervals."[22] C.P.E. Bach offered advice regarding the trill. He felt it should be "practiced diligently with all fingers so that they will become strong and dexterous."[23] Even Liszt suggested to Mason a two-note exercise which, he felt, was basic to all of his technique.[24] J.S. Bach's students, according to Forkel, had to "practice, for months together, nothing but isolated exercises for all the fingers of both hands, with constant regard to this clear and clean touch."[25] Mozart, Beethoven, and Chopin all utilized technical drills. Deppe, Caland, Mason, Brahms, Cortot, Long, Safonov, Roeder, Ganz, as well as Ortmann, Schultz, Newman, Whiteside, and many others have constructed pedagogical materials from which the student might judiciously

514

choose. But he could also well construct his own, making sure each lever is adequately exercised. Patterns which are modulatory and smoothly lead through all the keys are most beneficial. They are also good preparation for scale work.

Scales and arpeggios are universally accepted as essential technique. They must be thoroughly mastered. Both Rachmaninoff and Lhevinne wrote of their thorough development in the Russian schools. But scales and arpeggios, like all technical patterns, should be made imaginative, musical experiences—not dull, meaningless repetitions. Walter Robert has written:

> Scales are the free-hand drawing of the pianist's art. An even scale is the equivalent of a straight line. A scale rhythmically inflected, controlled in timbre and touch is the equivalent of the expressive brush stroke of the painter. A scale dashed off swiftly is the correlate of a bold curve in a sketch. Easy command of a succession of tones, control of sonority without emotional involvement, stockpiling of building material—those are the values of scale playing.[26]

Robert calls them primarily ear exercises.[27] They should be accented in groups of five, six, seven, etc., as well as two, three and four. The accents may be alternated between the hands. The hands may also be spaced at intervals other than an octave–a third, tenth, or sixth. Varieties of touches and dynamics are helpful, as Lhevinne has emphasized.[28] Staccato practice assures velocity coordination. The hands may be crossed. Cross rhythms may also be used. Practicing all scales with the standard C major fingering is a good technique builder.

Major and minor need not be the only modes practiced. Material helpful in breaking away from such traditional treatment would include Paul Emerich's *The Road to Modern Music,* with its modal and bi-tonal scales, and *Thesaurus of Scales and Melodic Patterns* by Nicolas Slonimsky. The latter collection contains well over 1300 traditional and contemporary scale and melodic patterns, many of Mr. Slonimsky's own construction. Maurice Dumesnil has pointed out that "Mr. Slonimsky is above all an explorer of new musical resources, an investigator of hitherto unknown possibilities, a scientist who can dissect the fundamental forms of scale-making and develop them into thousands upon thousands of permutations. In fact, he shows us that the number of possible scale patterns is practically inexhaustible."[29] Keyboard drill of many of these patterns would help the advanced pianist to

515

develop a superior technique particularly applicable to twentieth century literature.

All forms of seventh chord arpeggios as well as triads are also beneficial for technical drill. A profitable sequence can begin on C with a series of arpeggios executed in which C is first the root, then the third, fifth, and seventh of similar chords. The pattern can then be repeated upwards in chromatic sequence.

The more musical etude material has its place in building technique. Beethoven was fond of the Cramer Etudes as well as advocating the use of the C.P.E. Bach and Clementi method books. Chopin taught the etudes by Cramer, Clementi, and Moscheles. Although many fine studies have been written after Chopin (including Liszt, Scriabin, and Debussy), no better sets exist today than those by Chopin himself. A most useful present-day collection is Dohnányi's *Twelve Short Studies for the Advanced Pianist*. It is interesting to note that many of the pieces, especially the preludes and sets of variations from the *Fitzwilliam Virginal Book* and other pre-piano literature, are excellent technique builders. Irwin Freundlich has suggested that some of the virginal pieces might well be studied in place of a Czerny etude.[30] Although a certain amount of pure technical drill unrelated to pieces seems unavoidable, the more problems are solved by making technical patterns of difficult passages in the concert repertoire (with strong kinesthetic emphasis), the more beneficial and efficient will be one's practice and the more rapid the technical development. Astonishingly enough, Czerny himself voices some agreement:

> Useful as may be the practice of the numerous Exercises or Studies, now published; still the Teacher must not overload his Pupils with them. He must keep in mind, that each musical piece, even a Rondo, or an Air with Variations, etc. is an *Exercise in itself*, and often a much better one, than any professed study. . . .[31]

The teacher must also be concerned about the student's general physical health and well-being as this is a vital factor in technical development. A selection of gymnastics and isometrics can be employed for the strengthening of the muscles used in piano playing. But even more important to the pianist should be involvement in an exercise program which increases the oxygen supply to the body and builds the respiratory and circulatory systems.

Historical concepts and perspectives of piano technical thought. The student will be amply repaid for his efforts to search the literature. He will find that he is gaining an impartial, intellectual grasp of natural technique, molded and influenced by a wide range of historical teachings. In such a way, the pianist's own individuality is assured. Avoided is the danger of too much provincial influence, of the student's technique being formulated in an unbalanced manner. The kind of peril that Chopin was confronted with when he first came under the Kalkbrenner influence is still present today. Elsner's advice to Chopin ably sums up the objectives of this present study:

> One cannot advise a pupil to devote too much attention to a single method or manner or national taste, etc. What is true and beautiful must not be imitated but experienced according to its own individual and superior laws. No one man and no one nation must be taken as the unsurpassable, perfect model. Only eternal and invisible Nature can be *that,* and she contains it within herself. Men and nations can only offer us examples, more or less successful, to profit by. A final word: Those things by which an artist, always taking advantage of everything which surrounds and instructs him, arouses the admiration of his contemporaries must come from himself, thanks to the perfect cultivation of his powers.[32]

Surely the only right piano technique is the natural one. Every pianist, whether he be student, teacher, or concert performer, is a unique human being. In that he shares a common essence with all humanity, he cannot escape the basic natural principles that apply indiscriminately and justly within his art. But just as all of the seeds of a given species spring forth naturally into blossoms or fruit where no two are exactly alike, so should the pianist be encouraged to develop his own identity. He needs to embrace the natural laws of technique—the sunshine and rain that are basic to his growth; but the experience and knowledge of the many great pianists and teachers who went before him can also serve as the nutrients that enhance the flower and its uniqueness. The pianist's powers of intellectual curiosity should ally themselves wholeheartedly with his aesthetic nature in bringing his keyboard talents to full fruition.

Notes

[1] *Supra,* p. 98.

[2] *Supra,* p. 53.

[3] Frank Merrick, *Practising the Piano,* p. 1.

[4] William S. Newman, *The Pianist's Problems:* a modern approach

to efficient practice and musicianly performance, p. 106.

[5]*Supra,* p. 273.

[6]*Supra,* p. 168.

[7]*Supra,* p. 263.

[8]*Supra,* p. 11.

[9]*Supra,* p. 17.

[10]*Supra,* pp. 162, 165.

[11]*Supra,* p. 274.

[12]*Supra,* p. 256.

[13]*Supra,* p. 256.

[14]*Supra,* p. 11.

[15]*Supra,* p. 21.

[16]*Supra,* p. 20.

[17]*Supra,* p. 16.

[18]*Supra,* p. 91.

[19]*Supra,* p. 303.

[20]*Supra,* pp. 132, 267, 315.

[21]*Supra,* p. 363.

[22]*Supra,* p. 16.

[23]*Supra,* p. 29.

[24]*Supra,* p. 240.

[25]*Supra,* p. 23.

[26]Walter Rober, "In Defense of Scales," *Clavier,* Vol. I, No. 5 (November—December, 1962), p. 14.

[27]*Ibid.*

[28]Josef Lhevinne, *Basic Principles in Pianoforte Playing,* p. 45.

[29]Maurice Dumesnil, "Teacher's Round Table," *The Etude,* Vol. 67, September 1949, p. 14.

[30]James Friskin and Irwin Freundlich, *Music for the Piano: A Handbook of Concert and Teaching Material from 1580-1952,* p. 5.

[31]*Supra,* p. 115.

[32]*Supra,* p. 145.

Bibliography

Books

d'Abreu, Gerald. *Playing the Piano with Confidence:* An Analysis of Technique, Interpretation, Memory, and Performance. New York: St. Martin's Press, 1965. Paperback, 1971.

Adam, Louis. *Méthode ou Principe General du Doigte pour le Forte Piano*. Paris: Sieber, 1798.

American Composers on American Music. A Symposium edited by Henry Cowell. Stanford, California: Stanford University Press, 1933.

Apel, Willi. *Masters of the Keyboard:* A Brief Survey of Pianoforte Music. Cambridge, Mass.: Harvard University Press, 1947.

Arnold, Denis and Nigel Fortune, editors. *The Beethoven Reader*. New York: W. W. Norton & Co., 1971.

Bach, Carl Philipp Emanuel. *Essay on the True Art of Playing Keyboard Instruments*. Translated and edited by William J. Mitchell. New York: W. W. Norton & Company, Inc., 1949.

_____. *Versuch über die wahre Art, das Clavier zu spielen*. Facsimile edition of 1753 and 1762 editions. Leipzig: Breitkopf & Härtel, 1957.

Bach, Johann Sebastian. *The Bach Reader,* A Life of Johann Sebastian Bach in Letters and Documents. Edited by Hans T. David and Arthur Mendel. New York: W. W. Norton & Company, Inc., 1945. Revised edition, paperback, 1966.

_____. *Two and Three Part Inventions*. Preface translated by Alexander Lipsky. New York: Edwin F. Kalmus, 1943.

Bacon, Ernst. *Notes on the Piano*. Syracuse, New York: Syracuse University Press, 1963.

_____. *Words on Music*. Syracuse, New York: Syracuse University Press, 1960.

519

Badura-Skoda, Eva and Paul. *Interpreting Mozart on the Keyboard.* Translated by Leo Black. New York: St. Martin's Press, 1962.

Bardas, Willi. *Zur Psychologie der Klaviertechnik.* Berlin: Werkverlag, 1927.

Bartók, Béla and Sándor Reschovsky. *Bartók-Reschofsky Piano Method.* English edition revised and edited by Leslie Russel. London: Boosey & Hawkes Music Publishers, Ltd., 1967.

Bastien, James W., *How to Teach Piano Successfully.* Park Ridge, Ill., and La Jolla, Calif.: General Words and Music Co. Neil A. Kjos, Jr., Publishers, 1973.

Beethoven, Ludwig van. *Beethoven Letters, Journals and Conversations.* Translated and edited by Michael Hamburger. Garden City, New York: Doubleday & Company, Inc., 1960.

————. *The Letters of Beethoven.* Collected, translated and edited with an introduction, appendixes, notes and indexes by Emily Anderson. 3 vols. New York: St. Martin's Press, 1961.

————. *Impressions of Contemporaries.* Edited by O.G. Sonneck. Translated by Frederick H. Martens. New York: G. Schirmer, Inc., 1926.

Bidou, Henri. *Chopin.* Translated by Catherine Alison Phillips. New York: Tudor Publishing Co., 1927.

Bie, Oscar. *A History of the Pianoforte and Pianoforte Players.* Translated from the German by E.E. Kellett and E.W. Naylor. New York: E.P. Dutton, 1899. Reprint. New York: Da Capo Press, 1967.

Bodky, Erwin. *The Interpretation of Bach's Keyboard Works.* Cambridge, Mass.: Harvard University Press, 1960.

Boissier, Auguste. *Liszt Pédagogue: Leçons de piano données par Liszt à Mademoiselle Valérie Boissier à Paris en 1832.* Paris: Honoré Champion, 1927.

Bolton, Hetty. *On Teaching the Piano.* London: Novello and Company Limited, 1954.

Bonpensiere, Luigi. *New Pathways to Piano Technique:* A Study of the Relations between Mind and Body with Special Reference to Piano Playing. New York: Philosophical Library, 1952.

Bowen, Catherine Drinker. *"Free Artist": The Story of Anton and Nicholas Rubinstein.* New York: Random House, 1939.

Brée, Malwine. *The Groundwork of the Leschetizky Method.* Issued with his approval by his assistant Malwine Brée and translated from German by Theodore Baker. New York: G.

Schirmer, 1902.

Breithaupt, Rudolph M. *Die natürliche Klaviertechnik.* 2 vols. Leipzig: C.F. Kahnt Nachfolger, 1905.

_____. *Natural Piano-Technic.* Vol. II: *School of Weight-Touch.* A practical preliminary School of Technic teaching the natural manner of playing by utilizing the weight of the arm. Translated by John Bernhoff. Leipzig: C.F. Kahnt Nachfolger, 1909.

Briggs, G.A. *Pianos, Pianists and Sonics.* Bradford, England: Wharfedale Wireless Works, 1951.

Brinsmead, Edgar. *The History of the Pianoforte. With an Account of the Theory of Sound and Also of the Music and Musical Instruments of the Ancients.* London: Novello, Ewer, & Co., 1879. Reprint. Detroit: Singing Tree Press, 1969.

Brower, Harriette. *Piano Mastery:* Talks with Master Pianists and Teachers, and An Account of a von Bülow Class, Hints on Interpretation, by Two American Teachers (Dr. William Mason and William H. Sherwood) and a Summary by the Author. New York: Frederick A. Stokes Co., 1915.

_____. *Piano Mastery:* Second Series; Talks with Master Pianists and Teachers, including Conferences with Hofmann, Godowsky, Grainger, Powell, Novaes, Hutcheson, and Others; Also Hints on MacDowell's Teaching by Mrs. MacDowell and Reminiscences by Joseffy. New York: Frederick A. Stokes Co., 1917.

Burney, Charles. *A General History of Music, from the Earliest Ages to the Present Period (1789).* Vols. I and II. New York: Harcourt, Brace and Company, 1935.

Busoni, Ferruccio. *The Essence of Music and Other Papers.* Translated from the German by Rosamond Ley. New York: Philosophical Library, 1957.

John Cage. A Catalog of His Works. New York: Henmar Press, Inc., 1962.

Cage, John. *Amores.* New York: C.F. Peters Corporation, 1943. Copyright assigned to Henmar Press, Inc., New York, 1960.

_____. *Sonatas and Interludes.* New York: Henmar Press, Inc., 1960.

Caland, Elisabeth. *Artistic Piano Playing as taught by Ludwig Deppe.* Authorized translation of 1893 German edition by Evelyn Sutherland Stevenson. Nashville, Tenn.: The Olympian Publishing Co., 1903.

Campbell, LeRoy B. *The True Foundation of Relaxation in Piano Playing:* A Treatise on the Psycho-Physical Aspect of Piano

Playing with Exercises for Acquiring Relaxation. St. Louis: Art Publication Society, 1922.

_____, *Velocity Plus:* An Intensive Study of the Problems of Musical Velocity in Piano Playing and Teaching. New York: Creative Music Publishers, 1940.

Chasins, Abram. *Speaking of Pianists.* New York: Alfred A. Knopf, 2nd edition with supplementary chapter, 1961.

Ching, James. *The Amateur Pianist's Companion,* A Short, Precise Guide to Greater Progress and Greater Pleasure for all Sorts and Conditions of Pianists. London: Keith Prowse Music Publishing Co. Ltd., 1956.

_____, *Piano Playing,* A Practical Method, A Rationale of the Psychological and Practical Problems of Pianoforte Playing and Teaching in the Form of Twenty-five Lectures Originally Given in London in the Years 1944-1945. London: Bosworth & Co., Ltd., 1946.

_____. Piano Technique: Foundation Principles. London: Chappell, 1934.

Chopin, Fryderyk. *Selected Correspondence of Fryderyk Chopin.* Abridged from Fryderyk Chopin's Correspondence collected and annotated by Bronislaw Edward Sydow. Translated and edited with additional material and a commentary by Arthur Hedley. London: William Heinemann Ltd., 1962.

Clementi, Muzio. *Introduction to the Art of Playing the Pianoforte,* London: Clementi, Banger, Hyde, Colland, and Davis, 1803. Reprint: N.Y.: Da Capo Press 1973. New introduction by Sandra Rosenblum.

Closson, Ernest. *History of the Piano.* Translated by Delano Ames. London: P. Elek, 1947.

Cooke, Charles. *Playing the Piano for Pleasure.* New York: Simon and Schuster, 1941.

Cooke, James Francis. *Great Pianists on Piano Playing.* Philadelphia: Theodore Presser Co., 1917.

_____. *Mastering the Scales and Arpeggios.* Philadelphia: Theodore Presser Co., 1913.

Cortot, Alfred. *In Search of Chopin.* New York: Abelard Press, 1952.

_____. *Rational Principles of Pianoforte Playing.* Translated by R. le Roy-Métaxas. Paris: Editions Salabert, 1928.

Couperin, François. *The Art of Playing the Harpsichord.* Edited by Anna Linde, English translation by Mevanwy Roberts.

Wiesbaden: Breitkopf & Härtel, 1933.

Coviello, Ambrose. *Foundations of Piano Technique.* London: Oxford University Press, 1934.

_____. *What Matthay Meant,* His Musical and Technical Teachings Clearly Explained and Self-Indexed. London: Bosworth & Co., Ltd., *n.d.*

Cowell, Henry. *Piano Music of Henry Cowell.* New York: Associated Music Publishers, Inc., 1960.

Cramer, Johann Baptist, *Etudes for Piano,* edited by Shedlock and including Beethoven's annotations. London: Augener, Ltd., 1893.

Cramer, Johann Baptist. *Instructions for the Pianoforte in Which the First Rudiments of Music Are Clearly Explained and the Principal Rules on the Art of Fingering Illustrated with Numerous and Appropriate Exercises.* To which are added Lessons in Principal Major and Minor Keys with a Prelude to each Key. The fourth edition with additions and improvements. London: S. Chappell, *n.d.*

Czerny, Carl. *Complete Theoretical and Practical Piano Forte School,* From the First Rudiments of Playing, to the Highest and most Refined State of Cultivation; with the Requisite Numerous Examples, Newly and Expressly Composed for the Occasion. 3 vols. Opus 500. London: R. Cocks & Co., 1839.

_____. *Letters to a Young Lady on the Art of Playing the Pianoforte,* from the Earliest Rudiments to the Highest State of Cultivation. Translated by J.A. Hamilton. New York: S.T. Gordon, 1868.

_____. *Über den richtigen Vortrag der sämtlichen Beethovenschen Klavierwerke.* Czerny's "Remembrances of Beethoven" as well as chapters 2 and 3, volume 4, *Pianoforte School,* Op. 500. Editing and commentary by Paul Badura-Skoda. Vienna: Universal Edition, 1963.

Demuth, Norman. *Ravel.* London: J.M. Dent & Sons, Ltd., 1947.

Deutsch, Leonhard. *Guided Sight-Reading: a New Approach to Piano Study.* Chicago: Nelson-Hall Co., 1959.

Deutsch, Otto Erich. *Mozart, A Documentary Biography.* Translated by Eric Blom, Peter Branscombe, and Jeremy Noble. Stanford, Calif.: Stanford University Press, 1965.

Diruta, Girolamo. *Il Transilvano.* Venice: Appresso Alessandro Vincenti, Part 1, 1593; Part 2, 1609.

von Dittersdorf, Karl. *Autobiography.* Translated by A. D. Coleridge, London: Bentley, 1896. Reprint. New York: Da Capo Press, 1970.

von Dohnanyi, Ernst. *Essential Finger Exercises for Obtaining a Sure Piano Technique.* Preface translated by Norah Drewett. Budapest: Editio Musica, 1963.

Dolge, Alfred. *Pianos and Their Makers.* New York: Dover Publications, 1972. Unabridged reprinting of 1911 edition.

Dolmetsch, Arnold. *The Interpretation of the Music of the Seventeenth and Eighteenth Centuries.* London: Novello and Co., Lt., 1946.

Donington, Robert. *The Interpretation of Early Music.* New York: St. Martin's Press, 1963.

Drake, Kenneth. *The Sonatas of Beethoven, as he played and taught them.* Cincinnati: Music Teachers National Association Publications, 1972.

Dumesnil, Maurice. *How to Play and Teach Debussy.* New York: Schroeder and Gunther, Inc., 1932.

Dussek, Jan Ladislav. *Instructions on the Art of Playing the Pianoforte or Harpsichord.* London: no publisher given, 1796.

Ehrenfechter, C. A. *Technical Study in the Art of Pianoforte-playing (Deppe's Principles).* London: William Reeves, 1891.

Einstein, Alfred. *Mozart—His Character, His Work.* Translated by Arthur Mendel and Nathan Broder. New York: Oxford University Press, 1945.

_____. *Schubert, a Musical Portrait.* New York: Oxford University Press, 1951.

Emerich, Paul. *The Road to Modern Music.* New York: Southern Music Publishing Company, 1960.

Engel, Carl. *The Pianist's Hand-book, A Guide for the Right Comprehension and Performance of Our Best Pianoforte Music.* London: Hope & Co., 1853.

Fay, Amy. *The Deppe Finger Exercises for Rapidly Developing an Artistic Touch in Piano Forte Playing.* Carefully arranged, classified and explained by Amy Fay. Chicago: S. W. Straub & Co., 1890.

_____. *Music-Study in Germany,* from the Home Correspondence of Amy Fay. Edited by Mrs. Fay Pierce. Chicago: Jansen, McClurg & Company, 1880. Paperback reprint. New York: Dover Publications, Inc., 1965.

Fétis, Francois Joseph and Ignaz. Moscheles. *Méthode des*

524

Méthodes de Piano, ou Traité de l'Art de Jouer de cet Instrument. Paris: M. Schlesinger, 1837.

Fielden, Thomas. *The Science of Pianoforte Technique,* London: Macmillan and Co., Limited, 1927.

Foldes, Andor. *Keys to the Keyboard.* New York: E. P. Dutton & Co., 1948.

Forkel, Johann Nikolaus. *Johann Sebastian Bach. His Life, Art, and Work.* English translation by a Mr. Stephenson, 1820. Reprinted in *Bach Reader.* Edited by Hans T. David and Arthur Mendel. New York: W. W. Norton & Co., Inc., 1945.

Friedheim, Arthur. *Life and Liszt, The Recollections of a Concert Pianist,* New York: Taplinger Publishing Co., Inc., 1961.

Friskin, James. *The Principles of Pianoforte Practice.* New York: The H. W. Gray Co., 1921.

Friskin, James and Irwin Freundlich. *Music for the Piano:* A Handbook of Concert and Teaching Material from 1580 to 1952. New York: Rinehart & Co., Inc., 1954; Dover Reprint, 1974.

Galamian, Ivan. *Principles of Violin Playing & Teaching.* Englewood Cliffs, N.J.: Prentice-Hall, Inc., 1961.

Ganz, Rudolph. *Exercises for Piano, Contemporary and Special.* Evanston, Illinois: Summy-Birchard Co., 1967.

Gát, József. *The Techniques of Piano Playing.* 2nd edition completely rewritten by the author. English translation by Istvan Kleszky. London: Collet's Holdings, Ltd. 1965. 4th edition, 1974 reprint of revised 3rd edition.

Geiringer, Karl. *Haydn, A Creative Life in Music.* In collaboration with Irene Geiringer. Garden City, New York: Anchor Books, Doubleday & Company, Inc., 1963.

Gieseking, Walter and Karl Leimer. *Piano Technique.* Unabridged republication of *The Shortest Way to Pianistic Perfection* (1932) and *Rhythms, Dynamics, Pedal and Other Problems of Piano Playing* (1938). New York: Dover Publications, Inc., 1973.

Gillespie, John. *Five Centuries of Keyboard Music:* An Historical Survey of Music for Harpsichord and Piano. Belmont, Calif.: Wadsworth Publishing Company, Inc., 1965.

Gold, Arthur and Robert Fizdale. *Hanon Revisited, Contemporary Piano Exercises based on The Virtuoso Pianist.* New York: G. Schirmer, Inc., 1968.

Goss, Madeleine. *Bolero, The Life of Maurice Ravel.* New York: Henry Holt and Co., 1940.

Grove's Dictionary of Music and Musicians. 5th edition, edited by Eric Blom. New York: St. Martin's Press, Inc., 1954.

Grove's Dictionary of Music and Musicians. 2nd edition, edited by J.A. Fuller Maitland. New York: The Macmillan Co., 1910.

Hallé, Sir Charles. *Life and Letters of Sir Charles Hallé* being an autobiography (1819-1860) with correspondence and diaries. London: Smith, Elder and Co., 1896.

Handbook for Piano Teachers. Collected articles on subjects related to piano teaching. Evanston, Ill.: Summy-Birchard Publishing Co., 1958.

Hanon, Charles Louis. *The Virtuoso Pianist.* Translated by Theodore Baker. New York: G. Schirmer, 1900.

Harding, Bertita. *Concerto, the Glowing Story of Clara Schumann.* Indianapolis, Ind.: The Bobbs-Merrill Co., Inc., 1961.

Harding, E. M. Rosamond. *A History of the Pianoforte to 1851.* Cambridge: Cambridge University Press, 1933. Unabridged republication under title *The Piano-Forte. Its History Traced to the Great Exhibition of 1851.* New York: Da Capo Press, Inc., 1973.

Harich-Schneider, Eta. *The Harpsichord.* An Introduction to Technique, Style and the Historical Source. St. Louis, Mo.: Concordia Publishing House, 1954.

Harrison, Sidney. *Piano Technique.* London: Sir Isaac Pitman & Sons, Ltd., 1953.

Harvard Dictionary of Music. Edited by Willi Apel. Cambridge, Mass.: Harvard University Press, 1946. 2nd edition, revised and enlarged, 1969.

Haydn, Joseph. *The Collected Correspondence and London Notebooks of* Joseph Haydn. Edited by H. C. Robbins Landon. Fair Lawn, New Jersey: Essential Books, 1959.

Helm, Ernest Eugene. *Music at the Court of Frederick the Great.* Norman, Oklahoma: University of Oklahoma Press, 1960.

Helmholz, Hermann L. F. *On the Sensations of Tone as a Physiological Basic for the Theory of Music.* The second English edition, translated, thoroughly revised and corrected, rendered conformal to the fourth (and last) German edition of 1877, with numerous additional notes and a new additional appendix adapted to the use of music students by Alexander J. Ellis. New York: Dover Publications, Inc., 1954.

Hiller, Ferdinand. *Mendelssohn.* London: Macmillan & Co., 1874.

Hinson, Maurice. *Guide to the Pianist's Repertoire.* Edited by Irwin Freundlich. Bloomington, Ind.: Indiana University Press, 1973.

———. *Keyboard Bibliography.* Cincinnati: Music Teachers National Association Publications, 1968.

Hipkins, A. J. *A Description and History of the Pianoforte and of the Older Keyboard Stringed Instruments.* London: Novello, Ewer and Co., 1896.

Hipkins, Edith J. *How Chopin Played (Notes of A.J. Hipkins).* London: J.M. Dent and Sons, Ltd., 1937.

Hofmann, Josef. *Piano Playing with Piano Questions Answered by Josef Hofmann.* Philadelphia: Theodore Presser Co., 1920.

Hook, James. *Guida di Musica:* being a complete Book of Instructions for Beginners on the Harpsichord or Piano Forte entirely on a new plan, calculated to save a great deal of time, trouble both to master and Scholar to which is added Twenty-Four Progressive Lessons in Various Keys with the fingering marked, Op. 37. London: J. Preston, 1788.

Hullah, Annette. *Theodor Leschetizky.* London: John Lane, The Bodley Head Ltd., 1906.

Hummel, Johann Nepomuk. *A Complete Theoretical and Practical Course of Instructions,* on the Art of playing the Piano Forte commencing with the simplest elementary principles, and including every information requisite to the most finished style of performance. London: T. Boosey & Co., 1829.

Huneker, James. *Chopin, the Man and His Music.* New York: Charles Scribner's Sons, 1900. Paperback. New York: Dover Publications, 1966.

Hutcheson, Ernest. *The Elements of Piano Technique.* Baltimore, Md.: G. Fred Kranz Music Co., 1907.

———. *The Literature of the Piano.* New York: Alfred A. Knopf, 1948. 3rd edition, revised and brought up-to-date by Rudolph Ganz. New York: Alfred A. Knopf, 1964.

Jackson, Edwin War. *Gymnastics for the Fingers and Wrist.* London: N. Truebner & Co., 1865.

Jacob, Heinrich Eduard. *Felix Mendelssohn and His Times.* Translated from the German by Richard and Clara Winston. Englewood Cliffs, N.J.: Prentice-Hall, Inc., 1963.

James, Philip. *Early Keyboard Instruments from the Beginnings to the Year 1820.* New York: Frederick A. Stokes Co., 1930.

527

Kalkbrenner, Friedrich Wilhelm. *Méthode pour apprende le Piano á l'aide du Guide-Mains, Op. 108.* Paris: J. Meissonnier Fils, 1830.

Karasowski, Moritz. *Frederic Chopin, His Life and Letters.* Vol. I and II. Translated by Emily Hill. London: William Reeves, 1906.

Kirby, Frank Eugene. *A Short History of Keyboard Music.* New York: The Free Press, 1967.

Klose, Hermann. *Die Deppesche Lehre des Klavierspiels.* Hamburg: Nolte, 1886.

Kochevitsky, George. *The Art of Piano Playing: A Scientific Approach.* Contains excellent English, German, and Russian bibliographies. Evanston, Ill.; Summy-Birchard Co., 1967.

Kullak, Adolph. *The Aesthetics of Pianoforte-Playing.* Translated by Dr. Theodore Baker, from 3rd German edition, revised and edited by Dr. Hans Bischoff. New York: G. Schirmer, 1893. Reprint: N.Y.: Da Capo Press, 1972.

Kullak, Franz. *Beethoven's Piano Playing.* New York: G. Schirmer, Inc., 1901. Translated by Dr. Theodore Baker. Reprint. New York: Da Capo Press, 1973. Same title and with an *Essay on the Execution of the Trill.*

Lahee, Henry C. *Famous Pianists of Today and Yesterday.* Boston: The Page Co., 1900.

Landowska, Wanda. *Landowska on Music.* Collected, edited, and translated by Denise Restout, assisted by Robert Hawkins. New York: Stein and Day, 1964.

Last, Joan. *The Young Pianist:* A New Approach for Teachers and Students. London: Oxford University Press, 1954.

Lebert, Sigismund and Ludwig Stark. *Grand Theoretical and Practical Piano School for Systematic Instruction in All Branches of Piano Playing from the First Elements to the Highest Perfection.* 4 vols. Translated from the fifth German edition by C. E. R. Muller. New York: White-Smith Music Publishing Co., *n.d.*

Leimer, Karl and Walter Gieseking. *The Shortest Way to Pianistic Perfection.* Philadelphia: Theodore Presser Co., 1932.

Lenz, Wilhelm von. *The Great Piano Virtuosos of Our Time from Personal Acquaintance (Liszt, Chopin, Tansig, Henselt).* Translated from the German by Madeleine R. Baker. New York: G. Schirmer, Inc., 1899. Reprint. New York: Da Capo Press, 1973.

Levinskaya, Maria. *The Levinskaya System of Pianoforte Technique and Tone-Colour through Mental and Muscular Control.* London and Toronto: J. M. Dent and Sons, Ltd., 1930.

Lhevinne, Josef. *Basic Principles in Pianoforte Playing.* Philadelphia: Theodore Presser Co., 1924. Reprint in paperback. New York: Dover Publications, 1972.

Liszt, Franz. *Life of Chopin.* Translated with introduction by Edward N. Waters. New York: Free Press of Glencoe, Division of Macmillan Co., 1963.

_____. *The Liszt Studies. Essential Selections from the Original 12-Volume Set of Technical Studies for the Piano including the first English edition of the legendary Liszt Pedagogue—a lesson-diary of the master as teacher, as kept by Mme. Auguste Boissier, 1831-32.* Selections, editions, and English translation by Elyse Mach. New York: Associated Music Publishers, Inc., 1973.

Litzmann, Berthold. *Clara Schumann,* an artist's life based on material found in diaries and letters. Translated by Grace E. Hadow. London: Macmillan & Co., Ltd., 1913.

Lockspeiser, Edward. *Debussy: His Life and Mind.* Vols. I and II. New York: Macmillan Co., 1962.

Loesser, Arthur. *Men, Women and Pianos: A Social History.* New York: Simon and Schuster, 1954.

Loggins, Vernon. *Where the Word Ends. The Life of Louis Moreau Gottschalk.* Baton Rouge, La.: Louisiana State University Press, 1958.

Logier, Johann Bernhard. *An Explanation and Description of the Royal Patent Chiroplast or Hand-Director.* A newly invented apparatus for facilitating the acquirement of a proper execution on the pianoforte by J. B. Logier, Inventor, Professor of Music, Sackville Street, Dublin. London: Clementi & Co., 1816.

Long, Marguerite. *Au piano avec Claude Debussy.* Paris: R. Julliard, 1960.

Long, Marguerite. *Au piano avec Gabriel Fauré.* Paris: R. Julliard, 1963.

Long, Marguerite. *Le Piano.* Paris: Editions Salabert, 1959.

Lukacs-Schuk, Anna. *Reform of Piano Teaching.* Budapest: no publisher given, 1897.

Mackinnon, Lilias. *Musical Secrets.* London: Oxford University Press, 1936.

Maier, Guy. *The Piano Teacher's Companion.* Compiled and edited from his writings in the *Etude Magazine* by Lois Maier. New York: Mills Music, Inc., 1963.

Mainwaring, John. *Memoirs of the Life of the Late George Frederic Handel.* London: R. and J. Dodsley, 1760.

Marek, George R. *Beethoven, Biography of a Genius.* New York: Funk & Wagnalls, 1969.

Marmontel, Antoine François. *Les Pianistes célèbres.* Paris: (Heugel et fils) Imprimerie A. Chaix et cie., 1878.

Marpurg, Friedrich Wilhelm. *Anleitung zum Klavierspielen der schöneren Ausübung der heutigen Zeit gemäss entworfen.* Berlin: Haude & Spener, 1755.

_____. *Die Kunst das Klavier zu spielen.* Berlin: Haude & Spener, 1751.

Martienssen, Carl Adolf. *Die individuelle Klaviertechnik auf der Grundlage des schöpferischen Klangwillens.* Leipzig: Breitkopf & Hartel, 1930.

Marx, Adolf. *Introduction to the Interpretation of the Beethoven Piano Works.* Translated by F. L. Gwinner. Chicago: Clayton L. Summy Co., 1895.

Mason, Daniel Gregory, *Music in My Time and Other Reminiscences.* New York: The Macmillan Company, 1938.

Mason, William. *Memories of a Musical Life.* New York: The Century Co., 1901. Reprint. New York: Da Capo Press, 1970.

_____. *Touch and Technic: For Artistic Piano Playing, Op. 44.* Vols. I-IV. Philadelphia: Theodore Presser, 1897.

Matthay, Jessie Henderson. *The Life and Works of Tobias Matthay.* London: Boosey & Hawkes, Ltd., 1945.

Matthay, Tobias. *The Act of Touch in All Its Diversity,* An Analysis and Synthesis of Pianoforte Tone-Production. London: Bosworth & Co. Ltd., 1903.

_____. *The Child's First Steps in Pianoforte-Playing.* Boston: The Boston Music Co., 1912.

_____. *The First Principles of Pianoforte Playing,* Being an extract from the author's *The Act of Touch* designed for school use, and including two new chapters: Directions for Learners and Advice to Teachers. London: Bosworth & Co. Ltd., 1905.

_____. *Muscular Relaxation Studies,* Relaxation studies in the muscular discriminations required for touch, agility and expression in pianoforte playing. London: Bosworth & Co. Ltd., 1912.

_____. *Musical Interpretation,* its laws and principles, and their

530

application in teaching and performing. London: Joseph Williams, 1913.

———. *The Nine Steps towards "Finger Individualization" through Forearm Rotation,* A Supplement to the first book of *Pianist's First Music Making* and *Child's First Steps.* London: Oxford University Press, 1923. New and revised edition.

———. *Some Commentaries on the Teaching of Pianoforte Technique.* London: Bosworth & Co., Ltd., 1911.

———. *The Visible and Invisible in Pianoforte Technique,* being a digest of the author's technical teachings up to date. London: Oxford University Press, 1932.

Matthews, W. S. B. *Teacher's Manual of Mason's Pianoforte Technics;* a guide to the practical application of the Mason exercises for modifying touch and developing superior technique in every direction. Chicago: Music Magazine Publishing Co., 1901.

May, Florence. *The Girlhood of Clara Schumann.* London: Edward Arnold, 1912.

———. *The Life of Johannes Brahms.* Vols. I and II. London: William Reeves, 1905.

Mellers, Wilfrid. *François Couperin and the French Classical Tradition.* New York: Dover Publications, Inc., 1950.

Mendelssohn, Felix. *Letters of Felix Mendelssohn-Bartholdy from 1833 to 1847.* Edited by Paul Mendelssohn-Bartholdy, and Dr. Carl Mendelssohn-Bartholdy, with a catalogue of all his musical compositions compiled by Dr. Julius Rietz and translated by Lady Wallace. Boston: Oliver Ditson & Co., 1863.

Merrick, Frank. *Practising the Piano.* New York: Denman & Farrell, 1958.

Mikuli, Karol (Carl). *Introduction to the Complete Works for the Pianoforte by Frederic Chopin.* New York: G. Schirmer, 1915.

Milchmyer, Johann Peter. *Die wahr Art das Pianoforte zu Spielen.* Dresden, Germany: Gedruckt bie C. C. Meinhold, 1797.

Moreux, Serge. *Béla Bartók.* Translated from the French by G. S. Fraser and Erik de Mauny. London: Harvill Press, 1953.

Morgenstern, Sam, editor. *Composers on Music.* New York: Pantheon Books, Inc., 1956.

Moscheles, Ignace. *Life of Beethoven,* including the biography by Schindler, Beethoven's correspondence with his friends, numerous characteristic traits, and remarks on his musical works, edited by Ignace Moscheles. (Reprinted from the London edition, 1841) to which is added *The Life and Characteristics of*

Beethoven from the German of Dr. Heinrich Doring. Boston: Oliver Ditson Company, 1842.

_____. *Recent Music and Musicians* as described in the diaries and correspondence of Ignaz Moscheles. Edited by his wife and adapted from the original German by A. D. Coleridge. New York: Henry Holt and Company, 1873. Reprint: N.Y.: DaCapo Press 1970.

Mozart. *The Letters of Mozart and His Family.* Chronologically arranged, translated, and edited with an introduction, notes, and indexes by Emily Anderson. Second edition prepared by A. Hyatt King and Monica Carolan. New York: St. Martin's Press, 1966.

Müller, August Eberhard. *Klavier und Fortepiano Schule, oder Anweisung zur richtigen und geschmackvollen Spielart beyder Instrumente.* Jena, Germany. Fr. Frommann, 1804.

Murdoch, William. *Chopin: His Life.* New York: The Macmillan Company, 1935.

Myers, Rollo H. *Ravel, Life and Works.* London: Gerald Duckworth and Co., Ltd., 1960.

Nestyev, Israel V. *Prokofiev.* Translated from the Russian by Florence Jonas. Stanford, California: Stanford University Press, 1960.

Neuhaus, Heinrich. *Die Kunst des Klavierspiels.* Köln: Musikverlage Hans Gerig, 1967. English edition translated from the Russian by K.A. Leibovitch: *The Art of Piano Playing.* New York: Praeger Publishers, 1973.

Neupert, Hanns, *The Clavichord.* English translation from second German edition. Edited by Ann P. P. Feldberg. Kassel, Germany: Bärenreiter-Verlag, 1948.

Neupert, Hanns. *Harpsichord Manual:* a Historical and Technical Discussion. English translation by F. E. Kirby. Kassel, Germany: Bärenreiter-Verlag, 1960.

Newcomb, Ethel. *Leschetizky as I Knew Him.* New York: D. Appleton and Company, 1921. Reprint. New York: Da Capo Press, 1967.

Newman, Ernest. *The Man Liszt,* A Study of the Tragi-Comedy of a Soul Divided Against Itself. New York: Charles Scribner's Sons, 1935.

Newman, William S. *A History of the Sonata Idea.* Vol. I: *The Sonata in the Baroque Era,* Vol. II: *The Sonata in the Classic Era,* Vol. III: *The Sonata Since Beethoven.* New York: W. W. Norton & Co., 1972. Paperback.

_____. *Performance Practices in Beethoven's Piano Sonatas.* New York: W. W. Norton & Co., 1971.

_____. *The Pianist's Problems:* A modern approach to efficient practice and musicianly performance. Revised and enlarged. New York: Harper & Brothers, 1956, 1974.

Niecks, Frederick. *Frederick Chopin as a Man and Musician.* Vol. I and II. London: Novello, Ewer and Co., 1888.

Niemann, Walter. *Brahms.* Translated by Catherine Alison Phillips. New York: Tudor Publishing Company, 1937.

Nixon, William. *A Guide to Instruction on the Piano-Forte,* designed for the use of both parents and pupils in a series of short essays, dedicated to the young ladies of the Musical Seminary, Cincinnati, Ohio: Josiah Drake, 1834.

Olson, Harry F. *Music, Physics and Engineering.* Revised and enlarged version. New York: Dover Publications, Inc., 1966. . Originally published under title, *Musical Engineering.* New York: McGraw Hill, 1952.

Onren, Frank. *Maurice Ravel.* Stockholm, Sweden: The Continental Book Co., n.d. (after 1945).

Ortmann, Otto. *The Physical Basis of Piano Touch and Tone.* An experimental investigation of the effect of the player's touch upon the tone of the piano. London: Kegan Paul, Trench, Trubner & Co., Ltd., 1925.

_____. *The Physiological Mechanics of Piano Technique.* An experimental study of the nature of muscular action as used in piano playing, and of the effects thereof upon the piano key and the piano tone. London: Kegan Paul, Trench, Trubner & Co., Ltd., 1929. Paperback reprint. New York: E.P. Dutton and Co., Inc., 1962.

Palmer, H. R. *Palmer's Piano Primer.* New York: Palmer, 1895.

Philipp, Isidor. *Complete School of Technic for the Pianoforte.* Philadelphia: Theodore Presser Co., 1908.

_____. *Exercise for Independence of the Fingers.* Parts I and II. New York: G. Schirmer, Inc., 1917.

Potocka, Countesse Angéle. *Theodore Leschetizky.* An Intimate Study of the Man and the Musician. Translated from the French by Geneviève Seymour Lincoln. New York: The Century Co., 1903.

Prentice, Ridley. *Hand Gymnastics for the Scientific Development of the Muscles Used in Pianoforte Playing.* London: Novello and Co. Ltd., 1898.

533

Prentner, Marie. *The Modern Pianist,* being my experiences in the technic and execution of pianoforte playing, according to the principles of Prof. Theo. Leschetizky. English translation by M. DeKendler and A. Maddock. Philadelphia: Theodore Presser Co., 1903.

Prokofiev, S. *Autobiography, Articles, Reminiscences.* Compiled, Edited and Notes by S. Shlifstein. Translated from the Russian by Rose Prokofieva. Moscow: Foreign Languages Publishing House, n.d. (c. 1954).

Quantz, Johann Joachim. *Versuch einer Anweisung die Flöte traversiere zu spielen.* Berlin: 1752. Revised edition, Leipzig: Arnold Schering, 1906.

Rameau, Jean Philippe. *Code de Musique pratique, ou méthodes pour apprendre la musique.* Paris: De l'Imprimerie Royale, 1760.

_____. *Méthode sur la Mécanique des doigts sur le Clavessin.* Paris: Publisher unknown, 1724.

Richner, Thomas. *Orientation for Interpreting Mozart's Piano Sonatas.* New York: Bureau of Publications, Teachers College, Columbia University, 1953.

Rockstro, William Smyth. *Felix Mendelssohn-Bartholdy.* London: Sampson Low, Marston, Searle, and Rivington, 1884.

Roeder, Carl. *Liberation and Deliberation in Piano Technique:* how to develop ease and mastery through understanding correct processes and drill. New York: Schroeder and Gunther, 1941.

Rosen, Charles. *The Classical Style: Haydn, Mozart, Beethoven.* New York: The Viking Press, 1971.

Rothchild, Fritz. *Musical Performance in the Times of Mozart and Beethoven.* London: Adam and Charles Black, 1961.

Rubinstein, Beryl. *Outline of Piano Pedagogy.* New York: Carl Fischer, Inc., 1947.

Russell, Raymond. *The Harpsichord and Clavichord: An Introductory Study.* London: Faber and Faber, 1959.

Safonoff, Wassili. *New Formula for the Piano Teacher and Piano Student.* English edition. London: J. & W. Chester, Ltd., 1915.

St. Lambert, Michel de. *Les Principes du Clavecin.* Paris: C. Ballard, 1702.

Schenk, Erich. *Mozart and His Times.* Edited and translated from the German by Richard and Clara Winston. New York: Alfred A. Knopf, 1959.

Schindler, Anton Felix. *Beethoven as I Knew Him.* Edited by

Donald W. MacArdle and translated by Constance S. Jolly. Chapel Hill, N.C.: The University of North Carolina Press, 1966.

Schmitz, E. Robert. *The Capture of Inspiration.* Translated by Merle Armitage. New York: Carl Fischer, Inc., 1935.

Schnabel, Artur. *My Life and Music, with Reflections on Music.* New York: St. Martin's Press, 1963.

Schonberg, Harold C. *The Great Pianists from Mozart to the Present.* New York: Simon and Schuster, 1963.

Schott, Howard. *Playing the Harpsichord.* New York: St. Martin's Press, 1971.

Schultz, Arnold. *The Riddle of the Pianist's Finger and Its Relationship to a Touch-Scheme.* New York: Carl Fischer, Inc., 1936.

_____. *A Theory of Consciousness.* New York: Philosophical Library, 1973.

Schumann, Eugenie. *The Schumanns and Johannes Brahms.* New York: Lincoln MacVeagh, The Dial Press, 1927.

Schumann, Robert. *Early Letters of Robert Schumann originally published by his wife.* Translated by May Herbert. London: George Bell and Sons, 1888.

_____. *On Music and Musicians.* Edited by Konrad Wolff and translated by Paul Rosenfeld. Includes "House-Rules and Maxims for Young Musicians." New York: Pantheon Books Inc., 1946. Paperback. New York: W.W. Norton. 1969.

_____. "Preface to Studies for the Pianoforte on Caprices of Paganini, Op. 3," *Complete Works for Piano Solo.* Vol I. New York: Edwin F. Kalmus, n.d.

Seroff, Victor I. *Maurice Ravel.* New York: Henry Holt and Co., 1953.

Sitwell, Sacheverell. *Liszt.* New York: Philosophical Library, Inc., 1955.

Slenczynska, Ruth. *Music at Your Fingertips* with the collaboration of Ann M. Lingg. Garden City, N.Y.: Doubleday & Co., Inc., 1961.

Slonimsky, Nicholas. *Thesaurus of Scale and Melodic Patterns.* New York: Coleman-Ross Co., 1947.

Smith, Julia. *Master Pianist,* The Career and Teaching of Carl Friedberg. New York: Philosophical Library, 1963.

Sorel, Claudette. *A Compendium of Piano Technique.* New York: Marks Music Corporation, 1969.

Spohr, Ludwig. *Ludwig Spohr's Autobiography.* Translated from the German. London: Longman, Green, Longman, Roberts and Green, 1865. Reprint of 1878 edition. New York: Da Capo Press, 1969.

Steinhausen, Friedrich Adolf. *Die physiologischen Fehler und Umgestaltung der Klaviertechnik.* Leipzig: Breitkopf & Härtel, 1905.

Steinway, Theodore E. *People and Pianos,* A Century of Service to Music. New York: Steinway & Sons, 1953.

Stevens, Halsey. *The Life and Music of Béla Bartók.* New York: Oxford University Press, revised edition 1964.

Suchoff, Benjamin. *Guide to the Mikrokosmos.* New York and London: Boosey & Hawkes, 1969.

Sumner, William Leslie. *The Pianoforte.* London: Macdonald & Co., 1966.

Thalberg, Sigismond. *L'art du chant applique au piano. Op. 70.* Leipzig: Breitkopf & Härtel. c. 1860.

Thayer, Alexander Wheelock. *The Life of Ludwig van Beethoven.* Edited and translated by Henry Edward Krehbiel. Vol. I, II, and III. New York: The Beethoven Association Press of G. Schirmer, 1921. Two volume edition by Elliot Forbes. Princeton, N.J.: Princeton University Press, 1964.

Thompson, Oscar. *Debussy, Man and Artist.* New York: Dodd, Mead & Co., 1937.

Tomaschek, Johann Wenzel. *Autobiography and Reminiscences.* No publisher given.

Townsend, William. *Balance of Arm in Piano Technique.* London: Bosworth and Co. Ltd., 1890.

Tureck, Rosalyn. *An Introduction to the Performance of Bach.* 3 vols. London: Oxford University Press, 1960.

Türk, Daniel Gottlob. *Klavierschule oder Anweisung zum Klavierspielen für Lehrer und Lernende, mit kritischen Anmerkungen.* Leipzig and Hallé: Schwickert, 1789. Facsimile edition. Kassel, Germany: Barenreiter, 1962.

Turner, Walter James. *Mozart, the Man and His Works.* New York: Alfred A. Knopf, 1938.

Varro, Margit. *Der lebendige Klavierunterricht. Seine Methodik und Psychologie.* Hamburg: N. Simrock, 1929.

Virgil, A.K. *Foundation Exercises in Piano Playing* especially adapted to the Virgil practice clavier. New and enlarged edition. New York: The Virgil Piano School, 1895.

536

Virgil, Mrs. A.M. *The Virgil Method of Piano Technique.* New York: Mrs. A.M. Virgil, 1902.

Walker, Bettina. *My Musical Experiences.* London: Richard Bentley & Son, 1892.

Weitzmann, Carl Friedrich. *A History of Pianoforte-Playing and Piano Literature.* Translated by Theodore Baker. New York: G. Schirmer, 1897. Reprint. New York: Da Capo Press, 1969.

Wells, Howard. *Ears, Brain and Fingers.* Philadelphia: Oliver Ditson Company, 1914.

Whiteside, Abby. *Indispensables of Piano Playing.* New York: Coleman-Ross Company, Inc., 1955.

_____. *Mastering the Chopin Etudes and Other Essays.* Edited by Joseph Prostakoff and Sophia Rosoff. New York: Charles Scribner's Sons, 1969.

_____. *The Pianist's Mechanism:* A guide to the production and transmission of power in playing. New York: G. Schirmer, Inc., 1929.

Wierzynski, Casimir. *The Life and Death of Chopin.* Translated by Norbert Guterman with a foreward by Artur Rubinstein. New York: Simon and Schuster, 1949.

Wieck, Friedrich. *Piano and Song,* How to teach, how to learn, and how to form a judgment of musical performances. Boston: Oliver Ditson Company, 1875.

Wolff, Konrad. *The Teaching of Artur Schnabel: A Guide to Interpretation.* New York and Washington: Praeger Publications, 1971.

Zuckermann, Wolfgang Joachim. *The Modern Harpsichord. 20th Century Instruments and Their Makers.* New York: October House, Inc., 1969.

Articles and Periodicals

Apel, Willi. "Pianoforte Playing," *Harvard Dictionary of Music.* Cambridge, Mass.: Harvard University Press, 1946, 579-583. 2nd edition, revised and enlarged, 1969, 675-677.

Balogh, Erno. "BARTÓK, The Teacher—As I Know Him," *The Etude,* LXXIV, No. 1 (January, 1956), 20, 51.

Bauer, Harold. "Self-Portrait of the Artist as a Young Man," *The Musical Quarterly,* XXIX, No. 2 (April, 1943), 153-168.

Boise, Otis B. "An American Composer Visits Liszt," *The Musical*

Quarterly, XLIII, No. 3 (July, 1957), 316-325.

Boissier, Auguste. "Liszt as Pedagogue," *The Piano Teacher,* III, No. 5 (May-June, 1961), 12-14, III, No. 6 (July-August, 1961), 14-15. (Translated by Maurice Dumesnil).

Boulanger, Nadia. "Sayings of Great Teachers," *The Piano Quarterly,* No. 26 (Winter, 1958-1959), 26.

Breithaupt, Rudolph M. "The Idea of Weight-Playing—its Value and Practical Application," *The Musician,* Part I, Vol. 16, No. 1 (January, 1911), 12-13; Part II, Vol. 16, No. 2 (February, 1911), 90-91; Part III, Vol. 16, No. 3 (March, 1911), 232-233. (Translated by Florence Leonard).

Broder, Nathan. "What Was Mozart's Playing Like?" *Piano Quarterly,* No. 34 (Winter, 1960-1961), 13-18.

Brower, Harriette. "Where Technique and Mechanics Differ," An Interview with Leopold Godowsky, *The Musician,* XXVIII, No. 9 (September, 1923), 9, 24.

Campbell, LeRoy B. "Wischnegradzky's Quarter-Toned Piano, The Keyboard in Attempted Competition with the Violin Family in the Realm of Atonality," *The Musician,* XLII, No. 5 (May, 1937), 88, 93.

Canin, Martin. "A Rational Approach to Piano Technic," *The Piano Quarterly,* No. 65-73, (Fall, 1968 to Fall, 1970), 9 installments.

Chasins, Abram. "The Return of Horowitz," *The Saturday Evening Post,* 239th year, No. 22 (October 22, 1966), 102-104.

Copp, Laura Remick. "Should the Piano Have Two Keyboards? An Interview with the Distinguished Piano Virtuoso Winifred Christie," *The Etude,* XLIX, No. 4 (April, 1931), 239-240.

Couperin, François. "The Art of Playing the Harpsichord." Translated by Dorothy Packard. *Clavier.* VII, No. 4 (April, 1968), 20-25.

Crowder, Louis. "Debussy and Subtraction," *The Piano Teacher,* I, No. 4 (October, 1962), 10-14.

_____. "Relaxation Comes of Age," *The Piano Teacher,* Part I, Vol. 3, No. 5 (May-June, 1961), 2-9; Part II, Vol. 3, No. 6 (July-August, 1961), 6-13.

Czerny, Carl. "Recollections from my Life," *The Musical Quarterly,* XLII, No. 3 (July, 1956), 302-317. Translation by Ernest Sanders.

Deppe, Ludwig. "Armleiden des Klavierspielers," *Deutsche Musiker-Zeitung* (1855). Reprinted in *Neue Zeitschrift für Musik,*

Vol. 70 (1903), 315. (Translation by Helmut Zeifle).

Drake, Kenneth. "The Voice of a Contemporary," *Clavier,* II, No. 6 (November-December, 1963), 10-12.

Dumesnil, Maurice. "Coaching with Debussy," *The Piano Teacher,* V, No. 1, (September-October, 1962), 10-13.

Dumesnil, Maurice. "Teacher's Round Table," *The Etude,* LXVII, No. 9 (September 1949), 14.

Eisenberg, Jacob. "Horowitz Explains Accenting a Melody While Playing Chords, *The Musician,* XXXIII, No. 6 (June, 1928), 11.

Eitel, Luise. "Beethoven as a Piano Teacher," *The Piano Quarterly,* No. 35 (Spring, 1961), 21-24.

Farmer, John. "Josef Lhevinne on Ampico Piano Rolls," *The Juilliard Review Annual* (1966-1967), 25-28.

Fay, Amy. "Deppe and His Piano Method," *Music,* XIV, No. 6 (October, 1898), 581-588.

Fielden, Thomas. "Pianoforte Playing," *Grove's Dictionary of Music and Musicians.* 5th edition. Edited by Eric Blom. New York: St. Martin's Press, Inc., 1954, VI, 744-751.

Fleisher, Leon. "About Practicing and Making Music," *Clavier.* II, No. 4 (September, 1963), 12-16.

Fuller Maitland, J.A. and Franklin Taylor. "Gymnastics," *Grove's Dictionary of Music and Musicians.* 2nd edition. New York: The Macmillan Co., 1910, II, 263-266.

Fuller Maitland, J.A. "Pianoforte Playing." *Grove's Dictionary of Music and Musicians.* 2nd edition. New York: The Macmillan Co., 1910, III, 732-736.

Godowsky, Leopold. "The Best Method Is Eclectic," *The Etude,* Part I, LI, No. 10 (October, 1933), 645, 710; Part II, LI, No. 11 (November, 1933), 737, 784.

Goldberger, David. "Arthur Schnabel's Master Classes," *The Piano Teacher,* V, No. 4 (March-April, 1963), 5-7.

Hinderer, J.G. "We Attend Godowsky's Master Class," An Associate of the Eminent Pianist and Teacher Gives Us a Close-Up of What Happens There, *The Musician,* XXXVIII, No. 7 (July, 1933), 3-4.

Hoare, Rodney. "What Matthay Meant," *The Piano Teacher,* IV, No. 4 (March-April, 1962), 2-3.

Holcman, Jan. "An Interview with Horowitz," *The Saturday Review of Literature,* XLIII, No. 18 (April 30, 1960), 41-43, 60-61.

_____. "Keyboard Left to Right," Part I, *Saturday Review of*

Literature, XLII, July 25, 1959, 33-35.

Horowitz, Vladimir. "Technic the Outgrowth of Musical Thought," An Educational Conference with the Sensationally Successful Russian Piano Virtuoso, secured expressly for *The Etude* by Florence Leonard, *The Etude,* L, No. 3 (March, 1932), 163-164.

Hughes, Edwin. "Theodor Leschetizky: A Maker of Pianists," *The Musician,* XV, No. 9 (September, 1910), 580.

――――. "Theodore Leschetizky on Modern Pianoforte Study," *The Etude,* XXVIII, No. 4 (April, 1909), 227-228.

Jonas, Oswald. "Beethoven's Piano Technique," *The Piano Teacher,* III, No. 2 (November-December, 1960), 9-11.

Kamm, Henry. "The Grande Dame of French Music," *The New York Times,* Sunday, January 31, 1965, Section X, 11.

Lassimonne, Denise. "Tobias Matthay 1858-1945," *The Piano Quarterly,* No. 36 (Summer, 1961), 17-20.

Leonard, Florencee. "How Breithaupt Teaches," *The Musician,* XX, No. 4 (April, 1915), 225-227.

Lhevinne, Josef. "Good Tone Is Born in the Player's Mind," transcribed by Harriette Brower, *The Musician,* XXVIII, No. 7 (July, 1923), 7.

Limón, José. "Dancers Are Musicians Are Dancers," *The Juilliard Review Annual* (1966-1967), 5-10.

Ludden, Bennet. "My Broadwood," *The Piano Quarterly,* No. 34 (Winter, 1960-1961), 21-23.

Maffei, Scipione, "New Invention of a Harpsichord with the Soft and Loud," *Giornale der Letterati d'Italia,* V. Venice: Appresso G.G. Hertz, 1711.

Moszkowski, Moritz. "Methods and Customs of the Paris Conservatoire," *The Etude,* XXIX, No. 2 (February, 1910), 81.

Newman, William S. "A Little Matter of the Pianist's Anatomy" *The Piano Quarterly,* 36, (Summer, 1961), 20-21.

――――. "On the Special Problems of High-Speed Playing," *Clavier,* II, No. 3 (May-June, 1963), 11-15.

――――. "The Pianist's Anatomy Revisited. Department of the 4th Finger." *The Piano Quarterly,* 64, (Summer, 1968), 22.

――――. "Ten Ways to Exercise the Four Basic Touches and Keyboard Harmony, Too," *The Piano Quarterly,* No. 50 (Winter, 1963-1964), 13-16.

"New Piano Effects Created by Double-Keyboard," Winifred Christie will this season demonstrate in her recitals here, the

Bechstein-Moor Invention which increases the instrument's tonal possibilities, *The Musician*, XXXV, No. 8 (August, 1930), 7.

Ortmann, Otto. "Piano Technique in the Light of Experiment," *The American Mercury*, XII (December, 1927), 443-446.

_____. "What Is Tone Quality?" *The Musical Quarterly*, XXI (October, 1935), 442-450.

Parrish, Carl. "Criticisms of the Piano When It Was New," *The Musical Quarterly*, XXX, No. 4 (October, 1944), 428-440.

_____. "Haydn and the Piano," *Journal of the American Musicological Society*, I, No. 3 (Fall, 1948), 27-34.

Pecher, W. F. "The Emotional Legacy of the Classical School: Reminiscences of the Teaching of Moscheles," *The International Library of Music for Home and Studio*. Vol. III. New York: The University Society, 1948, III, 28-30.

"Piano on the Half Shell," TIME LXXXV (April 30, 1965), 52.

"Prepared Pianist," from "The Talk of the Town, *The New Yorker*, XXI (February 24, 1945), 18-19.

"Recording the Soul of Piano Playing," *Scientific American*, CXXXVII, No. 5 (November, 1927), 422-427.

Reinecke, Carl. "Mendelssohn and Schumann: Personal Recollections of Them as Teachers," *The Etude*, XXVIII, No. 12 (December, 1909), 803-804.

Rezits, Joseph. "The Interrelationship of Quantitative and Qualitative Elements in Piano Playing," *The American Music Teacher*, XXII, 6 (June-July 1973), 29-31 and XXIII, 1 (September-October 1973, 25-29.

Robert, Walter. "In Defense of Scales," *Clavier*, I, No. 5 (November-December, 1962), 13-16.

Sargeant, Winthrop. "The Leaves of a Tree," *The New Yorker*, XXXVIII, No. 47 (January 12, 1963), 37, 52.

Schmitz, E. Robert. "A Plea for the Real Debussy," A Conference secured expressly for *The Etude Music Magazine* by Lucille Fletcher, *The Etude*, LV, No. 12 (December, 1937), 781-782.

Schonberg, Harold C. "The Cluster Man." (Henry Cowell), *The New York Times*, Sunday, March 11, 1962, Section X, 11.

_____. "The Far-Out Pianist." David Tudor has made himself the No. 1 virtuoso of a new kind of music—or anyhow, noise, *Harper's Magazine*, Volume 220 (June, 1960), 49-54.

Schultz, Arnold. "Contest Standards—Are They Logical?" *The Piano Teacher*, V, No. 5 (May-June, 1963), 6-10.

Stone, Kurt. "The Piano and the Avant-Garde," *The Piano Quarterly,* No. 52 (Summer, 1965), 14-28.

"Syllabus of Special Classes in Piano for Music Schools," approved by the Department of Education of the Ministry of Culture of the Union of Soviet Socialist Republics. Moscow, 1960. Reprinted in *The Journal of Research in Music Education,* XII, No. 3 (Fall, 1964), 199-204. (Translated by Walter Robert).

Whiteside, Abby. "Successful Piano Teaching: The Physical Sensation Comes First," *Musical America,* LXXI, No. 16 (December 15, 1951), 25.

Proceedings of Musical Societies

Barrington, Daines. "Account of a Remarkable Young Musician," *Philosophical Transactions of the Royal Society,* XL (1770), 626.

Fielden, Thomas. "The History of the Evolution of Pianoforte Technique," *Proceedings of Royal Music Association,* Session 59 (January 17, 1933), 35-39.

Haake, Charles J. "Modern Piano Technic—How New Is It?" *Music Teachers National Association Proceedings,* 16th series (1921), 71-81.

Ortmann, Otto. "Tone Quality and the Pianist's Touch," *Music Teachers National Association Proceedings,* 31st series (1936), 127-132.

Schultz, Arnold. "The Riddle of the Pianist's Finger," *Music Teachers National Association Proceedings,* 31st series (1936), 138-143.

542

Glossary

Abduct   To lead a playing lever laterally away from its normal median line. Example: when the arms are engaged simultaneously in contrary motion scale work, the outward arm movement away from the body involves *abduction* at the shoulder. As the arms come together again, *adduction* takes place.

Antagonistic muscles   Muscles that directly oppose each other and create opposite directional movements of the same lever and joint. When working harmoniously, one muscle will relax at precisely the same rate as its antagonist contracts. Where the relaxation rate of one is greater than its antagonist's rate of contraction, a condition of *hyper-relaxation* exists. Where the relaxation rate is slower, *hypo-relaxation* is present. When the antagonistic muscles contract simultaneously, a relative state of fixation will occur in the joint concerned. Functional relaxation is directly related to the harmonious interaction and balancing of the antagonistic muscles. Freedom of movement or a quiet wrist or arm are not accurate indicators of the state of relaxation of the limb involved.

Base   The support or foundation to which a lever is attached at the fulcrum point.

Dorsal   Pertaining to the back side or surface of a body, such as the outer side of the hand or wrist (opposite the palm).

Extensor   A muscle that extends a lever in the direction of an 180 degree angle.

Fixation   The simultaneous contraction of a set or sets of antagonistic muscles so that a fulcrum point is firmly fixed and unmoving when its playing lever is in motion. The super-energetic action of the high-finger school resulted in excessively strong fixations of the wrist and forearm joints.

Flexibility   The ability to bend easily, to move freely at the various joints in the body.

Flexor   A muscle that contracts to bend a joint so as to form a smaller angle.

Force   The application of power to overcome resistance. Muscular effort will be reinforced or impeded by gravitational force.

Fulcrum   The point on which a lever pivots or turns. Example: the hand knuckle serves as the fulcrum for a finger movement.

Geometrics of Movement   Paths of physical movement traced by the fingers, hand, and arm during the act of playing. Properly functioning

543

arm movement, especially when controlled by a fundamental rhythm, tends to unite the notes played by the smaller movements of finger and hand into a long, unified phrase line. Sustained, flowing arm movement is most efficient when curvilinear and possessing a sense of continuity.

Inertia   Tendency of matter to stay in a fixed condition, whether at rest or in motion. Always present is the inclination to resist acceleration, until overcome by an external force.

Isolation   The movement of a lever, such as the finger, without any detectable reactionary movement on the part of its base.

Kinesthesia   Sensory awareness of physical position, presence, or movement caused by stimulation of the ends of the sensory nerves in joints, tendons, and muscles. Examples: horizontal distance perception by the arms and torso; the sense of key touch and resistance felt in the finger tips. Highly desirable is the *prepared* or *non-percussive* touch where the finger tip is in sensitive physical contact with the key-surface before the key descent has been initiated. The French touch school of the nineteenth century encouraged the stroking of the key in connection with the act of touch and termed it *carezzando*.

Lever   An unbending body operating as a machine engaged in work and turning or pivoting on a fixed fulcrum. In piano playing, finger, hand, forearm, and full arm all function as levers.

Mass   An integrated body of matter unspecified in shape or weight.

Momentum   Property of matter that makes a body tend to continue its forward motion and resist a slowing influence.

Muscular Coordination   Harmonious functioning and interacting of muscles or groups of muscles so as to activate the playing lever to the desired point of tone at the keyboard with the desired force and timing. Throughout, the right combination of contracting and relaxing muscles will be so balanced and graded that the expenditure of energy will be minimal, but consistent with the amount of work to be accomplished. When a rhythm of contraction and relaxation *(muscular breathing)* is properly set up and each muscle functions harmoniously in relation to every other one, a condition of *muscular synergy* exists.

Pronation   The rotating of the forearm so that the palm of the hand is downward and is clearly perceived as the underside of the hand.

Phalanx, pl. *Phalanges*   Any one of the finger bones.

Power   Possession of the ability to move effectively with muscular strength.

Power Arm   On a lever, the distance between the fulcrum and the point at which the force or power is applied.

Resistance Arm   On a lever, the distance between the fulcrum and the point of resistance to the force applied.

Supination   The rotating of the forearm so that the palm of the hand is in an upward and visible position.

Ventral   Pertaining to the under or lower side of a body surface, such as the wrist or hand.

Weight   The quantity of gravitational force exerted upon a mass.

Index

547

310

Prostakoff, Joseph, 472,475,476, 477-478
Prout, Ebenezer, 369
Pruckner, Dionys, 187
Psychology, 335,401-402,413,440, 441,462,463,464,465,466,509-510
Pugno, Raoul, 316
Pye, Kellow, 361

Quantz, Joachim, 18-19,33
Quarter-toned piano, Wishne-gradzky, 496

Rachmaninoff, Serge, 193,292,293, 302,436,437,515
Raff, Joachim, 187
Raieff, Josef, 300
Raif, Oscar, 463,509
Rameau, Jean Philippe, 17,18,31, 229,509,512
Ravel, Maurice, 319,326-327
Reeves, Henry, 172-173
Reicha, Anton, 171
Reichardt, Johann Friedrich, 27
Reinecke, Carl, 204
Reisenauer, Alfred, 185
Rellstab, Ludwig, 89,198,199
Reményi, Eduard, 215,216
Reschovsky, Sándor, 485
Resistance, 414,415
Resistance arm, 415
Revue et Gazette musicale de Paris, 500
Revue musicale, 152
Rhodesian Academy of Music, 399
Rhythm,
  bodily. *See* Movement
Richter, Georg Friedrich, 55
Richter, Sviatoslav, 293
Riemann, Hugo, 305
Ries, Ferdinand, 61,86,87,88,89,90, 98,115,118
Risler, Édouard, 318,320
Ritschl, Alexander, 329
Robert, Walter, 515
Robertson, Rae, 395
Rochlitz, Johann Friedrich, 25
Rockstro, W.S., 200-201
Roeder, Carl, 491,514

Roseingrave, Thomas, 23,24
Rosenthal, Moriz, 193,436,437
Rosoff, Sophia, 478
Rossini, Gioacchino, 205
Royal Academy of Music, 362
Royal College of Music, 362
Rubato, 161
Rubinstein, Anton, 229,263,274, 290-296,297,300,330,507,508, 509,512
Rubinstein, Artur, 293

Safonov, Vassily Ilyitch, 296-297, 300,514
St. Lambert, Michel de, 13,14,507
St. Petersburg Conservatory, 287, 292,293,307
St. Saëns, Camille, 136,316
Salaman, Charles, 177
Salieri, Antonio, 67,83,171
Sand, George. *See* Aurore Dudevant
Sandor, Gyorgy, 484
Sauer, Emil, 193
Sayn-Wittenstein, Carolyne von, 180
Scarlatti, Domenico, 18,23,24,116, 507
Schachtner, Andreas, 50
Schanz, J. Wenzel, 40,41
Schanz piano, 40,41
Scharer, Irene, 395
Scheibe, Johann Adolph, 18
Schenk, Johann, 83
Schindler, Anton, 59,61,67,83,513
Schmidt, Henry, 236
Schnabel, Artur, 4,271,272,275-276,278-279,288,330,333,467,494
Schonberg, Harold, 494
Schools
  English, 361-403,507
  French, 315-327
  national characteristics, 287-288
  Russian, 287-313
  Stuttgart, 230,288,508,510. *See also* Finger technique
  Survey of, 116-119
  Viennese, 52,65,507
Schroeder-Devrient, Wilhelmine, 179